EARLY CIVILIZATIONS
OF THE OLD WORLD

To the genius of Titus Lucretius Carus (99/95 BC–55 BC)
and his insight into the real nature of things.

EARLY CIVILIZATIONS OF THE OLD WORLD

The formative histories of
Egypt, the Levant, Mesopotamia,
India and China

Charles Keith Maisels

London and New York

First published 1999
by Routledge
11 New Fetter Lane, London EC4P 4EE

Simultaneously published in the USA and Canada
by Routledge
29 West 35th Street, New York, NY 10001

Typeset in Garamond by
The Florence Group, Stoodleigh, Devon
Printed and bound in Great Britain by
Biddles Ltd, Guildford and King's Lynn

British Library Cataloguing in Publication Data
A catalogue record for this book is available
from the British Library

Library of Congress Cataloguing in Publication Data
A catalogue record for this book has been requested

ISBN 0–415–10975–2

CONTENTS

CONTENTS

APPENDICES 360

FIGURES

TABLES

PREFACE

How the world's first civilizations came into existence is the subject of this book. It charts, analyses and compares the parallel paths followed in each of the seminal areas of the Old World (Africa and Asia), from the Old Stone Age (Palaeolithic) right through to historical times. It documents the circumstances that gave each region its distinctive cultural characteristics: settling down, the domestication of plants and animals, economic specialization, class stratification, city and state formation.

It is, then, a book about the processes by which hunter–gatherers became farmers (the Neolithic), villagers became townspeople with a complex division of labour (the Chalcolithic) and, beginning around 5000 years ago, cities, states, writing, calculation and institutional religion emerged (the Bronze Age).

ACKNOWLEDGEMENTS

This work stems from a series of lectures on Old World Archaeology that I gave during 1992–3 in the University of Bristol at the invitation of Caroline Malone and Simon Stoddart. Many thanks to them for the invitation, for their hospitality and for the suggestion that the lectures be written up for publication. They are, of course, not responsible for deficiencies of realization, and neither are Kenneth A. Kitchen, who read Chapter 2 (Egypt), Gary O. Rollefson, who read the section on the Levant, or John Brockington, who read Chapter 4 (Indus). Their encouragement is, however, greatly appreciated, as also is that of Alan Barnard, John Curtis and Andrew Sherratt. I am likewise indebted to Gina L. Barnes, Stuart Campbell, Kwang-chih Chang, M.K. Dhavalikar, Roger Matthews, Nicholas Postgate, Lech Kryzaniak at Poznan Archaeological Museum and, of course, all of those whose work I have cited.

The photographs in Chapter 2 have been supplied by the Ashmolean Museum, University of Oxford, whose assistance is appreciated.

GLOSSARY

(See also note 5.5 on climate. For some ethnographic terms, see Appendices; for definitions of myth, fantasy, religion and ritual, see notes 2.10 and 6(c).1 and for information on organizations/roles/statuses see note 6.3.)

Aggradation The 'building up' of the land surface (in Holocene times especially the lower reaches of river channels) by the *depositional* action of rivers, winds or seas (*see* alluvium, anastomosing and loess). Its opposite is *denudation*.

Alluvium Sedimentary deposits of eroded rock fragments laid by the action of rivers. Larger particles, notably gravels, are deposited upstream, while finer materials (usually called *silts*) are deposited downstream, sometimes right into waterbodies, where *alluvial fans* are formed. If offshore conditions are right, *deltas* are formed. As unconsolidated (though usually deep and mineral-rich) material, *alluvisols* are a type of *immature*, *skeletal* or *azonal* soil, manifesting poorly developed *horizons*, which are levels of different structure and organic activity.

Anastomosing A condition of rivers in which, due to excessive *deposition* (see alluvium above), there is little gradient (slope) in the rivercourse, encouraging the main stream to break up into a network of branches or braids, the number and location of which shift over quite short periods of time. *Levees*, which are broad raised banks, can also result.

Biome An ecosystem covering a significant proportion of the earth's surface, land or water. Tundra, boreal (i.e. northern coniferous) forests, tropical rainforests and savannahs are examples of biomes. A dominant life-form structures each – mosses and lichens in the case of tundra – hence their alternative designation as 'formation types'.

Caprid Goat. *Caprini* is the *tribe* including both sheep and goat. *Capra aegagrus* is the Bezoar goat, the wild progenitor of the domestic goat, while *Capra ibex* is a type of goat (the ibex) specializing in high altitude and desert conditions.

Climax Two senses: (1) the most massive species of plant that a territory can sustain, e.g. oak; (2) the final stable plant community, e.g. oak–ash forest, reached after a process of *succession* from simpler/lower/less massive/less woody plant types. Thus, primary succession from tundra to broadleaf and coniferous forests occurred in Britain after the last Ice Age, and secondary succession, which takes places after climax has been removed, is spontaneously toward renewed forest cover. Moisture, temperature, seasonality, light and soils are determinants, as also is the actual occurrence of species where particular combinations of those factors are optimal for them. *See* prairies.

Dendritic   Tree-like branching.

Dendrochronology   Tree-ring dating.

Distal   Situated farthest *away from* the point of attachment or connection, the converse of *proximal*, nearest.

Ecotone   The transitional zone between two biomes.

Epiphysis   Peculiar to mammalian vertebra and limb bones, this is the separately ossified end of a growing bone (the *diaphysis*). Separated by cartilage, the two become unified only at maturity.

Evapotranspiration   The rate of water loss from surfaces of (1) the ground, and (2) leaves and stems; a function of temperature and wind speeds. The water balance (positive or negative) of an area is the rate of evapotranspiration set against rainfall plus any exogenous supply.

Exogenous   Coming from without. Thus, the Nile in Egypt is fed from drainage basins that lie outside Egypt in areas of adequate rainfall. A substantially positive water balance is required for rivers to originate, otherwise only wadis form (q.v.).

Fractal   Describes similar forms repeated at different scales most often in natural phenomena. Thus trees, mountains, clouds and coastlines manifest fractal symmetry. Leaves have similar forms to branches and branches have similar forms to whole trees (by affine transformation). Small stones in close-up resemble large rocks and the forms of individual rocks resemble mountains. Coastlines have similar 'ragged edge' interactions between land and water at every scale from, say, a 1:4,000,000 map, down to that of rockpools.

Hydric/hygrophyte   Plants that require large amounts of moisture and which therefore thrive only in/by water or in humid regions (*see* mesic and xeric).

Isohyet   A line joining points that receive the same amount of rainfall. Analogous to isobars, which are lines of equal atmospheric pressure, and to contours which are lines of equal height. All are *isopleths:* lines joining points of equal value.

Loess soils   Sometimes called 'brickearth' soils from their sandy-yellow colour, hence the 'Yellow River' (Huang He) from the sediment it carries. Consisting mainly of fine quartz particles in deep layers, the loess soils of north China are rich in lime and form a good *loam* for agriculture. Loess soils are analogous to alluvial soils, but are primarily wind-deposited (aeolian), compacted and thus more cohesive, being able to sustain vertical banks when rivers cut down (as they always do in loess). Loess soils, being free-draining, do not waterlog. Russia's fertile 'black earth' (Chernozem) soil is loess with a high humus content. Such soils also occur in a long swathe from Saskatchewan through North Dakota to Texas.

Mesic/mesophyte Temperate climate plants requiring moderate amounts of moisture.

Metacarpal bones Corresponding to the palm-region in man, those are the rod-like bones of the fore-foot in tetrapod vertebrates, usually one corresponding to each digit (finger or toe). *Metatarsals* are the same bones in the hind foot (sole).

Nucleation A settlement type that has its buildings clustered tightly together, leaving little space in between (only squares, greens or plazas, not fields and farms).

Obsidian (Rhyolite) 'volcanic' glass in extrusive igneous (i.e. *magmatic*) rocks. Like glass, it takes a very sharp edge.

Ovicaprids Sheep (*Ovis*) and goat together, used as a term particularly where differentiation from skeletal remains is difficult. However, wild sheep (e.g. *Ovis orientalis*, or mouflon, the progenitor of domestic sheep) and goats have different environmental preferences and tolerances, goats being tougher and more versatile.

Palynology Pollen analysis. Since many pollens were originally airborne and all are different, identification and counting of different types in sedimentary and peaty deposits can reveal changing vegetation types over time, e.g. from woodlands to grasslands where man has cleared for farming and grazing.

Phytoliths Silica deposits in soil from plant cells, notably grasses. The morphology of the deposits is related to transpiration and so can indicate water availability.

Prairies Longer mid-latitude grasslands found in both North and South America (prairies and pampas). Natural grasslands are a function of 'interiority' (distance from coasts) and wind direction. However, much of the Argentine pampas is only situational climax (a function of species availability), as trees will thrive there when introduced. (See the discussion of grass as climax in Maisels 1993b:51–4.)

Savanna Low-latitude grassland, often containing trees such as baobab (*Adansonia digitata*), acacia and euphorbia. The llanos and campos of South America are savannas, and it covers much of Australia. However, the regime is often referred to as 'Sudan-type', as it extends right across sub-Saharan Africa from the White Nile to the Atlantic. *See* steppe.

Steppe Short grassland, most extensive in mid-latitudes. A belt extends all the way from the Ukraine to northern China.

System   The pattern of interaction between nodes or elements. Nodes can be anything from simple switches to complex sets of sub-systems, such as living cells. A system that seeks out its own energy is alive. Energy is the capacity to do work, and work is the capacity to produce changes of condition, that is, of state or position.

Wadi   An intermittent watercourse without baseflow and thus running only after rains or storms (carrying run-off). Not to be confused with a palaeochannel, which is a course abandoned by a river for geological or energetic reasons (*see* anastomosing). A wadi is more like a large erosion gully than a river.

Xeric/xerophilic/xerophyte   Trees like tamarisk and acacia ('gum', 'wattle' or 'thorn' trees) and other plants such as cactus (succulents) that can thrive in arid conditions. In addition to a simple lack of soil moisture, excessive transpiration caused by heat *or* wind (or both) produces xeric conditions. Thus, pines and marram grass (on dunes) are xerophytes. Responses to periods of intense or prolonged drought can have significant consequences for radiocarbon dating (cf. Chapter 2).

1

HOW DOES THE PAST
ILLUMINATE THE PRESENT?

> time by itself does not exist; but from things themselves there
> results a sense of what has already taken place, what is now going
> on and what is to ensue. It must not be claimed that anyone can
> sense time by itself apart from the movement of things or their
> restful immobility.
>
> (Lucretius *De Rerum Natura*, trans. R. Latham, 1951)

What are the operating principles upon which the world is based? How
do things in nature and society work and how do they inter-react? We
need to know this to make some sense of our lives. For consciousness itself
has a double aspect: self-awareness and awareness of environment: the inside
and the outside world. The comprehension of each is of course highly problematic and answers can be wrung only from their interrelation.

It is easy to see the relevance of anthropology to answering the question
of why the world is the way it is: anthropologists study other societies by
participating in them, so what is learned from one, or better still, several,
helps us to understand others.

But why bother with ancient societies if it is present and near-future
society you want to understand? For this it is surely politics and economics
you need, anthropology, plus a close watch on emerging technologies? What
have long-gone societies got to do with the here-and-now and the Internet?
A lot more than you might think.

In the first place, ancient societies are interesting as a form of anthropology. If we can get a fairly full picture of what any ancient society was
like and what went on there, from that we can learn the same sorts of
things about social organization and human motivation as we can from the
study of living societies: what forces shape them and what ongoing effects
those particular patterns have. In the second place, there is the role of
ancient societies in chains of cause and effect. Science consists of establishing chains of cause and effect – that is, of specifying mechanisms.

In Western Europe we are all at least vaguely aware that the modern
period was preceded by the medieval ('feudal') period, which was separated

by a Dark Age from the previous period of the Roman Empire. Most people also know that the Roman Empire existed for several centuries before and after the time of Christ, which, from the calendar, was obviously about 2,000 years ago. But we know too that 'the glory that was Greece' was a bit earlier than Rome and that one of the major glories of Greece was its remarkably broad breakthrough into rational science, philosophy and drama. But did it not do this on the basis of the newly acquired alphabetic script, and did this not come from the 'Phoenicians' who inhabited the Mediterranean's eastern shoreline (the Levant)? The Levant is halfway between the earlier civilizations on the Nile and the Tigris and Euphrates rivers (Mesopotamia). Egyptians and Mesopotamians had different ways of writing, with the Egyptian more or less pictorial, the Mesopotamian formed by marking wedges in wet clay using a stylus. Could it not be, therefore, that the alphabetic writing that has been so important in shaping the modern world was the outcome of the interaction of Mesopotamian and Egyptian civilizations?

Well, it is; archaeology tells us so. And if this is true of writing, what of other forms of culture, with culture defined as the cumulative intergenerational transmission of techniques (technology), beliefs and institutions?[1] In terms of formative beliefs and institutions, the Near East is the region in which the Old Testament, the New Testament and the Koran were written. This is something that could not have taken place without the prior existence of thousands of years of complex society and the state,[2] and indeed of recorded theological thinking (cf. Malamat 1989).

Archaeology shows us that recording and calculation techniques, which are essential for the progress of complex thought, have their origins around 3000 BC in Egypt and Sumer (Iraq). But this period is also the one when states had just recently come into existence in Egypt and Mesopotamia, so where did the state come from? It arose on the basis of a relatively dense population numerous enough to fill towns and cities. So how did that come about?

The basis was successful farming villages multiplying and expanding over previous millennia. But humankind had only quite recently become farmers – well within the last 10,000 years – before that all were hunter–gatherers. How did this transition occur and, more important, why? After all, farming marks a whole new way of life, employing new technologies and forms of organization, so it could not be a matter of chance discoveries. And anyway farming is both risky and hard, so why bother? What really happened? Did all the game animals die out, or what? The general answer lies in 'process', while the specific answer turns upon the way in which initially small human choices have cumulatively large and unintended consequences. In other words, it is all down to chains of cause and effect!

As we look about us it is clear that we are embedded within everlengthening chains of cause and effect. The origins of mathematics lie between 3000 BC and 2000 BC, and those of astronomy and physics too. The Sumerians developed the positional or place value notation, and, well beyond Pythagorean 'triples', knew the value of root-two accurate to six decimal places. Does this matter for where we are today as I type this into my PC?

It matters for several reasons, one of which is sheer intellectual curiosity concerning origins. A second, and related, reason is that to comprehend the world and our place in it we need to have an integrated mental map situating us in time and space. The spatial map has, of course, to be a good representation of what the surface of the earth looks like in terms of landmasses, oceans, mountain chains, rivers, forests and deserts. This tells us what is where. The time-map is, of course, about what went on, when and where. And without an integrated space–time grid relating events and processes to places, we are left wandering in the kaleidoscope world of myth where we are prey to all kinds of vapourings and fairy-stories. The twentieth century has, after all, been the century of hallucinatory fairy-stories for the masses – in other words of totalitarian political ideologies – intended, after a period of mass mobilization and war, to result in a closed society with a 'final' end to real, evolutionary change.

From a broad understanding of the past, by tracing linkages, we can learn about the processes of evolution, natural and social, to which we are all individually and collectively subject. And then maybe we can do something about it in the here and now. At the very least we will have satisfied our need to know how things came to be the way they are.

For this archaeology is essential. Historical accounts rely on texts and inscriptions. Writing is only 5,000 years old, and even where it survives (and can be read) it is so fragmentary that it cannot possibly answer the range of questions we need answered about the constitution of societies, their origins and dynamics. By going straight to the physical evidence of what nature has provided and what people have actually done – material remains of tools fashioned, earth dug, animals killed, structures built, pottery shaped and painted, meals eaten, and so forth – archaeology both circumvents and complements the partiality of texts. Those anyhow could never deal with early formative processes, such as the origins of farming, or, way back beyond this, to the very origins of culture itself (Knight and Maisels 1994; Knight et al. 1995).

It is, then, the task of this book, by employing archaeology, anthropology and some textual material, to try to answer those questions concerning the formative processes of the four originating civilizations of the Old World: Egypt, Levant/Mesopotamia, India and China.

First we must know how archaeology emerged and why only so comparatively recently.

THE EMERGENCE OF ARCHAEOLOGY AS A SCIENTIFIC DISCIPLINE

There are three basic requirements for a discipline to come into being: the social basis, the intellectual basis and the specific theoretical apparatus of the discipline (the latter is a set of linked operational concepts and methodology).

This set of requirements runs from the broadest and most encompassing – the social order – through the intellectual, to the most particular or technical, and of course back again to the social, changing as a consequence of new inputs from technical advances. Nonetheless, the major factor in social change is economic activity, and it is economic expansiveness which, if sustained, provides the social space that can then be occupied by a broad cultural, intellectual and technical dynamic.

The social basis

The technological package put together in northwestern Europe by the sixteenth century under expanding mercantile conditions meant that technology could expand in scope and develop in depth at an accelerating rate. As it did so, transforming not only the economy but the social order, ideas necessarily underwent sustained development. Empirical and technical information became sounder and denser. As the new knowledge was systematized, old disciplines were transformed and new ones emerged. So the broad cultural basis for archaeology was not just widespread literacy and numeracy, but the whole mind- and indeed universe-expanding enterprise of the post-Renaissance period, culminating in the Enlightenment of the eighteenth century.

The socio-political characteristics of the Georgian period in Britain are, of course, those of the ruling Whig aristocracy, themselves a product of trade (and closely allied to the London 'money interest', or financiers), in opposition to the 'country party' of traditional lesser gentry or 'squirearchy', who supported the Tory Party. A working and liberal aristocracy (Baugh 1975:8–13), Whig self-confidence and therefore openness to new ideas, were a consequence of 'the concentration of wealth and both political and social authority in the hands of one small, unchallenged class, sophisticated, civilised and, except for purposes of sport, urban in its inclinations' (Steegman 1986:xv).

Writing generally of 'the rule of taste' in the eighteenth century, Steegman observes that by the middle of the century antiquarianism had already become the fashion.

> Not that every squire or wealthy nabob who Gothicised his country seat during the 1750's and 1760's was a mediaeval scholar; but

there was certainly, after about 1740, a widespread interest among educated people in archaeology, and an interest in the past became a fashionable affectation.

(ibid.: 80–1)

Like the seventeenth century the eighteenth tended to think of itself as old in time. Only a few scientists and philosophers were beginning to think in terms of a time-scale so vast that the few millennia of recorded history became insignificant. But age now signified maturity rather than decay. Men compared their civilization with historical Greece and Rome, rather than with classical legend and the Old Testament and its uncompromising story of the Fall.

(Hampson 1968:147)

Although the likes of Samuel Johnson regarded contemporary writers as pale reflections of classical authors,

the fire had gone out of the controversy between 'ancients' and 'moderns'. Where civilizations, rather than individual authors, were concerned, most people – for the first time perhaps in modern history – preferred their own age to any that had gone before. Johnson himself could pontificate, in a different mood "I am always angry when I hear ancient times praised at the expense of modern times. There is now a great deal more learning in the world than there was formerly, and it is universally diffused".

(ibid.)

Thus classicism was used in a new unslavish way which had stimulating effects on the built, as well as the mental and natural landscapes. Ancient Greece and Rome, the latter championed against the former by the Venetian architect Piranesi (whose *Antiquita Romane* was published in 1748), provided architectural, artistic and political models for the Age of Enlightenment. One of the Enlightenment's political monuments was the United States Constitution. Logically, neo-classicism became the dominant architectural style.

The elegant neo-classical style and the buildings of Robert and James Adam are well known, especially to graduates of Edinburgh University. Less well known perhaps is that theirs was not a 'bookish' style drawn from Vitruvius and Palladio (or even Piranesi, whom Robert Adam greatly admired), but was developed from Robert's own studies in Rome and on the Dalmatian coast at Split. He made hundreds of drawings in Rome, where he also studied and was greatly influenced by the public baths of Caracalla and Diocletian (Bryant 1992:6). Working with assistants, Robert measured and drew Diocletian's enormous palace at Split (currently occupied by private dwellings) in July and August of 1757. This was published in 1764 as *The Ruins of the Palace of the*

Emperor Diocletian at Spalatro, in Dalmatia, with engravings supervised by the French architect Charles-Louis Clerisseau (ibid.:14).

The pre-Christian Graeco-Roman world was thus no longer filtered through Renaissance rediscovery. In addition to knowledge of Latin and Greek, first-hand experience of its monuments was expected, and was a prime purpose of the Grand Tour undertaken by gentlemen and aristocrats. Such travellers tended just to visit; scholars and artists stayed and recorded, as, for example, James 'Athenian' Stuart and Nicholas Revett, who spent the years 1751–1754 in Athens measuring, drawing and recording (Daniel 1975:21). Their first volume of the *Antiquities of Athens* was published in 1762, financed by the Society of Dilettanti. Formed in 1732, the Dilettanti also paid for the 'first Ionic expedition' of 1764 by Revett, Richard Chandler and William Pars, published as the *Antiquities of Ionia* between 1769 and 1797. In 1766, Chandler identified the site of ancient Olympia. Earlier, in 1753 and 1757, Robert Wood published scholarly accounts of his travels with James Dawkins through Greece, Asia Minor, Syria and Palestine. His *Ruins of Palmyra* (1753) and the *Ruins of Baalbek* (1757) by Wood and Dawkins was followed in 1758 by Le Roy's *Ruines des plus Beaux Monuments de la Grèce*.

As the Industrial Revolution flowed from the Mercantile Revolution over the following hundred years, all manner of things became possible, most importantly the nineteenth-century scientific revolution in which Charles Lyell and Charles Darwin are pre-eminent. In turn they helped provide further *intellectual* space for the emergence of archaeology by pushing back the time-span during which the earth and mankind had existed ('deep time') and which therefore made an evolutionary 'prehistory' of man inevitable. However, the term 'prehistory' was not even used in English until 1851, when Daniel Wilson published his work on *The Archaeology and Prehistoric Annals of Scotland*, though in French it had been used by d'Eichthal in a paper published in 1845 (Clermont and Smith 1990:98–9). Wilson also seems to have been the first to use the term 'archaeology' in its modern form and fully modern reference.

The intellectual basis

From the Renaissance to the Enlightenment, Europe contained a class of scholar peculiar to it, and those were the antiquarians, people who had an abiding curiosity about artefacts as such: who wanted to know who had made them, when, why and how (see Evans 1956). Those artefacts could be anything from henge monuments to barrows, other earthworks, worked stones – anything in fact for which the origins and use were not apparent. Now the usual approach of their time was to scan the ancient authors, preferably classical, for 'answers'. Since, however, few if any of the above remains were actually mentioned in any text, these artefacts were simply assigned to peoples and periods 'known' from ancient authors or the Bible, or, worse still, were assigned to mythical kings and conquests by 'infer-ence', for which read ignorance.

But the antiquarians were not content with this literary-speculative approach. Though they were often ultimately reduced to such modes of explanation, they got out and interrogated the monuments by measurement and comparative survey, and by the collection and association of artefacts. In other words, they provided wholly new and independent sources for the writing of history, and rationalist history at that. For antiquarianism was an aspect of the post-Renaissance enquiry into the world at large, which, associated centrally with map making, came to change qualitatively the mediaeval world-picture amongst the educated.

During the sixteenth century

> triangulation by means of compass, plane table and sight rule (the alidade), became commonplace, with numerous illustrated hand-books to enable amateurs to do it themselves. From hilltops and church towers, or towing measuring wheels along the roads, the recording of Europe's surface passed into the hands of hundreds of surveyors, highly skilled or merely enthusiastic. Distance scales began to be incorporated into maps. Symbols for towns, cities, castles, river-crossings made them easier to read.
>
> (Hale 1993:17)

By the latter half of the century,

> maps had become for the first time [in history], the spur to a rationally grasped personal location within a clearly defined contin-ental expanse. And this source of self-orientation on a flat surface was given depth by the parallel development of *chorography*: the descrip-tion in words of the topography, antiquities, customs and more recent history of the diverse regions of which Europe was composed.
>
> (ibid.: 27; my emphasis)

A major outcome of the chorographic impulse was William Camden's *Brit-annia*, published in Latin in 1586. However, John Aubrey (1626–97) – well known now for his posthumous *Brief Lives (Letters by Eminent Persons)* – and his friend Edward Lhwyd (1660–1708), author of the first volume of the *Archaeologia Britannica* (1707), were probably the first in Britain to study antiquities in their own right (Daniel 1975:19).

Complementary to fieldwork was the collection of 'curiosities' often kept together in 'cabinets'. Collections ranged from fossils and lithics and specimens of contemporary plants and animals to artefacts and coins. Each collection, some of which went on to form the core of our great museums, was as individual as the collectors' interests, pockets and contacts. This spirit of open-minded enquiry where everything is of interest and nothing is excluded because it has no present use is the true spirit of pure science.

This was all part of a broad scientific curiosity conducted by 'virtuosi': people with scientific interests and expertise. There were only a few professional scientists in the seventeenth century and not many until the nineteenth century. Not surprisingly therefore, 'men of science' were interested in just about everything.

In order to become archaeologists, antiquaries had first to become geologists. It was only under the aegis of geology that excavations could be conducted that would produce secure and thus compelling artefact associations within an objective temporal framework. The physical basis had first to be securely understood before human actions modifying aspects of the earth's surface could be realistically interpreted.

Uniformitarian geology, under which 'no processes are to be employed which are not natural to the globe; no action to be admitted except those of which we know the principle' commenced with James Hutton's (1788) revolutionary paper to the Royal Society of Edinburgh. His *Theory of the Earth; or an Investigation of the Laws Observable in the Composition, Dissolution and Restoration of Land Upon the Globe*[3] was the substantive launchpad for 'deep time', genuinely geological, with 'no vestige of a beginning – no prospect of an end'.

In the light of this, but perversely, perhaps because of the furore Hutton's enlightenment naturalism had caused, little notice was taken of the findings of John Frere. Frere wrote to the Secretary of the Society of Antiquaries in 1797, enclosing some Acheulian hand-axes from Hoxne, near Diss in Suffolk, remarking that they were apparently 'weapons of war, fabricated by and used by a people who had not the use of metals', and adding that 'the situation in which those weapons were found may tempt us to refer them to a very remote period indeed; even beyond that of the present world'. Frere had been rigorously careful in establishing the geological context, so the 'situation in which they were found' was really incontestable and the implications likewise.

This letter (reproduced in Maisels 1993a:10–11) was not published until 1800. But in 1816 there appeared the descriptively titled *Strata Identified by Organized Fossils*, wherein William 'stratification' Smith (1769–1839) applied classificatory methods analogous to those used by Thomsen in producing his 'Ages System' two decades later. As Daniel (1975:24) remarked, 'there could be no *real* archaeology before geology, [that is] before the doctrine of uniformitarianism was widely accepted' (my emphasis); and uniformitarianism turns on the concept of 'manifest causes now in operation' (actualism) being those also operating in the recent and distant past. 'Causes now in operation' form a key part of the very title of Charles Lyell's great three-volume work, *Principles of Geology* (1830–3), wherein uniformitarianism is demonstrated. Nonetheless, Lyell, like his predecessor Buckland, was so reluctant to accept a deep antiquity for man (with all it might imply for creationism) that both resisted the association of human bones and artefacts with those of extinct or 'pre-diluvial' animal species. This reluctance held even when the associations were well recorded in secure contexts at Paviland Cave ('Goat's Hole') by Swansea (where Buckland himself found human skeletal remains in 1822); at Hoxne in Suffolk and at Kent's Cavern in Torquay (carefully excavated by McEnery). At the last mentioned, the association was even locked into place beneath a dense layer of hard travertine. Indeed, Buckland prevailed upon McEnery to change his mind on the interpretation of his own excavations at Kent's Cavern. Sadly this induced a mental impasse in the Reverend McEnery, who, beset with the contradictions between evidence and 'acceptable' interpretation, proved unable to publish his reports on the site although they existed in manuscript for several decades (Grayson 1983:76). And when R.A.C. Godwin-Austen declared at the eleventh meeting of the British Association for the Advancement of Science in 1841 that, on the basis of his own excavations at Kent's Hole, 'arrows and knives of flint, with human bones, in the same condition as the elephant and other bones, were found in an undisturbed bed of clay, covered by nine feet of stalagmite' (cited Grayson 1983:77), Buckland still refused to believe it, claiming without any evidence that the human artefacts had been 'dug into' the animal material.[4] In general, those resisting a deep history for humankind used the acknowledged complexities of cave stratigraphy to dismiss everything. Hampson (1968:278) observes that the concept of evolution was a real bogey in the early nineteenth century.

Boucher de Perthes (1788–1868) was of course the archetypal antiquary, and without his decades-long campaign of insisting, in the light of his own excavations in the gravels of the River Somme, that the lithic artefacts found with 'antediluvial' animals were in fact those of man, no prehistory for mankind could be established (Cohen and Hublin 1989). Indeed, the first use of a 'prehistorical' term – megalithic – for specific chronological purposes appeared in *The Archaeological Journal* as late as 1870, and the full vindication of de Perthes' arguments did not take place until the 1860s, which in turn rehabilitated the earlier work of Frere, Schmerling, McEnery and others.

Only when Brixham Cave was excavated in 1858–9 by Hugh Falconer and William Pengelly, with the support of a committee of the prestigious Geological Society of London that included Lyell, Prestwich, Godwin-Austen and Richard Owen (the anatomist and palaeontologist), was the matter favourably resolved in scientific opinion. Though not published in detail until 1873, the status and findings of those involved at Brixham Cave led to a positive re-examination of earlier work, which prejudiced scepticism had kept from general acceptance. After 1860, however, in both Britain and France only those motivated by bad faith (as Lartet remarked) persisted with this false scepticism. By then, Boucher de Perthes had clearly won (Grayson 1983:194), thanks to his 'perseverant and fortunate zeal' as it was put at the time by Geoffroy Saint-Hilaire. Until the breakthrough of 1859, long-standing rejection, as Grayson (1983:207) explains,

> stemmed from the sheer belief that such things could not be. In addition, however, there was the problem that the right person had not made the discovery.
>
> With almost no exceptions, the people arguing for a great human antiquity were not influential scientists whose word alone could convince. Boucher de Perthes was a customs official, Rigollot and Schmerling physicians, Tournal a pharmacist, and so on. Unlike, for example, Lyell, who was trained for the law but did geology, these men worked full time at their chosen professions; their geological studies were done as time allowed.

As in technology, China had made a promising start in geology too. No floods and catastrophes as their explanatory mechanism, but a processual understanding of erosion, deposition, uplift and further erosion by water and wind. As the famous Neo-Confucian philosopher Zhu Xi (Chu Hsi AD 1130–1200) wrote:

> The waves roar and rock the world boundlessly, the frontiers of sea and land are always changing and moving, mountains suddenly arise and rivers are sunk and drowned. Human things are utterly extinguished and ancient traces entirely disappear; this is called the 'Great Waste-Land of the Generations'. I have seen on high mountains conchs and oyster shells, often embedded in the rocks. These rocks in ancient times were earth and mud, and the conchs and oysters lived in water. Subsequently everything that was at the bottom came to be at the top, and what was originally soft became solid and hard. One should meditate deeply on such matters, for these facts can be verified.
>
> (cited in Temple 1986:169)

Similarly, China led in antiquarianism in which great strides were made during the Sung Dynasty (AD 960–1279) but thereafter went into major decline (K.C. Chang 1986a.9). Many works were written during this period, beginning with *Kaogutu* published by Lu Dalin in 1092. Most, however, had a rather narrow focus on bronze vessels and jades. Why did this not broaden out into a topographic perspective and thence, with further advances in geology, become archaeology rather than a limited antiquarianism at the service of traditional historiography and collectors of ritual and art-objects?

The difference, of course, is situational: mere literary talk as against ideas informing action on a cumulative scale. Hutton was a medical doctor and an agronomist. Wilson was an engineer. The society to which they belonged was undergoing the world's first Industrial Revolution which itself was the consequence of an Agricultural and Mercantile Revolution that preceded and accompanied it.

It is thus a historical irony that archaeology came to China through the aegis of the Geological Survey of China, established by foreign geologists in Peking in 1916 (K.C. Chang 1986a:13–14). The members included a Swede, J.G. Andersson. In addition to several geological firsts, he had had, in 1921, in his own phrase, a red-letter year:

> the Neolithic dwelling site at Yangshaocun, the Eocene mammals in the Yellow River, the Shaguotun cave deposit in Fengtien and the still more remarkable cave discovery at Zhoukoudian, which became world famous by the work of those who followed after us.
> (Andersson 1934:xviii)

This was, of course, the excavation in 1929 revealing 'Peking Man' (*Sinanthropus pekinensis* or *Pithecanthropus sinensis* or *Homo erectus pekinensis*) at Zhoukoudian, southwest of Beijing in Hebei Province. Those highly important *Homo erectus* remains disappeared during the Japanese invasion. Meanwhile, in 1927 Andersson's work in Gansu province revealed a large group of painted-pottery culture sites (K.C. Chang 1986a:14). Those belonged to the widespread Yangshao Neolithic culture, and it was one of those, called Xiyincun in Xiaxan, Shanxi Province, that the 28-year-old Li Chi (1895–1979) excavated, making him the first Chinese archaeologist. From 1928 until 1937 he was director of excavations at Yinxu – the late Shang capital near Anyang – and came to be regarded as 'the father of Chinese archaeology', not least because so many Chinese archaeologists were trained there (K.C. Chang 1986a:17).

The specific theoretical apparatus of the discipline

The Three Ages system of Vedel-Simonsen and Thomsen belongs to the third requisite, namely the specific theoretical apparatus of the discipline. Demonstrated in the first three decades of the nineteenth century, the tripartite scheme did indeed provide the crucial organizing principle for archaeology – of necessity chronological – the Ages of Stone, Bronze and then Iron. However, the Ages System could not by itself establish the discipline: after all, a version not much different from Thomsen's appeared in Lucretius' (*c.* 99–55 BC) *De Rerum Natura*, and in China was approached by Yuan Kang in his *Yue jue shu*.

However indispensable such a classification was, it was not yet sufficient. For that to happen, as with any science, there would have to be experiments – in our case actual excavations – in the doing of which substantive information on prehistory and history would emerge. In gaining this knowledge, the methodological limitations and errors would become apparent and could be addressed. Additionally, since a theory is but a structure of linked operational concepts specifying the components of a mechanism, some necessary concepts could be derived from other disciplines, notably anthropology, geography and history, as they also developed, all of which would take time (for a full history see Trigger 1989).

The key experiments confirming Thomsen's classification came from the clear Neolithic to Chalcolithic/Bronze Age sequences manifested at Swiss lakeside pile villages. By 1879 the author of the first *Pile Dwelling Report* of 1854, Ferdinand Keller, the excavator of Obermeilen on Lake Zurich, could report no less than 161 authenticated sites in Switzerland, with others in surrounding countries also. And, although metal objects were few, the Three Age System received further validation from Jacob Messikommer's careful excavations, beginning in 1857, of the pile village of Robenhausen by the tiny Lake Pfaffikon, east of Zurich. He used 3 by 6 metre sections, controlled for depth, and kept accurate records of what was found and where (Bibby 1957:247). Gabriel de Mortillet accordingly adopted the term Robenhausen to designate the first period of the Neolithic, and the Swiss sites became a decades-long magnet for visitors with interests in prehistory, thereby serving as a catalyst for prehistoric research in continental Europe.[5]

The first scientific excavation seems, however, to have been not in Europe but in the New World. It was of a burial mound in Virginia, excavated in 1784 by its former Governor (1779–81) and future President of the United States (1801–9), none other than Thomas Jefferson. He

> describes the situation of the mound in relation to natural features and evidences of human occupation. He detects components of geological interest in its materials and traces their sources. He indicates the stratigraphical stages in the construction of the mound. He records certain significant features of the skeletal remains. And he relates his evidence objectively to current theories. No mean achievement for a busy statesman in 1784!
>
> (Wheeler 1954:58–9)

No mean achievement indeed for an academic in 1984! However, as the history of archaeology makes clear, instead of a steady advance on a broad front in the techniques of excavation, recording and publication, in every period from Jefferson onwards it has taken generations for best practice to become standard practice. In archaeology it seems, knowledge accumulation and dissemination have been particularly haphazard.[6] This is particularly troubling in our discipline, because in contrast to laboratory experiments, a badly dug or reported site cannot be restored for others to try again later! Consistency of funding and continuity of personnel are thus essential to good excavation and reporting.

In Europe, classical archaeologists were probably the first to employ extensive stratigraphic profiles, possibly the earliest being Giuseppe Fiorelli (1823–96) who took over from the wreckers of Pompeii in 1860 and began proper excavations, in this following in the footsteps of Carlo Fea in the Roman Forum (1803 and 1813–20). Fiorelli insisted on careful stratigraphic excavation to reconstruct buildings and their uses, and was probably also the first to declare that the recovery of works of art was not the prime purpose of archaeology. Instead he concentrated on the recovery of organic remains, especially human bodies, by filling in with plaster of Paris the forms they had left in the ash deposits. He also recognized the importance of proper publication, and accordingly started the *Journal of the Excavations of Pompeii*.

Plans and stratigraphy were drawn by Alexander Conze who began excavations on the island of Samothrace in 1873. His was also the first site to use both professional architects and photography. Similar standards were employed at Olympia between 1875 and 1881 by Ernst Curtius and Wilhelm Dorpfeld for the German Archaeological Institute, at which site they fortunately forestalled Schliemann (though a French team under Abel Blouet had dug there in 1829).

Of Schliemann, Wheeler wrote:

> We may be grateful to Schliemann for plunging his spade into Troy, Tiryns and Mycenae in the seventies of the last century, because he showed what a splendid book had in fact been buried there; but he tore it to pieces in snatching it from the earth, and it took us upwards of three-quarters of a century to stick it back together again and to read it aright, with the help of cribs from other places.
>
> (Wheeler 1954:59)

Before about 1860, then, excavations were essentially pre-archaeological, and most eighteenth-century digs, such as those conducted at Pompeii and Herculaneum by the execrable Alcubierre, were just plain horrifying.

A doubly promising start was, however, made in India, first by the efforts of Captain Meadows Taylor, an administrator in the employ of the Nizam of Hyderabad. According to Wheeler (1954:22–3), during the 1850s, 'Meadows Taylor dug into a number of the megalithic tombs characteristic of central and southern India, and drew and described sections which preserve an informative and convincing record of what he found, *with differentiated strata*' (my emphasis). Then, in 1862, General Alexander Cunningham was appointed (temporary) Director of Archaeology, becoming Director General of the Archaeological Survey of India in 1871 in order to conduct 'a complete search over the whole country and a systematic record and description of all architectural and other remains that are remarkable alike for their antiquity or their beauty, or their historic interest' (cited in Wheeler 1955:180). Cunningham, though outstandingly energetic and wide-ranging, concentrated on north India and the medieval period. He did, however, make three visits to the mounds of Harappa (1853, 1856, 1872–3), during the last of which he conducted a small excavation and drew a plan of the site (Possehl 1991:6).

Dr James Burgess became responsible for South India after 1874. He succeeded Cunningham as Director General in 1885, but retired in 1889, after which the Department fell into one of its periodic torpors from which it was only awakened by the appointment of John Marshall in 1902 through an initiative of Lord Curzon, the Viceroy, to get things moving. In a renewed burst of energy, Marshall tackled everything from classical Taxila to Moghul architecture, built up an epigraphic department of the highest calibre, according to Wheeler (1955:181), and drafted an Ancient Monuments Act. Most importantly, however, he oversaw the first systematic excavations at Harappa and Mohenjo-daro, fully revealing the importance of a major pristine civilization (Marshall 1926–7). Marshall's three volumes (1931) are the basic literature on Mohenjo-daro, followed by two reporting further excavations from E.J.H. Mackay (1938); while M.S. Vats reported on his work in progress from 1926 to 1934 in the *Annual Report of the Archaeological Survey of India*, publishing his full report of 'Excavations at Harappa' in two volumes in 1940.

Of those major reports, however, Mortimer Wheeler who took over directorship of the Archaeological Survey of India from 1944 until Independence in 1947, wrote scathingly:

> It is almost beyond belief that as recently as 1940 the Survey could publish in monumental form 'sections' . . . the one showing walls suspended, such as those of Bethel, in a featureless profile of the site, with neither building lines nor occupation strata, varied only by indications of the completely unmeaning piles of earth on which the excavator left some of his walls standing; the other showing the burials of two variant cultures floating, like a rather disorderly barrage-balloon, without hint of the strata and the gravelines which would have indicated their scientific inter-relationship. It is sad to compare these caricatures of science with the admirable sketch-records of Meadows Taylor, nearly a century earlier.
>
> (Wheeler 1954:34)

It was, however, the Archaeological Survey of India that promoted Aurel Stein's explorations in south-central Asia in 1900–1, 1906–8, 1916–18 and 1930. It was in 1907, while ranging into western China to the 'Caves of the Thousand Buddhas', that he discovered at Tunhuang a whole library of ancient Chinese texts, one of which – a Chinese translation from the sanskrit of the well-known Buddhist work, the *Diamond Sutra* – was actually block-printed in AD 868. In the form of a roll with a total length of 5.3 metres and 27 centimetres wide, this is the world's oldest surviving book printed on paper. It also contains the earliest woodcut illustration in a printed book (Temple 1986:111). Printing itself dates from the first half of the eighth century in China, the impetus coming from the needs of Buddhist proslytising (ibid.:113).

In sum, by the last quarter of the nineteenth century archaeology was becoming established as a scientific discipline, thanks to the efforts of such leading workers as Alexander Conze, and his meticulous work at Samothrace in 1873; Ernst Curtius, who led the German expedition to Olympia between 1875 and 1881; Petrie's individualist work in Egypt from 1880, and, of course, Pitt-Rivers at Cranborne Chase (beginning on 9 August 1880). Prior to that, digging was undertaken for one of four reasons: to find art for private collectors or museums; to extend the historicity of the wide and deep classical stream in European culture (which Schliemann notoriously tried to do for Homer); or to give substance to biblical accounts, of which, especially since the Enlightenment, educated opinion was beginning to doubt the literal veracity ('biblical archaeology' began, indeed, as the search for 'proofs'); or for nationalistic reasons, with the triumph of the nation-state across Europe in the nineteenth century and the first decades of the twentieth century.

THE LANDS OF THE BIBLE (= NEAR EAST)

Given the importance of the Bible to European cultures, it is then not surprising that the first permanent body anywhere for archaeological research was the Palestine Excavation Fund. The PEF was established in London in 1865 with the full support of the establishment by the amazingly multi-faceted George Grove (1820–1900): civil engineer, musicologist (he launched the *Dictionary of Music and Musicians* that still bears his name) and, of course, biblical scholar.

The inaugural meeting was presided over by the Archbishop of York, who declared that: 'This country of Palestine belongs to *you* and *me*, it is essentially ours. . . . It is the land to which we may look with as true a patriotism as we do this dear old England, which we love so much.' Not surprisingly, the PEF is still very much in existence, with Her Majesty the Queen as its patron and the Archbishop of Canterbury as President. Grove made sure that Austen Henry Layard was present and spoke at the inaugural meeting. This was because Layard was famous in public life and for his campaigns in Mesopotamia at Nimrud and Nineveh on the Tigris, between 1845 and 1851.

Now the presence of Layard tells us two important things: first, that the whole of the Near East, from Egypt to Mesopotamia, was necessarily included in the scope of biblical archaeology, and not merely Palestine itself; and second, that research and excavation beyond Europe in this period were not necessarily or even usually carried out by antiquarians and scholars, but by explorers whose cast of mind is best captured in Layard's own words:

> I had traversed Asia Minor and Syria, visiting the ancient seats of civilization, and the spots which religion has made holy. I now felt an irresistible desire to penetrate to the regions beyond the Euphrates, to which history and tradition point as the birthplace of the wisdom of the West. Most travellers, after a journey through the usually frequented parts of the East, have the same longing to cross the great river [Euphrates], and to explore those lands which are separated on the map from the confines of Syria *by a vast blank stretching from Aleppo to the banks of the Tigris.* A deep mystery hangs over Assyria, Babylonia and Chaldea. With these names are linked great nations and great cities dimly shadowed forth in history; mighty ruins, in the midst of deserts, defying, by their very desolation and lack of definite form, the description of the traveller; the remnants of mighty races still roving over the land; the fulfilling and fulfilment of prophesies; the plains to which the Jew and the gentile alike look as the cradle of their race. After a journey in Syria the thoughts naturally turn eastward; and without treading on the remains of Nineveh and Babylon our pilgrimage is incomplete.
>
> (Layard 1867:2; my emphasis)

So note that Syria was quite well known, being an interior extension of the Levantine seaboard. Someone as early as Francesco Petrarcha (Petrarch), from whose lifetime (1304–74) the Renaissance is conventionally dated, wrote a guidebook to the Holy Land, the *Itinerarium*. The 'unknown interior', reaching through to Persia, began as relatively far west as Aleppo, about half-way between the Mediterranean and the Euphrates.

Layard's pilgrimage originally had nothing at all to do with archaeology, but started out merely as a romantic overland adventure to Ceylon where, after six years legal training in Britain, he had been offered a job in a relative's law firm. Layard in fact made two such 'pilgrimages', described in two popular works – this one from which I have just quoted, namely: *Nineveh and its Remains: A Narrative of an Expedition to Assyria During the Years 1845, 1846 and 1847* (1867); and *Nineveh and Babylon: A Popular Narrative of a Second Expedition to Assyria, 1849–51* (1853) (this latter additionally containing ethnological accounts of Yezidis). Both were bestsellers and brilliantly capture the flavour of those times. If organizing to excavate abroad is difficult now, which it often is, imagine what it would have been like in the days of the backward and decaying Ottoman Empire, when travel was on foot or horseback and transport was by donkey.

Further, it is important to realize just how little *historically* was known of the Near East before Layard started digging, even of periods that were fully historical in the sense that written texts had existed there for millennia. Writing in 1851, Layard gives us this summary of what was then known:

> Although the names of Nineveh and Assyria have been familiar to us from childhood, and are connected with the earliest impressions we derive from the Bible, it is only when we ask ourselves what we really know concerning them that we discover our ignorance of all that relates to their history, *and even to their geographical position.*
>
> (Layard 1867, Introduction xix; my emphasis)

And he sets out what little was then known as:

> A few fragments scattered amongst ancient authors, and a list of kings of more than doubtful authenticity, is all that remains of a history of Assyria by Ctesias; whilst of that attributed to Herodotus not a trace has been preserved. Of later writers who have touched on Assyrian history, Diodorus Siculus, a mere compiler, is the principle. In Eusebius, and the Armenian historians, such as Moses of Chorene, may be found a few valuable details and hints, derived, in some instances, from original sources, not altogether devoid of authenticity.
>
> (ibid.:xvii)

But, whose authenticity could not be checked, still less extended, without excavation. And this despite the fact that northern Mesopotamia formed part of the Roman Empire during part of the second and third centuries. It was not even known that the biblical Tower of Babel was merely a folkloric memory of a standard Mesopotamian ziggurat.

The science of accidental survivals

The city of Bristol has a double connection with Mesopotamia and Persia, for *both* Claudius Rich (1787–1821) and Henry Rawlinson (1810–95), who jointly laid the basis for the work of Layard and Paul Emile Botta, were Bristol men. Not coincidentally, Bristol was Britain's first serious west-facing port, the one from which Cabot had sailed to Nova Scotia in 1497, and a first-rank mercantile centre and a centre for scholarship in the broadest sense.

Rich was appointed resident in Baghdad for the remarkable East India Company (cf. Keay 1991) when he was still only 21 years old, yet he arrived in Baghdad via travels at least as extensive and interesting as those undertaken decades later by Layard. The great pioneers were first of all

17

well-educated adventurous travellers. It was Rich who provided the first collection of Mesopotamian artefacts in Europe. Nonetheless, when deposited in the British Museum, this collection amounted to 'a case scarcely three feet square, enclos[ing] all that remained, not only of the great city of Nineveh, but of Babylon itself' (Layard op.cit.:xxii). However, what laid the specific basis and inspiration for subsequent excavation was the publication in London in 1815 of Rich's *Memoir on the Ruins of Babylon* and his expanded *Second Memoir on Babylon* in 1818 which, according to Seton Lloyd (1980:65), 'virtually exhausted the possibilities of inference without excavation'. They did, however, arouse interest all over Europe.

Nonetheless, it was not the British who first followed up the possibilities, but the French, sending the naturalist and oriental scholar Paul Emile Botta to represent them as consular agent in Mosul. It was he who discovered the site of Kuyunjik, where in December 1842 'the first modest trenches were cut in the summit of the palace-mound' (ibid.:96), thereby inaugurating over 150 years of excavation in Mesopotamia. Finding only some fragments of alabaster and inscribed bricks, in March of 1843 Botta transferred his excavations to Khorsabad, 22.5 kilometres to the north. There spectacular limestone slabs of sculptured figures were immediately, and gratifyingly, uncovered. This turned out to be the site of Dur Sharrukin, built *de novo* in the eighth century BC by Sargon II (722–705 BC) as the new capital of Assyria.

Those finds, which were exactly of the sort wanted at the time, namely spectacular museum exhibits, galvanized Layard. He was at that time employed as assistant to Stratford Canning, the British Ambassador to the Sublime Porte in Istanbul, capital of the Ottoman Empire, of which Mesopotamia, like most of the rest of the Eastern Mediterranean, was then a part. So, early in 1845, Canning put some money at Layard's disposal to allow him to dig at Nimrud, where he was convinced there were other Assyrian palaces. It took Layard only twelve days to reach Mosul (ibid.:100). He began digging on 9 November at the site of Nimrud, which was the ancient city of Kahlu, biblical Calah (Genesis). Located on the east bank of the Tigris at its junction with the Greater Zab, a major tributary, Nimrud was, from around 880 BC, the second capital of Assyria. The earliest, dating from at least the third millennium, was the eponymous city of Ashur. Khorsabad (Dur Sharrukin), about 20 kilometres northeast of Mosul, was built by Sargon II late in the eighth century but was only briefly capital before the move to Nineveh under Sennacherib.

In the very first day's digging two major palaces were discovered on the mound – the Northwest and the Southwest – exposing slabs containing long cuneiform inscriptions and others with inscriptions and scenes of battle. On 28 November the monumental slabs bearing bas-reliefs started coming to light, and from then on it was only a matter of time before the British Museum took over funding in exchange for all the major finds. This sensible arrangement nonetheless had to be pressed on reluctant Trustees by Canning and his friends in London. As usual, the BM was excessively parsimonious, and the amounts allocated did not even permit Layard to excavate to standards he would have wished. Instead he was driven 'to obtain the largest possible number of well preserved objects of art [sic!] at the least possible outlay of time and money' (ibid.:108). So it is not that all excavators of the time were blind to the necessity of rigorous methods; rather, then as now, they were painfully aware of the financial, temporal and political constraints upon them. As Layard himself lamented:

> The smallness of the sum placed at my disposal [by the BM] compelled me to follow the same plan in the excavations that I had hitherto adopted [when financed by Canning], viz. to dig trenches along the sides of the chambers, and to expose the whole of the slabs, without removing the earth from the centre. Thus, few of the chambers were fully explored, and many small objects of great interest may have been left undiscovered. As I was directed to bury the building with earth after I had explored it, to avoid unnecessary expense, I filled up the chambers with the rubbish [sic!] taken from those subsequently uncovered, having first examined the walls, copied the inscriptions and drawn the sculptures.
>
> (ibid.)

And for much of the time he had to do this copying himself for lack of a trained draughtsman or artist. By contrast, of Botta's *Monument de Nineve* (1849–50) in five large volumes, no less than four comprise drawings by the artist Flandin, specially sent by the French government to illustrate Botta's finds.

Botta's Khorsabad sculptures were dispatched to the Louvre in 1846. At Nimrud in that year Layard discovered the Black Obelisk of Shalmaneser III, sculpted into twenty small reliefs covering all four sides and bearing a long cuneiform inscription beneath. It includes a reference to the King of Judah bringing tribute.

By 1847, in addition to confirming the sites of both Nimrud and Nineveh, Layard had 'discovered the remains of no less than eight Assyrian palaces connected, as was subsequently proved, with such illustrious names as Assur-nasiripal, Sargon [II], Shalmaneser, Tiglath-pileser, Adad-nirari, Esarhaddon and Sennacherib' (Lloyd 1980:122). He shipped to the British Museum hundreds of tons of sculpture and the Black Obelisk. Layard's finds during his second season, from 1849 to 1851 are, if anything, more important, for it was during that campaign that he found Sennacherib's library: cuneiform clay tablets covering the floor of two large chambers to over 30 centimetres in depth. Three years later, Hormuzd Rassam, Layard's former assistant and successor, found the archive of Sennacherib's grandson Assur-banipal.

Despite large excavation losses, together they amounted to over 24,000 whole or largely intact tablets (Campbell-Thomson 1929, cited in Lloyd 1980:126). Much of what we know of Mesopotamian arts and sciences comes from copies lodged in those Assyrian libraries.

Fortunately, cuneiform could by now be read. It was, however, not Claudius Rich, but his successor from 1843 in the Baghdad Residency (replacing a certain Colonel Taylor), Henry Creswicke Rawlinson, who was the first to translate cuneiform. And he did this not from clay tablets, of which very few were known at that time, but from a great trilingual inscription carved into the rock at Behistun, 122 metres above the road from Hamadan to Kermanshah, about 35 kilometres east of Kermanshah, in what was then Persia. The Behistun inscriptions are the Rosetta Stone of Assyriology.

The Behistun inscriptions were copied by Rich between 1835 and 1837, when he was resident at Kermanshah as military adviser to the Shah's brother, the governor of Kurdistan. It is a declamation in Persian, Elamite and Babylonian by 'Darius, the King, son of Darius' trumpeting his genealogy and triumphs. As Persian is an Indo-European language, this and the titulary (the proper names and descent indications) assisted translation, so that as early as 1837 Rawlinson had succeeded in deciphering the first two paragraphs of the inscription, and this was sent as a paper to the Royal Asiatic Society. It is from this paper of 1837 and another in 1839 that Rawlinson was hailed as the 'father of cuneiform'. Babylonian, a semitic language, and Elamite, one, like Sumerian, without known associations, all remained to be tackled. But at least cuneiform script was no longer inscrutable by 1840. In 1846 a complete translation by Rawlinson was published in two volumes by the Royal Asiatic Society as *The Persian Cuneiform Inscription at Behistun*. Rawlinson later capped this with his famous memoir: *On the Babylonian Translation of the Great Persian Inscription at Behistun*.

The Rosetta Stone itself, discovered when the Napoleonic expedition was reinforcing the fort at Rosetta in the Delta, was immediately recognized as a major find by Pierre Bouchard, an engineering officer. Taken to Alexandria, French scholars immediately began to translate the Greek inscription, which occurred under two texts in unknown scripts. When the Egyptian campaign was lost, the stone passed into British hands and was sent to London, where the Society of Antiquaries made copies and casts for distribution to scholars in universities. It is now displayed in the British Museum.

Bearing inscriptions in Greek, Egyptian hieroglyphic and Egyptian demotic, this priestly decree of 196 BC 'deals with the honours heaped on Ptolemy V Epiphanes, by the temples of Egypt on the occasion of the first anniversary of his coronation' (James 1983:16). This stela enabled Jean François Champollion (1790–1832) of Figeac to translate Egyptian hiero-glyphs for the first time (1822–4). It was a most fitting culmination of the efforts of the scholars accompanying Napoleon's expedition, who conducted the first comprehensive scientific survey of Egyptian antiquities (as scholars had accompanied Alexander of Macedon's great eastern expedition). Their researches were lavishly published by the state between 1809 and 1828 as *Description de l'Egypt*, comprising nine volumes of text and eleven volumes of illustration, for which 200 artists prepared over 3,000 figures. They were not confined to monuments and topography, but showed the flora, fauna and ethnology also.

The whole project represents a great monument to the Enlightenment, as was the French archaeological work undertaken in Rome during the Napoleonic Wars (cf. Ridley 1992). There had been many expeditions to Egypt during the eighteenth century from a number of European countries. Indeed, one published in 1735 was also entitled 'Description of Egypt': 'containing many strange observations on the ancient and modern Geography of this country, on its ancient monuments, its morals, customs, the religion of its inhabitants, on its animals, trees, plants . . .' by Louis XIV's Consul General in Egypt, Benoit de Maillet, a great procurer of antiquities, but also a considerable scholar.

Egypt had never been cut off from the rest of the Mediterranean and Europe in the way that Mesopotamia had been. Ease of access up the Nile had made Egypt, with its distinctive geography, exotic culture and massive monuments, a favourite tourist resort for Greeks and then Romans. Scholars from both societies also visited and published invaluable accounts: Herodotus and Strabo, Didorus Siculus and Plutarch.

And so, after the Renaissance recovery of ancient Greece, Egypt was the first ancient civilization to be rediscovered. In a sense it had never been 'lost', embedded as it was in both biblical texts and classical authors, the twin pillars of western culture. From the early seventeenth century, Capuchin and Dominican monks and Jesuits had bases in Cairo from which to preach the Gospel. In a scientific spirit, just before the outbreak of the English Civil Wars, the astronomer John Greaves visited Giza and Saqqara in 1638–9. In 1646 he published a description of the pyramids, providing both measurements of them and references to earlier work including writers in Arabic. In 1726, Claude Sicard, the chief of the Jesuit mission in Cairo, who had travelled throughout Egypt and mapped it, published the first detailed geographical account, his *Geographical Comparison of Ancient and Modern Egypt*.

Temples and towns, pyramids and sphinx, the desert and the sown, the river and the sky; fabled antiquity amidst pressing immediacy. The sheer contrasts of Egypt, then as now, were irresistible to tourists as well as to scholars. Unfortunately, the country was thereby also open to vandalism and souvenir hunting. This ease of access by water, plus the ease of clearing away sand or sandy soil, made despoliation of Egyptian antiquities all too easy; not just by visitors, or even by treasure plunderers, but also by natives stripping stonework to build other structures, or by peasant *sebakh* digging, that is, seeking organic material for fertilizing fields. Grave and tomb robbing was also a native tradition reaching back to antiquity. Indeed, toward the end of the third millennium, during the First Intermediate Period, King Merikare of the Ninth/Tenth Dynasty (Herakleopolitan) admitted to his son that he had been guilty of looting tombs, and records of ancient trials for looting survive from more stable periods.

Nothing in Egypt was safe, and this is what prompted the novelist Amelia Edwards to call the Egypt Exploration Fund into being in 1882 (after 1919 Egypt Exploration Society), the task essentially being that of rescue or conservation archaeology. Broad support was, however, gained from the appeal to biblical archaeology, in particular, as the public announcement stated, to excavate in the Delta, for 'here must undoubtedly lie concealed the documents of a lost period of Biblical history – documents which we may confidently hope will furnish the key to a whole series of perplexing problems' (Drower 1982:9). Again the society's sponsors included the Archbishop of Canterbury, the Chief Rabbi, several bishops, Lord Carnarvon, energetic President of the Society of Antiquaries, in addition to Sir Henry Layard, Robert Browning and Professor Thomas Huxley, Darwin's associate.

The immensity of this challenge is what kept William Matthew Flinders Petrie (1853–1942) in the field for over 50 years from 1880, the longest period of fieldwork ever undertaken by any individual (cf. Drower 1985).

When he arrived in Egypt, even the official antiquities service established by Auguste Mariette was still really only interested in *objets d'art*, while some few scholars back in Europe were interested in texts. Indeed, Mariette had originally been sent out to find Coptic texts. Appointed Director of Excavations in 1858 by the Khedive, Said Pasha, Mariette exercised autocratic power, 'forbidding anyone but himself to excavate, he undertook far more than he could effectively control', for what his personal control might have been worth. Alas

> dynamite was employed to remove obstacles, and later buildings ruthlessly removed to reveal the earlier monuments beneath. The temples of Edfu and Dendera, and a part of Karnak were cleared; *mastaba* tombs in Maidum and Saqqara were cleared out by the dozen. No adequate record was made of most of his discoveries, and little attempt was made to conserve for posterity what had been exposed.
>
> (Drower 1982:11)

In showing, amongst much else, that sites cannot just be cleared of something regarded as mere overburden to reveal the glories of the artefacts and monuments beneath (as Mariette was wont to do), Petrie helped lay the basis for archaeology as such: that is, as a field discipline and as a branch of historical studies, one where empirical material had to be combined with imagination, and serve as a control upon it to provide genuine insights. For, as he wrote in the opening pages of *Methods and Aims in Archaeology*:

> The power of conserving material . . . of observing all that can be gleaned; of noticing trifling details which may imply a great deal else; of acquiring and building up a mental picture; of fitting everything into place and not losing or missing any possible clues – all this is the soul of the work, and without it excavating is mere dumb plodding.[7]
>
> (Petrie 1904:5)

He did this in part by stressing the key importance of pottery, hitherto only valued if intact and 'artistic'. On the contrary, Petrie argued that mundane pottery, everyday cheap, often homemade stuff, was in fact of higher value to archaeology. It would not form heirlooms, but in its immediate discard and replacement it would serve as temporal and cultural indicators, a view also shared by Worsaae (1821–85), the pioneer of palaeobotany, and by Pitt-Rivers (1827–1900). As 'the General' wrote in 1892: 'the value of relics, viewed as evidence, may . . . be said to be in an inverse ratio to their intrinsic value' (Bowden 1991:3). Indeed, like Worsaae (1849:156) before him, who had also emphasized the crucial importance of context, Pitt-Rivers (1887:xvii) stressed the importance of recording the apparently trivial: 'Every detail should, therefore, be recorded in the manner most conducing to facility of reference, and it ought to at all times to be the chief object of the excavator to reduce his own personal equation to a minimum.'

Further, by seriating pottery into evolutionary sequences, cultural continuity and development over time could be demonstrated, as Petrie famously did with Egyptian predynastic pottery. With their artefact-associations, this can be seen to be a powerful and flexible interpretive technique, not merely a substitute for absolute chronology. To this process of seriation (ardently advocated by Pitt-Rivers) Petrie gave the name 'sequence dating'. Stratigraphic relationships at a particular site are used to arrange the order of appearance of attributes in a class of objects. Similar finds from other sites can then be relatively dated by comparison. Each type in the Egyptian predynastic series received a number between 30 and 80, and the series commenced at number 30 to allow for the integration of earlier material when it would be found (Drower 1985:251–2). However, the term 'typology' seems to have been invented by the 'great sequencer' himself, Pitt-Rivers (Bowden 1991:55), although his later contemporary, the outstanding Swedish archaeologist Oscar Montelius (1843–1921), was also justly famous for his typological series.

Not for nothing then, was Petrie called by the Egyptians the 'father of pots'. As he wrote in 1891:

And once settle the pottery of a country, and the key is in our own hands for all future explorations. A single glance at the mound of ruins, even without dismounting, will show as much to anyone who knows the styles of pottery, as weeks of work may reveal to a beginner.

(cited in Moorey 1991:29)

But although he planned and recorded thoroughly, and published at the end of each season by dint of working seven-day weeks, Petrie did not record stratigraphic profiles in Egypt, since he was generally dealing with single-period sites, and/or ones swamped with blown sand. When, however, he did excavate a conventional tell (mound) site, as at Tell el-Hesy in Palestine (1890), he did indeed draw a profile, grasping 'precociously if crudely' the significance of stratigraphy (ibid.:28). Stratigraphic excavation techniques were introduced to Japan in 1917 by Hamada Kosaku, a Japanese art historian who had studied with Petrie in England (Barnes 1993:31).

We take pottery so seriously now, as an absolutely central component of the material record, that it is hard to appreciate that rigorous excavators of the first decades of the twentieth century – notably those from the Deutsche Orient-Gesellschaft[8] – despite their meticulous excavation and recording technique, nevertheless failed to use pottery properly as a sequencing tool.

In 1880, Colonel Augustus Lane Fox (1827–1900) became Pitt-Rivers, the change of surname a condition of his inheriting the estate of Cranborne Chase from his uncle Horace Pitt, sixth Baron Rivers, who died childless that year. The Colonel, later promoted to Lieutenant General, was now in possession of a property extending over 10,930 hectares and an annual income of around £20,000 (Bowden 1991:31). With prehistoric sites and Romano-British sites located on his own estate, and with the finances to be able to excavate and publish properly, we see the aforementioned advances coming together in his meticulous work. To the rigour of the military engineer he added considerable anthropological knowledge and research in material culture. And, as with Arthur Evans, the excavator of Knossos from 1900, his private wealth supported thorough and thus lengthy excavation with full three-dimensional recording of everything found. Pitt-Rivers' lavish, privately printed volumes are the worthy result (1887, 1888, 1892, 1898).

By the beginning of the twentieth century, then, archaeology as a discipline with its own distinctive and rigorous methodology had been formed. This is not to say that the rigour of 'best technique' was widely or consistently applied early in the century or even during most of it. 'Best technique' is in any event itself a moving target.

Although the pioneers practised excavation that we would not recognize as archaeology, without them there would be no archaeology; and without archaeology the greatest expanse of human experience would remain a blank and we would thereby be even more disoriented than we presently are as we tumble into the third millennium.

SOCIAL ARCHAEOLOGY

Archaeology, as it is practised toward the end of the twentieth century, is social archaeology, attempting to reconstruct from artefactual evidence the configuration of a previous society in order to discover how it functioned.[9]

The lead in this was given by Vere Gordon Childe (1892-1957), the greatest archaeological theorist of the first half of the twentieth century. He was the author of many major publications, professional and popular, and Director of the Institute of Archaeology at the University of London, when in 1950 he published a seminal article entitled 'The Urban Revolution'. It set out criteria identifying the advent of complex, state-ordered society across the Old World in the Bronze Age.

Consciously or not, all contemporary archaeologists use his interpretive criteria in some form. So much is this the case that his concepts have become the 'natural' and 'obvious' ways to think about early civilizations.[10] And it was Childe, after all, who most cogently pointed out that it is not the real world to which human beings adapt, but what they *imagine* the world to be like (Trigger 1989:261).

In what follows I use Childe's criteria as a grid to ensure that like is compared with like in each region examined. For each early civilization I first set out its unique trajectory from Late Palaeolithic to Neolithic, discussing in detail the sites that provide the evidence. From there I examine the Chalcolithic – the period of explosive specialization – urbanism and the rise of the state, in the process characterizing the society so formed.

Finally, in order to summarize what has been discovered and to enable cross-cultural comparisons to be made, I use Childe's criteria as a twelve-point checklist concluding each chapter. A summary table of checklist results begins the final chapter, which could be read with advantage before starting the chapters on specific areas.

CHILDE'S CHECKLIST

Childe's Checklist (1950) for the Urban Revolution, requires the presence of:

1 Cities that are 'more extensive and more densely settled than any previous settlements' . . .
2 Full-time specialists – craftsmen, transport workers, merchants, officials and priests – who 'did not secure their share directly by exchanging their products or services for grains or fish with individual peasants',

but instead worked for organizations that could command surplus from peasants.

3 Concentration of surplus (limited by low productivity) 'as tithe or tax to an imaginary deity or divine king'.

4 'Truly monumental public buildings [which] not only distinguish each known city from any village but also symbolize the concentration of the social surplus.'

5 The presence of a ruling class, including 'priests, civil and military leaders and officials [who] absorb a major share of the concentrated surplus'.

6 Members of this class develop technical expertise, particularly systems of writing and numerical notation, from which emerge:

7 'Exact and predictive sciences – arithmetic, geometry and astronomy. . . .'[11] Calendrical and mathematical sciences are common features of the earliest civilizations and they too are corollaries of the archaeologists' criterion [separating the historic from the prehistoric], writing.'

8 Specialists in representative art emerge – 'full-time sculptors, painters, or seal engravers [who] model or draw likenesses of persons or things, but no longer with the naive naturalism of the hunter, but according to conceptualized and sophisticated styles which differ in each of the four urban centres'.

9 Regular foreign trade, involving comparatively large volumes and long distances, emerges to exchange part of the concentrated social surplus for 'industrial materials'. 'To this extent the first cities were dependent for vital raw materials on long distance trade as no neolithic village ever was.'

10 'Peasants, craftsmen and rulers form a community. . . . In fact the earliest cities illustrate a first approximation to an organic solidarity based upon functional complementarity and interdependence between all its members such as subsist between the constituent cells of an organism. Of course this was only a very distant approximation.' In apparent contradiction to which:

11 This social solidarity is represented and misrepresented by ideological means 'as expressed in the pre-eminence of the temple or sepulchral shrine'.

12 State organization is dominant and permanent.

Criteria 10, 11 and 12 are all contained in Childe's lengthy point 10. As each is important in its own right, to the extent some would say of being pre-eminent characteristics, I have separated them out, so expanding Childe's 'ten traits' to a dozen. For an up-to-date discussion of Childe's life and work see Harris (1994).

Progress will be west to east – Egypt to China – from the world's oldest territorial state to the world's most populous. But before setting off, let me give a specific answer to the question 'How does the past illuminate the present?' Take China for example; or rather, for two examples, one particular, the other general.

THE PRESENT ILLUMINATED: PATHS OF THE PAST, SPIRALS TO THE FUTURE

The antiquity and continuities of Chinese society, comprising a quarter of mankind, are so well known as to be almost a cliché. It should not be thought that China is 'unchanging': its very borders have changed over the centuries and it has undergone many profound changes over lengthy periods. Against this background, however, it is possible to identify strong, structuring continuities which include: family organization; intensive peasant agriculture divided north/south; ancestor worship and nature veneration; social stratification, warfare, and territorial state organization employing literate administration.

Certain key facets of Chinese culture history have their origin in the Neolithic: animism (veneration of natural phenomena) and shamanism; hierarchical family structure ordained by ancestor worship; central importance of family, lineage and clan; and hierarchic ranking of lineages. A consequence was the early emergence of 'lords' with control of people and territory, sanctioned by genealogical rank plus ritual, and defended by force. This form of class domination produced the territorial state in the particular form of village state, an extensive agrarian regime with the bulk of the population living as peasants in villages dominated by a capital/garrison (Maisels 1987). There was not one, but a congeries of states in competition, alliance and conflict even during the Bronze Age. The Warring States Period (475–221 BC) which marked the final breakup of the formerly hegemonic Zhou regime saw interstate conflict, death and destruction on a scale not again met with until the First World War.

From it came three major ideological systems of enduring importance: Confucianism, Daoism and Legalism (though there were nominally 'Six Schools' of pre-Qin philosophy). Confucianism stressed rites and fitting behaviour; Daoism was a sort of nature religion (the folk basis) combined with poetic inscrutability (Laozi's elaboration); while Legalism, developed by Han Fei (c. 280–233 BC) and Shang Yang (executed 338 BC) emphasized harsh measures, including constant surveillance and control, restraining the populace for the greater freedom of the state to engage in economic and military development. This supposedly would result in benefits for all, eventually.

Why was Mao Ze Dong so pleased to compare himself in ferocity, autocracy and anti-intellectualism with the first Emperor (Qin Shihuangdi, 259–210 BC), who burned books, engaged in mass executions, buried intellectuals alive and instituted the *bao jia* method of total social control?

Mao led a party that espoused scientific socialism and which claimed to embody 'people's power'! Saying that power corrupts and that the claims to scientific socialism were just rhetoric does not explain the *form* that post-revolutionary power took in China, or for that matter in the USA after 1776, France after 1789, or in Russia after the squalid putsch of 1917.

King Zheng of the state of Qin was, of course, the unifier of China and an extreme centralizer, as are all totalitarians. It is most significant that Mao chose to identify himself with the first emperor Qin Shihuangdi (at, for instance, a Communist Party Central Committee meeting in 1958) and not with the commoner Liu Bang. At that 1958 meeting Mao bragged: 'What does Qin Shihuangdi amount to anyway? He buried only 460 scholars alive, while we have buried 46,000 counter-revolutionary scholars alive.' And this as early as 1958, well before the Cultural Revolution.

Liu Bang founded the subsequent Han Dynasty (206 BC–AD 220) of 400 years duration, a period popularly and historically regarded as China's golden age, and one whose official ideology was Confucianism, despised by Legalists (Daoism was despised by Buddhists).

In philosophy, Mao and the Communist Party utterly failed to identify with Mohism, the school founded by Mo Zi (*c.* 479–391 BC) – utilitarian, pragmatic, meritocratic and ethical-humanist – insisting on the greatest good of the greatest number through peace, efficiency and economic development. But although Mao's 'dialectics' owed everything to Mo Zi, in practice he identified with and indeed pursued the brutal Legalist principles embraced openly by the first Emperor (Qin Shihuangdi) and implicitly by most sub-sequent emperors. Why? Because, always stressing the 'Chineseness' of his revolution, Mao embraced an indigenous state ideology and practice that emerged from local conditions, rooted in the Chinese Neolithic, Chalcolithic and Bronze Ages. As such considerations still motivate his successors, and as they will have a major say in shaping the world of the twenty-first century, it is as well to understand those origins in some detail. Paradigmatic of a particular mindset or cultural disposition is the fact that the tomb of Shihuangdi is known to lie at Mount Li near Xi'an, defended by his famous 'terracotta army'. Yet no one in contemporary China dare excavate his tomb for fear of offending and unleashing so powerful a spirit!

Further, the scale, complexity and longevity of Chinese civilization can serve as a conceptual testbed for the processes of social evolution. The two centrally dominant Bronze Age states were the Shang (1575/54–1050/40 BC) and the Western Zhou (1040–771 BC). Centred in the Yellow River valley, they existed in a landscape composed of other polities of varying scales and sophistication and all in a state of flux, variously allied to, competing, at war with, or distant from others in this set of 'Chinese' inter-action spheres.

Amidst this, the hegemonic Shang ruling dynasty sent out branches to occupy distant territory. This would, as it were, secure its rear, hold corridors to allies, etc. One such was the site of Panlongcheng on a tributary of the Yangzi, dating to the Middle Shang period (Bagley 1977:168–9). It has a city-wall enclosing palatial constructions on stamped earth platforms, fine bronzes and rich burials with human sacrifice – all the signs of elite residence and territorial control. At the same period, 300 kilometres farther south, the site of Wucheng contrastingly indicates a local culture adopting Shang characteristics. In addition to direct bronze and ceramic imports, high-grade local versions of Shang products were made in large amounts, including high-fired stamp-impressed ware, 'proto-porcelain' and glazed ware (Bagley 1977:211). This is a local elite consolidating its position using Shang attributes, even attempting a local pictographic script inscribed on stone moulds and pottery (ibid.).

Later, 'peripheral' cultures such as Zhou would overthrow the (Shang) centre and for a time become the 'centre'. In its turn, the Zhou centre undertook direct colonization, spreading metropolitan culture and technology yet further afield (see Fig. 5.21). By the time of the Eastern Zhou, comprising the Spring and Autumn (770–476 BC) and the Warring States (475–221 BC) periods, there was only a nominal centre. The landscape was covered by large, mechanistic, fiercely competitive states with similar cultural and technological levels. All of them strove to come out on top by uniting the interaction sphere under their own leadership. As already mentioned, the state of Qin won, and that is why we call this sphere China.

This process tells us a great deal about 'peer-polity interaction' (Renfrew and Cherry 1986). Within an interaction sphere even of approximate equals, there is always one area in advance of others and it thereby serves as a general catalyst within its interaction sphere. For a while it is dominant, provoking others to strive to catch up. In time, one or several areas do overtake, becoming the leading element(s) and catalysts. The new synthesis brings new players into being as its effects spill over into other interaction spheres. Existing players are spurred on to make fundamental changes as they are overtaken by new players in newly dynamized interaction spheres. From this emerges a yet more advanced synthesis which acts as a further catalyst, and so on in an ever widening spiral that first embraces whole regions and then, since the nineteenth century AD, the whole world. Of course the process does not stop at that point, but is played out on a global scale. Indeed, the process is now known as 'globalization', with all that means for international competition and intercontinental flows of information, capital, skills, jobs and people.

One could not ask for a clearer or more important example of how the past illuminates the present.

Table 1.1 An evolutionary classification of sites and cultures from the Nile to the Yellow River

Sites and cultures representative of the named periods in:–

Period and characteristics	EGYPT			NEAR EAST		INDUS	CHINA
	UPPER (South)	LOWER (North)	FAYUM (North West)	LEVANT	MESOPOTAMIA		
LATE-PALAEOLITHIC (Microliths/ compound tools)	Wadi Kubbaniya Makhadma			KEBARAN	ZARZIAN	Sanghao Cave Rabat, Baghor I & III	Xibaijianfang, Xiaonanhai Xiaogushan, Xiachuan, Xueguan,# Daxianzhuang*
EPI – PALAEOLITHIC (Pounding/Grinding tools)			FAYUM B (Qarunian)	NATUFIAN	Zawi Chemi/ Karim Shahir	Chopani Mando Baghor II	Shayuan, Huduliang Xijiaoshan, Layihai, Zengpiyan
NEOLITHIC (Villages, agriculture)	BADARIAN	MERIMDE/ EL OMARI	FAYUM A	PPNA PPNB PPNC YARMOUKIAN JERICHO IX WADI RABA	PROTO-HASSUNA HASSUNA SAMARRA HALAF	Mehrgarh I (aceramic) Mehrgarh IIA (ceramic)	YANGSHAO (Zhongyuan) DAWENKOU (Shandong) HEMUDU (Zhejiang)
CHALCOLITHIC (Craft Specialization, Towns)	AMRATIAN (Naqada I) GERZEAN (Naq.II)	BUTO-MAADI	MOERIAN	GHASSULIAN	UBAID	Mehrgarh IIB-III	LONGSHAN (East Coast/ Zhongyuan) HONGSHAN (Dongbei) QUJIALING-SHIJIAHE (mid-Yangzi) LIANGZHU (Tai Hu Bandao)
EARLY STATE (Centralization of force, cult, and tribute/tax)	PROTODYNASTIC: unification process – Dynasty 0				URUK JEMDET NASR	KOT DIJI, SOTHI & AMRI-NAL synthesis = EARLY HARAPPAN	ERLITOU (= XIA?) LOWER XIAJIADIAN (Dongbei) Sanxingdui (2000–1000 BC)
BRONZE AGE STATES (Writing, calculation, cities, monumental building, warfare)	EARLY DYNASTIC: (Dynasties 1 + 2)			CITY-STATES (Early Dynastic I–III)		MATURE OR URBAN HARAPPAN OECUMENE	SHANG, WESTERN ZHOU (to 770 BC) EASTERN ZHOU
BRONZE AGE EMPIRES (Bureaucracy)	OLD KINGDOM (Dynasties 3–8)			SHORT-LIVED EMPIRES (Sargonic, Ur III, Hammurabic) (BABYLON 1763 BC – 539 BC)		LATE HARAPPAN (Devolution) Castes Develop	QIN UNIFICATION (221 BC) HAN EMPIRE

1) Cultures are shown in upper case, sites in lower case. 2) This is a classificatory, not a chronological chart. Alignment does not imply synchrony. 3) The Levant column stops with the

2

SEMA-TAWY: THE LAND OF THE PAPYRUS AND LOTUS[1]

A great lotus came out of the primordial waters; such was the cradle of the sun on the first morning.

(Hermopolitan creation myth)

THE PLACE

Iteru, 'the river' (*itr-aa*) is Egypt, and the Nile's floodplain is only 10 kilometres wide on average. The plain is a mere 2–3 kilometres wide at Aswan, reaching a maximum of 17 kilometres at Beni Suef, just south of the Fayum, a depression west of the Nile and with an area of some 12,000 square kilometres. The Fayum is Egypt's biggest oasis, containing a lake, Birket Qarun (ancient Moeris), 44 metres below sea level in the northwestern and deepest part of the depression. However, the whole Nile Valley with the Delta can be considered 'an extremely elongated oasis' (Close and Wendorf 1992:63). The area of the Nile Valley with that of the Delta is 37,540 square kilometres. Of 7.5 million acres of arable land in modern Egypt, no less than 6 million acres are in the Delta, the unofficial capital of which is El Mansura. So intensively is the Delta farmed that there is now little trace of the original vegetation, which comprised *Cyperaceae* (sedges) and *Graminae* (grasses) (Bottema 1992:123–4).

It is 1,360 kilometres by river from the granite barrier of the first cataract at Aswan to the Mediterranean. From the first to well beyond the second cataract (south of Wadi Halfa), Lake Nasser now stretches for an amazing 338 kilometres behind the Aswan High Dam. At 6,695 kilometres the Nile is the longest river in the world, the lower 2,690 kilometres being through desert. The Nile is formed from the junction of the White and Blue Niles at Khartoum. The Blue Nile rises at Lake Tana in the Ethiopian Highlands, the White originates in Lakes Albert and Victoria in Uganda. It then flows through the Sudd swamps to join with other tributaries, just south of the Sudanese town of Malakal, to form the main course of the river. Further north, but still in Sudan, the Nile receives the Atbara, a river that also rises in

Ethiopia, which is its only major tributary after unification. As a system, the Nile drains no less than 1,774,000 square kilometres, roughly one tenth of Africa (Roberts 1975, cited in Brewer 1989:70). From Aswan to the sea, the gradient of the Nile's bed is only 85 metres (Baines and Malek 1980:16). There are six cataracts numbered north to south from Aswan to Khartoum.

The sea is now reached by two branches, the western one called the Rosetta (Rashid) branch, the eastern the Damietta (Dumyat); though in antiquity there were three principal channels called 'the water of Pre', 'the water of Ptah' and 'the water of Amun'. Those distributaries form a low-lying alluvial delta (see Glossary, p. xiii). Indeed, so low-lying is the Delta that in Hellenistic times it necessitated the building of one of the ancient world's seven wonders – the lighthouse of Pharos at Alexandria in the western Delta. This is in marked contrast to that of the eastern Mediterranean seaboard, for Levant means 'uplifted', which is how the coastline appears when approached from the sea.

The distance from Alexandria to Port Said at the head of the Suez Canal is 135 miles (216 km). North to south, from Rosetta to Cairo at the apex of the Delta, the distance is a little over 100 miles (160 km).

The Delta was inhabited at least from the fourth millennium onward (Andres and Wunderlich 1992:164), with the western Delta 'characterized by vast vegetated plains free from inundation, settlements existing before the Predynastic period were not restricted to the few elevations represented by sand dunes or levees of former Nile branches', as was generally the case in the eastern Delta (ibid.).

The Delta is the core of Lower Egypt, while Upper Egypt is the long narrow valley stretching south into the Sudan. The junction of valley with delta was in the area of the Old Kingdom capital, Memphis (Hikuptah), just south of the present capital, Cairo (see Figure 2.1). Indeed, there have been two 'capital districts' for proto-historic and historic Egypt. The first comprises the 'Quena bend' area of Upper Egypt, containing Naqada, Armant, Qift (cult centre of Min), Luxor (Thebes, Waset), Karnak and the 'Valley of the Kings' (where in 1922 the tomb of Tutankamun was found) amongst other important prehistoric sites and historic monuments. Hierakonpolis ('Falcon City') lies south of the bend, Abydos to the north. The other capital district lies in the vicinity of Cairo; major sites include those of Saqqara, Helwan, Memphis and, of course, the Giza pyramid complex. Memphis, whose god was the creator Ptah, was supposedly built by the archaic King Menes (Meni, Min) on land he reclaimed from the Nile by deflecting it. There is much speculation about which king in Dynasty 0 the name Menes represents, if indeed it refers to a particular individual at all, rather than to formative kingship in general.

Though alluvial deposition has extended the Delta during historical time (until the advent of the Aswan High Dam in 1970, which blocks 98 per cent of sediment), the Mediterranean shore of the Delta held no

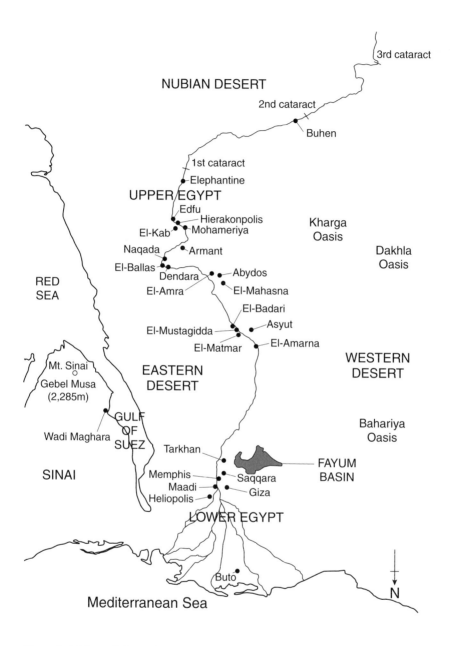

Figure 2.1 Map of the Nile Valley with some key sites

important settlements until late in the first millennium. Earlier ports such as Naucratis, Tanis and the Hyksos capital of Avaris (Tell el-Dab'a) were river ports (Montet 1965:6; Bietak 1975). A partial exception was the sacred port–city of Buto (Pe/Dep), home of the cobra-goddess Wadjet, the most northerly significant settlement and one that was only about 2 kilometres from the sea (Wunderlich 1989:93), later referred to as the 'Great Green'.[2] Tanis (ancient Dja'net) was founded on the highest point in the Delta in the eleventh century BC, supplanting Pi-Ramses and serving as a block against Assyria and Babylonia. Naucratis is the site at which Flinders Petrie, 1884–5, introduced the use of stratigraphy dated by index object.

To the west of the valley proper, whose sides are abrupt and red (*Deshret*, whence our word desert and their word for the Sahara) in stark contrast to the black river-valley soil (*Kemet*, 'the black'; the indigenous name for Egypt), lies the moist Fayum Depression (*Ta-she*, lake land) now about 2,200 square kilometres, at the northern end of which is Birket Qarun lake (anciently the much larger Lake Moeris) much favoured by the Pharaohs for hunting.[3] Farther west and south lie the oases, the 'fields of palm', roughly in a line north to south: Siwa, Bahariya, Farafra, Dakhla and Kharga, with the Kufra Oasis farthest west, well into 'Libya'. The least hospitable 'oasis' was the Wadi Natrun, the 'field of salt' (natron being hydrated sodium carbonate used for mummification, faience and glass making).

Central state administration was organized into 'nomes' (*Sepats*) or provinces; there were ultimately twenty for Lower Egypt (*Ta-meh*, 'the Flooded Land'), while the valley of Upper Egypt (*Ta-shema*) had twenty-two administrative districts, each under a 'nomarch', effectively a mini-monarch sitting in the province's capital city. Appointed by the king, his chief function was the maintenance of order and the gathering of taxes, levied according to the surface area of the nome and the height of the Nile in the tax year. The king, as normal in agrarian society, was the principal landowner, and had estates in all of the nomes. Nomes were symbolized by an emblem on a standard, a banner of territorial identity reaching back to the pre-unification period (See Figure 2.2).

It is well known that the Nile valley was a most fertile land, agriculture needing only the annual flood to replenish it (but not of course to accomplish it). Accordingly, the fields were not 'irrigated' but were inundated, this requiring a rise of river level (optimally) of 16 cubits (*c.* 8.36 metres) to cover all the (previously levelled) farmland. In addition to levelling, the construction of dykes and ditches/canals managed the inundation and ponded water back for thorough soaking of the soil,[4] as illustrated in Figure 2.3.

After fifteen to twenty days of soaking, the dykes surrounding the basins were breached and seed thrown onto the soft ground. Then a man with a hoe or a two-cow-powered plough went over the ground to cover the seed.

34

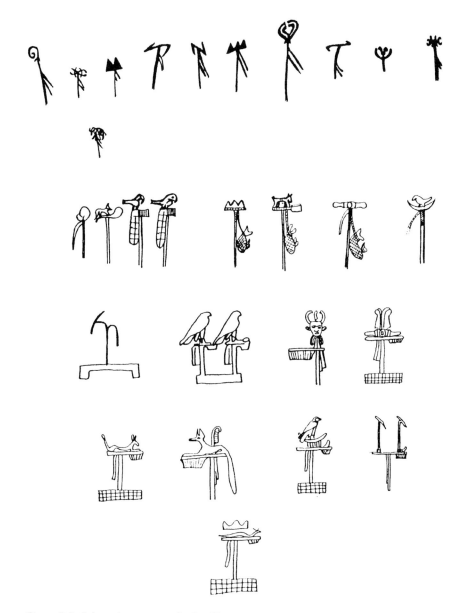

Figure 2.2 Selected nome standards of historic Egypt and possible proto- and prehistoric antecedents

Key: Top row: Late Gerzean 'ship standards'; middle row: protodynastic signs from the Narmer Palette; bottom row: Early Fourth Dynasty nome standards from the reign of Snefru

Source: Hoffman 1979:31

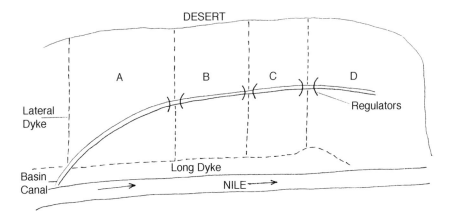

Figure 2.3 The developed Nilotic irrigation system (Late Period)
   Source: After Lloyd (1976)

Additionally or alternatively, pigs or sheep were turned out onto the field to trample the seed in and churn the soil (similar to the cultivation of rice paddy with water-buffalo).

Unlike Sumer and Akkad, there was thus no need for hydraulic engineering and no danger of salinization, so long as the land was inundated each year. Modern dams have, however, brought this ancient problem with them, as well as spreading the snail-borne parasitic worm disease bilharzia or schistosomiasis.[5] This is not just a modern problem. The Papyrus of Kahun (a site excavated by Petrie) dating from around 2000 BC and the Papyrus Ebers both describe schistosomiasis, the earlier referring to blood in the urine, the latter to worms in the stomach, and it honestly states that the worms are not killed by any remedy.

The Egyptian calendar had three 'seasons', each of four months, predicated on the Nile: *Akhet* inundation (autumn), *Peret* growing (winter) and *Shemu* harvest (summer). Thus, despite rainfall declining rapidly from 184 millimetres around Alexandria to only 29 millimetres at Cairo and 16 millimetres in the Fayum (1 millimetre at Siwa Oasis in the Libyan Desert!), flood-recession agriculture was possible along the Nile and at hydromorphic locations such as the Fayum and other oases. Rainfall occurs between November and April, but is most likely in December and January. Lying between the Tropic of Cancer and the Mediterranean, that is between latitudes 23.5 degrees North and 31 degrees North (almost identical in latitude-spread to Harappan civilization), December to February comprises the cool season or winter, March to May a warming period, June to August the hot season, while September to November is the cooling period (Brewer 1989a:135). For all crops, ploughing and planting commenced in October.

Ploughing and planting took place at the same time in the light friable alluvial soils; light enough, indeed, for the ploughs to be pulled by men or cows, rather than oxen (which were also used). Often the seed would be broadcast just in front of the ploughteam, so incorporating the seed into the new furrow without having to go over it again or use something as complex as the Sumerian seeder-plow.

Egypt was rich not only in crops (barley, *iot*, emmer wheat, *boti*, and flax [not cotton until the Coptic period] being the main ones) but also in animal (e.g. hippopotamus) and bird life. Originally the Delta, the Nile Valley and the Fayum teemed with fish and fowl. Later, fowl were reared in great numbers; while fish (notably carp and perch, eel, mullet and catfish) were/are the peasants' main source of protein.[6] Cattle were important, sheep and goats less so, given the limited amount of pasturage available (and the Egyptians' aversion to wool). Pigs and donkeys were significant. Indeed, the donkey (*Equus asinus*) is the only animal demonstrably domesticated in Egypt; the other domestic animals were domesticated in the Near East.

Valley edges supplied any amount of easily worked building stone, namely limestone (of which the cliffs from Cairo to Edfu are largely composed) and sandstone, but harder rock too: granite and basalt. In the deserts around, an abundance of semi-precious stones occurred: agate, amethyst (Wadi el-Hudi), carnelian, chalcedony, felspar, garnet, jasper in red, yellow and green, onyx, rock crystal and turquoise (Sinai) – even gold occurred in the Eastern Desert (but not pure silver, only electrum, a natural alloy). Flint was available along most of the valley, while copper was also present in the Eastern Desert, though its alloy metals, arsenic and tin, had to be imported from further afield, as did obsidian (Majer 1992:230). There were even different types of mud available (more or less organic content) for different purposes, building or pottery. Thus, again in contrast to Mesopotamia, Egypt lacked for little in the way of raw materials, with the exception (here as in Mesopotamia) of good building timber, which similarly was imported from the Levant. Oil, however, was locally available from *moringa* and *balanos* trees, in addition to the well-known linseed (flax plant) and sesame oils. Flax, of course, was the source of the dominant textile, linen, and it had the further advantage that it could be harvested at different times. Wool and cotton (and iron also) are very rare before Roman times, and cotton is not common until the late Coptic Period. Other local trees were the date and the dom palms, sycamore fig, willow, plus acacia and tamarisk.

Transportation of goods (and people) until this century was by boat, since linear distances are considerable and no settlement was far from the river bank. With the basic wind direction being from the Mediterranean, a rectangular sail drove the boat upstream (i.e. south), while to go north one simply folded the sails and went with the stream or rowed. Steering was by a single or a pair of stern-mounted oars, the top of which pivoted on a vertical post. Upstream/downstream were thus the cardinal directions for the Egyptians.[7]

Where it forces its way through the Gebel es-Silsileh, north of Kom Ombo, to enter Egypt proper, the River – *itr-aa* – bringer of all good things, had its vital spirit worshipped as *Hapi*, a naked, green and blue, long-haired, pot-bellied man with pendulous breasts. He is often shown with a bunch of lotus flowers on his head and holding an offering table on which are lotus flowers and libation vases. However, the relative paucity of representations of something as crucially important as the (deified) Nile in the person of Hapi suggests something of the tension between the religion of the peasantry, focusing upon their conditions of life, and state religion, concentrating upon the office of the king, his person and his descent. This tension between legitimacy and hegemony, wherein the king/state must try to incorporate the concerns of the peasantry while imposing their own agenda upon them, is discussed at some length in the final chapter on p. 353-4.

THE TIME

A chronology of Egypt in the form of a King List, based on temple archives, was written by a Graeco-Egyptian priest called Menetho during the third century BC, a period of Greek rule and culture in Egypt. Although the original has not survived (since the great Library of Alexandria was lost), enough remained in ancient copies to provide the basic framework that we still use, though decreasingly and with many qualifications (Kitchen 1987; Ward 1992). Indeed, until the advent of scientific dating methods, absolute dates in the Mediterranean and the Levant could be provided only by comparison with Egyptian chronology, and this in turn relied on finding Egyptian artefacts, notably scarabs (seals made of hard stone or faience) in secure contexts abroad. Conversely, of course, foreign items, Mycenaean or Sumerian, for example, could be found in datable contexts in Egypt itself.

Manetho listed thirty Dynasties (ruling families) and those are now grouped as shown.[8]

Early Dynastic Period or Archaic Period (1st–2nd Dynasties)	3050–2686 BC
Old Kingdom (3rd–8th Dynasties)	2686–2181 BC
First Intermediate Period (9th–11th Dynasties)	2181–1936 BC
Middle Kingdom (12th Dynasty)	1936–1786 BC
Second Intermediate Period (13th–17th Dynasties)	1786–1540 BC
New Kingdom (18th–20th Dynasties)	1540–1070 BC
Third Intermediate Period (21st–24th Dynasties)	1070–715 BC
Kushite (Sudanese)/Assyrian rule (25th Dynasty)	715–656 BC
Saite Period (26th Dynasty)	664–525 BC
Late Period (27th–31st Dynasties)	525–332 BC

Conquest by Alexander the Great of Macedonia	332 BC
Macedonian Kings	332–305 BC
Graeco-Roman Period:	
Ptolemaic Kings	305–30 BC
(Death of Queen Cleopatra VII – *the* Cleopatra)	30 BC
Roman Emperors	after 30 BC

Source: after Kitchen 1991a:14 and Kitchen pers. comm.

The best introduction to the difficulties of Egyptian historical chronology is Kitchen 1991a, which contains a full outline from prehistory to the Arab conquest in AD 641.

LATE PALAEOLITHIC

Wadi Kubbaniya in Upper Egypt, about 12 kilometres north of Aswan, provides by far the best evidence for Late Palaeolithic subsistence patterns. The food and faecal remains from 16,000 bc to 15,000 bc (uncalibrated radiocarbon) clearly indicate that the inhabitants of Wadi Kubbaniya successfully pursued a mixed subsistence, 'broad-spectrum' economy, enabling the site to be occupied on a year-round basis (Hillman 1989:233). The site covers a large area of fossil dunes and interfingering silt deposits about 3 kilometres from the mouth of the wadi. The special conditions at Wadi Kubbaniya are indicated by the fact that this period around the last glacial maximum in North Africa was one of hyper-aridity.

The plant carbohydrate staples were two sedges: wild nut-grass, *Cyperus rotundus*, and the papyrus reed, *Cyperus papyrus*. Wild nut-grass was the most used, though a range of other grasses were available, including those of the millet group, such as *Paspalidum germinatum* and *Panicum repens* (ibid.:219). Although the seeds and nutlets of the various grasses were exploited, nut-grass tubers were the main resource, even providing the basis for a baby-weaning mush. However, since mature nut-grass tubers are both fibrous and toxic, they require grinding prior to sifting and leaching of the toxins, which goes a long way in accounting for the large numbers of grinding stones and mortars discovered (ibid.:227).

In common with later Nile sites, only three large terrestrial mammals were hunted (available?): aurochs (*Bos primigenius*), hartebeest (*Alcelaphus buselaphus*) and dorcas gazelle (*Gazella dorcas*). This must be the most arid terrain in which aurochs have been found. However, the same three species were exploited by the Fayum B Qarunian (Upper Palaeolithic) culture, a period of more intense rains in Egypt than occurs today (Brewer 1989a:164).

The diet was balanced by fishing and fowling, with 90 per cent of the fishbones derived from one species of catfish, *Clarias*. It also accounts for approximately 66 per cent of the identifiable fauna recovered from the

Fayum A (Neolithic) site investigated by Wenke *et al.* (1988). Of the plants, it is important to recognize that none was in cultivation. Hillman (1989:214) is emphatic that 'Claims of pre-Neolithic cultivation at Wadi Kubbaniya can therefore be dismissed, as can equivalent suggestions for Epipalaeolithic Abu Hureyra, Ain Mallaha, El Wad (Nahal Oren) and Rakafet', sites in the Levant (Chapter 3). Indeed, Wenke *et al.* (1988:46–7) observe of the Neolithic Fayum populations that they did not invest in permanent architecture. Their subsistence was largely non-agricultural, relying on fish and the hunt. They suggest that the stability and success of this essentially Mesolithic lifestyle account for the absence of large permanent settlements in the Fayum until the Middle Kingdom.

A group of five Late Palaeolithic sites named after Makhadma near Qena in Upper Egypt has an odd emphasis on burins (mostly of dihedral technique) and a coherent group of radiocarbon dates ranging between 13,380 +−770 (years) b(efore) p(resent) and 12,060 +−280 bp (Vermeersch *et al.* 1989:105–6).

> From the faunal list it is evident that fishing must have been the main subsistence activity at both Makhadma 2 and 4. Hunting and fowling apparently were practised less intensively but the meat yield of each catch, especially of the ungulates, was much higher.
>
> (ibid.:107)

Those ungulates included *Hippopotamus amphibius*, *Bos primigenius* (aurochs) and *Alcelaphus buselaphus* (hartebeest). Of the fish, *Clarias sp.* (catfish) again predominated (Vermeersch *et al.* 1989, Table 2). Blackened shallow pits suggest that fish were smoked/dried, with or without salting (ibid.:111).

As in the Middle East as a whole, the immediate post-glacial climate of the Sahara became wetter as less water was locked up in the form of ice, and wind patterns altered. Indeed, until 11,000 years ago (or somewhat before) the Eastern Sahara was rainless, acquiring moisture only with the Early Holocene northward shift of the summer monsoon system (Wendorf and Close 1992:155).

Hassan (1986, 1988) postulates an Early Holocene greening of the Western Desert also, coupled with high Niles (and thus minimal flood-plain area), forcing some at least of the Nile Valley fisher–hunter population out into the now greener desert to hunt, subsequently to domesticate bovids. Increasing aridity in the Sahara around 5000–4500 BC drove those pastoralists back toward the Nile, there to merge with the resident fisher–hunter population.

Isabell Caneva, on the basis of her work in the Sahara, doubts this model:

> in this perspective, at about 6000bp, the Nile Valley would have been populated by a mixture of groups including agro-pastoral,

bovid herding people from the Western desert, agro-pastoral, ovicaprid herding people from the Levant and local, 'pre-adapted' fishers.

[However] no traces of ancient Saharan pottery from the Western Desert have been found in the northern Nile valley and all the elements indicate that the spread of Saharan pottery towards the Nile Valley, which is dated in the Sudan to about 6000bp, did not reach even the northern oases, but involved only the southern part of the Valley, down to the White Nile, well south of Khartoum.

Conversely, the simultaneous development of the agricultural communities in the Fayum and the southern Delta shows that a strong influence from the Levant at this time interested the northeastern part of the Valley, replacing the previous epipalaeolithic cultures. The chronological sequence of the cultures in the Fayum shows that the influences from the two regions reached the Fayum in separate times, first from the Levant and later from the Western Desert.

The new data from the Delta do not contradict this general picture.

(Caneva 1992:221–3)

Nonetheless, while there was clearly a qualitative transformation between late Pleistocene and Holocene environmental conditions, north of the 22nd parallel (the border with Sudan), Early and Middle Holocene conditions up to about 5500 bp were more moist than today's, then drier thereafter (Neumann 1989:154).

EPIPALAEOLITHIC TO NEOLITHIC

Childe's model of the Urban Revolution was based on the experience of Sumer, treated at length in his work *The Most Ancient East* (1928) and *New Light on the Most Ancient East* (1934). His model of Neolithic Revolution, involving the domestication of plants and animals, was generalized from what was then known of Egyptian experience. For his Neolithic model, Childe took over the 'propinquity or oasis theory' of Pumpelly (1908), reinforced by Caton-Thompson and Gardner's research (1926, 1928, 1929, 1934) in the Fayum. In the generalized model, increasing dessication at the end of the last Ice Age forced plants and animals into close proximity around the remaining water and food sources which were concentrated in the major river valleys of the Nile, Euphrates and Indus. In this restricted domain, mankind was able to get a sufficiently exact knowledge of plants and animals to exploit them by husbandry, and so to avoid wiping them out in such restricted habitats where his own population densities had become high by concentration.[9]

The evidence from Wadi Kubbaniya and elsewhere shows that excellent knowledge of a large variety of plants existed as early as the Upper Palaeolithic. Hunters usually have an excellent knowledge of the habits of their prey, which they spend much time stalking and watching.

Wenke *et al.*'s (1988) surveys and excavations on the northern and southern shores of the Fayum investigated both Upper Palaeolithic and Neolithic occupations around the lake (Birket Qarun), the level of which ('Protomoeris'), raised by 'high Niles', reached 17 metres above sea level at 7450 bp. Between 6950 bp and 5950 bp the lake may have dried up almost completely, for at this time there is an absence of archaeological remains. Recovering to 15 metres at 5860 bp (Brewer 1989a:19), Moeris was repopulated by the 'Neolithic' Fayum A folk. By the end of their occupation of the Kom W site, the lake probably stood around 20 metres above sea level, peaked at 23 metres during the Old Kingdom, and thereafter declined to reach its present level during the Hellenistic period (ibid.). Thus, there are two distinct periods of interest: the Upper Palaeolithic 'Fayum B' or 'Qarunian' cultures of the seventh and eight millennia BC; and, after an interval of at least 1,200 years (Wendorf and Schild 1975) – caused most likely by the drying of the Protomoeris Lake – the 'Fayum A' or 'Neolithic' occupations of the late sixth and fifth millennia BC. This is within the time range of the eastern Saharan Neolithic as defined by Wendorf *et al.* (1984).

The Qarunian occupations are those of small groups of hunter–collectors showing no evidence of cereal use and no ground stone or pottery, the most numerous artefact being a small backed bladelet (Brewer 1989a:37). Even the 'Neolithic' (Fayum A) of several millennia later show dominant fisher–hunter characteristics, with some Neolithic elements appended, notably evidence of cereal use from scores of 'grinding stones' and 'sickle blades', employed almost certainly to harvest cereals, sown broadcast or dibbled into the moist shoreline. The cereals maintained the calorific value of the diet, but the source of protein and calories shared by both Qarunian and Neolithic populations was obtained from the high consumption of catfish, genus *Clarias*, 'the most common animal represented in both Fayum A and B sites' (ibid.:28). This remarkable fish is specially adapted to shallow deoxygenated water, thanks to its ability to breathe atmospheric oxygen through accessory gill structures housed within an expansion of the gill chamber. More exceptionally, this feature enables the fish to be effectively amphibious, conferring the ability to cross land between bodies of water (ibid.:77–8). Similarly, both A and B populations exploited the range of waterfowl drawn to the lake. However, the Epipalaeolithic population ('B') exploited a much wider range, including great crested grebe (*Podiceps cristatus*), a larger variety of ducks (*Anas*), including shelduck (*Tadorna tadorna*) and even coot (*Fulica atra*) (Brewer 1989b:133). Nonetheless, both swan and Egyptian goose (*Alopochen aegyptiacus*) are absent from Fayum B avian remains, suggesting that the record is incomplete.

The 'Neolithic' aspect of Fayum A activities does *not*, however, include permanent housing. No stone or mud-brick dwellings were constructed, although materials for both were locally abundant. Indeed, neither Caton-Thomson nor Wenke *et al.* found any evidence for any kind of permanent dwellings even at the largest site, Kom W, which contained hundreds of hearths in association with great quantities of animal bones, flint tools and pottery sherds (Wenke *et al.* 1988:44).

Wenke *et al.*

> did extensive statistical analyses of the spatial distributions of pottery, animal bones, and other debris, but there is little in their distribution to suggest anything other than temporary encampments of people who relied heavily on fish and hunted animals in addition to (presumably) domesticated sheep and goats. . . . It may be significant in this context that apparently there were *no* large permanent settlements in the Fayum until the Middle Kingdom.
>
> (ibid.: 46)

According to Hassan:

> The earliest good evidence of these early 'Neolithic' or 'Neolithicized' folk is the lower levels at Merimda Beni Salama on the southwestern fringe of the Nile Delta, 60 km north of Cairo, and in several sites in the Fayum depression. Neolithic sites in the Fayum have not produced any evidence for substantial architectural remains. . . . The only evidence for a 'built environment' are post-holes discovered by the Polish Mission. . . . Even at Kom W . . . the largest Fayum Neolithic site, dating to about 4700 BC or 5800 bp . . . there is no evidence of permanent dwellings even though there are hundreds of hearths, basket-lined granary pits, and masses of food refuse, potsherds, and lithic debris. The dwellings were most probably wigwams or wickiups of rounded or oval shape formed of poles overlaid with reeds or mats. Such structures are still common among the Ababda in the Eastern Desert and are sometimes built by beduins.
>
> (Hassan 1988: 147–8)

Although in the Fayum there is no evidence for dependence upon agriculture until historic times, Merimda, a 20-hectare site on the edge of the Delta, shows a succession of occupation spanning nearly all of the fifth millennium (ibid.:151). Early in the millennium the settlement consisted of insubstantial oval huts, wigwams or wickiups (as in the Fayum Neolithic, with which, Hawass *et al.* 1987:38 claim, Merimda was closely associated in its early stages) with the entrances facing away from the prevailing westerly or northwesterly wind (ibid.). Prominent were hearths, which could either be simple round or oval fire-pits, grooved hearths hollowed in the middle to receive a cooking pot, or fire trays above which a cooking pot rested on firedogs or andirons of conical mud.

Toward the end of the millennium, however, perhaps by 4300 BC, semi-subterranean types of permanent dwelling characterized Merimda (also seen in the earliest Pre-Pottery Neolithic of the Levant). This is sunk below ground level, the living floor being a mud-plastered oval pit 1.5–3.2 metres in diameter, with walls made of layers of Nile mud or rough blocks of mud containing straw as binder, and roofed with reed or rushes supported on posts. The houses were arranged in ragged rows, with workspaces, on either side of winding alleys (Hassan op. cit.) and had both pottery jars and storage bins sunk into the ground. The cordiform, flat-topped pithoi, about 1 metre deep and 60 centimetres in diameter had a capacity of about 60 kilograms of grain, while both fruit and emmer wheat were held in the hemispherical mud-lined bins. Also embedded in the floor or placed against a wall was a pottery jar for water. Subsistence relied upon wheat and barley, with sheep/goats, cattle and pigs. Hawass et al. (1987:74) state that this subsistence base, shared with the Predynastic of Upper Egypt at Naqada and Hierakonpolis, depended little upon game, with the exception of aquatic resources and birds. However, the excavations of Hawass et al. (1987:35), though limited, also produced fragmentary (tooth) remains of hippopotamus, and Hassan (1988:148) reminds us that 'the exploitation of hippo must not be underemphasised as a substantial food resource' until of course, like the otter, they were totally wiped out in Egypt.

Taking the full area covered by Merimda as around 180,000 square metres, and using some alternative assumptions, (ibid.:152) estimates put the population of late Merimda in the order of 1,000 to 2,000 persons.

The Badarian

Like much else in the Egyptian Neolithic, the chronology and even the lithic typology of the Badarian are uncertain due to the collecting and excavating circumstances 'of the late 19th Century and early 20th Century investigators who are responsible for the excavation of almost all Predynastic cemeteries' (Holmes 1988:84):

Badarian	c. 5000–4000 BC
Amratian (or Naqada I)	4000–3650 BC
Gerzean (or Naqada II)	3650–3150 BC
Dynasty 0	3150–3050 BC
Dynasty 1	3050–2890 BC
Dynasty 2	2890–2686 BC

The Badari district lies on the east bank of the Nile about 30km south of Assyut. Badarian settlements and graves extend over a distance of 33km southward in the Mostagedda and Matmar region. . . . The survey by Brunton and Caton-Thompson revealed 41 cemeteries and 40 habitation sites in the low desert overlooking the floodplain under the cliffs of the high desert limestone plateau. One site, Hemamieh has a 2 metre sequence from the earliest confirmed Predynastic in Middle/Upper Egypt to the late Predynastic.

(Hassan 1988:153)

Thus, this site has good late *Amratian* (Naqada I) evidence from the early fourth millennium. Caton-Thompson found there the remains of several circular huts, built of mud and limestone rubble, and very likely covered by a domed roof of straw and reeds. Either the roof had an opening or more likely there was an opening between (low) wall and roof, since no doorways were found.

Excavation by Gabra (1930) at the Badarian site of Deir Tasa revealed a settlement of around 5,000 square metres, but the cultural deposits were very uneven in depth, ranging from only a few centimetres to a few tens of centimetres. As previously, the habitations were huts or windbreaks, associated with hearths. Large, well-shaped granary pits of up to 3 metres deep and 2.7 metres in diameter were present, probably for holding barley and emmer, which were recovered from the graves at Matmar and Mostagedda. In striking echoes of the Upper Palaeolithic staple at Wadi Kubbaniya, the Badarians also ate the tubers of *Cyperus* sedges, and lentils (*Lens esculentia*). Layers 20–25 centimetres thick of sheep and goat droppings indicate that they were kept in enclosures, like the present-day *zeriba* (Hassan 1988:154). Hunting (gazelle) and fishing are also indicated.

The shallowness of cultural debris, coupled with the relatively high numbers of small settlements, suggest to Hassan that the sites were occupied for short periods, with large settlements unlikely to emerge here because of the narrowness of the floodplain. As a consequence, he envisages a relatively fluid grouping of population into 'three large communities, each consisting of several villages, hamlets and homesteads', where individual settlements were short-lived, reflecting, most likely, an interplay between ecological and social factors.

Also attributed to the Badarian on 'cultural' grounds are the several sites at El Khattara (Hayes 1984); but the use of blocky, rectangular, unfired mud-bricks for housing and their association with zeribas – hornless domesticated ewes predominating (ibid.:68) – rather indicates Amratian. Even Hayes' radiocarbon dates place these sites within the early Amratian.

El Khattara is a group of sites a few kilometres north of Naqada, on the western side of the river opposite Qus. They lie therefore in the 'cockpit' region on the west bank of the Nile, midway between Qena and Luxor,

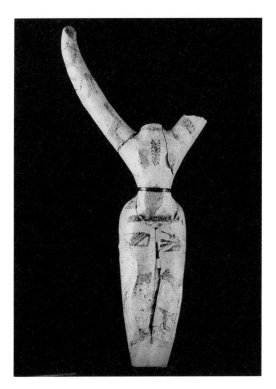

Figure 2.4 Amratian dancing figurine possibly representing/invoking a bird deity
Source: With kind permission of the Ashmolean Museum, University of Oxford

the bend where the Nile takes a loop toward the Red Sea, and from which the Wadi Hammamat leads off due east toward the Red Sea coast. Roughly equidistant, to the south lies Hierakonpolis, to the north Abydos. Location might help explain the perplexity of the findings.

El Khattara sites provide an *average* MASCA calibrated (BC) date of 3715+−25 (Hayes 1984:72) from no less than seven good charcoal samples taken from three mounds and examined at Southern Methodist University and the University of Texas. The subsistence pattern, which included sheep, pig, possibly goat, plus domesticated emmer and barley, with *panicum* and *manisuris* grasses also present (ibid.:69), taken together with the radiocarbon dates seem to put Hayes' El Khattara sites into the Amratian category; but he claims otherwise.

As Hayes reminds us, it is traditionally held that: 'the black-top red "rippled" pottery is characteristic of the Badarian; the white-cross line ware is exclusive to the Amratian; and the Gerzean is characterized by the presence of light-coloured pottery, some painted and others with "wavy" handles (ibid.:72). However, Hayes (ibid.) reports that his El Khattara sites do not fit this scheme: much of El Khattara pottery being a brown 'rough' ware, the burnished pottery usually black-topped red, or, occasionally, brown ware (ibid.). Most significantly, he maintains, no white-cross line ware characteristic of the Amratian or light-coloured pottery characteristic of the Gerzean was found at El Khattara, either on the surface or in excavations (ibid.).

So despite satisfactory dates at El Khattara and only two seasons' fieldwork there (1975 and 1977) which were devoted to survey and the digging of test pits, he concludes 'on the basis of previous ceramic schemes . . . the El Khattara sites should be described as part of the Badarian culture. . . . At El Khattara, at least, the Badarian was coeval with the Gerzean', the differences between them, he suggests, a matter of political organization and social status (ibid.:73).

However, even the anomalous radiocarbon dates affecting Badarian/Amratian/Gerzean classification can now be explained, and its implications go much wider. Hoffman and Mills found at Hierakonpolis that Gerzean dates were falling squarely within the range of Amratian dates from nearby sites. They suggest that in times of heightened stress upon xerophytic trees like tamarisk and acacia,

> they stopped taking in C14 during periods of extreme stress (i.e. drought) but either survived in dormancy for a long time or eventually died but remained standing in the desert. They were subsequently harvested by local peoples and used as construction elements in light wattle and daub type superstructures or as fuel. [This] helps explain the failure, to date, of radiocarbon dating to differentiate Amratian and Gerzean periods at settlements *which are clearly (stratigraphically and seriationally) distinct* as well as their anomalous date on the C-Group site at HK64.
>
> (Hoffman and Mills 1993: 368–9, my emphasis)

As such xerophytes (see Glossary p. xvi) are a major source of radiocarbon dates right across the Near East, the consequences for possible radiocarbon anomalies are obvious. What the radiocarbon indications from such highly stressed/overstressed xerophytes would in fact be dating is the 'normal' period before the onset of drought. Reading from the wood after its subsequent human use would thus give dates that were too early.

Holmes maintains that

> there is no single Amratian [lithic] industry or Gerzean industry; different industries were produced in different regions, and essentially the same lithic tradition would be carried on from the Amratian to the Gerzean in each area with only a certain amount of modification through time.
>
> (Holmes 1988:83)

Hayes (1984:69) reports that lithic artefacts he excavated from the El Khattara sites showed a high degree of similarity. 'Stone tools included bifacially flaked axes, planes, large numbers of burins (especially dihedral), scrapers, notches, truncations, perforators and denticulates. All sites contained the same tool types, but in somewhat different frequencies', although those variations have no statistical significance. And though none of the ripple-flaked and polished flint knives characteristic of the Amratian and Gerzean *grave goods* (my emphasis) was found, 'the El Khattara tool typology shows great similarity with the later Gerzean' (ibid.:70), notably with regard to the most common tool from Gerzean settlement, oval flint axes. It seems therefore that the El Khattara sites span the Amratian *and* the Gerzean, not the Badarian.

During the late Amratian/Gerzean transition, a new rectangular form of dwelling and a new form of settlement are apparent. In a Gerzean grave at El-Amirah, Petrie (1902) found a clay model of a rectangular house resembling typical dynastic mud-brick dwellings, while Baumgartel (1970:484)

Figure 2.5 Naqada I grave goods of superior quality

Key: Right to left: elaborately worked flint knife; black-topped redware pot with incised design; statuette of a woman with her right hand under her left breast

Source: With kind permission of the Ashmolean Museum, University of Oxford

uncovered the remnants of such a house under the temple at Badari. Similarly, Hoffman (1980:129) found a rectangular dwelling in Locality 29 at Hierankopolis (Nekhen) where the ceramics and other artefacts also indicate a late Amratian/Gerzean date.

> The house consists of a roughly rectangular pit (4 × 3.5 metres and 80–45 centimetres deep) dug into Nile silt. The pit sides were plastered with a mixture of mud, mud clods, and mudbrick debris and mudbricks were used for a freestanding wall. The roof was supported on eight posts, two of which were at the centre of the dwelling. The entrance was on the eastern side and shows minor rebuilding connected with the construction of a reed zeriba fence. Features associated with the house include an oven, a storage pot, and an upright pottery slab that may have served as a heat baffle.
>
> (Hassan 1988:156)

In Locality 49A, Hoffman (1982) also uncovered the plans of two adjacent complexes of rectangular houses, with shared walls.

Subsistence showed much continuity with preceding periods, barley and emmer wheat being cultivated, sheep, goats and pigs raised, peas and bitter vetch grown. Fishing is, naturally, still a mainstay (notably of the excellent Nile perch and catfish, and also of bivalves), but hunting is only of marginal importance, perhaps literally on the valley edges for gazelle. Wild mendicago or trigonella were collected, as were the fruits of *Nabq* (*Zizyphus spina-christi*), the jujube tree (Wetterstrom in Hassan 1988:156).

Gerzean or Naqada II

Not only does Naqada II lead on directly to the state formation period, but culturally similar settlements spread from Upper Egypt into the Delta and come to dominate it. Indeed,

> Naqada II forms the turning point in the development of pre-dynastic Egypt, spreading over the entire Nile valley north of Gebel el-Silsila and into the Delta. There is also social stratification and a development of significant population centres, notably Hierakonpolis (Kom el-Ahmar), Koptos (Qift), Naqada and Abydos. It is, on the other hand, the last period during which there was some cultural uniformity extending south of the first cataract.
>
> (Baines and Malek 1980:30)

Maadi is probably the best site illustrative of the Delta culture tradition. As Figure 2.6 shows, Delta culture sites are by no means confined to the Delta. Maadi (No. 8) is located not within the Delta but to the south,

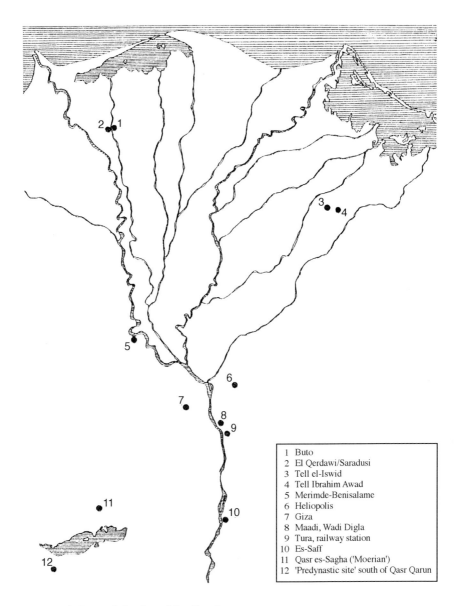

Figure 2.6 Sites of the Buto/Maadi culture
Source: Schmidt 1993:274

on the outskirts of Cairo, and there are sites well to the south and west of the capital. Maadi is a Naqada II period settlement that commenced during Naqada I (Rizkana and Seeher 1984:252).

First, however, something has to be said about this system of periodization based upon Kaiser's system of *Stufen* (using tables of *Leittypen*) first published in 1957. It derives from Kaiser's analysis of a single site in Upper Egypt: Armant Cemetery 1400–1500. Despite its widespread use since then, there are some fundamental problems with his scheme (Naqada I, II, III and its ever finer sub-divisions). The problems derive from, but are not confined to, the facts that from the ceramics of a single cemetery in Upper Egypt a chronological framework is derived for the whole of predynastic Egypt and latterly for the transition to the dynastic period, in the process confounding the cultural with the political. A new and more thorough approach has recently been launched by Toby A.H. Wilkinson (1994–5) utilizing data from eight cemeteries: Tura, Tarkhan, Matmar, Mostagedda, Mahasna, El-Amrah b, the Hierakonpolis Fort cemetery and, of course, Armant Cemetery 1400–1500. Seriating their pottery systematically, building on Kemp's (1975, 1982a) earlier work in this direction and processing his data with the Bonn Seriation and Archaeological Statistics Package (developed at the Rheinisches Landesmuseum), Wilkinson (1994–5:23) summarizes his present understanding in Table 2.1. It incorporates

> Petrie's basic idea that the political chronology runs in parallel with the cultural sequence, without either affecting the other . . . [and it] correlates the individual site-based sequences with national developments and the known sequence of early kings. The bold lines indicate major breaks in the sequence, corresponding to the Naqada I-II and Naqada II-III transitions.
>
> (ibid.:24)

A 'delta-culture' site in what was to become the capital district after unification (and is today), Maadi originally extended for 1.5 kilometres along a Pleistocene terrace between the mouths of Wadi Digla and Wadi El Tih. Both settlement and part of a cemetery have been dug, no less than 40,000 square metres of the settlement having been excavated in the early 1930s by Mustapha Amer, Oswald Mengin and Ibrahim Rizkana. Indeed, its very extent would indicate a multi-period site. Now a suburb of Cairo, Maadi has four reliable, MASCA calibrated dates clustering around 3650 BC (Caneva *et al.* 1987:106). This represents the beginning of the Late Predynastic in Egypt, and falls within the Uruk Period of Mesopotamia (i.e. 4000–3200 BC).

It is not merely contemporaneous, however; there are direct Sumerian imports via Buto at this time (Buto layer 1–Naqada IIb) most notably solid and hollow-headed 'clay-nails' – *Grubenkopfnagel* – pressed head outwards into mud-brick buildings for decorative and protective purposes (Von der Way 1991:55–6). At Buto during Naqada IIa/b-IIc, 'we encounter Mesopotamian influence upon the building(s) with mosaic decoration and

Table 2.1 A new cultural and political chronology for the Pre-Dynastic–Early Dynastic transition as derived from the seriations

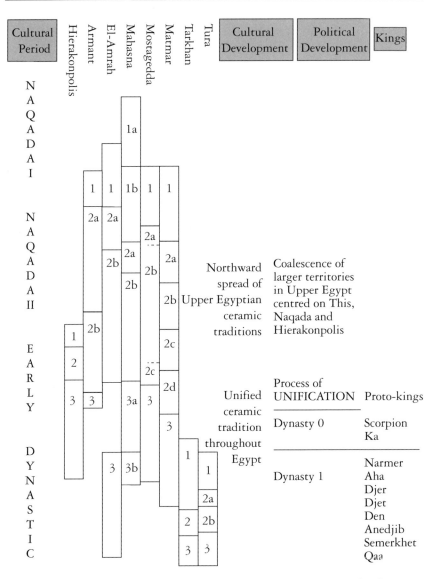

Note: 'Early Dynastic' in the first column is equivalent to Naqada III. Cf. Table 2.2.
Source: Wilkinson 1994–5:23.

niched facade' (Von der Way 1992a:5). Indeed, he suggests (1992b:220) a direct presence of Mesopotamians in Egypt that was earlier than usually supposed: not during Late Uruk/Jemdet Nasr, but when the colonies on the Balikh, Habur and Upper Euphrates *floruit*, namely the Middle Uruk periods (Eanna VIII-VI).

Gerzean pottery types are found at Maadi, and Maadi-ware has also been recovered from es-Saf, 50 kilometres south of Cairo (ibid.). This is 'usually either black, brown, or reddish with grit and organic temper, or with grit temper only, covered with a red slip' (Rizkana and Seeher 1984:238).

The centre of Maadi consisted of both underground houses ('probably intended for communal use'; Caneva *et al.* 1987:107) and flimsy post houses, surrounding which was a periphery of 'commercial' structures, namely silos and storage shelters. Hassan concludes that

> there is overwhelming evidence that the site had active and strong contacts with Palestine and Syria and that, indeed, it may have provided accommodation for 'merchants' from there. This is indicated by cavelike subterranean dwellings unknown in Egypt but well attested in Palestine and by huge, burial store-jars also alien to Egyptian practices. . . . The separation of the stores and magazines from the dwellings suggest a commercial enterprise. The size of the stores is unmatched by any other site in Egypt.
>
> (Hassan 1988:160–1)

Copper was found in the form of a poor copper ore, as ingots and as manufactured items: small pins, chisels, fishhooks and pieces of wire (Rizkana and Seeher 1984:238). Only two copper axes were recovered. Remarking on a distinct trade orientation, Caneva *et al.* (1989:291–2) observe that 'the Maadi site reveals a marked craft specialization in different sectors of activity such as metallurgy, lithic industry, stone vase production and, above all, pottery manufacturing'.

Caneva *et al.* (1987:106; 1989:288–9) have also recovered a wide range of cereals from around 380 square metres, about all of the site that remained undisturbed. They included einkorn (*Triticum monococcum*), emmer (*Triticum dicoccum*), hexaploid or bread wheat (*Triticum aestivum*), spelt (*Triticum spelta*), and cultivated barley (*Hordeum vulgare*), plus lentils and peas. Large quantities of animal bones, with more than 15,000 so far identified, plus horn, skin and hair have also been found. Those come overwhelmingly from domesticated sheep and goats, cattle, pigs, donkeys and dogs; wild animal bones were rare (Caneva *et al.* 1987:107), but fish, turtle and bird remains were not. Furthermore, remains of donkey found here are the earliest for domesticated donkey anywhere in Africa (Caneva *et al.* 1989:289).

The Palestinian connection is certain at Maadi, as are links to the Upper Euphrates, for there occurs at Maadi late-Uruk-style fan scrapers of tabular flint, according to Caneva. This has nothing in common with the Maadi toolkit, which is never made of tabular flint, but consists 'mostly of borers and scrapers made on flakes and blades struck from fairly small pebbles' (Caneva *et al.* 1989:291). However, the fan scrapers at Maadi are most likely to be Ghassulian (Palestinian Chalcolithic).

Furthermore, at Buto there are many examples of North Syrian Amuq F phase, 'spiral reserved slip', wheel-made ware (Kohler 1992:201), with the presence of pots characteristic of the Palestinian Chalcolithic and EB I period. Those are 'relatively tall vases with a wide flat base, a globular body and a more or less pronounced neck, and furnished with lug or ledge handles, better named as "wavy-handled jars"' (Rizkana and Seeher 1984:238). They are light coloured, mostly yellowish to light red and contain a large amount of grit temper (ibid.). Recent work in the interior highlands of Palestine – an area best suited to horticulture – demonstrates that those settlements were already established during Palestinian EBIA (eastern part of the central hill country) and EBIB (western flank, including Samaria) (Finkelstein and Gophna 1993:14). This specialization, in a hill zone without enough flat land for grain growing, was in the production of olives and grapes, a process referred to by Finkelstein and Gophna (op. cit.) as 'the indust-rialization of the orchards' products [which] came only during EBI'. Although Egyptian overland trade to Palestine using the northern Sinai route lasted only during EBI, shifting to sea-borne trade through the port–cities of the northern Levant during EBII-III, the Egyptian demand brought about 'agricultural specialization [that] stimulated intraregional trade [in Palestine] and brought about the emergence of administrative institutions, social stratification, and large market centres', mainly centred in the lowlands (ibid.).

The local pottery seems to be hand-made using a tournette ('slow-wheel') but remarkably,

> A kind of primitive assembly-line was probably used for the red jars. assembling parts which had been made separately. . . . Furthermore, the examples show such a uniformity of shape, size and colour, that they seem to document the first standardized, non-domestic production, probably intended for a specific product and related to an internal exchange.
>
> (Caneva *et al.* 1987:107)

Canaanite pottery with features like indented rims and knobs was also found at Buto by the German Institute of Archaeology in Cairo.

In addition to several types of stone vases, notably in basalt, maceheads of metamorphic rock and palettes of limestone and slate were also found in the original excavations (Rizkana and Seeher 1984:244). Those become very important for dynastic state iconography, where 'representation was a scarce, centrally controlled resource' (Baines 1995b:107). Here Von der Way's concept of cultural assimilation preceding political unification should be mentioned.

In the thirteen seasons of excavations at Buto (Tell el-Fara'in), which seems to have been the capital and principal port of Lower Egypt prior to unification (Von der Way 1991:47), a lengthy process of cultural domination of Lower by Upper Egypt is seen from the replacement of local ware (especially the characteristic fibre-tempered fabric) by the characteristic wavy-handled group, a process commencing from Naqada IIc/d contexts, and resulting, as Friedman (1992a:199) has observed of the Mendes ceramics, in a 'pottery that is essentially identical in shape, techniques and finish . . . found throughout the country by the beginning of Dynasty I'. This registers the total takeover of the north by the south.

Buto stratigraphy has seven main layers, with Stratum IIIa marking the actual transition phase. The transition layer

> is characterized by an increasing amount of pottery made in Upper Egyptian tradition according to its shape and manufacture while pottery of the Lower Egyptian tradition gradually disappears. During this stage, at parts of the excavated area, mud-brick buildings were built while at other parts of the settlement the construction of traditional dwellings made out of posts was continued. The mud-brick buildings at this stage inside the habitation area were certainly introduced by the people of the Naqada culture.
>
> (Von der Way 1992a:3)

The whole domination/unification process is clearly illustrated by Thomas Von der Way's *Scheme of Cultural and Political Progression*, as shown in Table 2.2.

In contrast to Maadi, where the southern takeover – manifested in new hard pottery and rectilinear mud-brick architecture – appears sudden, Von der Way (1991:54) postulates a process of elite elimination at Buto, but of incorporation of the 'commoners'. Indeed,

> sites south of the apex of the Delta come to an end through the northerly expansion of the Naqada culture. For Maadi, for instance, a timespan between late Naqada I and Naqada IIb is evident, meaning that this place was abandoned about the time Naqada culture reached the nearby sites of the Fayum (Gerzeh, Haraga and Abusir el-Meleq).
>
> (ibid.)

Thus it was not only the Fayum that was well populated prior to this. In conflict with traditional assumptions about the Delta being an almost

Table 2.2 Scheme of cultural and political progression

Century	King	Naqada sequence	Process
2900	Adjib Udimu	IIIc$_3$	
3000	Djet Djer Aha	IIIc$_2$	1st Dynasty
	Narmer	IIIc$_1$	Dynasty 0
	Scorpion Ka		↑
		IIIb$_2$	Political unification
3100	Jrj-Hor	IIIb$_1$	
	First king attested so far at Abydos	IIIa$_2$	
3200		IIIa$_1$	
		IId$_2$	Cultural superposition
3300		IId$_1$	
3400		IIc	

Source: Von der Way 1992a:4.

uninhabitable swamp in Predynastic times, other sites in the Delta such as those at Faqus, Tell el-Iswid, Tell Ibrahim Awad and Tell el-Farkha, in addition to Mendes (Tell el-Rub'a and Tell Timai) and those near to Buto itself (Ezbet el-Qerdahi and Konayiset es-Saradusi), indicate a dense population across the Delta in this period. Accordingly, from the fact that the settlement structures, pottery and flint artefacts of the Delta show strong affinities to one another and strong differences from Naqada examples, Von der Way (1991:54) contends that 'those linkages entitle us to call the Lower Egyptian culture the Buto–Maadi culture: there is much more specific to this culture than had previously been known from Maadi only'.

The discovery of trade loci at Buto and Maadi in this predynastic period would normally confirm the prejudices of those who see the rise of the state as triggered by trade or as crucially dependent upon it. After all, the

Uruk 'colony' of Habuba Kabira, on the Upper Euphrates at its nearest approach to the Mediterranean and to its ports, would seem to 'assure' such an explanation.

But not so fast. Evidence from Badarian burials (c. 5000–4000 BC) shows that social ranking and incipient stratification were already present. Wendy Anderson (1992:54) made a detailed study of 262 burials in the seven cemeteries at El Badari. She looked at variables such as size of grave, placement and grouping, plus, of course, grave goods, to see whether they were randomly distributed or exhibited some pattern. Being statistically able to dismiss the 'null hypothesis' that there was no association, she proceeded to see whether it could be explained merely by age or sex differences. This too did not adequately explain the patterning, and in her own words:

> The discovery that the dispersion of grave goods amongst the Badarian graves is non-random; the finding that 35 of the grave occupants had been entombed with more than ten grave goods each, while ninety had received only one burial offering and fifty-one had received none; the discovery that there was an association between the number of burial goods recovered from the various tombs and (a) the sizes of graves, (b) the condition of graves and (c) grave occupants listed as 'subadults'; the finding that the data do not indicate an association between the sex of a grave occupant and the number of grave goods retrieved from any particular grave; the detection of difference in the quantity and quality of grave offerings both *between* and *within* cemeteries; the detection that the most richly furnished graves were restricted to a minority of the mortuary population, and furthermore that such tombs were subject to plundering [during the Badarian!] – all may be interpreted as a manifestation of the unequal distribution of material wealth amongst the grave occupants and thus an indication of differential access to resources.
>
> (ibid.:61, original emphasis)

The resources may only have been those appropriate to rank rather than class, but Anderson's analysis does tend to support Park's hypothesis (below), that natural and human ecology under a chaotic flooding regime will tend to see ranking (hierarchy of access) instituted early to secure the livelihood of a 'core' population.

Following on from the work of Kathryn Bard (1988, 1989) at Armant – a site on the west bank of the Nile in Upper Egypt between Hierakonpolis and Naqada – Griswold (1992), on the basis of Mond and Myers' (1937) excavation data, used grave volumes as a measure of labour expended and thus of social inequality during Predynastic/Early Dynastic phases. A principal advantage of comparing grave volumes is that they are hardly affected by grave robbing. Lorenz Curves/Gini Indexes were used to provide invariant measures from the raw data.

Plotting this from Ic to IIIa–3c, Griswold (1992:196) observes that

> one can see the apparent jump in inequality at the end of the Predynastic when Dynasty I graves, especially 1207 and 1208, are added in. . . . This analysis also supports Bard's conclusion that social stratification did not increase in complexity beyond simple ranked population until very late [Bard 1988:53–54]

that is, until the 'dynastic takeover' occurred. Armant, a farming village located between the power centres of Naqada and Hierakonpolis, actually experienced an overall decline in inequality from period Ic onwards, as elite functions and personnel were concentrated in the major centres. Indeed, the graphed line reaches a low point at period IIIa, just before shooting up almost vertically toward IIIc (Griswold op. cit.: Fig. 2).

The dynastic process

Gunter Dreyer (1992a:295) excavated Cemetery U at Abydos – an elite burial ground from Naqada IId onward. Abydos is the third formative power centre, along with Hierakonpolis and Naqada (Nubt) itself (cf. Payne 1992). The most imposing tomb discovered was U-j, a twelve-chambered tomb measuring 9.1 by 7.3 metres, brick lined and expensively roofed with wooden beams, mud-bricks and matwork. Three types of pots were discovered in U-j:

1   Egyptian wavy-handled pots (Petrie's type W 50/51), containing oil and fat;
2   rough Nile-silt ware: beer jars, bread moulds and plates;
3   imported Canaanite jars originally for shipping wine.

There are more than 400 Canaanite pots of a form specialized for the export trade.

Tomb U-j seems to have belonged to a 'King Scorpion' preceding the Dynasty 0 King Scorpion (II) of the famous macehead (Figure 2.7 below).

Traditional Egyptian accounts, such as are contained in the text called the *Memphite Theology* (*Shabaka Stone*), spoke of (the falcon god) Horus as the ruler of Lower Egypt, while his brother (the jackal god) Seth ruled Upper Egypt. Partly on account of their quarrels and partly because Horus was 'the son of the firstborn son', Seth's portion was given by Geb (lord of gods) to Horus and Upper and Lower Egypt were thereby united. Scholars have seen in this a mythic representation of the conquest of Upper by Lower Egypt, and Menes as the king who first achieved this to become the first dynast. Certainly Horus is unambiguously associated with Early Dynastic kingship; Horus did not just 'stand for' the king, the king was Horus, or as John Baines (1995b:123) put it, 'manifested Horus'. For things are not so simple as they used to be in the realm of 'divine kingship' or in the field of territorial unification.

The consensus of modern Egyptology (O'Connor and Silverman 1995:xxv) is that the king, known to be just a human being, gained divinity from his supreme office, which was the embodiment of the divine state (there being no separate term for the state in Egyptian), while as a person he functioned as prime ritualist, mediating between heaven and earth.[10] The office accordingly embodied and transmitted order itself, and such a constraining power (over chaos) was obviously a transcendental power. As O'Connor and Silverman eloquently put it:

> When the king took part in the roles of his office, especially in rituals and ceremonies, his being became suffused with the same divinity manifest in his office and the gods themselves. With this capacity, the king would be empowered to carry out the actual and symbolic acts that contributed to the maintenance and rebirth of cosmos. Indeed, in these contexts, the king acted as a creator deity and *became* the sun-god. On these occasions pharaoh would be recognized by those who saw him as imbued with divinity, characteristically radiant and giving off a fragrant aroma.
>
> (ibid.)

Unity of Egypt as a whole was represented by the wearing – first perhaps by Narmer – of two crowns (often shown as hieroglyphs), the red of the Delta and the white of Upper Egypt, two thrones at key ceremonies, the intertwining of two animals, and so forth.

In this game of dualities, the king was portrayed as the pivotal player in a cosmic balancing act of order against chaos, the known against the unknown, the green ribbon against the red desert, the domestic against the wild and insiders against outsiders, such that the Pharaoh could be seen as the 'master of all polarities'. Early Dynastic kings even had two names which could be used independently, the principal one of which was known as his 'Horus name', an epithet or title assumed on coming to the throne (Baines 1995b:122). It was contained in a cartouche representing the (niched facade of a) palace, indicating 'Horus in the Palace' (*serekh*). During the third millennium another four names were acquired, one being the dual or 'Two Ladies' title (*nebty*), which referred to protection by goddesses at either end of the country: Nekhbet of Hierakonpolis and Wadjet of Buto (Baines 1995b:127). A third title was what later became known as the 'Golden Horus' name, probably referring to the sunlit sky. Another cartouched title was an oval representing the universe and suggesting the king's central place in it. With the addition of yet another cartouche in the Fifth Dynasty, the king had acquired five titled names.

Thus, Tuthmosis I of the Eighteenth Dynasty bore the titles: 'The Falcon, Mighty-Bull-beloved-of Maat; the Vulture-Cobra-who-appears-in-the-Uraeus; the all-powerful; the Golden Falcon, Blessed-in-Years-who-makes-all-hearts-live; he of the (Upper-Egyptian) Reed and he of the (Lower-Egyptian) Reed, Akheperre, Son-of-Ra-Tuthmosis' (the last two in a cartouche) (Montet 1965:42; Kitchen pers. comm.). From the Eighteenth Dynasty too the king is often shown wearing the *khepresh* or Blue Crown, a wrapping of cloth with circular sequins (Quirke and Spencer 1992:70–1).

Amidst all those oppositions in which the king's office was pivotal, the 'two-lands' seen simply as an expression of the distinctness of Upper and Lower Egypt and of their unification under the former, may be more cognitive than historical reality. Undoubtedly the south did come to dominate the north in Early Dynastic times. However, the continuation of the 'Two Lands' terminology may be more a case of 'good-to-think' geographical complementarity (like 'above and below') than a matter of continual political restatement of conquest.

STATE FORMATION PROCESS

The archaeological evidence, especially as interpreted by Barry Kemp (1989) reveals a complex evolutionary path. Rather than there being simply a northern and a southern chiefdom or kingdom, one of which conquers the other, this new view, supported by comparative anthropological and archaeological evidence, posits the Predynastic period of the later fourth millennium as one in which small territorial states (which Kemp calls 'incipient city-states'), centred on a capital town, emerge in parallel, sharing a common culture but competing politically in an 'interaction sphere'. Those are Colin Renfrew's *peer-polity interactions of Early State Modules*, which he developed to model the rise of the Bronze Age states of Greece. In Egypt, the proto-states of Upper Egypt, centred on Hierakonpolis (Nekhen), Nagada and This, come to be dominated by the Kingdom of Hierakonpolis. Upper Egypt then destroyed the kingdoms/chiefdoms of Lower Egypt, uniting Egypt by conquest, as already indicated by the archaeology of the Delta. The *Narmer Palette*, which dates from the Dynasty 0 to Dynasty 1 transition[11] bears the imagery of the king smiting enemies with a mace, and reviewing decapitated bodies. It becomes a standard and lasting theme of royal power from this time onwards.

Scorpion King's macehead indicates that while emergent kingship had much need of force, it could not actually be based upon naked force. Rather, force had to be subsumed within the category of *power*, and this in turn had to be rendered as power-for-good or *potency*. Conquest was involved, but it was not just a simple matter of a series of conquests; the central position of the king, as he moved towards supreme and indeed divine power, had to be rooted in the soil. To agricultural societies, farming success is everything, and the potency of the leader was imagined to assure this. Thus, King Scorpion, a (white) crowned king before the unification of Egypt, is shown undertaking a crucial ritual, that of 'opening the ground' in preparation for the building of a new temple. Such a demonstrative act could just as well be annual, with the king breaching a dyke with a pick or hoe to 'open the new agricultural season' at the recession of the Nile flood (see Figure 2.7).

Barry Kemp (1989:34–5) has located the roots of hierarchy in the very territoriality of the (egalitarian) farming village, which allows 'a powerful urge to dominate [to] come to the fore'. He illustrates (ibid.:33) the process with graphic models, commencing from small, egalitarian communities in competition with each other and in possession of their own territories, which vary in resources from river bank to desert-edge.

Figure 2.7 Ceremonial macehead in limestone showing Scorpion King with hoe

Source: With kind permission of the Ashmolean Museum, University of Oxford

The next step is the emergence at the valley edge of a 'large low-density farming town', essentially a large village, the function of which is to facilitate exchanges across the area, and which also supplies to the whole area services that no village-district could provide for itself, e.g. religious ones. By the third stage, some of those 'farming towns' have become larger, fortified and dominant over the immediate farming landscape. They extract taxes to support an 'urban elite', whose tombs are located on the valley-edge.

This is, as it were, a stepwise view. In terms of evolution, Kemp asks us to imagine

> a board game of the 'Monopoly' kind. At the start we have a number of players of roughly equal potential. They compete (to some extent unconsciously) by exchanges of different commodities, and later more openly by conflict. The game proceeds by means of a combination of chances (e.g. environmental or locational factors) and personal decisions [and demography]. The game unfolds slowly at first, in an egalitarian atmosphere and with the element of competition only latent, the advantage swinging first to one player and then to another. But although hypothetically each player's loss could later be balanced by his gains, the essence of gaming, both as a personal experience and in theoretical consideration, is that the initial equality amongst the players does not last indefinitely. An advantage which at the time may escape notice upsets the equilibrium enough to distort the whole subsequent progress of the game. It has a 'knock-on' effect out of all proportion to its original importance. Thus the game inexorably follows a trajectory towards a critical point where one player has accumulated sufficient assets to outweigh threats posed by other players and so becomes unstoppable. It becomes only a matter of time before he wins by monopolising the assets of all, although the inevitability of his win belongs only to a later stage in the game.
>
> (ibid.:32)

But what if the starting point is not egalitarian villages but ones that are internally stratified from the outset as the very condition of their permanence? The idea of an egalitarian village acting in unity in competition with others is not well founded ethnographically. What is well founded, however, is a 'leading lineage' or family inducing the village to act as a unit, ostensibly in the interests of the whole village.

As mentioned earlier, Thomas Park (1992) has argued, on the basis of Chaos Theory and his own fieldwork amongst flood-recession agriculturalists on the Senegal River (which has a regime similar to that of the Nile), that where the height and duration of floods are crucial to agriculture, and where, as also on the Nile, the extent of flooding is unpredictable ('chaotic'), with year-to-year fluctuations in flood crest elevation and flood duration (Butzer 1984:105), then the sort of flexibility required of the human population will involve hierarchy. This gives the 'original'/best-established families or minimal lineages preferential access to village lands, such that in good years they have rights to the best, which here are the sectors of flood basin between the levees and the lowest depressions. 'These were the prime areas for cultivation of the single annual crop of barley, emmer wheat, beans, chickpeas and other vegetables' (ibid.)

In runs of bad years, there is insufficient land of satisfactory quality (wetness + structure) for 'non-priority users', requiring those family groups to take up other means of livelihood: fishing, hunting, mining, trading, pastoralism, etc. (Park 1992:106). Those so 'extruded' retain claims to land when better floods return, but are likely to be reincorporated as agriculturalists under a double disability: access only to poorer quality or more insecure land, coupled with social disabilities. As 'returnees' they would, for instance, not be permitted the central cultic roles available to the 'true natives', coupled with which may be liabilities to extra tribute, corvee, etc.

Thus, social evolution is like natural evolution, for both require only a source of variation, an independent source of selection, plus a means of transmission of advantageous traits. Here, unpredictably variable river-flow[12] plus differential land quality, present themselves to the human population. It selectively employs aspects of environmental conditions to serve material and psychological ends through a social framework; the framework organizationally and normatively serves to transmit practices found to be efficacious in the continuity of core village lineages.

A way of integrating Kemp's game-theory with his three-step model and Park's stochastic-hierarchic one, is by means of my processual model, which, however, requires more than three levels:

1. Farming villages form as internally stratified settlements with leading lineages which:

   a   compete for prestige
   b   which comes from success in farming, and
   c   which proves the ritual power of its representative
   d   which proves his overall 'leadership qualities'

2. Agricultural towns

   e   form from expanded successful farming villages
   f   compete for the leadership of villages in their hinterlands
   g   fight to control hinterlands and fortify themselves

3. Fortified towns

    h   dominate the landscape
    i   fight for predominance in a given region
    j   their predominance is that of the dominant lineage

4. Regional capitals

    k   the likes of Hierakonpolis (Nekhen) emerges, dominating a region
    l   it conquers other regions of Upper Egypt (Dynasty 0 period begins)

5. It unites Upper and Lower Egypt by conquest (demonstrated at Maadi and Buto archaeologically). That is, the 'Theban' kings of the south conquer the area north of Cairo.

That conquest was central to the formative political processes, while the imagery of conquest was to become central to the ideology of the king's power (= potency), is indicated by the iconography of the Narmer mace-head, his slate palette and the 'Battlefield Palette' from Abydos of the thirty-second century.

The first states were the city-states of Sumer, but the first territorial state was Egypt. No doubt the linear constriction of arable land along the Nile facilitated this at a physical, organizational and indeed military level, with royal armies able to arrive quickly by land and by boat. The large example shown in Figure 2.8, from Naqada – one of Petrie's wonders – obviously had many rowers (cf. Berger 1992).

Topography also helps to explain the peculiar form taken by the central-izing ideology, that of funeral cult and its memorialization of which Hoffman (1979:335) states that 'with the unification of Egypt, therefore, emerged about the royal death cult a series of institutions that formed the central core of the state'. But not only the royal death cult. 'Nowhere are the imme-diate consequences of royal patronage [in the first two dynasties] more clearly reflected than in the 10,000-plus tombs of courtiers excavated by Zaki Saud at Helwan' (ibid.:321). Of course all courts dispense and are supported by patronage, but why did royal ideology centre upon the tomb, the most visible manifestation of which is of course the pyramid, containing both a secure tomb for its builder and a 'public' mortuary temple on the east side where offerings would be made for the king's soul (a multi-faceted entity in Egyptian belief)?

Such 'level 4' explanations (in the Hawkes Ladder of archaeological infer-ence; cf. Maisels 1990:5) must remain conjectural, but a plausible guess (suggested earlier) would invoke the peculiarly stark contrast in Egypt between the desert and the sown, between lifegiving flood and 'low water', between land and sky, between order and chaos. In addition to the forces affecting all agrarian societies – drought and flood, plague and war, feast and famine – the geographical contrasts along the Nile pose peculiarly sharp

Figure 2.8 Naqada II pot – D45B in Petrie's corpus – showing large boat with superstructure and many oars

Source: With kind permission of the Ashmolean Museum, University of Oxford

liminalities or boundaries highlighting the ultimate human liminality: that between life itself and death, with the possibility of further life. This impression would be reinforced by climatic conditions, according to a suggestion of A.J. Spencer (1982:29–30). Since Predynastic burials consisted of shallow circular or oval pits dug into the low desert spurs away from, and higher than, valley cultivation, where the corpse was placed in a contracted fetal position, subsequent exposure of the dessicated but very realistically preserved body could convey the suggestion that the deceased was 'only sleeping', awaiting the right conditions for 'awakening'.

First and Second Dynasties

This is where the Abydos and Saqqara cemeteries, built between 3100 and 2700 BC, loom so large. Abydos (the cemetery site is actually behind it at Umm el-Qa'ab, the 'mother of pots') is located in Upper Egypt on the west bank of the Nile, just after the river does a 180 degree bend beginning at

Armant. It was excavated famously by Flinders Petrie in 1899 as rescue archaeology in the immediate wake (sic) of the depredations between 1894 and 1898 of the execrable Emile Amelineau, a supposed archaeologist, but actually a student of Coptic (Kemp 1982b:71). By contrast, Saqqara lies in the 'capital district' south of Cairo; indeed, Saqqara is just outside the new capital of Memphis built by the kings of the First Dynasty. It was excavated from 1935–9 by Walter Emery.

The key feature of the tombs at both cemeteries is the *mastaba* (meaning 'bench' in Arabic): a large deep pit, the edges of which were supported by retaining walls in thick mud-brick, with internal partition walls also made of mud-brick. At the centre of the tomb was the royal burial chamber cased in costly imported timber, planks of which were also used to support roof-packing of rubble, mud-brick and mud. The effect was to produce a low benchlike building, or rather platform, since the side-retaining walls with their packing projected as much as five metres above ground level. Those above-ground walls were not sheer, but decorated by regular recessing (vertical panelling) and patterning on the brick. Some archaeologists have seen the recessing, so characteristic of Mesopotamian monumental building, as an indication of eastern influence. However, in Mesopotamia recessing (actually building *out* to provide reinforcement by vertical buttressing) evolved from the structural requirements of efficient building in mud-brick, and the same might just as well be true in Egypt. Indeed, the prototype of the structure, as of the decoration, is probably the recessing of matting panels behind the timber uprights supporting them.

The significance of such *mastabas*, quite apart from the valuable grave goods they contain, is that, with their associated temples, they mark the beginning of truly monumental architecture in Egypt, predating the pyramids by three centuries. Starting quite modestly at 103.4 square metres of floor area with Narmer (= Menes), founder of the First Dynasty, the Abydos list provided by Hoffman (1979:270) and reproduced here in Table 2.3 shows floor area to have increased tenfold (though unevenly) by the time of Khasekhemwy of the Second Dynasty (*c.* 2890–2686 BC). His tomb equipment includes the first bronze vessels found in Egypt.

Even larger tombs occur at Saqqara, leading Emery to argue that here was the graveyard of the First Dynasty kings, while Abydos contained their ceremonial cenotaphs. However, as Abydos lies deep in the traditional home-lands of the dynasty, it seems possible that the roles were actually reversed, since a more strictly ceremonial context seems appropriate to a new royal foundation such as the city of Memphis was. This is, of course, only circumstantial; what is not is the presence of the associated 'valley temples' (on the edge of the cultivated land) exclusively at Abydos and absent at Saqqara. Since memorialization of the ruler and his dynasty was the very purpose of the *mastaba*, with family, nobles' and courtiers' tombs clustered around, it was not enough that pre-eminence be marked by sumptuous grave goods

Table 2.3 List and comparative sizes of royal tombs found by Petrie at Abydos

Ruler's Horus[1] (Throne) name	*Principal variants of name*	*Petrie's tomb designation*	*Dynasty*	*Total floor area (sq.m.) (After Reisner 1936)*
Narmer	Narmer	B-10	O	103.4
Aha	Aha-Mena,[1]	B-19	I	110.0
	Aha Menes,[2]		I	
	Hor-aha[3]		I	
Djer	Zer[1]	O		311.1 (or 313.0)
	(Queen) Merneit,[1]	Y		229.0
	Merneith,[2]			
	Meryet-nit[3]		I	
Wadji	Zet[1], Uadji,[3]Djet[4]	Z	I	158.7
De(we)n	Den,[1] Wedymuw,[2]	T		341.6 (or 346.0)
	Udimu[3]			
Anedjib	Azab,[1] Az-ib,[2]	X	I	109.0
	Enezib-Merbapen[3]			
Semerkhet	Mersekha[1]	U	I	209.0
Qaa	Qa,[1] Qay'a,[2] Ka'a,[3]	Q	I	385.9 (or 369.0)
Peribsen	Perabsen-Sekhemib[3]	P	II	270.0
Khasekhemwy (Khasekhem)	Khasekhemwy (Khasekhem)	V	II	1001.88

Source: Hoffman (1979:270)
Notes
*Information provided by Prof. Klaus Baer
[1] After Petrie 1900, 1901
[2] After Reiser 1936
[3] After Emery 1961
[4] After Kemp 1966

for use in the next life. Temples served by a priestly staff were charged with ensuring the transition to new life for the monarch and thereafter his perpetual bliss.

Mastabas were, then, imposing monuments, even though most of their structure was below ground. The subterranean aspect was their function as a tomb; the 'platform' above ground, containing the mortuary chapel with its declarations of ownership, titulary and accomplishments, was a political declaration of pre-eminence (or just eminence for the non-royal examples). They form a long line along the eastern edge of the escarpment at Saqqara. The more transcendent the ruler became, the more his memorial would have to ascend to the heavens. Physically, this meant 'raising up' his tomb to be a stunning monument, while still keeping it as a tomb. The pyramids were the answer to this functional/political problem, and logically enough the breakthrough is also sited at Saqqara, in the form of Djoser's (Zoser) Step-Pyramid, or rather Im-hotep's, for he was the architect. This first pyramid was built for the first king of the Third Dynasty (*c.* 2686–2613 BC) a period in which the Early Dynastic period becomes the mature Old Kingdom. Until the Third Dynasty the principal luxury product was a genre of stone vessels which had originated in Predynastic times (Baines and Malek 1980:32).

Third and Fourth Dynasties

Djoser's (Third Dynasty) pyramid rises in six steps, attaining a height of around 60 metres. Beneath is the master burial chamber amid a network of passages and small chambers, containing the burials of members of the royal family and their funeral goods. Over 40,000 stone vases alone have been recovered from Djoser's chambers – just one of the many types of item present there.

Djoser's complex was the first to be wholly built of stone, which is somewhat surprising, given that the valley cliffs were made of some excellent rock. Limestone was used, faced with fine white Tura limestone from the Mukattam hills.

At 110 metres north to south and 125 metres east to west, the Step-Pyramid is not square; neither is it isolated as a monument. Still a most imposing pile dominating the Saqqara skyline, it forms part of a grand funeral complex contained within a walled enclosure, at the south end of which is

> a great mastaba beneath which is a duplicate set of chambers reproducing those immediately connected with the burial chamber beneath the pyramid. The walls of some of the rooms under the mastaba and pyramid are decorated with blue glazed composition tiles, arranged to represent primitive hangings of matting, and fine low reliefs showing Djoser performing various religious ceremonies. On the north side of the Step Pyramid is a mortuary temple and a small chamber containing a statue of the dead king. The former was intended for the practice of the funerary cult of the king and the latter as substitute for the body for the reception of offerings.
>
> (James 1979:176–7)

Matting designs were also standard decoration on the exterior mud-brick walls of *mastabas*. But the great plaza formed by the enclosure represented probably the most important ceremony undertaken by the king in his lifetime, or fervently to be wished. This was the *Sed* festival, 'a great jubilee celebration of the king's earthly rule', to be continued in the next life, 'over a period which was ideally thirty years, although second and third celebrations could subsequently take place at shorter intervals' (Kemp 1989:59). Dressed in special robes,[13] the king sat under a special canopy on a double-stepped, double-throned dais (symbolizing Upper and Lower Egypt), from whence he reviewed a line of temporary shrines in timber and matting which represented the provinces and their submission to him. At the Step-Pyramid a rectangular sub-enclosure contains a double row in stone (like the whole complex), for eternity, of those formerly temporary shrines. Though built for Djoser by Im-hotep (deified in Ptolemaic times), the wood and wattle originals were favoured for the subsequent two millennia of *Sed* festivals.

Another territorial-claim ritual, which was logically held more frequently that *Sed* ceremonies, but was assimilated to it from the Third Dynasty onwards, had the king running around a series of cairns (here memorialized in the main plaza of the enclosure). It possibly involved striking the cairns with a ceremonial flail grasped in his right hand, signifying 'smiting', power, and thus control. This is present in ceremonies held from before the First Dynasty. They are the 'Appearance of the King of Lower Egypt', the complementary 'Appearance of the King of Upper Egypt' and the 'Appearances of the King of Upper Egypt and the King of Lower Egypt' at which the Double Crown is worn (Millet 1990:56). What may be a forerunner in use from Gerzean (Naqada IIb-d) times until early in the First Dynasty, is the site Hk29A described as a 'temple-workshop-complex' (Hoffman 1987). Discovered by the Hierakonpolis Expedition in 1985–6, it lies in the desert and consists of a large parabolic courtyard, over 32 metres long by about 13 metres wide, surrounded by a mud-covered reed fence, and later by a mud-brick wall (Holmes 1992a:37). Adjoining the northern (long) side are at least five rectangular buildings, some of which were specialized production centres for flint tools and carnelian beads. On the facing (south) side are a line of four enormous post holes, with a maximum diameter of 1–1.5 metres. Their ceremonial role is suggested by the occurrence of another, serving as a flag or totem pole, located at the 'top' or apex end of the enclosure, while the entry gate is at the other end, on the north fence/wall (ibid.).

At Saqqara, in addition to the graves of ordinary folk (also provided with food and drink for their journey) located at the south-western edge of the necropolis near the Serapeum (catacombs at the centre of the later animal cults), there are at least three other Third Dynasty enclosures. The best preserved is that of Sekhemkhet, partially excavated by Zakaria Goneim. It too has a stepped pyramid, a 'southern tomb' and a fine enclosure. Amazingly, the others have not been excavated, even here in what is probably the most archaeologically rich part of the earth's surface; hence my call for a coordinated global programme of rigorous excavations before yet more is lost (Maisels 1993a:201–6).

Saqqara is also the site of the pyramid complexes of Userkaf and Unas, the first and last kings of the Fifth Dynasty (*c.* 2494–2345 BC) and Teti, first king of the Sixth Dynasty (*c.* 2345–2181 BC). From the late Sixth, through Seventh and Eighth Dynasties, Egypt seems to have been afflicted by several famine periods, caused by a combination of abnormal Niles and poor leadership. Thereafter, unified leadership broke down into the First Intermediate Period (2160–1936 BC) when rival nomarchs at Herakleopolis (Middle Egypt) and Thebes (Upper Egypt) struggled for ascendency.[14]

However, the Fourth Dynasty (c. 2613–2494 BC) was the first period in which true mummification – involving the removal of the body's soft internal organs – commenced. It was still not a very successful process of preservation, but was an advance on the use merely of linen bandages and resin moulding of features which had been the practice during the earlier dynasties (Spencer 1982:35).

The Fourth Dynasty also marked the peak of pyramid building, notably that of the Great Pyramid of Cheops, at Giza, by Memphis. Cheops, whose Egyptian name is Khufu, an abbreviation of Khnum-khuefui meaning 'Khnum is protecting me', was the second king of this dynasty. But it was the first king of the Fourth Dynasty, Snefru, who was responsible for the first 'true', plane-sided pyramid, made at Medum, about 53 kilometres south of Saqqara, by 'filling-in' an eight-step pyramid. However, *mastabas* continued to be built for the elite, not only in brick but now in stone, their superstructures faced in fine limestone from the 'royal' Tura quarry. Such prestigious stone was available during but not after the Fourth Dynasty, for this arrangement was part of the 'new dispensation' of royal/elite accommodation occurring at that time. Quarrying stone was, after all, a royal prerogative, as was gold mining.

> The advent of the Fourth Dynasty of Pharaonic Egypt marked a radical break with the first three dynasties. The break is most visible in the new shape of the era's most substantial archaeological remains, the royal pyramids and their surrounding mortuary complexes. In the Third Dynasty, royal tombs took the form of stepped pyramids, surrounded by dummy buildings and enclosed in a rectangle of high, niched walls, with its long axis north–south. During the reign of Snefru, royal tombs became true pyramids of vastly increased size [and cost!], built at the western end of a complex of new components and proportions, which extended in an east west line from the border of the cultivation.
>
> (Roth 1993:33)

As Roth further argues, this was the most visible aspect of a new relationship between king and elite and between the king and the gods, for now the king was identified with Ra, the sun, even more than Horus, the falcon. The falcon was a narrowly dynastic symbol, while the sun (like Utu/Shamash in Sumer, 'whom Enki placed in charge of the entire universe') was the god of justice and friend to mankind. More than this, at his principle sanctuary at Heliopolis, Ra took the name of Atum, 'the All', from whom all creation issued including the first nine deities, the Enead or Nine of Heliopolis (Quirke and Spencer 1992:60).

In exchange for a form of deficit financing of his monuments, whereby the elite made resources available from their own estates, the king made both his name and his 'mana' accessible to the elite, especially after death, simultaneously 're-valuing the currency' by both assimilating himself to the gods while allowing the use of his name, like a theophoric, in the names of his subjects. Similarly, the coupling of the king 'with Anubis in granting boons in the afterlife, associated the living king with a divinity and granted him divine powers' (Roth 1993:53).

What all of this seems to represent, pointed by Snefru's adoption of the title 'ntr nfr', 'the good god' and the Horus name 'possessor of Maat' (good conduct: truth/fairness/rightness) is 'his ability to maintain an ideal world order based on justice, truth, and traditionally prescribed behaviour' (ibid.), in place of the early dynasties' emphasis on armed might and the state. With the unified state long and well established, the emphasis could now be on community, family and shared benefits. Indeed, as Roth observes, the king's family first appears together in royal iconography in Djoser's temple to Ra at Heliopolis, and Fourth Dynasty tombs are the first in which husbands, wives and children appear together in tomb relief decoration and statuary (ibid.:54).

CHILDE'S CHECKLIST

We now have enough information to let Childe's model summarize the discussion, and conversely to assess the model itself for understanding Egyptian conditions.

Childe's model requires the presence of:

1 *Cities that are 'more extensive and more densely settled than any previous settlement'.*
This condition is met with the appearance of Hierakonpolis, Memphis and Thebes. However, cities are not the determining features of the social and economic landscape in Egypt that they are in Mesopotamia. They are primarily political centres.

2 *Full-time specialists: craftsmen. transport workers, merchants, officials and priests.*
None of the artefacts, from pyramids to scarabs, would have been possible without the skills of craftsmen; the materials required, local or foreign, could not have been obtained in the amounts required without the work of transport workers, merchants and, sometimes, officials. This relates to point 8 below.

Cemetery T at Nagada was established at the beginning of
Nagada II (times) and was used throughout the whole period
and in the early First Dynasty.

. . . Items of material culture from Cemetery T that are shared
with the great cemetery [of Nagada] are various pendants and
in the rich graves quantities of beads of carnelian, ivory, lapis
lazuli, rock crystal, steatite, shell, pottery, and possibly copper
(Tombs 690, 1848)

(Davis 1983:25–6)

3 *Concentration of surplus.*

Provinces, towns, landowners and peasants were taxed very methodi-
cally, everything from cattle to canals being continually assessed and
reassessed for state revenue purposes. The Palermo Stone records bien-
nial assessments of wealth from as early as the beginning of the Second
Dynasty. Peasants either paid directly, or the estates, temple and secular,
paid, which of course meant that their peasant labour force paid. Again,
as in Mesopotamia, there was corvee, the obligation to seasonal or peri-
odical work on state projects, organized through the provincial or nome
capitals.

4 *Truly monumental public buildings.*

They do not come any more monumental than pyramids, built by corvee
labour in the slack farming season under the direction of expert architects, surveyor-managers and scribes.

5 *The presence of a ruling class, including 'priests, civil and military leaders and
officials [who] absorb a major share of the concentrated surplus'.*

They mobilized it, collected it and consumed it in temples, palaces,
pyramids and other activities, notably interment. Many of the objects
and structures were for use by priests, who lived from products of
temple lands.

6 *Technical expertise, specifically systems of writing and numerical notation.*

The structures already mentioned could not have been built, nor the
taxation system developed, without systems of writing and numerical
notation which emerged at least as early as the First Dynasty. Bard
observes that

the earliest hieroglyphs appear with royal names on tags and
sealings of Dynasty 0, to identify goods and materials of the
state, and although there is no evidence, writing was probably
used to record the economic activities of the state. . . . Early
writing developed in Egypt, then, to serve the state: for justifying its political organization, and for facilitating its economic,
administrative and religious control.

(Bard 1992:304)

Further, ink on paper (papyrus, the symbol of the Delta) was Egypt's major gift to civilization. Papyrus was in use as early as the First Dynasty (Emery 1961:235), and ink inscriptions on stone vases occur in Dynasty 0 (Ray 1986:315). Indeed, the ink used with a pen on 'paper' was 'modern' ink: pigment and gum arabic made into cakes and dissolved with water for use.

Although the earliest alphabetic scripts are not on papyrus (and were developed in the Levant), without the model of ink on some type of paper[15] the enormous potential of alphabetic script for systematic theoretical knowledge, higher mathematics and literature, could not have been realized as it was in the last millennium BC (Iron Age) and subsequently. In any event, Egyptian writing was instrumental in the evolution of alphabetic scripts. Figure 2.9 is an example of Hieratic, a cursive form of writing (usually right to left) distinct from but parallel to the more famous and pictorial hieroglyphic (usually in columns) and utterly different from cuneiform.

The alphabet emerged in the Levant where the Egyptian writing system interacted with the Mesopotamian, notably at Byblos. Catalytic in this process was the acrophonic principle, in which the sound value of the sign corresponds to the value of the first syllable of the name of the thing the sign represents. Thus, the sign for a dog = the phonemic

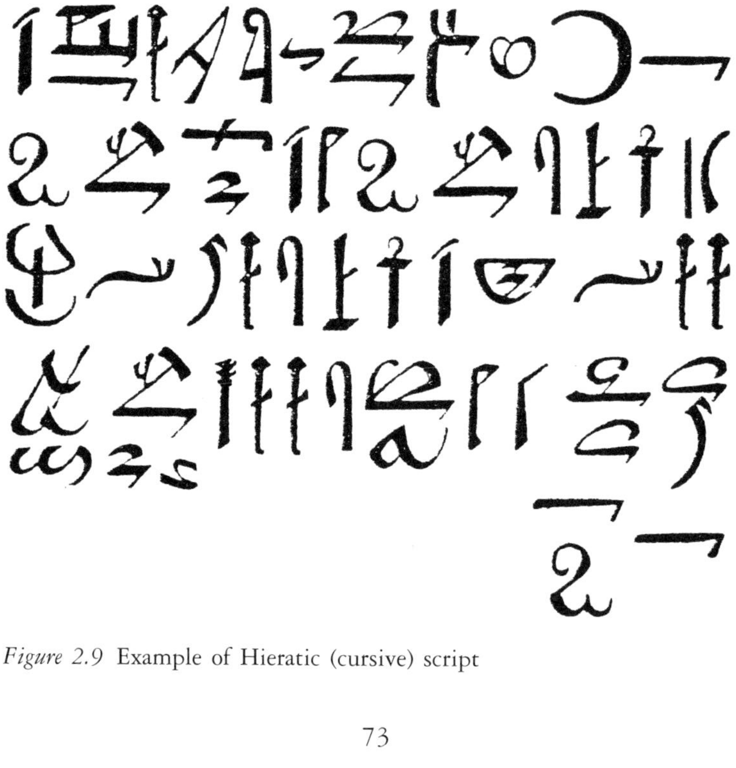

Figure 2.9 Example of Hieratic (cursive) script

name 'dog' = the first syllable 'do'.[16] Repeated, this produces a syllabary, from which an alphabet is but two more steps, both restrictions: in the number used and in separating consonants from vowels.

7 *Exact and predictive sciences: arithmetic, geometry, astronomy and a calendar.* Taking the latter first:

> The basic building blocks that made up the Egyptian system of measuring time were the agricultural, lunar, stellar, and civil years. Since they were never in synchronism, there was never a unified calendrical system; it is this which causes the difficulties encountered in modern chronological studies.
>
> (Ward 1992:57)

First the 'Nile Year' from commencement of inundation to inundation, could range between 336 and 415 days (Neugebauer 1938:185–7). Though scarcely a calendar, such reckoning would be all the early agriculturalists required. A more precise agricultural calendar ties this flood cycle to phases of the moon, resulting in a calendar of 4 lunar months spanning the three 120-day seasons mentioned earlier: inundation, emergence and harvest. However, as twelve lunar months of 29.5 days from full moon to full moon produces a year only 354 days long, every three years or so an extra lunar month has to be added, making that year 384 days long, but bringing the following year back into line with the stellar year of 365.25 days (Ward op. cit.).

The stellar year was tied to the heliacal rising (that is, just before sunrise) of the star Sirius, which the Greeks called Sothis and the Egyptians personified as the goddess *Sepdet*. Accordingly, New Year's Day was known as 'the emergence of *Sepdet*'.

> It seems most likely that the reappearance of Sirius [after its 70 days invisibility] was originally chosen as New Year's day [July 17–19 if observed from Memphis or Heliopolis] since this event took place within the period of several weeks during which the inundation of the Nile began each year. This meant that the lunar years, beginning with the first lunar month after the heliacal rising of Sirius, could be kept in approximate synchronism with the agricultural seasons by the periodic intercalation of a 13th lunar month.
>
> (ibid.)

Although adequate for agricultural and religious purposes, such calendars were neither consistent nor coherent enough for the purposes of civil administration, issuing documents and keeping records. The 'civil calendar' of 365 days was originated by 'averaging' either a series of lunar years or agricultural years. Accordingly, the civil calendar retained the three seasons, held to consist of four 30-day months, with five extra – epagomenal – days added to make the total of 365 days.[17] But this still produced a 'wandering year'. The true, or sidereal (stellar) year, is slightly more than a quarter-day longer than 365 days, and so the civil calendar fell behind ('progressed backward') every year. This had the consequence that the civil New Year's Day eventually fell on every single day of the sidereal year, only re-occurring on the same day once in 1460 years (365 × 4). This period of the coincidence of New Year's Day in civil and stellar years every 1460 years (or less), is called the Sothic Cycle.

The day itself had twenty-four hours, divided equally into twelve hours of day and night. As the length of daytime and darkness vary according to season (and latitude), the length of an hour of day or night varied according to season.

Areas, weights and volumes are, of course, central to the operations of an agrarian society: areas for allocating fields, weights and volumes for exchange, the payment of taxes (rendered in kind) and for construction projects. Thus the mathematical literature consists of practical trial problems with their solutions, and no theoretical apparatus. Here are two examples (from James 1979:122):

- 'A circular container of 9 cubits in its height and 6 in its breadth. What is the amount that will go into it in corn?'
- 'A pyramid 140 (units) in length of side, and five palms and a finger in slope. What is the vertical height thereof?'

There were 7 palms or 28 fingers in the royal cubit of 52.3 centimetres.

For such purposes, arithmetic and geometry were adequate, and so until the Ptolemaic period this was all the mathematics Egypt had. It did, however, employ a decimal system with a million as its highest unit (represented by a god holding up the sky with his raised arms) and had an approximation (3.16) to pi (true: 3.14159 . . .) obtained by squaring ⅞ of the circle's diameter. There was, however, no sign for zero, but sometimes a blank space represented it. Long distances were measured by the *atour* of 20,000 cubits, using the previously mentioned 'royal' or 'long' cubit of 52.3 centimetres (the 'short' cubit was *c.* 45 centimetres: 6 palms or 24 fingers). By this 'river measure' (Greek *schoinos*) using the long cubit, Upper Egypt was indigenously and fairly accurately reckoned to be 86 *atours* in length, Lower Egypt 20 *atour*, respectively almost 900 kilometres and 209 kilometres.

8 *Full-time sculptors, painters or seal engravers.*

The visual arts of ancient Egypt are probably the most striking of any of the pristine civilizations. Wall-painting in particular must be singled out for its sheer scale, realism, colour and comprehensiveness. This does not mean that it was not highly stylized; but it does mean that many aspects of daily life were portrayed in such a vivid and accurate way that one could imagine that the intention was to leave a record for subsequent generations. Life-size and extremely life-like statuary was also produced, as also striking model-tableaux, and very many small items, such as scarab seals (of highly variable workmanship) mounted in a ring or as a pendant. Experts even portrayed themselves at work sculpting, painting and constructing, as they also portrayed agricultural, domestic and scribal activities.

9 *Regular foreign trade, involving comparatively large volumes.*

It is necessary to keep reminding ourselves that all the pristine civilizations were agrarian. The Egyptian staples were bread and beer, as were the Mesopotamian (cf. Millard 1988). The vast majority of the population were engaged in basic agriculture, with only a narrow stratum above them engaged in crafts; above the artisans were specialists in trade, administration and cult; above them the thinnest stratum of all, that of the rulers. Such a society thus divides fundamentally into two – those who work with their hands (land or raw materials) and those who do not, but who 'direct' those who do – a cleavage still of fundamental importance in the culture of contemporary societies emerging from the agrarian stage.

The fact that most of the population worked the land, with bulk transport very costly (except where, as with the Nile, the whole country was accessible by water up to Aswan), made agrarian civilizations autarkic: they routinely and necessarily produced the food, clothing and building materials required (even in a resource-poor area like Mesopotamia) locally or not at all. Speaking of Egypt, Kemp (1977:198) states that 'it would be forcing the evidence to suggest that the growth of an urban structure in Egypt was significantly dependent on the methods of distribution of material goods'.

However, items that set the elites apart from the rest of the population were by definition something exotic, either because they came from afar, or because their production demanded much more labour than any peasant or craftsperson could command, even when that labour was local (see Chapter 6).

Materials like obsidian and shell were traded even prior to the Neolithic, let alone the advent of the state, so it is not trade itself but the 'comparatively large volumes' that would be significant where they existed. Trade in large(ish) volumes is a product of a developed state system, not the cause of its rise. The centrality of the Egyptian state in trade expeditions, undertaken for political reasons, makes this clear.

Egypt's major trading connections were with the Levant (overland or by sea), notably with the city-state of Byblos (*Keben*) with which

Egypt had long had a 'special relationship' and to whose ruler it accorded the high rank of prince – *hati-a*. From this 'Land of the Forests', Egypt obtained principally woods: pine (*uan*), fir (*ash*) and cedar (*mer*), variously used for priest's coffins, temple and tomb doors, furniture and sacred barges. Finished seagoing ships – *kebenit* – were also sold to Egypt in exchange for manufactured items such as gold and silver vases, flax, papyrus, ox-hides, rope, lentils and dried fish (Montet 1965:110).

From the Sinai at the Wadi Maghara or Serabit el-Khadim (where Egyptians constructed a rock-temple to Astarte identified with Hathor – the goddess of anywhere 'abroad', as Kitchen [1993:594] nicely puts it) turquoise (*mefaket*) was obtained from the First Dynasty until the Late Period. The high desert peninsula of Sinai (in the south Mt Sinai reaches 2,637 metres), also supplied copper and malachite. The much prized lapis lazuli (*tefrer*) reached Egypt by onward trade through Sippar, which locus, as was usual in ancient Egyptian, gave its name to the material supplied.

Visited at least from the Fifth Dynasty onward (*c.*2500–1170 BC), Punt was the location of the 'terraces of incense', supplying not only incense trees (especially live myrrh shrubs, for replanting), but also ebony, ostrich plumes and eggs, perfume, baboons, monkeys, plus leopard (Arabic: *nimr*, cf. Nimrod) and cheetah skins. Gold (of Amau) in rings was also sought. Note that there is no such animal as a 'panther', only a range of cats whose proper names begin *Panthera*, including lions and jaguars. A 'panther' can no more supply skins than can a unicorn.

Punt was reached by expedition from Koptos, on the east bank of the Theban Nile, via the Wadi Gasus to the coast of the Red Sea at *Sa'waw* harbour (now Mersa Gawasis), where the ships were reassembled for their southward journey to Punt (Kitchen 1993:591). Expeditions bearing trade goods also went from Punt to Egypt using raft-like boats driven by a single black triangular sail, quite different from the well-known Egyptian craft (ibid.:599, illustrated). Other routes to the Red Sea from the Nile Valley are: Wadi Hammamat to Quseir; Wadi 'Abbad to Berenike; Wadi el-Quash, leading from Koptos to Berenike. 'There is also a minor route from about 80km south of Cairo to the Gulf of Suez, attested from the reign of Ramesses II' (Baines and Malek 1980:19).

Having reviewed the evidence, Kitchen concludes that

> there is seemingly a virtually conclusive case for placing Punt between the Red Sea and the Middle Nile, straddling the latter and the former's coasts, occupying a large area on (and from) the north and northwest flanks of the Ethiopian Highlands, in east Sudan; the supposed location of Somalia becomes increasingly impossible to sustain.
>
> (Kitchen op. cit.:604)

Other southern trade was along the Nile beyond the second cataract (by Wadi Halfa) to Nubia. This cataract, which marked the political frontier as early as the First Dynasty (Djer), lay in the land of the *Nehesiu*, effectively colonial territory (the southernmost nome, Elephantine, was originally Nubian). Nubia, extending from First to Fourth cataracts, supplied diorite and amethyst, cattle, hardwood, ivory, ostrich feathers and animal skins, but principally human resources of labourers and soldiers. It is overstretching the term to call those relationships trade, in contrast to relations with Punt and the Levant. In sum, products deriving from within the Egyptian domain do not represent trade; those from beyond the borders do represent trade (Kitchen, pers. comm.).

To the immediate west of and roughly parallel to the Nile valley were the oases (from *uhat*, cauldron, through the Greek) forming the 'land of the Temihu', also under continuous Egyptian domination and later incorporation. The Egyptians reckoned there were seven of those 'fields of the *ima-trees*', though not all were what we now call oases, for it included the Wadi Natrun. True oases supplied vines, wines and small donkeys, and were also a place of banishment. The Delta, however, was a more important vine-growing area.

Oasis dwellers – *Sekhetiu imu* (*sekhet*: meadow) – were originally quite separate from the more western pastoralists of the land of the Tehenu. During the Old Kingdom at least, Tehenu supplied Egypt with asses, oxen, sheep and goats (Montet 1965:125). Like the kings of Byblos, their chiefs also had the title of prince – *hati-a*. However, during the New Kingdom period the Tehenu and indeed the Temihu of the oases were swamped by pastoral incursions from further west. The dominant newcomers were called Libu, and it is from this name that the (increasingly loose) term Libya became applied to the land to the west of the Nile. Merenptah II and Ramses III only just managed to prevent the Libyans overrunning Egypt.

Childe's criteria Nos 10, 11 and 12 cover the apparent contradiction that while the state is run by, and to a large extent for, a privileged elite, it nonetheless functions to knit up the society into 'a first approximation to an organic solidarity'. As Childe himself notes, part of this is simply the interdependence resulting from a division of labour, where everyone has a role to play. This, of course, pure (but relevant) Durkheimianism, as is Childe's invocation of 'collective representations' of society to itself, mediated by religion in general and 'temple or sepulchral shrine' in particular. Those two aspects of social solidarity – division of labour and common (though not totally shared) culture – are obviously parts of the explanation of how the majority of any population, who comprise the lower classes of every society, nonetheless still identify with it and regard it as theirs.

However, a missing or third part of the explanation is simple habitude: being raised in a particular society and having no experience of an alternative. Culture, after all, is just a summary word for a way of life.

There is, finally, a fourth aspect of social cohesion that is of particular relevance to ancient Egypt, but is also of general importance. Just as any currency, especially a paper one, needs some 'sovereign' standing, so to speak, behind it and guaranteeing its value, so to validate the myriad interpersonal transactions of which social life consists, some ultimate guarantor of the worth of people's activities is required, especially by those without acclaim, wealth or power. This is because in the contingencies of everyday life and the pressures of subsistence getting, it is all too easy to lose a sense of its intrinsic value. That is, the means tend to defeat the ends of living. Accordingly, someone 'divine' is needed to keep score, confer significance upon and thus validate existence, thereby turning it into 'a life worth living'. In the modern world we are still trying to come to terms with the loss of such agents.

However, as the Pharaoh lived in society but due to his divine aspects was not of it, who better to validate interpersonal activity and an individual's biographical trajectory than the eternal representative of heaven on earth? It is not that he personally issued certificates of merit; the king had nothing to do with commoners. It is that he is the centre of a structure in the lower part of which one is embedded; and as the structure itself possesses transcendental value, it confers worth on one's own existence. Thus, the way things are is the way they have to be. This sense gains extra, not lesser, strength from the fact that the ruler was not always revered by everyone. Indeed, tombs could be robbed even shortly after interment. Deviations from the norm serve to highlight the value of the norm unless it is replaced by something of greater overall value. Thus the system cohered for millennia despite declines, invasions, famines, civil wars and interregnums.

Egypt's 'second wind' came during the New Kingdom (1540–1070 BC: Eighteenth to Twentieth Dynasties) in the wake of the Second Intermediate Period. The wheel and the pulley were introduced, bronze supplanted copper for implements, rock-cut tombs replaced pyramids for kings, and Amun, 'the hidden one' associated with wind, became pre-eminent. The Eighteenth Dynasty is the time, after all, of the water-clock (invented by Amenemhat in the reign of Amenophis I); of the Amarna Letters and the induction of the spoken language to written forms (Amenophis IV/Akhenaten); also the engagement with 'Asia', where Tuthmosis III – a considerable intellectual – fought no less than seventeen campaigns and built an empire.

3

THE LEVANT AND
MESOPOTAMIA[1]

THE PLACE

The Levant comprises the states of Syria, Lebanon, Israel, Palestine and Jordan (plus the Sinai peninsula), while Mesopotamia is largely synonymous with Iraq. When Turkey, Iran, Arabia and Egypt are added, the larger region is known as the Near or Middle East, extending no farther east than the Gulf of Oman.

It is a region framed by five seas: Red, Mediterranean, Black, Caspian and the Arabian/Persian Gulf, hereafter referred to simply as the Gulf. Major mountain massifs run due east across southern Turkey to the foot of the Caucasus around Mount Ararat, situated between Lakes Van, Sevan and Urmia. There the mountain masses turn southeast to become the western flank of Iran and then the northern side of the Gulf. But the 'Fertile Crescent' of foothills and plains enclosed by this great mountain arc commences in the Jordan Valley and the coastal plains of the southern Levant, thence to the Lebanon and Anti-Lebanon ranges trending northeast, roughly parallel to the Mediterranean coastline (see Figure 3.1 and back endpapers).

Continuing northwards into Turkey across the fissure in which the River Orontes (Nahr el Assi) runs and where ancient Antioch, modern Antakya is located, the Amanus hills merge into the Taurus Mountains. Having formed the southern coastline of Turkey, the Taurus range arcs northeastwards to become, around Lake Van, the Zagros mountain chain of Kurdistan and Luristan that then reach southeastwards all the way to the Straits of Hormuz, the entrance to the Gulf from the Arabian Sea.

The Levant and Mesopotamia are dominated by three rivers, east to west – Jordan, Euphrates and Tigris – crucial in a region that has some of the world's highest amounts of sunshine and levels of temperature. Away from Turkey and the Levantine coast (c. 800 millimetres, for instance around Ras Shamra/Ugarit) low overall rainfall,[2] generally diminishing north to south and west to east, characterizes the region. Most of the Near East thus has a negative water balance, making much of the terrain semi-arid or arid. Evapotranspiration rates in Iraq are such that around 250 millimetres of

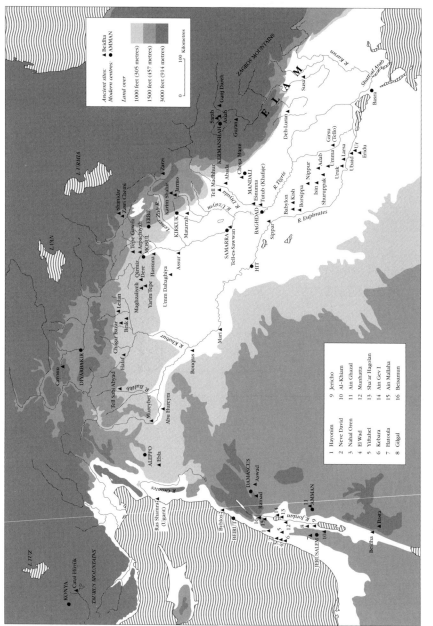

Figure 3.1 Map of the Levant, Mesopotamia and Western Iran with some prehistoric, protohistoric and historical sites

Source: Maisels 1993a

reliable rainfall is required for a viable cereal crop, unless irrigation is used. This requirement is met by farming within the 300 millimetres isohyet in order to accommodate the highly variable level and distribution of rainfall.[3]

River banks and lakesides were thus the sites of the earliest permanent settlements (hamlets and villages) occupied for some of the year by populations that were still hunters and gatherers. Under such conditions lakes, marshes and springs (the last referred to as 'living water' in Arabic) played a crucial part in providing concentrated resources for hunters, and subsequently moist soils for early agriculturalists. Indeed, the preference for such locations made *Falciparum malaria* a major killer in many Neolithic settlements, according to Hershkovitz and Gopher (1990:40).

Amongst the largest were the lakes in the Damascus Basin, where a number of Early Neolithic sites are located, notably Tell Aswad. Jericho, right down in the Jordan Valley, is located on the spring of Ain es-Sultan. Netiv Hagdud and Gilgal in Israel are also sited on springs. So too is Jerusalem high in the Judean Hills, here forming the west flank of the Jordan Valley, with the Hills of Moab constituting the valley's east flank. On the coast, at the now submerged Pre-Pottery Neolithic (phase C) hunting, fishing and farming site of Atlit-Yam 'it is suggested that the wheat types, either as separate crops or mixed ones, were cultivated in wet alluvial soils on the banks of the Oren River or on low ground with a high water table' (Galili *et al.* 1993:153).

The northernmost extension (and termination) of the East African/Dead Sea/Jordan Valley Rift system is the Ghab Valley, through which the Orontes (Asi) flows to the sea. The Syrian capital Damascus, northeast of the snowcapped Mount Hermon (at 2,814 metres the highest peak in the Anti-Lebanon range), is in the extreme southwest of the country, backing onto the Hamad (stony desert), thanks to the River Barada, its distributaries and lakes. This is why Damascus has been graced by orchards, vineyards and gardens for millennia and is one of the world's very oldest continuously inhabited sites.

The other large towns of Syria are located on the Orontes (Homs, ancient Emessa, and Hama) or, in the case of the second largest city, Aleppo, on the Quweiq. Between Lebanon and Anti-Lebanon (Jebel esh Sharqi) mountains runs, almost for the whole length of Lebanon, a long, high interior valley, extending for some 112 kilometres (Schroeder 1991:44). At about the middle of the valley, the highpoint of the valley floor (1,000 metres) produces a watershed near the Roman (and modern) town of Baalbek. The watershed generates two rivers, the northward-flowing Orontes and the southward-flowing Litani.

Aleppo (Halab), Syria's second city and principal industrial centre, is twice favoured. In addition to its riverside location, Aleppo is also situated in the 'Syrian saddle' or gap of low hills (centred about Latakia on the coast) that enables the westerly rain-bearing winds from the Mediterranean to penetrate in winter right through to the western slopes of the Zagros range separating

Iraq from Iran. Accordingly, Aleppo, and the northern Jezira beyond, are favoured with a reliable rainfall of about 250 millimetres, sufficient to grow cereals without irrigation.

East of the Orontes and south of Aleppo lies the great third millennium city of Ebla. In Table 3.1, Gelb has contrasted its situation – adequate rainfall for extensive grazing and relatively moderate temperate ranges – with that of Lagash in southeastern Sumer (Iraq), which has deep and irrigable alluvial soils but climatic extremes, indicating the economic consequences. The economic consequences of the ecological differences are a concentration on textile and metal manufacturing in the north (Syria), where few texts relate to agriculture, contrasting with the southern alluvium where large-scale grain-growing is the basis of the economy. (As the world's first commercial state, one imagines that Ebla was also the main Near Eastern centre for entrepot trade. For a detailed view of the region-wide importance of Ebla [Tell Mardikh], see Pettinato 1991, in addition to Gelb's article already cited. For Mari on the Euphrates see Young 1992, and for the second millennium, Dalley 1984.)

Only the Litani River, flowing south out of the fertile Bekaa Valley, the granary of Lebanon, and then west into the Mediterranean just north of Tyre, has no sizeable modern settlement anywhere along its length. This is explained by the disrupted drainage pattern of the narrow trough (graben) seen in the gorges south of the Bekaa, and its difficult access, there being no way down the Litani beyond the bend of Merj Ayun.

The Yarmuk River, a tributary of the Jordan, is the only other significant river in the Levant. The Jordan Valley, a trough hundreds of metres below sea level, is part of a great rift system reaching right down into the southern hemisphere (southeast Africa). The River Jordan has neither cut the valley nor does it begin to fill it, a condition called 'underfit'.

The main rivers of agriculture in the Near East are, of course, the Euphrates and the Tigris, rising in Turkey (around Lake Van) and running southwards for 2,430 kilometres and 1,850 kilometres, respectively. The Euphrates makes a big swing west across northern Syria, but the Tigris, running a fairly straight north–south course, enters Iraq directly from Turkey.

On entry to Iraq, the two rivers form a Jezira, or 'island', between them, roughly a triangle of land pointing down the alluvium. Having entered the alluvial lowlands in the vicinity of the towns of Hit and Tikrit, the two rivers make a close approach in ancient Akkad. Here, between Baghdad on the Tigris and the nearest loop of the Euphrates, the rivers are only 35 kilometres apart. South of Baghdad the rivers flow apart again to encircle an area of low alluvium that was the land of Sumer, the heartland of cities. East of the most ancient cities of Eridu and Ur, the rivers unite at Al Qurna for their final stretch to the sea as the tidal Shatt al-Arab, 160 kilometres long.

Table 3.1 Ecological features of Ebla and Lagash and their exploitation

	Latitude	Temp.	Rainfall	Hydro-graphy	Soil	Hydro-graphy	Produce	Pastures	Animal husbandry	Produce	Main imports	exports
NORTH Syria (Ebla)	36° N	Summer 25°C Winter 8°C (aver.)	22 cm variable	small rivers	middling	only ¹/₄₀ irrigated	middling (self-sufficient)	extensive	sheep = 25 × cattle (grass- + hay-fed)	wool (surplus)	metals	textiles
SOUTH Meso-potamia (Lagash)	32° N	Summer 35°C Winter 12°C (aver.)	12 cm variable (irrelevant)	large rivers	alluvial, very rich	all irrigated	high (surplus)	very limited	sheep = 5 × cattle (grain- + plant-fed)	wool (self-sufficient)	metals, stone, timber	grain

Source: Gelb 1986:164

Such is the amount of material deposited by the rivers that the gradient from Nasariyah (the nearest modern city to Tell Al-Ubaid, Ur and Eridu) to the sea, is but 2.4 metres.

As just mentioned, the Tigris and Euphrates unite at the town of Qurna to form the tidal Shatt al-Arab, on which lies Basra, Iraq's principal port, 97 kilometres from the Gulf. Until the recent eco-genocide perpetrated by the Baghdad regime on the Marsh Arabs, by cutting off the water and attacking the exposed population, Qurna lay at the centre of a 15,000-square kilometre marsh 'sealand', of which there is no better description than that of Wilfred Thesiger:

> they consist of permanent marsh where *gasab* (Phragmites communis) is the predominant vegetation; seasonal marsh, most of which is covered with bullrushes (Typha augustata) and dries up in the autumn and winter; and temporary marsh, which is only inundated during the floods and is later overgrown with a sedge (Scirpus brachyceras). This area can be conveniently divided into the eastern Marshes, east of the Tigris; the Central Marshes, west of the Tigris and north of the Euphrates; and the Southern Marshes south of the Euphrates and west of the Shatt al Arab. There is also some permanent marsh below Shatra on the Shatt al Gharraf, a river that leaves the Tigris at Kut and flows south-west in the direction of Nasariya; some seasonal marsh on the plains to the north-east of Amara, where the floods from the Tib and Duarij flow down from the Persian foothills and disperse; and a little seasonal marsh in the Al bu Daraj country, fifteen miles north of Amara to the west of the Tigris. At the height of the floods great tracts of desert adjoining the Marshes are covered by sheets of open water that vary each year in size but can extend for a distance of more than two hundred miles from the outskirts of Basra almost to Kut. As the floods recede the land reverts to desert.
>
> (Thesiger 1964:13)

Like the Nile in Eygpt, the Euphrates (Sumerian: **Buranum**) in Iraq can be considered a desert or exogenous river, receiving no tributaries or base-flow contributions there, only the seasonal/periodical surface-flow from wadis. This helps to make the Euphrates slow, meandering and thus aggrading, raising its bed above the surrounding land surface.[4] While ideal for gravity-flow irrigation, this also makes the Euphrates prone to flooding and, more importantly, to shifts in its bed, with at least four main courses known, the branching location being north of ancient Sippar. The major ancient levees of both the Euphrates and the Tigris and of the canals they fed are identifiable in Landsat imagery (Figure 3.2).

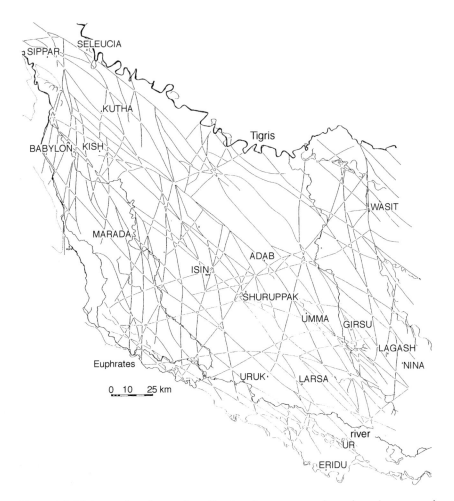

Figure 3.2 Major ancient levees from Landsat imagery revealing the primary canal
network

Source: Adams 1981:34

The Tigris (Sum.: **Idiglat/Idigina**), by contrast, can be regarded as a
'mountain river', with a relatively good gradient and receiving major tributaries such as the Diyala (Sum.: **Durul**) plus perennial streams, making it
turbulent and incised along much of its length. However, at Kut, where
Sumer begins, it does indeed meander, with three channels known: the
modern one, the Shatt al-Gharraf (now a canal) and the Dujail. North of
Kut, then, water from the Tigris has to be lifted by machine (such as the
shaduf), but gravity canals can easily be cut from the Euphrates. Accordingly,

major settlements are located on the levees (naturally raised banks, which can be a kilometre wide) of the Euphrates channels. Their fields lie 'behind' them and are irrigated by canal systems in a four-part hierarchy: the major canal (i₇/id/*narum*; which also means river) feeds into smaller canals, each of which irrigates a whole district (pa₅/*atappum*); thence to a channel feeding a field, which internally uses the water in narrow irrigation furrows (Mauer 1986:67). This dendritic or multi-branching pattern was not, of course, a 'straight-through' system operating under gravity alone, but one that relied upon divertors on the main channel, head regulators at the 'take-off' to the canal system, cross regulators/canal falls down-system and, in the fields themselves, bunds or boundary dykes called **eg**/*ikum*, nominally enclosing an **iku**, 60×60 metres approximately.[5] The bunds contain the water and make it soak into the soil (Pemberton *et al.* 1988:214).

Logically then, 'in sales contracts the general location of fields (or orchards) is – in numerous cases – expressed by the Sumerian word **a.gàr** (Akkadian *ugārum*) 'irrigation district' (Renger 1990:41). Thus **pa₅**-Kuruttum, the name of a canal irrigating such a district, and íd-Urim(ki) 'the Ur canal' (ibid.:33). The crucial importance attached to the king digging/restoring the major canals, and the responsibility of the users (**dumu.meš a.gàr**/*mārū ugārim* 'sons of the irrigation district', through their town (ibid.:39)) maintaining their lower-level channels, is indicated by kings' year formulae (relating to the previous year's accomplishments) and to their stream of instructions to officials to ensure that the users did their part. Thus, in the Old Babylonian period, Hammurabi with justified pride declares in regard to this Year Formula 33:

> Hammurabi has dug the canal [called] 'Hammurabi is the prosperity of the people' – the canal for which [the gods] An and Enlil take care – and thus provided the cities Nippur, Eridu, Ur, Larsa, Uruk and Isin with a steady supply of water for their prosperity and made it possible for the inhabitants of (the lands) Sumer and Akkad, who had been scattered (by war), to return to their settlements.
>
> (ibid.:34)[6]

THE TIME

The argument here is both temporal and spatial. It turns on the ending of Ice Age conditions (the Pleistocene) and the onset of warm contemporary conditions (the Holocene). The transition process as it affected life in the Near East lasted several millennia, from about 13,000 to around 10,000 years Before Present, a period of human culture emerging from the Palaeolithic (Old Stone Age) and accordingly referred to as (Late)

Table 3.2 Chronological scheme of cultural developments in the Southern Levant during the Terminal Pleistocene and Early Holocene

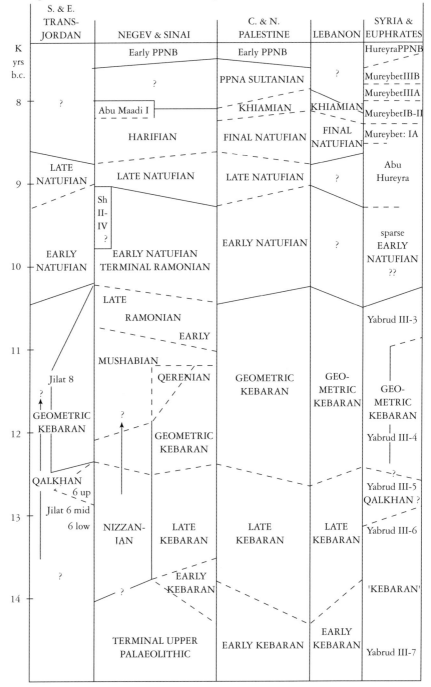

Source: After Goring-Morris 1989:11

Epipalaeolithic. Table 3.2 makes relationships clear for the various parts of the Levant.

The argument, which I have made previously for the Near East (1984, 1987, 1990, 1993a), is that the long-term post-Pleistocene trend was (despite zonal and temporal fluctuations) for raised biomass levels in the Near East, with higher temperatures and higher overall rainfall (though it diminished in northeastern Africa and the Negev). With this improvement in growing conditions, a wider variety of plants (certainly) and animals (almost certainly) became available to hunter–gatherer populations, especially the cereal grasses which spread from lowland refuges into upland areas ahead of expanding oak-pistacio woodland after about 15,000 bp, the period of Late Glacial warming. From a ratio of 20 per cent of tree to other pollens at the end of the pleniglacial (c. 17,000 bp), this had risen to a maximum of 75 per cent at 11,540+- 100 bp, according to the new pollen core extracted from Lake Huleh by Baruch and Bottema (1991). However, by 10,650 bp, tree pollen had fallen right back to 25 per cent, recovering to 50 per cent at 10,440+-120 bp, but declining again over the next few centuries, to improve thereafter.

Natufian populations extended their subsistence repertoire by storing highly seasonal resources – acorns, legumes and seeds – in order to provide a greater range of food during the year and/or to cover any lean periods. Thus with Jack Harlan,

> we may conclude that wild grass seed harvests are not necessarily measures to avert starvation. On the contrary, they may provide an easily obtained staple for people living where appropriate species thrive. Whole grass seeds are generally nutritious, but higher in fibre than the highly-processed flours used in modern societies.[7]
>
> (Harlan 1992:22)

In a rigorous review of the environmental implications of pollen-bearing cores from the Ghab valley (through which the Orontes flows in northwest Syria), and another from the Hula valley in the north of the Israeli part of the Rift Valley (through which the Jordan flows), Baruch and Bottema conclude that:

> As far as cultural developments are concerned it may be inferred from the Hula Diagram that the origins of the Natufian complex in the region referred to as its 'core area' (largely overlapping with the Mediterranean territory of the southern Levant) occurred under the most favourable climatic conditions prevailing throughout the final Pleistocene–Early Holocene timespan. This calls for revision of models suggesting that the emergence of the Natufian culture may have resulted from environmental stress (Bar Yosef 1987; Bar

Yosef and Vogel 1987; Goring-Morris 1987, 1989). Rather it seems that the success of the Natufian subsistence strategies, largely based on sedentism, at least in the Mediterranean territory (Bar Yosef 1983, 1987), was underlined by the improved climatic conditions. One wonders therefore whether the paucity of Natufian 'base camps' in the northern Levant, especially in the Early Natufian, (Bar Yosef 1987; Byrd 1989) has to do with unfavourable climatic conditions prevailing there during most of the Late Glacial period.

(Baruch and Bottema 1991:18)

Conversely, it might have much more to do with limited archaeological survey.

As to the ending of the Natufian culture, the picture now emerging is this:

1 From the middle of the thirteenth millennium bp, Natufian groups exploited two basic types of terrain: the oak forests between the coast and the Jordan Valley, and steppic areas further inland. In the oak forests the major resource was acorns; in the steppic areas, legumes and seeds (Olszowski 1993) in both cases supplemented by gazelle, deer and other species. In particularly favoured sites the laying down of stores produced a kind of sedentism.

2 The Younger Dryas drying episode, spanning the eleventh millennium bp, imposed changes on human subsistence strategies as forests retreated and thinned and the steppe became more desertic.

3 A premium is placed on sites with permanent moisture. It is in their vicinity that grass cereals are manipulated or to which they are moved.

4 This survival strategy of the Terminal Epipalaeolithic becomes fully-fledged cultivation under the improving climatic conditions of the Holocene. Bigger reserves and larger populations now result in true, year-long sedentism. This is the Pre-Pottery Neolithic.

The Pleistocene/Holocene transition, 16000–7000 BC, from cold relatively dry to warm wet conditions, is also seen in Anatolia, at Okuzini cave in the Taurus foothills inland from Antalya (Otte et al. 1995). It is manifested there by the increased presence of forest (including oak and ash) and forest animals such as fallow, roe and red deer, plus pigs. Indeed, the excavators (op. cit.:922) state that 'in particular, one should note the increasing wetness at the top of the sequence'.

But for human populations precipitation alone is not sufficient: a good source of potable water is also required. So sites with a good water supply and around which substantial plant and animal resources could be depended upon (such as Ohalo II discussed below) induced formerly mobile populations to reduce their mobility until they were spending most if not all of the year at such naturally favoured sites. Sedentism, by reducing mobility stresses on women (and so reducing child spacing) and by making available a better year-round supply of palatable – not necessarily dairy – foodstuffs (Maisels 1990:121–30; Hershkovitz and Gopher 1990:35), permitted population growth fed by intensified hunting and gathering. Nonetheless, growth could continue only so far in any particular location, leading after a time to the establishment of settlements at other sites also favoured by suitable combinations of natural resources, including wild stands of wheat and/or barley.

But such sites were limited, and so upon further population expansion other sites had to be found where the resources could be combined only by human activity. This involved moving the cereal grasses to sites already favoured by the presence of streams, springs or marshes, which latter could also offer fish, wildfowl and other sources of protein. Indeed, *only* removal of seed grains from their zones of natural occurrence and their introduction to new habitats could have led to the formation of domestic variants, for otherwise the 'self (re)sowing' characteristics of the brittle (i.e. shattering) rachis would merely have caused wild stands to perpetuate themselves (Anderson 1991:551–2).

In the moist(er) soil the cereals would thrive; tillage would not have been necessary or even desirable (ibid.). Population levels rose, but cereals alone do not farming make. The early cultivating populations still depended on game, fowl and fish for their protein requirements. This put far too much pressure on ungulates, especially gazelle and deer, forcing the expanded human population first to exploit a wider range of terrestrial animals, plus fish and birds, then, once the animals' 'reservoir areas' were filled by settlements, forcing animal keeping and (incipient) domestication upon the cultivators during the seventh millennium (Pre-Pottery Neolithic B).

Davis (1991:385) provides a bar diagram illustrating that while the species of large ruminant killed around Hatula did not vary significantly between Natufian and the succeeding Pre-Pottery Neolithic A period there, the number of gazelle (*Gazella gazella*) killed declined by two-thirds, while the exploitation of hare, fish and birds more than tripled. Further, the killing of gazelle at younger ages[8] indicates heavy human pressure on the animals' reproductive cycle (ibid.:386). This was not, as some have argued, a kind of selective culling that functions as 'proto-husbandry', but a strong depleting pressure. He concludes (ibid.:388) that continuing demographic pressure into the PPNB forced the domestication of sheep and goats during the seventh millennium.

This is not at odds with Horwitz's model (1989) which has four major components: (A) generalized hunting; (B) incipient domestication; (C) domestication and (D) husbandry. On this model the seventh millennium is the era of only incipient domestication, something comprising two parts: 'intensive hunting' and then 'population isolation', only after which does 'domestication' exist (by control of breeding), followed in turn by 'husbandry'. This developed condition, 'husbandry', Horwitz does not see being in place until the Pottery Neolithic (ibid.:170).

While Belfer-Cohen *et al.* (1991:422), after a thoroughgoing review of the skeletal evidence, 'suggest that some portions of the population were responding to environmental stress during the Late Natufian', overall they see 'no indication of substantial health deterioration from the Early to the Late Natufian'. From her review of the dental evidence, Patricia Smith, (1991:427–8) concludes that while 'the incidence of dental disease, and specifically ante-mortem tooth loss, increases in the later phases of the Natufian', caused largely by an increased reliance on cereals which are more abrasive and cariogenic, the higher frequency of dental hypoplasia in succeeding agricultural populations relative to the Natufian and Mousterian of the same region 'supports the evidence presented elsewhere for relatively good nutritional and health status [amongst] the Natufians'.

The adoption of a securely based farming way of life depended on an integrated suite of plant and animal domesticates, something that took several millennia to develop (Garfinkel 1987a:212; Hershkovitz and Gopher 1990:38–9) and in the absence of which, (plus the requisite husbandry skills) the earliest farmers, those of the Pre-Pottery Neolithic of the Levant, were highly vulnerable. Very few PPN sites survive beyond 6000 BC.

Thus priority was lost by the Levant for reasons that will emerge below. Nonetheless, the sweep of developments right across the Zagrosian Arc must be included in the explanation of Mesopotamia's trajectory into the first urbanism and state-structures, and this is what is seen in the *flow-chart of social evolution in the Near East* shown in Figure 3.3.

SYRIA AND THE LEVANT

Late Upper Palaeolithic: Early Kebaran[9]

A most significant Early Kebaran (*c.* 19,300 bp) site was revealed in the autumn of 1989 when the level of the Sea of Galilee dropped to an unusually low level of −212.45 metres below mean sea level, thereby uncovering what is probably the world's lowest archaeological site. The site has since been re-submerged. Called Ohalo II, it is situated 9 kilometres south of Tiberias on the southwestern shore of the freshwater lake (Kislev *et al.* 1992:161). Covering 1,500 square metres, the central area of 160 square metres was systematically excavated in addition to test trenches (Nadel and Hershkovitz 1991:632). Altogether 325 square metres have been exposed (Nadel *et al.* 1994:451). A well-preserved male skeleton belonging to this period was also recovered. About 35 years old, he was disabled.

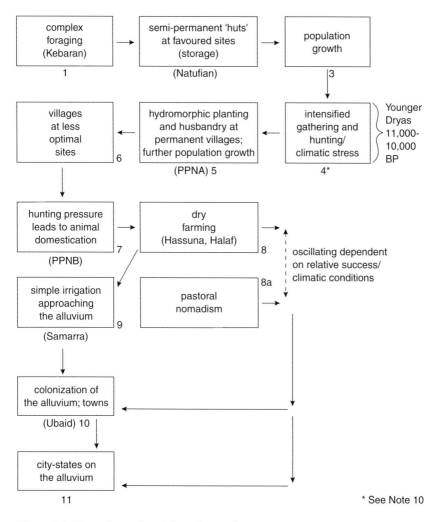

Figure 3.3 Flow chart of social evolution from hunter–gathering to city-states in the Near East

Source: Maisels 1990:70

In situ, and in good (even 'mint') condition thanks to the protective silt, were found 'typical flint tools, stone objects and beads made of Mediterranean shells. In the rich faunal assemblage remnants of fish, tortoise, birds, hare, fox, gazelle, deer and other species were identified' (ibid.). Plant species include wild barley (*Hordeum spontaneum*), wild emmer (*Triticum dicoccoides*), wild almond (*Amydalus communis*), wild olive (*Olea europea var. sylvestris*), wild pistachio (*Pistacia atlantica*) and wild grape (*Vitis vinifera ssp. sylvestris*) plus two types of oats and large acorn fragments. Thousands of fish bones were found, some still articulated, and fibres probably representing the nets used for catching and storing them (Nadel *et al.* 1994:457).

Of the plant seeds, barley grains were by far the most plentiful, which is not surprising as

> dense stands of wild barley are common in the Spring within a few hundred metres of the site, on the piedmonts of the Lower Galilee. If its distribution was similar to that found today, the grains could have been collected close to the site.
>
> (Kislev *et al.* 1992:164)

Situated in an area today receiving 400 millimetres of winter rain, Ohalo II was obviously a 'milk and honey' site for its inhabitants as well as for archaeologists, for whom really early food resources are almost never preserved in such a range to such a standard.[11] Also found were many Natufian-like major artefacts, notably basalt mortars and pestles and worked bone tools, along with the more obvious microliths, accompanied by burins, end-scrapers, awls, notches, retouched flakes and blades, plus Falita points (Nadel and Hershkovitz 1991:632).

Not only the major subsistence categories present – grains, fruits, nuts, edible plants, game, fish, fowl and reptiles – but the diversity within each is striking. Even now, 19,000 years later in a period of climatic optimum, only a small minority of the world's population have regular access to such a quality of diet. With such a diversity of high value resources available around the site, it is not surprising that Nadel and Hershkovitz (1991:633) and Kislev *et al.* (1992:164–5) suggest that the site was occupied at least during the spring and autumn (when, respectively, the grains and then the fruits/nuts become ripe). It is even possible that Ohalo II functioned as a permanent settlement provisioned logistically (Binford 1980) by means of task groups sent to fetch specific resources back to the settlement, only lacking durable structures. But there were structures. At Ohalo II three kidney-shaped 'pits' 3 to 4.5 metres wide and 0.5 metre deep were found to contain much flint, animal bone, carbonized seeds and other debris (Nadel and Hershkovitz 1991:632). These are house floors (cf. the late Epipalaeolithic site of Abu Hureyra, below); the largest had a dark perimeter with clear indications of the stems, straw and wood used for walling (Nadel *et al.* 1994:451). The huts occur in association with stone installations, graves, hearths, a pit and a trash dump (ibid.:453). Prior to the development of agriculture, however, sites as bountiful as Ohalo would have been few, and even semi-permanent settlement not generally possible.

In the schematic model of the settling down process in the Levant shown in Figure 3.4, we see that provisioning and thus mobility were usually logistic, which predisposes towards permanent settlement.

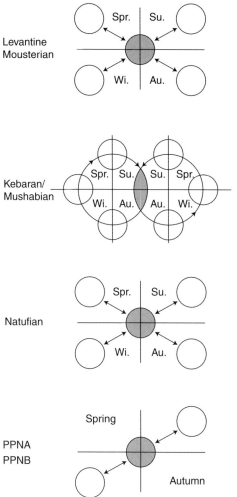

Levantine Mousterian

Kebaran/ Mushabian

Natufian

PPNA
PPNB

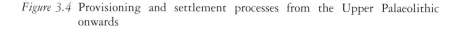

Circles indicate the relative location of campsites. Dark circles / intersections indicate sites occupied for longer and which accordingly tend to be larger.

Figure 3.4 Provisioning and settlement processes from the Upper Palaeolithic onwards

Epipalaeolithic: The Natufian

Originally identified in Palestine by Garrod, the Natufian was characterized by:

1   A toolkit in which lunates are a dominant element.
2   A well-developed bone industry.

3   A variety of heavy grinding equipment.
4   Circular dwellings and other structures in stone.
5   A high number of burials relative to preceding periods.
6   The first appearance in the Levant of art objects and items of personal adornment.

The question then arises as to which sites should be called 'Natufian', since not all sites even in the Carmel-Galilee 'heartland' will meet all six criteria, as a consequence of functional specialization. Perles and Phillips (1991: 638–9) have raised the potentially qualitative distinction between sites that have had the 'full' kit *attenuated* for functional-locational reasons (below) and those where the kit has been added to or substituted for, that is, where there are substantial differences of presence and absence. In this case, while we may still be dealing with an Epipalaeolithic culture having some interaction with the Natufian (and/or common derivation from the Kebaran), finer resolution can be obtained by *not lumping* into the Natufian those sites/cultures such as Mureybet and Hureyra on the Euphrates.

Brian F. Byrd, by applying cluster analysis to chipped stone tool group percentages from thirty-eight Natufian occupation horizons, found (and confirmed by Mann-Whitney tests) that they formed three major clusters:

> Cluster 1 is characterized by higher percentages of non-geometric backed tools, while cluster 2 has higher percentages of notches and denticulates, scrapers, and the 'various' tool group which is composed primarily of simple retouched pieces. Higher frequencies of geometric and lower percentages of burins differentiate cluster 3. In general, broad environmental differences exist between clusters. The cluster 1 sites are highly correlated with the forest and coastal environments, while sites of clusters 2 and 3 more closely correlate with the steppe and desert environments.
>
> (Byrd 1989:179)

One expects and generally finds that there is a greater thickness of occupational horizons in cluster 1 sites (woodland/coastal) as against cluster 3 (Byrd 1989:184), as well as variation in the frequency of tool types and the presence of architectural and storage structures. However, it is still an open question whether the same group of people centred upon a cluster 1 type site, move out seasonally to occupy type 2 and type 3 sites, from which to exploit steppe and desert environments; or whether either or both steppe and desert populations were specialists in those environments and thus detached from the woodland/coastal populations, sharing nothing perhaps but a common material and mental toolkit. In the latter case, relationships could have been sustained by periodic (annual?) ceremonial events (cf. Perles and Phillips 1991:637–44).

Certainly from the Geometric Kebaran onwards large aggregation sites are now well known, such as Neve David and Hefziba, the former covering over 1,000 square metres, the latter about 1,500 square metres (Kaufman 1989:278–9). Kaufman also observes that Nahal Oren and Hayonim Terrace seem to represent similar kinds of site in the Natufian period, and stresses 'continuity in ritual behaviour between the Geometric Kebaran and the Natufian' (ibid.).

The multi-period site of Hatula (Natufian, Khiamian, Sultanian) on the Nahal Nashon, just south of the famous Latrun monastery about 20 kilometres west of Jerusalem, is within the coastal/woodland belt as mapped by Byrd (1989:162 and 1991:266), and presently receives 500 millimetres of rainfall. However, the excavators Ronen and Lechevallier observe after eight seasons that, while Hatula has typical Natufian lithics and an elaborate bone industry, it has none of the characteristics indicative of sedentism, grinding implements being particularly notable by their absence. Indeed,

> not only structures and walls are wanting, but even isolated building materials – stones and pebbles – are strikingly missing. . . . The absence of even scattered building materials is taken to indicate that no Natufian structures existed at Hatula. The Natufian of Hatula also lacks art objects and burials.
>
> (Ronen and Lechevallier 1991:158)

They conclude (1991:159) that

> the Natufian at Hatula must be viewed . . . as an accumulation of short term halts in a specialized site, probably for hunting gazelle. It may mark a regressive shift from intensive to simple foraging, suggested by Henry (1989) to have occurred in the late Natufian because of climatic deterioration.

Or it may signify nothing of the sort: just a site about 15 metres above the river bed on the edge of a rocky slope in the upper reaches of the alluvial valley, which was excellent for the specialized task of intercepting gazelle herds and less than ideal for other subsistence purposes, even though located near a group of perennial springs (ibid.).

Conversely, Wadi Hammeh 27, an Early Natufian site near ancient Pella, Jordan, lies in the central Jordan valley, and as such is placed in the 'cleft' between the woodlands to east and west of the valley. The site takes its name from its location on an interfluvial ridge near the mouth of the Wadi al Hammeh, a tributary to the Jordan which enters the Rift opposite the Marj ibn al-Amr Plain (Edwards 1991:123). This site does indeed have permanent architecture (with internal hearths) in the form of three large oval structures: a concentric walled complex and a u-shaped structure, plus one that is about 14 metres across (ibid.:125). It has yielded three radio-carbon dates:

11,920+–150 bp (Humic acid from seeds)
12,200+–160 bp (Charred seeds)
11,950+–160 bp (Charred seeds)

(ibid.:128)

The site is also rich in heavy grinding equipment: no less than 77 pestles, some decorated, 48 mortars and 28 mullers (for use with open querns) in fine-grained basalt (mostly) and limestone from only two locations (ibid.:129–30). Additionally, there are hammer stones and arrow-shaft straighteners in the same material.

Hunting equipment was used on a range of large herbivores, including cattle, pigs, equids, deer, goat and gazelle (ibid.:144) with fox, hare, fresh-water crab (*Potamon potamon*) and tortoise still found in the vicinity of the site, but tortoise are the only reptilian remains from the Natufian. As usual, gazelle was the most exploited species (65.7 per cent of remains), with at least seven bird species contributing no less than 10 per cent of identified bone fragments (ibid.:145).

Only wild barley (*Hordeum spontaneum*) is as yet positively identified of the *Graminae*, though *Aegilops* and *Avena* (oats) seem to be present (ibid.). *Stipa* (steppe grass) is represented, as are several legume species, plus *Cruciferae*; this is particularly interesting as their roots can be used (Colledge 1991:392).

The type-indicating lunates (geometric microliths) are well represented, with Helwan retouched lunates occurring in the ratio of 4:1 to total lunates in Natufian Phase 1 levels. Other tools include chert picks and a 'prodigious number of flaked chert artefacts' (ibid.:129; 71,000 pieces from Plot XX D alone, of which over half are chunks and chips!), but no lumps of raw material, so the tools were probably fashioned where the lunates were extracted.

Helwan retouched bladelets were used in sickles, made of bone and horn core, slotted into v-shaped grooves 2 to 6 millimetres in width. No less than six sickle shapes, ranging from narrow straight-shafted examples to broad scimitar-like ones, were found virtually complete, with fragments of others (Edwards 1991:136–7). Bone (distal epiphyses) was also extensively used for beads, often strung together with *Dentalium (vulgare)* shell spacers. Long bone pieces served to fashion pendants and tubular beads (ibid.). Pendants were also made in non-organic rock crystal and schist, and polished agate also occurs. Further personal ornamentation derived from the use of red and yellow ochre, plus red and mauve ferruginous limestone (ibid.:137).

Burial pits were dug during the earliest phases of the site, and grave goods accompanied the dead, including red ochre and bead necklaces. Bone scatters represent at least three mature individuals, plus sub-adults and infants (ibid.:146).

Here at Wadi Hammeh 27 is a site with all the criteria for permanence, but which is not located on the coastal plains/densest woodland zone. Its location at the 'juxtaposition of riverine, crag, open-forest and savannah like habitats in close proximity to the site, all of which would have been centred on abundant freshwater resources' (ibid.:144) explains its year-round occupation, in common with Ohalo II and Abu Hureyra. As argued above, most-favoured sites are those where major resources intersect, and this is not necessarily in the midst of woodland. In the Near East, aquatic resources are more likely to be the key to diversity and thus plenty. Abu Hureyra's position on the inexhaustible Euphrates meant that it was the only Levantine site so far excavated to have been inhabited throughout the Younger Dryas drying episode of the eleventh millennium (Moore and Hillman 1992:490).

Mallaha (Eynan), for instance, one of the 'classic' Natufian sites with probably the best house remains, is located in a difficult position hard against the western cliffs of the northern rift valley because this gives it prime access to the resources of Lake Hula and the adjoining areas of marsh.

Terminal Epipalaeolithic: Hureyra on the Euphrates

In north-central Syria, only about 90 kilometres east of Aleppo (which is 110 kilometres east of the mouth of the Orontes), the Euphrates makes its closest approach to the sea. This stretch of the Middle Euphrates, the southern bend of which is now under Lake Assad (formed in 1972 by the Tabqa Dam), was the locus of two important Epipalaeolithic/ Pre-Pottery Neolithic sites, Tell Mureybet and Tell Abu Hureyra. Mureybet, which is not far north of Hureyra, but on the opposite bank and in a slightly wetter zone (with more emphasis on onager hunting), represents a later stage of the terminal Epipalaeolithic. Its beginning (Mureybet 1A) just overlaps the end of phase 3 of Hureyra 1 (Olszewski 1991:441). Hureyra 1 is thus broadly contemporary with the Natufian, and at a similar evolutionary level, though different in adaptive specifics (Moore 1991:289).

> Abu Hureyra 1 was located in the steppe and its economy reflects that strongly, above all in the dependence on seasonal hunting of gazelle and the exploitation of steppe grasses, cereals and other small-seeded plants. It was also a riverine site that looked out over the Euphrates flood-plain. The wild foods from the valley bottom [notably roots, rhizomes and tubers] contributed much to the diet of the inhabitants, especially in the later phases of occupation. Yet the steppe aspect of the economy remained of fundamental

importance throughout, and continued to contribute to the livelihood of the farmer-villagers of Abu Hureyra 2.

(ibid.:290)[12]

The tell, half a kilometre in diameter (11.5 hectares) had two distinct occupation periods, with a clear hiatus between the Epipalaeolithic and Neolithic.
The earlier, Abu Hureyra 1, was exposed over only 49 square metres at the
bottom of a trench 3 metres deep, from which level the strata containing
Hureyra 1 material descend another 1.4 metres. Cultural remains of Hureyra
1 divide into three phases, extending between 11,500 and 10,000 bp, and
perhaps beyond (ibid.:282). Architecture and subsistence opportunities
suggest a permanent (year-round) settlement of hunter–gatherers. Three
ecological zones were within walking distance: valley floor, steppe and forest
edge, which from the species associated with it, is assumed to have been
close to the site until early in Phase 2 (ibid.:286). Thereafter, the forest
retreated northwards and westwards in response to a drying episode.[13]

The habitations began (Phase 1: 11,500–11,000 bp) as grouped or interlocking pit dwellings reaching 2 to 2.5 metres in diameter and up to
0.7 metres deep, with post holes at their centres and also around the peripheries. 'The postholes would have contained vertical posts, probably of
poplar, that would have supported walls and roofs of brushwood and reeds,
or perhaps, gazelle skins' (ibid.:279). Associated with them were storage
pits reaching 1 metre in diameter (ibid.). The dwelling complexes, of which
three were dug, were probably family groupings. Amongst other artefacts,
they contained two basalt querns (in 470), other ground-stone tools, animal
bones and carbonized seeds.

Phase 2 houses (11,000–10,400 bp) were still tightly grouped, but above
ground, with clay-reinforced floor surfaces in some cases (ibid.). Hearths
were still being placed on the bench area across the centre of this site, while
around the hearths numerous groundstone and other tools were dropped.

By phase 3 (10,400–10,000 bp), 'the bench and [screening] bank [on
the south side] were completely covered with occupation debris . . . the hut
floors were more widely spaced as the village opened up and there were
numerous hearths all over the excavated area' (ibid.). Nonetheless, these
were still huts based on wooden posts with cladding between; mud-brick
architecture did not occur on the site until the Neolithic of Hureyra 2,
after the break. Charcoal from the hearths resulted from burning the gallery
woodlands, consisting of willow, poplar, maple and tamarisk (Hillman
et al. 1989:259).

The major initial attraction seems to have been that in the vicinity Persian
(or goitered) gazelle (*Gazella subgutterosa*) concentrated to cross the river at
the northernmost limit of their spring migrations from the Jordanian Desert
(Legge and Rowley-Conwy 1987:93). Gazelle bones, from mass kills just
after the April/May birthing, formed 80 per cent of the total (ibid.:94),

falling to 70 per cent in the early Neolithic though some onagers, sheep and hares were also taken (Moore 1991:285). Even this, however, would not by itself permit year-round settlement. The large-scale flotation methods employed by Hillman, Colledge and Harris (1989:259) enabled them to establish that there were at least 157 edible seed species represented at the site, although only a few were consumed in quantity. This indicates, in contrast to many sites where year-round occupation is merely assumed or conjectured, that at Hureyra 1 permanent occupation is highly probable, given the abundance and variety of plant species known to be available throughout the year. Forty-five flat or slightly concave basalt grinding dishes and twenty-one rubbers, also basalt, were recovered from Hureyra 1 (Moore 1991:281). While some basalt could have been imported from 80 kilometres away, most common were ground stone tools such as grinding stones and rubbers made of river pebbles (ibid.). However obsidian was also imported, with thirty pieces found.

Although settlement size and population are reckoned to have increased over the three phases of Hureyra 1 (ibid.:279), no major change occurred in tool types, the flint being largely flakes, and their main classes scrapers, notched pieces and microlithic lunates (ibid.). Of around one hundred bone artefacts recovered, most were awls, bipoints, needles and pins, with the bipoints most probably used to arm arrows (ibid.:281). Further,

> Olzewski's analysis has demonstrated quite clearly the important difference in flint working between Abu Hureyra 1 and Natufian sites. Our ground stone tools were mainly open dishes and rubbers with a few querns, while on Natufian sites mortars and pestles predominated. This hints at a difference in subsistence patterns, the grinding of seeds at Abu Hureyra and the processing of acorns, perhaps, on Natufian sites.
>
> (ibid.:289)

To me, however, it suggests more than this. Hureyra was not just geographically out on a limb. Its year-round occupation and permanence over the centuries rather set it apart from Natufian sites, even the largest and longest established. Relatively isolated, Hureyra was fortunate enough to occupy a stable niche by a major river with its three resource zones: stream, bankside/floodplain and hinterland.

Pre-Pottery Neolithic: Netiv Hagdud (PPNA) and 'Ain Ghazal (PPNB/PPNC)

Netiv Hagdud is a 1.5 hectare site situated at the outlet of the Wadi Bakar (and partially buried in its alluvial fan) which descends eastwards from the Judean hills into the Jordan Valley. A low mound, it is just 13 kilometres

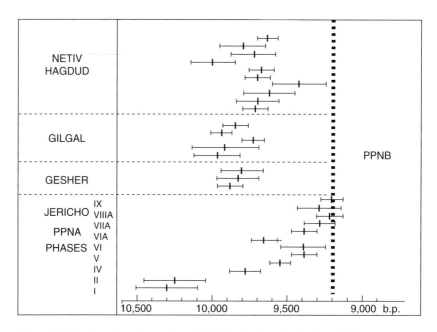

Figure 3.5 Radiocarbon dates from PPNA sites in the Jordan Valley
Source: Bar-Yosef *et al.* 1991:421

north of the mound of Jericho and within 2 kilometres of the related sites of Gilgal and Salibiya IX. Radiocarbon dates for those PPNA sites are shown in Figure 3.5.

Only Jericho seems to make it into the PPNB after 9,200 bp. Netiv Hagdud radiocarbon dates cluster around 9,700+−150 bp. A wood charcoal sample (RT-762 C) from Loc. 1004 gives 9970+−150 bp, but this was probably because the tree was old or dead when used for fuel. Barley seeds, by contrast, give 9700+−150 bp (see Table 6 in Bar-Yosef *et al.* 1991).

Though a relatively large exposure for sites discovered in the last two decades, even Netiv Hagdud has only been excavated over 500 square metres, and is effectively a rescue project caused by the building of a reservoir, whose fence cuts off the northernmost part. About 15 per cent of the site's total surface area has been damaged. This is particularly ironical, since the high frequency of Epipalaeolithic sites in the Salibiya basin is explained by the (then) presence of a shallow freshwater lake. Situated near 'copious springs' in an area then receiving around 300 millimetres of rainfall, Netiv Hagdud lay within the Mediterranean woodland belt (ibid.:418–19).

Despite belonging to the earliest Neolithic and still highly dependent on hunting gazelle, fowl and a wide range of other game, Netiv Hagdud is an archetypal Neolithic site to contrast with Natufian examples. It contains

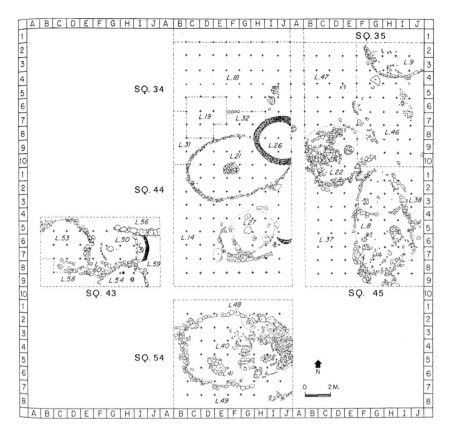

Figure 3.6 Composite map of the upper layers in the Upper Area of Netiv Hagdud
mound

Source: Bar-Yosef *et al.* 1991:407

permanent architecture of mud-brick on limestone foundations, storage silos
for gathered grains, and some of the very earliest examples of clay female
figurines. The site was occupied only during the Early Neolithic, and was
abandoned around 9500–9400 bp (ibid.:407).

Like their Natufian forebears, the houseforms at Netiv Hagdud are circular
or oval (rectilinear walls are later in the Neolithic), as shown in Figure 3.6.
Buildings are of two types: large oval ones 8–9 metres in length (e.g.: Locs
21, 8, 10, 23) and small circular ones of 4–5 metres in diameter (Locs 27,
50, 55, 57, 26, 51) (ibid.:408). A couple of houses seem to have been
constructed entirely of mud-brick, later coated with plaster to form continuous cover across floors and walls. The rest had foundations of limestone
slabs placed upright, standing to an average height of half a metre,

supporting walls of unbaked, plano-convex mud-brick like those of Jericho (ibid.). Wooden posts reinforced those walls and no doubt helped to support the weight of roofs made heavy by mud-plastered reeds on top of what were probably tree branches with twigs and leaves attached.

Only Loc. 8, an oval house, had its interior space sub-divided by a partition wall, and this one was anomalous in its contents. Containing a four cup-hole slab near the entrance (examples also at Locs 27 and 50), two further slabs with four and five cup-holes were found in the main room of the building. Common during the PPNA, those receptacles used with (usually basalt) pestles for pounding are probably the reason for the absence of deep mortars at the site (ibid.:415). In this anomalous house,

> Near the eastern wall, an unexpected, rectangular cobble-covered installation about 1 metre long was exposed. On its southern side, the remains of at least three fragmentary skulls of adults were found. The entire house contained numerous grinding implements such as pestles, broken mortars and bowls, and many flat polished pebbles: 70 items altogether. Only one flint axe was found, and only a very few other lithic artefacts. Undoubtedly this structure had a different function from most other habitations at the site.
>
> (ibid.:411)

The excavators do not suggest what this function may have been, but from the description Loc. 8 appears to be a communal meeting house for the preparing and sharing of ceremonially important meals, either life-cyclical (wakes?) or seasonal. It is also likely that the 'skull cult' was a means of promoting community cohesion by stressing ancestral roots. Slightly concave cobbled floors seem to have served as hearths in various loci, such that 'the number of fire-cracked rocks in the deposits is one of the major sedimentological attributes of this mound' (ibid.:409).

Bins and silos provided storage, probably for dry grains (ibid.:411). Three small bins formed from flat limestone slabs each of 40 centimetres diameter and about 40–50 centimetres deep were encountered, and under Locus 40, two round 1-metre deep silos built of mud (ibid.). No doubt the small number reflects limited exposure, limited storage at so early a site and related reliance upon an 'amazingly rich diversity of vertebrate species', though not just vertebrates. The mosaic of ecotypes in the vicinity provided an enormous range of species, ranging from carp-like fish, through snails, crabs, frogs, lizards (including chameleon) and tortoise, to hare, ibex, gazelle (*Gazella gazella*, 130 bones so far, making it the most abundant species among the *Bovidae*), wild pig and fallow deer (*Dama mesopotamica*), most of which would have been consumed fresh (ibid.:418–19). Even a few fragmentary bones of hartebeest (*Alcelaphus buselaphus*) were recovered. However, the greatest variety of species and individuals derives from no less than

2,000 birds, most of which are ducks (*Anas* spp.) but also including quail (*Coturnix coturnix*) and birds of prey (for feathers?).

Nearby woodland is also reflected in the presence of bifacial axes and adzes, including the type called 'Tahunian tranchets' which have an edge shaped by transverse removal (ibid.:412). Also included amongst the axes are polished celts in limestone and basalt, the two common materials at the site. Thirty pieces of obsidian from Golu Dag in the Ciftlik region of central Anatolia were found, contrasting with Gilgal, where none was discovered. At Jericho, however, the number of pieces recovered per cubic metre, without proper sieving, was actually higher (ibid.:417). Arrowheads are mostly El-Khiam points: a small projectile with a notch on either side separating point from base, which is concave retouched (ibid.:414, Figure 9). Also present is the 'Hagdud truncation': a 'special tool' formed from the segment of a blade (ibid.:414–15). The use of arrows is further indicated by the finding or a cache of 'arrow straighteners': smoothed oblong stones with deep grooves running lengthwise.

> Grinding stones include flat stone bowls or *metates* (11.0%) and handstones or *manos* (8.7%). The former are made of limestone and are generally broken, while the handstones are limestone, occasionally basalt, and even less often sandstone.
>
> Included in the group of grinding or food processing tools are flat limestone slabs (1.1%) and small limestone bowls that exhibit fine workmanship by their slender, curved profiles.
>
> (ibid.:415)

However, there is a large category of miscellaneous objects (43.3 per cent of 329 ground stone items), some of which represent fragments (e.g. of pestles) and others semi-processed materials, such as pebbles, a flat example of which bears a decorative meander pattern between multiple horizontal lines (ibid.: Figure 12). Similar and more complex patterns also occur at Jerf el-Ahmar, a new Mureybetian (PPNA) site on the Middle Euphrates (Stordeur *et al.* 1996: Figure 2).

The excavators of Netiv Hagdud (Bar-Yosef *et al.* 1991:420) suggest that the cup-holes were used to crush the spiny pods of the wild legume sainfoin (*Onobrychis* sp.) with a pestle. Employing flotation methods, over 50 plant species were identified, ranging from goat grass (*Aegilops geniculata/peregrina*), oats, emmer and barley (thousands of grains and rachis fragments of *H. spontaneum* recovered) through legumes, including lentil and plaintain (*Plantago* sp.), to tree crops: fig (*Ficus caria*), pistachio (*Pistacia atlantica*), and almond (*Amygdalus communis/korchinskii*), plus acorns of Tabor oak (*Quercus ithaburensis*). The fruits of both *Pistacia* species, *atlantica* and *palaestina*, are edible.

Truly the inhabitants of this Garden of Eden wanted for nothing. A mix of aquatic, terrestrial and avian species were available throughout the year, while barley became available in spring and early autumn, the fruits, nuts and acorns from September until December. The excavators consider that 'the evidence from Netiv Hagdud represents an early phase of field-crop agriculture, *a monoculture of wild, pre-domesticated barley*. Only in Pre-Pottery Neolithic B (9,200–8,000 bp) sites is there good morphological evidence for domesticated cereals' (ibid.:420, my emphasis). Indeed, Kislev (1992: 91–2) has on this basis developed a model for the onset of agriculture which posits (a) that domesticated cereals were *not* the staple during the eighth millennium, and (b) that pulses, fig and other tree fruits, with possibly flax, were in fact the first crops to be cultivated, but only 'locally and on a small scale'. Only in the seventh millennium would extensive cultivation employing domesticated cereals have emerged.

At Ras Shamra the pulses, especially lentil, were at least as widely grown as grain (emmer and two-row barley) in the early phases. Thereafter the proportion of pulses fell continuously to very low values in the Halaf levels, which terminate here around 4300 BC. The wild olive was an important food at Ras Shamra and at Atlit Yam, also on the coast (now submerged). At this more southerly site the olive may even have been domesticated as early as the sixth millennium BC (Galili *et al*. 1993:154). This is, of course, at least a thousand years earlier than the Chalcolithic Ghassulian indications (discussed below), though both olive and flax appear for the first time in PPNB (Willcox 1996:151). Willcox (ibid.) also reports that the first fully morphologically domesticated cereals occur at Halula in the middle Euphrates Valley (north of Mureybet) during the middle PPNB. A similar decline of pulses relative to cereals was also observed at Aswad and Ghoraife (Van Zeist and Bakker-Heeres (1984/86a:166). However, this relationship is far from straightforward, as the survival chances of grains are so much higher than pulses.[14]

Kislev's model reinforces my earlier argument (1990:65–77) that hunter–gatherers became farmers accidentally and piecemeal, for what they actually intended to do was to extend their subsistence repertoire by storing the newly abundant wild grains (in the late Epipalaeolithic/Early Holocene). Achieving success in bolstering food supplies allowed population to increase, in turn forcing intensified food procurement. This is the earliest stage at which plants would have been cultivated (stage 5 in Figure 3.3) and this is probably when the pulse/tree-fruit/flax complex became established (in the eighth millennium).

Actual planting of the grains would not occur until, with the expansion of population, new villages had to bud-off to new sites where wild stands were either absent or insufficient. Provision at such sub-optimal sites necessitated the planting of fields of cereal (no longer merely harvesting wild stands) and the rearing of animals when predatory pressures made species locally scarce. As discussed below, only planting puts selection pressures on wild cereals rendering them domesticated,[15] for wild cereals have brittle spikelets which shatter, and self-sow, on ripening. Only interference with this mechanism puts selection pressure upon wild populations. This pressure can amount to ca. 60 per cent per generation (year) against the wild-type spikelets, where the four criteria below are present (Hillman and Davies 1992:151). From computer modelling, Hillman and Davies estimate the length of time needed for the fixation of the semi-tough rachis (i.e. the emergence of populations of fully domestic einkorn, and by extension emmer and barley), to be of the order of only twenty to 200 years (ibid.).

From their long-term experimental/theoretical work, Hillman and Davies (ibid.:124) derive two plus two prerequisites for the emergence of domesticated cereals from wild stands by unconscious selection. The first is that grains would have to harvested by sickling or uprooting, not by beating. Beating ripe grains into a basket minimizes effort and time in harvest, but has high grain losses due to brittle spikelets on necessarily ripe ears. Further, the unevenness of ripening calls for several passes through the stand which results in serious trampling of the stems. Indeed, P.C. Anderson (1992a:187) found the method so wasteful as to be impractical at the Jales experimental station in Mediterranean France. Accordingly, she suggests that beating might be suitable only for panicled grasses, not for the 'spike' grasses like wild einkorn and wild barley.

Sickling, by contrast, maximizes output per unit area, which would be important with rising human populations. This second prerequisite demands, therefore, that ears be harvested in the pre-ripe, semi-green (or even unripe green) state. Not only does the still firm attachment of the grains prevent harvesting losses, but those grains are reckoned to have superior flavour (Hillman and Davies 1992:128), which is particularly important when they are to be used in types of gruel or roasted. Laboratory germination tests showed that grains harvested green or semi-green are still viable for use as seed stocks, with germination success rates ranging between 85 per cent and 95 per cent (Anderson 1992a:191). Further, the classical crescentic sickle with three to four microlithic blade inserts and a fairly long handle was found to be the most practical sickle form, and 'was used for year to year without retouching or renewing blades' (ibid.:185).

If two further conditions are not met, namely that the grains must be sown on new land each year and they must be taken from last year's *new* plots, around a century more must be added to the domestication process. For the first requirement, Hillman and Davies suggest either shifting cultivation or field-extension. I have already proposed the mechanism to be field-extensions and wholly new fields at new villages in response to population pressure consequent upon sedentism itself. However, the 'shifting cultivation' could consist of 'short fallow' of three to four years, discussed in detail elsewhere (Maisels 1990:31–9). Briefly, the sort of 'shifting cultivation' envisageable in the Near East is actually not shifting but rotational cultivation around a fixed site.

The second requirement, of using 'last year's new plots' to supply the seed grains, could have been met, since older plots tend to become quickly weed infested (resulting in 'mixed seeds' being planted) whereas last year's plot would still be relatively clean. Further, 'by sowing early and densely, the weed problem can be greatly reduced' (Willcox 1992b:168). Unsurprisingly, for it mimics Nature, the densest and most evenly ripening stands are obtained by early or summer sowing, as against late or autumn sowing (Anderson 1992a:206). Spring sowing gives such poor results that it was probably employed only as a last resort.

Hillman and Davies (op. cit.:151) estimate that once the process of unconscious selection had become visible around the 1–5 per cent level, then conscious selection could have played a part. However, below 5 per cent the domestic type rachis cannot have been very visible. On the assumption that harvesting when green produces much more sickle-sheen or gloss than harvesting dry, fully ripe grains, evidence from 'Ain Ghazal indicates that unripe ears were harvested until the pattern was

> drastically altered in the LPPNB (c. 8,500–8,000 bp), which contains few heavily glossed blades, a small proportion of moderately glossed blades, and an abundance of those that are lightly glossed. These findings suggest that by the LPPNB the reaping of cereal grains occurred when the plants were dry and the crops were fully ripened.
>
> (Qintero et al. 1997)

The village of 'Ain Ghazal at the 'spring of the gazelles'

The PPNB in general is best seen at the site of 'Ain Ghazal, some 14 kilometres to the northeast of the centre of Amman, capital of Jordan. It is situated on both sides of the Zarqa River, the western slope averaging 10 per cent and the eastern 35 per cent, as can be seen from the close grouping of the contour lines. The plateau above the east slope/bank of the Wadi Zarqa has a slope of 4 per cent, and it likely that this plateau was the location of the bulk of the farmland cultivated from the MPPNB through to the Yarmoukian Period. 'Ain Ghazal is situated near 'an abundant spring' and Kafafi (1993:104) observes that all five Yarmoukian sites that have been excavated in Jordan – 'Ain Rahub, Jebel Abu Thawwab, 'Ain Ghazal, Wadi Shu'eib and Tell Wadi Feinan – 'are all located on the banks of wadis, most of them sloping and all are close to perennial water sources'.

At 700–740 metres above sea level, 'Ain Ghazal is a large settlement of town dimensions (>15 hectares) founded in the MPPNB and extending through the PPNC to the late Yarmoukian (early Pottery Neolithic) period without a break (Rollefson n.d.). The site presently receives annual precipitation of 250 millimetres, which is just adequate (in reliable years) for cereal farming. It is located between two phytogeographical zones, that of Mediterranean scrub and Indoturanian vegetation, with true forest and true desert well within a day's walk (Kafafi 1993:103). The MPPNB agricultural suite included wheat, barley, peas, lentils and chickpeas, with almonds, figs and pistachios.

'Ain Ghazal is one of the very largest Neolithic settlements known in the Near East, extending over at least 15 hectares, not including the area of the river itself (Rollefson and Kafafi 1996b:1). The right side (northern end) of the settlement has been truncated by road development.

Excavation has proceeded since 1982 at a site already reduced by building development and due to be virtually obliterated, but still excavated over less than 1 per cent of its area. Fortunately, the core of the site at least is to be preserved for research and tourism (Rollefson 1996:6). It is probable that 'Ain Ghazal's population peaked, near the end of the LPPNB (c. 6100 BC),

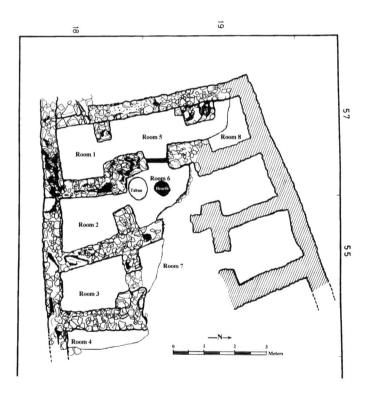

Figure 3.7 LLPNB house at 'Ain Ghazal. The structure had two storeys at least over the western half of the building (Rooms 1–2, 5–6, and 8–9). Rooms 1–2 and 5–6 had hundreds of thousands of charred lentils in the fill, fallen from the rooms above.

Source: Drawing and description by special courtesy of G.O. Rollefson.

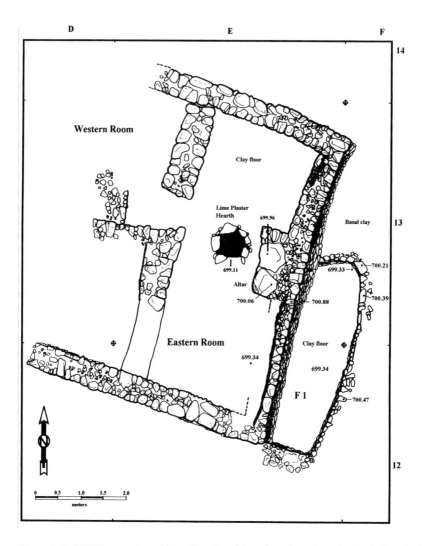

Figure 3.8 PPNC temple at 'Ain Ghazal, with a floor hearth and raised altar (*c.* 1m
high) in the east room. F1 is a semi-subterranean storage (?) facility outside
the temple. The western room was destroyed by erosion and bulldozers,
but there was a doorway near the centre, with a wall that made a 90° turn,
blocking off view into this forerunner of the 'holy of holies'.

Source: Drawing and description by special courtesy of G.O. Rollefson.

at between 2,500 and 3,000 people, requiring a support area of 1,000 hectares
(G. Rollefson, pers. comm.).

Houses were rectangular constructions in stone with, of course, plastered
floors, 'finger-painted' with red ochre in dense, parallel lines. The main

room of each house during the early MPPNB phase measured 5 × 5 metres, with a central hearth. The roof was supported on two or four posts, the holes for which at this time were 50–60 centimetres in diameter, later shrinking to only 15–20 centimetres (Rollefson *et al.* 1992:448). Further indicating that ever smaller timbers were being used, room size also shrank during the MPPNB, and into the LPPNB also (ibid.:449). In common with several other Jordanian LPPNB sites such as Basta and 'Ain Jammam, at least two two-storey buildings occur at 'Ain Ghazal in this period. Figure 3.7 shows just such a two-storey LPPNB house.

By the PPNC in the first part of the sixth millennium, a marked change in architecture occurs:

> Room sizes changed little from the preceding LPPNB period, but room shapes altered considerably. Rather than small square chambers (which could be roofed using only branches) the PPNC spaces were rectangular, separated by a central corridor leading from the front entrance to the back wall. The restricted confinement of the cells argues against 'normal' domestic use, such as living/reception rooms or sleeping chambers.
>
> (ibid.)

Taken with the fact that rooms were semi-subterranean with walls of PPNC structures never exceeding a metre in height, Rollefson *et al.* (op. cit.) argue that those were not houses at all, but storage facilities for a significant proportion of the village population. This substantial part of the population effectively detached itself for much of the year to pursue a pastoralist way of life grazing goats. They maintain (1992:452) that goats had been domesticated by the end of the MPPNB[16] and did enormous ecological damage when herded in the vicinity of the village. According to Alex Wasse (1997), in the MPPNB the ratio of sheep to goats was 5:95 per cent, a proportion that reversed in the PPNC to 85:15 per cent.

Domesticated cattle were exploited by the beginning of the sixth millennium (Rollefson *et al.* 1992:452). Indeed, by the Yarmoukian, domesticated animals provided over 90 per cent of the meat consumed at 'Ain Ghazal (ibid.:453). Crucially though, the percentage of domestic ovicaprids among the identified faunal elements rose from around 50 per cent during the PPNB to 70 per cent in the PPNC at 'Ain Ghazal, with similar proportions reported from roughly contemporary Jericho, Beidha and Basta (Rollefson and Rollefson 1993:39). Given the devastating effects of goat husbandry on vegetation, especially semi-arid vegetation which cannot tolerate year-round grazing, Rollefson and Rollefson (ibid.) argue that 'it was the PPNC that witnessed the emergence of nomadic pastoralism', whereby ovicaprid herds were taken right away from the village on long annual circuits. This enabled 'Ain Ghazal to sustain a settlement in the PPNC of more than 10 hectares.

The PPNC was itself a period of flux such that by the Yarmoukian 'a fully segregated pastoral vs farming strategy had been adopted' (Rollefson *et al.* 1992:468) at least in the drier, southern Levant, where deforestation had been most serious. This is seen in the move from oak to tamarisk in the charcoal remains from the MPPNB forwards, and in the use of dung and/or brush for fuel by the mid-PPNC (ibid.:453–4).

Although PPNC room size had shrunk to 4 × 4.5 metres on a poor quality *huwwar* surface (i.e. a mechanical mixture of chalk/marl and mud, requiring no firing, as opposed to lime plaster which does), a broad and long courtyard wall separating two *huwwar*-plastered outdoor areas (Rollefson 1993:94) suggests that investments were still being made in village installations during the PPNC. However, this wall, preserved to *c.* 60 centimetres (five courses), 1.4 metres wide and running NW–SE for well over 11 metres in the Central Field, may simply have existed to 'privatize' family spaces or to separate settled from the mobile parts of the population with their animals. So during the PPNC there were two different kinds of structures at 'Ain Ghazal: the semi-subterranean storage bunkers for pastoralist use and normal dwellings inhabited by farmers who lived at 'Ain Ghazal all year round (Rollefson and Kohler-Rollefson 1993). The houses are, however, simple and small (4 × 4.5 metres) in comparison to earlier houses at 'Ain Ghazal.

The significance of the ancestor/skull cult during the PPNB under the conditions of egalitarianism obtaining, seems to have lain in the attempt to produce community cohesion by symbolic elaboration of 'corporate belonging' (McIntosh 1991), since integration by hierarchical assignment had not yet evolved. When intensification of the ideological domain would no longer suffice, due to demographic/ecological or political pressures, communities diminished and or/dispersed, marking either the failure of this mode of integration, or its irrelevance under changed conditions.[17]

Certainly, the 'ancestor cult' embodied in skull veneration, symbolizing rootedness and continuity, was no longer practised even during the PPNC:

> In contrast to the 7th millennium burials the semiflexed and flexed PPNC bodies retained the skull intact with the rest of the skeleton; indisputably, the 'skull cult' form of ancestor veneration was no longer practiced. Two of the adult burial pits included immature pig skulls in their graves, and a third included other kinds of pig bones.
>
> (Rollefson and Rollefson 1993:38)

Yarmoukian burials, in contrast to the PPNC practice of subfloor or courtyard interments, were placed outside the villages (Rollefson 1993:97). Neither have interments within the settlement boundaries been reported from Tell Abu Thawwab, 'Ain Rahub, Wadi Shu'eib or Munhata (ibid.). Although about 1,150 square metres have been excavated of the Yarmoukian at 'Ain Ghazal, so far (1996) not a single burial has been found there.

From China we can clearly see the political-organizational possibilities of ancestor worship, reinforcing reverence for senior categories of kin: parents, their parents, elders (the parental/grand-parental generation), elder brothers, etc. By such means a finely structured 'natural' hierarchy is established with asymmetric rights and obligations. The 'balance' of the reciprocation deficit due to juniors is restored when (if) one becomes senior oneself (or a mother-in-law). And one cannot become more senior than by becoming an ancestor: a deceased senior who continues to live in and through his descendants, kept alive by their worship. The ancestor reciprocates by his paternal care of them, now that he has influence in the spirit world. Ancestors should receive detailed reports of descendants' activities. A disregarded or disrespected ancestor is a dangerous enemy; it then becomes a malevolent spirit. In societies of ancestor worship when misfortunes become serious, one immediately asks how the ancestors might have been offended. Beyond the familial hierarchy is the general order that is established by such means.

It looks as if, beyond the MPPNB, ancestor worship could not by itself provide the 'manifest community focus' required. Accordingly, by LPPNB, PPNC and Yarmoukian times, community focus took the form of shrines or temples (today the mosque) not only at 'Ain Ghazal, but also at other LPPNB settlements such as Beidha, Jericho and Ghwair I, with others in Turkey also. Ancestor worship began to fade in the LPPNB, disappearing completely by the PPNC. The later LPPNB period (when the shrines and LPPNB temple were in use) have not produced any plastered skulls or even decapitated skeletons, and the same is generally true at Basta, 'Ain Jammam and Es-Sufiya, indicating that the older practices were dying out even before the end of the PPNB (Rollefson pers. comm.).

No longer the main focus, the deceased could now be removed to a collective burying place away from the community. Perhaps related to this transition is the occurrence at 'Ain Ghazal of two caches of statuettes, consisting of those about 35 centimetres high (called 'dumpies') and others 90 centimetres tall (called 'figures'), made of lime plaster modelled around a reed/brush core serving as an armature (Tubb 1985:117). Quite different from the usual Neolithic pregnant-woman fecundity blobs (which also occur at 'Ain Ghazal where they wear a sort of linear tattoo), the MPPNB figures show particularly realistic human torsos modelled in the round, perhaps the earliest anywhere. They also have particularly clearly modelled eyes, noses and ears, and indeed other anatomical details such as toenails. The 'dumpies', by contrast, possibly later, are busts only (ibid.:123). Perhaps what the stare of the figures signifies is that the ancestors are watching over their descendants and/or watching out for correct/reverential behaviour from them (Figure 3.9).

Two temples have been found in East Field, one LPPNB, the other possibly early PPNC (Figure 3.8).

The axis of the earlier temple is oriented southeast–northwest, but its full dimensions are unknown due to erosion. What survives is a dressed-

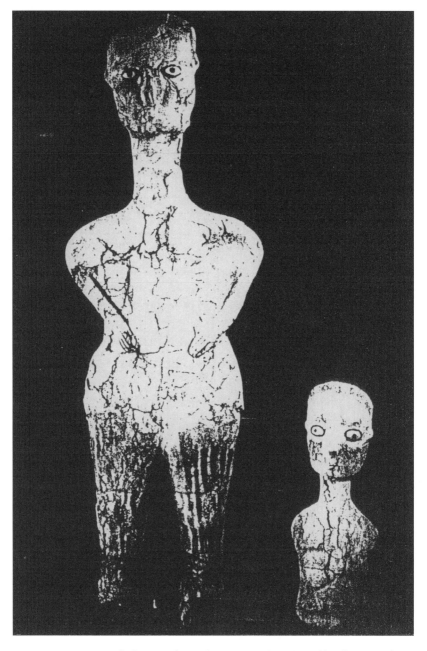

Figure 3.9 Figure and 'dumpy' from the 1983 cache. The taller figure is about 90 cm high

Source: Rollefson, Simmons and Kafafi 1992:467. Photo: P. Dorrel and S. Laidlaw

114

Figure 3.10 Lifted deposit of statues at 'Ain Ghazal in the course of laboratory excavation and separation. Letters designate individual pieces referred to in the catalogue

Source: K. Tubb in Rollefson *et al*. 1985:118

stone construction measuring about 5 metres E/W by 4 metres N/S (Rollefson and Kafafi 1996a:2). This room has five features that mark its purposes as cultic:

1   At its centre three 'standing stones' about 70 centimetres high, oriented N/S.
2   A floor-level platform at the southwestern edge of the room, made of two rectangular stone blocks of about a metre in length, oriented E/W. They partially enclose a layer of clay burned to the colour and consistency of fired ceramics.
3   About midway between the standing stones and the eastern wall is a circular hearth of red-painted plaster showing evidence of burning, about 50 centimetres in diameter and surrounded by seven flat limestone slabs.
4   A large, brilliant white, chalky limestone orthostat over a metre high and about 50 centimetres thick was built into the centre of the eastern wall. Projecting from the centre-top of the orthostat is a natural knob-like projection, lending it an anthropomorphic shape. However, it is not known whether this was a desired feature. The excavators (Rollefson and Kafafi 1996a:2) suggest that 'the presence of this orthostat may indicate that the walls were built only to this height and that the structure may have been open to the sky'.
5   During a later phase, a single-leaf wall closed off the space between the northernmost standing stone and the north wall. Inside the alcove thus formed, a low platform of large and small limestone slabs was constructed (ibid.).

The PPNC temple is situated about 75 metres to the south and is also rectangular or sub-square. Erosion has destroyed its western limits. This building consists of two interior rooms connected by a metre-wide doorway. The damaged western room would have measured at least 6.5 metres N/S and 2 metres E/W. As its floor is largely destroyed, the eastern room supplies most information. Measuring 6.5 metres N/S × 3.5 metres E/W, its long axis, N/S, thus contrasts with that of the PPNB temple. However, this eastern temple room is also marked by five features:

1   The floor is made of uncharacteristic sterile yellowish clay and was kept scrupulously clean. This floor does not extend to the west room.
2   In the centre of the eastern wall is a construction some 2 metres long and 60 centimetres wide, made of two large flat limestone slabs resting on three pairs of standing stones. As those standing stones vary in height between 45 and 70 centimetres, smaller stones fill the uneven spaces. Rollefson and Kafafi (1996a:3) logically call this construction an altar. (See Figure 3.8.)

3   'Directly in front of the central pair of standing stones supporting the altar was a lime plaster hearth surrounded by seven flat limestone slabs, altogether about 1 metre in diameter. While this parallels the LPPNB temple hearth, the PPNC example was not painted red, although there was clear evidence of burning on the plaster surface' (Rollefson and Kafafi 1996:3).

4   Adjacent to the centre of the northern wall is a small feature made of limestone slabs set onto the clay floor, thereby forming a roughly square 'cubicle'. Empty of any artefacts or refuse, its function remains unknown (ibid.).

5   When the door between the two rooms was opened, a narrow 'screen-wall' built westward from the door for about 60 centimetres before making a right-angled turn to the north was seen. This had the effect of blocking the line-of-sight from the western room into the eastern, so preventing any view of the altar and associated hearth. This effectively marks off the eastern room as an inner sanctum, with the western room serving as the meeting hall or antechamber (Rollefson and Kafafi 1996a:3).

Two shrines, used successively, were found in the North Field, where a four-phase LPPNB cult building was discovered in 1993.

> Phase 1, like its successor, consisted of an apsidal building. All of the phases utilized a courtyard behind (west) the building, which originally was an abandoned MPPNB house with a lime plaster floor and walls modified by the LPPNB inheritors. Five metres to the south of this (ultimately) circular shrine, a virtual twin circular shrine was exposed, presumably the successor to the original circular building after it was abandoned; the more recent shrine was quickly erected and lasted only a short time. PPNC exposures in the North Field showed considerable re-use of earlier LPPNB structures, but severe post-depositional damage (especially by twentieth century agriculture) make reconstructing the PPNC situation very difficult.
>
> (Rollefson 1996:5)

An apsidal structure also occurs at Abu Thawwab (Kafafi 1993:108).

'Ain Ghazal was one of the few settlements to survive the PPNB collapse, which it did by becoming a 'fluctuating population centre'. This

> is associated with a socioeconomic base in which agriculture and pastoralism are semi-integrated such that herd animals are kept away from the village fields and settlement for extensive parts of the year. Modern examples of this settlement type are Qrein and

Suweimra, settled Howeitat Bedouin villages approximately 20 km WSW of Ma'an in southern Jordan.

(Rollefson and Kohler-Rollefson 1989:85)

At their peak from May to October, the populations of those villages are respectively 3,000 and 800. However, once the winter rains have come, the flocks are removed to the steppe and desert for grazing, there to remain until the spring. During this 'detached' period, the human population falls to 500 and 250 (ibid.), which of course also makes fewer demands on the environment.

In the PPNC period there seems to have been a 'fluctuating' population at 'Ain Ghazal, with some families leaving the town with their herds of sheep/goat for the steppe and desert at the start of the rains, staying away until after the grain harvest. When they returned home they exchanged the sheep/goat products for the grain and pulses that had been harvested and stored for them in the corridor buildings. This periodic movement away from and back to the permanent settlement is what Kohler-Rollefson has termed 'Incipient Migratory Pastoralism' (Bar-Yosef and Khazanov 1992:11).

In the Yarmoukian it appears that farming and pastoralism had become completely separated at 'Ain Ghazal. Although a few sheep/goats may have been owned by residents, most ovicaprids were in the hands of full-time pastoralists who visited, but did not live at 'Ain Ghazal. Eventually the farmland within a reasonable distance of the settlement gave out, and the farmers went elsewhere. It was then that pastoralists began erecting temporary, circular structures at 'Ain Ghazal (Rollefson and Kafafi 1994).

Both rounded and rectilinear structures are found at Yarmoukian sites: rounded ones at Munhata, Megiddo and Jebel Abu Thawwab, rectangular ones at Sha'ar Hagolan and 'Ain Ghazal (Garfinkel 1993:129; Gopher and Gophna 1993:311).

Mid to late Neolithic

First identified as a distinct cultural phase by Stekelis at Sha'ar Hagolan, the Yarmoukian culture was characterized by him as manifesting: '1. Pottery decorated with incised herring-bone pattern; 2. Sickleblades with course denticulation; 3. A rich assemblage of art objects, which included large numbers of schematic anthropomorphic pebble figurines' (Garfinkel 1993:115). However, more intensive excavations of the Yarmoukian site of Munhata by J. Perrot from 1962–7 make Munhata the key site for a fuller understanding of that culture. Further, 'Art objects have been found in almost every Yarmoukian site, but two sites, Sha'ar Hagolan and Munhata, are unparalleled in the quantity and quality of their artistic inventory' (ibid.:126). As to the pottery of this first phase of the Pottery Neolithic, there is an earlier stratum of pottery than the 'classic' herring-bone or chevron incised, namely red painted or red slipped ware, which, at 'Ain Ghazal is stratified beneath the herring-bone. Red painted/red slipped ware is, of course, later than the very crude 'experimental' pottery sherds in the PPNC layers at 'Ain Ghazal and Basta (Kafafi 1993:110).

More detail on Sha'ar Hagolan can be found in Maisels 1993a:100–1. In a recent major review of the Pottery Neolithic, Gopher and Gophna observe that

> the major distribution of Yarmukian . . . lies in an east–west band across central Israel and Jordan, spanning all the topographical units of the southern Levant: the coastal plain, the mountainous ridges and valleys, the Jordan valley, and the Jordanian Plateau. This band is very narrow from north to south, reaching from the Nahal Soreq area to the Nahal Hadera in the coastal plain and from the Dead Sea to the River Yarmuk in the Jordan Valley and the Jordanian Plateau.
>
> (Gopher and Gophna 1993:315)

They also (ibid.: Figure 10) identify a somewhat later distinctive ceramic style, Jericho IX (= Lodian). This ware has innovatory slip, paint and burnish, plus different shapes and technology from the Yarmoukian. It occurs at sites with a more westerly and southerly distribution, obviously including Jericho itself, with Jericho near the eastern margins. As yet 'no Jericho IX material is reported from the hilly area of Israel' (ibid.:322).

Jericho IX assemblages are followed by those of the Wadi Raba culture,

> a major entity which consisted of an array of generally contempor-aneous and interrelated variants, spanning much of the seventh millennium bp and occupying the Mediterranean zones of the southern Levant. . . . Geographically, the Wadi Raba sensu lato, including all variants, is larger than the Yarmoukian or Jericho IX. It also displays more diversity and spatial segregation.
>
> (ibid.:339)

By this period, they suggest, hunting had almost disappeared, olives were being used, while the increased importance of dairy products is indicated by the presence of early churns, along with higher frequencies of cattle (and pig). 'Overall', they conclude (ibid.:344), 'the Wadi Raba economy reflects an established rural society.'

The Chalcolithic

The Ghassulian culture is the local Chalcolithic of the southern Levant. It is the one in which the domesticated olive (more flesh and oil) makes an unmistakable appearance as an important crop (Zohary and Spiegel-Roy

1975:319). Churns are prominent in Ghassulian iconography, lending support to Sherratt's (1981) concept of a 'secondary products revolution' exploiting animals for purposes other than meat, from ploughing and transport to dairy products, some four millennia after their original domestication.

Well beyond this, however, the explosive specialization characterizing the Chalcolithic is the cause of a wider technological and social revolution of which the 'secondary-products' revolution is merely a part, although in the Levant a particularly important part. It is commonplace since Childe to speak of a Bronze Age 'urban revolution', but we can now speak of a 'Chalcolithic technological revolution'. Alternatively, stressing its social aspect we can just as well call it the Chalcolithic 'specialization revolution'. Its profound consequences for the political economy have already been discussed in Chapter 1.

As described in the previous chapter, the Ghassulian-Beersheba had important connections with Buto-Maadi culture (cf. Perrot 1955), indicated by the presence at Maadi of 'fan-scrapers' on tabular flint (Caneva et al. 1989:291). Here, again, in both Egypt and Palestine, we encounter the Chalcolithic (= Eneolithique) defined not merely by copper usage, but rather by a system of production in which specialization *and diversification* have increased relative to the Neolithic (Levy 1986). The specialists need not be full-time, though some are likely to be. Here in the Levant 'fourth millennium crafts were practiced by part-time specialists and this seems to be the case for trade too' (Gilead 1988:427) and also priestcraft, as indicated by the shrine at En Gedi (ibid.:434). Located on the western shores of the Dead Sea, distant from any settlement, it probably served as a cult centre for a number of communities, as Gilat seems to have done for the whole of southern Palestine. It is the specialization itself that matters, not the materials utilized or whether the practitioners also engage in other activities. Not only will an increasingly wide range of goods be produced under specialization, but 'services' too. This said, the quantity and quality of copper artefacts produced by Ghassul-Beersheba culture, most notably the hoard found in the Cave of the Treasure, Nahal Mismar, do indicate that metal casting here (as in China) had particular significance.

However, Teleilat Ghassul's flint industries reflect specialization in woodworking (Elliott 1978:46), as at Byblos, the largest Levantine Chalcolithic site. The size of Byblos and also the extent of specialization at the Ghassulian-Beersheba sites are probably a consequence of strong connections with Egypt (Gilead 1988:415), by sea from Byblos, overland from the southern sites. Chisels, which are bifacially flaked, are unsurprisingly Ghassul's most characteristic artefact (Hennessey 1969:17). Like the 'fan-scrapers', they use apparently imported brown tabular flint (cf. Rosen 1983).

Ghassulian houseforms should be compared with the qualitatively different ones from Ubaid Mesopotamia (Figure 3.11). Located to the south of the Amman–Jerusalem highway, only 5 kilometres east of the Abdullah

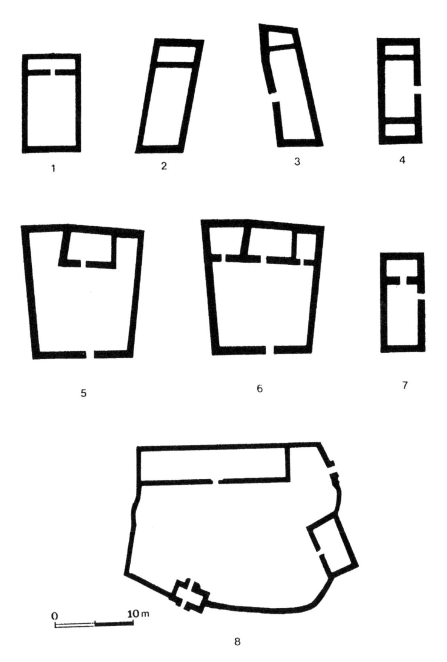

Figure 3.11 Ghassulian house-forms compared with the En-Gedi temple compound
(no. 8). (1,2) Teleilat Ghassul; (3,4) Golan sites; (5,6) Fazael; (7) Meser

Source: Gilead 1988:417

121

Bridge over the River Jordan (Hennessey 1969:1), the type-site of Teleilat Ghassul was used from the Palaeolithic (Stockton 1971:80–1). It is situated 305 metres below sea level on what was originally a sandy island surrounded by slow-moving water (Webley 1969:21). This is indicated not only by the pedology, but also by pollen: alder (*Alnus* spp.), sedge (*Scirpus* spp.), reed mace (*Typha latifolia*), water chestnut (*Trapa natans*), club moss (*Lycopodium* spp.) spores and another fern-like plant (*Selaginella* spp.). Reed and alder were by far the most common (ibid.).

Built of mud-brick on stone foundations (where a footing was required on uneven ground), the rectangular houses comprise a large and a small room with an adjoining courtyard. All of Henessey's houses contained a series of post holes along the longitudinal axis to support the roof of thick reeds, almost certainly pitched (Hennessey 1969:5). Sometimes the roof was supported on mud-brick columns. Floors were of tamped earth or a thick lime plaster (ibid.).

The village contains striking polychrome murals in green, black, red, yellow and white (confined to Phase B in Hennessey's excavations). There was much repainting (ibid.:7), probably necessitated by seismic activity, which would have been particularly destructive on such an unconsolidated site.

> A marked feature of the excavations was a series of camp settlements after each destruction of the village. All phases yielded evidence that during rebuilding the inhabitants camped on the remains of their destroyed houses. Such camp sites helped to distinguish successive building phases.
>
> (ibid.)

Though the site of Teleilat Ghassul itself is a large one, comprising a number of mounds spanning some 24 hectares (Hennessey 1969:1), modest farming villages are the norm. Ghassulian settlements did not directly lead on to urbanism in Palestine, as did the Ubaid in Mesopotamia.[18] Indeed, the development of Bronze Age urbanism in the Levant is a decidedly secondary (non-pristine) phenomenon (Gilead 1988:427) stimulated in part at least by Egyptian trade (Finkelstein 1995).

Paradoxically, it seems that environmental fragility was the reason why urbanism was delayed in Palestine *and also* the spur to its occurrence in the first part of the third millennium (Early Bronze Ib/EB II), according to Portugali and Gophna (1993:166–7). This impetus is also hypothesized by Weiss *et al.* to be the explanation of urbanization on the northern, Subarian plains (formerly Halaf heartlands) of the Habur triangle:

> The centrally administered urban economies and mixed land use strategies that developed in Period IIId [at Tell Leilan] may have presented adaptive advantages by facilitating maximum

agricultural production under increased variability of rainfall. The sudden growth of Tell Leilan, Tell Mozan, and Tell Brak, each 75 to 100 hectares, transformed the Habur Plains into an urban landscape dominated by three equidistant centres with approximately equivalent territorial control extending up to 25 km around each centre.

(Weiss *et al.* 1993:997–8)

In a stimulating review, Portugali and Gophna (op. cit.) argue that agricultural systems are inherently risky and thus prone to collapse, dispersing the population through nomadism and emigration. By subsuming hitherto autonomous agricultural systems within a larger urban system, however, greater stability can be achieved, for

> the urban system, due to accumulation, planning, long-distance trade and other features of urbanism, enabled the regional agricultural sub-systems to absorb, or overcome their local instabilities, previously fatal during the agricultural era. Only when several local instabilities coincided did the urban system as a whole, or major parts in it, collapse or undergo a major crisis. Thus, relative to the agricultural era, the urban system was characterized by relatively long periods of socio-spatial stability, followed by short, but very intensive environmental crises. Urbanism thus reduced the *frequency* of socio-environmental crises, but increased their *intensity*.

(original emphases)

Thus, crisis produced early urbanism in Palestine, most likely, they suggest, brought on by the collapse of the Uruk commercial system that had hitherto stabilized north Syria, at Habuba Kabira, Jebel Aruda (both on the Euphrates between Mureybet and Carchemish) and beyond.

There were three categories of Urukian settlement in the north: those actually containing many southerners, those with mixed populations, and those merely part of the economic network. As Surenhagen puts it:

> Habuba Kabira-South and Jebel Aruda belonged to colony-like settlement clusters along outer-Babylonian trade routes, presumably controlled by the South [of the alluvium]. Hassek Hoyuk is a characteristic example of borderland conditions, while Arslantepe VIA probably was one of the centres for the metal trade, which was never controlled by the South, but stood in loose, caravan-like contact with genuine Uruk sites south of the Taurus Mountains.

(Surenhagen 1986a:30)

There is no evidence for the existence of genuine Uruk settlements in the north before Gawra XI (ibid.). From the pottery, Surenhagen (ibid.:32) places the inception of the northern Uruk sites roughly contemporary with Uruk VII–VI levels, and possessing a duration of only about a century.

Populations formerly benefiting from Urukian presence in the north migrated into Palestine, there probably overloading the agricultural potential. Ceramic affinities between Uruk and EB I pottery in Palestine (Amiran 1970:85–8) are not confined to the southern Levant, nor are the influences limited to ceramics. Surenhagen states that:

> Uruk-related, wheel-made pottery (plain simple ware, true reserved-slip), cylinder seals, and other Uruk-related artefacts became common in northwestern Syria, the Levant, and southeastern Anatolia *after the collapse of the Euphratean Uruk settlements*. This know-how was probably transmitted by emigrants from these cities. Uruk culture was no longer the property and privilege of southern colonists.
>
> (Surenhagen 1986a:30, my emphasis)

Whether or not actual migrants spread elements of Uruk culture or whether it was a matter of cultural diffusion, Steinkeller (1993:115–16) argues that the *cause* of the collapse of the fragile Urukian commercial network was the arrival of new Semitic populations (including the 'proto-Akkadians') in Syria and northern Mesopotamia.[19]

Steinkeller sees this as occurring in several waves, beginning in Uruk IV (*c.* 3100 BC) and continuing through Uruk III into the Early Dynastic I (EDI) period of Sumer in the early centuries of the third millennium. In addition to settling upon the north of the alluvium proper (the Akkadian province which they called *Wari* or *War* and the Sumerians called Uri), this population was that which, under Sumerian influence, produced what has become known (following I.J. Gelb) as 'Kish Civilization', a single political configuration with shared language, culture and writing extending from Babylonia to western Syria (Steinkeller 1993:117). Its centres were the city of Kish itself (on the north/central alluvium), Akshak, and in Syria, Ebla and Mari.

It is to an examination of those cities and the processes that produced them that we now turn.[20]

TO THE HEARTLAND OF CITIES IN SUMER, VIA HUSSUNA, SAMARRA AND HALAF VILLAGE FARMING CULTURES

Hassuna is a Pottery Neolithic society of northeastern Mesopotamia in the first half of the sixth millennium. It is preceded for half a millennium by the proto-Hassuna and succeeded for less than half a millennium by the derivative Samarran culture. This culture, by developing irrigation techniques, pioneered the colonization of the rain-starved alluvium south of a putative line drawn between the modern towns of Hit and Samarra in Iraq. In its advance to the south toward the head of the Gulf, Samarran became Ubaidian. By the early fifth millennium, Ubaid culture sites were vigorously expanding northwards out of the alluvium to incorporate the Halaf dry farming culture that had spread in a broad band right across northern Mesopotamia and into the Levant.

This is a simplified chronology:

Years BC		
6500–6000	Proto-Hassuna	
6000–5000	Hassuna/Samarra	
5000–4000	Halaf/Ubaid	
4000–3200	Uruk	Protoliterate period
3200–3000	Jemdet Nasr	
3000–2750	Early Dynastic I	
2750–2600	Early Dynastic II	Pre-Sargonic period
2600–2350	Early Dynastic III	
2350–2150	Dynasty of Akkad	
2150–2000	3rd Dynasty of Ur	
2000–1800	Isin-Larsa Dynasties	Old Babylonian period
1800–1600	1st Dynasty of Babylon	

Proto-Hassuna – Aceramic (Tell Maghzalia)

Prior to the classical Hassuna are both aceramic and ceramic sites in that critical area between the Upper Zab tributary to the Tigris and the Jebel Sinjar in the middle of the Jezirah. On the right bank of the Abra River on one of the hilly flanks of the Jebel Sinjar (and 7.5 kilometres northwest of Yarim Tepe) lies Tell Maghzalia. It is a big, permanent, aceramic settlement just 1 kilometre north of the junction of the uplands with the plains and at an elevation of 50–70 metres above them (Bader 1993a:8). This is a zone of rocky limestone hillocks, today not really suitable for farming, yet there is plentiful evidence of it here. The original settlement proceeded in a southerly direction along the river, which is here in a deep canyon (ibid.:27).

A tenth of Maghzalia's original 0.65 hectare extent has been excavated (Munchaev et al. 1984:45), though only 4,500 square metres survive. The Russian excavators Bader, Merpert and Munchaev (1981:62) see in it similarities with Mureybet (cf. Maisels 1990:82–94), Bouqras and Abu Hureyra on the Euphrates and also Cayonu Tepesi. The last is a site almost equidistant between the upper courses of the Tigris and Euphrates, just below the mountain front. At Maghzalia, 40 per cent of faunal remains are those of domesticated sheep and goat, though the morphological indicators of domestication are, as would be expected, 'only in their initial stages' (Bader 1993a:39).

Today annual precipitation around Tell Maghzalia is about 350 millimetres. E.M. Zelikson interpreted the natural conditions in the seventh to sixth millennia as being 'sparse xerophilic wooded areas and savannas, and on the adjacent slopes of the mountains (Jebel Sinjar) strips of oak forests in combination with steppe flora; ie, the natural conditions of the time were more favourable than today' (Munchaev *et al.* 1984:53). Even today, however, localized oak woods have survived in the more inaccessible parts of the Sinjar range, clearly indicating that cutting and grazing are the main producers of 'less favourable conditions'.

Wild faunal remains from the sites studied in this part of the Sinjar Valley include common fallow deer, wild ass, aurochs, bezoar goat, mouflon, wild boar, deer and fox (ibid.). Bezoar goat and mouflon are, of course, the wild ancestors of herded goat and sheep. However, the authors (op. cit.) see the Maghzalian economy as characterized by 'a combination of agriculture and cattle-breeding with hunting and gathering'. The primary game species were, apparently, onager, with Bader (1993d:67) remarking that aurochs, deer, common gazelle, bezoar and mouflon were hunted.

Material culture is highly uniform throughout no less than sixteen building levels, with an average thickness of 50–60 centimetres. Grouping into three major periods and resulting in a cultural deposit exceeding 8 metres (ibid.), the first period comprises Levels 1–5, the second Levels 6–12, the third levels 13–16 at the top of the tell (ibid.:65). The first period is that of the houses along the riverbank, while in the second the dwellings run at an angle to the river. The third period again has its houses aligned along the riverbank, and in Levels 13–14 was surrounded by a protective wall of which 60 metres has been exposed (ibid.). Its base consists of limestone blocks, some upright and as long as 1.5 metres, with some stretches in irregular fieldstone, others of regular rectangular blocks (photographs in Bader 1993a:34). By this (third) period, houses had grown to attain a floor area of up to 100 square metres:

> The settlement behind the wall occupied about 1500 sq. metres. That territory included eight to ten multiroom houses. Each of these would have accommodated from 10–15 people. The population of the settlement probably did not exceed 100–150 persons, including children.
>
> (Bader 1993d:66)

Earlier houses could be as small as 10–12 square metres, consisting of a single rectangular room, though they coexisted with larger structures. The standard constructional technique throughout was of pisé on stone bases (usually surface) which are 60–80 centimetres wide and about the same high (see plan in Munchaev *et al.* 1984:48).

Much use is made of gypsum plaster for lining bins and troughs ('citerne' water tanks?) and it is used throughout the largest structure so far excavated at the site, a dwelling in Level 4. Oriented, like the others, north–south along the river and, like them, rectangular and constructed of pisé on stone foundations, it has been excavated over 75 square metres, but is thought to cover around 100 square metres (Bader 1993a:32). This large structure, which contains an oven and storerooms less than a metre wide, is associated with the earliest phase of defensive building (ibid.).

Wickerwork, bags, baskets and mats are much in evidence (Munchaev *et al.* 1984:52), including what looks like the predecessor of the classic Hassuna 'husking tray', something that occurs in the later 'Sotto' phase (see below). As at Kultepe (below), fine polished marble vessels are common, some of it bichrome (Bader 1993a:34). With simple rims and flat bases, the shapes of the shallow bowls and goblets at Maghzalia seem less elaborated than at Kultepe, but were none the less already highly accomplished, something also seen in the making of bracelets from marble and pendants from pebbles and obsidian.

By contrast, the only major use for clay in small artefacts was for moulding figurines, zoomorphic (some horned) and some female fecundity objects. Highly stylized, the body

> has the form of a high cone, and the breasts are represented by oval-shaped protrusions. The top of the figurine is pinched to indicate its head. The bodies of these figurines have parallels at Telul eth-Thalathat and Jarmo, and the legs and torsos are identical with those found at Tell Sotto.
>
> (Bader 1993d:67)

The only clay storage vessel found was unbaked. An anthropomorphic figurine in soft white stone was found on the floor of a structure in the uppermost stratum and a small conical pestle in white marble with red veins bears a stylized human head (Bader 1993a:22–3).

All strata at Maghzalia are characterized both by rectangular structures and by a remarkable preponderance of obsidian, accounting for nearly three-quarters of all the chipped stone (tools plus waste) in phase I, two-thirds in the middle period, and parity in the last, until Level 14, when flint predominated for the first time (Bader 1993d:66). Used for items as diverse as sickle blades and pendants, the obsidian used for the former has a slightly bevelled retouch, but the working edge is often left unretouched. Geometric microliths are rarely encountered (Bader 1993a:13–14). Knives, drills, scrapers, including massive examples in tabular flint (as at Hassuna sites), are well represented at Maghzalia (ibid.:15). Bone carving is prominent, with fine needles and awls produced (ibid.:16). Found in sealed stratigraphic contexts in the walled settlement were two pieces of copper ore or malachite, and a cold forged chisel ('awl', so-called, but has a square cross-section) in native copper from Talmesi in central Iran (ibid.:37).

> Grain grinders, milling stones, and pestles make up a distinctive category of tools from the site. In most cases, as is the case at Tell Hassuna, they are made from basalt. Milling stones are oval-shaped, with a flat or slightly convex working surface. In contrast to this the grain grinders have a concave working surface.
>
> (ibid.:16)

Mortars and pestles are, however, the most common items of ground-stone equipment, and some show traces of ochre (Bader 1993d:67).

Merpert *et al.* (1981:31) observe that while

> a greater number of tanged arrowheads on blades and animal bones, apparently wild bulls, indicate hunting activity . . . at the same time the permanent character of the habitation, the numerous querns, sickle knives, grain bins and other finds suggest that farming predominated.

Whatever 'predomination' might mean in this context, we now accept that the term 'farming' should be reserved for the cultivation of domesticated plants, and yet the harvesting, storing and processing equipment found at Maghzalia could have been applied to wild stands. However, one hundred fragmentary and complete grains analysed by G.N. Lisitsina indicated the presence of wild *and* domesticated plants including einkorn, emmer and spelt wheat (and *Triticum compactum* Host.), two and six-row barley, plus flax, lentils and vetch (Merpert and Munchaev 1987:18). They remark that 'the domesticated cereal grains are small and appear to represent early forms. Sickles and reaping knives further attest the presence of early farmers at Maghzalia.'

Proto-Hassuna - ceramic (Tells Sotto and Kultepe)

Sotto

The ceramic pre-Hassuna stage is represented by the 'Sotto' phase, named by the Russians from an 80-metre long (elliptical) mound, 2.5 metres above the modern Sinjar plain, 3 kilometres west of Yarim Tepe, which was excavated over 475 square metres. There are seven building levels, with the eighth being the top surface. 'Levels 1–6 yielded a type of very archaic carinated[21] cooking ware with organic temper, which developed successively from one level to the next, until in the seventh level were found some archaic Hassuna vessels' (Bader 1993d:68). Until Levels 7 and 8, when several fragments of dense and highly fired Hassuna ceramics occur, all previous ceramics are poorly fired (ibid.:69).

In 3.8 metres of cultural strata, the lowest, Level 1, contains more than a dozen pits of various sizes, one of which, pit 11, contained fragments of grain-grinders. Pit 10 was filled with ashes and ceramic slag, while many sherds occurred in the charcoal and fill layers at the bottom of pit 19. Bader (ibid.:68) surmises that some of the pits may have been dwellings.

Level 2 has three rectangular one-room houses in tauf (mud-brick) with areas between 12 and 15 square metres. Not only did they have the usual facilities of ovens, hearths, compartments for storing grain and storage vessels dug into the floors, but they were also linked to a complex of 'reservoirs', made of shallow plaster-coated pits between parallel mud-brick walls (ibid.). One had a plaster-coated drain at one end.

Levels 3–6 are generally unclear, though the evolution from carinated to spherical vessel forms can be followed. Level 7 yielded several large, crude, spherical pots characteristic of archaic Hassuna (ibid.:69). Overall, the ceramic assemblage of Tell Sotto can be categorized into twelve basic forms:

1 carinated vessels;
2 spherical vessels with a straight vertical rim;
3 flat oval troughs for winnowing;
4 troughs with corrugated bottoms;
5 oval troughs with smooth bottoms;
6 flat platters;
7 carinated bowls;
8 rounded bowls;
9 straight-walled basins;
10 round basins;
11 carinated cups and
12 round cups.

(ibid.)

Clay was also used for sling balls, spindle whorls and female figurines, while the crude pots of the earliest strata have anthropomorphic and zoo-morphic figurines moulded onto them (ibid.).

Although the site may not have been inhabited year-round during Level 6, Level 7 contains the remains of a large, rectilinear and well-preserved multi-roomed house in mud-brick, with residential surfaces adjoining it (Bader 1993b:43). It was maintained and remodelled over a lengthy period.

However confused, the earliest levels at Sotto are certainly no 'campsite' and in fact show a number of close parallels with Umm Dabaghiya (Kirkbride 1972, 1973a, 1973b, 1974, 1975). It also shows numerous links to Jarmo, notably in sharing a repertoire of appliqué designs on crude vessels, which include large oval troughs (Bader 1993b:48–9).

> At Jarmo, one of the most ubiquitous forms of the ceramic assem-
> blage are vessels with carinated sides, both of the crude cookware
> variety, and small delicate vessels and platters made from well-
> levigated clay. At Tell Sotto carinated forms are also common. The
> form and proportions of the vessels may differ, but the carinated
> side itself is common at both sites.
>
> (ibid.)

Other similarities include burnished pots to which ochre is applied after firing. Stone vessels at both Jarmo and Sotto share horizontally everted rims, but most important is the moulded decoration applied to vessels at both sites. Some are produced by pressing outwards from the inside to form knobs; in some, from Sotto, zoomorphic and anthropomorphic projections are applied as already mentioned (ibid.:51). Cylindrical stone beads also occur at both sites, one from Jarmo inscribed with straight lines suggested as serving as the prototype for clay and stone Hassuna seals from Yarim Tepe I (ibid.:52). Further, some of the range of stone bracelets at Jarmo also occur at Sotto, while the small, wedge-shaped stone axes that are quite frequent in both Jarmo and Sotto are practically indistinguishable between the two sites (for more detail on Jarmo, see Maisels 1993b:109–12).

In conclusion, 'Tell Sotto represents an unknown early stage of Hassuna, perhaps a Proto-Hassuna. Tell Hassuna, Tell Sotto and Umm Dabaghiya constitute early agricultural settlements within a single cultural sphere' (ibid.:48).

Kultepe

Kultepe I ('ash mound') is a 2.5 metre high, 60 × 80 metre site only 100 metres from the right bank of the Wadi Sharai, about 6 kilometres due west of the Yarim Tepe group (Bader 1993c:55). One hundred and twenty metres to the northwest lies Kultepe II, with a diameter of about 60 metres, partly eroded by the watercourse and revealing a Hassuna assemblage.

In the excavated mound of Kultepe I there are a minimum of four building levels. The thick, lowest level contains material of Sotto type, while the three above contain archaic Hassuna materials, without obvious breaks in settlement at the site (Bader 1993c:56).

The four building levels have a depth of 2.25 metres; 125 square metres have been exposed so far. The lowest level has a preponderance of undecorated coarse pottery with barely discernible rims and moulded decoration (ibid.:58–9). 'The entire ceramic assemblage in the lowest level of Kultepe is closely related to that found in the earliest layer of Tell Sotto' (ibid.).

Although the surface of the mound has been frequently ploughed and Hassuna pottery can be collected on the surface, Kultepe I is otherwise intact (ibid.:55).

The lowest level is the most interesting, as it contains a well-preserved residence with adjoining rectangular storage structures, on the floor of one of which three striking marble vessels were found (below). This complex was built on sterile soil at one time (except for the internal partition walls). The structural walls already mentioned form a bipartite rectangular structure whose main chamber's dimensions are 2.5 × 5.5. metres. This 'main chamber', containing the metre-wide entrance on its short southern wall, is narrowed on the immediate right of entry by a sub-square storage bin (mud-plastered, with traces of burning and carbonized grain), beyond which the chamber proper opens out. Adjoining (at right angles) is what appears to be a rectangular block consisting of a number of cellular compartments, suggesting either that this was a storage complex, or that we are simply seeing substructure. Only further excavation can clarify this. Nonetheless, Bader (ibid.:58) maintains that 'the residence is reminiscent, in its dimensions and the details of its household assemblage, of the dwellings in the lowest level of Tell Sotto', while the assemblage is comparable with that of the lowest stratum at Umm Dabaghiyah.

Level 2 contains a number of circular ovens, plus their associated charcoal and ash deposits. The absence of space for houses on the tell at this time leads Bader (1993d:69) to suggest that the site was visited only during the agricultural season (or the hunting season?), like Level 6 at Tell Sotto. Level 3 consists of several small one-room houses with storage vessels, compartments for grain storage and querns. They apparently had well-defined plaster floors (1993c:56), while by contrast, the floor and walls of the building in Level 1 are mud-plastered. The fill within the structures of Level 3 is wind-deposited. Level 4 is a layer as much as a metre thick, containing the fragmentary remains of small rectangular structures, several times rebuilt. Bader (ibid.:58) sees 'uninterrupted development' from Level 1 through to Level 4. And Levels 1–4 at Kultepe correspond to Levels 3–6 of Tell Sotto. Further, 'the inventory of tools at Tell Sotto and Kultepe are very close typologically. The stone vessels found at Kultepe have direct analogues at Tell Sotto and Umm Dabaghiyah' (Bader 1993d:70).

Those are three intact marble vessels from Level 1, 'found together in a well-defined stratigraphic context on the floor in the easternmost subdivision of the large house' (Bader 1993c:59). They comprise:

1   a deep bowl in yellowish marble, with slightly flaring walls and a simple rim on a well-defined flat base; 7.2 centimetres high, the vessel's diameter is 7.8 centimetres at the bottom, 18 centimetres at the rim;
2   a globular vessel only 10 centimetres high in pink marble with a round base of approx. 11 centimetres in diameter, thin convex walls and a

very narrow flaring rim, the diameter of which is 13 centimetres;

3 the third, described (ibid.:59) as the most distinctive, is a flat-based oval bowl in white marble. The base, also oval, is 9.5 × 7.5 centimetres and its height 11 centimetres to an oval rim of 12 × 8.5 centimetres, defined by a small groove. 'The vessel is asymmetrical and massive, with thick walls and base' (ibid.).

The real importance of the three vessels is that they have close analogues not only at Sotto and Umm Dabaghiyah, but also in the white marble example at Tell es-Sawwan. Bader observes:

> The yellow marble bowl from Kultepe is analogous to examples from Tell Sotto and Umm Dabaghiyah. Certain stone vessels of red marble or of pink marble with red veins, identical to vessels found at Kultepe, are well known from Umm Dhabaghiyah and Tell Sotto. All have practically identical forms of this type, but it is not encountered at Tell es-Sawwan. However, the oval white marble vessel from Kultepe is reminiscent of oval vessels frequently found at Tell es-Sawwan. At Umm Dabaghiyah, one whole vessel of a similar shape was found.
> . . . Although the early Hassuna sites in the Jezira yield one type of stone vessel, the lowest stratum of Tell es-Sawwan apparently yields an entirely different assemblage. However, both assemblages are seen at Kultepe, suggesting that they came from a common tradition.
>
> (Bader 1993c:59)

A shared tradition with zonal variation on themes seen first at Maghzalia might be a better expression. Sites with the Tell Sotto/Umm Dabaghiya assemblage on the west bank of the Tigris (i.e. in the Jezira) gave rise to the classic Hassuna culture, while those more southerly sites (closely Jarmo related) on the east bank of the Tigris engendered Samarra culture (Bader 1993d:71).

Hassuna

The ensuing Hassuna stage is the fully-fledged, mature Neolithic originally seen at the eponymous site, reported in 1945 by Seton Lloyd and Faud Safar.[22] Hassuna standard painted wares are illustrated in Figure 3.12 (right) from their report. On the left are samples of Samarra painted wares, with the famous 'face pots' at the top-right. Figure 3.13 shows Hassuna standard incised and painted-and-incised ware (a Hassuna 'trademark') and likewise, at the bottom, the famous pottery 'husking trays'.

Hassuna was a rainfed plus groundwater agricultural regime. Not much later, Samarrans along the Tigris between Lower Zab and Adhem Rivers

Figure 3.12 Hassuna and Samarra wares

Key: On the left, Levels IV-VI, Samarra painted ware and the famous 'face pots'; on the right, Levels II-VI, Hassuna standard painted ware; bowl with cross at bottom centre, is Hassuna archaic ware, Level II.

Source: Lloyd and Safar 1945

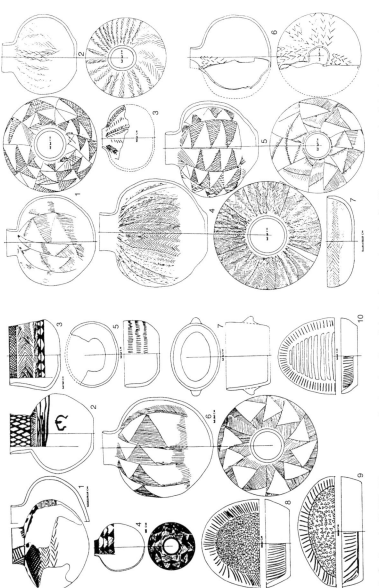

Figure 3.13 Left: Levels II–VI; Hassuna standard painted-and-incised ware (nos 1–4); Hassuna standard incised ware (nos 5–6); 'milk jar' coarse ware (no. 7) and 'husking trays' (nos 8–10). Right: Levels Ic–VI; Hassuna standard incised ware.

Source: Lloyd and Safar 1945

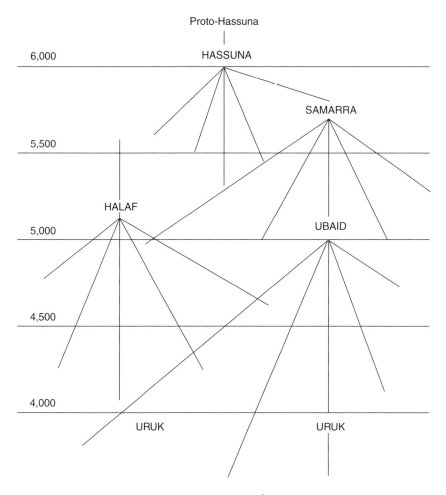

Figure 3.14 Interdigitation and succession of prehistoric and protohistoric Mesopotamian cultures, showing descent of Sumerian Culture from Samarra through Ubaid. Uruk is a *period* named from the city

were becoming irrigation specialists with enormous consequences for the peopling of the southern plains. Somewhat later, other rain-dependent agriculturalists, Halaf, spread widely from the well-watered Habur headwaters/Balikh area across all of northern Mesopotamia. The Halaf oecumene will be discussed next before turning to Samarra, since the latter leads on directly to the colonization of the alluvium with the Ubaid, which is the immediate precurser of Sumerian civilization.

The relationships between Proto-Hassuna, Hassuna, Samarra and Halaf are illustrated in Figure 3.14 above.

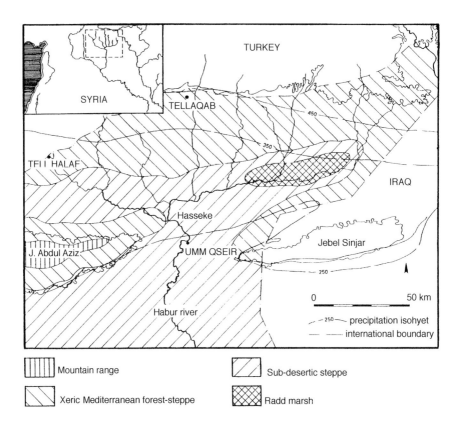

Figure 3.15 Location of some Halaf sites, with modern precipitation levels and
vegetation zones in the Habur headwaters, Syria

Source: McCorriston 1992:316

Halaf

Halaf villages, specializing in rainfed agriculture,[23] occupied a sweep of
territory from the hinterland of Mosul west to that of Aleppo, and north
from both to the hinterlands of Diyarbakir in Turkey, the area so enclosed
forming an isosceles triangle with a base between Mosul and Aleppo of
nearly 600 kilometres. Between the three hinterlands mentioned lies the
Habur Headwaters triangle, and to its west the Upper Balikh area, both
well supplied with rainfall and thus possessing many known Halafian sites.
On the margins of adequate rainfall (<250 millimetres), sites like Umm
Qseir relied on hunting for a large part of their subsistence requirements
(Zeder 1994a). The Habur Headwaters area in Syria, north of Jebels Sinjar
and Abd-Al-Aziz, is shown with modern isohyets and vegetation types in
Figure 3.15.

As I have previously discussed Halaf sites in considerable detail (1993a:124–40), particularly the extensive Russian excavations at Yarim Tepe, I shall not repeat this here, but will instead consider a village site for which a full monograph has recently been published by Patty Jo Watson and Steven LeBlanc (1990). This is Girikihaciyan, in the Tigris headwaters area of southeastern Turkey, about 25 kilometres from the earlier site of Cayonu. It is a roughly circular mound of about 175 metres in diameter, rising about 3 metres above the surrounding plain, and receives about 500 millimetres of rain annually. A single-period site, its life extended, at a maximum, between 5000 BC and 4500 BC, uncalibrated radiocarbon dates based on Libby half-life (Watson and LeBlanc 1990:4). With a surface area of between 2.4 and 3.4 hectares, the excavators suggest a maximal population of between two and three hundred (ibid.:134). Even this range, however, may be too high (Aurenche 1981; Akkermans 1990). Girikihaciyan is a marginal site in a non-optimal situation (Watson and LeBlanc 1990:1).

Four attributes characterize Halaf sites clearly: pottery (including incised pendants and female figurines), architecture, a common food complex and participation in an egalitarian exchange network.

Halaf painted pottery is aesthetically superb in both form and decoration, as is shown in the examples as Figures 3.16 and 3.17. The pottery at Girikihaciyan, as elsewhere, falls into the category of either Plain Ware or Fine Ware, the latter including painted pottery. The former comprises 'a relatively thick-walled ware with tan to very dark brown, almost black, smoothed or lightly burnished surfaces' (Watson and LeBlanc 1990:77). Lightly burnished plain ware seems to precede painted ware at most sites, something confirmed by Davidson (1977:161) at Tell Halaf itself. The proportion of plain to painted ware at Girikihaciyan, at 87 per cent plain to 13 per cent painted, is the reverse of the situation at Tell Aqab, just north of Chagar Bazar, and at Arpachiya. It seems that the proportion of fine ware rises as one goes from the margins toward the nodal centres of production and network distribution, the significance of which will be developed below.

The distinguishing architectural feature of Halaf settlements is the *tholos* a round domed structure with or without rectangular antechambers (the *dromos*). Materials are various, reflecting the enormous spread of Halaf sites, and include limestone boulders, rock fragments, tauf and mud-brick.

With an almost uniform wall diameter of 0.35 metres at Girikihaciyan, the inside diameters of the *tholoi* range from 2.25 to 4.50 metres (ibid.:Table 3.8). One of the largest and most complete in groundplan (house 1, Operation A), which consisted of mud walls on a stone foundation on top of 50–60 centimetres of earlier trash, is shown in the plan view in Figure 3.18. The large *dromos* (rectangular annexe) can be seen adjoining in the southwest.

Figure 3.16 Halaf polychrome plate from Arpachiya

Source: Mallowan and Rose 1935

The subsistence complex includes emmer wheat and two-row barley (*Hordeum distichum*) and perhaps hard wheat/bread wheat (*Triticum durum/ aestivum*), the pulses chickpea (*Cicer arietinum*) and lentil (*Lens culinaris*), the latter most common, plus vetches and borages (Van Zeist 1979–80). Six seeds of flax (*Linum usitatissimum*) were recovered and measurement made

1. A 144 (B)

2. A 117 (B)   Scale ⅜

Figure 3.17 Halaf painted pottery from Arpachiya
   Source: Mallowan and Rose 1935

on the three best preserved. From this, Van Zeist (ibid.:80) concluded that flax was cultivated. It also occurs at the other Halafian sites of Arpachiya and Tell Brak. Though pea (*Pisum sativum*) is conspicuously absent at Girikihaciyan, use was made of wild tree crops: pistachio, almond and even, apparently, hawthorn (*Cretaegus* sp., *tanacetifolia*? – it has large nutlets).

139

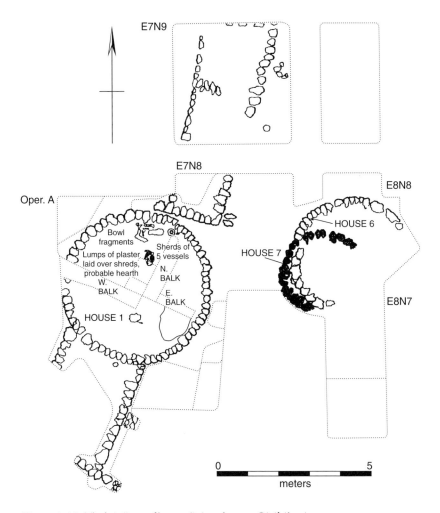

Figure 3.18 Tholoi ('roundhouses') in plan at Girikihaciyan

Source: Watson and LeBlanc 1990:28. Reprinted courtesy of the UCLA
Institute of Archaeology

McArdle (1990:119) reports that domestic sheep and goats were the most
common animals found at Girikihaciyan, with *Ovis* predominating in a ratio
of about 2:1. 'In this respect, the flocks of Girikihaciyan resemble those
found in the area today, which comprise predominantly sheep' (ibid.:111).

McArdle further observes that both domestic and wild caprines are present
at the site, which he ascribes to the proximity of the Taurus mountains.
As southern Anatolia has long been thought to be the area in which cattle
were domesticated,[24] the presence of clearly domesticated cattle is not unex-

pected, although the Halafian examples at Girikihaciyan were slightly larger than later domestic breeds (ibid.:115). At least as important as cattle, however, were domestic pigs.

Ovicaprids and pigs were killed young, predominantly in their first two years, but cattle were not, being allowed to live considerably longer. Thus either they were kept for milk, ploughing or ritual slaughter, or for some combination of these. Despite the proximity of the River Tigris, there is no evidence that fish or fowl were exploited, nor indeed that hunting played much of a role, except for some red deer (*Cervus elaphus*) (ibid.:120). Indeed, the uses made of both domesticated and wild resources is remarkably similar to that obtaining at Tell Sabi Abyad on the Upper Balikh (Akkermans 1989c, 1990).

It can be seen that throughout its wide range across the great northern bow of the Zagrosian Arc, Halafian culture was remarkably (but not totally) homogeneous. This was achieved *not* by the imposition of uniformity from above, not even by the existence of a 'Chiefdom' encompassing the area. Patty Jo Watson (Watson and LeBlanc 1990:136–7) has now withdrawn that suggestion in the Girikihaciyan monograph. It seems that the pattern of Halafian settlement was of small villages of 1–2 hectares, at some distance from a larger settlement (<8 hectares) that provided central place functions. The best known of such 'central places' are, of course, Tell Arpachiya and Tell Brak in Iraq.

The largest so far known are in southeastern Turkey. This includes the unexcavated site of Takyan Hoyuk (still only 12 hectares) just into Turkey over the Iraq/Turkish border; Kazane, a site of about the same size on which excavations have recently commenced (by Bernbeck, Coursey and Pollock); and Domuztepe some 30 kilometres south of Kahramanmaras and about the same distance north of Sakce Gozu, being jointly excavated by Prof. Elizabeth Carter of UCLA and Stuart Campbell of Manchester University. Domuztepe, founded around 6000 BC, a millennium later reached its maximum size of more than 18 hectares, declined toward 4000 BC and was then abandoned.

> Among the more notable finds were several Halaf stamp seals. A considerable number have now been discovered from the site, including ten from the surface, two in a pit in Operation I, one from Operation III and six from stratified contexts in Operation II; in addition a fragmentary seal impression came from the sounding in Operation I. This is an exceptionally high number given the very limited excavation and may correlate with a greater complexity of interaction within the settlement and with neighbouring settlements.
>
> (Campbell and Healey 1996:4)

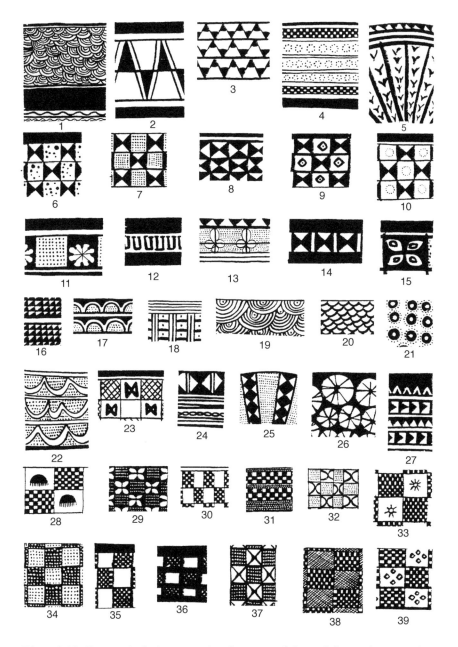

Figure 3.19 Geometric designs on painted pottery of the Halaf Period at Arpachiya
Source: Mallowan and Rose 1935

It looks as if central places like those served to knit-up the whole Halaf culture-area into an oecumene (commonwealth), through the exchange of fine pottery (in my view unsurpassed aesthetically), obsidian (bowls and decorative links as well as blades), and perhaps even animals, oils and fibres, dyes and medicines, as suggested by McCorriston (1992:330).

At any event, what appears crucial is the existence of the network itself: a network of nodes (central settlements) linked by exchange relationships of mutual advantage. Indeed, the very lack of domination in such a network – and indeed the lack of any centre to it – may be the secret of its success; it did, after all, thrive for seven centuries (according to Campbell 1992:187), extending from the Zagros to the Mediterranean. Such a distributed network may have had 'heartlands' – in terms either of an originating cluster or a zone of higher settlement density. There is a site every 15–16 kilometres in the Mosul-Sinjar region, according to Hijara et al. (1980:244). But a distributed network is inherently centreless: it is the existence of the network itself that matters. Accordingly, anyone could join an open system like this, which may well explain Campbell's (1992:183) finding that 'the Halaf seems to have evolved from localized Neolithic cultures, more or less simultan-eously, over much of its later range, negating any attempt to isolate its origins'.[25] Further 'Halaf-influenced' sites, containing only Halafian pottery perhaps, such as those in the Keban area, become explicable as settlements that partly joined the network or limited their participation in it to par-ticular requirements. As Watkins and Campbell (1987:430) observe, 'there may be highly localized inter-site variation on very specific details, and a hierarchy of participation in cultural traits'.

Thus, disparate Neolithic societies 'became' Halaf by 'networking' a shared lifestyle for themselves. By this means 'one can envision a series of asym-metric local or subregional exchange patterns of relatively low intensity operating at the same time as much more symmetric, or reciprocal, exchange at the regional level' (Watson and LeBlanc 1990:136). The famous, and so far anomalous, burned building of level TT 6 at Arpachiya, excavated by Mallowan, could in such an egalitarian scenario have served as a kind of 'central emporium' where settlements 'in credit', or at least creditworthy, could have drawn on resources coming from any part of the network. That this might not be too fanciful is suggested by the stamp seals, bullae and sealings found at Arpachiya and elsewhere. Though seals, tokens and calculi originate in the Neolithic, Halafian examples are the earliest large groupings found anywhere (Mallowan and Rose 1935: plate IXb; Von Wickede 1990:54–66; Akkermans 1995:23–4). From the burnt TT6 building at Arpachiya, Mallowan and Rose (1935:98) found spindle-shaped dockets with a string-hole at each end, and three more ovoid-shaped examples in the British Museum 'have been repeatedly impressed with a single stamp-seal' (Collon and Reade 1983:35). The function of the dockets was obviously to 'keep tabs' on goods or records of goods.

Thanks to the 1991 and 1992 field seasons conducted by Peter Akkermans at Sabi Abyad,[26] it is now actually possible to see the system coming into existence in what might be called the Proto-Halaf period. Tell Sabi Abyad is the largest mound in a cluster called Khirbet Sabi Abyad in the valley of the Balikh, about 30 kilometres south of the Syro-Turkish border. Another tributary of the Euphrates to the immediate west of the Habur system, the Balikh today flows 5 kilometres west of the mound cluster (Akkermans 1995:5).

Tell Sabi Abyad shows unbroken development of the Halaf *in situ* from a local Neolithic basis (Akkermans 1991:124; 1995:21). There is a substantial late Neolithic settlement into the early sixth millennium. Then, after what appears to be a hiatus between levels 11 and 10 (Akkermans 1995:8), there is an unbroken sequence during which an 'intermediate' settlement emerges in Level 6, *c.* 5200/5100 BC (uncalibrated). Indicative of its transitional nature (from Late Neolithic to Halaf) is the presence of a Fine Ware, comprising around 6 per cent of local ceramic production, the Dark-Faced Burnished Ware present being, of course, an import from the west (Braidwood and Braidwood 1960). Showing the expected close parallels with Hassuna and Samarra wares, the Fine Ware is so called because it has a finely textured, mineral tempered fabric, and because the majority of what are various kinds of bowls and small jars of angle-necked type (often burnished) are decorated either by painting or, less commonly, incised work, or painted and incised (Akkermans 1995:20). Geometric designs predominate, and naturalistic designs of horned animals are present in very small numbers.

This proto-Halaf settlement with its contents is very well preserved because it was destroyed by fire, probably spreading through the roofing materials (beams supporting mud-covered reeds), remnants of which were clearly recognizable in building V (Akkermans 1995:15). The 'burnt village' of Sabi Abyad, as presently known, comprises five rectangular multi-roomed structures, four *tholoi* and seven ovens, one huge, all built in pisé, replacing the mud-brick used previously in the Balikh region. It is terraced, tightly clustered, and thus has predominantly roof-entry to the 'houses' (Akkermans 1995:9) on the pattern of Catal Huyuk.

I have put 'houses' in quotation marks for several reasons:

1   Although none are presently fully exposed, they consist of very many, very small compartments quite unsuited to domestic purposes: 'basic-ally, the oblong structures seem to have been divided in three rows or wings, each of which consisted of a series of small rooms. Some of these houses must have had 15 or more rooms, all very small and varying in size between about 3 and 5 m^2' (Akkermans 1995:10).

2   They contain relatively few domestic necessities, with, for example, no domestic installations at all in building V other than a small tanour oven in room 5 (Akkermans 1995:15).

3   Building III, measuring *c.* 7 × 3.5 metres consists of three rooms,
all accessible from the north where they open onto a series of ovens,
the largest of which, S, is beehive-shaped, 1.5 metres high, has a
maximum diameter of 2.9 metres, walls 35 centimetres thick and is
fed through an opening 70 centimetres wide at its base (Akkermans
1995:13).

The function of building IV remains somewhat enigmatic. In terms
of shape, size, and room partitioning the structure closely resembles the nearby building II, which seems to have served largely
for storage and food processing. Similar activities may have been
pursued in building IV. The absence of ovens, bins, or other
domestic installations may point in this direction.

(Akkermans 1995:15)

Obviously people must have lived at the site, but what we seem to have
at the burnt village of Sabi Abyad is a major processing centre, and one
located in an extensive network.

The most noteworthy finds came from rooms 6 and 7 [of structure
V, a ten-roomed building as presently known]. Here, in addition
to ceramics and various kinds of stone tools, hundred of small
objects of sun-dried clay were found, including jar-stoppers, loom-
weights, sling missiles, figurines, tokens, and sealings that usually
carried stamp-seal impressions. These finds closely resemble those
in room 6 of building II.

(ibid.)

This is easily the largest and earliest collection of sealings and tokens yet
found anywhere. So far there are 275 clay sealings made by at least 61
different stamp seals (Akkermans 1995:23). Sealings bearing designs that
were mostly geometric – zigzags, triangles, concentric circles, diamonds,
crosshatching, etc. – were applied principally to ceramics and baskets, but
also to stone bowls, sacks and mats (ibid.:22).
  Clay tokens or calculi were of various shapes and sizes to indicate type
of goods as well as quantity. All are very small and have simple geometric
shapes: balls, cylinders, discs and cones (ibid.:24).

The sealings and tokens were found in three buildings: the rectangular features II and V and the circular structure VI. They were
not mere refuse randomly distributed throughout these structures
but seem to have been deliberately taken out of circulation and
stored, together with numerous other small items, in specific rooms

(room 6 in building II; rooms 6 and 7 in building V and compartments 2, 3 and 4 in tholos VI).

(ibid.:24)

So the sealings functioned not as badges of ownership or status, but kept
with the calculi formed archives tracking exchanges.

Sealings and other exchange devices originate in the Neolithic, not the
Chalcolithic. Seals are known from Archaic Hassuna, Catal Huyuk and
Amuq A and B (Buchanan 1967a:265–6), while clay tokens are known even
earlier from Zagros sites including Jarmo, Asiab and Ganj Dareh (Jasim
and Oates 1986:355). Interestingly, those sites span the area that was later
to become the Halafian oecumene.

When we encounter the later Sumero-Akkadian accounting devices
they are clearly aspects of social control and stratification, centred on
the 'great households' known to have been the condition of Sumer
from the Uruk Period of the fourth millennium onward (Maisels 1990;
Crawford 1991; Postgate 1992). And the Late Uruk is the period of
transition from stamp to cylinder seals (Buchanan 1967b:535). From
the well-known historical situation, some might wrongly conclude that
the Halaf accounting rationale would be less like that of an egalitarian
credit-union and more akin either to the relationship between consumers
and capitalists, or subordinates rendering dues to superiors. However, there
are no indications of a Halafian social hierarchy, and the nature of the
exchange process is too dispersed and reciprocal for it to be a matter
of traders and purchasers. Prior to the discovery of the Burnt Village,
Akkermans (1990:290–3) suspected that 'chiefdom' was a misplaced description of Halaf social organization. On the basis of the wide variety of
seals in use in a mere village and other considerations, he now (1995:25)
states that

> access to the trade network was not restricted to a few individuals
> only but was open to the community at Sabi Abyad as a whole.
> In other words, receipt of the sealed goods or objects at Sabi Abyad
> seems not to have been centrally organized but, on the contrary
> was in the hands of many persons.

In stark contrast, the Uruk Period is well known to be a watershed in social
evolution, the time of the first emergence of the state. Further, accounting
bullae and tokens in steatite, faience and terracotta have been identified at
Harappa[27] and I have argued on other grounds (see Chapter 4) that Harappan
Civilization was an essentially egalitarian oecumene integrated by community of interest: economic, political and cultural.[28]

Samarra

Samarran sites had nothing like the wide spread of Halaf, being concentrated in the middle reaches of the Tigris, where irrigation techniques were developed (as at Choga Mami; Oates and Oates 1976). At sites such as Choga Mami, 'transitional' characteristics to those obtaining in the Ubaid are found. The process must therefore be, that, having learned their irrigation skills as 'Samarrans', in colonizing the alluvium they 'became' Ubaid. If, as now is generally accepted, the Ubaid is the very basis of Uruk urbanism and later Sumerian culture, then there can be no 'Sumerian problem', by which was formerly (mis-)understood the so-called 'appearance' of Sumerian culture, either 'suddenly' or 'from elsewhere'. There are many real problems of reconstructing Sumerian culture and society, but their 'origins' are certainly not one of those problems.

The type site is not actually at Samarra but at Tell es-Sawwan, some 10 kilometres to the south on the left bank of the Tigris, just where the river enters the alluvial plain. A line drawn eastwards to the town of Hit (an ancient source of asphalt) on the Euphrates is conventionally reckoned to indicate the start of alluvium proper. The site of Tell es-Sawwan covers $230 \times 110 \times 3$ metres, but is presently separated into three tells (A, B and C) by wadis or erosional gullies, as shown on the site map in Figure 3.20.

What is particularly interesting about Sawwan appears immediately from this map: for the first time in Mesopotamia a nucleated settlement or township exists. It consists of a cluster of large independent houses of tripartite plan (central hall with lateral rooms), surrounded by a wall and ditch, as is so clearly seen on the plan of Sawwan in Figure 3.21, which superimposes Level III (with its wall and ditch) onto the earliest level, I.

Five main building levels are known, with Level I the earliest. A radiocarbon sample (P. 855) from a Level I floor gives a date of 5506+−73 BC (el-Wailly and es-Soof 1965:19). The four remaining houses of Levels I/II have surface areas of 162, 166, 173 and 167 square metres (J.-D. Forest 1983:11). When, in Levels III–IV, surface area reduces to only 60–80 square metres, J.-D. Forest (ibid.:16) postulates major rooms on an upper floor or landing, which, he thinks, is indicated by a larger stairwell in buildings of this later period. An upper storey would take the floor area of each house up to the Samarran/Ubaidian general average.

Levels I and II provided relatively little pottery, and the grave goods suggest that alabaster was more commonly used. What little pottery there is at those levels closely resembles late archaic Hassuna Ib–II (el-Wailly and es-Soof 1965:21). Pottery in Levels I and II is coarse, being made from clay with large extraneous particles and poorly fired, producing a black unoxidized core. Surface colour is buff or light brown, decorated with a self slip, and sometimes burnished. Fragments of very crude hemispherical bowls were found on a Level I floor, and fragments of red slipped and grey wares also occur in Level II (ibid.).

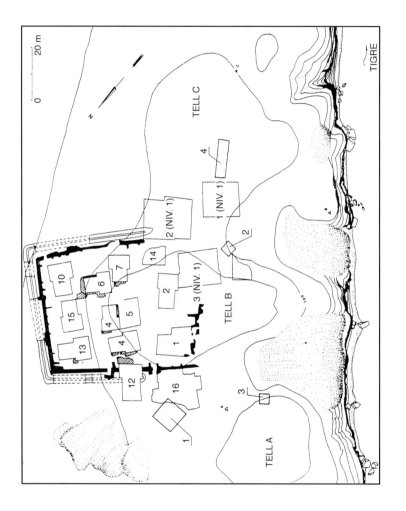

Figure 3.20 The Samarran site of Tell es-Sawwan on the Tigris, indicating tells A, B and C

Source: Breniquet 1992:6

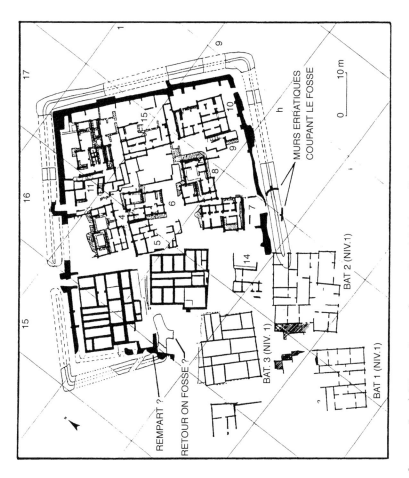

Figure 3.21 Tell es-Sawwan, Level III superimposed upon Level I (the earliest)

Source: Breniquet 1992:78

In Level II the incised Hassuna ware becomes very popular and the crude archaic type disappears. Painted Samarra ware makes its appearance in considerable quantities, and a few examples which were painted after firing are found. ... In Level IV the incised Hassuna pottery appears for the last time, and the painted, and painted and incised, Samarra ware now predominates. Very little is left of Sawwan V, but it suffices to show continuity in pottery: Samarra wares are the only ceramic product of this level.

(ibid.)

Catherine Breniquet (1991:79), who has done much to clarify the difficult stratigraphy of the site and its internal evolution as a settlement, summarizes the levels as follows:

- Level I: tripartite buildings
- Level II: reconstruction of those buildings
- Level IIIA: fortified installations and T-shaped buildings
- Level IIIB–IV: extension of the T-shaped buildings to the exterior of the ramparted zone and transformation of certain buildings into granaries, indicated by heavy buttressing and internal plastering
- Level V: Halafian installation on the western part of the site: a large circular construction on pebble foundations.

So a local evolution from Hassuna origins to Samarra is indicated. Also a product of local evolution is the development of irrigation techniques, vital in a zone that receives only 200 millimetres of rainfall. Concerning the presence (*inter alia*) of linseed and six-row hulled and naked barley, Helbaek remarks that

most probably agriculture was conducted on the basis of the seasonal flood of the river, spill pools were exploited, run-off checked in favourable spots by primitive damming – and generally the activities which we may visualize as the forerunners of later fully-fledged canal irrigation.

(Helbaek 1965:47)

However, we do not have to be content with mere visualization, for at the site of Choga Mami, by Mandali (in the piedmont zone, south of Sawwan and east of Baghdad), Joan Oates (1969, 1982) found evidence of fully-fledged canal irrigation, although not, of course, the four-level hierarchy later developed on the alluvium. Just as Sawwan is a settlement that can be seen to evolve from Hassuna to Samarra, so at Choga Mami the 'Transitional' pottery shows Samarrans transforming themselves into Ubaidians. In my scenario (1993a:191), Samarrans moved down the levees

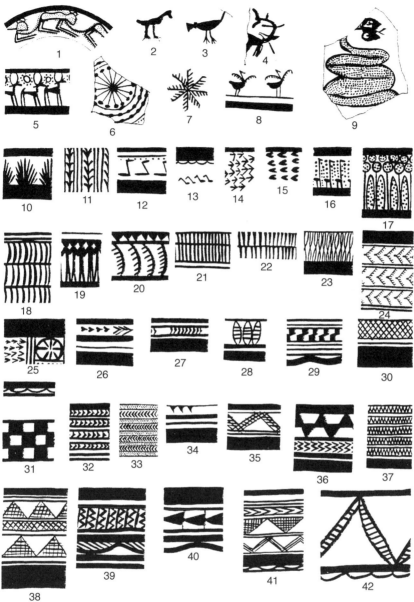

Nos. 4, 10-24, 29, Samarra ware; Nos. 25-28, 30-42, Al 'Ubaid ware; the remainder
Tall Halaf ware

Figure 3.22 Naturalistic and geometric designs from the classic trio: Halaf, Samarra
and Ubaid

Source: Mallowan and Rose 1935:fig. 77

onto the southernmost alluvium, 'becoming Ubaid' in the process. They then reflexed north to occupy the width of the central alluvium and expanded further north again, replacing the Halaf. A selection of their mutually influential designs are reproduced in Figure 3.22.

Ubaid

In accord with this model – Samarra → Ubaid (south) → Ubaid (central and north) – is the fact that the earliest Ubaid site so far discovered is that of Tell el-Oueili in the far south, only 3.5 kilometres from the historic Sumerian city of Larsa. Oueili lies on the northern side of the Euphrates not far from the type site of al-Ubaid. At Oueili, Ubaid levels even earlier than those of Eridu, farther south, have been explored (though modern excavations at Eridu might well find earlier strata there). The earliest level at Oueili, just above the water-table (which is 4.5 metres below modern plain level – Huot 1992:192) has accordingly been designated Ubaid 0, since the earliest Eridu level (c. 5500–5000 BC) is called Ubaid 1. Ubaid 2 with 3 extends from 5000–4500 BC, while Ubaid 4 runs from 4500 to 4000 BC.

Jean-Louis Huot states that

> pottery from Ubaid 0 shows close parallels with the Choga Mami Transitional Ware and ceramics from Choga Sefid in the Deh Luran Plain of southwest Iran. Ubaid 0 is thus clearly derived from the earliest culture to move into lower Mesopotamia, the Samarra.

> (ibid.)

Also similar to Choga Mami are small painted 'lizard head' humans from the Ubaid 0 level at 'Oueili (ibid.:194). Bitumen objects – spindle-whorls, small sticks, beads, etc., – are present too. Bitumen was very popular at 'Oueili for a wide range of uses (in addition to the common 'glueing' one of mounting sickle-blades): from impregnating shrouds, waterproofing baskets and wicker doors, to modelling the hair on alabaster female figurines. Laid under a layer of plaster, bitumen served as a damp-proof course against 'rising damp' (Connan and Deschesene 1992:47–8), no doubt another world-first.[29]

The usual 'Samarran' range of crops was grown, including six-row hulled barley (*Hordeum vulgare*), the main crop, and einkorn wheat (*Triticum monococcum*), with the tending of date palm (*Phoenix dactylifera*). However, given the permanent drought conditions of the southern alluvium, 'it is clear that irrigation was used from the very beginning of our sequence at 'Oueili and continued to be used from that time forth' (Huot 1992:193). Flax (*Linum usitatissimum*) is indicated but not yet conclusively demonstrated.

The hydromorphic nature of the site is indicated by the presence of date palm (fruit kernels found also at Eridu), *Cyperus rotundus* and *Phragmites australis* reeds. However, clearly recalling Thesiger's description of the southern marshes (cited earlier) is the emphasis on cattle keeping: no less than 45.5 per cent in Ubaid 0, rising to 57.9 per cent in Ubaid 4. Next most important were pigs, their proportion almost constant in all periods at around 37 per cent (Huot 1989:27). Sheep and goats, only 16.8 per cent in Ubaid 0, were obviously unsuited to the wet conditions and fell to a mere 5.6 per cent of recovered bones by Ubaid 4 (ibid.). The marsh/high water table this indicates would indeed have given the 'Oueilians a strong need for the 'damp-proof course' technology pioneered at Sawwan. But the solution in the deep south seems to have been an underfloor platform of reed and wood on which to mount the main rooms (Huot 1992:192). Nonetheless, bitumen was extensively used as a barrier.

Grand tripartite buildings in moulded-brick akin to those of Sawwan I–II occur at 'Oueili from late Ubaid 0 onwards. However, with access to more/older timber than in the north, 'Oueilians were able to support the roofs on columns and so provide more flexibility to room space. According to the summary of Matthews and Wilkinson (1991:179), during phase II a building covered an area of 233 square metres. Huot (1989:29) remarks that 'the architectural units at 'Oueili are without doubt larger than 200 square metres', and he reports an Ubaid 0 granary as covering an area of at least 80 square metres. One house has a central room 7.3 metres long and 4 to 4.6 metres wide, or approximately 32 square metres (Huot 1992:192). This is only slightly larger than the average size of the central hall (29 square metres) in Ubaidian houses, and the 30.5 square metres in Levels I–II of Samarran Sawwan (Forest 1983:11).

The continuity of the Samarran/Ubaidian building tradition, and the evolution of the latter from the former, are thus well attested, as is made abundantly clear from the pottery at 'Oueili, where even what appear to be 'Hassuna throwbacks' occur (Huot 1989:41) as well as the much more common Choga Mami Transitional type (cf. Oates 1982: Plate 2a).

Tell Abada, in the Hamrin along the Zagros foothills, is a Ubaid 2–3 settlement comparable to that of Sawwan, as is clear from the plan in Figure 3.23. Figure 3.24 shows household layout and access at Kheit Qasim III (Ubaid).

Though of different periods, both Sawwan and Abada (and Tell Qalinj Agha) consisted of large houses tightly nucleated. In addition to stressing the industrial specialization at Adaba, Jasim (1989:79) states that 'the carefully constructed buildings found in the upper two levels (I & II) show unequivocal evidence for the tripartite plan with T-shaped or cruciform hall which shows its finest development in the Uruk Inanna precinct at Warka'.

Kheit Qasim III, which is only a few kilometres to the north of Tell Abada, also contains an early Ubaid building of striking symmetry. There

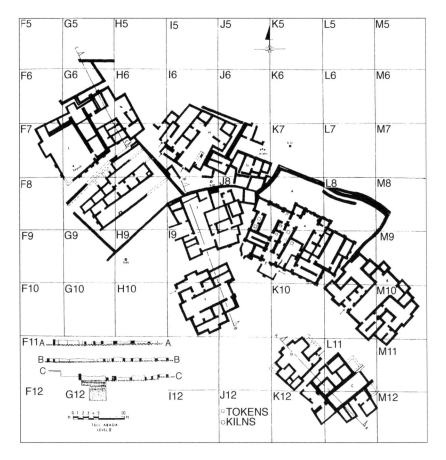

Figure 3.23 Plan of the Level II settlement at Tell Abada showing large houses tightly nucleated (early Ubaid 3)

Source: Jasim 1985, pt 2: fig. 13

each of the T-units contains its own hearth and storage bin, suggesting a household formed of separate domestic units, the key indicator of which in ethnology is the separate hearth. As Chantal Forest-Foucault (1980:224) remarked of this building: 'Cependant, la répétition du même type d'installations (foyers et compartiments) dans les trois unités, semblerait indiquer que le trois halls étaient le siège d'activités du même ordre.' [However, the repetition of the same sort of installations (hearths and compartments) in the three units would seem to suggest that the three halls were the scene of activities of the same order.] Symmetry in Figure 3.24 is very clear.

So down the eastern flank of the Tigris, from Tell es-Sawwan through Choga Mami to the marshlands of the deep south, we find structures of a

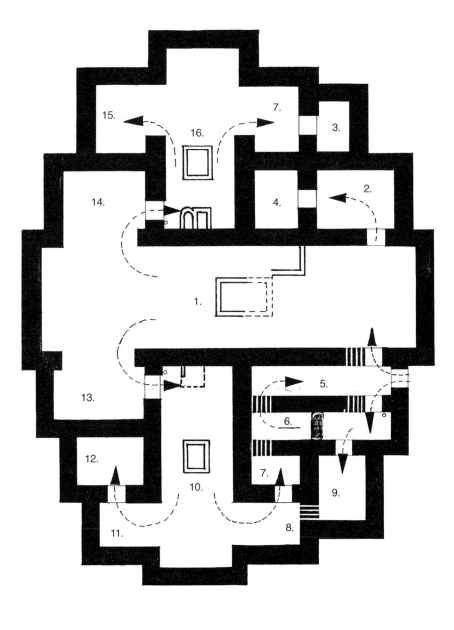

Figure 3.24 The house at Kheit Qasim III (Ubaid 3) showing circulation
Source: Forest 1984:119 and 1980:222

155

size and symmetry comprising settlements of a type occurring nowhere else in the Near East, or indeed the world. What does this actually tell us about the social arrangements of the people who lived in them? According to Huot:

> it remains to be understood how a specialized agricultural society, well adapted to its environment, like 'Oueili in its final phase, was able to evolve sufficiently to emerge a few centuries later into a far more complex culture [Uruk]. Today, we can hardly see why and how this transition from one to other occurs.
>
> (Huot 1989:40)

On the contrary, I have long thought that the key to this evolutionary process lay in the very architecture of those large, independent, tripartite buildings, or rather in the ecological demands to which they were a response.

THE SOCIAL ORDER

This household would, then, be one of parents and married children each with their own quarters, or, after the death of the parents, of siblings and their children. Only thus would the size and repetitive aspects of the Samarran/Ubaidian houses make sense. My explanation (1984, 1987, 1990, 1993b) therefore has been that what such a household represents is an organization specially adapted to pioneering colonization of the alluvium. Such a household (referred to using the Greek term *oikos*) would come into being with the necessity of having to marshal all possible resources, particularly the human ones, in an efficient unit, leaving as little as possible to chance faced with the vagaries of river-regime and climate. This implies tight managerial control under a household head, and, reflexively, hierarchy within the household. I have previously termed this sort of arrangement an *augmented and stratified household*, in which subordination was especially applicable to distant relations or those with no family connection. Such dependants could either live within the house or in adjoining barn-type buildings, as seen at Kheit Qasim III and at Abada (Jasim 1989:83; the building north of H9).

Such a household would be self-sufficient over all the subsistence products and in the processing of raw materials into finished products. Additionally each would undertake a particular specialization (again seen at Abada), such as in fine pottery, leather goods or textiles, in order to have the means of exchange for necessary imports such as bitumen, obsidian and metal, and for luxuries also. All this was labour-intensive, requiring an extensive, diverse and multi-skilled labour force. This is supplied by

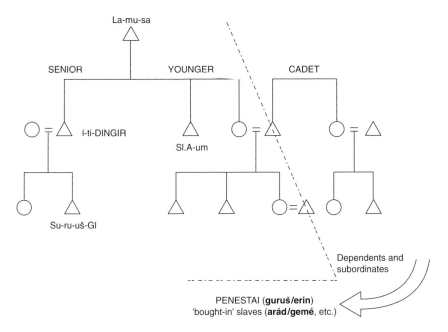

Figure 3.25 The internal structure of the Lamusa oikos showing its augmented and stratified character

Source: Maisels 1990

the augmented and stratified (or *oikos*) household. What it is an 'extended' form of is the joint-household of siblings, who 'own it', and become its 'proprietor-managers'. Building on Gelb's work (especially 1979) I have previously (1984, 1990, 1993a) been able to delineate the core of two such (related) households of the Sargonic Period, as shown in Figures 3.25 and 3.26.

Thus Stein's (1994:40–1) suggestion that 'Ubaid Mesopotamia consisted of a series of small localized chiefdoms based on staple finance' which is 'the mobilization of surplus staples such as cereals to support the elite' is totally misconceived. Stratification was internal to the household, the settlement and the settlement cluster. There is just no role for a 'chief'. The Eridu 'baked clay figurine of [a] male holding a mace or scepter', (illustrated on his p. 41), taken by Stein as a representation of a chief, is, as I have indicated (1990:313–14) proto-'Dumuzi of the Dates', and the 'scepter' he is holding is a phallus-shaped date-pollinator. He also has date-stone eyes and ripe dates across his shoulders. His role could not be more explicit unless he had his name and duties inscribed across his chest in pictographic script! Head, eyes, genitals and 'wand' all declare 'date-pollinator'.

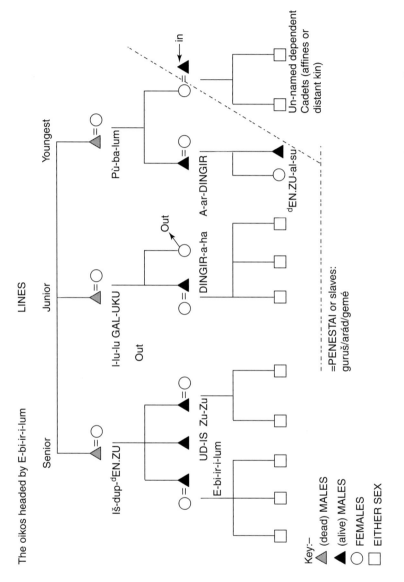

The oikos headed by E-bi-ir-i-lum

LINES

Senior   Junior   Youngest

Iš-dup-ᵈEN.ZU

E-bi-ir-i-lum   UD-IS Zu-Zu

I-lu-lu GAL-UKU

Out

DINGIR-a-ha

Pù-ba-lum

A-ar-DINGIR

ᵈEN.ZU-al-su-

— in

Out

Un-named dependent
Cadets (affines or
distant kin)

Key:-

◣ (dead) MALES
▲ (alive) MALES
◯ FEMALES
☐ EITHER SEX

----- =PENESTAI or slaves:
guruš/aråd/gemé

Figure 3.26 The Iš-dup-ᵈEN.ZU oikos led by Ebiirilum, showing its augmented and stratified character; full clan structure appears in Maisels 1993b:157

Source: Maisels 1993

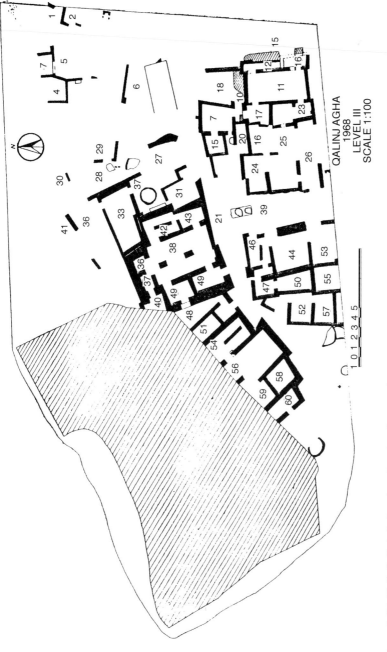

QALINJ AGHA
1968
LEVEL III
SCALE 1:100

Figure 3.27 Tell Qalinj Agha site plan (Uruk Period)

Source: Al-Soof 1969:39

Kalam – 'the land'[30]

Nucleated settlements of large tripartite buildings similar to Tell es-Sawwan and Abada exist also in the succeeding Uruk[31] and Jemdet Nasr Periods, which together span the fourth millennium; an example is the Uruk period site of Tell Qalinj Agha by Erbil, as shown in Figure 3.27.

The Jemdet Nasr Period takes us into historical Sumer. In the south-central alluvium at Fara, ancient Shuruppak (the original city of Noah, called Ziusudra in Sumerian), from the Jemdet Nasr to Early Dynastic III periods, similar clusters of house-types have been observed by Martin (1988) and confirmed by Matthews (1991) from architectural and glyptic evidence. Further confirmation is found in the Diyala (east of Baghdad) by Henrickson (1981, 1982, 1994) for the Early Dynastic II period through the pre-Sargonic period, and in Ur during the Isin-Larsa period. Postgate (1982:59), at his site of Abu Salabikh in the north-central alluvium, 'suggests that at

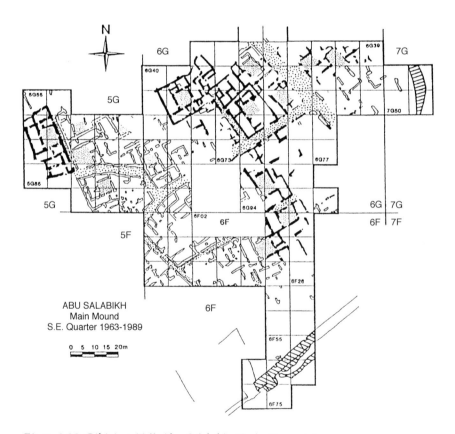

Figure 3.28 Oikioi at Tell Abu Salabikh (Early Dynastic)
Source: Postgate 1990:98

the beginning of the Early Dynastic I period we should envisage a city composed of large, self-contained compounds, and socially of corresponding groups of persons'. For the EDIII period he exposed building 6H82 at Abu Salabikh which can be seen with others of the same type on the map of the Main Mound shown in Figure 3.28.

On the basis of textual evidence, Sumerologists, notably I.M. Diakonoff and I.J. Gelb, had noted and discussed peculiar households. Here ancient *kudurrus* (Sum: Na-du-a) – public records in (valuable) stone –

> enable us to see the structure of the ancient family and clan much better than at any other time of Mesopotamian history. Texts such as the Manishtushu Obelisk describe the ancestry of sellers which is often as long as six generations. These long lists of generations provide us with evidence that there were also extended families besides nuclear families, which in turn were grouped into larger social configurations up to the level of 'clans'.
>
> (Gelb *et al.* 1991:2)

The Manishtushu Obelisk text (in Akkadian: ibid.:116–40) records the sale by several sellers of a descent grouping ('clan' = imru) of eight parcels of land totalling 9,723 iku (= 3,430 hectares), situated around the four Akkadian cities of Dûr-Sin, Girtab, Marda and Kish, to king Manishtushu, elder son of Sargon 'the great' (ibid.:116). From descent lines of the principal participants previously set out by Gelb (1979:76–7), I constructed (1990:159; 1993:174) two *oikos* households under the paterfamiliae I-ti-DINGIR and E-bi-ir-i-lum, being those in their respective branches who received significant gifts (= payment) for alienating their patrimony.

Kudurrus (almost certainly placed in temples) publicized the alienations, while sale documents in clay were the buyers' receipt. The most comprehensive and authoritative work on kudurrus is the product of the great scholarship of I.J. Gelb, supplemented by Gelb *et al.* (1991). They provide the invaluable summary of Table 3.3.

From such alienations – which are recorded as early as the Uruk III period shortly after the (pictographic) beginnings of writing – there arose private landholdings as a third category, alongside *oikos* and temple holdings. But the situation was neither simple nor uniform. Indeed, and this is a most important consideration, the relative importance of temple estates, as against palace and private landholdings, seem, from the provenance of kudurrus and other texts, to be inversely proportional as between the Sumerian south and the Akkadian north:

> These facts seem to indicate that during the Fara, Pre-Sargonic, and Sargonic periods the 'private' ownership of land was considerably more widespread in the north than in the south. As for the

Table 3.3 Main characteristics of ancient kudurrus and sale documents

	Ancient kudurrus	*Sale documents*
Time:	From Uruk III to Sargonic	From Fara to Ur III
Place:	Sumer, Akkad, Diyala Region, Assyria	
Form:	Tablet, stela, statuette, animal figurine	Clay tablet (very rarely brick or cone)
Language:	Sumerian, Akkadian	Sumerian, Akkadian
Contents:	Purchases of multiple parcels of land, each from one or more sellers by one buyer	Purchase of a single piece of property (field, orchard, house, slave, animal, etc.) from one or more sellers by one buyer
Purpose:	Publicity of the purchases	Record of the purchase, prepared for the buyer

Source: Gelb *et al.* 1991:3

south, 'private' land holdings appear to have been insignificant in the far south, their importance gradually increasing in the near south as one moves in the northerly direction.

Coupled with the decreasing significance of 'private' land holdings as one passes from northern Babylonia into the south, is the complementary phenomenon of the increasing importance of temple households and temple estates within the same geographical area. As is abundantly shown by the third millennium economic sources, temple households and temple domains were most prevalent in the far south and in the lower section of the near south, at Lagash and Umma. Their importance was markedly less in the places located farther north, such as Adab, Isin, and Nippur, decreasing even further in northern Babylonia, where the dominant forms of economic organization were the royal and private households.

On the basis of these data it can be tentatively suggested that the institution of private/alienable landed property originated in the north from where it spread to the south. Conversely, the institution of the temple household and its peculiar system of land tenancy appears to have been originally a southern phenomenon, which was eventually transmitted to the north, though never superseding in importance the royal and private households.

(Gelb *et al.* 1991:25)

In the north, the temple estate never even approached the importance of royal and private estates. In short, private property in land was a fundamental northern characteristic that spread through the south in the second half of the third millennium.

The north/south, **Uri/Ki-en-gir** or Akkad/Sumer contrasts are rooted not merely in cultural but also in the geomorphological differences between what Liverani (1996:13) refers to as the river 'valley' and the 'delta' zones of the alluvium. In the valley, including not only the area around Kish but also the Diyala basin, large-scale/long-distance irrigation is difficult, while in the delta it is not only highly practicable but highly necessary to sustain high density populations.

Paradigmatically this resulted in small, variously shaped and basically family-owned fields in the north, with the south characterised by huge (40 hectares), markedly rectangular, institutionally worked fields parcelled into long narrow strips for ease of ploughing (ibid.:14–15).

He illustrates the north–south differences in irrigation practice, land use (field size and shape) and ownership/control as shown in Figures 3.29a and 3.29b. The differences in both scale and intensity of land use are immediately apparent: localized and relatively small-scale in the north; extensive, institutional, 'mass-production' in the south. 'The difference was so marked and deeply rooted in the agricultural and topographical thought of ancient Mesopotamia, that it gave rise to two different terminological systems designating the sides of the fields' (ibid.). Though the north–south economic differences tended to reduce from the Sargonic period onwards, some still existed even during the Old Babylonian period. And while a Sargonic king (probably Naram-Sin) is known to have seized large areas of land (444,505.25 *iku*) in Lagash to give to his dependants (there were doubtless other extensive seizures), the Ur III kings effectively 'nationalized' the temple estates and ran them as an integrated whole.

The basis of Sumerian society lay in the estates, owned and operated by augmented family households, plus, most augmented and stratified of all, temple and palace households. This form of social organization, permitting the integrated control of labour and capital, land of different uses, livestock and water, was a response to management demands imposed by the environment, especially by the hydrological conditions.

Temples as large institutional landowners had their origins in the 'community reserve' for a cluster of *oikos* households as they expanded from a township to become a town and then a city. Presumably their role became more critical in the 'deep south' of the alluvium, where the earliest pioneers established the first true cities. This would also account for the temples' location (there was usually more than one) at the centre of southern cities, most visibly at Uruk and Ur (cf: Roaf 1990:60, 63, 101).

However, even in the 'near south', at Al-Hiba, the capital city of Lagash state (which includes the cities of Girsu [Tello] *c*.25 kilometres to the southeast and Nina [Surghul]), Hansen states that:

Although this capital city of the Sumerian city-state of Lagash is exceedingly large [600 hectares in the late Early Dynastic] in

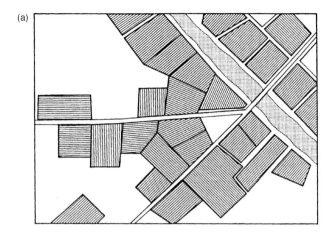

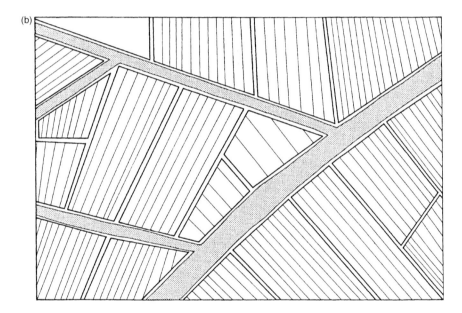

Figure 3.29   Schematic representation of the irrigation regimes in (a) northern and (b) southern Mesopotamia, the latter more extensive and more complex

Source: Liverani 1996:18

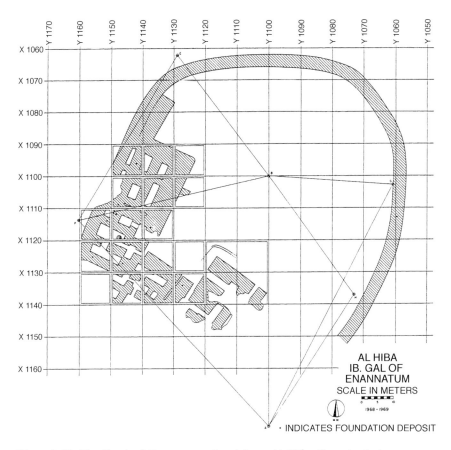

Figure 3.30 The Ibgal of Enannatum, Level I, at Al Hiba (Lagash city)

Source: D.P. Hansen 1970:251

comparison with other contemporary Sumerian sites [e.g. Shuruppak, *c*.100 hectares] the excavations have already revealed that a good portion of the area was devoted to the manors of the major gods.[32]

(D.P. Hansen 1992:210)

Those temple establishments included (at the highest point of the mound) the Bagara, belonging to Ningirsu, 'Lord of Girsu', the god of Lagash; Gatumdug, the 'Mother of Lagash'; Shagepada, the precinct of Nanshe; the establishment of the goddess Bau (which has supplied so many documents); and the Ibgal of the goddess of fecundity, Inanna, who with An, Enlil and Enki is one of the supreme gods of the Sumero-Akkadian pantheon.[33] Enannatum's reconstruction of the Ibgal (originally built by his grand-

165

father Urnanshe) within its 'temple oval' formed by a platform and enclosing wall, is seen in Figure 3.30. It was built at the extreme southwestern edge of the city (which today, like Nippur in the late nineteenth century AD, can only be reached by water), indicating that the Ibgal was a relatively late addition (during ED III), since space to build on this scale could only be found on the outskirts.

Within the Bagara precinct D.P. Hansen (1992:209) found the second oldest brewery so far known anywhere in the world. The earliest, discovered by Jeremy Geller as part (Hk24A) of the Hierakonpolis complex in Egypt, has radiocarbon dates of 4719+−34 bp, calibrated (according to Stuiver and Reimer 1986) at 3,500–3,400 BC (Geller 1992:23). Egyptian beer (hnqt), made of partially baked loaves of coarsely ground wheat or barley (ibid.:19), and therefore associated with ovens, was a staple there as in Sumer.[34] The Al-Hiba brewery – ebappir – had a dedicated building given over to grain storage rooms, ovens, tanks and vats. One room was filled by a huge oven whose dome in corbelled mud-brick had a diameter of no less that 5 metres (Hansen 1992:209).

Agricultural lands belonging to and supporting the temples would, of course, be outside the city. As a community (later state) institution, the temples were run by elders: ab-ba-ab-ba-me ('fathers'). But those elders functioned also as 'city-fathers', sitting in council (AB+AS-uru), and I have already (1987, 1990, 1993) proposed that the Elders Council consisted of paterfamiliae, such as Itidingir and Ebiirilum.[35]

From a synopsis of ten texts from Lagash in the Ur III period, Gelb provides the following hierarchy of temple functionaries:

1. ab-ba-ab-ba-me, 'elders', in the sense of top officials.
    a) Managers:
        1 sanga, 'priest', or 1 sabra, 'temple steward'.
    b) Officials, Class 1:
        1   GA-dub-ba, 'archivist'.
        1   sag-du$_5$, 'field surveyor'.
        1   ka-gur7, 'grain-store supervisor'.
        1   nu-banda erin-na, 'overseer of workers/soldiers'.
    c) Officials, Class 2:
        1   dub-sar gud-apin, 'scribe of the plough animals'.
        1   sár-ra-ab-du, 'treasurer(?)'.
2. engar nu-banda gud-me, 'chiefs of plough teams and overseers of plough animals'.
    2-28 nu-banda gud, 'overseers of plough animals'.
    4-100 engar, 'chiefs of plough teams'.
3. 8–450 erin-me, 'workers/soldiers'.
4. Miscellaneous personnel.

(Gelb 1979:14)

Here we find 'high managerialism' of an order that did not reappear until the twentieth century AD. The engar is, of course, middle management.

The temple of Nin-dara (Nanse's husband) in the Lagash area had 292 estate personnel 'present' (gub-ba), according to an Ur III inscription upon a stone statuette, as studied and interpreted by Civil (1989:52). Nineteen were high officials (ab-ba-ab-ba) and their aides (šeš-tab-ba); fifty-seven were farming experts and management (sag-apin-me); over one hundred and ten were sheep and cattle personnel, under a superintendent with two overseers (ugula), each with an assistant; the rest were miscellaneous personnel, whose high degree of specialization is most revealing:

> three people in charge of arboriculture, two for tamarisks and for giš-ab-ba trees, one chief of boatmen (ugula mah$_2$[lah$_4$]) with one aide, the overseer of the residents (ugula gan-tuš-u$_3$[ne]), one vegetable grower (lu$_2$-nis[igx(SAR)]), six people taking care of oil, two chief porters, and assorted workers with no activities given. Among them there must be the domestics (doormen, firewood carriers, fishermen etc.) listed in a text [AAS 178] studied by Gregoire.
>
> (ibid.)

The sanga is a priest only in the sense that an abbot is a priest; actually they were administrators, as Maekawa's (1987a:90) table of the lands of all the public households in Ur III Lagash (Girsu) makes plain. The first half of the table encompasses six households (é) with a total area amounting to 1488 bur 13 ¾ iku or 9,647.19 hectares. The full dozen establishments have an agricultural area amounting to 4030 bur, 17 ¾ iku, or 26,120.79 hectares (Maekawa 1987a:91).

While everyone in the 'public sector', whether working full or part time, received (some) rations, they were by no means equal. As ever, those 'in charge' were entitled to huge incomes reflecting their 'responsibility', and so the sanga or temple steward received twice the rations of the higher officials, with the lowest levels of Grade 1 receiving only a fifth of the barley (še) rations received by the šabra/sanga (Gelb 1979:16–17). In turn, those in Grade 2 had at least as great differentials over the workers in Grade 3, while they were better provided for than the members of Grade 4: 'widows, old people, especially old women, sterile and childless women, cripples, especially the blind and the deaf, beggars and vagabonds, prostitutes, fatherless children, orphans, bastards, foundlings, and the ex-voto personnel' (ibid.:22; cf. Gelb 1972:10 ff).

Ordinary workers' rations – fairly constant during Sargonic and Ur III periods – were as indicated in Table 3.4.

For cereal cultivation, the basic pattern of land use is simply set out in Table 3.5, on the assumption that each field was put to fallow in alternate years.

At least in the historical periods, temple lands were by no means all worked as demesne (gán-gu$_4$-$^{(giš)}$apin) that is, directly by the temple

Table 3.4 Ordinary workers' rations

Kind	Time	Men	Women	Children	Measure
barley	once a month	60	30	25, 20, 15, 10	quarts (sila)
oil	once a year	4	4	2, 1.5, 1	quarts
wool	once a year	4	3	2, 2.5, 1	pounds = (453.6gm)

Source: Gelb 1965:233

Notes: 1 *sila* is about 1 litre; 300 sila = 1 gur. For a set of length/mass/volume/area equivalences see Postgate (1992:xix), Snell (1982:xix–xx) and Friberg (1984:79–81). The child's wool-ration of about 2 minas is roughly equivalent to the annual clipping of one sheep. Milk yields were also low.

Table 3.5 The basic pattern of land use in cereal cultivation

Cultivation year	Activity	Harvest-fallow year	Activity
spring-summer:	flooding/leaching	spring-summer:	harvest
summer-fall:	ploughing/sowing	summer-fall-winter:	fallow

Source: La Placa and Powell 1990:75

workforce. Some was assigned to temple functionaries and private citizens for their subsistence ((gán-)ŠUKU/gándab₅-ba), and some fields, gán apin-lá/gán níg-gál-la, always the smallest category, were rented to tenants on a share-cropping basis. Towards the end of the third millennium, in Ur III Lagash, the proportions of domain to allotment to tenant farmed land stood in the ratio of 67 per cent:25 per cent:8 per cent (Maekawa 1987a:97).

From such economic bases, Gelb has categorized the social status of household members for the last half of the third millennium (see Table 3.6). The intricacies of the occupational/class structure have still to be fully delineated; for a concise statement of the present understanding see Postgate (1992:234–40); for some of the intricacies see Maekawa (1976 etc.). One of the very first things recorded in Sumer (in the archaic, still pictographic, Uruk texts) is a list of professions (Nissen 1993:61–3, illustrated on p. 62) and although this list is headed by kings/high officials/priests/under-officials (collectively 'managers'), it appears from this and much other evidence that non-agricultural labour falls into three broad categories generally applicable from the Uruk until the Old Babylonian period:

1 Communal labour that is both seasonal (harvest, canal maintenance) and episodic (war and defence: construction/maintenance of city walls) and civic (temple building, etc.).
2 Artisanal, notably smithing, from basic work such as moulding copper sickles to the making of fine statuary, and work in gold, silver, lapis, etc.

Table 3.6 Economic dependency and family life

---

1   Officials and supervisors
    –   lead a full family life
    –   work full-time for the household
    –   have means of production in land
    –   may receive additional rations.
2   Craftsmen and persons with various occupations
    –   lead a full family life
    –   if they have means of production in land, they work only
        part-time for the household, during which they receive
        rations
    –   if they have no means of production in land, they work full-
        time for the household and receive rations throughout the year.
3   Workers/soldiers (settlers, colonists)
    –   lead a full family life
    –   have means of production in land
    –   work part-time for the household, during which time they
        receive rations.
4   Women and children without family and other 'rejects of the society'
    have no family life
    –   work full-time for the household
    –   have no means of production
    –   receive rations throughout the year.

Source: Gelb 1979:23–4

Note: Sumerian for rations is še-ba, wages are á, for craftsmen gašam.

3   Manufacture of woollen textiles (and pottery?) in large workshops
    employing scores or even hundreds of workers, producing the principal
    export commodity of the alluvium: fine 'Akkadian' textiles.

This last category was exclusively an institutional activity, organized by
temple and palace. However, the 'ration system' indicates that the recipient was expected to make up their own clothes, prepare their own food,
build their own houses and so forth. Likewise much agricultural cooperation and exchange was 'privately' organized and so of little interest to the
institutions. So although the overwhelming majority of texts are institutional records, this should not deceive us into thinking that their activities
comprise anything like the entirety of economic activity.

The state

In the texts we also hear of an Assembly completing the 'circle of the
people' (ukkin/*puhrum*) of each city-state. For the want of explicit texts, my
conjecture is that the Elders' Council was the more or less permanent city

government, and that 'juniors' were admitted to form an Assembly when assent was wanted for decisions of the Elders' Council. This Assembly would accordingly comprise the lú-tur-mah (*sahir rabi*), the 'small and the great' (literally young and old). The small [people] would be the dependants of households, private and public. Most prominent in this category were the guruš (pronounced gurush), who functioned as both the basic labour and military force (as the erín did later).[36]

The stories surrounding Gilgamesh, third king of the First Dynasty of Uruk in the Early Dynastic period, existed in Sumerian long before they were written down in Akkadian as a connected developmental narrative (see Dalley 1989). He tried to mobilize the citizens of Uruk for a war against the overlordship of Me-salim of Kish. The 'senate' or Elders' Council refused his request, so he appealed to a 'general assembly' to overturn their decision. In this sense, city-state government was consensual. Nonetheless, the fact that Gilgamesh appealed to the guruš against the elders does not itself justify belief in the existence of a duly constituted second chamber of 'commons'. It seems to me that rather than constituting an autonomous chamber of a bicameral Assembly – each with its own rights of initiative, debate and decision – the guruš were merely part of the 'commons' assembled when debate was complete and decision made, to hear and endorse the consensus emerging from the Elders in council.

By going from the Council of Elders to the guruš in order to bypass a firm decision of theirs, Gilgamesh was acting more than illegally, he was effectively conducting a *coup d'état*, something suggested by the Sumerian King List (Jacobsen 1939:88–90). He may, by reacting opportunistically and ruthlessly against 'Kish kingship' and mobilizing a personal following (Jacobsen 1980:76) have been able to turn himself into a king (*lugal*) on the northern model (Diakonoff 1969c:181–2).

At least until the time of Sargon, the city-state's army was composed of foot-soldiers in phalanx formation, attacking with bronze-tipped spears and protecting themselves as a unit with a barrier of shields, as shown on the Stele of the Vultures from Lagash in the mid-third millennium. Those 'hoplite' troops seem to be wearing thick plucked-wool garments. By contrast, the 'Royal Standard of Ur', of about the same period, shows heavy four- (solid) wheeled battle-wagons drawn by equids, accompanied by lines of infantry carrying battle-axes and wearing studded leather cloaks as armour.[37]

As in Greece, inter-city warfare was endemic from earliest times. City walls existed at Uruk itself as early as the Uruk period, and also at Chogha Mish (Boehmer 1991:468–9) and Abu Salabikh (S. Pollock, cited in Postgate 1992: n.441). Boehmer (op. cit.) illustrates a seal impression from Uruk in the Uruk period clearly showing a manned city wall. Given the competitive relations between cities, walls cannot have been confined to those named. Once an arms race starts, only a 'neutral' holy city like Nippur could afford to be left out.

But there was another, more venerable, source of leadership, which continued where there had not been such a *coup d'état*. Thus the pious kings of Lagash (some of whom were indeed *lugal*), Isin, Larsa and especially Assur, referred to themselves as ensi for 'the ensi was the man who functioned as the "steward" of the god, entrusted with the duty to manage the demesne of the [city] god, and thus acting as the intermediary between the human community and its divine ruler [the city-god]' (Larsen 1976:113). Jacobsen (1957:123 n.71) suggested an origin in en-si-ak, 'manager of the arable lands', the title applicable to the person who was 'the leader of the seasonal organization of the townspeople for work on the fields'. This either means that joint work teams cultivate all the *oikos* lands in some kind of rota, including the temple lands; or it may just refer to the 'collective' temple lands. As a term for kingship, however, Jacobsen (1980:77) suggests that *ensi* arose in the smaller of the city-states.

Later, more dominant kings tended to refer to themselves as **lugal** (indeed in Sumerian lugal has the general meaning of domination or ownership), going as far in wider claims as **lugal-kalam-ma**, 'king of the land', and **lugal-KIŠ**, 'king of Kish', both titles claiming wider territorial power or hegemony, and referring to subordinate rulers as **ensi**. But titulary reflected local traditions and religious sentiment[38] as well as the more obvious external politico-military circumstances in the constantly shifting power relations between the various city-states.

The ensi seems to have emerged from the ranks of the gal or 'greats' and/or from the ranks of the temple establishment in the smaller cities of the Sumerian south. The third leadership office, bearing the title **en**, is, however, more definitely associated with the temple, and has strong associations with divinity. The **en** was the leading priestly position of the early historic period, with the sense of 'possession of a power to make things thrive, to produce abundance and prosperity, and from this power the authority to command the affairs of the community' (Weadock 1975:102) – accordingly a title and status that later rulers could annex. Truly pious kings, however, such as Gudea of Lagash (2141–2122 BC) could in all humility refer to themselves as 'the great en of Ningirsu'.[39] En was also the title of supreme authority at Ebla, where the several lugals were subordinate officials (Pettinato 1991:114).

En, the high priestship, is known as a title as early as the Jemdet Nasr period, by which time it had probably already assumed the significance of 'priest-king', given, Jacobsen (1980:77) postulates, the general warlike conditions. While sanga, 'chief administrator', appears as early as Uruk IV texts (as does the sign for 'smith' along with over two thousand others), the title **lugal** is only known about half a millennium later, the first secure instance being from Kish (Tell Ingharra/Tell Uhaimir) around 2700 BC. This agrees well with the Sumerian King List (Jacobsen 1939), which states

1

2

3

Figure 3.31 The EN in action: four glyptic images (Late Uruk/Jemdet Nasr)
Panels 1–3: offerings to the temple(s);
Panel 4: defending the city, or campaigning to glorify the temple(s).
Source: Antonova 1992:Fig. C

that when kingship was lowered from heaven after the Flood, it was centred in Kish. However, not only in Kish during the ED III period is there archaeological evidence for a royal palace (Moorey 1964, 1978), but also at Eridu (Safar *et al.* 1981), al-Hiba/Lagash (Hansen 1973) and possibly on the South Mound of Abu Salabikh too (Postgate 1990). Kings lived in palaces (**é-gal** = 'great house'), while the en lived in a giparu, part of a temple complex, such as the large building (at least 92 × 48 metres overall) so identified at Jemdet Nasr by Moorey (1976:106). There the collective city-seals illustrated in Figure 3.32 were found.

The gipar, as famously at Ur, could also be the abode of an **en** priestess (*entum* in Akkadian). The outstanding example is the world's first named author – high priestess Enheduanna ('En, ornament of the heavens') Sargon's daughter. Enheduanna compiled and redacted forty-two hymns addressed to all the temples of Sumer and Akkad. No. 5, praising 'the house (*Ešumeša* temple) of Ninurta in Nibru' (= Nippur), is translated by Sjoberg and Bergmann in their standard work:

> House with the gathered **me**'s of heaven standing on a great place,
> With the true **me**'s which the hero . . .
> Arm of battle, heroic(?) meddu-weapon, carrier of the quiver,
> Valiant (?) brickwork which endures, your foundation is eternal,
> Founded by the primeval lord, (temple which makes) a decision through(?) the princely **me**'s,
> Holy soil which fills the mountain, lifting its head among the princes,
> Lofty house, your . . . is like the sunlight whose glow radiates,
> Eshumesha, Enlil has clad your name in awe-inspiring splendour,
> Your prince, the great [. . .], the hero whose strength is unsurpassed,
> The great ensi of Enlil, the sovereign(?) who rivals heaven and earth,
> The. . . . sealkeeper of father Enlil, he who makes the great **me**'s perfect. . . .
>
> (Sjoberg and Bergmann 1969:20–1)

Clearly **me**'s [always plural and pronounced *may*] are the norms and techniques of civilization; the apotheosis of the components of Sumerian culture.[40] It is the complement of the term **nam**, 'mode of being' or 'existence' (Jacobsen 1993:122), though according to Diakonoff (1983b:84) **nam** can be translated as an abstract term, 'fate'. Jeremy Black and Anthony Green (1992:130) state that 'the **me** are the powers which make possible the implementation of the ğiš-hur and which ensure the continuation of civilized life', with ğiš-hur meaning plan or design.

Ninurta is elsewhere referred to as the farmer and first-born son of Enlil. Inanna has many aspects, those of great power in agriculture (fecundity), sex and war. Indeed, Enheduanna goes so far as to describe Inanna/ Ishtar as 'Queen of all the **me**', mistress of the world and everything in it (Westenholz 1989).

The *entum*'s most important role was as the human wife of the god in the rite of sacred marriage. She, 'whose loins were suitable by their purity for the en-ship', represented Inanna at Nippur, and Ningal, the divine wife of Nanna the moon god, at Ur (Weadock 1975:101–2). The union of Nanna and Ninlil produced Utu, the sun-god. Gipars are also known at Uruk, Khafaje and Agrab in the southern corner of the Shara temple, which last seems to have been the residence of the en (Weadock 1975:126).

Kings supplanted ens or ens became kings during the Early Dynastic Period. Kings then placed their sisters/daughters in the *giparu* to attend to cultic matters and to pray for the king's life and success. In Enheduanna's case, it seems, also to render the new dispensation wrought by her father ideologically acceptable to the Sumerian south.

Piotr Steinkeller (1993), in the most important analysis of Mesopotamian political structures since Jacobsen's (1957) seminal work, has convincingly argued that kingship itself and the territorial state (with its intrin-sic pressures toward expansion) were the form of organization that the Sem-itic population of Syria and Northern Mesopotamia adopted when they became urbanized as 'Kish civilization' in the first part of the third millennium. Mari was founded as a completely new site in EDI or EDII (Steinkeller 1993:128). Early Dynastic texts from Ebla and Mari are only slightly later than those from Fara (ancient Shuruppak) around 2600 BC (Michalowski 1990:67). Contrasting with the Sumerian notion of the king as a dutiful servant, the head of a bureaucratic structure of dutiful servants, the notion of kingship founded on genealogy, patrimony and might initially gave the 'Kishite' north hegemony over the Sumerian city-states in the Early Dynastic Period. Might prevailed over proper procedure and cultic duty.

It will be remembered that in 'Gilgamesh and Akka', the initial hege-mony lies with Kish; indeed, Jacobsen (1980:76) suggests that Gilgamesh was originally installed by Akka, 'only to have him eventually rebel'. Akka's father, the penultimate king of the First Dynasty of Kish, whom the King List states was strong enough to ravage Elam, was called En-mebaragesi, of whom Jacobsen observes:

> in the city-states where the priest-king (en) retained himself in power, the constant war-like conditions forced him to take on the duties of a warrior-king. A striking example of this fusion of ori-ginally distinct offices is Me-barage-si, with whose name the title en 'priest king' became so closely associated that later tradition knows him only as En-mebarage-si even though he is remembered simply as a warrior king.

(ibid.)

He is also the earliest king with a surviving royal inscription.[41]

Thus, the development of the titulary and scope of kingship can be

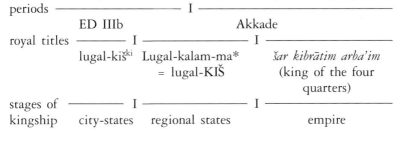

related as follows (after Maeda 1984:81):

CONCLUSION

By the end of the Ubaid period, Eridu had reached about 12 hectares, Ur around 10 hectares and Uruk a massive 70 hectares (Jacobsen 1980:73–4). In the Late Uruk period, at the end of which writing appears, the city of Uruk encompassed an area of at least 2.5 square kilometres, or 250 hectares. Of this, Nissen (1993a:56) estimates 230 hectares were occupied, suggesting to him a population for Uruk at the end of the fourth millennium of between 25,000 and 50,000. For comparison he cites the area of Jerusalem at the time of Herod as c.120 hectares, Athens when Themistocles built the Long Wall to include its seaport of Piraeus at c.210 hectares, and even Rome, as late as the time of Augustus, at only about 360 hectares. This is all the more remarkable since within two to three hundred years the size of Uruk had more than doubled again, approaching 600 hectares by around 2900–2800 BC (ibid.).

Just prior to this in the Jemdet Nasr (or Eanna III) period (3200–3000 BC) there is evidence of a 'league' (Jacobsen's [1957] Kengir League) between cities of the alluvium – including Ur, Larsa, Nippur, Uruk, Kish, Zabala and Urum, amongst others (Matthews 1992:199) – demonstrated by the 'city-seals' illustrated in Figure 3.32 that recorded probably only token amounts of goods sent between the cooperating cities (for rotational festivals?) to foster their cultural unity and possible military alliance.

The examples shown – see Matthews 1993 for extended discussion – are from Jemdet Nasr itself, which Moorey (1976:105) has further suggested functioned as a kind of 'clearing house' in the circulation network, given that settlement's central location. Such 'collective sealings' are also known from Ur.

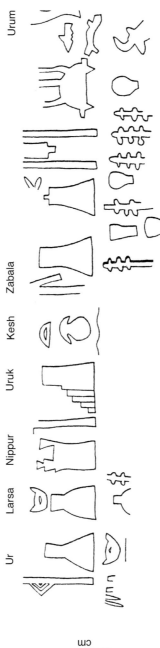

Figure 3.32 Impressions of city-seals from Jemdet Nasr

Source: Matthews 1992:200

In the seals and sealing, methods of accounting and means of account-ability, we see continuities in Mesopotamian social organization from pre-history to the late Bronze Age, political changes notwithstanding. Thus, as early as the Ubaid at Abada, token groups ('geometric' clay objects) used for the purposes of accounting have been recovered from Levels I and II of Building A, the most imposing (Jasim 1985:Part II, Figs 25 and 279). But the functions of seals and sealing are, of course, best known in proto/historic Sumer and Akkad, where cylinder seals rolled their incised images onto wet clay to seal goods for despatch or storage, to acknowledge receipt and accept responsibility. Doors of storerooms were similarly 'sealed' in the Jemdet Nasr period (Matthews 1991). All of this was part of an intricate system accounting not only for goods in store, outstanding or in transit, but also for surplus and deficit owed by/to other institutions and indi-viduals. Indeed, the complexities of such accounts led to the world's earliest systematic permanent recording, namely the 'tablets with signs' found in the Eanna IV levels at Uruk (Nissen 1993a:67). This was done through or in parallel with (Jasim and Oates 1986) the clay balls or *bullae* which contained differentially shaped clay tokens (*calculi*) that represented quantities of commodities indicated on the outside of the envelope. Liverani (1996:13) captures this whole process brilliantly and succinctly when he observes that 'the first known bureaucratic states – namely the "late Uruk" state(s) – produced the first known administrative landscape, a "sexages-imal landscape" as it were, modulated according to the arithmetic needs of the scribes'.

Finally, at the other end of the Bronze Age in the thirteenth and twelfth centuries BC, real estate sales and other legal agreements in the city of Emar, of the 'land of Aštata' on the Middle Euphrates in Syria, were witnessed and solemnized by two official seals: Ninurta's Seal and the Dynastic Seal. The former was the seal of the city, that is, the corporate body of Ninurta (city god) and the city Elders (Yamada 1994:61), while the latter was the seal of the ruling house. The seals could be applied separately to tablets, since each body – city and ruling house – had its own area of autonomy, or both applied together when 'the king and Emar' (*LUGAL ù URU.e-mar*) acted in concert (ibid.:59).

From this, Yamada concludes that

> the Dynastic Seal and Ninurta's Seal are perceived as official seals of the royal palace and the city-community respectively. The usage of those seals clearly shows that the city-community, represented by Ninurta and the city elders, held its own authority, which was distinguished from that of the royal palace in Emar.
>
> (Yamada 1994:61–2)

Figure 3.33 shows impressions from a pair of particularly fine seals from

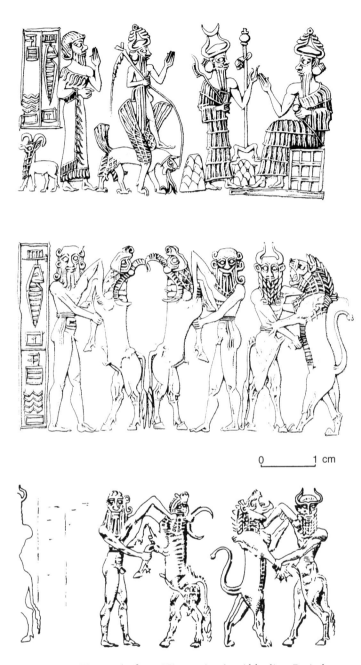

Figure 3.33 Fine seals from Nippur in the Akkadian Period: presentation (top) and contest/mastery scenes

Source: Gibson and McMahon 1995:15

Nippur in the Akkadian Period. Panel 1 shows a 'presentation scene' whereby a mortal (on the left) is presented by a personal deity (riding a prototype winged dragon) to the high gods in conference (on the right). Note that in addition to their horned headpieces, the high deities wear 'classical' plucked-wool garments, while the mortal's is merely wool-fringed. The other two panels bear the usual bull-man and hero 'contest' scenes, which specifically represent the mastering of Nature, but stand for 'mastery' in general.

CHILDE'S CHECKLIST

1   *Cities that are 'more extensive and more densely settled than any previous settlement'.*
    In the final centuries of the fourth millennium, that is in the Jemdet Nasr period, the alluvium contained cities spread all the way from Urum in the north through Kish and Nippur to Ur in the south. Although Shuruppak covered 70 hectares at this time, it was only one of the five largest settlements south of Nippur (Martin 1988:125). Not only does the alluvium contain strings of cities that were of the same order of magnitude as, say, Harappa, but each settlement was also tightly nucleated behind city walls. Further, the city agricultural lands were tightly clustered around the cities, which were themselves strung along watercourses, usually channels of the Euphrates.
2   *Full-time specialists: craftsmen, transport workers, merchants, officials and priests.*
    Seals in steatite (and probably also in wood) obviously played a key role in the organization of Sumerian society. Equally obviously, craftsmen carved them. Officials and priests have featured prominently in the discussion above, in roles from that of lowly scribe (= clerk) to that of city leadership (the *en*). The cities' 'merchants' were, at least until the Isin-Larsa period, rather 'agents' of the temple and palace. Transport workers existed in considerable numbers, given the movement of staples in bulk between country and city, between cities and between institutions. This can best be illustrated when taken with:
3   *Concentration of surplus.*
    In Mesopotamian society management structures were everything. This began, as we have seen, in the Samarran *oikos*, the large households that engendered the even larger 'great households', namely temples and palaces. The title of the official at the head of temple administration, sanga, which appears with the earliest texts in Uruk IV (Eanna IV), can be interpreted as 'accountant'. Thus, in contrast to the other archaic agrarian societies (notably Egypt), surplus was not concentrated after the fact by taxing peasant smallholder production. In Mesopotamia, the šub-lugal, guruš, erín, arád and gemé (the last female), semi-free to unfree

dependants, were organized on a large scale with infrastructure needed for large-scale production. It employed, for example, a seeder-plough requiring a team of three to use it, but which was extremely efficient in seed application (broadcast-sowing is chronically inefficient). Large numbers of labourers were employed in quasi-military 'brigades' for cultivation, and there was mass mobilization for the harvest. Corvee was regularly used for major canal and road projects.

4 *Truly monumental public buildings.*
   Temples were very large buildings and their precincts many times larger. Spread through the city, with or without high ziggurats attached, their monumentality was archetypal, even legendary ('tower of Babel', 'hanging gardens'; cf. Finkel 1988). So too palaces and other state buildings. The Early Dynastic Palace A complex at Kish, for example, was minimally 120 × 80 metres, and would not have been lacking in height or decoration (cf. Moorey 1964; Leick 1988).

5 *The presence of a ruling class, including 'priests, civil and military leaders and officials {who} absorb a major share of the concentrated surplus'.*
   Yes. But like ancient Athens and unlike, for instance, China, city-state society does not consist merely of a royal family, the court, administrative and military hierarchy ruling over a mass of peasants (Maisels 1990). Emergent during the third millennium there was indeed palace, administrative and military apparatus at the top and a stratum of slaves at the bottom. Between top and bottom there was the overwhelming majority of the population, consisting of major household heads, their families and dependants, ranked temple functionaries and their dependants, craftsmen, scribes, boat crews, fishermen, and so on, constituting numerically, economically and politically significant strata.

6 *Technical expertise, specifically systems of writing and numerical notation.*
   Enough has been said concerning the primacy of writing in Mesopotamia, where it existed as a system by about 3200 BC. Writing did not exist for its own sake, for literary purposes, but to expedite accountancy for the exact management of labour-time in farming, herding, fishing, canal digging, transportation and canal work. This is an Ur III-Dynasty tablet from Umma, translated by Goetze:

> 50 (volume) SAR of earth (to be) removed, the wages for the hired men (being) 5 sila of barley each;
> installing fascines(?) in the irrigation ditch of the field Zur. (gis.)ad
> 10 (volume) SAR of earth (to be removed) from the unused(???) canal branching off from the Royal Canal.
> Wages therefore (amount to) 360 man-days.
> Foreman (i.e. ugula) Ur-Enunna.
> Seal (kisib) Akalla.

Year (Amar-Sin 3): 'The throne of Enlil was fashioned'
[Year Name].

(Goetze 1962:13)

The year name indicates that a particularly important cultic artefact
was made in that year. The throne with the god's statue would have
been the focal point of the temple sanctuary, where offerings were laid
out and the principal prayers recited.

7   *Exact and predictive sciences: arithmetic, geometry, astronomy and a calendar.*
While each city-state had its own calendar, the basis was common:
from the end of the fourth millennium, a 12-month, 360-day year was
used, a rationalization of natural lunistellar divisions (Englund
1988:122). The 360-day (u_4) calendar was then a bureaucratic system-
ization of the position in which

> the moon cult dictated the de facto division of the year (mu) into
> 12 synodical months (iti), each consisting of 29.53 days. The
> resulting year of approximately 354⅓ days consequently fell
> short of the 365¼ days of the tropical year (equinox to corre-
> sponding equinox), so that an intercalation of the so-called diri-
> month was necessary, on average, every three years.
>
> (ibid.:123)

It could be inserted after the first, sixth or twelfth month. Synodic
months began on the evening of the first sighting of the lunar crescent after a conjunction of the sun and the moon (Pingree 1989:441).
The Sumerian scribe (dub.sar) had to be as numerate as he was
literate – exceptional for scribes in most periods and places. (For such
'school' training in the 'tablet-house', the é.dub.ba, see Kramer 1949 and
Sjoberg 1976.) Sumerian accountancy had equivalences for everything:
time into work into rations for men and animals and back again into
time and production; all of which was achieved by rigorous arithmetic,
employing fractions and a place system. Arithmetic and arithmetical
ratios are, of course, adequate for simple geometry, which in turn
is adequate for field mensuration and monumental construction.
'Babylonian astronomy', which so impressed others, was a product of the
second millennium. Since our knowledge of Old Sumerian mathematics
and astronomy is miniscule, Neugebauer (1969:29–30) suggests that the
famed mathematics of the Old Babylonian period – which included
quadratics and Pythagorean prime numbers or 'triples'[42] – might well be
a product of just that period, and not (as, for example, so much of the
literary canon) an inheritance from the third millennium (on which see
Friberg 1978–9). However, Pingree (1989:445), concluding his discussion of the influence of the MUL.APIN and other astronomical texts

on Vedic astronomy early in the first millennium BC, remarks that

> MUL.APIN, written in about 1000 B.C., summarizes the astro-
> nomical knowledge that had accumulated in Mesopotamia in
> the previous half millennium, but whose roots presumably lie
> in the civilization of Sumer, since so much of the technical
> vocabulary of MUL.APIN and other Akkadian astronomical
> texts is, in fact, Sumerian.

Since the mathematics were essentially problem-based, and since the
physical problems of quantities, areas and angles go right back to
the late fourth millennium (to cope with which writing and notation
were developed), then a third-millennium Sumerian mathematics is
almost certain. Friberg in fact concludes his first volume with the statement that

> It is a remarkable and distressing fact that although almost the
> entire vocabulary used in Babylonian mathematical texts is of
> an unmistakable Sumerian origin, practically no Sumerian
> mathematical texts have been preserved. . . . It is therefore
> inconceivable that Sumerian 'mathematical texts' have never
> existed. It is just that we have not yet had the luck to find
> more than a few texts of this type.
>
> (Friberg 1978–9: Part I, 51–2)

Sumero-Akkadian medicine also has claims to scientific status, for at
its best it aimed at cures by technique,[43] without recourse to magic
and prayer (cf. Limet 1986; and see Larsen 1987), though as today,
those too were present. But magical and medical practitioners were
separate individuals with independent traditions, the physician regarded
as a craftsman (Biggs 1969:96–8). There can be no doubt, however,
that the advances of Mesopotamian mathematics beyond mere arithmetic were not paralleled by a similar distance of its therapeutic practices beyond folk medicine. Herodotus' unfavourable comparison of
Mesopotamian with Egyptian medicine seems to be correct.

Much more significant than science for everyday life, was, however,
engineering. The construction and maintenance of long trunk canals,
their headworks and other installations being major feats that involved
precise quantitative measures.

8   *Full-time sculptors, painters or seal engravers.*
Seal engravers were crucial to the organization of Mesopotamian
society from the Uruk period onwards, that is, in the earliest state
formation processes. Seals were the crucial control devices regulating
the flow of goods and energy through the system. Whether working

in hard stone or wood (Matthews 1992), expertise was demanded, especially since the basic form was that of a cylinder (which had to leave a clear even image when rolled) and not the rectangular flat stamp (though such were also known).[44] Their technical and artistic accomplishment is clear (sic) and their imagery is a major source of information on Sumero-Akkadian society, from everyday life to mythology and cult (Collon 1987; Antonova 1992). This is just as well, since in Mesopotamia we do not have the extensive and realistic mural painting and model making so characteristic of Egypt (though the early second-millennium Mari palace has murals). However, other artistic expressions, such as pictorial and decorative inlaying, were highly developed as early as ED III, and strikingly apparent in a diverse range of elite goods from the Royal Cemeteries of Ur (Pollock 1991). There were found the funeral goods which famously include lyres or harps, inlaid gaming boards, the so-called 'standard of Ur' (which may have been the sounding box for another musical instrument) inlaid with war-scenes and a banquet, a wooden land sledge decorated with mosaic and golden lions' heads, and the glorious 'ram-in-a-thicket': a billy-goat standing erect on his hind legs to eat the foliage of a small tree (superb colour illustrations and text in Roaf 1990). All this in addition to stacks of gold, silver and copper vessels, plus jewellery in gold, silver, lapis lazuli and carnelian (Moorey 1982:77–8). Seals too were part of the tomb contents, one of which was inscribed 'Meskalamdug lugal', and no less than three referring to queen Puabi ((Shudi-ad(.anak) 'Praying for her father').

In addition to bas-reliefs, three-dimensional sculpture in hard stone and bearing descriptive/dedicatory inscriptions were commissioned by rulers (Cooper 1990).

9 *Regular foreign trade, involving comparatively large volumes.*
A whole issue of Iraq (Hawkins: 1977) was devoted to this subject, and there is a large and fast-growing volume of literature on it (cf. J. Oates: 1993b; J. Curtis: 1993). Copper/tin, timber, lapis lazuli, etc. were indeed imported in significant quantities – the alluvium proper is deficient in mineral and timber resources, amongst most others. However, if I have demonstrated anything about Sumero-Akkadian civilization it is that internal production and distribution systems are determinant of its formation and structure, and that foreign trade, while present, was merely an adjunct. Actual administrative texts almost never mention foreign trade, but are given over to internal production of staples and their distribution. Kingly rhetoric, however, often claims negative trade, that is the seizure of booty and the imposition of tribute in regions to the east and the northeast (for lists of such claims see Maeda 1984).

The best up-to-date summary is that of Moorey (1993:43), who

observes that 'the place of Iran in Sumerian literature from an early
date is indicative of the relationship's centrality and vitality'. Yet 'taken
together the evidence of artifacts and texts sustains a minimalist rather
than a maximalist view of the overland trade between them, a trade in
luxuries for the privileged rather than in staples for the masses' (ibid.).
Those luxury items were not trivial, however, for

> the role of this flow of luxuries in sustaining Sumer's great
> organizations of state and their hierarchies is everywhere
> apparent. It is far less clear how it affected the local highland
> communities engaged in the extraction, processing and distri-
> bution of minerals, since so little is known of their subsistence
> technologies, their social structures, and the extent to which
> their economies were geared to production for export.
>
> (ibid.)

Indeed, until much more excavation takes place in Iran, there is no
way of knowing.

For the north, up to and including the southern edges of the Taurus,
Oates (1993a:416–17) has formed a similar view, encompassing the
Ubaid through to the Early Dynastic period. Apparently Uruk 'agen-
cies' were able to plug into existing local hierarchies in the north. By
this means both elites were thereby able to serve their own interests
in procuring status goods. However, as to the central tenet concerning
'comparatively large volumes', this is not substantiated even where most
likely, namely, waterborne trade in the Gulf to Dilmun (Bahrain, classical Tylos), Magan and Meluhha.[45] Potts (1993:424–5) categorically
states that 'the putative mass export of Mesopotamian cereals to Magan
is illusory', for not only is there no inscriptional evidence for such
exports during the third millennium, but the anthropological evidence
is that 'cereals played no part in the diet of these coastal populations
[in the Oman peninsula], who were largely dependent on fish, turtle
and dugong for their protein'. Interior populations such as those at Hili
8, had their own agricultural regimes. Sumer and Akkad did import
copper from Magan, but the bulkiest thing exported to pay for it would
have been wool and/or linen textiles and also sesame oil. Oil exports
reminds us that olive oil and wine were the most valuable traded
commodities in the classical Mediterranean: relatively low bulk, high
value items.

Accordingly, Potts concludes that

> the arguments raised against P.L. Kohl's suggestion that surplus
> grain was being exported en masse from Mesopotamia to the
> Iranian Plateau in the third millennium (Potts 1982:40–1;

Carter 1990:94) are just as appropriate in the case of alleged cereal exports from Mesopotamia to Magan.

(ibid.)

Indeed, Edens (1992:121) sums it up well when he says that 'to analyze precapitalist complex societies, and the place of long-distance trade in those societies, as economic configurations is to misplace basic social forces in these societies'.

10 *Peasants, craftsmen and rulers form a community.*

Peasants are generally absent from the ancient Mesopotamian scene, or at least are none too visible in the documentary record. Highly visible are the dependent labour that Gelb refers to as 'semi-free'. That they were 'structured in' to Mesopotamian society without (so far as can be seen) the use of force by the rulers, indicates a certain social solidarity. That this was a genuine civic solidarity with the city under its own god is strongly suggested by the stubborn, long and bloody resistance of the individual city-states to incorporation into the territorial states of Sargon and later Hammurabi.

11 *Social solidarity is expressed in the pre-eminence of the temple or sepulchral shrine.*

Indeed, not one but several temples in a city, with a number of shrines in each.

12 *State organization is dominant and permanent.*

Cities vied with each other for hegemony and in the process strengthened kingship, the tendency of which is always toward the territorial state. In Mesopotamia it achieved permanence under Hammurabi in the Old Babylonian period.

4

THE INDUS/'HARAPPAN'/
SARASVATI CIVILIZATION

THE PLACE

A fundamental contrast between the Mesopotamian and Harappan situation is in matters of scale. The occupied area of the alluvium between the Tigris and Euphrates in about the middle of the third millennium – when Harappan civilization entered its urban stage – was around 65,000 square kilometres, while the cultivated valley of the Nile, at 34,440 square kilometres, amounts to only half that (Kees 1961:17). By contrast, Indus Civilization extended roughly 1,100 kilometres north to south and east to west, covering an area of around 1,210,000 square kilometres. This is nearly twenty times the area of Egypt, and over a dozen times the settled area of Egypt and Mesopotamia combined.

To get some feel for the distances involved, Harappa, located by the south bank of the River Ravi, an Indus tributary, is some 625 kilometres from the other major centre, Mohenjo-daro on the lower Indus (and it is some 500 kilometres from Delhi, around 850 kilometres from Karachi). Harappa to Ganweriwala is 280 kilometres, Ganweriwala to Mohenjo-daro 308 kilometres. By comparison, virtually the whole length of the settled Mesopotamian alluvium is spanned by a straight line of 440 kilometres, drawn from Eridu northward through Uruk, Isin and Kish to Samarra. At Baghdad the Tigris and Euphrates are only 35 kilometres apart, while the longest transect between the rivers – a southwest–northeast line passing between Shuruppak and Umma – amounts to only 240 kilometres, much of which in the east is or was marsh.

In the southeastern alluvium adjoining Umma (its traditional rival) lay the important state of Lagaš, which contained in addition to its name city of Lagash (al-Hiba), the city of Girsu (Tello) in the north, five other towns and a southern province around Guabba, 'the seashore', with a port on the Tigris (Ur used the Euphrates channel to the sea). Although the long axis northwest–southeast of Lagash state was only about 60 kilometres, this represented a great area for a Mesopotamian city-state on the alluvium. Accordingly, at the time of unification under the Third Dynasty

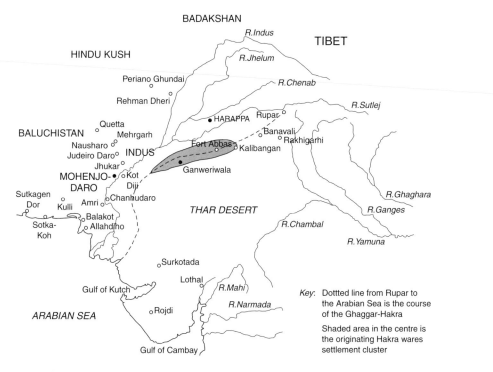

BADAKSHAN

HINDU KUSH

TIBET

R.Indus

R.Jhelum

Periano Ghundai

R.Chenab

Rehman Dheri

R.Sutlej

BALUCHISTAN

Quetta

Mehrgarh

Nausharo

Judeiro Daro

INDUS

Jhukar

MOHENJO-
DARO

Kot

Diji

HARAPPA

Rupar

Banavali

Fort Abbas

Kalibangan

Rakhigarhi

Ganweriwala

Sutkagen
Dor

Kulli

Amri

Chanhudaro

Balakot

Allahdiho

THAR DESERT

R.Ghaghara

R.Ganges

R.Chambal

Sotka-
Koh

R.Yamuna

Surkotada

Lothal

Gulf of Kutch

R.Mahi

ARABIAN SEA

Rojdi

R.Narmada

Key: Dottted line from Rupar to
the Arabian Sea is the course
of the Ghaggar-Hakra

Shaded area in the centre is
the originating Hakra wares
settlement cluster

Gulf of Cambay

Figure 4.1 Map of the Greater Indus drainage

of Ur (Ur III), Lagash was assessed contributions in support of Enlil's temple (the Ekur) at Nippur four times that of any other city-region.[1]

Allchin and Allchin (1982:180) report population estimates for Mohenjo-daro and Harappa of around 30,000 and 40,000, respectively, which is in the same order of magnitude as Mesopotamian cities. The difference, however, lies in the sheer number of Mesopotamian cities, which on the southern alluvium could even be in sight of one another, in turn reflecting fundamental differences in the relationships between centres and hinterland. The consequence is a different level and type of urbanization, as between Sumer and Harappa, with nearly double the percentage (78 per cent) of the Sumerian population living in settlements above 40 hectares as the Harappan (44 per cent). Synoecism is the key: the number of people living and working together in a dense interactive network. Sumerian society was composed of just such nodes. Accordingly, Sumer was a society of city-states whose populations had a strong civic consciousness. Harappan society consisted of an extensive oecumene or commonwealth, with a largely village-based population which the cities helped to integrate economically and culturally.

The contrasts have been well made by Ratnagar's comparison of fifty Mature Harappan sites (whose areas are known) with fifty-six Early Dynastic II–III site areas surveyed by Adams (1981), as shown in Table 4.1. It will be seen that Indus has only three sites above 40 hectares against Sumer's eleven. In the next size category, exceeding 200 hectares, Indus has no representative at all, while Uruk reached 450 hectares in ED I (see also Chakrabarti 1979, 1995).

With the Thar desert to the east and the Baluchistan hills to the west – the nearest of which, the Khirthar Range, are only about 65 kilometres from Mohenjo-daro, from where they are visible in winter – Harappan settlements are concentrated as in a funnel (the floodplains) along the rivers flowing south to the sea.

The River Indus flows for no less than 3,200 kilometres and is estimated to drain an area of 372,000 kilometres. 'The average annual inflow of the Indus and its tributaries is about twice the flow of the Nile and over ten times that of the Colorado River . . . During floods the river in the plains of Sind can be over 16km wide' (Allchin *et al.* 1978:16–17). The reason for this is that, with a gradient of only about 4.8 cm per kilometre in Sind the river 'is so markedly aggrading [see Glossary] that its own bed is above the general level of the plain' (ibid.). The Indus annually transports 150 million tons of silt to the sea. The high sediment load – which here is laid down at the rate of 1–2 metres per millennium – is a most important

Table 4.1 Number and size of Harappan cities compared with those of broadly contemporary Sumer

	Settlement sizes in hectares						
	< 4	4.1–10	10.1–20	20.1–40	40.1–200	> 200	Total
ED Sumer							
No. of sites	19	16	5	4	11	1	56
Total area (hectares)	52.0	112.0	75.0	120.0	1,100.0	200.0	1,659.0
Percentage of total settled area	3.13	6.75	4.52	7.23	66.30	12.05	
Harappa							
No. of sites	21	18	4	4	3	0	50
Total area (hectares)	38.3	117.9	59.5	109.1	251.5	0	576.3
Percentage of total settled area	6.64	20.45	10.32	18.93	43.64	0	

Source: Ratnagar 1986:151

Note: Lagash city, being outside Adams' survey area, is not accounted for in this table, which understates Sumerian urbanization.

feature of the rivers in the area, since rivers with beds that are not cut into groundrock are easily deflected by floods (channel instability, as in Mesopotamia) or by tectonic movements. Crustal activity is continually active in the northern subcontinent, as the peninsula, driving northwards against the continent of Asia, produces the compression upthrusts that have caused (and are still causing) the Himalayas to rise ('orogeny' or mountain building). Only the high rate of erosion of such fold mountains made of sedimentary rocks keeps them from rising ever higher. The mountains' height, extent and recent origin have greatly affected the climate of southern and eastern Asia and turned the interior behind the massifs into cold high deserts.

Thus, topographically, the Indus culture area appears as a larger, reversed analogue of Mesopotamia, with a desert, the Thar, on the eastern flank, hills (Baluchi) on the west, and with two main rivers (Indus and the now dry Sarasvati) flowing from mountains in the north across alluvial plains to the sea in the south. The most pronounced similarity, though highly unsurprising, is that settlement followed river courses in both regions.

The mouths of the Indus open to the Arabian Sea southeast of Karachi (Pakistan's main port and largest city), while the Makran ranges of mountains extend westwards along the coast to the Straits of Hormuz, the 'Gates' of the Gulf, which extends northwest to terminate as the southern shores of Mesopotamia.

Between the twin cities of Sukkur and Rohri, some 90 kilometres upstream from Mohenjo-daro (and with only an erratic 90 millimetres of rainfall), the Indus cuts a gorge through predominantly limestone hills. This Sukkur Gorge (containing the Lloyd Barrage) in the Rohri Hills supplied the light-buff chert that provided the vast majority of stone blades for Mohenjo-daro and other urban centres (Allchin 1979:188–9).

Although termed 'Indus' Civilization on account of the location of Mohenjo-daro on that river and Harappa on the Ravi, its tributary, this is a most misleading name which actually obscures the ecological and geological processes fundamental to the civilization's evolution and its devolution at the end of the third millennium.

Of the 1,399 Harappan sites presently known (917 in India, 481 in Pakistan, 1 in Afghanistan: Misra 1994:512), only 44 sites are actually on or near the River Indus. However, around 1,000 lie along the course(s) of the Ghaggar-Hakra/Sarasvati in Cholistan and, most importantly, those include the Hakra-ware sites, the earliest of the pre-Early Harappan wares. Hakra wares are the core ceramics on the core sites of Harappan origins, 'mark[ing] the oldest or earliest human habitation in Cholistan, which could have begun sometime during the first half of the fourth millennium B.C.' (Mughal 1992a:106).

The Ghaggar-Hakra (or the Ghaggar, Hakra [or Sotra] and Nara as the ancient Sarasvati is called in different parts of its north–south course) flowed for more than 1,000 kilometres east of and roughly parallel to the Indus, through Punjab, Haryana, Rajastan, Bawalpur and Sind to its mouth in the Rann of Kutch (ibid.:482), now part of the Indian state of Gujarat. Originating in the Siwalik Hills, now the only live part of a dead river system, it failed because it had no feed from snowmelt in the Himalayas, making its flow dependent on the monsoon rainfall. Thus 'Harappan' as a synonym for Indus Civilization is doubly unfortunate: the city of Harappa is later than Mohenjo-daro, and while Mohenjo-daro, situated on the middle stretch of the Indus, is indeed catalytic, it does not lie in or near the originating centre, which title belongs to the Hakra-Ghaggar/Sarasvati cluster, with its key unexcavated cities of Ganweriwala (in Bahawalpur) and Rakhigarhi (in Haryana, not far from Banawali). After a decade's research at Mohenjo-daro, Jansen is forced to admit that

> the actual process of development from the 'Pre- or Proto-Urban' cultures in the Greater Indus Valley to the 'Urban' Harappa Culture has not yet been proved for any of the sites explored, including Mohenjo-daro; the *genius loci*, as it seems, is still missing.
>
> (Jansen 1994:271)

And it is still missing because the cities, towns and villages of the Hakra-Ghaggar/Sarasvati cluster remain unexcavated.

The model of collapse that I shall present later in full is introduced now in brief: with the Harappan agricultural heartland clustered along the Sarasvati, when this river began to dry up, the density of population that had made complex civilization possible dwindled, shrank to those on the Indus proper, and could not be sustained in that fashion. Accordingly, Post-Harappans reverted to something like their previous socio-economic basis, that is, to a relatively restricted post-Neolithic condition without urban centres. The drying of the Sarasvati is the simplest explanation. But other factors may be involved in the collapse of a civilization that spanned only half a millennium: major vagrancy by the Indus; a sequence of disastrous floods, perhaps alternating with years of poor flow (critical, given the floodwater agricultural regime); a final possibility being the spread of cholera, perhaps brought on by an erratic river regime. Whatever the underlying cause(s), the civilization that, in the words of Bridget Allchin (1979:209), manifested 'a higher degree of uniformity over a wider area than we see in any of the contemporary cultures of the ancient world', lost its coherency and 'devolved'. Nothing like the military pressures implicated in the collapse of Rome, west or east (Byzantium), are present around the Indus. Harappan Civilization is truly unique in both its mode of formation and dissolution.

The highly arid conditions prevailing away from the river environs made the subsistence system of the oecumene a set of variations on a theme: permanent agriculture with some herding of cattle in the floodplains, and pastoralism, again mostly of cattle, but with some sheep and goats too, in the more arid and/or hilly areas. The principal ranges of accessible hills lie to the west of the alluvial plains (Baluchistan, merging into Iran), and to the east, where the bare Aravalli Range, which although low, extends from Ahmedabad in (largely peninsular) Gujarat northeast to Delhi.

As in contemporary Pakistan, the principal areas of Harappan settlement lie in the provinces of Sind and Panjab (Punjab, whose major city is Lahore); Panjab means in Sanskrit the 'Five Waters' feeding the Indus. The five rivers are the Jhelum, Chenab, Ravi, Beas and Sutlej. Without the rivers, agricultural settlement in the 800 kilometres northeast of the mouths of the Indus would not have been possible. Most of Baluchistan, Sind and southwest Punjab receive precipitation of less than 200 millimetres annually (Meadow 1989b:62), which is at least 50 per cent less than the amount required for dependable agriculture. By contrast, the plains stretching from the Jhelum to the Yamuna, north of a line between Delhi and Multan (just east of the Ravi), which are all 'of one piece, environmentally speaking', receive from 200 to 700 millimetres of rainfall annually (Fentress 1982:245).

Shereen Ratnagar (1982:261) has pointed out that neither Harappa nor Mohenjo-daro are sited where we should expect the major cities to be, namely functioning as 'central places' in the midst of the most densely settled areas. On the contrary, both cities are marginal to the major agricultural clusters, to the extent that, where Harappa is concerned, 'the nearest known cluster of settlements lies in Cholistan, some 150 kilometres to the south', with which, however, Harappa has good lines of communication. Accordingly, Ratnagar (ibid.:263) postulates that both cities were in fact 'gateway cities' linked 'by dendritic networks where lower level centres are tributary to only one higher level centre – not to more than one as in central place systems'. This is a most important observation in view of what I have already said about networks in the previous chapter and the extended discussion to come.

In central place systems there are rings of settlements at varying radii from the centre. But here, 'with primate cities functioning as "gateways" the networks connecting the settlement points are like elongated fans radiating from the primate city' (ibid.). As a 'primate city' is one that is many times larger than any other in the country, and thus dominates the rest economically and/or politically, it is logical that routes tend to converge directly upon the primate city (like railways and roads do upon London and Paris), rather than the primate simply lying at the centre of a web of routes connecting other cities and towns. 'One may thus imagine a dendritic fan with its apex at Harappa. This fan spreads out from northwest to northeast, and in turn feeds the core Harappan regions in the lower Sarasvati and Sind' (ibid.). What it feeds them with includes

lapis lazuli from Badakshan (via the Gomal Valley), deodar wood from the Himalayan temperate forests, pine wood from the Himalayan ranges east of Kashmir, elm wood from the subtropical Himalayas east of Dehra Dun, copper and steatite from the Zhob Valley (Mughal 1970:194), placer gold from the upper reaches of the Chenab, and perhaps copper from scattered deposits in the Simla and Kangra regions.

(ibid.)

Harappa and Mohenjo-daro contained many workshops, for they were not merely procurement centres or entrepots, but manufacturing centres producing for export as well as (but overwhelmingly for) internal consumption. Fentress (1982:248) has estimated that Harappa had in its immediate vicinity, notably in the Kamalia Plain, around 6,600 square kilometres of farmland for its own support, employing flow irrigation and exploiting low-lying hydromorphic (permanently damp) soils. Given the high levels of rainfall in the *northern* part of the Jhelum-Yamuna Plain, which today ranges between 500 millimetres and 700 millimetres of *dependable* rainfall annually, Fentress (ibid.:250) states that those plains north of Harappa were then covered in thick forest 'and could only have been inhabited by mobile pastoral groups'. Like the Deccan and other forested areas to this day, it could of course also have been inhabited by many groups of hunter–gatherers.

THE TIME

Indus Civilization was the shortest lived of all the Old World pristine or seminal civilizations, entering its urban period (whose area largely coincides with that of the Early Period) around 2500 BC and the Late Period around 2100 BC. A total span for urban Indus Civilization would thus be from about 2550 until 2000/1900 BC, the extra century or so not sustained at all sites (Lal 1994:23). Interestingly, from a thorough re-evaluation of Mohenjo-daro stratigraphy, Franke-Vogt (1994:45) concludes not only that so far there is no evidence of Early Period occupation at that site, but that the great city was occupied only between 2350 BC and 2000/1900 BC.[2]

Lal (1994:24) provides a comprehensive and up-to-date sequence of Indus radiocarbon dates, along with a most incisive discussion of the chronology.

SOCIAL EVOLUTION: NEOLITHIC TO CHALCOLITHIC AT MEHRGARH

The only site we presently have with extensive exposures and a stratigraphic sequence extending back into the aceramic Neolithic is that of Mehrgarh, which is why it is treated in such detail. Mehrgarh lies at the foot of the Bolan Pass, the route from Sibi and Dadhar to Quetta. It is situated in foothills at the northwestern end of the Kachi Plain which, part of the Indus drainage, extends southeastwards for all of 200 kilometres to the Indus River (Jarrige and Meadow 1980:102). The site, extending over 200 hectares, is not in fact a single settlement, but a group of successive settlements divided into six areas, all lying on the western banks of the Bolan River. (For an equivalent long sequence in Khuzistan, S.W. Iran, see Maisels 1993b:96–108).

Excavation, by a French CNRS and Pakistani team, started in December 1974 with the oldest area, MR3 (mound three), which has 12–14 metres of aceramic deposits. Those are framed by the successive remains of rectilinear mud-brick structures, comprising multi-room dwellings separated by open spaces that are used both for domestic activities and for burials (Jarrige and Meadow 1980:104; Jarrige 1984:24). Significantly for later social patterns,

> the reconstruction phases of the settlement were planned in respect to the orientation and spacing between the houses. Such planning, the quality of crafts, as shown by the fine ornaments from the graves, and the presence of buildings such as a monumental funerary platform exposed in 1979–80, are all elements which suggest an already complex social organisation by the end of the seventh millennium BC and the early sixth millennium BC, supported by skilled artisans and successful farmers.
>
> (Jarrige 1984:24)

That such developments are no flash in the pan is clear from area MR4, corresponding to Period II, which covers the last part of the sixth and early part of the fifth millennium. For Period IIA, described as that of 'neolithic with coarse ware', already contains three rectilinear, compartmented, storage/workshop buildings on foundations of hard clay (ibid.). They were reproduced in Period IIB (fifth millennium), examples of which are illustrated by Jarrige (ibid.:25).

Two things stand out in particular concerning both the craft use of the buildings and the agricultural storage function:

1 One of the buildings contained a terracotta bead, 'which, when rolled on clay, makes a cylinder-like imprint showing a vegetal motif' (ibid.:24).

2 Within the cell-units, and in ashy dumps, seeds of the barley *Hordeum sphaerococcum* were found. According to Constantini as reported by Jarrige (op. cit.), this grows (well?) only under irrigation conditions. This barley is absent in the earliest Neolithic levels.

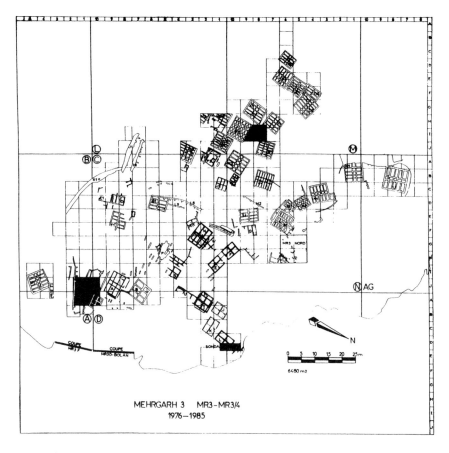

Figure 4.2 Plan of Mehrgarh 3, Area MR3-MR3-4

Source: Meadow 1989:168

Jarrige (op. cit.) sees the continuity and complexity of uses with its implied division of labour as evidence of 'a degree of social control'. But this can just as readily be seen as a high degree of social integration based on the division of labour itself.

The Period II tool-kit is still of bone and stone, with some copper (a small ingot, ring and bead) present by IIB (ibid.).

Mehrgarh Period III, commencing shortly before 4000 BC, is fully Chalcolithic in the literal sense: a number of crucibles containing traces of copper were recovered. More importantly, it is Chalcolithic in my usage of *professional craft specialization*, one aspect of which at Mehrgarh is the use of the bow-drill (ibid.:28). Survey suggests that the settlement by this period is not only much larger (pottery scattered over 75 hectares) but more

194

densely occupied (ibid.:26). Some of this pottery is wheel-thrown, but the earlier hand-made and basket-marked ware is similar in style to Kili Gul Mohammad II (KGM II). Nonetheless, 'technically, the potters of Period III at Mehrgarh were producing a pottery of superior fabric when compared to the pottery of Sialk II and of the early phases of Sialk III or Namazga I and II, which were hand-made' (ibid.:27). At Mehrgarh they were also mass-producing it.

Jarrige concludes with two important observations. First, that pottery typical of Period III, which includes Togau A Style, KGM III, Loralai Striped or Jangal painted, extends over the whole highland valley system surrounding the Kachi Plain – Zhob, Loralai, Quetta, Kalat and Surab. 'We have also pointed out (Jarrige 1981:107) that the first settlement at Mundigak has a cultural assemblage showing an almost total identity with Mehrgarh Period III.' This forms a 'vast cultural complex' comprising sites whose remains indicate a high degree of similarity over the plains and hills around 4000 BC.

Second, he stresses that 'the rather impressive urban developments of the south of the Kachi Plain, adjoining the Indus Valley and the region of Mohenjo-daro, are linked to a continuous cultural tradition starting at least as early as the Period III of Mehrgarh around 4000 BC'. The craft specialization and its accompanying socio-political organization are the key to the type of urbanization seen in the third millennium (ibid.:27–8).

Figure 4.3 is a comparative pottery typology and chronology after Dani (1988:52–3). It covers sites in Iran, Baluchistan and the Indus Valley using as a framework the original Mehrgarh chronology of Jarrige and Lechevallier (1979).

Flora and fauna

The top levels of MR3 are dated by radiocarbon with MASCA calibrations to around 5000 BC (Jarrige 1982:82). The lower layers are assumed by the excavators to commence in the seventh millennium (ibid.), which would make the origins of the site broadly contemporary with the proto-Hassuna villages of northern Mesopotamia. However, radiocarbon dates from the lowest levels of Mehrgarh are unreliable. Certainly the suite of plant domesticates identified at Mehrgarh is not far different from Hassuna and Samarra at least by the late sixth millennium, when impressions register: two-row hulled ('pearl') barley (*Hordeum distichum*), six-row barley hulled and naked (*H. vulgare* and *H. vulgare v. nudum*), einkorn wheat (*Triticum monococcum*), emmer wheat (*T. dicoccum*) and bread wheat (*T. durum/aestivum*). Naked six-row barley in a local adaptation referred to as *Hordeum sphaerococcum* – a type with a short compact spike with shortened internodes and small rounded seeds (Constantini 1984:31) – was the dominant cereal (91 per cent of nearly 5,956 identified impressions). Similar mutations in tetraploid/

Period I	Sixth and fifth millennia BC. Area: MR3. Neolithic settlement. *Parallel:* Kili Gul Mohammad I.
Period IIA	End of the fifth millennium BC. Area MR4. First occurrence of potsherds in a very limited number. *Parallel:* Kili Gul Mohammad II.
Period IIIB	Beginning of the fourth millennium BC. Area MR4 (upper layers). Wheel turned ware painted with geometric motifs, straw-tempered handmade ware. *Parallels:* Kili Gul Mohammad III: Mundigak I.1–3.
Period III	First half of the fourth millennium BC. Area MR2. Wheel-turned ware with painted caprids, birds and geometric motifs. *Parallels:* Kili Gul Mohammad III; Mundigak I.3; Togau A.
Period IV	Middle of the fourth millennium BC. Area MR1 (main mound). Wheel-turned pottery with monochrome and polychrome geometric decorations, terracotta female figurines. *Parallels:* Damb Sadaat I; Togau B; Amri 1A.
Period V	Third quarter of the fourth millennium BC. Area MR1 (main mound). Pottery with white pigment, monochrome pottery with geometric motifs, human figurines, first grey ware at the end of the period. *Parallels:* Togau D; Mundigak II.
Period VI	End of the fourth millennium and beginning of the third millennium BC. Area MR1 (main mound). Black-on-grey ware, Quetta ware, Nal polychrome, red ware with painted pipal leaves, human figurines, compartmented stamp seals, lapis lazuli. *Parallels:* Damb Sadat II; Mundigak III; Shahr-i-Sokhta I; Rehman Dheri I: Amri IIA.
Period VII	Middle of the third millennium BC. Area MR1 (main mound). Black-on-grey ware, late Quetta style, mass production of female and male figurines. Monumental platform. Upper layers: so-called Zhob figurines, a few Kot Dijian style sherds. *Parallels:* Damb Sadaat III; monochrome geometric style of Nal; Mundigak IV; Shahr-i-Sokhta II; Kot Diji; Amri IIB.

Figure 4.3 Mehrgarh in comparative context

Source: Dani 1988:52–3

hexaploid wheats resulted in *Triticum sphaerococcum* becoming the dominant wheat type by Period V. Sphaerococcoid forms of both wheat and barley are also found in the Caucasus, Armenia and southern Turkmenia (ibid.).

Richard Meadow, who has been largely responsible for the faunal assemblages, reports the following trends:

> First, a shift during the aceramic Neolithic from the hunting of wild animals to the keeping of domestic sheep, goats and cattle; second, an increase in the importance of zebu cattle in relation to sheep and goats during the course of the aceramic and early ceramic periods; third, a reversal of this trend during later occupations at this site; and fourth, a decrease in the size of the individual domestic animals through time.
>
> (Meadow 1984:34)

In the first levels 17 to 4 of Period I, namely the aceramic Neolithic, ending no later than the middle of the sixth millennium, the majority of taxa represented in a standardized bone count are from wild species: gazelle (*Gazella dorcas*), swamp deer (*Cervus duvauceli*), nilgai (*Boselaphus tragocamelus*), blackbuck (*Antilope cervicapra*), onager (*Equus hemionus*), chital or spotted deer (*Axis axis*), water buffalo (*Bubalus bubalis*), wild cattle (*Bos ?namadicus*), wild sheep (*Ovis ?orientalis*), wild goat (*Capra ?aegagrus*), wild pig (*Sus scrofa*) and elephant (*Elephas maximus*) (ibid.:35). It is obvious that those species come from the entire range of local habitats, hill and river valley, woodland and open plain, indicating a diversity no longer extant. Meadow comments that 'of these animals only gazelle, sheep, goat, and pigs are found in the general area of the site today, the other forms being no longer present west of the Indus River or else extinct' (ibid.).

In the very earliest levels (17–13), domesticated sheep, goat and cattle were already present, with *Capra* the most numerous. This of course suggests that the Near Eastern suite of domesticates was received. By Level 4, sheep, goat and cattle pass the 50 per cent level, and by the end of the aceramic at Mehrgarh (*c*.5500 BC), almost all identifiable faunal remains come from sheep, goat and cattle, the latter ranging as high as 65 per cent in Period II and not falling below 35 per cent (ibid.). As Meadow observes, the proportions are quite unlike those obtaining in the Neolithic or post-Neolithic Near East. Further, given that the cattle in question are zebu, or humped cattle which do not occur in the Near East, local domestication is certain.

Lithics and ceramics

Lithics are overwhelmingly of flint, found as rocks in the Bolan River. The industry is a blade one, in which microliths, used for hunting, were also employed as blade segments in sickles (all periods), set obliquely into the groove of the sickle as a series of pointed teeth, and glued in place with a thick layer of bitumen (Lechevalier 1984:43). Microliths disappear in Period III, replaced by true arrow-heads and in sickles by backed elements such as lunates and triangles, more resistant to fracture than thin bladelets (ibid.). Until Period III, burins are exceptional, while borers are characteristic of the first three periods. Lechevalier identifies this with the needs of bead manufacture, for this activity is well attested at MR3 in nearly all levels, where some of the dead were buried with necklaces, bracelets and belts made of stone, bone and shell beads (ibid.:46). Indeed

> a workshop [for] calcite beads has been found at MR3 (phase Ib) and another [for] steatite beads at MR4 (phase IIb) along with small borers and plain bladelets, probably ready to be retouched into borers and drills. [However] the number of flint borers falls off to almost zero in Periods IV to VI, and to a few pieces in Period VII, as if piercing had then been achieved with other hard stones, easier to round off than flint.
>
> (ibid.)

Jasper drills found in large numbers in Period III, and associated with fragments of lapis lazuli and carnelian for beadmaking, indicate an early start to what became the most characteristic Harappan industry.

Another industry is the mass-production of pottery, much of it fast-wheel thrown, seen in Periods VI and VII, dating to the early–middle third millennium. Indeed, the southern half of mound MR1, in which a whole potters' sector was uncovered, contained not only single- and double-chambered ovens (in addition to the tandur type, fired by cow-dung which was also used as temper for the pottery), but also developed two-chamber kilns with seven or more internal flues. This in addition to the use of large open firing areas for the production of larger jars and common pottery (Santoni 1989:176). Indeed, Jarrige and Meadow state that the same technique is still in use today, a matter of relevance to the devolutionary processes described below:

> The potters first spread a layer of straw on the ground and put on it as many as 500 to 1000 unfired pots. There are covered with more straw, a layer of broken pottery and finally a roof of clay. The straw is ignited, the fire burns for about 24 hours and then the pile is allowed to cool for a week. In analysing the spoiled wares [at Mehrgarh] Audouze and Catherine Jarrige found that the identical procedure had been followed some five millenniums earlier. This is significant evidence for the semi-industrial manufacture of standardized vessels by that time [c. 2900 BC]. The pots were prob-

ably intended for regional distribution, just as the pots made in the area today are.

(Jarrige and Meadow 1980:109)

At Mehrgarh the range of pottery types made is remarkable. A sample includes: rough, undecorated, wide-mouthed jars and common buff ware; decorated wet-ware, decorated narrow-mouthed and wide-mouthed pots, decorated buff ware with stamped dotted circles on the shoulder; decorated common ware, namely plates with fingernail incised decoration, and green-ware (using dung temper). The range of painted pottery is even larger, ranging from monochrome, black or brown designs on a natural buff background, through bichrome to polychrome, such as, 'in Period VI: geometric black and white motifs on red painted background (carinated or ovoid pots, jars); in Period VII: red, black and yellow, or black and yellow, on buff or white background (miniature vessel and lids, jars)' (Santoni 1989:178–9).

Also present by Period VII in the painted category are 'Kot Diji style' jars and pots, plus black or red burnished pedestalled goblets. The examples shown in Figures 4.5 and 4.6 are from Kot Diji itself in Khan's excavations. A small example of Mehrgarh Period VII pottery is reproduced in Figure 4.7.

Of the succeeding Period VIII, Santoni remarks that mass production has led to

a kind of uninterest in finishing and decoration . . . that reaches its climax at the end of the third and the beginning of the second millennium B.C. The process continues later, into a lack of interest even for the quality of the pottery, which becomes strictly utilitarian and probably loses favour to bronze and copper vessels.

(Santoni 1989:185)

This should be compared to the quality of the work done in the Early Indus ('pre-Mature') Periods (Id and II) at Nausharo, as shown in Figures 4.8a and 4.8b.

In general, the corpus of Harappan pottery is well fired, wheel-turned, thick textured and heavy, often with a bright and glossy deep-red slip. Common types include dish-on-stand, beakers, bowls, goblets, basins, storage jars, cups, saucers, jar-covers and lids. Designs are 'pipal-leaf, fish-scale, intersecting circles, linked balls, peacock, antelope, sun-symbol and other patterns in black paint . . . executed in the usual bold, free and assured but conventional style, clearly the product of long usage' (Khan 1965:39); cf. Figs 4.10 and 4.11. The contrast with the Chinese style of decoration could not be more marked.

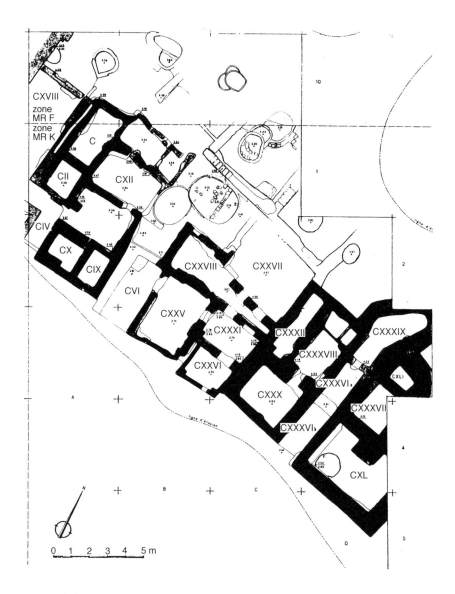

Figure 4.4 Storage/workshop buildings at Mehrgarh, Period IIB
Source: Santoni 1989:177

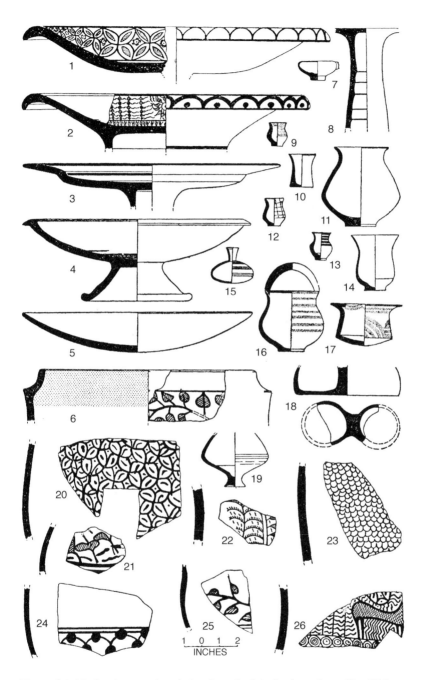

Figure 4.5 Neck pieces, painted sherds and plain beakers from Kot Diji
Source: Khan 1965:fig.11

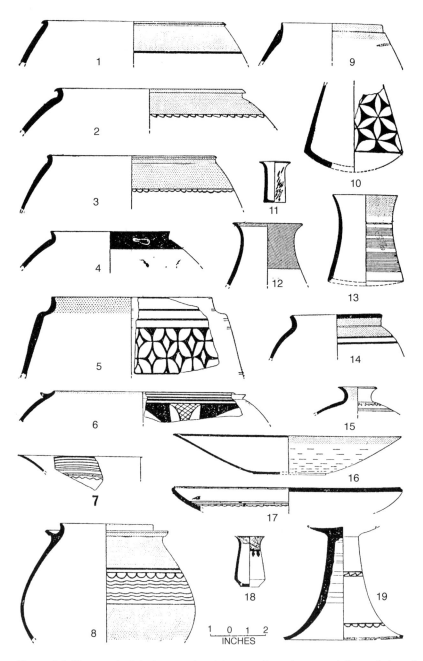

Figure 4.6 Vases and globular vessels with everted, undercut and flanged rims from Kot Diji

Source: Khan 1965:fig. 14

202

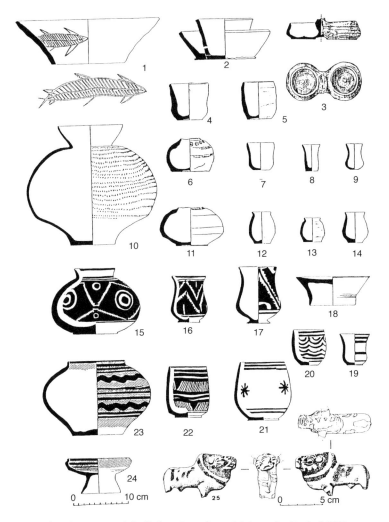

Figure 4.7 Pottery and bull figurines from Mehrgarh, Period VII

Notes: 1 is a mould-made, 'built up' dish with an inscribed fish; 2 is a two-part pot in which a conical goblet, with two holes near the base, is inserted into a bowl. For separating ghee? Examples occur in deposits of Period IV, V and VI also (Santoni 1989:184); 3 is a small double pot, with only the handle missing; 10 is a wet-ware high-necked jar, with stamped dotted circles on the shoulder; 15/16/17 are in the striking (monochrome) 'Quetta style'; while 18, namely two lids in reddish micaceous paste, painted in red and black, are examples of 'Kot Dijian style'; 24 is the pedestalled goblet referred to on p.199; 25 bull zebu or buffalo. Human figurines, including a female with baby, are also found in terracotta, as are round and rectangular stamp seals from Periods VI and VII. Male figurines first appear in Period VII (Jarrige and Meadow 1980:103). See Fig. 4.24.

Source: Santoni 1989:183

Figure 4.8a Early Indus painted jar of Period ID ('Pre-Harappan')
Source: Quivron 1994:634

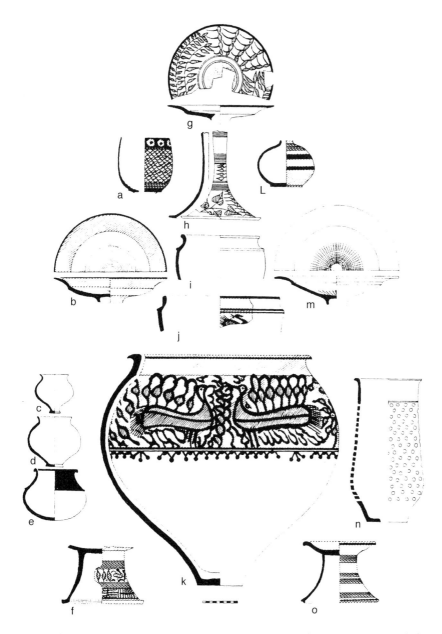

Figure 4.8b Period II pottery at Nausharo, with peacocks, pipal leaves and dish-on-stand

Source: Quivron 1994:637

Figure 4.9 Painted potsherd of the Harappa Period at Kot Diji
Source: Khan 1965:plate XIV

LATER AGRICULTURAL SUBSISTENCE

Neither Nilotic nor ancient Indic society employed irrigation, defined as permanent canals with control works. They had no need to, for the source of moisture in both places was simple river inundation of its own flood-plain.[3] At certain times of year, run-off from the mountain sources swelled the river sufficiently to flood a relatively narrow strip along the banks. Seed was sown directly into the fresh silt when the rivers began dropping back to their dry-season levels. In the case of the Indus, the spate occurs between June and September, after which time wheat and barley are winter-sown, *without ploughing*, as rabi crops for harvesting in spring during March–April. This is in contrast to the kharif (autumn) crops, such as sesame and cotton, planted at the beginning of the inundation for harvesting at its close in the autumn (Lambrick, cited in Allchin and Allchin 1982:217). However, kharif crops were not common prior to the second millennium (Jarrige and Meadow 1992:165).

206

A schematic diagram (Figure 4.12) of this river regime, which relied upon *sailaba* (inundation) illustrates three land-use zones: *bet* land, *kadir* and *bhangar*. Leshnik (1973:73) from whom this information is taken, observes that 'the land of Zone A clearly benefits most directly from seasonal floods and the rich deposits of alluvial soil they bring. This is the most favoured land and is therefore given over mainly to the favoured crop, wheat.' But Zone A is not simply a narrow strip adjoining the margins. There are several methods of maximizing the extent of fields in Zone A, and a method of doing the same in Zone B also is illustrated in Figure 4.13. They involve flow or flood-water irrigation.

The first technique applicable in Zone A is called *budh* (1 in Figure 4.13). There

> the dry beds lying above the cold weather level of the main river are filled during the floods (which reach a high level in mid-August–September). When the rivers fall (subsidence begins toward the end of October, and a low-water level is reached in January) these short arms are transformed into lakes, sometimes with the aid of weirs at take off. But before that, they frequently spill over and flood the adjacent low-lying land. Thereafter, the remaining water is used for irrigation through lifting devices.
>
> (ibid.:74)

The second technique applicable to Zone A is called *dhak*, for this 'spill' method works on land located at the apex of a sharp bend in the river (2 in Figure 4.13). This requires even less attention, for 'if the level of the adjacent ground is suitable, the high river jumps its banks and spills for many miles downstream' (ibid.).

> Next there is the *sailaba* technique applied to the inland Zone B of the Punjab [3 in the diagram]. This is an extension of the *budh* system, using natural channels but with artificial courses (*chhar*, ie, small cuts) leading off from them. Where possible, the water surface is kept above ground level for at least a few miles beyond the head, although the alignment of the canals is influenced more by the needs of the individual villages than topography. Hence their courses are tortuous like the river itself. . . . On these canals, too, lifts are used to bring the water onto the fields. The devices now employed are the *shaduf* [beam lift] and Persian wheel, but only the former can be dated to the Harappan period. The canals in Sind are generally wider than those in the Punjab and also differ from them in being aligned obliquely with the river, to take advantage of the fall of the plains. These courses are entirely seasonal and carry almost no water in the winter months. But during the

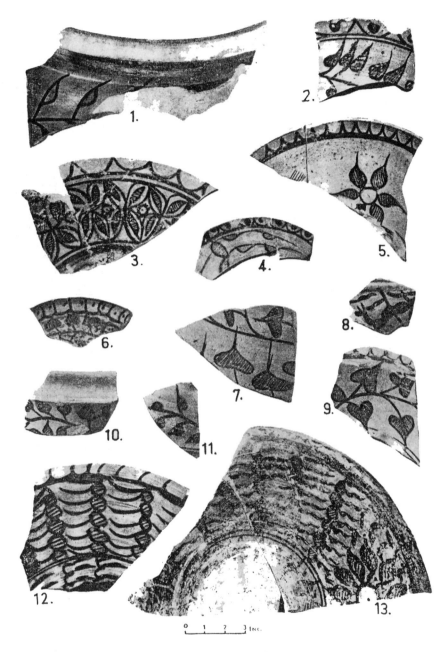

Figure 4.10 Painted incised and plain pottery of the Harappa Period at Kot Diji
Source: Khan 1965:plate XV

Figure 4.11 Small, thin-textured jars with bright red slip and finely drawn motifs of peacocks and fish scales

Source: Khan 1965:plate XVI

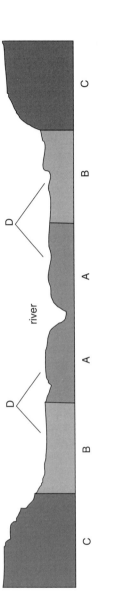

Figure 4.12 Diagram of the river regime; land-use zones of the Punjab in cross-section

Note: A: *Bet* land, parallel and close to the rivers, is thus the most favoured land for cultivation. B: *Kadir* low-lying areas beyond zone A are still suitable for cultivation, especially when taken with wells, which in this zone are intended to be permanent, whereas in zone A they are merely hollows. C: Called *bhangar* in the Punjab, those are uplands used for grazing and the cultivation of some rain-fed (*barani*) crops such as barley, but of most value to nomadic pastoralists for its good grass cover. D: Represents depressions and marshes in zones A and B.

Source: After Leshnik 1973:73

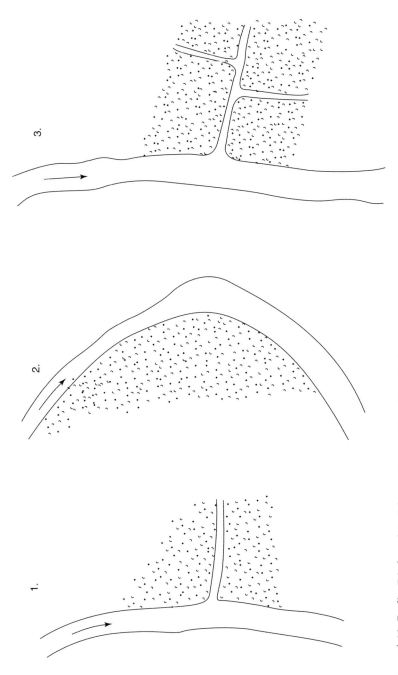

Figure 4.13 Budh, Dhak and Sailaba methods of flow/flood irrigation (respectively).

Source: After Leshnik 1973:74

flood season the low river banks are easily topped by the swollen waters, making the use the lifting machines less common than in the Punjab.

(ibid.: 74–5)

Table 4.2, based on late nineteenth-century data from the Punjab Government (at which time agricultural modernization had scarcely begun), correlates crop seasons (rabi and kharif) with the type of irrigation and cultivation used.

The cross-ploughed field found at Kalibangan, where a closely spaced set of furrows runs east–west, while another widely spaced set runs north–south, is remarkably similar to modern practice in the area, where, for instance, pulses can be found in one direction and mustard in the other (Lal 1970–1:1–3). This sort of evidence leads Leshnik to conclude that,

> so far as the actual implements of cultivation are concerned, those employed today [i.e. pre-mechanization], can all reasonably be assigned an antiquity stretching back to Harappan times. For tillage, the plough and harrow are used, a seed-drill sometimes facilitates sowing, weeding is done with a hoe, harvesting with a sickle, threshing requires only a team of bullocks to stamp out the grains, and winnowing is done with the aid of a wooden stool and a plaited basket.
>
> (ibid.:71)

A model/toy draught plough has been found at Mohenjo-daro and at Banawali,[4] where many model carts also occur.

More detail on the Harappan agricultural regime is provided by Constantini (1990:323), who has examined seeds from Pirak, Mehrgarh and Nausharo. He confirms wheat and barley to be the principal Harappan crops 'as shown by the quantity and quality of the recovered seeds, and by the diversity of the cultivated species'. Those include no less than three species of hexaploid free-threshing wheats – *Triticum aestivum*, *T. compactum* and *T. sphaerococcum* – the latter two, club wheat and short wheat, respectively, being adaptations to local conditions and peculiarly 'Harappan'. Accordingly,

> in such an agricultural landscape dominated by naked wheat, in which there evidently appears the tendency to cultivate/select small seeded plants, the role of hulled wheats, *Triticum monococcum* [einkorn] and *T. dicoccum* [emmer], appears to have been marginal. At Nausharo only a few grains of einkorn and emmer were found.
>
> (ibid.:325)

Table 4.2 Crop types and the agricultural cycle in Punjab

River condition	Crop season	Months	Ploughing	Sown	Harvest
LOW		MID-MARCH MID-APRIL	–	–	BARLEY, PULSES, VEGETABLES
		MID-APRIL MID-MAY	X*	COTTON, RICE, MELONS	WHEAT, GOURDS, PULSES
RISE		MID-MAY MID-JUNE	X	COTTON, RICE, (BROADCAST)	GOURDS, ROWAN
	KHARIF	MID-JUNE MID-JULY	X	RICE (BROADCAST) SORGHUM, BAJRA	–
		MID-JULY MID-AUGUST	WHEAT, BARLEY	MAIZE, RICE, (BROADCAST), SORGHUM, SESAMUM, MILLET	–
HIGH		MID-AUGUST MID-SEPTEMBER	WHEAT, BARLEY	PULSES	ROWAN
		MID-SEPTEMBER MID-OCTOBER	X	VEGETABLES, PULSES	COTTON, RICE, MAIZE
		MID-OCTOBER MID-NOVEMBER	X	WHEAT, BARLEY, VEGETABLES	RICE, COTTON, MILLET, MAIZE, SORGHUM, PULSES
SUBSIDENCE	RABI	MID-NOVEMBER MID-DECEMBER	X	WHEAT, BARLEY	SORGHUM, PULSES, COTTON
		MID-DECEMBER MID-JANUARY	COTTON	–	COTTON
LOWEST		MID-JANUARY MID-FEBRUARY	COTTON	–	ROOTS (TURNIPS)
LOW		MID-FEBRUARY MID-MARCH	–	MELONS, VEGETABLES	ROOTS

*represents ploughing for crop shown after

Source: Punjab Government 1889:88

Source: Leshnik 1973:77

Constantini (1990:329) confirms previous identifications of cultivated date palm (*Phoenix dactilifera*) and grape vine (*Vitis vinifera*) and of the former declares that 'the date palm was certainly well known to the Harappans', as indeed would be expected from the name 'Sind', which in Dravidian (the probable language of Indus Civilization) means 'land of dates' (Southworth 1992:83). At Nausharo both date and jujube (*Ziziphus jujuba*) fruit-stones as well as grape pips were found in large numbers in all four excavated sectors, leaving Constantini (ibid.) in no doubt concerning the importance of such fruits in the human diet.

Legumes seem to have played a minor role in subsistence, although Weber (1992:286) suggests that this paucity might be an artefact of previously weak archaeobotanical research in South Asia. However, lentils (*Lens culinaris*) have been identified at Nausharo, and peas (*Pisum arvense*) at Harappa itself. Chickpeas (*Cicer arietinum*) are recorded from Kalibangan, but so far nowhere else. The absence of Near Eastern pulses at certain South Asian sites may, however, be an artefact not of preservation or recovery, but of the difficulty of introducing *Leguminosae* as seed, thus lacking the symbiotic bacteria (*Rhizobium* spp.) required at the roots for nitrogen fixation (Willcox 1992a:293).

Flax (*Linum usitatissimum*), cotton (*Gossypium arboreum*), mustard (*Brassica juncea*) and sesame (*Sesamum indicum*) supplied the oil and clothing fibres needed. Their find locations, as well as those of the other plants mentioned, are summarized in Table 4.3.

'Based on the environmental parameters within which these plants flourish, the climate was not different from today's' (Weber 1992:287). This is important for what will be said with regard to theories of the collapse of urban Indus society.

Willcox (1992a:294) envisages a three-stage process for the development of agriculture in India, beginning with 'primary Middle East domesticates [which] were all self-fertilizing, giving multiple pure lines of homozygous plants which can undergo rapid selection under the pressures of cultivation'. Those primary domesticates then trigger the domestication of indigenous tropical plants (notably rice, cotton, mustard and broom-corn millet) which provide the summer crops, as tropical plants require no vernalization, relying only on the presence of moisture for germination. Finally, 'once the indigenous tropical crops were in use, farmers were pre-adapted to receive exotic African cultivars' (ibid.:298). Amongst the latter group are: *Sorghum bicolor*, *jowar*, the large or great millet, referred to by Jack Harlan (1989:336) as 'one of the great cereals of the world'; *Pennisetum typhoides*, *bajra*, 'pearl' or bullrush millet; *Eleusine corocana*, *ragi* or finger millet; and the cowpea, *Vigna unguiculata* – *gram* (although the term 'gram' includes other legumes).

Table 4.3 Find sites of food, oil and fibre plants in the Harappa Period

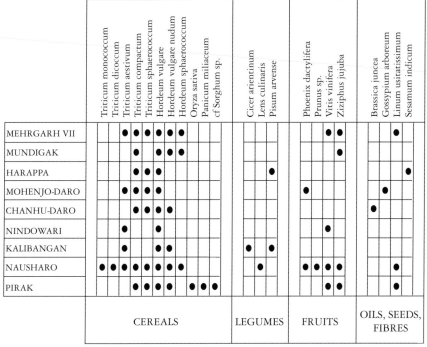

	Triticum monococcum	Triticum dicoccum	Triticum aestivum	Triticum compactum	Triticum sphaerococcum	Hordeum vulgare	Hordeum vulgare nudum	Hordeum sphaerococcum	Oryza sativa	Panicum miliaceum	cf Sorghum sp.	Cicer arientinum	Lens culinaris	Pisum arvense	Phoenix dactylifera	Prunus sp.	Vitis vinifera	Ziziphus jujuba	Brassica juncea	Gossypium arboreum	Linum usitatissimum	Sesamum indicum
MEHRGARH VII		●	●	●	●	●	●	●								●	●				●	
MUNDIGAK		●		●	●	●											●					
HARAPPA		●	●	●										●								●
MOHENJO-DARO		●	●	●	●										●						●	
CHANHU-DARO		●	●	●	●	●														●		
NINDOWARI		●			●												●					
KALIBANGAN		●			●	●						●		●								
NAUSHARO	●	●	●	●	●	●	●	●	●								●		●	●	●	●
PIRAK		●	●	●	●	●			●	●	●					●	●					●
	CEREALS											LEGUMES			FRUITS				OILS, SEEDS, FIBRES			

Source: Constantini 1990:326

URBAN SOCIETY

Kalibangan lies on the southern bank of the Ghaggar in the Ganganagar district of Rajastan, about 310 kilometres northwest of Delhi. It was excavated by B.B. Lal (cf. 1973, 1979) in nine seasons throughout the 1960s. Fairly well preserved, it can stand as a clear example of Harappan cities, or more exactly towns, as can be seen in Figure 4.16 (p.225).

While some Amrian pottery is found at Kot Dijian sites and vice versa (Flam 1987:75), from the end of the fourth millennium to the middle of the third, Flam's settlement maps show a diminution in the number of settlements in the Sind Kohistan and Kirthar regions, associated with a movement east to the Lower Indus Basin, there to fuse with people of the (Cholistan) Kot Diji tradition (ibid.:76–9). The type-site Kot Diji, representing one of the component cultures of the Harappan oecumene, lies on a Ghaggar channel, only about 50 kilometres southeast of Mohenjo-daro. The alluvial fan that is the Kachi Plain, in which the Bolan and Nara Rivers are prominent, merges into the Indus Valley not far from Mohenjo-daro.

The Harappan oecumene formed from a Kot Dijian/Amri-Nal synthesis. Excavations at those sites clearly show that indigenous levels (e.g. 3A at Kot Diji, II at Amri, I at Banawali) *receive* developed Harappan (actually Mohenjo-daran) cultural material and in a short time *become* Harappan. Kot Diji, Amri and other regional Chalcolithic cultures no doubt already shared many attributes, making integration easier. In the development of complexity it is also clear that Mohenjo-daro has priority over other sites so far excavated, with the exception of the Hakra-Ghaggar cluster referred to above, where Hakra wares actually *precede* the Kot Diji related material.[5] So certain areas were *catalytic* in producing the *fusion* from Hakra, Kot Dijian and Amri-Nal cultural elements that resulted in the gestalt we recognize as Early Harappan (Early Indus). Since this is a process of uneven development, the new gestalt was then *transmitted back* to sites representative of its pre-synthesis cultural origins. As previously indicated, the catalytic areas must lie along the Ghaggar-Hakra and in the vicinity of Mohenjo-daro.

Kot Diji artefacts, which include miniature carts, female figurines, copper/bronze tools, personal ornaments in stone, shell and ivory, everted-rim globular jars, flanged/double rimmed jars and the most characteristic dish-on-stand, make its culture directly ancestral to the Harappan. But at such sites as Rehman Dheri on the Gomal Plain there is a pre-Kot Diji phase (RHD I, 3300–2800 BC) and two Kot Diji phases (RHD II and III) that continue into and alongside the Mature Harappan (2500–2100 BC).

Rehman Dheri is a remarkable rectangular site of 21 hectares, rising gradually to 6 metres above the bare plain about 16 kilometres west of the Indus; 'like a battleship anchored in the midst of a calm sea' (Durrani 1981b:196). Its location is shown in Figure 4.14. So far it is the earliest urban site to be excavated in the sub-continent, with dates (above) placing it in the late fourth and early third millennia (Durrani 1981:205). The excavator (ibid.:200) suggests a population of 10,000, but this is excessive even for a densely built-up town site which Rehman Dheri seems to have been. It is, after all, only 520 × 390 metres. Instead 3–5,000 (150–200 hectares) seems more reasonable. What is not in doubt is that Rehman Dheri is a harbinger of Mature Indus urbanism, with planned or at least regular layout, compartmented stamp seals, bronze rods, chisels, nail files, needles, axes and a large amount of lapis lazuli. The bead industry was already important, with carnelian, agate and turquoise also present, as were micro-drills and half-finished beads. A carnelian bead even has a stone drill-bit jammed in it.

Altogether, 'Rehman Dheri possesses the richest bead industry of the contemporary sites on the subcontinent' in Durrani's opinion (ibid.). It also has a very rich repertoire of potter's marks, engraved and painted, the former occurring near the bases, the latter appearing on the neck below the rim. Many of the marks are strikingly similar to those appearing in the Mature Indus symbol system. The wares themselves in the lowest phase (RHD I) *pre-date* the Kot Diji-Sothi complex.

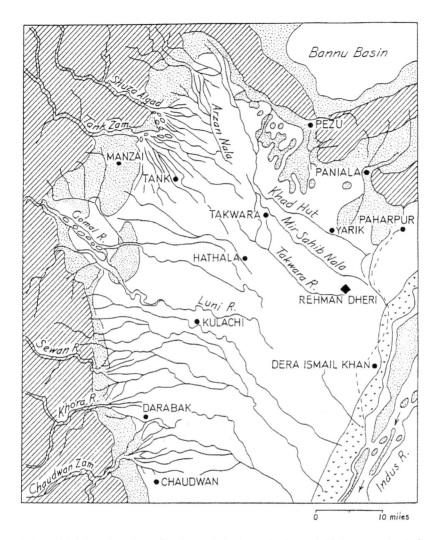

Figure 4.14 The location of Rehman Dheri on the Gomal Plain; near the Indus
Source: Durrani 1981b:194

Predominant types of this phase are cups, bowls, and jars with very
fine thin fabrics and elegant ring bases. They have fine painted
designs drawn in black or chocolate on a red background. Most
striking are those in black or chocolate outline filled with white
paste; the filling seems to be fugitive or superficial and tends to
fade out the moment it is exposed to the sun or touched with the
hand. It is just possible that the same was applied after the firing

217

of the pot. Besides some linear and geometric designs, this type of decoration is found in fish and animal motifs.

(ibid.:201)

Fish, pipal leaves and geometrics are features of the sign system in this early phase at Rehman Dheri and in the Mature Indus phase throughout the oecumene.

The ecology of Sind Kohistan and Kirthar, with its hilly, broken topography, short of both water and extensive soils and reliant on springs ('a prehistoric site [occurs] at almost every known spring in Sind Kohistan'; ibid.:69) obviously could not support an expanding society, which the alluvial plains of a major river system could readily do.

During the first half of the third millennium, people of the Amri, Nal, Kot Diji and Sothi traditions became Harappan together, with centrally placed Mohenjo-daro as a catalyst. Kulli, while interacting with the oecumene, never seems to have become an organic part of it. Flam sees the emergence of the acro-sanctum as the advent of hierarchy and control. No doubt in an ideological form this is so. But it is the minimum sort of essentially normative control required to allow individual settlements to grow, and beyond this, to integrate with others similarly motivated. Indeed, it can be argued that the 'skull-cult' of the Levantine Pre-Pottery Neolithic was an attempt to fashion just such an integrative set of ideological mechanisms, whose failure resulted in the disintegration of those communities when they came under pressure. As far as I am aware, no one has suggested that the 'skull-cult' was an attempt at chiefly or, risibly, 'state-control'.

That productive specialization was the basis of Harappan social integration has already been argued at some length by Bridget Allchin for whom:

> our observations on the lithic industries of early settlements in Sind, and upon the palaeogeography of the lower Indus region strengthen the case for intercommunity specialization, and for the essential interdependence of specialized communities, and hence a wider organization utilizing and maintaining this interdependence.
>
> (Allchin 1979:209)

Kuntasi is one of the many sites established at the 'high-tide' of the Mature Period, which here commenced around 2,220 BC, and lasted until about 1900 BC.

> This is evident from the occurrence of many mature forms of ceramics such as the 'S' shaped jars, highly decorated step-sided dishes, short-stemmed stud-handled bowls and ledge-necked jars,

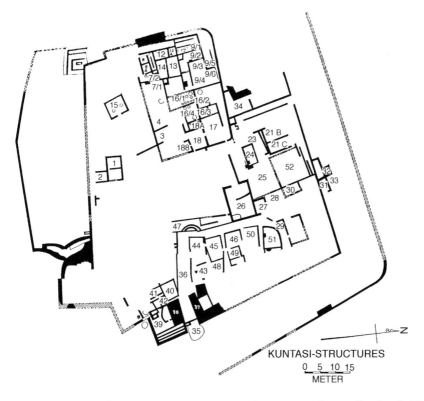

Figure 4.15 Plan of Kuntasi, a Harappan manufacturing settlement by the Gulf of Kutch in Gujarat

Source: Dhavalikar 1992:77

etc. The design repertoire consists of a range of geometric patterns as well as a variety of floral motifs. There is also a bichrome ware which has a red and buff surface painted with black or brown.

(Dhavalikar 1992:75)

Established specifically as a manufacturing centre by the Gulf of Kutch in Gujarat, an area with low agricultural potential and largely brackish water, the settlement of Kuntasi covers 2 hectares, one hectare of which is walled, indeed double-walled, as can be seen from the plan in Figure 4.15.

Manifestly its goods were valuable. Kuntasi's manufacturing role is positively indicated by the workshop complex concentrated on the west of the settlement. It contained kilns and furnaces, granary and storerooms (ibid.). Dhavalikar maintains that 'the structure to the north of this granary was the largest room in the entire complex, and must therefore have belonged to the most important person in the settlement' (ibid.). Goods were loaded onto boats from a long loading platform (12.5 × 3.2 metres) on the river-bank. This complex, like the whole settlement, is constructed of limestone rubble set in mud, or made of standard Harappan mud-brick (38 × 19 × 9.5 centimetres) with stone foundations.

Dhavalikar (ibid.:78) identifies the 20.3 × 3.8 metre feature emanating from structure 26 in the centre of the settlement as a ritual platform, akin to the one numbered 15 in area L at Mohenjo-daro.

> Equally interesting is the fact that it faces towards the open quad-rangle in the centre of the settlement. This certainly cannot be without significance, and we may not be far off the mark in infer-ring that the congregation occupied the open quadrangle and was addressed by the priest-chief from the platform.
>
> (ibid.)

Also paralleled, but this time at Harappa, is a faience seal which Dhavalikar thinks belonged to the manager of the site's industrial complex (ibid.:75). By contrast, the 'badge of office' of either the ritual leader or the chief of the security personnel (or both, two found) may have been the large double-scroll ('spiral') copper ring. The rings occurred in a structure near the entrance gateway which comprised a large squarish room opening out onto a veranda to the north. Dhavalikar thinks it highly likely that this was the security chief's dwelling, facing that of the chief priest (ibid.).

Kuntasi thus seems to represent Harappan Civilization in microcosm: trade, industry and cult serve to integrate society more or less spontaneously, without the emergence of a state. There is order and organization, but it comes not from power-imposed top-down management, rather from the complementarity of specialized roles. At Kuntasi, for example, one such role seems to be that of preventing valuable commodities from 'disappearing' without an equivalent being received in exchange. The 'police' function of town walls doubtless had this function too, for the absence or presence of a state doesn't mean the absence of theft. Nor does it imply the absence of local administrations funded by tolls or market taxes.

THE MISREPRESENTATION OF THE GREATER INDUS OECUMENE

Because of its scale, urbanism, iconography and other attributes (including its peer treatment by Babylonia), Indus Civilization has been forced into the classificatory straitjacket of 'state' or even 'empire'. This last is no doubt induced by the extent of Indus Civilization, extending over about 1,200,000 square kilometres in its Mature, or urban, period. The major cities of

Mohenjo-daro, Harappa and the unfortunately unexcavated Ganweriwala had populations in the region of 20 to 30,000 (if current size estimates are sustained), on a par with medium-sized cities in Mesopotamia, as we have seen above.

Jacobsen declares as much in the very title of his article 'The Harappan Civilization: An Early State'. His conclusion is that

> two general characteristics of the Harappan complex fulfil the key functional criteria of states, as concluded by Claessen and Skalnik (1978a:630) after their exhaustive study: (1) decision-making by some centrally operating authority or group consistently 'affected behaviour in lower order settlements' ... and (2) this central force maintained this vast system and prevented any centripetally fractioning tendencies for some five centuries. Briefly, then, the Harappan Civilization would seem to have passed the tests of 'long-term effectiveness and cohesion' which Webb would suggest distinguishes states from non-state systems.
>
> (Jacobson 1987a:163)

Long-term effectiveness and cohesion there certainly was, but it was not brought about by state organization. On the contrary, I contend that when the evidence is examined in depth, every single state-defining criterion is absent, *especially* the 'central force' or commanding centre, and that what produced social integration was the existence of a commonwealth, the developed form of the mutually beneficial interaction network first seen in the Halafian sphere.

A state resides in the control over people and territory exercised from a centre through specialized apparatuses of power:

1   military
2   administrative (mostly tax-raising)
3   legal and
4   ideological.

A fifth element is the centre itself, possessing a double aspect: the ruling engine (palace, elite establishments, etc.) which is situated within a settlement and hinterland that provide core resources.

I will review the evidence by way of countering the explicit arguments put forward by proponents of a Harappan state, in the course of which each of the four apparatuses and the matter of a ruling centre will be covered. Finally, the issue of class stratification will be tackled.

Defining state characteristics

Military

Offensive

There is no Harappan evidence for armies, either in terms of imagery or equipment, in complete contrast to the contemporary Near East. There, for instance, Eannatum's 'Stela of the Vultures' (*c.*2450 BC) shows a phalanx formation of locked shields and spears at the charge, while Naram Sin's Stela (twenty-third century BC) graphically shows conquest and death, as, in most graphic fashion, does Horus Narmer's famous palette of some eight centuries earlier. Mesopotamian seals also show many agonistic scenes of struggle and conquest, often centred on a kind of Gilgamesh hero figure. Quite apart from the imagery, Mesopotamia provides us with many explicit texts concerning military matters. Indus script (which cannot be read and may not even be a conventional script but rather a series of icons) appears on seals. Those seals never show combat scenes but only naturalistic represen-tations of animals, plants, rituals and cultic equipment.

In the rest of Bronze Age Eurasia, bronze itself was a scarce, expensive and politically important commodity controlled by the elite. Weapons were expensive for two reasons: materials were costly as also was the highly skilled labour of artificers. Weapons were therefore issued by the palace when necessary, and then taken back into the armoury. Those damaged would be remelted and recycled. The same process held for metal farming equipment in Mesopotamia, where temples and other 'great households' were the controlling agency (Maisels 1987, 1990). None of this obtained in the Greater Indus region where, unique amongst major Bronze Age civil-izations, copper/bronze was available to all, as indeed copper items are in India to this day.

Defensive

City walls are apparent in Mesopotamia from as early as the state formation period in the late fourth millennium, and one of the key indications of emer-gent class stratification in the Chinese Chalcolithic are the *hangtu* or stamped earth town walls (Underhill 1994). *Hangtu* also provided a platform on which elite residences and whole compounds were 'raised up' above the earth, into which the houses of their servitors were often dug (Thorp 1983:32).

But city walls in the Indus context have different purposes. The city walls traced by Meadow and Kenoyer at Harappa are too low or weak or poorly maintained to serve as defensive structures. As they observe,

> walls serve to exclude unwanted elements, enclose what people want
> to keep inside, and channel formal movement through a restricted

number of openings. Walls can also act to physically separate different social units, and as retaining structures, to stabilize construction.

(Meadow and Kenoyer 1994:468)

Harappan gateways are not defensive structures. Kesarwani (1984:67, 71), who has made a comparative study of Harappan gateways and defences, concludes that although 'the practice of erecting fortifications and gateways existed even in pre-Harappan times, as is clear from the evidence of Kot Diji and Kalibangan', it is apparent that 'the simple design of the citadel and the lower-town gateways of Kalibangan had no strategic importance. They were ordinary entrances for the free movement of people and goods.' Details of entrances at Kalibangan are seen in Figure 4.16 beneath a plan view of the town (from Kesarwani 1984:66).

Part of the problem is semantic, turning on bipartite layout of Harappan settlements, each separately walled. The 'hightown' area is conventionally referred to as 'the citadel', and the larger part the 'lower town'. Taken with assumed evidence for 'town planning', it is usual to see in this the controlling hand of a state.

At Kalibangan not only is there an 'upper town/lower town' contrast, but the very 'citadel' is divided into two. The northern section (or 'rhomb') contains mud-brick houses (probably for priests) on a street going from the southeast entrance diagonally across to a northwest exit. The southern section contains streets or lanes but no house structures, instead a minimum of five mud-brick platforms, which Wheeler (e.g. 1968) had assumed to be working or threshing areas of granaries. At Kalibangan, however, there is no evidence for granaries, but one of the citadel platforms did contain seven 'fire-altars' arranged in a north–south row. Consisting of clay-lined pits, they measured 75×55 centimetres, within which were found ash, charcoal, the characteristic 'terracotta cakes' and the remains of clay stele. From the complete examples found in the residential buildings of the lower town, stele were 30–40 centimetres in height and 10–15 centimetres in diameter, and formed the centrepoint of the hearths (Lal 1984:57).

The same platform contained a well, plus the remains of a few bath-pavements with attached drains, all in fired brick, indicating the importance of bathing rituals. (Ritual is repeated, conventionalized, symbolic behaviour, externally [publicly] and internally [psychologically] actualizing aspects of the belief system [ideology].) Another platform contained, in addition to a well and a fire-altar, a rectangular pit, 1.25×1 metre, lined also with kiln-fired bricks, within which

lay bovine bones and antlers, evidently representing some kind of a sacrifice. That the offering of animals in sacrifice was a Harappan practice is also suggested by certain seals, for example from

Mohenjo-daro. It depicts a deity in front of whom kneels a devotee. Behind the latter is an animal, in all likelihood brought as an offering.

(ibid.)

The so-called 'citadels' at all the Harappan sites[6] thus appear to be 'ceremonial precincts' for the population of the 'lower town', whose spacious and well laid out houses contained domestic equivalents of the 'fire and water' installations (ibid.:58). As Lal (1979:85) observed of the 'lower town' houses at Kalibangan: 'it further appears that in almost every house a room was reserved for the "fire-altars" which had their characteristic shape and other features including central stele. In a few cases these were lined with mud-bricks.' It is indeed odd that a 'granary' should be located right alongside a 'great bath' and other cultic installations, seen in Wheeler's (1968:39) reconstruction of the 'citadel' at Mohenjo-daro (Figure 4.17).

Instead, the 'citadels' are best referred to, following Flam (1987:81–2), as *acro-sanctums*, or community ritual precincts. Their scale and openness both to the elements and to the populace make Indus ritual precincts quite unlike temples elsewhere in the Old World, where access to the really potent interior was highly restricted.

Acro-sanctums have their origins in Amri- tradition settlements in Sind Kohistan, where thirteen of the forty known sites possess 'high places' adjoining a 'lower town'.

> The most conspicuous prehistoric settlement type in Sind Kohistan consists in part of an artificially built, conically-shaped hill which rises to an average height of 25 metres above its surrounding plain. These conically-shaped hills (known as *buthi* in Sindhi) vary in circumference, but each one exhibits the remains of a series (2–4) of encircling, terraced stone walls on its slopes, and remnants of inclined stairways or ramps ascend its southern side. Below these conically-shaped hills lie the remains of numerous stone foundation walls indicative of domestic structures.
>
> (Flam 1987:74–5)

The Indus oecumene was formed by the fusion of Kot Diji, Sothi and Amri-Nal traditions, as already mentioned several times.

Administrative, mostly tax-raising

Across Eurasia the origins of writing and accounting lie in tax-raising and the tracking of revenue flows (Postgate *et al.* 1995). The partial exceptions are China, where scapulimancy was a key early motive (but where lists of goods on perishable material like silk and bamboo existed), and the Halaf which, as we have seen, had a recording but no developed writing system

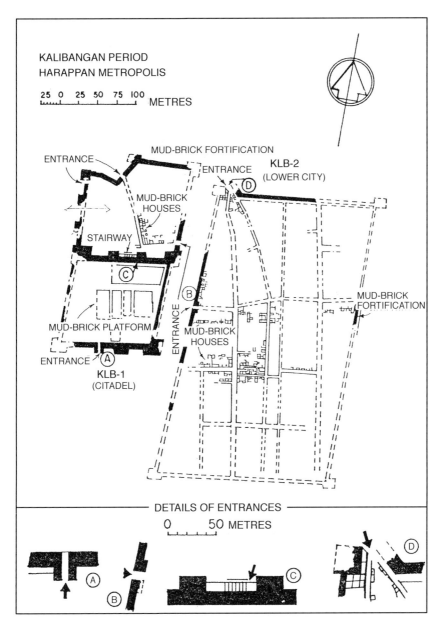

Figure 4.16 Layout and entrances at Kalibangan on the Ghaggar (Kesarwani 1984:66)

because there was no central authority that needed one. Similarly, in the Greater Indus area, there was a great deal of economic activity, a clear manifestation of which are the finely made and highly standardized weights. Some of it even involved foreign trade, but nowhere is there evidence of a controlling authority (Asthana 1979:33).

There is no doubt that Mohenjo-daro was an integrative centre, and with Atre (1989:50) I think that its importance was primarily as a religious, ceremonial, cultural and economic centre, while Harappa's eminence was due to trade. Furthermore, Atre (ibid.:58) argues that, alongside Mohenjo-daro, 'Kalibangan is the only other centre, though devoid of similar grandeur, where an exclusively ritual complex of public nature existed.' All the other excavated Harappan settlements, from village-sized and over, seem to be craft and/or trade loci, lacking any local manifestations of state control or central administration. Even an acculturation site such as that of Padri in southeastern Saurashtra seems to represent the (entirely peaceful) extension of the Harappan oecumene by means of economic integration, in this case the supply of salt northwards, for which the remarkable globular 'Sturdy Red' storage jars were employed. One bears the striking image of the Harappan 'Horned Deity' (Shinde 1992:64–5), seen as proto-Siva in his later aspect, that of *pasupati*, Lord of the Beasts. It is seen in Figures 4.18b and c in the overall design of the jar and in detail in Figure 4.18a.

This should be compared with the horned creature with double floral emblem on jars from Kot Diji shown in Figure 4.19b.

Larger, more central sites, such as Allahdino and Balakot, evidence craft specialization, while

> it is apparent that centres like Chanhu-daro, Lothal [also in Saurashtra], Desalpur and also Shortugai on the Oxus, were each located at a vantage point to carry out trade transactions smoothly and efficiently. Sutkagen-dor and Sotka-koh on the Makran coast also indicate the commercial acumen of the Harappans in selecting strategic points from which to trade. From these examples it can be easily observed that every Harappan settlement had its own specific function, and town planning in each instance differed according to the demands of the local environment and the original function of the settlement. Several common features were maintained as a matter of natural adherence to some inherently accepted norms but no rigidity was to be observed.
>
> (Atre 1989:50; cf. Mughal 1990c:38)

In concluding her detailed examination of private houses at Mohenjo-daro, Anna Sarcina (1979:446) observes that 'the continuity and the uniformity of building make evident this structural logic [north–south orientation, courtyards, few windows, thick walls, many ablution platforms;

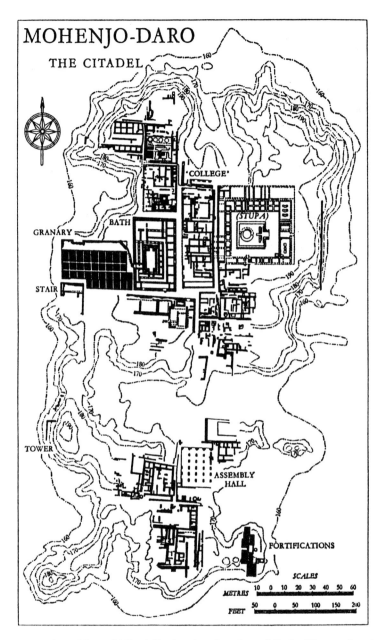

Figure 4.17 Plan of 'Citadel', showing location of Bath, 'Granary' and other installations, Mohenjo-daro

Source: Wheeler 1968:39

all well adapted to the continental climate]. It is because of this uniformity that a government was often suggested who had been able to impose their direction on a people without imagination. It is obvious that a government must have existed [?] but it is more prudent to talk of coordination than imposition.'

Legal control

Neither in the sense of a monopoly on the legitimate use of force, nor in the civil sense of dispute resolution between rights holders is there any evidence of a 'Harappan' legal system or code. Rather, the evidence presented

Figure 4.18a Horned deity, detail
Source: Shinde 1992:62

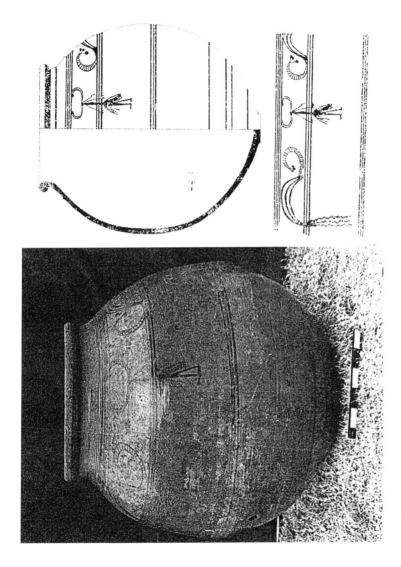

Figure 4.18b and c Horned deity on jar

Source: Shinde 1992:59

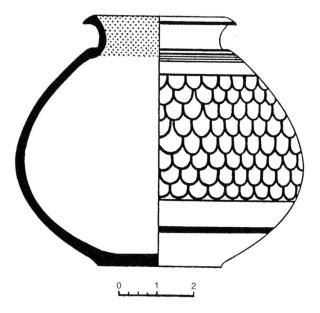

Figure 4.19a Jar painted with fish-scale pattern. Kot Diji culture

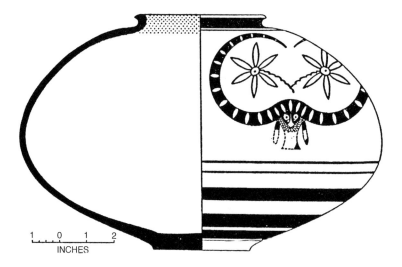

Figure 4.19b Horned creature with double floral emblem on jar from Kot Diji,
Kot Diji level

Source: Khan 1965:58

under the military and administrative headings (above) indicates a negoti-
ated, ideologically constrained and consensual understanding of 'law': not
a 'legal process' established through the courts of a central authority, but
a localized, relatively informal, dispute resolution process.

Ideology

With Atre (1989) and Miller (1985a), I have previously argued (1991) for
strong normative 'controls' on behaviour in Harappan Civilization. Ideology
certainly had a central place in the functioning of Harappan society. What
are not present, however, are temples on Egyptian, Mesopotamian or even
Chinese lines. They just do not exist here as the houses of a god, as monu-
mentally imposing buildings. Installations are not monuments, still less
dominating ones, as are the deliberately intimidatory structures of Albi and
the Sacré Cœur in Paris. Further, there is no evidence that they were 'great
households' on Mesopotamian or Egyptian lines, supporting themselves as
establishments by controlling people and property.

The artefact conventionally assumed to be evidence of a state religion,
personified by the existence of a supposed 'priest-king' (Wheeler 1968:86–7),
is an incomplete stone sculpture of a seated male wearing a trefoil-patterned
garment (conveniently in ibid., cover, and Plate XVIII, an important
side-view). Whatever or whomever the bust represents, there is evidence
that it is both late and atypical, such that J.-F. Jarrige (1994:312)
refers to it as having 'some connection with an intrusive iconographical
tradition', though probably locally produced. Further, 'the trefoil is almost
absent on Harappan ceramic: only two polychrome pottery sherds from
Mohenjo-daro are known which bear "red trefoils with white borders on an
apple-green ground"' (Ardeleanu-Jansen 1989:205, citing Mackay 1938:
227). In fact the 'priest-king' fragment on which so much has been predicated belongs to a category of miniature (and apparently ritualistic)
statuettes that can be found from Elam through Shahdad (with its echoes
of Tell Asmar statuary) to Bactria and the Indus Valley, as Winkelmann's
(1994) pathbreaking synthesis clearly shows. Wheeler (1968:87) had
already indicated that the trefoil pattern possessed extensive western connections.

Lacking either textual or architectural evidence, Kenoyer (1991a:364)
declares that 'at present, we cannot clearly associate the stone sculptures,
seals, or any other set of symbols with a "state religion" as opposed to a
less structured cult'. Quite! Jansen (1994:272) puts it most succinctly: 'not
a single monumental representation in sculptural art of rulers, gods or
priests has been discovered'.

In sum, there is no evidence whatever for a state Church, but much
evidence for diffuse, diverse and often domestic ritual practices, unified by
a set of shared themes ('cardinal tenets') and beliefs.

Dominant centres and ruling engines

Concerning the eerie absence of 'ruling engines', Kenoyer claims that 'Many of the complex and sometimes massive structures at Mohenjo-daro and Harappa could have been elite residences, centralized administrative structures or even temples, but later disturbances obscured their primary function.' When later? During the lifetime of Indus Civilization? In the immediate post-Harappan Period or perhaps during nineteenth-century railway construction? And why should their 'primary function' be so obscure if universal state forms or indicators are indeed present? Nineteenth-century excavation standards in the Near East left a great deal to be desired, but palaces and temples, seals and texts quickly became apparent (cf. Maisels 1993a:33–50).

Great caution is urged by Jansen (1979:405) in the light of the assumptions of earlier excavators, who 'searched for "Fortifications", "Granaries", "Temples", residences of "Priest-Kings", "Grid Patterns" in the layout of the towns', etc., and [unsurprisingly] they seemed to find what they were looking for'. The more Jansen looks at the physical evidence in the field, the more those established categories dissolve. As we saw above, 'fortifications' on close examination have a habit of turning into flood defences, platforms and retaining walls, 'citadels' into acro-sancta.

In the north of Mohenjo-daro Mackay (1935:59–60) found a large building 74 metres long and 34 metres wide, with outer walls over 1.5 metres thick and bounded on the south and west by two very important thoroughfares.

> A short distance south of it is what appears to be a palace – a large straggling building of excellent masonry, arranged around two spacious courtyards, with servants' quarters (sic), a number of storerooms and, in its earlier days, accommodation for metal-workers as well.
>
> (ibid.)

The complex contains three wells and at least one bread oven. This 'palace', about 67 metres long by 35 metres wide with walls 1 to 2 metres thick, had a major entrance 2.5 metres wide from 'Crooked Lane' and two more from 'Fore Lane'. To Mackay it 'seems to form an island in an otherwise undistinguished quarter of the [lower] city', and its alignment is unaltered from the surface down 6.5 metres (the maximum he had reached), suggesting to him that 'this building was occupied for some three to five hundred years' (ibid.).

Even if this turns out to be a 'proper' palace with a king rather than an administrative/trade/artisan centre, the case for a 'stateless' Indus Civilization is not affected *unless* it can be shown that the whole region was *ruled* from Mohenjo-daro or some other centre. Otherwise the writ of such a 'ruler' would not have extended very far outside of the city, and in any event he

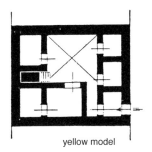

yellow model

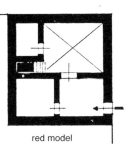

red model

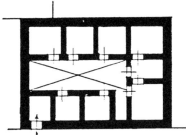

blue model

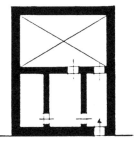

brown model

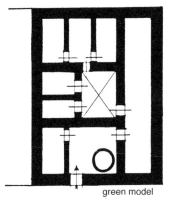

green model

Figure 4.20 Modular house-forms at Mohenjo-daro
Source: Sarcina 1979:437

may have had no more real power than the Doge of Venice. This putative palace is located in an 'undistinguished quarter of the city' without the usual accompaniment of other elite residences, compounds, ceremonial areas, temples, defences, etc. From its workaday location and its mundane interior, I see this large building as having an economic function, artisanal and/or commercial, analogous to the large, imposing structures housing 'wool' or 'piece' halls in early modern England.

CLASS STRATIFICATION

Fairservis (1994:178) maintained until the end of his life that Harappan Civilization was most likely a series of interlocking chiefdoms. Kenoyer (1991a:371) maintains that a Harappan state properly so-called did indeed exist, though he nowhere defines what he understands a state to be, that is, what control/ideological mechanisms have to exist for a society to be categorized as state ordered. Instead he just

> propose[s] that the Indus state was composed of several competing classes of elites who maintained different levels of control over the vast regions of the Indus and Ghaggar-Hakra Valley. Instead of one social group with absolute control, the rulers or dominant members in the various cities would have included merchants, ritual specialists, and individuals who controlled resources such as land, livestock, and raw materials. These groups may have had different means of control, but they shared a common ideology and economic system as represented by seals, ornaments, ceramics, and other artifacts. This ideology would have been shared by occupational specialists and service communities, who appear to have been organised in loosely stratified groups.

It is self-contradictory to restate one's position, as Kenoyer does (1994a:77), again mentioning 'competing classes of elites', with 'the largest cities relatively independent, possibly organized as city states', the whole integrated by economic, ideological and cultural means, and yet still claim that a Harappan state existed, which we could see if only we were able to 'break out of inappropriate older models and develop more complex frameworks that can be refined through problem oriented archaeological research'. On the contrary, it is Kenoyer who is trapped within older and now inappropriate models which assume that every complex society is by that very fact state ordered.

The condition of Indus Civilization as described by Kenoyer is such a clear example of organic solidarity/social integration based on complementarity in the division of labour, that Durkheim would have regarded it as archetypal had he known of it. My contention is that the organic division of labour was itself structuring.

The complexities described by Kenoyer are indeed remarkable, but nowhere does he identify a ruling centre or apparatus. Indeed, he specifically excludes a unified ruling class! What he actually describes are competing and collaborating, but essentially diffused, loci of power. The corporative units seem to be something like family/lineage ones (Maisels 1991), the familial entities sharing a world view of common values and distributed religious powers, both in the organizational sense and in the sense in which pantheism is a complex of distributed powers with no hegemonic centre. So shared values and ideology would seem to produce social cohesion with a minimum of coercion. Nonetheless, Kenoyer (1991a:367) cavalierly dismisses such considerations when raised by Miller (1985a).

Kenoyer counters that

> certain segments of Indus society were trying to differentiate themselves from the rest. These individuals used distinctive pottery styles and wore elaborate ornaments made from carefully worked raw materials, including gold,[7] silver, electrum, carnelian, lapis lazuli, turquoise and shell. They also required ornaments and symbolic objects made from manufactured substances such as bronze, faience, stoneware and fired steatite.
>
> (Kenoyer 1991a:367)

While the rest of the population imitated with poorer materials. But who said that there could be no differences in wealth? The acephalous condition does not demand homogeneity and cannot command it. Over such a vast area and within each part of it, differences in fertility, productivity, organization, skills and occupations, as well as family size, structure, sickness rates and life-cycles, are bound to produce differences of wealth and rank. None of those differentiating factors owes anything to a ruling centre or even a dominant elite.

Though (like Kenoyer) he seems not to know of Mackay's 'palace' (Mackay is not even cited in the bibliography), Jacobson (1987a) makes by far the strongest case for Harappan Civilization taking the form of an early state. Using comparative anthropology and some archaeological evidence, he argues that is possible to construe Indus Civilization in this fashion, even though,

> while evidence for socio-economic stratification in the Harappan Civilization does not reveal the same marked differences found in some other ancient urban cultures, the evidence is not incompatible with the relatively limited degree of economic stratification which characterizes *early* states.
>
> (his emphasis)

However, with regard to the evidence from Kalibangan, Jacobson concedes (ibid.:148) that 'nothing, for example, is presented concerning any differential nature of the houses or their artifactual contents'; nor overall can he see any differentials in health standards or general standards of living (ibid.:150).

Although Kenoyer does not mention it, there is nonetheless some evidence from Kalibangan of a proto-*varna* system in what B.B. Lal (1979:85–6), the excavator, sees as distinct quarters for a priestly class (northern half of the citadel mound), merchant and cultivator classes (the lower city on the main mound) and to the south of the citadel complex (unexcavated) probably the artisans' quarter.[8] As I have argued elsewhere (1991), caste stratification is an *alternative* to state-ordering, providing integration through hierarchy without a compelling and administering centre, which is not to say that oppression is absent from the system. I have provided a mechanism by which the caste order arose from kinship/occupational groups upon the devolution from urban Harappan society (p.250). And while the devolutionary process was relatively slow, the onset of Harappan social organization was so sudden that Bisht and Asthana (1979:227) speak of 'the suddenness by which it happened [as] the most baffling issue of Harappan studies'. Obviously this is an instance of 'switching' as seen in the formation of the Halaf network.

Jacobson (1987a:144–5) admits that his conclusions must be 'highly tentative', and he rightly declares that we need much more in the way of horizontal exposures in villages and towns (and particularly at the unexcavated cities of Lurewala and Ganweriwala) before anything more definite can be said.

He cites Trigger (1974:103) as stating that Indus art 'appears to be singularly poor in information about political subjects'. Perhaps that is really telling us something about political subjects? After all, Jacobson (op. cit.:147) does concede that 'Indus Civilization was at least culturally – if not politically – unified'. And contrary to traditional views of 'state planning' of the built environment, Bisht and Asthana, reviewing six (then) recently excavated sites, conclude that

> Banawali is yet another site of Kalibangan type but with certain items of town-planning which are similar not to Kalibangan but to the coastal sites like Surkotada. In fact, the dynamism of the Harappa Culture lies in its town-planning; one city was *similar* to the other but never *identical* since each one was conceived separately by the genius of its own citizens.
>
> (Bisht and Asthana 1979:230, original emphasis)

From all of this I conclude that there was no Harappan territorial state, but an oecumene (commonwealth) consisting of an economically integrated commerce-and-culture area (Mughal 1990c:38). Such a view is reinforced by Asthana's (1979:33) contention that Harappan overseas trade, 'by and large, appears to have been the joint-venture of merchants, agents, expert sailors, port authorities and others. . . . ' He sees Harappan trade, internal as well as external, as essentially non-administered, with commercial agents therefore assuming a pivotal role (ibid.:54).

I envisage the Harappan oecumene to consist of disparate, overlapping and interactive spheres of authority: economic, political, religious and, only derivatively, territorial. Perhaps it is the identity of limited territoriality that the seals with their inscriptions represent. And one of the functions of the 'Doge of Mohenjo-daro' (if such a person there was) could have been the establishment and monitoring of the famously standardized system of weights and measures.

As to the elite monopolization of prestigious raw materials, Harappan Civilization is the only one of the major Bronze Age societies in which copper/bronze artefacts were very widely distributed throughout the population, *and were actually used primarily for production and decoration rather than for warfare and ritual*. The *locus classicus* of the latter, showing total elite control, was of course China, where metal did not enter the productive process until the Iron Age. With regard to craft specialization, technological and stylistic uniformity and the supply of raw materials around the Indus, Kenoyer himself has stated that,

> based on an ethnographic model of similar craft communities in South Asia today, this uniformity can be explained, not as the result of centralized authority but on the basis of networks for supply and distribution that were defined by kin-ties or socio-economic alliances between the distant groups. These kin relations or alliances involve the sharing of resources, technology and stylistic expressions. Hereditary, kin related learning processes and alliances have resulted in standardization and uniformity in technology, raw material and stylistic features of the finished objects.
>
> (Kenoyer 1989a:186)

Further still, so far there is precious little evidence of Harappan soldiery in any form, or even of walled towns, let alone the professional warriors and mass levees that are so characteristic of the other major civilizations. Lacking state religion, state administration and state armed forces, of what then does Kenoyer's or Jacobson's Harappan state consist? Only of the word itself stretched far beyond utility, where social complexity is tautologically equated to a reification entitled 'The State'. Not all inegalities imply the state; even hunter–gatherers have them (Maisels 1990:221–30). Neither do all personal and social status markers imply dominance. Differentiation is certainly necessary to an eventual elite dominance but is not itself sufficient to produce it. So the existence of some marks of differentiation does not prove that a ruling elite has already emerged and imposed itself upon society, controlling it. Differentiation of social categories and the distinguishing of individuals are, however, central to competition between structural units, such as between lineages and clans. Only if one or a few could establish such ascendency over the rest that they could impose their wishes upon the others by legitimated force, would the state have emerged. That just such a clan-based differentiation could produce a ruling class is evident in China (see Chapter 5 and Appendix A, this volume).

If, however, we accept that Indus Civilization was *not* one in which the state as a controlling centre acted in the interests of a dominant class, but one in which there were very strong normative controls underpinning economic integration (organic solidarity), then the subsequent emergence of caste in particular, and historical Hindu society in general, becomes more readily explicable. If there was no tradition of the state in Harappan and post-Harappan society (as there manifestly was in post-Roman European society), then the forms of social integration that caste represents – namely of occupationally based and metaphysically sanctioned stratification without an encompassing state and state religion – simultaneously explain the uniqueness of caste and the 'churchlessness' of Hindu religion.

A society structured by (sub-) caste (*jati*) exists nowhere else in the world. The distributed social network and the complex but egalitarian commonwealth that were the social organization of Chalcolithic Halaf and Bronze Age Indus is also historically unique. Nothing like it is known elsewhere or subsequently, no models of such societies exist, and so scholars have persisted in trying to force recalcitrant information into categories of social explanation derived from societies encountered over recent centuries.

THE FALL

It might be thought that if there was some 'central authority', when this was lost the system fell apart. Of course what caused the centre to collapse would also have to be explained. However, since so far no evidence for a controlling centre exists, the 'centre' could have been just that: an area of the highest interaction density, serving as the motor of the system.

Attenuate this and thereby make mutual reliance more difficult or uncertain, or just less beneficial in economic terms, and then people begin to concentrate on local production of subsistence necessities. Diminished interaction and specialization then cause the whole to disintegrate in a cascade of defections to self-subsistence and localized exchange.

Thus the rise and early fall of Harappan Civilization is the story of successful settlements on the Ghaggar–Hakra system for as long as it flowed, but of progressive collapse into basic post-Neolithic village farming when the essential perennial Himalayan feeders to the Ghaggar–Hakra, namely the Sutlej and the Yamuna, became tributaries of the Indus and the Ganges, respectively.[9]

The reasons for the diversion of the Sutlej and the Yamuna away from the Ghaggar–Hakra, as Pal *et al.* (1984:497) argue from Landsat imagery, seem to lie in 'neotectionism shown by the enechelon nature of the structural control along the main river systems in this area'; that is, since the river courses are already determined by parallel overlapping geological structures, any further geological movement has sharp disruptive effects. Indeed, the Sutlej now takes a sharp, almost right-angled turn to the west near Ropar, away from its old channel into the Ghaggar south of Patiala, where there is a sudden widening of the river bed. Then from Shatrana, just downstream, to Marot, the now dry bed of the Hakra is from 6 to 8 kilometres wide (ibid.:495). Accordingly, 'there are no Harappan sites on the Sutlej except in its upper course near the Siwaliks' (Misra 1984:476). Similarly, 'the total absence of Harappan sites along the present course on the Yamuna shows that the river was not flowing in its present course during the Harappan period' (ibid.:480).

River vagrancy (sideways displacement, e.g. of the Indus to the west) had been noted for a long time before the advent of satellite imagery. Alexander Burnes, when crossing the Punjab in 1832, noted a wide, dry 80-kilometre stretch of the bed of the Sutlej where maps indicated an active river. He further discovered that this displacement had taken place within living memory, that is, only fifty years previously (Allchin *et al.* 1978:17). Throughout the later nineteenth century, as Allchin *et al.* note, surveys and historical references accumulated concerning the high level of vagrancy of rivers in the Punjab. (Indeed, since the times of British control, many of the relict beds have been used for irrigation canals.) In 1893 Surgeon Major Oldham published a survey of this material, combining it with his own extensive field observations. In particular he noted the migration of the Sarasvati, resulting in its eventually becoming nothing more than a tributary of the Indus. In 1969 Wilhemy re-examined the whole question and concluded that the upthrust caused by the northward movement of the Indian Plate against the Asian caused the entire drainage of North India to vary greatly in very recent geological time. He illustrated the consequences with seven maps reconstructing the rivers feeding the Hakra.

Here four of his maps are reproduced. Figures 4.21a and b contrast the positions at 2000 BC and 1500–1000 BC. By the latter period, the Ur-Jumna (original Jumna) has left only a dry bed, for the live river has been captured by the headwaters of the Delhi stream, turning it into a major river feeding the Ganges system. Thus begins the drying of the whole Ghaggar–Hakra system, completed between 500 BC and 1100 AD (Figure 4.22). By then, the Sutlej flows into the Indus and the Ghaggar–Hakra system had ceased to exist. The diversions of the Sutlej and the Jumna were of crucial significance because they were the only original Ghaggar–Hakra tributaries that were fed by Himalayan meltwaters, so guaranteeing substantial and perennial flow. The headwaters of the Sarasvati itself lay in the Siwalik foothills, which could not generate enough moisture to provide perennial flow.

Aurel Stein's opinion, based on extensive survey and some excavation, was that

> archaeological facts prove cultivation, and with it settled occupation, to have been abandoned much earlier on the Hakra than on the Ghaggar. Prehistoric mounds with pottery of the Chalcolithic period appear first near Fort Abbas. Thence they were traced down the Hakra as far as my survey extended west of Derawar. . . .
>
> I suggest that prehistoric occupation along the Hakra had stopped lower down after the branch of the Sutlej has ceased to join it, but for a time the floods of the Ghaggar may still have sufficed for cultivation in a stretch of the bed, until later settled agriculture became restricted to the Ghaggar higher up in Bikaner territory.
>
> (Stein 1942:180)

See also Suraj Bhan (1972, 1973) and, for a short history of surveys on the Sarasvati, Dalal (1980).

However, another potential cause of 'decline and fall' has been suggested by the biologist Paul Ewald of Amherst (1991a and pers. comm. 1993). He considers Harappan Civilization to be the very first in which extensive waterborne transmission of virulent disease could be expected – the disease in question being cholera or a cholera-like disease – precisely because the Harappans made great efforts to pipe their sewage away, something not seen in the other pristine civilizations. His argument is that:

> Inhabitants of Harappan cities obtained water from public wells in streets or from private wells within the densely distributed houses. The rims of these open wells were typically within a few inches of the surface of the road or floor (Mackay 1931; Marshall 1931: Plates 41b, 51b, 73b). Open wells of this type are notorious for spreading waterborne diseases when they lie within a network of leaky drainage lines, especially when flooding distributes surface contamination and allows backflow from drainage lines.
>
> The Harappan cities were the first urban areas to have networks for transporting wastewater, which flowed through bricklined drainpipes, typically a few inches to two feet below the surface of each street or lane. Wastewater would pass into soak pits (each approximately 100 cu. ft) within which it would gradually seep into the ground (Mackay 1931; Marshall 1931: Plate 43c). This drainage

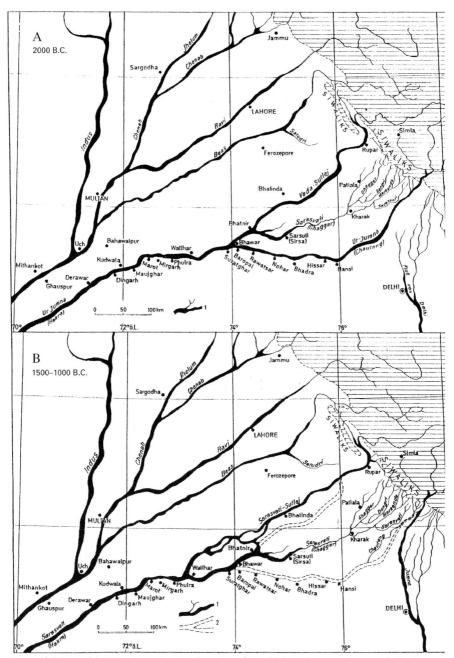

Figure 4.21a and b The rivers in the domain of the Hakra: Jumna, Sarasvati, Sutlej
A: flowing at 2000 BC; B: diverted/drying by 1500–1000 BC

system formed a network around the open wells (Gokhale 1959), and drain openings were often situated near well openings (Mackay 1931).

(Ewald 1991a:11)

Confounding their considerable efforts, the Harappans violated the iron rule of sanitation: waste and fresh-water cycles must be absolutely closed off from one another. Rigid demarcation of the cycles by engineering are what made such great public health advances possible in Britain during the nine-teenth century. Even in the twentieth century, with all its advances in medicine, this mode of supplying clean water remains the biggest single contribution to a population's health that can be made.

The consequences of cross-contamination, affecting the largest cities first and hardest, would then have been the explosive spread of illness, causing a high proportion of those affected to die in a matter of hours to days from the onset of the first symptoms. Ewald continues:

> It wouldn't take a statistician to notice hundreds of city-dwellers dying suddenly and the absence of this mortality in rural areas. Given the hysteria that typically surrounds epidemics and the tendencies to interpret pestilence as an omen or divine wrath, one could easily imagine wholesale emigration from a city no matter how much a centre of culture it was.

(ibid.:13)

Thus a frightened and diminished population seeks refuge in rural areas where human density and sanitary arrangements do not result in such epidemics. Attempts to recolonize the city meet with similar disastrous consequences, since public health engineering has not improved, and indeed may be compromised further by decay or flooding. After a number of tries at recolonization, the attempts cease and the cities are abandoned, the largest first.

This is a very powerful, parsimonious and persuasive model which accounts well for the run-down of a complex civilization to a village culture ('Great' to a 'Little' Tradition; see Chapter 6) in a short period of time like a century or so. Indeed, of all the proposed explanations for the surprisingly short span of Harappan high civilization other than by river drying – invasions, floods, climatic changes etc. – only this one of waterborne infectious diseases stands up to scrutiny, for it embraces all the archaeological evidence and violates none. Indeed, the possibility of cholera outbreaks was clearly recognized by Ernest Mackay, an excavator of Mohenjo-daro, who observed:

> Like all systems, however, the method of drainage adopted by the people of Mohenjo-daro had its limitations. In some cases it has

been found that a drain was placed much too close to a well, so that a certain amount of seepage from one to the other must inevitably have taken place. Perhaps this was not so serious a matter as it sounds, especially if the well was in constant use, for the people of the city were, no doubt, more or less immune to typhoid; *but a case of cholera in the vicinity of a well would have produced very serious results.*

(Mackay 1935:49–50; my emphasis)

Furthermore, recent work by Richard Meadow on faunal remains from Harappa indicates that streets could be used as organic garbage dumps and open sewers. In Street NS2355, Area C, Harappa Mound E South:

the olive green staining of the bone-rich deposits is an indication that organic sludge was a component of this stratum, suggesting that drains or sump pits were no longer operational in this part of the site when the deposits were formed and that sewage was allowed to run in the streets. Like Lot 3171, this concreted rubble may represent a kind of natural pavement formed as the street served traffic and, in this case, as an open sewer.

(Meadow 1991a:100)

This is all very suggestive but does not by itself indicate the presence of cholera, still less in epidemic proportions. Thus, although Ewald's cholera hypothesis is both parsimonious and precise, the evidence is all circumstantial, none is direct. Indeed, circumstantially, one could even postulate (though Ewald does not) that the later obsession with ritual purity as defining the place of a caste in the hierarchy, was a hypostatized recognition of the connection between impurities (waste) and devastating disease, something most visible in the tropics. This is sheer speculation, however, in contrast to which we do know that the rivers changed their courses and that the most densely settled one, the Sarasvati, diminished greatly in its flow during the time in question.

For populations dependent upon the natural flood regime of the river and thus not used to employing irrigation, a diminution in water volume would have been sufficient to undermine the agricultural regime, and that in relatively few seasons. In this (geological) model, the size and number of villages along the Sarasvati should diminish first, undermining the *raison d'être* of the cities and perhaps their food supplies. By contrast, in the epidemic model, the cities collapse first while the villages continue to thrive, augmented in number or size by the refugee populations. Only excavation of Ganweriwala and a number of associated village sites in Cholistan can settle this matter. Presently it looks as though Cholistan shrank first, with a retreat to the Indus. On the other hand, it could be argued that the density of villages along the Sarasvati represents a fugitive population from the cities. However, both settlement-size distributions and dating are against this (Mughal 1992a:108–9). It is certainly possible that the real body blow was the simultaneous action of the diminution of river flow coupled with or compounded by outbreaks of cholera or cholera-like diseases in the cities and major towns. Nonetheless, until major re-survey and excavation of the lost Sarasvati villages and Ganweriwala take place, the known vagrancy of the rivers in the area is the simplest and strongest explanation we have.

Mughal (1990c:64–5) sees two river vagrancy episodes as shaping Harappan Civilization. The first, taking place around 2500 BC, caused relocation and concentration of the Early Harappan (Kot Dijian) population, as a consequence of which Ganweriwala expanded to become a central focus. The second occurred around 2100 BC, at which time

> there was a reduction in the water supply through a channel from the Sutlej River causing a relocation of settlements into a much more restricted area than that of the Mature [Urban] Harappan. . . . It would therefore seem that in the case of Cholistan (or Hakra-Ghaggar region) in the Punjab, cultural and settlement changes in size, density and hierarchy were directly related to the hydrographical changes of the river regimes.
>
> (ibid.)

'Contingency and change' may thus have been denied by artefactual, built-environment and cultic continuities, as Miller (1985a) suggests, but Nature cannot be controlled by ideological means. The drying up of the Ghaggar-Hakra right at the civilization's centre cannot be denied by, nor would it respond to, any amount of purification or sacrifice, including the presumed asceticism of the 'priests'. Two responses are available to a population thus affected. One is to try to restore the status quo ante using technology, in this case by constructing long artificial irrigation canals from the Indus, which had extra water from the captured Sutlej. However, in contrast to Mesopotamia, which had over two millennia of incremental experience before the full urban period, India had no tradition of major canal construction. Leading water is one thing; hydraulic engineering is quite another. As Mughal observes:

> along the Hakra River where the original settlement pattern has not been seriously disturbed, no evidence of an ancient canal system has yet been found. It is possible that abandoned channels of the rivers were used to direct or store water for irrigation after the monsoon rain since a single cereal cropping was practiced until the Mature Harappan Period (Meadow 1989).
>
> (Mughal 1990c:35–6)

There was a very obvious alternative, however, and that was simply to move to areas that were unaffected. This was the simpler because village society was the basis of Harappan Civilization, and the role of urban centres was essentially integrative, not directorial. The production and reproduction of the 'little communities' were not dependent upon there being a high-level cognitive or material culture. Certainly no 'state coordination' or integration was required and neither was craft production skewed by elite demand. Accordingly,

> A considerable decrease in the number of settlements in Sind, Punjab (Pakistan) and Cholistan and a much higher increase in their number in Gujarat, Punjab (India), Haryana and north-western Uttar Pradesh during the Late Harappan phase can only be explained by large scale migration of Harappan populations from the former to the latter regions.
>
> (Misra 1984:473)

The cities on the Indus were abandoned not because that river was drying up, but because the society of which they were the foci simply changed its distribution and density and thus broke with tradition. Material production in the relocated villages could continue essentially as before, but overall social reproduction was profoundly affected and would need new structures. Of course, re-adaptation could be effected only on the basis of what went before.

High civilization by specialization

In the Early Harappan Period the degree of specialization undoubtedly intensified. Mughal characterizes the Early Harappan Period along the 480 kilometres he surveyed of the (now dry) Hakra river bed in Cholistan (the desert tract of the former state of Bahawalpur, now in Pakistan), as

> marked by an increase in the size and number of functionally articulated sites, at least as compared to the preceding Hakra Wares Period. There is a very sharp decline in the number of camp sites; 7.5% of the total during the Early Harappan period against 52.5% during the Hakra period. There is a slight increase (57.5%) in the frequency of purely settlement sites. But, the interesting change is an increase to 35% in multifunctional settlements, that is, those combining residential functions with specialized/industrial activities. In the Hakra Wares Period only 2% of the sites were of this type. This shift seems to be significant in terms of socio-cultural changes that occurred by the beginning of the Early Harappan period in Cholistan.
>
> (Mughal 1982:91)

Unfortunately, Mughal does not suggest what those changes might imply but observes that around 60 per cent of Early Harappan sites in Cholistan are less than 5 hectares in size, and that 25 per cent are medium sized, that is, range between 5 and 10 hectares. One site, however, is outstanding, that of Gamanwala, at 27.3 hectares the largest Early Harappan period site so far known anywhere in the Greater Indus Valley, and half the area of Harappa itself (65 hectares without cemeteries). Another northern early site is that of Jalwali at 22.5 hectares, and Mughal concludes that

> It is thus evident that during the Early Harappan period, large settlements – towns, if not large cities – emerged amidst a cluster of smaller settlements. This is a distinctive feature of Harappan settlement patterns, especially *in Cholistan, where original cultural patterns have remained largely intact.*
>
> (ibid., my emphasis)

This is due to the desertification of this part of Cholistan with the drying of the Hakra. However, most germane to the argument is the occurrence of such a high proportion of sites combining residential with specialist occupational functions at this formative period.

Although the ensuing Mature Period (post-2,500 BC) is best represented in the cities of the Indus, the Hakra sites were still flourishing, seen in a quadrupling of sites to 174, with no less than *two* of equal size to Mohenjo-daro: Ganweriwala (located between Mohenjo-daro and Harappa) at 85.5 hectares, and Rakhigarhi (Rakhi Shahpur), located on one of the ancient courses of the Ghaggar and extending over 80 hectares (Mughal 1990c:40). Thus

> the most striking aspects of the Mature Harappan period in Cholistan are: (1) a general shift of sites from the northeast to the southwest, around and beyond Derawar Fort, (2) an increase in the number (47.7% of the total), size and height of settlement sites . . . (3) a profusion of industrial sites (45.4%) and their clear separation from habitation areas. However, sites combining both residential and industrial functions (19% out of 47.7% total settlements) also occur. In the preceding Early Harappan Period industrial areas were located close to, but outside the residential area at fourteen sites or 35% of the total number in that period. Although this feature persists in the Mature Harappan Period, some industrial areas at this time were demarcated exclusively for craft activities such as the firing of pottery, bricks, small terracotta objects, the glazing of faience objects and the melting, if not smelting, of copper.
>
> (Mughal 1982:92)

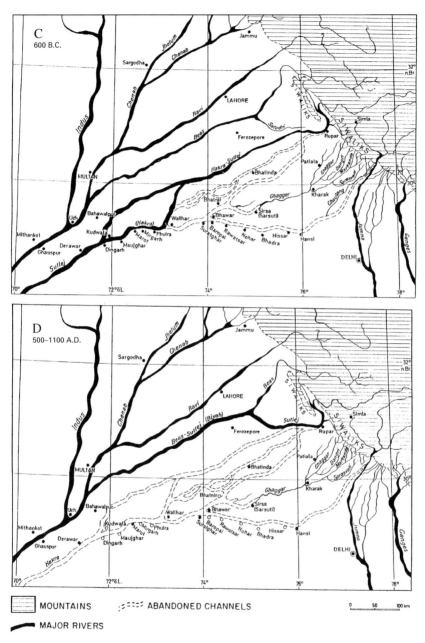

Figure 4.22c and d   The Sarasvati nexus: C: Ghaggar and Hakra-Sutlej at 600 BC, with Ghaggar system dead, D: Ghaggar-Hakra and Beas-Sutlej between 500 BC and 1100 AD, showing headwaters capture and system drying: entire Ghaggar-Hakra system now dry

Table 4.4 Number of sites in the Cholistan Desert by period

Approx. time range	Cultural association	No. of sites
4th millennium BC	Hakra wares (Jalilipur 1 related)	99
3100/3000–2500 BC	Early Harappan (Kot Diji related)	40
2500–2000/1900 BC	Mature Harappan (Mohenjo-daro and Harappa related)	174
1900 . . . 1500 BC	Late Harappan (Cemetery H related)	50
1100/1000–500 BC	Painted grey wares	14

Note: Some sites have more than one cultural phase.
Source: Mughal 1982:82 and 1990a:143

The numbers of sites of the various periods are shown in Table 4.4.

> The Mature Harappan sites were also concentrated around Yazman, an area where a channel from the Sutlej joined the Hakra River. Further eastward, there was only one site, Sandhanawala Ther, which represented both the Early and Mature Harappan periods. *It is evident that the Hakra stream east of Yazman ceased to be perennial, accounting for the abandonment of that stretch between Fort Abbas and Kudwala during the Mature Harappan period.*
>
> (1990a:149–51; my emphasis)

Kudwala, however, at 38 hectares in Late Harappan times (from 2100–1900 BC), functioned as the 'metropolitan centre' of an area that saw an increase in the number of camp sites (to 26 per cent of the total), a decline in the number of dedicated industrial sites and the retrenchment of manufactures back into the village – all strongly indicating de-specialization.

In the Late Harappan Period, then, population in Cholistan clustered nearer to the river, while sites of the Post-Harappan (or Painted Gray Ware) Period are located right in the river-bed itself, a starkly clear proof of drying. By this (Post-Harappan) time, with one single exception (Satwali, 13.7 hectares) all fourteen remaining sites are of less than 4 hectares. Indeed, three are of less than 1 hectare in size, while six are between 1 and 2 hectares, the other five ranging between 2 and 4 hectares (Mughal 1984:501). In the preceding Late Period, camp sites had increased to 26 per cent (against only 5.7 per cent in the Mature Period), while exclusively industrial sites account for only 18 per cent of the total. In this Late Period, settlements combining residential and specialized manufacturing functions are at 14 per cent of the total (as against 45.4 per cent of all sites during the Mature Harappan Period), with another 14 per cent representing purely habitation sites (ibid.:502).

Harappan Civilization did not so much collapse as devolve into another configuration. This necessarily had its own division of labour, but one rooted in what was known and established. The extent and density of exchange networks reduced to relatively localized ones that concentrated upon subsistence requirements (Bisht 1984:122).

Late newcomers

It seems a reasonable conjecture that a minority incoming population, especially if pastoralists as the Aryans predominantly were, would adopt the occupational pattern of a majority population in settled agricultural villages. There can be no doubt that the newcomers imposed themselves as dominant classes, but the peculiar elaborations of caste based on occupation could not simply be the outcome of a ruling class imposing itself.[10]

Berreman (1983:242–3) sees the caste system as emerging 'at the watershed between kin-based, unstratified, pre-state institutions of inequality and class-based, stratified state-organized institutions of inequality', as do I. This time has to be post Late Harappan, but with its full form emerging only after the Aryan invasion. Accordingly, the system's roots must lie in Post-Harappan 'Dark Age' social circumstances of 'coexisting, culturally distinct, largely endogamous groupings with perhaps a degree of economic specialization and interdependence within regions', as Berreman puts it. Encountering this, the

> Indo-Aryans placed themselves and those they could not dispossess of their land in the elite castes – those in the three 'twice-born' *varnas* at the top of the hierarchy – appropriating to themselves the land and labour of those they dispossessed. The latter, in turn, had little choice but to assume their assigned, economically enforced, and ritually endorsed social roles and statuses, to perform their assigned tasks, and to contribute the corvee (*begar*) labour, clientship [*jajmani*], rents, and taxes imposed upon them in the peasant economy of the emerging state.
>
> (Berreman 1983:242–3)

Contemporary ethnography should help confirm this, since here we have the strongest form of ethnographic inference ('analogy'), namely that which is 'direct-historic' or 'continuous' in the area of interest (Maisels 1990:4). One indication that we are dealing with continuities in culture, and not just in environment or subsistence practices, lies in evidence that in Harappan times 'girls were adversely stressed during growth and development due to the cultural practice of son preference/daughter neglect'. Lukacs

(1994:153) has established this pattern from clear evidence of dental pathology in the form of Linear Enamel Hypoplasia (LEH), which is the failure of tooth enamel to form properly during growth and development as a consequence of nutritional deprivation and/or serious illness. Significant LEH differences between the sexes were found on skeletons at Harappa itself (Lukacs 1992a; 1992b). The association of LEH with son preference/ daughter neglect is very strong, being supported by cross-cultural comparison. And son preference/daughter neglect is still the pattern in much of village India today.

PALAEOETHNOLOGY: KINSHIP TO CASTE

An evolutionary-transformative mechanism is needed to account for the emergence of caste society. The model below shows development from single or multi-clan villages to the caste system known historically. However, the conventional conception of the advent of caste (the four *varna* categories) is through a form of conquest theory. In it the Aryans, who arrived at the Indus region around the middle of the second millennium, were characterized by three social categories: warriors/aristocracy (*kshatriyas*), priests (*brahmins*) and the rest (*vaisyas*), which became a four-caste system on subjugation of the indigenous population, the *dasa*, incorporated as the fourth *varna* of cultivators (*sudras*). Some see the very term *varna*, meaning colour, taken in reference to the dark indigenes excluded from *dvija* (twice-born) purity, as supporting this view. Varnas, however, are just schematic categories. The everyday operational reality of 'caste' is as *jati* – sub-castes – with *jat* having the literal meaning of birth or species. Indeed, Fox (1969:28) declares that 'it is the *jati* or local endogamous group which is the foundation of the caste system'.

The process for the emergence of caste would in outline be thus:

> Clan villages → lineages specialize → clan name supplanted by occupational name (e.g. Smith, Tanner, Weaver, Barber, Potter) → specialized lineages relate through endogamy/non-competition with similar occupations in neighbouring villages → a common ritual and economic position emerges in a static society → castes (*jati*) have formed.

Indeed, in contemporary Hindu villages, such as the one in central India studied by Mayer (1960:161), 'Clans are said to have an origin contemporaneous with the mythical founding of the caste.' On the above model this would be an inversion of the evolutionary process, but it is the indigenous identity of clan and caste that is of interest. This transformation process may actually have been triggered by the Aryan incursion; or, much more

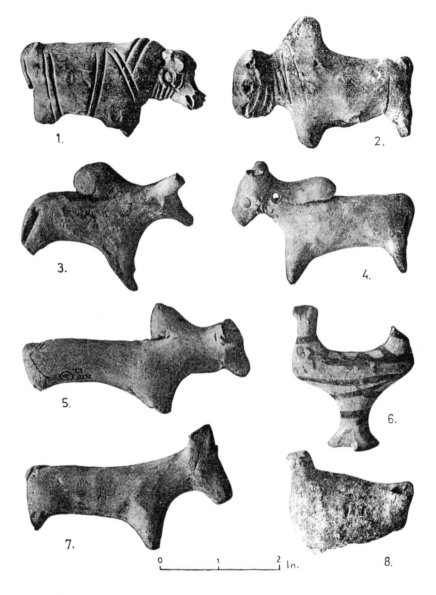

Figure 4.23 Terracotta animals, Harappan culture at Kot Diji. Note chicken.
Source: Khan 1965, Plate xxvi

251

likely, it was an ongoing evolutionary transformation that the invaders plugged into, putting themselves at the top of finely graduated strata, and justifying their position by an excessive concentration upon occupational/ritual purity. So we should see the *jati* system as emerging spontaneously upon Harappan devolution (post Late Harappan), with the Aryans merely imposing top and tail strata to the occupational layering already present. The other main Aryan input was to imbue the system with its obsession with ritual purity, a consequence of their own justificatory rhetoric ('twice-born' etc.).

The transformatory process (descent-derived, occupation-based integrative mechanism) certainly accords with the ethnographic record of the Hindu heartlands. As McKim Marriott reports of the old Hindu village of Kishan Garhi, located between Yamuna and Ganges rivers, 160 kilometres southeast of Delhi:

> At least 24 caste groups are represented locally; *each caste is perfectly exclusive in marriage*. There are 46 local lineage groups in Kishan Garhi, each wholly separate from every other in descent. There is no marriage inside the village within or among any of those groups. Daughters of the village move out and wives of the village move in at marriage, moving to and from more than a hundred other villages. Fifty-seven marriages currently connect Kishan Garhi with sixteen towns and cities. Half of the marriage ties of groups in Kishan Garhi connect them with places more than 14 miles away, while 5% connect them with places more than 40 miles distant.
>
> (Marriott 1955b:175; my emphasis)

In sum, 'families are inclosed within lineage groups and lineage groups are enclosed within caste groups' (ibid.:180).

CONCLUSION

So-called Indus Civilization (sometimes called 'Harappan Civilization') came into its 'Mature' or urban Phase in the middle of the third millennium, and by the time of Hammurabi of Babylon (1792–1750) had come to an end as a complex civilization. The last substantive contacts with Mesopotamia, to whom the Indus area was known as Meluhha, seem to have been in the early part of the preceding Isin-Larsa Period (2017–1763).

Indus Civilization in its developed form is the shortest lived of the seminal Bronze Age civilizations of the Old World. Nonetheless, as a civilization it is doubly remarkable: first, because it was the only complex society *of either Antiquity or the modern world*, that operated without social stratification and the state; and, second, in what must be a related phenomenon, because it was an agrarian society in which the villages were not oppressed by the towns. Doubtless the absence of royal or state capitals is significant in this; which is certainly not to say that towns and cities were absent, rather that they were not politically dominant.

Indus or Harappan Civilization is also the one that covered by far the widest area in the third millennium, exploiting a cultivable area approximately the size of France (544,000 square kilometres) from terrain over twice that extent. This is against an area of 33,657 square kilometres for the cultivable valley of the Nile, and about double that in Mesopotamia. Of the four originating civilizations considered here, the Harappan is the second most urbanized, as seen in the comparison made by Ratnagar on p. 188.

But the name Indus Civilization (which is used synonymously with Harappan) is a misnomer. It is so-called from the excavations initiated in the 1920s by Sir John Marshall, at the sites of Harappa and Mohenjo-daro located on the Indus river system. However, work in the last two decades has shown that those cities do not lie at the centre of maximum density of early village settlement, but rather at peripheries. This is especially true of Harappa, which stands in relative isolation and functions as a gateway city for exchanges with pastoralists and for the import of minerals such as carnelian and lapis lazuli from Afghanistan.

The greatest density of villages are clustered along a rivercourse east of but parallel to the Indus called the Sarasvati (the Ghaggar-Hakra drainage system) in Cholistan. Sarasvati is a major Hindu goddess representing abundance and nourishment. It is striking to see her fully clothed and bejewelled effigy being lowered into the now sacred Ganges to ensure those blessings. At the northern end of the Sarasvati village concentration lies the major site of Kalibangan, while at the southern end lies Ganweriwala, unexcavated. At 81.5 hectares, Ganweriwala is almost identical in size to Mohenjodaro (83 hectares) and significantly larger than Harappa (only 65 hectares). Both of the excavated cities are constructed of fired brick. By contrast it should be remembered that half a millennium earlier Uruk had reached 400 hectares and Shuruppak, one of about thirty city-states of early Sumer, reached 100 hectares at about the same time. Nonetheless, given the association of Ganweriwala with the originating village heartlands, when excavations belatedly take place there it may be more accurate to refer to Harappan Civilization as Ganweriwalan Civilization. Indeed, Shaffer and Lichtenstein (1989:123) point out that 'Harappan Culture represents a fusion of Bagor, Hakra and Kot Diji ethnic groups in the Ghaggar-Hakra Valley'. Sarasvati culture is thus the basis of Ganweriwalan Civilization.

That there are so few cities in such a large area of the Indus drainage and that none of them even attains 100 hectares in extent tells us a great deal about the nature of the civilization there. The most important points are that:

1 With the partial exceptions noted below, the cities contain no palaces or temples, only cultic facilities for fire and water on high platforms in the so-called 'citadel' areas, no doubt sources of ritual purification for the whole settlement.

2 The cities only contain a small fraction of the total population, who lived in villages.

3 Within the cities there are few disparities of wealth or power and this is reflected in the architecture of households; instead, differences in size are functional, reflecting family size.

4 Skeletal studies show no health disparities such as would indicate depressed or oppressed classes, but only male/female inequalities which are even present in hunter-gatherer societies (Maisels 1990:221–30).

5 The use of copper implements is very widespread and indeed standardized in form, indicating a general availability, something un-typical of other Bronze Age civilizations. In China, for example, bronze objects, especially tripods, are associated with only the most powerful lineages.

In sum, Indus Civilization is by far the most egalitarian of any of the pris-tine Old or New World Civilizations, and that by a long way and by any measure. This must be correlated with the archaeological absence of Harappan state power, which I have previously (1990:10) defined as 'central-ized social power deployed through specialised apparatuses'; where social power is the ability to make actors do what they would not otherwise do, by the threat of force, other sanctions (e.g. ostracism, excommunication) or inducements.

The fact is that Indus Civilization fits none of the established sociolog-ical or ethnographic models. Walter A. Fairservis, partly basing himself upon his own provisional decipherment of Indus graphs, hypothesizes that Indus Civilization remained at the sociocultural level of the chiefdom, failing to attain what he calls the 'second level of civilization', namely that characterized by 'higher abstract thought'. However that may be, in anthro-pological theory it is the state that is seen as the next advance in complexity, and indeed there is a distinct lack of evidence for the presence of a state at any, even the fully urban, stage of Indus Civilization.

Although H.-P. Francfort (1989:260) reports traces of canals that 'belong to different periods' from his team's work in Harayana and Rajasthan (respectively the areas north and south/southwest of Delhi), agriculture along the main courses of the Indus and Sarasvati Rivers was not by canal irri-gation. Damming and the use of localized canals occurred in the piedmont areas. But in the major river valleys, annual flooding was relied upon to renew fertility and to render the soil soft enough to sow seed into it without the long preparation required in Mesopotamia. In the Indus regime, the spate occurs between June and September, immediately after which wheat and barley are winter-sown *without ploughing*, as *rabi* crops for harvesting during March–April.

This is in contrast to the *kharif* (summer-grown, autumn harvested) crops, such as sesame and cotton, planted *at the beginning of inundation*, for harvesting at its close in the autumn. Rice is exclusively a summer crop (Meadow 1989b:68), but important summer-growth crops – rice (*Oryza sativa*) and finger millet/*ragi* (*Eleusine coracana*) – are not recorded in the Indus Valley proper until the Late Harappan Period, according to plant opal analysis at Harappa by Fujiwara *et al.* (1992). Richard Meadow observes that

> the 'millets' could be planted immediately after summer and, in frost-free areas, winter floods throughout the Greater Indus valley, thus enabling farmers to take advantage of situations where wheat and barley would have had only marginal changes of success. Similarly rice cultivation could be carried out in areas previously too wet for cereal agriculture, such a practice employing another agriculturally unused or under-utilized habitat. Another benefit particularly of 'millet' growing was the production of animal fodder. Zebu cattle are particularly well adapted to feeding in areas of marginal vegetation, but traditionally in South Asia today are fed 'millet' stalks and even grain from second-growth harvests.
>
> (Meadow 1989b:69)

The drying of the Ghaggar-Hakra system did not remove half the agricultural base, but two-thirds, putting society into a cycle of devolution during which castes emerged as the retrenchment of occupational specialization. Urban civilization had depended upon an organic division of labour; the *jati* system (of sub-castes) became its Dark Age transformation, like feudalism was that of the Roman Empire. With a shrunken agricultural base, the cities and their culture could not be sustained, and no cities existed in India until the first millennium BC, when they appeared in the Ganges area (cf. F.R. Allchin, 1992, 1995; Brockington 1993).

CHILDE'S CHECKLIST

1   *Cities that are 'more extensive and more densely settled than any previous settlement'.*
    The relative suddenness of the appearance of Harappa, Mohenjo-daro, Ganweriwala and Rakhigarhi, to name only the largest, and the nature of their street plans leave no doubt about an affirmative answer.
2   *Full-time specialists: craftsmen, transport workers, merchants, officials and priests.*
    The Harappan is the only civilization in which this proposition is

problematic. The state elite promote specialisms for their own sumptuary requirements and for reasons of state, e.g. chariotmakers and armourers, scribes and courtiers. Harappan full-time specialists obviously existed, given the quantity and high quality of pottery, figurines, copper artefacts and indeed the famous weights. Also, given that town-sized settlements possessed an acro-sanctum, the so-called acropolis manned most likely by professional priests, this area and its servitors had obviously to be built, maintained and provisioned. Nonetheless, the wealth of cultic and status artefacts associated with temples in other Bronze Age civilizations is not apparent in the Harappan. Other than the 'administrative' building at Mohenjo-daro, there is not a central secular institution, notably a palace or fortress, that would assume the role of direct surplus extraction and its disbursement to supporting specialists. On the contrary, the (limited) evidence suggests relationships between direct producers and institutions based on voluntary giving. If this is so, then some of the surplus could commission craft specialists. But more likely families, lineages or individuals would themselves commission works for temples and other public purposes.[11]

3 *Concentration of surplus.*
The figurine with the head fillet and trefoil garment has been interpreted as that of a divine king or priest king, but as discussed earlier the comparative evidence seems to rule this out. Neither is there any good evidence for a tithe or tax. Some form of communal labour built the public or cultic areas of the cities, but tithing, taxing or corvee imply systematic imposts, centrally controlled. There is no sign of the detailed tax investigations, censuses and inventories that are so marked in Egypt, for example. Some surplus was undoubtedly concentrated in Harappan society, but probably by voluntary contributions and cultural cooperation.

4 *Truly monumental public buildings.*
Childe's connection between surplus and monumentalism is certainly sound, but in Harappan society there is remarkably little monumental building as distinct from large utilitarian building. This, of course, reinforces the previous point about the seeming absence of a concentrating authority concerned to protect its position by overawing the populace.

5 *The presence of a ruling class, including 'priests, civil and military leaders and officials {who} absorb a major share of the concentrated surplus'.*
Everything does indeed turn on the presence of a concentrated surplus in the hands of a small elite. Again the absence of one is indicative of the absence of the other. No doubt there was a leading class, or rather, categories of people exercising leadership, such as priests, clan elders, etc.; but in the absence of a state apparatus which they command, such categories do not form a ruling class.

6   *Technical expertise, specifically systems of writing and numerical notation.*
The writing system, as so far known, consists of only short groups of characters or icons. Its extent, refinement and deployment seem far too limited to develop much in the way of abstract (i.e. non-craft) technical expertise, and with it the conceptual notation that would go beyond counting to mathematics. Indeed, the limited development of script and notation strongly reinforce the impression that no Harappan state existed. Elsewhere in the Old World the economic, administrative, political and ideological functions of writing were indispensable for focusing the emergent power of the dominating elite. Accordingly, writing makes the qualitative leap from potters' marks and other simple inscriptional techniques to a fully-fledged, flexible recording system when the elite institutionalizes its power as the state: centralized, transcendent and usually unchallengeable except by other states or strong factions within the elite.

7   *Exact and predictive sciences: arithmetic, geometry, astronomy and a calendar.*
So limited is our knowledge of Harappan Civilization that what sort of calendar was used is not known. There must have been one, but its degree of astronomic/mathematical sophistication is unknown. There may not even have been a single unitary calendar. In the light of what was said above, it seems extremely unlikely that there existed any degree of mathematical or scientific sophistication. What is known is that Vedic astronomy owed a great deal to Mesopotamian astronomy.[12]

8   *Full-time sculptors, painters or seal engravers.*
The examples already shown leave no doubt about the degree of specialism attained in representative art, particularly on seals. However, in this society, as has already been suggested, a broad swathe of specialists existed, and not merely palace or temple dependants. Indeed, like quality housing, such artefacts appear to have been available to all.

9   *Regular foreign trade, involving comparatively large volumes.*
There are surprisingly few items of demonstrably 'Harappan' manufacture to be found overseas, even in Mesopotamia, where the documentary evidence for trading links seems strong (cf. Ratnagar 1981). Clear instances do exist, such as the 'long-barrel cylinder beads' of carnelian excavated by Mackay at Mohenjo-daro (1938) and Chanhu-daro (1943) and previously identified by him (1929, 1931) in Mesopotamia at Kish and Ur, where they were found in Pre-Sargonic contexts. Even in this case, however, the number of items involved scarcely reaches double figures. Much more important than any such trade in artefacts was the introduction during the Akkadian period of sesame (*še.giš.ià/šamaššamū*) and water-buffalo (*Bubalus bubalis*) to Mesopotamia from Meluhha (Postgate 1992:171). Sesame became a fundamental part of the Mesopotamian agricultural regime – it grows right through the summer heat. Water-buffalo were not significant until a later period. Nonethe-

less, only trading functions can account for the number of Harappan settlements beyond, often well beyond, the Indus drainage basin, from Shortugai on the Oxus, in the Gomal and Zhob valleys, to the coastal port towns of the Makran.

There are settlements only explicable as having manufacturing/trading functions or ports like Lothal (Rao 1973) in Kutch, and the recently extensively excavated river port of Kuntasi. Presently 5 kilometres from the Arabian Sea, and in antiquity a tidal or estuarial port, Kuntasi lies on the other, western, side of the peninsula from Lothal, with Rojdi due south in the interior (cf. Possehl and Raval 1989). This area of Gujarat is rich in raw materials such as high-quality 'ball' clay (for faience as well as pottery), carnelian, chert, agate, chank shell and ivory (Dhavalikar 1992:80). More than a thousand microbeads of steatite were recovered at Kuntasi.

10 *Peasants, craftsmen and rulers form a community.*
This is truest of all for Harappan society where there are few if any signs of social stratification or indeed of the state as a dominant centre with palaces, temples and royal tombs. Points 11, concerning state religion/hegemonic ideology, and 12, on permanent state apparatuses, therefore become redundant.

Apart from the gender differences already noted, there is no evidence from skeletal remains of differential health status that would indicate superordinate and subordinate social classes. Lovell and Kennedy report

> low incidences of [dental] enamel hypoplasia and Harris lines in skeletal series from Harappan centres suggest[ing] that fluctuations in the food resource base may have been infrequent. No obvious distinction between social groups at these sites can be made on the evidence for interrupted skeletal growth and development (Kennedy 1978). These data are in accord with the absence of royal tombs and other archaeological indicators of preferential treatment of the dead in Harappan cemeteries.
> (Lovell and Kennedy 1989:91)

I postulate that Harappan society was constituted by occupationally specialized lineages and clans, producing a truly organic solidarity that operated regionally, spontaneously, without compulsion and therefore without a state. This accounts for the absence both of a dominant ruling centre and the extremes of power and wealth seen in the other formative Old World civilizations. This need not mean that formal coordination and leadership were entirely lacking, only that a coercive state serving a ruling class was absent.

The largest excavated centres, Harappa and Mohenjo-daro, seem to be functionally specialized to serve their regions and integrate with the broader society on an economic and cultural basis, not a politico-military-ideological basis. Thus I see Indus Civilization as an oecumene, or commonwealth, not a state-ordered society. Accordingly, it is the only complex society known to history that truly merits the name of 'civilization' in the proper, non-technical sense (Maisels 1993:205–6). This is the condition of serving the greatest good of the greatest number through advances in knowledge, civility and economic wellbeing shared by all.

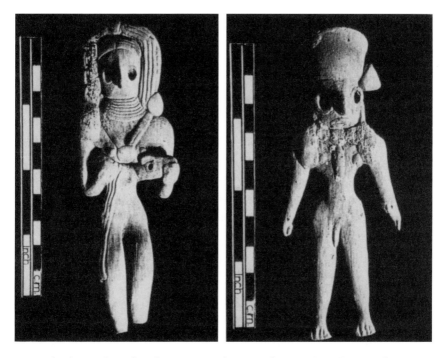

Figure 4.24 Female and male terracotta figurines from Mehrgarh, Period VII. (Dept of Archaeology and Museums, Karachi, Pakistan)

5

THE CENTRAL KINGDOM, ZHONG-GUO[1]

THE PLACE

The first thing to know about China is its continental proportions: 9,597,000 square kilometres against 10,614,900 square kilometres for Europe, 9,359,235 square kilometres for the United States and only 3,163,758 square kilometres for India. That is why Chinese always refer to areas of their country as provinces,[2] for some of them are the size of countries in Europe or states in North America with populations to match. They were, of course, separate and often warring states, so the provinces were instituted in 221 BC by the First Emperor, Ch'in Shih Huang Ti (Qin Shi Huang Di) 259–210 BC.

The present boundaries of China extend from the latitude of London (51°30′N) as far south (18°N) as Nouakchott in Mauretania, and from London as far east as the Ural Mountains and the Aral Sea, which line of longitude (61°E) is farther east than Oman on the Arabian Sea. Of course China has not always had this extent; Taiwan, for example, was first conquered in AD 1683. Nonetheless, from early historic times it has always had large populations organized into territorial states.[3] The present borders of China enclose a quarter of mankind's total numbers, an astounding proportion. According to computation from traditional accounts and (later) official censuses (Chen Zhucai 1985: 10–11), China's population in the first state period, that of the Xia, was an amazing 13.55 million in the twenty-first century BC. Ostensibly[4] this level had not increased even by Zhou times in the eleventh century BC (when the Zhou themselves were but a small fraction of the population). By the Warring States period (475–221 BC), population was estimated at 40 million, with millions of casualties per generation in the unceasing warfare. However, by AD 2 (Western Han Dynasty), 60 million had been reached (similar in magnitude to the Roman Empire), collapsing to only 7.7 million in AD 263 (the Three Kingdoms period: AD 221–280). By AD 280, first year of the Daikang reign of Emperor Wu Di of the Western Jin, population had more than doubled to reach 16 million, bounding upwards again to 46 million in Sui times (AD 589–617) and 52 million in the Tang (AD 618–906). In Yuan times (the Mongol dynasty, 1279–1368), 60 million was again reached, over 65 million in 1486 (Ming).

By 1741, 143.5 millions were recorded and a staggering 475 million in 1931, the twentieth year of the Republic of China. Population has nearly tripled since then to 1,008,175,288 in 1982 (State Statistical Bureau of the PRC), excluding Taiwan, Hong Kong, Macao and other islands. It now exceeds 1.2 billion, necessitating the 'one child per couple' population control policy. Population density in the eleven coastal provinces municipalities and autonomous region was 320.6 per square kilometre in 1982, an increase of 37.8 per cent from 1964. By contrast, the density of the eighteen inland provinces and autonomous regions (which include Inner Mongolia, Tibet, etc.), though only 71.4 per square kilometre in 1982, rose by 51 per cent from 1964 (Chen Zhucai 1985:3). Sichuan Province alone contained almost 100 million people in 1982, Henan 74.4 million, Guandong 59.3 million, Hunan just over 54 million, Hebei just over 53 million and Hubei 47.8 million (ibid.). All of those figures must now be increased.

The second major factor to know, namely the enormous range of geographical and climatic variation, is best caught by a distinction between north, centre and south. Though technically in the north, the Huanghe ('Huang Ho'), Yellow River, 4,840 kilometres long, called 'China's Sorrow' from its propensity to disastrous flooding, runs through the 'yellow earth' of the central plain (Zhong Yuan). Two rivers dominate the geography and history of China: the Huanghe in the north, already mentioned, and the Yangzi in the south. The Yellow River makes a great loop in its eastward passage from the mountains to the sea. In the northern part of this loop lies the Ordos Plateau, while the centre is cut by part of the Great Wall, a late feature. To the north of the loop lies Inner Mongolia and the Gobi Desert.

As ever, temperature (a function of latitude and altitude) and rainfall (a function of wind direction, distance from oceans and topography) are determinant.[5] Thus Mongolia in the 'north' – distant from oceans – is natural grassland, while Manchuria (Dongbei, the 'Northeast') is naturally forested. Actually the eastern margins of Asia originally provided the world's only complete and unbroken continuum of forest types, ranging from sub-arctic taiga (boreal forest: spruce and hemlock, birch and poplar) through cool-temperate mixed and warm-temperate deciduous broadleaf forest, to moist sub-tropical evergreen forests in southern China. Along the coast of the South China Sea was a thick band of moonsoon rainforest, extending westwards to Burma and northeast India. It is now largely confined to the Southeast Asian Peninsula. The archipelagoes (Malaysia, Indonesia) straddle the Equator and contain(ed) full-scale tropical rainforests. The Tropic of Cancer (23°32′N) cuts across the middle of Taiwan and crosses the coast just north of Hong Kong.

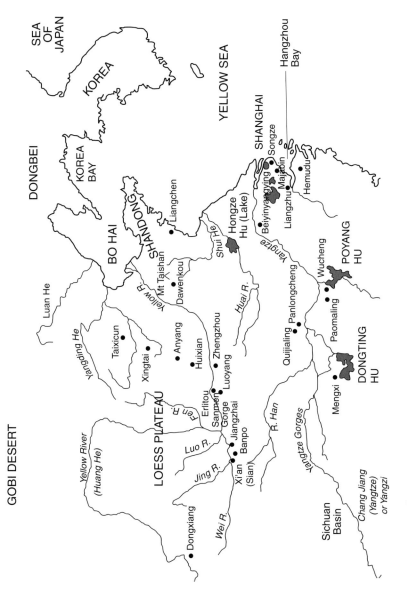

Figure 5.1 Outline map of China locating some key sites in relation to the major river systems

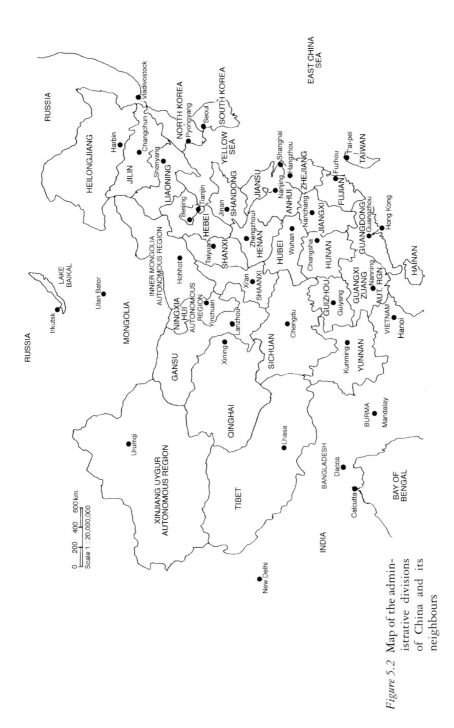

Figure 5.2 Map of the administrative divisions of China and its neighbours

A good idea of the diversity of biomes occurring in East Asia, which also includes steppe, desert (cold) and mountain vegetation (plus transitional mixes or ecotones), can be gained from the map shown in Figure 5.3.

To the immediate south of the Yellow River, so-called from the amount of silt it carries,[6] from around the 33rd parallel (the crest of the Jinling Mountains) is the region of deciduous woodland, lakes, wetlands and low ranges of hills. This is the classic rice country long associated with China, although the formative periods on the central plains in Shandong and the northeast, from the Neolithic to the early states and beyond, were dependent on dry grains, particularly the millets, foxtail and broomcorn. It is, however, in the south that the major rivers of China are grouped: (north to south) the Huai, Yangzi (Chang Jiang, 6,380 kilometres long) and the Hongshui/Xi Jiang (Pearl River) draining the extreme south are the main ones, all of which have tributaries and lesser rivers that make the Thames look like a brook. The course of the Yangzi is remarkable for

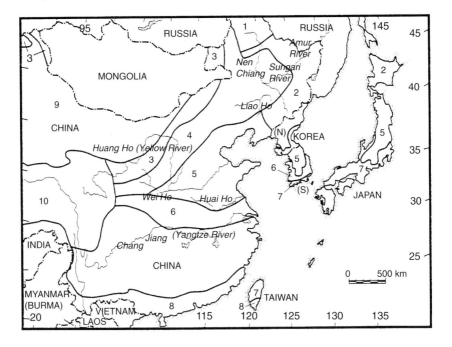

Figure 5.3 Vegetation zones of East Asia

Key: 1. boreal; 2. mixed conifer–deciduous; 3. steppe; 4. forest-steppe; 5. deciduous broadleaf; 6. mixed deciduous and broadleaf evergreen; 7. subtropical broadleaf evergreen; 8. tropical monsoon rainforest; 9. desert; 10. highland

Source: Crawford 1992:10

the number of large lakes its waters sustain. Virtually all the rivers of China (still) cause flooding, some disastrous. And despite many control works, one can even speak of a 'summer flooding season', or rather a summer flooding sequence.

The four major rivers flow west to east and do so because of the massive highlands to the west, which form the greatest mountain mass in the world, and include the Himalaya Range. The Yellow River *presently* flows into Bo Hai Gulf *north* of the Shandong (Shantung) Peninsula (in the past it entered the sea *south* of the peninsula) and the Yangzi empties into the East China Sea. In the triangular wedge of the Great Plains lying north, south and southwest of Shandong Peninsula (i.e. between Beijing, Hangzhou and Changsha), the physical barriers between the river valleys forming those 'plains' were mainly lakes and marshes.

The mountain massifs to the west point to the third basic thing that has to be known, namely that China is effectively cut off in East Asia, with easy access only to Japan and Korea, and to a lesser extent Southeast Asia (Indo-China). This is not to say that all communication westward is barred – after all, Buddhism was brought from India, and in about AD 112 the Silk Route to the Mediterranean opened – a Roman embassy arrived in China in AD 166. Nonetheless, contacts to or from mainland East Asia were difficult, intermittent or for long stretches non-existent. Its geography (and thus economic history) are utterly different from Europe, which is best regarded as a large peninsula with no natural barrier between it and the rest of Asia. Indeed, much of the history of Russia, Poland, Prussia and Central Europe has been determined by their location on plains extending into the heart of Asia with only the Urals between.

In marked contrast, the way westward from China is barred by deserts and even more by the world's highest and longest mountain massif, easily exceeding 4,000 metres in average elevation, and which, by intercepting the rain-bearing winds on such a broad front, generates most of Asia's great rivers.

The fourth basic point is really a consequence of the other three, namely that the geography and ecology of China, its great area and huge population induced a cultural orientation that was overwhelmingly inward-looking. China saw itself as the 'central kingdom' (Zhong Guo), effectively the centre of the world with the imperial capital as its pivot point (the 'pivot of the four quarters') around which turned heaven and earth with its lesser peoples and kingdoms (all called barbarians until they adopted Chinese lifestyles). The Emperor, the son of heaven, might graciously condescend to receive tribute from barbarians, but was certainly not disposed to reach out to make foreign contacts.

Geography thus plays a determining role not only in the earliest transition to agriculture in China but throughout its subsequent history.

Table 5.1 Principal cultivated plants of China

	North China	South China/Southeast Asia
Cereals	Broom-corn millet (*Panicum miliaceum*) Foxtail millet (*Setaria italica*)	Rice (*Oryza sativa*) Job's-tears (*Coix lacryma-jobi*)
Roots/tubers	Chinese artichoke (*Stachys sieboldii*)	Chinese yam (*Dioscorea batatas*) Taro (*Colocasia antiquorum*) Greater yam (*Dioscorea alata*) Yam (*D. esculenta*)
Legumes	Soybean (*Glycine max*)	Red beans (*Phaseolus angularis*)
Vegetables	Garlic (*Allium sativum*) Mallow (*Malva verticillata*) Knotweed (*Polygonum hydropiper*) Welsh onion (*Allium fisulosum*) Chinese cabbage (*Brassica chinensis, B.pekinensis*)	Amaranth (*Amaranthus mangostanus*) White gourd (*Benincasa cerifera*) Luffa (*Luffa acutangula*) Water spinach (*Ipomoea aquatica*) Lily (*Lilium tigrinium*) Manchurian water-rice (*Zizania latifolia*)
Fruit trees	Peach (*Prunus persica*) Chinese plum (*P. salicina*) Apricot (*P. armeniaca*) Hawthorn (*Crataegus pinnatifida*) Persimmon (*Diospyros kaki*) Chinese jujube (*Zizphus vulgaris*)	Oranges (*Citrus aurantium, C. sinensis, C. reticulata*) Kumquat (*Fortunella japonica*) Loquat (*Eriobotrya japonica*) Litchi (*Litchi chinensis*) Longan (*Euphoria longana*) Chinese olive (*Canarium pimela*)
Beverages and masticatories		Tea (*Thea sinensis*)
Fibre crops	Hemp (*Cannabis sativa*)	Ramie (*Boehmeria nivea*) Chinese jute (*Abutilon avicinnae*)
Other industrial crops	Mulberry (*Morus alba*) Varnish tree (*Rhus verniciflua*)	Tea oil (*Camellia oleifera*) Tung oil tree (*Aleurites cordata, A. fordii*)

Source: Based on H.L.Li, 1966
Source: Chang 1986:80

THE TIME

The Chinese was the latest of the seminal cultural centres to produce the state. State formation took place around 2000 BC and according to tradition was that of the Xia. It or some other early bronze regime flourished on fertile plains between the rivers Luo and Yi in central Henan, an area traditionally referred to as 'the wastes of Xia'. It may be that a seminal Xia state is real, as tradition has it, and can be identified with Erlitou sites and phases, of which well over a hundred are known.

On the other hand, a Xia state may be mythical, a product of political historiography (Falkenhausen 1993). State formation may then take place as late as the Shang. However that may be, complex and stratified society certainly had a long development in the Longshan Chalcolithic cultures of the Dawenkou (East Coast) ceramic tradition. Human sacrifice, ritual bronzes and scapulimancy are all present there (though by no means confined to it).

In the traditional scheme, the Xia state (traditional dates 2205–1760 BC) was supplanted by the Shang in 1760 BC when Tang, leader of the Shang, defeated the infamous King Jie of the Xia. Shang was conquered by the Zhou under King Wu around 1050 BC (1122 traditional). For the uncertainties of dating the conquest see Hsu and Linduff (1988:387–90). Shang hegemony (conquest) is now dated from the first part of the sixteenth century BC: at 1575 by Nivison (1983:562; for whom 1040 is the date of the Zhou conquest of Shang; cf. esp. pp. 568–80), and at 1554 BC by Pankenier (1981–82:21).[7]

The Zhou capital moved in 770 BC east to Luoyang from Xi'an and the Eastern Zhou commenced (and with it the extensive use of iron tools, including ploughshares). The remnants of Eastern Zhou hegemony were overthrown in 256 BC by the short-lived but unifying Qin regime, the ultimate victor in the struggle of the 'Warring States' (475–221 BC). Whereas the Zhou regime had been essentially feudal, predicated on ranked elite lineages with the king *primus inter pares*, this broke down during the Spring and Autumn Period (770–476 BC). What emerged during the subsequent Warring States period (between the state of Qin, the ultimate victor, and Qi, Yan, Qiao, Wei, Han and Chu) was the fully territorial state consolidated by mass mobilization. The individual family had now become the unit of responsibility to a state which regulated the lives of its subjects ever more closely and was, if possible, even more wasteful of their lives.

The political chronology of historical China is best seen in the dynastic/state sequence shown in Table 5.2, the background on Table 5.3.

It is a commonplace (especially for Han chauvinists – Thorp 1991) to remark on the continuities of historical China, but as we shall see, some continuities can indeed be traced all the way back to the widespread Yangshao Middle Neolithic. On the other hand, the present picture of the Neolithic or of any other period in China is far from complete or even comprehensive.

Table 5.2 Dynastic/state sequence of Chinese history

DYNASTY/period/states	DATES		
夏 Xia Dynasty	约前 21世纪 — 约前 16世纪 —	北 齐 Northern Qi	550–577
商 Shang Dynasty	约前 16世纪 — 约前 11世纪 —	西 魏 Western Wei	535–556
西 周 Western Zhou Dynasty	约前 11世纪 — 前 771	北 周 Northern Zhou	557–581
周 Zhou Dynasty · 东 周 Eastern Zhou Dynasty	前770–前 256	隋 Sui Dynasty	581–618
春 秋 Spring & Autumn period	前770–前 476	唐 Tang Dynasty	618–907
战 国 Warring States	前475–前 221	后 梁 Later Liang	907–923
秦 Qin Dynasty	前221–前 207	后 唐 Later Tang	923–936
BC 汉 西 汉 Western Han	前206–公元 24	五 代 Five Dynasties · 后 晋 Later Jin	936–946
AD Han Dynasty · 东 汉 Eastern Han	25–220	后 汉 Later Han	947–950
三 国 Three Kingdoms · 魏 Wei	220–265	后 周 Later Zhou	951–960
蜀 汉 Shu Han	221–263	宋 Song Dynasty · 北 宋 Northern Song Dynasty	960–1127
吴 Wu	222–280	南 宋 Southern Song Dynasty	1127–1279
西 晋 Western Jin Dynasty	265–316	辽 Liao Dynasty	916–1125
东 晋 Eastern Jin Dynasty	317–420	金 Jin Dynasty	1115–1234
南 朝 Southern Dynasties · 宋 Song	420–479	元 Yuan Dynasty	1271–1368
齐 Qi	479–502	明 Ming Dynasty	1368–1644
梁 Liang	502–557	清 Qing Dynasty	1644–1911
陈 Chen	557–589	中 华 民 国 Republic of China	1912–1949
南 北 朝 Northern and Southern Dynasties · 北 朝 Northern Dynasties · 北 魏 Northern Wei	386–534	中华人民和国 People's Republic of China	1949 成立
东 魏 Eastern Wei	534–550		

Source: *Chinese–English Dictionary* 1978:972 (Beijing). *dates to 771 BC are millennial approximations

A striking example of the major gaps in our knowledge has been the discoveries at Sanxingdui, 40 kilometres northwest of Chengdu, the provincial capital of Sichuan, China's most populous province. The site, which covers 17 square kilometres overall, includes a large city wall with buildings, pits and tombs inside. The walls, forming a rectangle against the southern bank of the Yazi River, 'were begun during the second phase of the development of Sanxingdui, that is, around the time of the Erlitou period (*c.*1700–1500 BC) in Henan, and they protected a town of 2.6 square kilometres until it was abandoned about 1000 BC' (Zhao 1996:233).

The pits contain, in addition to pottery, objects of jade, gold, stone and bronze, plus cowrie shells, more than 60 elephant tusks and over 3 cubic metres of burnt and broken animal bones. The presence only of exceptional items and the absence of ordinary ones strongly suggest the pits were ritual features. Indeed, the whole area may be a ritual centre.

Actually the site was first recognized in 1928 when a number of jade objects were discovered there (Feng and Tong 1979:21). In 1980–81 eighteen house foundations, three ash pits and four tombs were found. Although neither coffins nor burial objects were discovered in the tombs, Carbon 14 and seriation methods were used to date ceramics and establish a chronology for the site, extending from 2700 to 1000 BC (Ge and Linduff 1990:506). There are four phases. The first, between 2700 and 2000 BC, is approximately contemporary with the (Chalcolithic) Longshan of the Yellow River Basin. The second and third, between 2000 and 1500 BC, are roughly contemporary with Xia and early Shang dynasties, while the fourth, dated 1500 to 1000 BC, is broadly contemporary with Shang and early Zhou developed Bronze Age states.

The first phase is artefactually characterized by *guan*, jars of simple shape and decoration, plus *dou*, a high-stemmed goblet with a circular foot (Ge and Linduff 1990:506). There is a sharp change from first to second phases: *guan* with small pointed bottoms appear; a *shao* or ladle with birdhead handle; a thin-necked *hu* and a bugle-shaped vessel. Changes also occur in the shape of the hollowed out *dou* (ibid.) No discovery of bronze or gold has yet been reported from the first and second phases. In the third phase, shapes of the *guan*, *du* and *shao* further diversify. While cordmarked designs still dominate the pottery in this phase, some Central Plain derived motifs, notably the *ruding* and *yunlei*, appear (ibid.).

In the summer of 1986 two large rectangular pits were opened in the southwest quadrant of the town. Pit no. 1 (the more southerly) is 1.64 metres deep, 3.48 metres wide and 4.64 metres long, a ratio of 9:6:3 (Zhao 1996:234). This pit, the sides of which were in good order,

> was filled in with earth compacted in layers, the middle one containing a high proportion of burnt bones, probably of animals sacrificed by burning. The floor of the pit was covered with ritual jades such as various sceptres, known by their later names of *zhang*, *ge*, *fu*, *gui*, and *zuo*, ritual bronzes of the *zun* and *lei* types, and bronze heads and masks, intermingled with a few ceramic vessels. Some heads and other articles, such as a rod, a tiger and a face protector, are decorated with gold leaf. This pit has been dated to the end of the second phase at Sanxingdui, *c.*1300–1200 BC.
>
> (ibid.)

Pit no. 2 lies 30 metres southeast of pit 1 and is somewhat later, perhaps 1200–1100 BC. Also rectangular, it is almost identically deep, at 1.68 metres. However, its proportions are approximately 10:4:3, with a width of 2.3 metres and a length of 5.3 metres.

> This pit was filled with yellowish soil and the finds were distributed in three layers. The top layer contained over sixty elephant tusks, while the middle layer yielded the large bronze items such as the complete standing figure, the human-like heads, the mask, the tree and the ritual vessels [all brilliantly illustrated in Rawson 1996]. In the bottom layer were jade and stone implements, jade blades and discs, small animal masks, small bronze birds and animals, and seashells.
>
> (ibid.)

Both the number and variety of pit finds are remarkable. In pit 1 more than 300 artefacts were found; in 2 more than 600 objects of bronze, gold, jade, ivory, stone and pottery. As already stated, pits also contained burnt animal bones and shells, the bones burnt and broken before being put into the pits. Although all the objects were placed in the pits in an orderly manner, the bronzes too show evidence of burning. All of this may be evidence of *liaoji* or the 'Burning Ritual' used to worship/propitiate hills, rivers and earth, as recorded in Shang oracle bones (Ge and Linduff 1990:507).

From pit 2, three bronze trees were reconstructed, approximately 1, 2 and 4.2 metres high, the last the 'tallest bronze sculpture contemporaneous with the Shang' (Zhao 1996:238). They have nine branches with nine fruits, leaves and nine birds perching. The birds have large, curved, toucan-like fruit-eating bills, quite different from the bronze eagle heads also found in this pit and discussed below. Perhaps the trees represent the 'tree of life', or are particularly sacred. The largest has kneeling figures round its base. (The largest is illustrated in Rawson 1996b:19; bird-in-tree detail in Zhao op. cit.:237.)

Over 40 highly stylized human heads were found in both pits. The (comparatively) naturalistic 'heads' (with necks) wear a variety of hairstyles, including pigtails, and some have headgear. The 'faces' by contrast are 'fantastic', with flattened tops to the head, no hair or headgear (or necks) and grossly exaggerated features: huge wing-like ears, cylinders for eyeballs, etc.

Most of the 'heads' facial features are shared by a bronze standing statue, arms upraised to chest and head height for the loop hands to hold a (missing) elephant tusk (probably). The stunning figure, with columnar body and trunk-like lower legs and feet, is 172 centimetres high and stands on a decorated four-legged stool on a plinth, together 90 centimetres high. Thus the full height is 262 centimetres and the total weight more than 180 kilo-grams! Such striking figures look like bronze totem poles. This association is reinforced by the presence of bronze heads (one 43.3 centimetres high, socketed and drilled for attachment, the other a bell) representing what must be eagles from their powerful, recurved raptor's beaks and large, well-delineated eyes. Another bronze, only 12 centimetres high, shows an entire, though highly fanciful bird, perching. The facial features of this perching bird are almost identical (though much reduced in scale) to the faces on the columnar figures ('totem poles'), strongly suggesting that eagles here play a significant mythological role, perhaps as the archetypal birds of the mountains. Sichuan is surrounded by mountains and Chengdu, in the far west, is close to the mountain front.

Other, apparently earlier and similarly sized pits, though less spectacular in their contents, have been found elsewhere. Examples are Gaopianxiang to the west of Sanxingdui and in the north of Sichuan Province at Mayangxiang in Yanting county. In the latter a set of ten jade *bi* discs was discovered. At Gaopianxiang, lozenge-shaped jades, axes (*fu*), stone spear-heads, knives and a bronze plaque with animal mask and geometric patterns in turquoise inlay were found (ibid.:235).

The 'heads', 'faces', 'figures' and much else are unique to Sanxingdui, demonstrating that a complex Bronze Age society arose upon an indigen-ous basis far to the west of the so-called Central Plains. This was the first suggestion of an early Bronze Age culture contemporary with and at least as advanced as the Shang, but 1,000 kilometres distant. Indeed, its bronze statuary is larger, finer and much more arresting than anything from the Shang. What are the antecedents of this remarkable culture and what became of it? Is it ancestral to Early Shu civilization, as Yan Ge (1989) has suggested? Why are the finds smashed and mixed up in sacrificial pits or dumps? And why is there no mention in the 'classical' texts? Zhongyuan-centrism, lack of communication, or just the limited development of the script for narrat-ive purposes in the Shang period may be the answer. Given the extent of the archaeological region and the fact that archaeology is not even a century old in China, such discoveries are scarcely surprising. Major surprises are thus guaranteed for decades to come.

'Mesolithic'

This is a category used by Chinese archaeologists for sites that seem to be permanent but which are transitional from hunting and gathering, upon which there is still heavy reliance. Agriculture is still in its infancy and essentially supplementary at this stage.

There are at least three such groups known: Cishan in Hebei Province, Peiligang Culture south of the Yellow River in central Henan, and the Laoguantai Culture in the Weishui valley of Shaanxi. Cishan has three dates that, calibrated, range between 6005 and 5794 BC. Calibrated dates for the Peiligang Culture site of Beigang in Egou range between 5916 and 5737 BC (Rodwell 1984a:56), remarkably close to the Cishan dates.

The Cishan type-site can stand for all, though Peiligang is also discussed below. It is located in the foothills of the Taihang Mountains, on a terrace of the Ming River 20 kilometres southwest of Wuan, the county town of Hebei Province. The present climate is one of hot humid summers (30–35°C) and cold dry winters with temperatures below freezing. Annual rainfall is low and yet winter wheat, millet, cotton and kaoliang are presently grown. However, evidence of the palaeofauna, which are subtropical, indicates a warmer and wetter regime in the sixth millennium, when the environment at Cishan would have been broad-leaved forest and marshy river valley (Rodwell 1984a:59).

Wild animal remains identified by Zhou Ben Xiong (1981) include: moles, hares, monkeys, badgers, masked civets, leopards, sika deer, red deer, David's deer, roe deer, water deer, mountjack, short-horned oxen, wild boar, wolves, bean goose, turtle, carp and bivalves. With six related species favouring rather different wooded habitats present around the site, deer remains were the most common (Rodwell 1984a:57). This heavy emphasis on deer is a reminder of a similarly heavy reliance on gazelle in the Levant. From the fact that all stages of antler growth were represented on site, Zhou reckons that the site was occupied year-round.

From measurements of body, jaw and tooth size, Zhou assesses the dog to have been domesticated and pigs also. Their lower third molars had similar dimensions to the domesticated pigs at Yangshao sites. Pig figurines dating to this period have been found at Peiligang sites (ibid.:59). Many chicken bones occur at Cishan. Zhou compared spurred and non-spurred metatarsals with those from a range of pheasants, jungle fowl and modern domestic chickens. He found them to be larger than those of Red junglefowl (*Gallus gallus*) but smaller than those of modern Chinese domestic chickens (which are large and heavy in bone), leading him to conclude that the birds were most likely at an early stage of domestication (ibid.:60).

Wild nuts and fruits were gathered, including walnuts (*Juglans regia*), hazelnuts (*Corylus leteraphylea*) and hackberry seeds (*Celtis bunseana*).

Eighty pits, round, rectangular or irregular, were found, some rectangular ones over 5 metres deep (An Zhimin 1980:37). They contained heaps of rotted grain ranging from 30 centimetres to 200 centimetres deep (ibid.:61). This was identified as domesticated foxtail millet (*Setaria italica*) whose wild ancestor is reckoned to be *Setaria viridis* (de Wet cited in Rodwell 1984a:61).

Logically enough, sickles were found at the site, in addition to footed querns, grindstones and narrow, flat and elongated stone spades with two convex edges (Rodwell op. cit.). Three-legged bowls are present as are double-lugged jars and wide-mouthed pots in a range of low-fired, hand-thrown pottery producing coarse-textured walls of uneven thickness. Patterns were either comb impressed or cord-marked, though there was some painted pottery (ibid.).

The pottery, grinding equipment and the existence of the classic 'Yangshao' domesticates complex of millet, (dog), pig and chicken, all suggest that 'Mesolithic' is an inappropriate designation for the likes of Cishan, and that it actually represents the Early Pottery Neolithic of the region.

THE NEOLITHIC CLUSTERS

More Neolithic sites are known in China than in the rest of the world put together! However, relatively few have been properly studied and published, though some have been made into museums. What is clear is that there existed regionally evolved Neolithic cultures across what became China, and on into Indo-China. Within China, the key formative traditions are the Yangshao of the northern interior and the Dawenkou of the coastal areas. The latter originated the Late Neolithic/Chalcolithic Longshan complex which became the successor tradition to Yangshao.

Yangshao

The most widespread and best known of the Neolithic cultures after 5000 BC is the Yangshao of the middle Yellow River valley in the modern provinces of Shanxi, Shaanxi, southern Hebei, the western half of Henan, the eastern half of Gansu, and the eastern portion of Qinghai. Yang Shao village in Mianchi County, western Henan Province, was excavated by J.G. Andersson in 1921. Often referred to as the Painted Pottery Culture, red clay is hand formed and painted while still drying, before firing at temperatures between 1000 and 1400°C. Most common forms are jars and deep bowls with designs in red or black, as shown from Lanzhou, Gansu (Fig. 5.4 and Fig. 5.5). They are obviously not utilitarian wares.

There are two stages of Yangshao Culture. The earlier, dating from around 5000 BC and concentrated in the area of the Wei River, is called Banpo type; the later, the Miaodigou type. 'The main Banpo pottery types are bottles with hole mouths and pointed bottoms, coarse grit-tempered pots with grooves around the vessel and cord impressions, bowls and basins painted with rectilinear geometric designs, or with fish, deer, or human faces in black colour' (Zhang 1985:32). Indeed, the later 'western' Yangshao of Gansu and eastern Qinghai, especially those centred on the Tao River valley (including Majiayao, Banshan and Machang), contain primitive metal implements.

The core of the Yangshao distribution (centred on Xi'an and extending eastwards into Henan Province, westwards to Baoji) is identical to the known area of distribution of the earlier Peiligang and related Neolithic cultures, and the descent of Yangshao from those cultures is unmistakable.

Figure 5.4 Gansu Yangshao: red pottery amphora with whorl design in black

There is even clear indication that some of the regional phases of Yangshao directly descended from the regional clusters of the earlier Neolithic. Yangshao is, then, a generalizing name for a cluster of regional/sequential Middle Neolithic cultures: Banpo, Miaodigou, Xiwang cun, Hougang and Dasikong (Wang 1988–9:13). Yangshao in Gansu Province (*c.*3500–*c.*1500 BC) is later than in central parts, but there is a temporal overlap of about half a millennium.

'Longshan' is a portmanteau term for a range of late east-coast Neolithic cultures (the Dawenkou tradition). Most confusingly, 'Longshan' is also

Figure 5.5 Gansu Yangshao: red pottery jar painted with eight groups of rhomboids in black; neck decoration and saw-edged bands are in olive green

applied to interior Yangshao successor cultures under strong east-coast influence: the Henan, Shaanxi and Gansu 'Longshan', represented respectively at such sites as Hougang II, Kexingzhuang II and Qijia.

Table 5.3 is an outline chronology covering the regional Neolithics and Chalcolithics through to the end of the Han period.

Yangshao sites are densely distributed on the lower loessic terraces along the banks of the three major rivers of the north-central region: Yellow River, Wei River and Fen River or, to be even more precise, along the tributaries to those three major rivers. It is impossible to overstate the importance to Chinese culture/history of drainage basins, and the silty, fertile, easily worked loessic soils, which are aeolian (wind-deposited) in origin and subsequently cut (often very steeply) or eroded by watercourses. South of the Huai the most important soils are alluvial, and the key crop is rice.

On the northern plains the Yangshao phases (with over fifty Carbon-14 dates) extend from 5150 to 2960 BC calibrated (An Zhimin 1982–3:54; uncalibrated 4515–2460 BC). Prior to *c.*5000 BC the Early Neolithic cultures

Table 5.3 Outline chronology: Neolithic to Han

Neolithic and Chalcolithic	*c.* 6000–*c.* 1700 BC
North-eastern China	
Xinglongwa	*c.* 5000 BC
Chahai	*c.* 4500 BC
Zhaobaogou	*c.* 4500–*c.* 4000 BC
Hongshan	*c.* 3500–*c.* 2500 BC
North-central China	
Central Yangshao	*c.* 5000–*c.* 3000 BC
Gansu Yangshao	*c.* 3500–*c.* 1500 BC
Eastern China	
Dawenkou	*c.* 4500–*c.* 2500 BC
Longshan	*c.* 2500–*c.* 1700 BC
South-eastern China	
Hemudu	*c.* 5000–*c.* 4500 BC
Majiabang	*c.* 5000–*c.* 4000 BC
Songze	*c.* 4000–*c.* 3000 BC
Liangzhu	*c.* 3500–*c.* 2500 BC
South-central China	
Daxi	*c.* 5000–*c.* 3000 BC
Qujialing	*c.* 4000–*c.* 3000 BC
Shijiahe	*c.* 2500–*c.* 2000 BC
Erlitou period	*c.* 1700–*c.* 1500 BC
Western China	
Sanxingdui	*c.* 2700–*c.* 1000 BC
Great dynasties	
Shang	*c.* 1500–*c.* 1050 BC
Erligang period	*c.* 1500–*c.* 1300 BC
Anyang period	*c.* 1300–*c.* 1050 BC
Western Zhou	*c.* 1050–771 BC
Eastern Zhou	770–221 BC
Spring and Autumn Period	770–475 BC
Warring States Period	475–221 BC
Imperial China	
Qin	221–206 BC
Han	206 BC–AD 220
Western Han	206 BC–AD 9
Xin	AD 9–25
Eastern Han	AD 25–220

After: Rawson 1996a:284

were highly localized, such as the Peiligang. This site on the middle reaches of the Huanghe, near Xinzheng, south of Zhengzhou, was discovered only in 1977. At Peiligang

> there are polished stone implements . . . including 'spades', sickle-like objects, and milling stones, suggesting the use of cereal grasses. There is pottery – red, coarse, mostly plain, occasionally comb-impressed or rocker-stamped – in the form of jugs, jars, bowls, and *ting*-tripods. There is no stratigraphic evidence at the site for the culture's great antiquity, but one carbon-14 date of 7885+–480 bp (based on half-life of 5730+–40) has been determined. Another site that has yielded similar pottery has been reported from Cishan in Wuan in southern Hebei, and there two carbon dates of similar antiquity (7355+–100 and 7330+–105 bp) corroborate the early Neolithic status of cultural assemblages of this kind.
>
> (Chang 1980:284–5)

Like all later rural regimes in China, Yangshao villages were overwhelmingly agricultural, arable not animal based. Ho (1977:455) for instance, speaks of 'the Chinese agricultural system [as being] lopsided in favour of grain production at the expense of animal production'. The principal grains were foxtail millet, *su* (*Setaria italica*) and broom-corn millet (*Panicum miliaceum*), which, with its two subspecies, *shu* and *chi*, was the more important (Ho 1977:437). They were cultivated with digging sticks, hoes and spades, the deep loose soil requiring nothing more complex. Grain storage was in pottery jars and prepared with grinding stones.

Additionally, the seeds of chestnut, hazelnut, pine and Chinese hackberry trees were gathered, indicating the presence of temperate woodlands. Then, as now, anything that could be caught was eaten, whatever the size of the fauna: Chinese bamboo rat, mole rat, macaque (monkey), badger, racoon, fox, brown bear, wild boar, elaphure, musk deer, water deer, turtles, fish, snails, molluscs, leopard, wild horse, rhino, antelope, rabbit and marmot. This long list of prey is not found at any one site but is composite of finds from several.

The importance of fish, however, is indicated by the Yangshao decorative elements on pottery from the Banpo site at Xi'an, Shaanxi, as shown in Figure 5.6.

The most important domesticated animals were dogs and pigs, whose bones have been found at almost every site. Cattle, sheep and goats were present, but again, then as now, were not very important. This indicates that a type of Neolithic agriculture set in early, which, once established, basically did not alter for seven millennia (despite the incorporation of additional cultigens). There must be eco-cultural reasons for this, despite or because of the fact that early Yangshao villages employed a form of

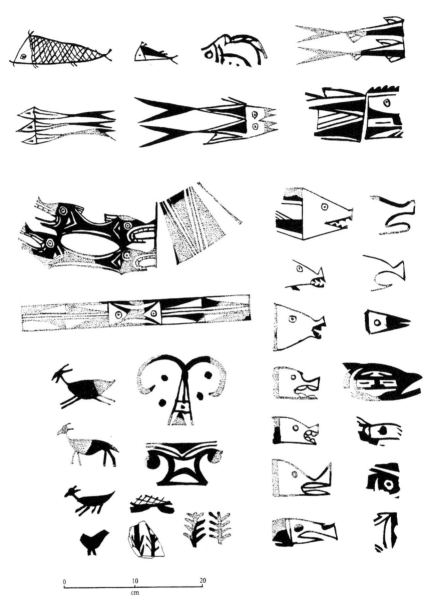

Figure 5.6 Yangshao decorative motifs, predominantly fish, from Banpo village, Xian, Shaanxi Province

Source: Chang 1977c

shifting cultivation. Villages were identical in layout and from 50,000–60,000 square metres in area, because minimally nucleated. In the area of the historic and modern city of Xi'an, where the Wei River with its many tributaries approaches the Yellow River, there are scores of Yangshao villages, including Jiangzhai, Beishouling and Banpo.

The last mentioned, Banpo, is the earliest phase of Yangshao. In 1958–59, Zhong-pei Zhang excavated a cemetery of this period at Yuanjunmiao in Shaanxi Province. It contained 51 graves arranged in six rows oriented north-south. Pottery enabled 46 of the graves to be sequenced chronologically, 18 in the first period, 17 in the second and 11 in the third. The entire cemetery is divided into a Section (I) running east to west, from the first to the third row (plus M428 at the end of the fourth row), while Section II includes the fourth to sixth rows. The graves in those two sections are so arranged that dates of the graves become more recent from north to south in the same row and from east to west in different rows (Zhang 1985:20).

Collective tombs containing up to three generations of adults of both sexes and children of both sexes account for two-thirds of the total graves. However, in terms of numbers, the overwhelming majority of the dead, 92 per cent, were buried in collective tombs. The numbers in each range between two and twenty-five, with more than four occupants in the majority of cases. Burials are overwhelmingly secondary. An example are the burials in Tomb M405, as shown in Table 5.4.

The two groupings seem to represent two clans, perhaps operating a moiety system of spouse exchange. Within each clan, each collective tomb seems to represent a single lineage, the different numbers present a reflection of the depth and economic/demographic success of the particular lineage (see Appendix A). However, each lineage has its members buried by minimal

Table 5.4 Three-generation tomb (M405) at Yuanjunmiao

Burial number	Sex	Age	Burial type
1	Male	Adult	Secondary
2	?	7+	Secondary
3	?	15–18	Secondary
4	Female	30	Secondary
5	Male	40	Secondary
6	Male	30	Secondary
7	Female	50	Secondary
8	Male	18	Secondary
9	Male	40	Secondary
10	Male	30	Secondary
11	Female	30	Secondary
12	?	c.10	Primary

lineage, that is, by family. There are no indicators of social stratification present. There is, however, evidence of differential prestige or ranking, and for once this does not attach to men.

> Out of 10 men's single or collective tombs there are 6 tombs with less than four pieces of burial pottery in each; there are only four tombs which have more than six pieces, and the owners of those tombs were males over 40 years old. In 10 women's tombs, single and collective, there are nine graves with more than six pieces of burial pottery in each. It is thus clear to me that women's positions were generally higher than men's.
>
> (ibid.)

Also some girls were accorded rich burials (beads, hairpins, knives) while no boys were; and, at least as important, some girls were buried according to adults' customs, namely they had a tomb of their own (M429 with two girls having a special red clay floor). This in contrast to the usual Banpo burial practice for children, which is in jars, pots, bowls and basins placed around the houses (ibid.:33).

Grave M420 is a collective tomb containing a mother with her two daughters: 'There are up to 25 pieces of pottery in the tomb, the most found in any tomb in the cemetery, and this tomb is the richest tomb of Banpo type found so far' (ibid.:31). Zhang hypothesizes that the reason why girl number 3 in tomb M420 received such a rich burial is due to her mother's wealth and high position in the family/lineage. From this he is drawn to the conclusion that the social structure we see here is 'matriarchal'.

In twentieth-century anthropology such a concept (here deriving from L.H. Morgan) has long been reinterpreted as matriliny, of which there is a strong and a weak form. In the weak form, descent is simply traced through the female line, mother to daughter succession. In the strong form, not only is descent traced through the female line, but real property is vested in females: houses, the control of certain lands and other resources. Here the permanent unit is the mother and her daughters in the maternal home and lands, rights to which the matrilineal unit holds exclusively. It is permanently retained and cannot be acquired by spouses. In the weak form, by contrast, power and property are effectively vested in 'mothers' brothers', who thus wield male power even though descent is traced through females, who may still hold important rights.

It is the strong form of matriliny that Zhang (ibid.) sees in the mortuary data, and it is hard not to agree with his interpretation. Such clear archaeological information is very rare and it lends itself to no other really plausible interpretation concerning social structure.

In terms of the relationships between a Yangshao cemetery, village and situation, Jiangzhai, excavated in 1972–79 and 15 kilometres east of Banpo,

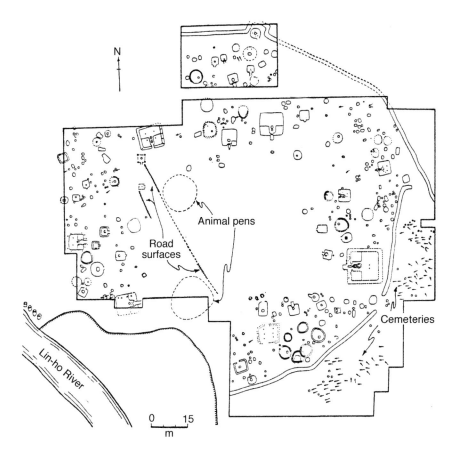

Figure 5.7 Layout of the Yangshao village of Jiangzhai
Source: Chang 1986b:118

displays this best (Figure 5.7). Like other Yangshao settlements, Jiangzhai has three components: a dwelling area consisting of more than 100 houses with over 300 storage pits, separated by a central plaza of about 4,000 square metres from burial areas to the east and south beyond the ditch and palisade. Kilns were located in a separate area to the southwest. The houses which could be either round or square, were semi-subterranean, with wattle and daub walls covered by a thatched roof. At Jiangzhai the houses were clustered into five groups arranged around the plaza, each group being headed by a large house and with the entrances of all the houses facing onto the plaza. Presumably this indicates five lineage groupings each led by a headman, but since burials were grouped into three discrete sections, they may have formed only three clans. Jiangzhai, however, may have been

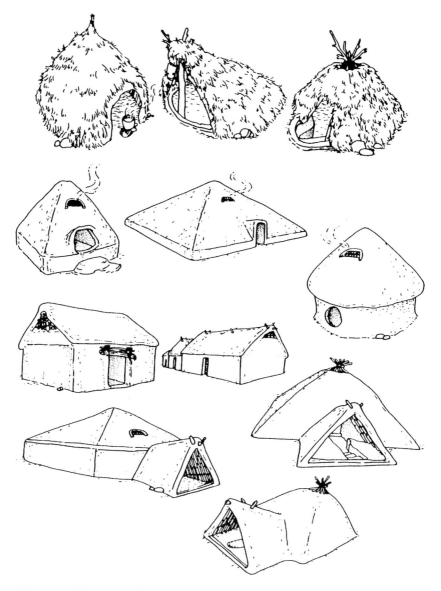

Figure 5.8 The range of Yangshao house types

Source: Chang 1977c:107

exceptionally large, for Wang (1988–9:12) argues that Yangshao villages typically contained 50–100 houses each of 20–30 square metres, which therefore, 'generally containing' five to six people, gives a village population of from 200 to 300. However, 300 to 400 better accommodate his figures.

Figure 5.8 shows the variety of house types characteristic of Yangshao culture, ranging from a kind of small thatched tepee through 'tukul'-like round structures and pyramid shapes, to rectangular houses with pitched roofs.

Dawenkou

The second regional Neolithic culture that had taken shape by about 5000 BC or a little after is the Dawenkou Culture of Shandong – the peninsula already referred to which sticks out into the Yellow Sea (Huanghai) toward Korea – separated from the Yangshao by the extensive wetlands of the Yellow River alluvium.[8] Initially at least dependent upon millet growing, fishing and hunting, Dawenkou sites are found on the low hills and terraces around the Shandong highlands and the sea coasts, extending south to the periphery of the Yangzi Delta. This area had a Palaeolithic stratum, but the earliest phase of the Dawenkou, the Beixin phase, was a member of the Peiligang horizon (Table 5.5). For the two and a half millennia of its existence the Dawenkou was, however, in a dynamic interchange with the Yangshao Culture, in which process of interaction it sometimes had the lead role, notably in generating the Longshan. The full importance of Dawenkou's influence and innovatory dynamism is only now being realized. For instance, the earliest coherent script, and one clearly related to subsequent scripts, notably Shang, is found as graphs etched into the sides of Dawenkou black pottery dating to the second half of the third millennium BC (Hsu and Linduff 1988:7). And Gina Barnes for one sees the Dawenkou as the culture in which elites first clearly emerge through differential resource investment in burials (pers. comm.). She further sees this cultural tradition as the one in which drinking rituals lay the basis for the ancestor rites of historical China:

> The east coast ceramic repertoire from the Middle Neolithic onwards included many vessels for the pouring and serving of liquids. The occurrence of these in rich burials confirms that they played a role in elite activities. Feasting or the ritual sharing of food and drink is generally recognized as an important stage for political manoeuvering, and to have one's rivals convert to and participate in one's own rituals is a strategic *coup d'état*. This seems to be what happened at the end of the Neolithic [my Chalcolithic] when one particular group of elites in the Erlitou culture co-opted bronze for the

production of their ritual vessels. The cult that developed from their activities was widely adopted throughout the north China Mainland, integrating competing elites into what is now recognized as the Shang cultural sphere.

(Barnes 1993:118)

Those competing elites were in a position to adopt bronze as their pre-eminent status marker because they comprised those lineages at the apex of conical clans (discussed below). They had already assumed control over territory through control over their clans, which they obtained through control over spirit access. Such control, with its beginnings early in the Neolithic, was fostered by shamanism (Chang 1983a; 1986a). Only lineage heads could sacrifice to ancestors, securing their blessings. Much later, ancestor veneration was at the core of all three of the classic Chinese belief systems: Buddhism, Confucianism and Daoism.

LIAOHE VALLEY

North of the Yangshao and Dawenkou spheres we have by 5000 BC the Xinlo Culture of the lower Liaohe River valley, followed by the Hongshan and Fuhe cultures. The Liaohe valley was a major centre of Palaeolithic cultures and the Xinlo Culture was undoubtedly a regional development, although important elements of its ceramics can be traced to the Peiligang. Hongshan and Fuhe Cultures are discussed extensively below.

Majiabang

In south China the earlier cord-marked pottery cultures may have been ancestral to most of the 5000 BC Neolithic cultures, but the continuity is not always clear. Nonetheless, Hemudu Neolithic culture (below) is preponderantly cord-marked. The most important Neolithic region in terms of subsequent development is the southern Huai River valley and the lower Yangzi valley – the region of the Majiabang Culture – c.3310–2250 BC – sharing numerous important features with the Dawenkou of Shandong. Indeed, there seems to be a continuum of coastal cultures with important common characteristics in both Neolithic and Chalcolithic periods, contrasting with the interior or Central Plains cultures.

Majiabang, as would be expected from the location, was a rice-growing, (low-fired) pottery culture. It was succeeded by the Liangzhu Culture making black-based and black-burnished pottery and growing *keng* rice. Liangzhu Culture, which represents the earliest Chalcolithic Culture in southeast China, is roughly contemporary with Longshan in the north and Hongshan in the northeast. It is also broadly contemporary with Majiayao in the (western) interior, with Daxi and Xuejiagang on the upper and lower reaches of the Yangzi, respectively, and with Shixia in the 'deep south', near Guangzhou (Canton) on the Xi Jiang (Pearl River). Majiabang is also, and most importantly, broadly contemporary with Dawenkou to its immediate north, and with Xiaozhushan Culture across Bohai Bay from the Shandong Peninsula.

Radiocarbon dated between 3310+−135 BC and 2250 BC (Xia 1977:225), over 100 Liangzhu Culture sites are presently known, and of these 30 have been excavated (Huang 1992:76). They are located to the south and east of Lake Tai, which occupies the centre of the important peninsula formed by the Yangzi River and Hangzhou Bay to the south. At the seaward end of the peninsula lies Shanghai, to the southwest the city of Hangzhou. This large peninsula – Tai Hu Bandao – is turning out to have been as important to the formative stages of China as it presently is to its transformative stages.

Liangzhu sites are remarkable for a number of things: the quality and quantity of jades; their ritual significance; clear evidence of pronounced social stratification; the profligate consumption of labour; extensive human sacrifice; and the iconography of power. Most of Liangzhu's contemporaries have some jades, but 90 per cent of all the *cong* and *bi* jades recovered, and by far the best in quality, are from Liangzhu sites (Huang 1992:78).

Bi and *cong* jades are, respectively, rings and elongated tubes. They have the historically known significance that the circular *bi* were used to worship heaven, the (sub)-square profiled, highly decorated *cong* to worship earth. The jades, of which well over 5,000 pieces have been recovered so far (Huang 1992:75), also bear the earliest *taotie* mask designs. This theriomorphic (monster-like) inscribed design has the form of a face, or rather a face is intended to be read from it. One on a *cong* tube (in Wenwu 1988(1):12), for instance, is formed from the pattern made by a figure with long arms bent back to play a pair of drums strapped about the waist (or the figure is supporting a pair of breasts). In the macro image, the hair of this figure becomes the forehead, the curving upper arms the eyebrows/ridges, the drums (or breasts) the eyes and their centres (nipples?) pupils. The lower body forms the nose and the turned out feet nostrils, while the (original) incised background becomes skin. This powerful illusion of transformation was eagerly seized upon and further stylized as the *taotie* image by Shang and Zhou elites, who rendered it much more 'beastlike', usually in bronze vessels. A particularly grim *taotie* spans a Shang executioner's bronze axe. An aperture at the centre of the blade forms a gaping, fanged mouth, waiting to devour its victims (cf. Rawson 1996a on *yue*: pp.103–5 for executions; 224 shamanism; 244 *taotie* origins).

But devouring victims was also pioneered by Liangzhu Culture, as Huang (1992:77) relates:

During 1982–6, over 700 jade objects were excavated from 22 Late Liangzhu tombs at Fuquanshan, a great mound raised exclusively for the construction of Liangzhu tombs, in Qingpu on the outskirts of Shanghai. These tombs also contained the remains of massive burned sacrifices and immolated slaves. . . . Tomb 144 in the centre of Fuquanshan was surmounted by three earth mounds which had been scorched by fire. The tomb enclosed an outer and an inner coffin, inside which lay a skeleton surrounded by numerous fine jades. The remains of a sacrificial victim were on top of the outer coffin.

Work during 1986 produced over 1,100 *bi/cong* sets (2,200 pieces) from eleven burials in another artificial hill at Fanshan in Zhejiang Province. In the following year, 635 sets were found in twelve burials cut into a rectangular ceremonial platform atop Yaoshan hill 5 kilometres to the northeast of Fanshan, and like it artificially constructed.

Other luxury products for the elite include silks and fine black wares. The Liangzhu type site was first excavated in 1936, but not until the excavation of the Caoxieshan site was Liangzhu Culture recognized as pre-Bronze Age (Huang 1992:76). Chinese archaeologists call this period late Neolithic and I call it Chalcolithic. In terms of its social stratification, craft elaboration and alienation of power, Liangzhu Culture seems to me just like the 'classic' Bronze Age of the Zhongyuan, only without the bronzes.

Hemudu

Hemudu is an early rice-growing, pottery-using, east-coast Neolithic site located on the northern bank of the east-flowing Yaojiang River in the peninsula immediately *south* of Hangzhou Bay (Hangzhou Wan). It lies 35 kilometres east of the town of Yuyao and 30 kilometres west of the city of Ningbo, with the Siming Mountains to the south and the Ningshao Plain to the north (Liu 1985:40). The site covers 40,000 square metres, of which 2,630 square metres were excavated in 1973–4 and 1977–8, when more than 7,000 artefacts were recovered (ibid.). It is the type site for other Neolithic settlements in the Ningbo-Shaoxing Plain of northern Zhejiang Province and the Zhoushan Archipelago (Liu 1985:43).

Stratification is in four clear layers of which the two lowest, 3 and 4, lie below the present water table and represent Hemudu Culture proper. Levels 1 and 2 correspond to the two phases of Majiabang Culture. Proximity to the river has eroded some of the site, but soil acidity has made for good organic preservation, the leaves and stalks of rice, for example, still having a fresh colour (ibid.). The lowest level is particularly rich in remains due to waterlogging. Those include deposits of rice grains, husks, straw and leaves averaging 40–50 centimetres thick. Both *indica* and *japonica* (*sinica*) varieties seem to be present in degrees of variation from the wild forms.

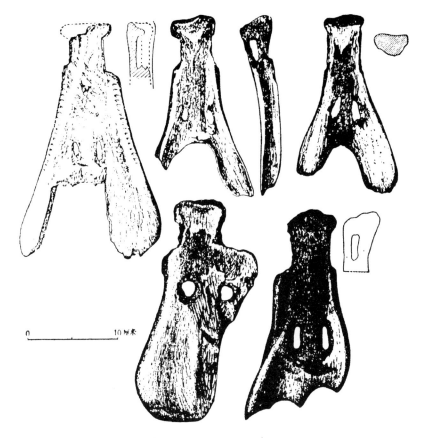

Figure 5.9 Scapula blades from Hemudu layer 4

In marked contrast to the stone hoes characteristic of Yangshao sites, at Hemudu rice was cultivated using specialized bone *si*-blades, hardwood picks and simple, pointed sticks. The spades, made on scapulae, have two holes made through the blades on either side of a shallow slot, made to take a T-shaped handle tied by rattan through the holes. They are illustrated in Figure 5.9. The remains of elephant, rhinocerus and red-faced monkey at this level, and also the plant species *Liquidambar formosana*, *Altingia chinensis* and *Castanopsis farg.*, indicate a significantly warmer climate in this area in the first part of the fifth millennium at least. The dense forest species *Lygodium microstachyum* and *Lygodium salicifolium* grow today only in Guangdong and Taiwan (ibid.:42).

This fourth or bottom layer, which is dated between 5000 and 4600 BC, contains houses constructed on piles. One house was over 23 metres long, 7 metres wide and had a porch 1.3 metres deep. It was constructed using

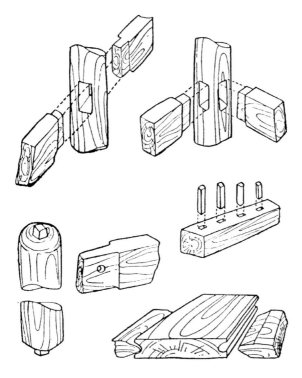

Figure 5.10 Mortice and tenon joints from Hemudu layer 4

Source: Kaogu Xuebao 1978 (1)

remarkably advanced mortice and tenon joints and dowelling, and is illustrated as Figure 5.10. Floors were covered with reed mats. The dimensions and form of this house, plus the terrain in which it is situated, suggest neither a private nor a chief's dwelling, but the sort of communal 'longhouse' still found, for example, in Borneo. Drying of the site is indicated by houses in the upper levels being built at ground level. Posts were either sharpened and driven into the ground or set into postholes packed with stones, sherds and clay (ibid.:43).

Echoing the Natufian in its extensive use of bone, arrowheads, whistles, chisels, awls and needles occur in this material. Jade ornaments are also present. The rather sculptural pottery, with forms that include *fu* cauldrons, two-eared jars, plates, deep basins and flat-bottomed *bo*, is cord-marked and sometimes incised with geometric, plant or animal designs (Liu 1985:41). This rather accomplished ware, illustrated in Figure 5.11 is certainly not beginners' work, although it is from layer 4. Some of the *fu* cauldrons have burnt rice crusts still adhering to their bottoms (ibid.:42).

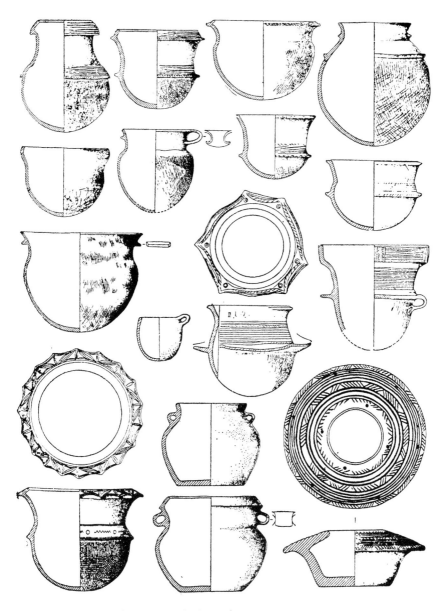

Figure 5.11 Pottery from Hemudu layer 4

The third layer, dating from *c.*4300 to 4000 BC, contains wooden house piles, wooden looms and painted bowls. The same bone inventory is in use, including the *si*-spades. Some butterfly-shaped ivory objects appear. Pottery quality declines somewhat, still mainly cord-marked but fired at only 850°C (ibid.:41). However, forms continue to include *fu* cauldrons, *bo*, *dou* and *zeng* and a portable pottery stove, plates, deep basins and flat-bottomed *bo*.

The second layer, *c.*3900–3700 BC, is chronologically and artefactually thin. Bone arrowheads and *si*-spades continue and one occurs with its handle attached.

The first or upper layer has a calibrated date of *c.*3400 BC (Liu 1985:40). It has produced twelve extended burials, a number of postholes, but no traces of wood or bone, most likely due to preservation conditions. However, stone implements include axes with central perforations and adzes with rectangular plans and cross-sections (ibid.). Jades include *huang*, which have a square shape and a central hole, and *jue*, a penannular ring. Pottery is now fired at 1000°C and is usually handmade, but some sherds may indicate the use of a wheel (ibid.). Decoration is still mainly cord-impressed and there are baked clay spindle whorls. Vessel types include *fu* cauldrons as previously, (rare) *ding* with three or four legs, *dou*, *hu* and *yi*. *Dou* with perforated stands are common, as are *fu* cauldrons with the greatest width at their shoulders (ibid.).

A remarkable range of animal species have been identified at Hemudu, amounting to well over 50. This testifies to a great diversity of habitats, from hill forests to riverine swamps and open water. Pelicans, egrets and ducks indicate the latter, carp, catfish, tortoise and turtle the former. Equally diverse is the range of pollens and spores, an amazing mix at one site, which includes *Quercus myrsinaefolia*, *Cinnamomum chingii* and *Prunus persica*, with *Typha augustifolia*, *Potamogeton distinctus* and *Nelumbo nucifera*, with *Artemisia* sp. and *Polygonum* spp. (Liu 1985:41). With such a range of flora and fauna available one wonders why the villagers would bother cultivating rice. Perhaps they were attracted to the site by the presence of wild rice, or by the possibility of growing it there. Other food resources included gourds, acorn and water chestnut. The dog and pig were domesticated and so, possibly were water buffalo (Liu 1985:42). Domestication of water buffalo would certainly allow for rice cultivation on a larger scale and in a more controlled way by preparing paddy fields. The Chinese character for 'field' and farmland, *tián*, shows a rectangular paddy-field divided by dykes in a cross pattern, thus: 田

And the basic unit of area 亩 (mu = 0.0667 ha) incorporates it (cf. *ikum* = 0.36 ha). The smallness of the unit shows how intensively farmed China was/is.

Yangzi Valley

Up the Yangzi Valley we encounter the Daxi Culture of western Hubei and eastern Sichuan and, much later, the Qujialing Culture of eastern and central Hubei. Finally, the southeastern coasts and inland southwest each had its distinctive Neolithic tradition.

The succession is chronologically ordered by An (1991:194) in Table 5.5, in which the Yangshao Culture(s) form a central bloc, and indicate the broad spread of Longshan Cultures, extending from the middle and lower reaches of the Yellow River to the Upper Yangzi. Longshan are, however, not Neolithic but Chalcolithic, as also Liangzhu on the Lower Yangzi.

So by the late Neolithic of around 3000 BC, we see that the situation is not fundamentally different from that of 2,000 years earlier: widespread but distinct Neolithics ranging from the northeast (Dongbei) through the central plains (Zhongyuan) and Shandong Peninsula, in the lower valleys of the Huai and Yangzi rivers, and along the southern coasts between Taiwan and Hainan islands. They can be categorized on a north/south and east/west set of axes, as by Gina Barnes (1993). The north/south axis occurs, as already mentioned, at the Qinling Mountains/Huai River, dividing the millet-growing north from the rice-growing south. The east/west dimension is seen in the different artefact traditions of the inland (Yangshao) and the East Coast (Dawenkou), the former best known for flat or ring-based painted pottery of relatively simple form; notably bowls and two-handled jars. The latter is best known for developing the characteristic tripod vessels, solid-legged examples appearing early in the Neolithic.

FINAL NEOLITHIC TO CHALCOLITHIC

Like the Yangshao, Longshan is a generic term covering a number of sub-phases and regional particularities. Indeed, within the Yellow River plains drainage alone, from the Wei River (Shaanxi) to Bohai Gulf (Shandong), no less than seven distinct regional variants (*leixing*) of Longshan culture have been identified (on the basis of similarity of artefacts, especially pottery) spanning the period from *c.*2600 BC to 1900 BC (Underhill 1994:198). The seven are: (west to east) Kexingzhuang II; Taosi; Wangwan III; Hougang II; Wangyoufang; Chengziyai; Liangcheng (ibid.:199). Five of the *leixing* have so far produced nine 'large' sites with walls of rammed earth (*hangtu*), containing large structures indicative of their centrality to some kind of settlement hierarchy, as yet undetermined for lack of rigorous survey. Underhill argues that here in the Huanghe Longshan we are seeing the emergence of complex societies still at the pre-urban chiefdom stage, with towns but not cities (ibid.:201).[9] Wangwan III and Taosi regional variants are evidently the direct predecessors of the Erlitou Culture, Period III, which some consider the reality of the Xia Dynasty (see below).

Table 5.5 Chronological table and phase division of Neolithic cultures in the Yellow River and Yangzi River basins

Period	Upper Yellow River	Middle Yellow River	Upper Yangzi	Lower Yellow River	Lower Yangzi	bc (5730 half-life)	Approx. cal. BC
BRONZE AGE	SIBA / QIJIA	SHANG	SHANG	SHANG	SHANG		
		LONGSHAN	LONGSHAN / QUJIALING	LONGSHAN	LIANGZHU	2000	2000
NEOLITHIC	MAJIAYAO	YANGSHAO	DAXI	DAWENKOU	SONGZE	3000	3000
					MAJIABANG		4000
	DADIWAN		ZAOSHI	BEIXIN	HEMUDU	4000	
		PEILI-GANG / CISHAN				5000	5000
	? ?	? ?	? ?	? ?	? ?	6000	6000

Source: An Zhimin 1991:194

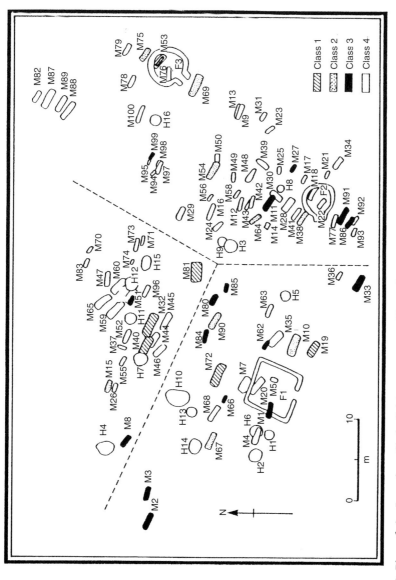

Figure 5.12 Plan of the Longshan Chalcolithic cemetery at Chengzi

Source: Chang 1986:251

The major distinction in material culture of the Longshan (so-called from the type site of Zhengziyai in western Shandong and meaning 'Dragon Mountain') compared with the Yangshao is that some house structures are no longer semi-subterranean but literally 'raised-up' on stamped-earth platforms (a technique identical to that used in building the town walls mentioned above). That technique is used, for example at the site of Chengzi, to construct massive city walls and long, deep ditches.

The occupants of the 'raised-up' houses, even where, as at Donghaiyou they were only 6 × 6 metres, were socially 'raised-up' also. Now there are perfectly clear signs of social stratification, and it is occurring *within lineages* as well as between them. The eighty-seven burials at Chengzi excavated between 1976 and 1977 lay in rectangular pit graves and were grouped into four distinct classes:

1   large graves, with second-level ledge, wooden caskets, and many grave goods, including invariably the thin cup on high stem and pig mandible;
2   smaller pits, with second-level ledge, some caskets, and a significant number of goods, sometimes including the thin cup on high stem and pig mandible;
3   small pits, with no second-level ledge or caskets, and very few goods;
4   very narrow pits, barely large enough to place the body inside, with no furnishings and no caskets.

There are altogether only five first-class graves, eleven second-class graves, seventeen third-class graves, and fifty-four fourth-class graves. Significantly, the burials were clustered in three well-defined areas of the cemetery, but most significantly *each* cluster had all four classes of grave, as shown in Figure 5.12.

This is the earliest clear example of a burial pattern associated with the stratified lineage society of ancient China. It is indeed the very framework of class stratification there and the basis of state formation in the ensuing Xia, Shang and Zhou periods.

> Clans and [their component] lineages, as shown both in inscriptions, when available, and in the layout of cemeteries and the association of emblems on vessels buried in the graves, not only continued to serve as primary groups governing social interaction but also provided a genealogical basis for the differentiation of their members into political and economic classes through the mechanism of hierarchical segmentation. Within each clan there were major and minor lineages determined by genealogical distance, and the lineage hierarchy was coupled with the hierarchy of the settlements.
>
> (Chang 1986:364–5)

A clan consists of a number of lineages all supposedly descended from a common ancestor, but not all the lineages are of equal standing or rank. Indeed, Chang (1983a:35) states that 'The lineage (zu) was probably the most important social framework for coercion; zu rules were the society's fundamental law.' Those deemed to be nearest to the founding ancestor of the clan arc the most senior and politically powerful. They control the most important fecundity rituals because they are invested with potency by dint of proximity to the ancestors who are the locus of crucial power, mediating as they do between divinities and men.[10] Paul Kirchhoff (1935) called the resulting social framework *the conical clan*, wherein one lineage gets promoted to the apex of a cone formed, as it were by the branching away (by hierarchical segmentation) of other related lineages. It is important to realize that all lineages have similar time-depth and number of members; it is just that the majority of lineages come to count for little while one or two tend to monopolize the bulk of social surpluses because their pivotal mediation between heaven and earth is supposedly the condition for the survival of their fellow clansmen.

The process of state-formation thus takes place when the apical lineages (at the top of the cones) no longer mix and marry with their clansmen. Instead they interact with other elevated lineages from other clans, who likewise draw their support and revenues from, but are no longer answerable to, inferior lineages. Thus the conical principle, in the words of Kirchhoff,

> results in a group in which every single member, except brothers and sisters, has a different standing: the concept of the degree of relationship leads to different degrees of membership in the clan. In other words, some are members to a higher degree than others.
>
> (Kirchhoff 1968:266)

This is illustrated in Figure 5.13, where the head of the 'central' or senior lineage becomes king (*wang*) because he has the most direct relationship with the ancestors and they with Shang Di (or just Di), the supreme being, the 'Lord on High'. Some Shang royal endogamy is known, as in the marriage of King Wu Ding, fourth Shang king at Anyang, to the celebrated Fu Hao, both being members of the ruling Tzu (Zi) clan (P.C. Chang 1986:130).

Her position in the dominant clan explains how she was able to take leadership roles in political and military affairs, something a 'married in' queen could not do. It also explains the incredible wealth of her tomb, whose items include:

Wooden chamber and lacquered wooden coffin
16 sacrificial victims

Stratification in the structure of the Conical Clan

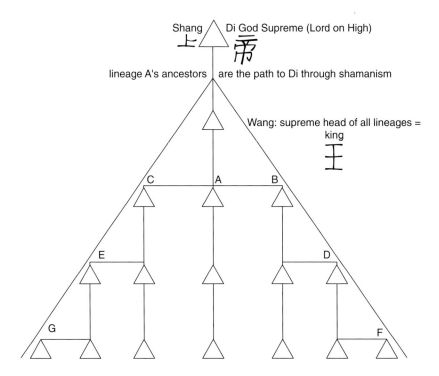

Figure 5.13 Stratification in the structure of the Conical Clan

Source: Maisels

6 sacrificial dogs
almost 7,000 cowries
more than 200 bronze ritual vessels
5 large bronze bells and 18 small bronze bells
44 bronze implements (27 of them knives)
4 bronze mirrors
1 bronze spatula
more than 130 bronze weapons
4 bronze tigers or tiger heads
more than 20 bronze artefacts of other descriptions
more than 590 jade and jadelike objects
more than 100 jade beads, discs and pieces
more than 20 opal beads
2 quartz crystal objects
5 bone implements

more than 20 bone arrowheads
more than 490 bone hairpins
3 ivory carvings
4 pottery vessels and 3 clay whistles

(Chang 1980b:42)

In the process of lineage promotion, the majority become 'the mass', *zhong* = 众, a term synonymous with peasant. Though still organized by clan, they were subject to agricultural corvee and military levee under aristocratic supervision. Indeed, with others, Chang (1980a:163) sees the original oracle bone graph character for *zu* as being composed of an arrow beneath a flag, indicating that it served as the basic military unit, composed of 100 adult men from 100 households. As Chang succinctly describes the formation of the Shang elite:

> The *zu*, by virtue of the incessant ramifications of its member units was the seed of social stratification within itself and among one another. Within each *zu* there were high and lowly members and among the various *zu* there were high and lowly *zus*. *Zhongren* were probably the lowly members of each *zu*, especially of each lowly *zu*, with in the various clans within the Shang state.
>
> (Chang 1980a:227)

How this worked in subsequent Zhou expansion is spelled out by Lewis:

> The kingship itself was transmitted from eldest son to eldest son, forming the so-called 'great lineage' (da zōng = 大宗) of the Zhou court. The brothers, younger sons, and allies of the king held hereditary offices in the Zhou court or were enfeoffed in distant cities to act as peripheral foci of Zhou power. The eldest sons of those enfeoffed would inherit the rule of those cities, where they established their own temples and thus formed a 'small lineage' (xiao zōng) 小宗 which replicated the royal line and the royal court in reduced form. The younger sons of these 'small lineages' received hereditary offices at the court of the lineage, or they might in turn be enfeoffed in a smaller city within the sphere of influence of the lineage's capital. These lesser fiefs were likewise inherited by primogeniture, and they then established their own ancestral temples and became new 'small lineages'. Thus the courts of the feudal lords formed a 'small lineage' which was a reduced replica of the 'great lineage' of the feudal state.
>
> (Lewis 1990:33–4)[11]

Figure 5.14 Shandong Longshan: white pottery tripod pitcher (*gui*) with hollow
legs; for boiling water

Figure 5.15 Shang (Huangbi, Hubei): bronze vessel for heating wine (*he*) with *gui* dragon design

Figure 5.16 Shang (Huangbi, Hubei): bronze battle-axe (*yue*) with *gui* dragon design

Figure 5.17 Shang (Anyang, Henan): bronze food container marked with the inscription 'Bei Gan Ge'

THE CHALCOLITHIC: LONGSHAN

Longshan pottery, in contrast to both Dawenkou and Yangshao, is predominantly grey and black, with a small percentage of brown, red and white pastes. The pottery was wheel-made and hard-fired. Often the vessels are plain, but decorations such as bow-strings, incisions, appliqués, and hollow-outs are also common. Most significantly, in the light of their later ritual importance, the types include the *ding* tripod cooking vessel, *xian* steamer, *gui* pitcher, *dou* on pedestals, cup with a handle, and a lidded vessel.[12]

Interestingly, Underhill (1991:23) concludes that 'there is no evidence for change in the mode of production [of pottery] over time' and that the 'complex household industry mode' characterizes the Longshan Period rather than the individual workshop industrial mode. 'Complex household industry mode', where the producers tend to be men for whom pottery-making is their major source of income, is intermediate between 'simple household industry', which takes place within the household, probably by women for domestic use, and the more specialized, exchange-oriented production in a detached and dedicated workshop, which can be either individual or, with urbanism, nucleated (ibid.:13–14).

Underhill (1994) has compared five large walled sites of the Longshan Period in Henan (Table 1) with four of the same period in Shandong Province, and contrasts them with four major Early Dynastic sites from the Huanghe Valley (Table 3). That is, Chalcolithic sites dating from the middle to the end of the third millennium are compared with settlements of the first part of the second millennium. Despite the patchy excavation evidence, three things stand out: first, the second-millennium sites (Erlitou, Shixianggou, Zhengzhou and Anyang) are at least ten times larger in area that those of the third millennium. Second, the Longshan settlements are characterized by a proliferation of craft activity. Third, none of the Longshan settlements exceeds 20 hectares, and even this extent is reached only at Chengziyai in Shandong. So despite the fact that the walled settlements of the Longshan Period functioned as regional centres and alone contained relatively large structures representing either elite residences or public buildings, they were still only towns rather than cities (ibid.:201, 223). Thus, the Chalcolithic in China has the same key attributes as in the other areas examined. It is characterized by towns and crafts, in contrast to the cities and states of the Bronze Age.

A conspicuous component of the Longshan wares is the eggshell-thin, lustrous-black ware.[13] Sometimes looking more like a candlestick than a drinking vessel, is a long-necked cup, on a slender hollow stem with open-work or fretwork. With similarly fine box and jar, those are presumably ritual vessels. Another common Longshan ritual item is the oracle bone: deer or other large mammalian scapulae (hence the term scapulimancy) or tortoise plastrons, burned to produce cracks. The egg-shell black pottery, scapulimancy, and the animal mask decorations on jade axes and black pottery all suggest a ritual intensity previously unattained. And it is ritual and clanship that are at the origin of the Chinese writing system, the earliest grouping so far known being those putting questions on the scapulae, the cracks formed on burning being the answers. Characters also appear as clan identification marks on ritual vessels at this time.

Extensive metal working commences with the Longshan, but bronze casting belongs to the next cultural phase. Early Dynastic Strata 3 and 4 at the Erlitou site have the earliest bronze vessels yet discovered in 'core' China (An Zhimin 1982–3:68). However, this certainly does not mean that the Zhongyuan owes its Bronze Age primacy to technological superiority.

> For instance, in the Qijia culture in the northwest region, which is contemporaneous with the Longshan culture, and at Lower Xiajiadian culture in the northern regions, there are also metal artifacts most of which are true bronze. Bronze artifacts were found much earlier beyond the Zhongyuan, such as the bronze knife discovered at Majiayao in Donglin town, Gansu province, with a date of about 3000 BC. The discovery of related bronze-casting in the

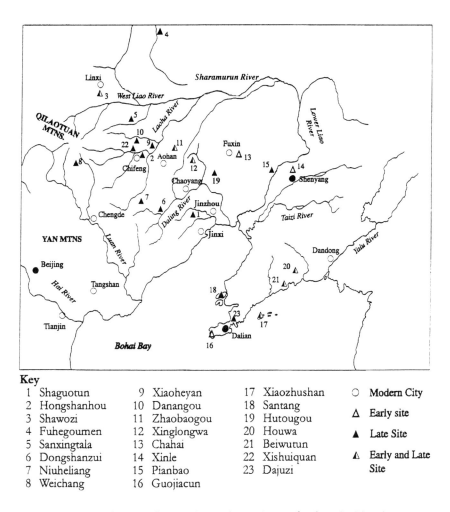

Key

1 Shaguotun	9 Xiaoheyan	17 Xiaozhushan	○ Modern City
2 Hongshanhou	10 Danangou	18 Santang	
3 Shawozi	11 Zhaobaogou	19 Hutougou	△ Early site
4 Fuhegoumen	12 Xinglongwa	20 Houwa	
5 Sanxingtala	13 Chahai	21 Beiwutun	▲ Late Site
6 Dongshanzui	14 Xinle	22 Xishuiquan	
7 Niuheliang	15 Pianbao	23 Dajuzi	◮ Early and Late
8 Weichang	16 Guojiacun		Site

Figure 5.18 Distribution of Hongshan culture sites and others in Liaoning
    Source: Guo Da-shun 1995:26

> Hongshan culture [Liaoning province] is therefore one of the earli-
> est, and in addition, the two-piece mould was already in use. Thus
> bronze casting already existed around 3500 BC or so, and bronze-
> casting technology in this place was already quite impressive.
>
>   (Guo 1995a:42)

However, not everyone is convinced that the bronzeworking materials found
at Niuheliang can as yet be reliably assigned to the Hongshan (Barnes,
pers. comm.). Figure 5.18 (above) maps Hongshan and other sites in
Liaoning.

THE CHALCOLITHIC: HONGSHAN

It is now becoming abundantly clear that the cultures north of Bohai Gulf across the Yan mountains (northeast from Beijing), in the large rectangle formed by the Luan, Sharamurun and Yalu Rivers, were at least as advanced in Neolithic and Chalcolithic periods as was the Zhongyuan. In Hongshan culture, indeed, there is evidence for the use of heavy plough, something rare in China at any period. In general, the Neolithic basis is indigenous to the region, as seen at the village sites of Chahai, minimally 5712–c.5530 BC, and Xinglongwa, 6032–c.5760 BC (Guo 1995a:48).

> The bronze-casting, pottery-making and jade carving . . . are the three major industrial accomplishments of the Hongshan culture. Large scale production and specialized division of labour suggest that in addition to farming and animal husbandry, a large group of people was already engaged independently in handicraft industries. As this group of people understood the technology and organized and managed it, they became a special class which arose from primitive agriculture. Since these three industries all made products which were closely related to rituals, it is possible that those who organized, understood, and managed the key technologies became the elite of society.
>
> (ibid.:43)

Of course, it is at least as possible that, as in the Zhongyuan, those who managed the rituals also managed society, despite or in accord with the presence of a medium of exchange in shell-pattern jade money. Hongshan Culture centred on the Liao River drainage of the lower Manchurian Basin. Its major centres were the ritual sites of Dongshanzui and Niuheliang, especially the latter. At Niuheliang a major Goddess Temple occurs at the centre of cairn clusters and altars associated with size-stratified graves in an area distant from any dwelling sites (ibid.:45). Stratification seems manifestly present, because

> one of the most salient features of the cairns is the central tomb. This tomb is huge in scale, and required a great deal of labour and expense. It contains superior-quality jade objects, and is surrounded by small graves with clear differentiation into primary and secondary. The covering earth, stones and dividing stones as well as the cylindrical pots, are designed specifically to make the large grave more outstanding, thus forming a 'mountainous tomb', and fully indicating the authority and power of one individual who was superior over all others.
>
> (ibid.:46)

In this pattern of altar, temple with multiple differentiated chambers and cairns, Guo (ibid.:46) sees the pattern being set for subsequent Chinese culture: 'the pattern is identical to that of the Ming Heavenly Altar, Temple, and Ming Shishan tomb several thousand years later'. Further, Hongshan jades set the pattern for Shang usage (Nelson 1995b:252).

One hundred and fifty kilometres north of the Sharamurun River, on the east bank of the Wuerjimulun River, lies the 150-house village of Fuhegoumen, type site of the Fuhe culture practising a mixed hunting/farming economy. A pottery Neolithic culture, Fuhe interacted with Hongshan along the Sharamurun River (Guo 1995a:52). One of many such regional interactions, it is clear that the northeastern group (in Liaoxi [western Liaoning], the Shenyang region [eastern Liaoning] and the Liaodong peninsula to the south) had their own set of interactions, while in turn interacting with both Yangshao and Longshan cultures. Thus it is not a simple matter of influences flowing to and from those latter cultures – which anyhow are not monolithic entities – but of cross-currents, circuits and derivations, intra and extra regional, sometimes from unexpected sources. One such is the use of polished oracle bones by the steppe culture people of Zhukaigou in southern Inner Mongolia, within the Ordos Loop of the Yellow River. A Longshan-type culture with a pastoral emphasis, it flourished between the late third and mid-second millennia. In Phases III and IV of Zhukaigou, polished, burned and drilled oracle bones occur that pre-date similar treatments at Shang sites of the Erligang Period (Linduff 1995:140). This also points up what a 'holdall' term Longshan really is. As the sites and sequences become better known they will be used instead.

Probably the most important post-Hongshan culture is the Early Bronze Age Lower Xiajiadian (c.2000–2500 BC), extending over the original area of the Hongshan and also into adjacent Inner Mongolia (hence its original designation as Chifeng Phase II). Two thousand sites of this culture are already known, revealing villages of close-packed, semi-subterranean houses with mud-brick walls. The majority of dwellings are round in plan, but the grander ones are rounded-square, the settlements, occurring in clusters, protected by stone and earth walls, both individual and linked (Guo 1995b:168).

Social stratification, based on intensive millet (broomcorn and foxtail) agriculture as indicated by specialized equipment, is marked by differences in the size and quality of housing, and also in housing for the dead. Most clearly at Dadianzi (which has rammed-earth walls), depth of burial, the use of a wooden coffin, the size of the artefact niche and the quality of the ceremonial objects are the key variables (ibid.:172). Further, 'the battle-axe is found only in large male burials, representing a special warrior class' (ibid.:173).

In conclusion, Guo goes so far as to declare that 'the origin of ancient China's civilization as well as the national culture' was first synthesized

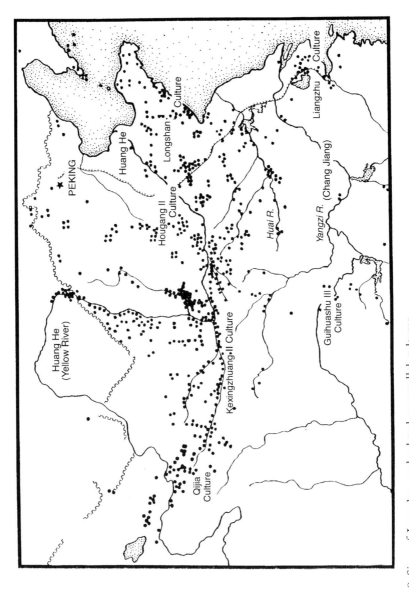

Figure 5.19 Sites of Longshan and related or parallel cultures

Source: Yen Wen-ming, W.W. 1981, No. 6:42

in the region north of Bohai Bay, and not in the Zhongyuan as is traditionally assumed. *Inter alia*, he points out that many of the motifs, such as the politico-symbolically important *taotie* animal mask design taken to be so characteristically Shang (and Western Zhou, see Figure 5.27), are first seen in fine painted pottery of the Lower Xiajiadian. On the basis of bronzeware designs as well as pottery, and in particular the *li* with pot-like body and three baggy legs shared by Lower Xiajiadian, Yan and Shang, Guo (1995b:179) concludes that 'Lower Xiajiadian culture, in the process of its development, was divided into several branches, one of which moved south and originated the Shang culture, while another remained in the same place for a long time and became the antecedent of [the historical] Yan.'

However that may be (cf. Keightley 1995; Meacham 1990), it is now clear that the Zhongyuan by no means pioneered all the significant technological and social developments. Its 'central' position (originally at the Wei/Fen/Huanghe intersection) was merely an important location within one of many East Asian interaction spheres. As mentioned above, there has recently come to light at Sanxingdui in the west, a major, highly accomplished bronze-casting culture, the later phases of which are contemporary with the Shang. Although some Shang-inspired pieces occur at Sanxingdui the latter is fundamentally distinct, with its own individual Chalcolithic basis. Neither Shang nor Zhou sources even refer to this western culture. It must have been part of a separate interaction sphere, although its wealth and lavish use of bronze led Ge and Linduff (1990:513) to speculate that Sanxingdui lay on an important trade route in metal from Yunnan to the central plains. Of course the two possibilities are not in conflict, as interaction spheres overlap and their composition varies over time.

Further, on the 'central plains' not just mutual influence but also population was much more mobile than is usually assumed. This enabled the Zhongyuan, over prolonged periods, to be the recipient of innovations and population derived from north, south, east and west. Its own main innovation may thus have been ongoing syncretism, the results of which it re-exported in a series of transformed packages to the various areas of origin (peaceably or forcibly). Thus in the use of *drilled* oracle bones, held to be so characteristic of Shang scapulimancy, we now find that drilling prior to heating originated with the Lower Xiajiadian culture (Shelagh 1994:282), while polishing and drilling are found earlier in Zhukaigou (Linduff 1995:140).

Similarly, they did not 'invent' the script, but employed graphs already in existence elsewhere. No doubt the more research that is done beyond the Zhongyuan, the less will that area's innovations appear to be its own, and the more they will be seen as deriving from a central location in a number of interaction networks.

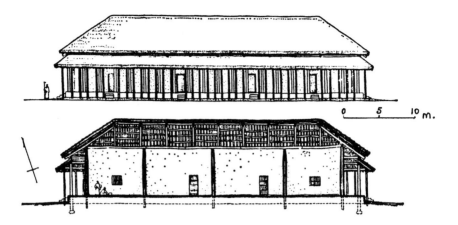

Figure 5.20 Restoration of hall F1, Panlongcheng site, Huangpi district, Hubei, by Yang Hongxun. Mid to late second millennium BC (from Wenwu No. 2, 1976:23)

STATE (guo 國) EXPANSION BY COLONIZATION AND CONQUEST

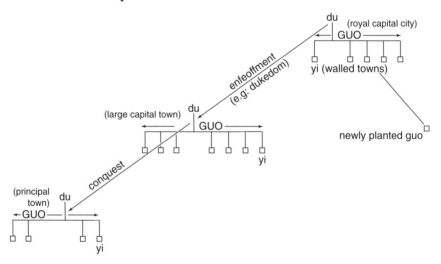

Figure 5.21 Zhou state expansion by colonization and conquest

CLANSHIP AND THE TERRITORIAL STATE

Longshanoid cultures underwent parallel development. For example, the Hemudu and the Liangzhu cultures of the lower Yangzi valley, evolving into the historic Wuyue groups. Figure 5.19 is a map of Longshan and related cultures, based on Yen Wen-ming (WW 1981, No. 6:42).

Chang selectively categorizes their evolution as follows:

The Longshanoid cultures, illustrated above, formed the basis of the *huaxia* – or (northern) Chinese culture area – under the three dynasties, because they shared social-structural properties from the Neolithic onward.[14] The defining relationships were between lineages (*shi*) and clans (*xing*) not between people and land. The *shi* were corporate units and members owed them, in the person of their head, absolute loyalty. 'Thus the surname plus *shi* was not only used to designate the *shi* but also its head. It is often impossible to determine, for instance, whether *Jishi* means "the Ji shi" or "the head of the Ji shi" ' (Creel 1964:181).

The king (*wang*) could assign particular lineages to be the military and economic retainers of an individual, usually a prince, queen or high aristocrat. Clans could be assigned territory many hundreds of kilometres away to serve strategic purposes of the Zhou state, by forming new reliable states in sensitive areas. The mechanism can be represented graphically, as shown in Figure 5.21.

This was, of course, to secure territory, but the *means* was that of agnatic segmentation and personal subordination, that is, of receiving land and people from the monarch in return for loyalty and contributions. Paraphrasing Yang Hsi-mei, Hsu and Linduff state that

the people were bestowed, the domain was assigned, and the authority designated in the manner of creation of a new state. Yang interpreted the term *zixing*, customarily understood as the bestowal of a surname, to be the bestowal of the 'people', who provided a base for the newly institutionalized ruling class. The ritual of creating a name for the new vassal state, *mingshi*, according to Yang, should be regarded as part of the process of segmentation of the dominating group, that is, that of the lord. New units were created that remained subordinate to the old unit. Thus distribution of power was created in the hierarchic manner of continuous segmentation.

(Hsu and Linduff 1988:157–8)

The branching lineage system (*zōngfǎ*) provided the perfect framework for feudal land-holding, since each state-forming bequest (*fengjian*) was in exchange for personal loyalty to the king. Individuals from elite lineages were enfeoffed by being granted a subordinate population already settled in the area to be ruled, plus from the core area lineages of specialists (the *renli*) in ritual and crafts, attached to the new courts for their immediate household and garrison functions. This vassalage of the recipients was marked by conferring ritual articles upon the newly created ruler, notably clothing, flags, horses and chariots. The *Zuo-zhuan* classic text records (in the Fourth year of Duke Ding) the establishment of the state of Lu. The Duke of Lu was given the above regalia, plus a great bow from an ancient state and six *zu* of Yin (the Shang population) as followers. Their clan heads were ordered 'to lead the chiefs of their kin, to collect their branches in the remote as well as the near (land), to conduct the multitude of their connection', in following the Duke to his new state (ibid.:188). Here the ramifications of the *zu* are of such extent as to refer to a clan.

Typically, the first task of a major vassal such as Duke Lu would be to build a *guo* or fortified settlement, which would become his capital city, then to expand the boundaries of this capital district (perhaps behind walls) until a territorial state, also referred to as *guo*, was attained. By this time the state would incorporate subsidiary settlements, villages and towns, called *yi*

> maintained by the sub-enfeoffed great officials and ranked lower than the capital city, not only because of their subordinated position politically, but also because the capital [of the new state] was entitled to have temples for the deceased lords and thus was endowed with the blessings and protection of the ancestral spirits.
>
> (ibid.:270)

Since this was very much a process serving the interests of the centre, states could be moved even several times to fill strategic gaps. As the peasantry were largely indigenes, with their own separate kinship and religious structures, and since also agricultural technique was largely uniform across the central plains, it was unnecessary and unwise to uproot the peasantry to create a new state. Although structures of bureaucratic administration did emerge during the Western Zhou, notably the Three (civil) Offices of *situ*, *sikong* and *sikou*, respectively the Ministries of Agriculture, Works and Crime, the centralized bureaucratic administration was a creation of the great southern state of Chu, later generalized throughout the empire by the Qin and Han regimes. The Zhou, by contrast, ruled by enfeoffment, delegation and accommodation. Accordingly,

> The general pattern of Zhou expansionism ... was for the population to follow a vassal prince to a new locality and then form the bulk (?) of his subjects. These populations, either the [dominant] Jhi or the Jhiang [their allies], generally moved from Shaanxi or Henan to the east or south, where new supporting powers were formed by them 'to screen and to protect' the new Zhou world

order. In the new land, where these immigrants constituted one stratum [the core?] of the ruling class, they superseded and were superimposed on the native population.

(ibid.:163)

Thereby reinforcing the distinction between 'state people' (*guo-ren*) and 'field people' (*ye-ren*), the former were either members of the ruling class or at least of citizen status, the latter lacking that status, formed 'the multitude'. The *guo-ren* were the population of the city upon whom military duties fell during the Western Zhou. The rest, the 'field people', were not generally mobilized until the Spring and Autumn/Warring States periods, when state control over the multitude became rigorous.

BRONZE AGE URBANISM

Capitals dominated their territories through a network of subsidiary towns occupied by subsidiary lineages or allied clans. Indeed, Chang (1983b: 362) states that 'The fundamental social unit throughout the Bronze Age [*c.*2200 to *c.*500 BC] was the walled town [yi] thousands of which dotted the loessic landscape of north China. Physically, all these towns were similar.' Founded by political fiat, they originated in a coordinated building event and

> were enclosed by earthen walls on four sides. The walls were built by the ramming technique [hangtu]: long planks were bound together to form a trough, earth was put in and then rammed solid with stone or metal pounders, and then the planks were untied and moved to form another trough, into which earth was put to form another wall section at a higher level. The town enclosure was mostly square or rectangular, with north, south, east, and west walls. Because of the use of planks, walls were straight, and corners were right-angled. Gates opened on the walls; the south gate was the main opening and the enclosure may be said to 'face' the south with its back to the north. This orientation is not unusual for north China, with the sun, the source of all life, shining in from the south.
>
> (Chang 1983b:362)

Accordingly, the situation at about 2000 BC, when the earliest state-level civilization was emerging, was that of a landscape dotted with walled towns, *yi*, populated by a single clan, *xing*, but actually ruled by a dominant lineage, *zu*. A state, *guo*, consisted of a network of towns, *yi*, under a royal capital, *du*.[15]

As discussed and illustrated earlier, the towns were politico-military constructs, their economic functions being secondary:

It is the power of the lineage that the Bronze Age town was built to maintain. . . . The agnatic clan of ancient China was actually composed of a number of genealogically real lineages, whose propagation in time led to major and minor branches, with major and minor political and economic powers, depending on genealogical distance from the founding father. When lineages became segmented, the head of each of the branches would lead his members to new walled towns, with their attendant land and other political resources. The lineage hierarchy would, normatively, coincide with the hierarchy of walled towns.

(Chang 1983b:364)

In about 2000 BC there were several thousand such 'states' (*guo*). In the succeeding Shang Period (1750–1100 BC), a couple of thousand remained, while in the Western Zhou Period (1100–771 BC) there were said to be still 1,800 states (as mentioned above, some newly created), and after the move of the Zhou capital to the east (i.e. to Luoyang, above, so inaugurating the Eastern Zhou), 1,200 states remained. It is this condition that prompts some writers to speak of the early Chinese 'city-state'. But neither socially nor economically, militarily nor in terms of settlement structure is this a useful description. They began as small territorial states and either expanded to become or were absorbed by larger territorial states of the 'village-state' type (Maisels 1987, 1990).

At the other pole socially, economically, culturally and politically is the city-state. A city-state is characterized by a common citizenship shared by the urban dwellers and the city's sustaining area. Citizens have the right and duty of participation in directing the affairs of the city-state, something clearly seen in the classic city-states of Greece, Pre-Roman Italy and, of course, Mesopotamia. Those rights and duties are signally absent from China at any period, including the present.

At the time of the Zhou conquest under King Wu, 800 'states' were said (by the *Shi Ji*) to be allies of the Zhou and a similar number of Shang allies were claimed as having been subjugated by the victors. As the average population of those 'states' was said to be about 5,000 persons, the 'states' accordingly seem to be little more than the territory inhabited by a particular clan, and ruled over by its dominant lineage.

Indeed, in the wake of the conquest, although Shang usages and elite personnel were retained, population redistribution was undertaken for strategic reasons. Typically, 'the Shang people who moved to Shensi went in groups of *zu*, a social and political entity consisting of a ruling lineage and their relatives and subordinates. Such a unit remained intact throughout the Zhou period' (Hsu and Linduff 1988:117). This, despite the fact that the Zhou were more genuinely 'universalist' in political practice and ideology than the descent- and ritual-obsessed Shang.

Hsu and Linduff (op. cit.:110–11) argue that the initial breakthrough to the humanist worldview that came to dominate Chinese thought was made as the correlate of developing the concept 'Mandate of Heaven', justifying (initially Zhou) rule not merely by legitimate succession (from the Xia) but far beyond this by the utilitarian principle of effecting the best governance for the population as a whole. By ruling incompetently and oppressively, the Shang had lost their Mandate to the Ji house of the Zhou, who promised to ensure the greatest good of the greatest number.[16]

Chinese history down to unification in 221 BC thus consisted of the continual reduction by intrigue and warfare of what had been semi-independent clan territories and states to a position in which a single, imperial lineage theoretically 'owned' the entire land of China, the borders of which are still expanding.

Presumably because the San Dai interaction sphere did not include civilizations beyond the central and coastal plains (cf. Huber 1988),

> no significantly new technological invention has been archaeologically documented from the Neolithic into the Bronze Age: the same stone, bone, shell, and presumably wooden digging, earth turning, weeding and harvesting implements were used during both periods. The emergence of Bronze Age civilizations in China was not accompanied, insofar as our available archaeological record suggests, by a significant use of metal farming implements, irrigation networks, any use of draft animals, or [even] the use of the plough. For a breakthrough in agricultural technology in China we will have to wait until about 500 or 600 BC, when cast iron began to be used widely and for agricultural implements.
>
> (K.C. Chang 1986a:364)

This was under pressure of continual warfare and social upheaval. Thoroughgoing technological and industrial changes had to await the Middle Empire, comprising the Sui (AD 589–617) and Tang (AD 618–906) Dynasties.

STATES: THE THREE DYNASTIES

As should be clear by now, traditional Chinese historiography mentions three dynasties – successively Xia, Shang and Zhou – as spanning the two millennia until the Eastern Zhou collapsed in 256 BC. The real existence of Shang and Zhou hegemonies was easily accepted in modern times, as archaeological and inscriptional evidence came to light during the twentieth century. However, there has always been some doubt concerning the existence of Xia, given its proximity to culture-heroic stories.

Kwang-chih Chang (K.C. Chang) has long been a proponent of the historical reality of a Xia dynasty which the tradition had localized in the Sanhe, that stretch of the Yellow River valley just after it is joined by the Wei and Fen rivers in the loessic terrain of western Henan. Certainly Erlitou, Erligang and Xiaotun, key ruling centres, are all within that Province.

Since the Survey of 1959 which identified it, excavations have uncovered remains of the Erlitou culture at a site of *ca.*1.5 × 2.5 kilometres on the Luo River, just 20 kilometres east of the modern city of Luoyang. Four kilometres to the south is the Yi River (which joins the Luo just before both join the Huanghe from the south). Five strata, in places together exceeding 3 metres in depth, are distinguished, but as yet no general plan of Erlitou is available. In the sketch map in Figure 5.22 (by John A. Wysocki) the solid blobs and rectangles are modern villages – Erlitou (112° 42′ E, 34° 42′N), Gedangtou, Sijiaolou, etc.

Five periods, namely Erlitou I–V, are recognized. Stratum 2 has both very rich deposits and stamped-earth house foundations, while Stratum 3 has remains of large buildings and tombs. The fourth stratum, which contains a large number of storage pits, corresponds culturally to the Lower Erligang Phase of the Shang Culture site at Zhengzhou (K.C. Chang 1986a:310). The last, fifth stratum (Erlitou V), is now recognized as equivalent to the Upper Erligang Period at Zhengzhou.

The most impressive of the house foundations belong to two rectangular palatial (*gongdian*) buildings in Stratum 3. Oriented north–south:

> Palace [compound] No:1, excavated in 1960, was 108 by 100 metres in size. The foundation, from over 1 to 2 metres thick, was built on sterile loessic ground of layers about 4.5 centimetres thick to a height of about 80 centimetres above the surrounding ground. At the northern centre of the foundation was built a rectangular platform 36 by 25 metres in size. On top of this low platform are postholes forming the rectangular outline of a hall measuring 30.4 by 11.4 metres. The walls and the roof of the hall were long gone, but enough remains are left to suggest timber framework, wattle-and-daub walls, and gabled roof. Some of the posts rested upon foundation boulders. Along the rims of the whole foundation were found fragments of stamped-earth walls about 45–60 centimetres wide.
>
> (Chang 1986a:310)

About 150 metres northeast of palace No. 1 is a second palace foundation, smaller but better preserved. About 58 metres east–west and 73 metres north–south, it too had a hall in its north central section. Here the hall, about 33 metres square, was clearly divided into three equal spaces, and extended externally by verandas. North of the hall a large pit-grave tomb, 5 metres long by 4 metres wide, had a second-level platform formed by a

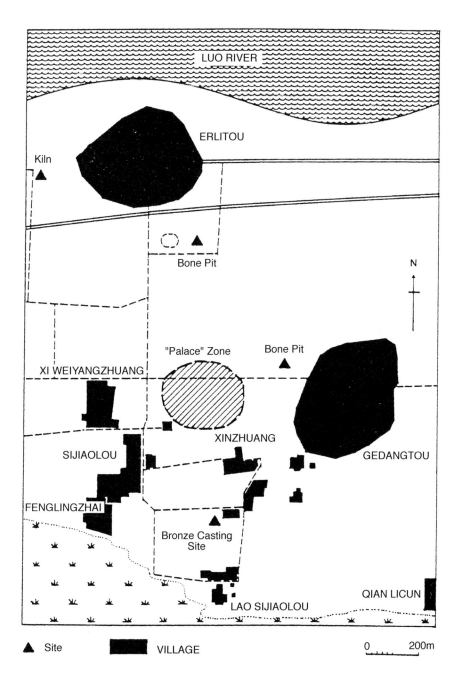

Figure 5.22 Erlitou area map

Source: Thorp 1991:6

315

smaller pit dug in the floor of the larger. Even the fill of this pit was stamped in layers, and the remaining elements of the original grave goods show that this was indeed a very elite burial construction. Other burials in the vicinity were accompanied by no grave goods at all. A veranda gate to the whole compound faced south, as also in palace No. 1 (ibid.).

The palace compounds (of the dominant clans?), as would be expected, were surrounded by many smaller houses, most of which were built on rectangular foundations of various sizes, while others were semi-subterranean. It is tempting to hypothesize that above-ground houses belonged to fellow-clan members, while the below-ground dwellings were occupied by retainers, dependants or even slaves. Some of the tombs, such as those associated with palace No. 1, show signs of ritual slaughter (ibid.:312), a standard feature of elite practice in subsequent Chinese history. Certainly the profligate use of labour was long established.

The artefact pattern is also characteristic of Shang and Zhou periods:

> Stone, shell and bone remained the only materials for agricultural implements: stone and shell knives and sickles and stone, shell and bone hoes. Stone was also the primary material for the axe, adze, chisel and arrowhead, but a few bronze tools have been found – knife, awl, chisel and adze. (The adze turned out to be 98% copper and only 1% tin). There were also bronze arrowheads, a bronze fishook, and bronze disks, probably ornaments on wooden or fabric products. But the major categories of bronzes in terms of quantity and size are ritual vessels, weapons and musical instruments.
>
> (ibid.)

All, indeed, 'instruments' of political control! It is characteristic that the basic productive equipment, used in agriculture, had to rely (and continued to rely) on low-status materials. Metals only 'leaked through' to some artisanal tools, no doubt for the production of expensive or restricted high-status items, such as the lacquered coffins, turquoise-inlaid plate and jades also found at Erlitou. Characteristic pottery types with tripod bases are well represented, mostly of grey fabric, of sandy or fine paste, and made by coiling, moulding, or upon the wheel, although most of the same forms also occur in bronze, either contemporaneously or later.

Another distinctive vessel occurring here is the four-legged *ding*, but by far the most significant artefact finds at Erlitou were shoulder blades of pig, sheep and cattle used for divination. However, no inscriptions occur on those scapulae, supporting Chang's assignment of Erlitou and its related sites, such as Lodamiao, Donggangou, Youcun and many others in central and western Henan, to a position intermediate between Longshan, from which it is manifestly derived (demonstrated by stratified sites such as Cuoli in Luoyang and Xinzhai in Mixian) and Shang, with which it shares so many characteristics. Finally, the radiocarbon profile from the five sites, but mostly from Erlitou and Dongxiafeng (ibid.:318) grouping between 1800 and 2100 BC are too early for Shang (c.1700–1100 BC) but just right for Xia.

Certainly the earliest palatial buildings so far known are found here at Erlitou, and, according to later texts Xia was the first regime to institute dynastic (father–son) succession, supplanting selection or election, and indicating the final dominance of the leading lineage in the conical clan. In tradition, so far reliable, this was initiated by the Great Yu, the First Lord of the Xia, convening the other lords and securing their agreement that his son would succeed him. He did, despite competition from a previously (traditionally?) designated successor, and the dynastic principle was established. Thereafter the supreme title was not lord, *hóu* 侯 but king, *wang*.

Yin Wei-Chang (Yin 1986) has undertaken an examination of Erlitou Culture, looking in detail at the artefacts of each of the four phases. He finds that they fall into two groupings, phases I and II, and phases III and IV, and that the second grouping of artefacts are in large measure identical with those of early Shang levels at Erligang. For instance, 'the large-mouthed *zun* {a vase-shaped wine vessel] so characteristic of Erligang period Shang culture had already appeared by Erlitou III, conspicuous in the manner of an index fossil' (Yin 1986:6). Other manifest differences occur between the vessels of period I and II at Erlitou and periods III and IV. He therefore concludes that

> the ashy pits, pottery kilns, crucibles used in bronze casting, oracle bones and other remains of Erlitou III and IV are identical to comparable remains of the Erlingang period. In addition rammed earth platform foundations and other types of building construction technology, the appearance of regular dented patterns resulting from *hangtu* construction, and methods of platform posthole insertion discovered at Erlitou sites are all identical to comparable remains from [Shang] sites such as Zhengzhou and Anyang.
>
> (ibid.:7)

For Yin, then, the upper levels at Erlitou are indeed Shang, while the lower two levels must represent the Xia regime, given that this site is (at least part of) a ruling centre (Thorp 1991:16). With its elite residences, temples to house the ancestral tablets of the ruling lineage and ceremonial compounds, Erlitou looks very much like a *du* capital (see Figure 5.22) possibly Zhenzin, the residence of the last Xia ruler (Huber 1988:53).

The likelihood of this was greatly strengthened by excavations during the 1980s of a city site at Yanshi Shixianggou, which is both contemporary with Zhengzhou and comparable in size. The walls of Yanshi are roughly 1,700 metres north–south and 1,215 metres across the north side. It encloses a *dian* or palatial structure 36.5 metres in length, its south side opening onto a rectangular courtyard 41 metres across (Figure 5.23a). A slightly later *dian* is even larger, with a length of 54 metres. While Erlitou has produced the earliest cast bronzes so far found in China, 'Zhengzhou has yielded a vast number of bronze vessels in a wide variety of shapes representing a very broad range in their evolution' (ibid.:49), spanning the terminal Erlitou and early Shang. It was here that the four massive square *fang ding* (for the preparation of sacrificial food) were found, one a metre tall and weighing 86.4 kilograms, another 87 centimetres high and weighing 64.3 kilograms. So it seems that Zhengzhou and Yanshi are the immediate post-conquest 'twin' capitals of Shang, namely Bo and Xi-Bo (West Bo), the latter specially walled by the Shang on conquest as a kind of 'garrison town' (ibid.:52–3). For, according to traditional accounts, around 1700 BC, Jie, the last king of Xia, was defeated by Cheng Tang, the first king of the Shang Dynasty. He established his capital called Bo near present-day Boxian in Anhui and Shangqiu in eastern Henan. Apparently twenty-nine kings followed Tang in the Shang Dynasty and the capital city moved five times to Xiao (or Ao), Xiang, Geng, Bi and Yan – and finally, under King Pan Geng, to Yin, the name of which has become synonymous with Shang in Chinese historical writing. At least Shang reign-lengths are realistic.

However, in reviewing the historical reliability of the Bamboo Annals, Keightley (1978b) established that it was composed during the Eastern Zhou Period and is particularly unreliable for the pre-conquest Shang Period. For instance, 'it generally refers to the capital and dynasty as Yin rather than Shang . . ., yet so far as we can tell from the bone-inscriptions the Shang did not call their dynasty Yin and they did call their capital or cult centre Shang' (1978b:429). The mere continuity of tradition and lore is no guarantee of historical accuracy, and the Chinese King Lists suffer problems as least as great as the Sumerian and Egyptian. The final arbiter in such matters is thus not textual exegesis but archaeology.

Archaeological illumination began at the turn of the twentieth century with the recovery of oracle bones from the site of Yinxu (Ruins of Yin) on the Huan River. Localized to the village of Xiaotun northwest of the city of Anyang in northern Henan, fifteen years of rigorous work was conducted by the Academia Sinica at Anyang until stopped by the Sino-Japanese War (K.C. Chang 1986a:317). This is the work that made possible tests of the validity of traditional historiography of the earliest periods. Accurate historical reconstruction demands references to events written down at the time of their occurrence, preferably by those participating in them. Weaker are contemporary references to events based upon the accounts of others, and progressively weaker still are references to events made as they recede in time from the writer. Thus there are two conjoined problems: the quality of the original reference or account, and the integrity of the transmission of that account to later generations (cf. Gardner 1961).

THE LATE SHANG CAPITAL AT ANYANG

Anyang is not a single site but the capital district extending over about 24 square kilometres in which seventeen sites are known so far. Such capital districts are what is usually meant when Shang 'urbanism' is referred to, but those 'cities' lack both nucleation and synoecism. Around it lay the Shang core territory or 'inner capital', an approximately elliptical area, the long axis of which would not exceed 200 kilometres. Surrounding the core territory, but mostly lying west and east of it, was the 'outer domain', consisting of the Daihang Mountains, the Huanghe Corridor and the Yellow River flood zone (Barnes 1993:133). Only the 'inner capital' was directly administered by the Shang bureaucracy, the 'outer domain' perhaps by detached members of the royal lineage or its affines. Surrounding the 'outer domain' buffer zone were many smaller-scale polities, referred as 'lordships', variously allied or opposed to the Shang centre as suited their shifting interests.

The ruling centre of the capital district was located at Xiaotun which, like the rest of the area, was only partly excavated and patchily published. The area of the Xiaotun settlement covers about 10,000 square metres, and, both north to south and earliest to latest falls into three sections. Section A, separated from B by a square stamped-earth foundation of pure loess, is thought to be a ceremonial altar (Chang 1986:322). Section A itself consists of fifteen parallel, rectangular houses on stamped-earth foundations, while Section B includes twenty-one rectangular or square houses on similar foundations. The houses here are arranged in three rows on a north–south axis, the central row consisting of three large houses and five gates (ibid.), and are accompanied by burials which include horse chariots (and horse skeletons) with their multi-spoked (18–28) wheels flanking a small wicker-walled platform.[17] Section C, the latest, consists of seventeen stamped-earth foundations accompanied by burials (ibid.).

Dominating the site, then, were the palaces of Section A with their stamped-earth foundations, pillar supports of stone, timber frames, wattle and daub walls and thatched roofs characteristic of the *tang*-hall building type seen at Erlitou and Fengchu. (see Figs 5.24a and 5.24b).

Section B is thought to comprise the royal temple sector, while C, in the southwest, forms the ceremonial quarter. Nearby are the semi-subterranean houses of the servitors, often in fact 'living on the job', for their dwellings, with diameter of about 4 metres, include large round or rectangular storage bins. The service area includes bronze foundries, stone and bone workshops and pottery kilns (ibid.:325–6). Experiment has conclusively demonstrated that bronze casting was by the piece-mould method (which uses a pottery intermediate mould) and not by *cire perdue*, i.e. lost wax (Li Chi 1977:205–6). Furthermore, Li Chi, the key figure in the Anyang excavations of 1928 to 1937, is of the firm opinion that spearheads in bronze and socketed axes, having no indigenous history, 'could definitely

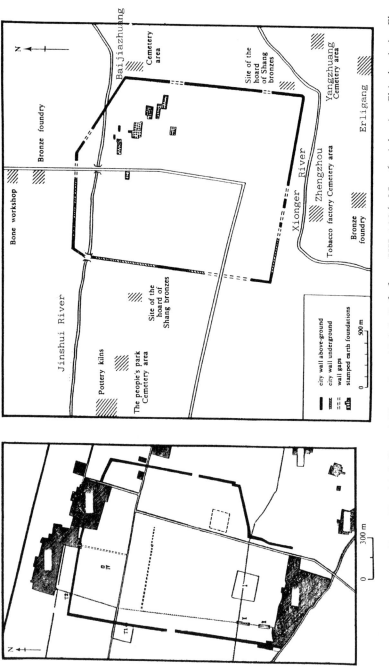

Figure 5.23 Shang city walls in Yanshi (left) and Zhengzhou (right). Left from KK 1984, No. 6; right An Chin-huai, in Chang 1986b:39

be identified with foreign origins' (ibid.), as could the 'wheeled carriages' or chariots.

North of the river at Xibeigang is the royal cemetery of eleven large graves, accompanied by over 1,000 small graves, and, of course, more servitors' dwellings and workshops. 'The eleven large tombs are grouped into a western cluster of seven and an eastern cluster of four, happily coinciding in number with the eleven kings from P'an Geng to Ti Yi who ruled from An-Yang' (K.C. Chang 1986a:326), according to traditional accounts (see above). Li Chi[18] estimated that at least 7,000 working days would be required just to excavate the pits for the major graves, which have long approach ramps north–south and shorter, narrower ones east–west. Major tombs were abundantly furnished with artefacts of stone, jade, shell, bone, antler, tooth, pottery and bronze, and many sacrificial victims, often with heads separated from torso. Chang (ibid.:331) describes the finds here as including many of the very best examples of Shang art. Indeed, their 'overwroughtness' of detail, decoration, modelling and compound imagery is such that one can readily accept Chang's argument (1983a) concerning the pivotal role of art, ritual and shamanism in the wielding of political power.[19] Figure 5.23 shows an oracle bone (ox shoulder blade) on which the Shang Emperor Wen Ding has recorded, in 134 characters in sixteen groups (lower left part missing), a human sacrifice to his ancestors.

'In this sense', Chang (1986a:365) observes, 'the first Chinese civilizations were shamanistic; their art was in fact shamanistic paraphenalia, which were not only the trappings but also the very instruments of political power.' And that is why an artistic representation of a shaman appears on the jacket of this work.

THE EARLIER SHANG CAPITAL AT ZHENGZHOU

But Anyang is a late capital. In 1950 an earlier Shang capital, most probably Bo (see above), was discovered at Zhengzhou, 150 kilometres south of Anyang. Located immediately south of the Yellow River in an industrial city of that name, Zhengzhou has been the provincial capital since 1954. All the early capital cities were located on high ground near a river, preferably in the angle between several rivers, and here the walled area of about 1.75 kilometres north–south and 1.5 kilometres east–west is situated between the Jinshui and Xionger rivers. For much of China's history, Zhengzhou (Cheng-Chou) has been a capital site, and the reason for this is its situation, for, as Chang states:

North China is divided into western highlands and the eastern plains [extending to the sea and to the Shandong Peninsula]. The Yellow River flows out of the western loess highlands in northern Henan and has poured into the eastern plains along several different courses throughout history. Zhengzhou is located near the Yellow River's exit from the highlands, at the meeting place between the west and the east.

(Chang 1980a:263)

It is indeed the presence of all this loess that provides not only a deep, fertile and too easily eroded farming soil, but also the material for the stamped-earth house platforms and city-walls that are such a notable feature of Zhengzhou. As with Anyang, the walled city is but the ruling centre of a large *capital district* extending over no less than 25 square kilometres (An 1986:17). As this lies within the modern built-up area of a city containing well over a million people, excavation has so far been confined to open spaces such as the 'People's Park' (Renmin Gongyuan). However, more than enough evidence has been found at Erligang, a mound about 1 kilometre southeast of the old town, to define and thus give its name to the early period of Middle Shang. The relationships are as shown in Table 5.6.

Similar to Anyang, the palatial area lies in the northeast of the walled city and covers in excess of 300,000 square metres (An Chin-huai 1986:38). The largest of the *hangtu* foundation platforms there measures about 1,000 square metres, the smallest only tens of square metres (ibid.:39). The rammed-earth technique used for building foundations is identical to that employed in constructing the city-walls – the east, south and west walls oriented to the cardinal directions – and indeed were constructed at the same time, according to An (op. cit.).

> As shown in the *jiagu* [oracle bone] scripts, the world was considered square, and each of the four directions probably had its own symbolic colour and certainly its own deity with its own name; winds blown from the four directions were the deities' agents, and countries beyond the kingdom were grouped into four directional classes.
>
> (Chang 1977c:291)

Architecture was likewise almost identical to that found better preserved at Anyang. At Zhengzhou all the major buildings so far excavated are

Table 5.6 The sequence of Shang sites at Zhengzhou

Early Shang	Early Period of Middle Shang	Late Shang
Lodamiao Period Nanguanwai Period (= Late Erlitou Culture)	Erligang Period	Renmin Gongyuan Period* (= Yinxu Period at Anyang)

Source: An 1986:19

Note: *'People's park'; see Figure 5.23, p. 320

framed and clad wooden structures with external pillars 30–40 centimetres in diameter and about 2 metres apart, supporting a veranda covering the edge of the platform (cf. Fig. 5.20).

Given the similarities to Anyang, most likely the rest of the walled area contains a temple complex in the centre and a burial complex at the southern end. Within the walls in the northeast, 'on elevated land, some middle to small slaveowners' tombs have been excavated', the grave goods including the ritual bronzes: *jue* (for heating wine), *ding* (cooking vessel), *li* (cooking vessel), *jia* (for heating wine), *ku* (for wine tasting) and *pan* (water utensils), in addition to jade artefacts such as hairpins, which are also found in bronze (An 1986:40–1).

Certainly, the overall structure of the settlement complex is similar, with workshops for bronze, bone (including human), ceramics, etc., and of course the dwellings of the artisans themselves at some distance from the walled centre, the palace part of which seems to have been surrounded by a moat 5 to 6 metres wide (ibid.:41). Indeed, from the scale of the installations at the manufacturing sites, An (ibid.:45) postulates that production was not merely to satisfy the needs of the Zhengzhou elite, but provided a surplus of goods for wider exchange. The goods manufactured were similar in materials and technique to Anyang.

A cache of thirteen bronzes found outside the southeast corner of the city wall comprised a large square *ding*, a large round *ding*, and round *ding* with flat feet and shallow body; also *gu*, *you*, *lei* and *zun* (ibid.). This cache includes the largest bronze vessels so far discovered at any early Shang site, probably for use by the royal lineage, with, as mentioned above, a square (*fang*) *ding* 1 metre high, weighing 86.4 kilograms. A round companion piece is 87 centimetres high and weighs 64.3 kilograms, while two others stand 81 centimetres high and weigh 75 and 52 kilograms (Huber 1988:49–50). Generally, round *ding* have three legs, square *ding* have four legs.

WESTERN ZHOU

The successor state to Shang, that of Zhou, which assumed hegemony in the central plains after about 1100 BC, repeats the three fundamental characteristics of Chinese prehistory and history:

1   domination by an elite lineage;
2   a common Chalcolithic (Longshan) basis;
3   relative fluidity of settlements.

The state of Zhou moved its centre of gravity several times, initially from the pre-dynastic Zhouyuan (Plain of Zhou) to Feng/Hao the pre-conquest centres, and thence to Luoyang in western Henan (the ancient centre of Erlitou culture) to secure the Shang heartlands after the Zhou conquest. Abandonment of the west and the forced concentration around Luoyang in 771 BC upon the sacking of the western capital by the 'barbarians', marked the end of Western Zhou and set in train the period of decline known as Eastern Zhou.

Zhou were the most westerly of the San Dai in origin and are still poorly known archaeologically, although well known from later texts and inscribed bronzes (mostly from the Zhouyuan, the 'Plains of Zhou', in central Shaanxi). Indeed, to later thinkers the Zhou was the model of good governance and moral rectitude. Three batches of their oracle bone inscriptions, which were not previously known to have been used by them in this early period, have been found since 1977 in the Zhouyuan, indicating that the Zhou court was literate before the conquest and in other respects also the equal of the Shang.

One site which provided a cache of oracle bones and which dates from the Zhou predynastic of the eleventh century BC (thus later than Erlitou but earlier than the conquest of Shang) is this elite compound at Fenchu village in Qishan district, Shaanxi, excavated in 1976. Built as usual on a pounded-earth (*hangtu*) platform raised 1.3 metres, and measuring 45 metres north–south and 32 metres east–west, are symmetrical components of hall, courtyards, perimeter chambers and gatehouses. All were differentially raised above the basic platform level and surrounded by a solid wall pierced by a southfacing gate with barrier screen (Figures 5.24a and 5.24b).

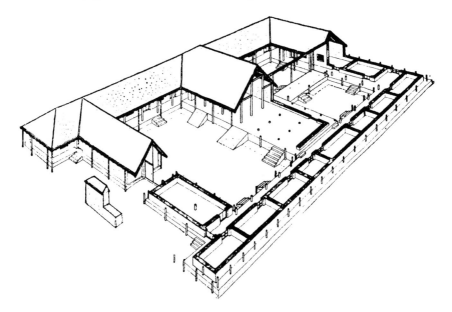

Figure 5.24a Reconstruction of Fenchu elite buildings, Qishan district, Shaanxi, late second millennium BC

Source: Thorp 1983:27

The fullest study of the Western Zhou is that of Hsu and Linduff, who write of this period:

> The proto-Zhou were first located in the Shaanxi-Shanxi highland, where they absorbed elements from the Guangshe culture and from the steppe dwellers. King Liu moved his people to the lower Fen Valley and to the western bank of the Yellow River, where they resumed agriculture. His son Qing Jie, led the Zhou to the upper valley of the Jing River. They stayed there until Dan Fu (or Tai Wang) moved again to the Wei Valley in order to avoid incursion by the Rongdi nomads. During this period, the Zhou mingled with

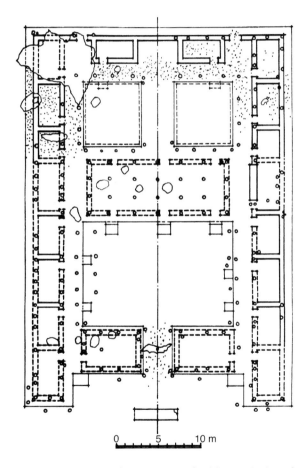

0   5   10 m

Figure 5.24b Plan of Fenchu elite buildings, Qishan district, Shaanxi, late second millennium BC

Source: Thorp 1983:27

the Qiang people, who provided them with a cultural inheritance from the Siwa and Anguo peoples and formed a political alliance with them. In all these stages, the advanced Shang bronze culture constantly imparted its influence on the Zhou.

The Qi area was the region in which all these influences would come to fruition. The contact among the proto-Zhou, the native Shaanxi Longshan, the Qiang, and the northern steppe traditions, plus the tradition of the Shang produced momentum for change and development.

(Hsu and Linduff 1988:66–7)

Shang contained the Zhou for a time, but ultimately they were unable to resist. The cultural diversity acquired by the Zhou gave them the flexibility to overcome the much more populous and well-established Shang. It also conferred on the Zhou a certain breadth and tolerance that were to produce the beginnings of a humanist outlook.

The synthesis occurred on the plains of Zhouyuan in the counties of Qishan (Qi mountain) and Fufeng in central Shaanxi (middle reaches of the River Wei) where, according to traditional accounts, a centre was established by King Tai Wang (or Tan Fu). Those accounts of the seminal role of the Zhouyuan are now supported by the concentration of archaeological sites that lie around the Weihe River, a tributary flowing south into the Weishui River which joins the Huanghe. The capital district of Zhouyuan covers about 15 square kilometres.

Roof-tiles make their appearance for the first time in China, and are probably a Zhou invention, as also are fired bricks, which were used to protect exposed faces of tamped-earth structures. The tile-like bricks found in the ruins at Yuntang of Fufeng, and measuring 36 centimetres by 25 centimetres by only 2.5 centimetres, had four knobs on the back that enabled them to be securely lodged in packed earth (Hsu and Linduff 1988:300).

Initially only used for ridge-tiling, after the mid-Zhou period stretches of important buildings received tile cover. At Fengchu, extensive use was made of plaster covering platforms, walls and rooftops. To ensure stability, drainage was taken care of by clay pipes and pebble layers. Other than this, innovations are confined to variations on a common artefactual scheme shared with Shang and Xia, as would be expected from a shared Neolithic/Chalcolithic background and sustained interaction. For instance, bronze knives of early Western Zhou are characteristically bent with a concave back and have a square loop at the end of the handle, something not found elsewhere. Arrowheads, too, differ in minor ways from Shang types. But like them, the Zhou cast a similar range of bronze ritual vessels and employed the horse-and-chariot in warfare. The Zhou did, however, improve on Shang body armour and this conferred an advantage on their troops when it came to the final battles.

> At the centre of this palatial locus, from Yuntang to Qizhen and
> Qijia, were Western Zhou workshops and the residential areas of
> the commoners. Among the workshops recovered were those where
> bone tools, bronzes, and pottery were manufactured. In the southern
> portions and elsewhere, especially near Hejia, Licun and Zhuangbai,
> more than a hundred human burials have been uncovered.
>
> (K.C. Chang 1986a:353)

All of this indicates a similar (dispersed) settlement pattern to Xia and
Shang. Widely spread around a palace and cult centre are workshop areas
and the houses of the artisans and other retainers. Clearly a common social
structure is determining physical layout, technology, economy and ideology
in all three cases (cf. Fig. 5.23).

This is even clearer at the immediately pre-conquest capital district around
the Feng River by the major modern city of Xi'an whither the Zhou rulers
had been forced to move from Zhouyuan under 'barbarian' pressure. Here
the cities of Feng and Hao were established from which the conquest of
Shang was launched. Feng lies southwest of Xi'an, on the east bank of the
River Feng; while Hao, Wen Wang's capital for only fifteen years and thereafter a centre for royal temples, lies on the opposite bank.

The capitals Feng and Hao were served, *inter alia*, by the village of
Zhangjiapo, the dwellings so far excavated consisting of fifteen semi-
subterranean pit-houses, some shallow, some deep. The living-space of a
shallow one measured 2.2 by 4.2 metres, the depth from the surface being
1.4 metres (Hsu and Linduff 1988:303). The circular thatched roof was
supported on a central pole, and the perimeter rim wall was made of stamped
earth. The dwelling was accessed by a ramp, and contained only a hearth,
sleeping area and storage niche. Despite the fire-hardening of walls and floor,
the dwellings were wet during rain (ibid.:308 citing the *Zhuangzi*). Deep
dwellings could have floors as deep as 3 metres below ground level. They
were oval in shape and from 7.8 to 9.5 metres in diameter, divided into two
rooms by a sectional wall pierced by a door opening of 1.2 metres (ibid.:304).
Dwelling pits were accompanied by pits that were both narrower and deeper,
and those were storage pits and wells. Similar dwelling pits, standard for the
'lower' classes, were also found at Cixian (illustrated in ibid.:306–7).

The inhabitants of Zhangjiapo village seem to have undertaken all the
elite-support tasks from farming to handicrafts, and/or they supplied
the tools for those who provided that range of services, for farming and
hunting implements occur alongside bone tools and bronze knives. Of sixty-
five bladed tools most were of stone, and of fifty-one axes only seven were
polished. Additionally there were ten polished stone chisels, a small bronze
axe and fifteen short (20 centimetres) bronze knives with end-loop handles.
Farm spades were predominantly of bone (eighty-two examples on scapulae
or lower jaw bones of horses and cattle); twenty-three of stone and seven

of seashell. For harvesting there were no less than 246 knives and ninety sickles, mostly of shell, something very common at other Western Zhou sites (ibid.:74). The rather thick knives were polished to give rectangular single- or doubled-edged blades, while the sickle blades were drilled at the rear for fastening to a handle by leather thongs, a method of sickle construction still used in the Chinese countryside.

The small bone implements were awls and needles, which more rarely occur in bronze and horn. Made of deer antler and other bone were no less than 310 arrowheads. Clay moulds for casting bronze bulbs were found, as were clay pressers for potting and spinning wheels for yarn (ibid.).

There was nothing here to give the Zhou a technological advantage. Zhou overcame Shang in a rolling process, surrounding the Shang state with Zhou allies, formerly allies of Shang. Even after the conquest, with a population in the homeland of only about 60,000 to 70,000 people (ibid.:113), the Zhou elite were obliged to seek accommodations and rule through allies, that is by agreement. Although a new Zhou capital was established to the west of the Shang capital at Luoyang, the Shang elite were encouraged to move to it and continued to rule over the indigenous Shang population on behalf of the new masters, with whom the old Shang elite merged. Political flexibility and accommodation are thus the key to Zhou's initial success.

Luoyang was the eastern capital built by Zhou Gong at the site of an existing Shang settlement to secure the territories of the middle Yellow River. By the time that it had become the (refugium) capital of the Eastern Zhou after 771 BC, reliable dates for Chinese history were less than a century old. The first such reliable date is 841 BC and it relates to the exile (to Zhi) of the despised King Li from the capital by the great lords of the realm, who formed a regency for fourteen years, and then handed over to the crown prince, enthroned as King Xuan. However, his son, King Yu, was not up to the crisis affecting the Zhou empire in the eighth century, and he was the last king to rule the west, that is, the area encompassing the original Zhou homeland. After 841 BC Chinese history is accountable annually (ibid.:144). The Zhou court included a corps of archivists, *zuoce*, whose functions ranged from preparing 'memorials' (documents of ceremony) to writing historiographic records.

Another fundamental distinction was external, namely between the plains agriculturalists, amongst whom Zhou overlordship would be culturally acceptable and thus stable, and the pastoral nomads to the north of the Yellow River. Thus the Rong (or the Shanrong) people, the ancient Tungus, were dominant over much of the present province of Hebei (where Beijing is situated), and the Xiajiadian steppe culture proved both very influential in its own right and highly resistant to Shang/Zhou influence. Indeed, the Western Zhou, like the Roman Empire, had great difficulty in maintaining its northern borders, as Hsu and Linduff observe:

The Zhou states, including Jin, could barely hold the defense lines along the north bank of the Yellow River. That area formed a buffer zone in southern Shanxi and shielded the Zhou from the non-Zhou who inhabited much of the Shanxi plateau.

(ibid.:211)

But pressure came from the west as well as the north, and by the eighth century BC it forced the abandonment of the original Zhou lands in the west and the retreat to Luoyang in the east. However, as with all ancient empires, the fall was not due to a single cause. The nomads administered the *coup de grâce* because the regime had been weakened by a combination of natural disasters, notably earthquake and famine, producing vagrancy, crime, maladministration and general impoverishment, even of high officials.

Centuries of peace had produced a routinized ruling class that could not cope with sudden excursions from normality which included spiralling elite revenge warfare (Lewis 1990), further aggravating the social and economic problems of the multitude. The western capital was invaded by groups of Rong, assisted by disaffected members of the elite, notably the Marquis of Shen (whose sister had been set aside as Queen). King Yu was killed, the capital looted, and the former heir-apparent, Shen's nephew Yijiu, fled to Luoyang. There he set up court as King Ping, the first monarch of the Eastern Zhou. However, the old domination was lost and what remained was just a variable authority. The increasingly nominal hegemony of the Eastern Zhou is traditionally divided into the Spring and Autumn Period (771–476 BC) and the Warring States Period (475–255 BC), brought to a close by the victory of King Zheng of Qin over Chao and Qi in 221 BC. He thereby became Emperor (Huangdi, Universal Ruler) Qin Shi, and China thereafter was not a single state but an empire, ever tending to pull apart into its diverse regions. Ironically, Qin was a state established by the Quan Rong who had, by taking over the territory around Xi'an, overthrown the Western Zhou regime.

Luoyang remained the capital for the Eastern Han (AD 25–221), Western Jin (AD 266–316) and the Northern Wei (AD 494–534). It served further as secondary capital of the Tang (AD 618–906) in the Middle Empire Period (see Table 5.2).

CHILDE'S CHECKLIST

1 *Cities that are more extensive and more densely settled than any previous settlements.*

The Longshan cultures produced many large, walled towns with evidence of social stratification, but no cities until the Xia centre at Erlitou in Henan (where there are dozens of sites of this period) around the beginning of the second millennium. The layout of Erlitou became characteristic of the Shang and Zhou cities that followed, namely, a dispersed city of districts: palace, temple, tomb, workshop, and servitor housing, all spatially distinct and in parts even walled off. Although the areal extent of cities grew over time, the dispersed structure barely altered. Thus the San Dai 'city' was more a collection of functionally distinct villages forming a *settlement cluster* than a city in its usual sense: that of a large nucleated settlement comprising a continuously built-up area. The population density that goes with nucleation is the key to sustained social intercourse in a face-to-face society. Nucleation requires that, in addition to public/ceremonial spaces, the only spaces within a city are the lines of communication, namely streets and lanes, with roads linking different parts of the city. Lanes, streets and roads together form a dendritic network integrating the whole. The Bronze Age city in China was not like this nor was it like the cities of India, Mesopotamia or Egypt.

2 *Full-time specialists: craftsmen, transport workers, merchants, officials and priests.*

Longshan fine-black ware, jade, lacquer and other fine work were obviously made by specialist craftsmen. Immediately above we have also noted that craftsmen's 'villages' were an intrinsic part of ruling centres.

The role of bronze craftsmen and the importance of their products in ritual and war are such as to need no further comment. This is also the case with the role of transport workers. However, the presence of merchants in the second millennium is not clear, except during the final centuries of Western Zhou (first millennium) when some merchant families could be richer than noble ones. Also, according to Hsu and Linduff (1988:331–2), from the mid Western Zhou Period onward the bronze industry was secularized and commercialized. All of this occurs toward the end of the San Dai Period, however, and there is no evidence so far for merchants playing a role in early periods, even of the Western Zhou.

3 *Concentration of surplus.*

In China much of this was in the form of 'living labour': capital districts contained many settlements of artisans working in bronze for ritual and military purposes and employing a wide range of materials for luxury goods. Everything from stamped-earth foundations to the decoration and maintenance of wooden buildings was labour-intensive, and a general corvee existed in addition to the tax-rent that peasants on Zhou fedual holdings were obliged to provide. Per-capita agricultural productivity in the central plains was probably always low, given the soils, climate and the restricted range of domesticates available.

4 *Truly monumental public buildings.*

It has to be conceded that of the four civilizations examined, China has the least 'truly monumental public buildings'. This is for three reasons.

Figure 5.25 Emblems that may be related to professions
Source: Chang 1980a:232

   i   What is categorized as 'public' is highly problematic in a Chinese cultural context. Thus the Forbidden City in Beijing and its fore-runners elsewhere were indeed forbidden to all but a tiny minority. Perhaps one reason why roofs can be so decorative in China is because the rest of the building is often hidden behind blank walls.

   ii   The absence of nucleated cities during the San Dai period, the dispersed layout of which

   iii mirrors a 'social dispersion' reflecting in the built environment rather extreme social distance between the tops and bottoms of clans, between clans, and between *guoren*, the politically enfran-chised, and the rest, namely the mass of the peasantry. This may seem ironical given the premium placed on cultural cohesion and homogeneity in both early, historical and modern China. The need to overcome such contradictions has given rites and rhetoric a partic-ular importance, seen so clearly in Confucianism and in the public temples/shrines discussed under Point 11.

5   *The presence of a ruling class, including 'priests, civil and military leaders and officials {who} absorb a major share of the concentrated surplus'.*
The Xia regime represents the stabilization of a ruling class and with it a rudimentary state apparatus. Further developed under the Shang, by Western Zhou times a government centred upon but distinguished from the court exists, and with it Departments of State, civil and mil-itary, staffed by a hierarchy of officials. The capital(s) and the armies did indeed require the concentration of surplus to construct and sustain them, even to the sacrifice of 'surplus' people, notably war-captives. However, the peasantry at large (the *zhong*) had to surrender a large proportion of their produce and time in taxes and state projects, although much of this was consumed by the local lords. The situation is well described by the ancient saying, cited by Hsu (1965:8): 'Dukes live on tribute, ministers on their estates, *shi* ['gentlemen'] on the land, and peasants on their toil.' Of course, of those named, the peasants were the *only* ones who lived from their own toil.

6   *Technical expertise, specifically systems of writing and numerical notation.*
For reasons that will become apparent, I am going to consider point 6 with point 7 'exact and predictive sciences: arithmetic, geometry, astronomy and a calendar'.

    Visible by Shang times are occupationally specialized lineages (*zu*) – potters, tanners, smiths, etc. – with those supplying non-productive goods and services, such as *ding*-tripod maker, flag maker, *li*-tripod maker, especially chariot maker or executioner, necessarily attached to elite centres. Chang (1980a:232) provides illustrations of emblems that he thinks may be related to professions (Figure 5.25, p. 331).

the probable fact that Chinese writing had its roots in the marking of pottery for social identification, in marked contrast to the roots of Near Eastern writing in an accounting system, may give us a strong hint of ancient Chinese priorities: membership in one's kin group was the first thing that the first writing recorded, because it was key to the ancient Chinese social order. Information that was essential to the working of an economic network . . . was transmitted within the network of lineages. We cannot say that records of economic transactions were unnecessary under such a framework, but the fact is that archaeological records of Shang writing . . . consist of group identification marks (pottery marks and bronze emblems), divination records (oracle bone inscriptions) and records of gift exchanges. . . . Only the last kind of written records can be called economical, but even here their explicit purpose was possibly political.

(ibid.:247–8)

Indeed, the very expression for civilization in Chinese (Mandarin) – *wen hua* – actually refers to 'the transformative power of writing'.[20] Under the Shang there was a large overlap of priests with officials, particularly in the key shamanistic roles that involved literacy. Under the Zhou, government became secularized and feudalized with the emergence of regular corps of officials, military (*shi* or *shi shi*, 'commanders') and civilian, notably the *si* 'directors' (i.e. chief ministers), the *zuoce* (archivists) and the *shi* (scribes).

There is no doubt that the San Dai Chinese were numerate and could record numbers and quantities. Computation was positional and decimal (base ten). However, there is no evidence for technical expertise at this time in the likes of geometry, which the Egyptians had been routinely deploying in pyramid and temple construction and in field mensuration since the third millennium, and which is required for other technical procedures, notably mathematical astronomy.

Like their hunter–gatherer predecessors, the early agrarian societies' calendar was lunar or monthly (twelve per year) and China was no exception. Monthly differences took adequate account of seasonal changes and were regional, the best known probably being the Xia and Zhou calendars, as recorded in the *Qi Yue*, section of the *Book of Poetry*. In those calendars reference was made to 'star' positions (especially the 'Fire Star') and meridians, of air temperatures and animal behaviour, and, of course, to the growth of plants. Not only agricultural tasks, but economic and cultural behaviour too are accounted on a monthly basis.[21] Seasonality and weather are, of course, basic to an agricultural regime, something seen particularly clearly in the traditional list of

二 十 四 节 气

The Twenty-four Solar Terms

立春 the Beginning of Spring (1st solar term)	立秋 the Beginning of Autumn (13th solar term)
雨水 Rain Water (2nd solar term)	处暑 the Limit of Heat (14th solar term)
惊蛰 the Walking of Insects (3rd solar term)	白露 White Dew (15th solar term)
春分 the Spring Equinox (4th solar term)	秋分 the Autumnal Equinox (16th solar term)
清明 Pure Brightness (5th solar term)	寒露 Cold Dew (17th solar term)
谷雨 Grain Rain (6th solar term)	霜降 Frost's Descent (18th solar term)
立夏 the Beginning of Summer (7th solar term)	立冬 the Beginning of Winter (19th solar term)
小满 Grain Full (8th solar term)	小雪 Slight Snow (20th solar term)
芒种 Grain in Ear (9th solar term)	大雪 Great Snow (21st solar term)
夏至 the Summer Solstice (10th solar term)	冬至 the Winter Solstice (22nd solar term)
小暑 Slight Heat (11th solar term)	小寒 Slight Cold (23rd solar term)
大暑 Great Heat (12th solar term)	大寒 Great Cold (24th solar term)

Figure 5.26 Formalised agricultural calendar (of the northern interior)

Source: Peking Dictionary 1978:976

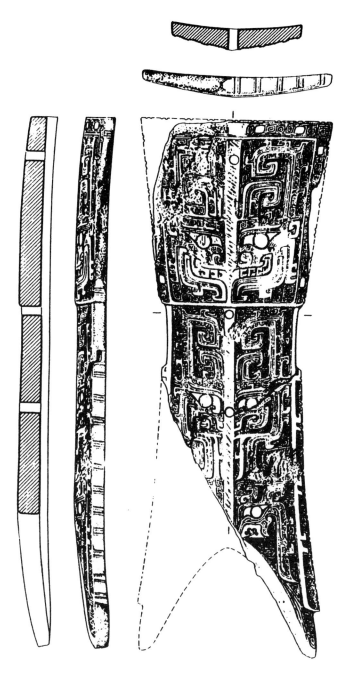

Figure 5.27   Carved bone plates bearing three stacked *taoties*
Source: Li Chi (1977:218)

'Twenty-Four Solar Terms' appended to the *Chinese–English Dictionary* published by Beijing in 1978 (see Figure 5.26, p. 334). It is significant that the main state publisher of such texts regarded something as traditional as the Twenty-Four Solar Terms (Fig. 5.26) as significant enough to append to this major work of reference.

According to tradition, imperial concerns with the calendar reached right back to the culture-heroic times that preceded and accompanied the foundation of the Xia state. Thus Emperor Yao, the fourth emperor of the prehistoric Wu-Di or 'Five Emperor' Period, whose traditional reign was the twenty-fourth century and who was held up by Confucians as an ideal ruler and sage, is said to have appointed the Xi and He families to 'fix the time' calendrically. Incorporated into the famous *Shang Shu* (*The Book of Documents*) is the *Yao Dian* (*The Canon of Yao*), approximately a third of which is devoted to astronomical topics such as the determination of seasons and calendar-making (Chen and Xi 1993:32–3). 'According to the Yao Dian, during the time of Yao the seasons were determined by the meridian passage of four star-groups, known later as *xiu*, the "equatorial compartments"' (ibid.). This important concept is developed in Chen and Xi's important article on the origins of astronomy in China, convincingly disposing of much misinformation, such as that Chinese astronomy owed much to Babylonian. It does indeed seem that Chinese calendrics have significant roots in the third millennium and that subsequent developments both proceeded in parallel with those of the Near East and generally kept pace with advances there.

According to Chen and Xi,

> By the fourteenth century BC the Chinese calendar was a lunisolar one in which the moon's phase and seasonal changes were reconciled by expressing the twelve-month year in terms of combinations of short and long months and by the occasional use of an intercalated month. The Yin [Shang] calendar revealed by the shell-bone inscriptions is consistent with the account of the Yao calendar given in the Yao Dian. . . . By the tenth century BC systematic sun-shadow measurements using a gnomon [rod] had become available for the accurate determination of the seasons.
>
> (Chen and Xi 1993:40–1)

From the Shang Dynasty onward to the end of the Qing there existed astronomical bureaux to determine 'when the civil year of each dynasty or ruler would commence, and [to try] with varying degrees of success, to reconcile the incommensurable calendrical interests of emperors, bureaucrats, farmers and philosophers' (Smith 1992:3–4). One key sort of reconciliation would have to be of the lunar (synodic) months (29.53059 days) with the solar year (365.2422 days) which, with a 10.87512 days annual discrepancy, meant the insertion of an intercalary lunar month. Since Han times (206 BC–AD 221) at the latest, an extra, thirteenth, month was inserted about every three years or rather twenty-two times in every sixty-year cycle, producing a thirteen lunar month year for the year of correction (and reduplicating a month number), subject to definite restrictions:

> It cannot be inserted after the first, eleventh or twelfth month, and its location is determined by the rule that the vernal equinox must occur in the second month, the summer solstice in the fifth, the autumnal equinox in the eighth, and the winter solstice in the eleventh. There is a further provision that the intercalary month shall be one in which the sun enters no sign of the zodiac.
>
> (O'Neill 1987:20)

Obviously, the calendar, solar or lunar, was no mere technical matter, but a means of providing regularity amidst flux:

> From the earliest times the Chinese calendar exemplified the notion of cosmological kingship. According to long-standing political beliefs in China, a sovereign had to understand the processes of change in the universe so as to assure that the social order and the natural way (dao), would be fully congruent. An inaccurate calendar, like the failure of designated officials to predict cosmic events such as eclipses, became a sign of moral imperfection, a warning that the monarch's virtue was not adequate to keep him in touch with celestial rhythms. . . . This accounts for the seemingly insatiable demand on the part of Chinese rulers for precision in calendrical calculations that far exceeded normal agricultural, bureaucratic and economic requirements.
>
> (Smith 1992:2)

For purposes of cultivation the seasonal/lunar calendar was adequate, and likewise for the economic and bureaucratic order dependent upon it. But to 'tune in' to the cosmos and thus be ritually alert, the king needed continuous astronomical ministration. Further, new dynasties required new calendars, while the commoners, at least from the Han Dynasty onwards, had recourse to almanacs, as they still do today.

8   *Full-time sculptors, painters or seal engravers.*

In historical times painting, especially landscape painting, with the

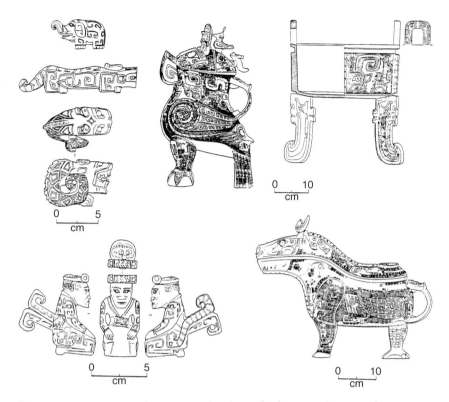

Figure 5.28 Bronze vessels (right) and jades (left) from Fu Hao's tomb at Xiaotun. Top right is a *fang ding*.

Source: Yinxu Fu Hao mu 1980

maobi or hair brush of the sort traditionally used for writing, became a widespread accomplishment of the scholar-gentleman, along with the writing of poetry. How early and how common painting was is unclear, given the perishability of the media: silk, wood, bamboo and later paper. This is also the case with personal name seals that stamped with ink, and are still common today. Highly accomplished tomb murals survive from Han and Tang periods, a technique that must have begun earlier.[22] Han painting probably owes a great deal to, or was derived from, the state of Chu (Creel 1964:175). For earlier periods, Rawson (1996b:19) observes that 'both the Shang and the Zhou relied upon ritual practice and ceremony, rather than images in paintings or sculpture, to proclaim their powers and view of the universe'.

Li Chi conjectures (1977:170) that the absence of early Shang writing on oracle bones is due to the lack of permanence of brush-applied ink on bone, stone[23] and pottery. In contrast the readable Shang records are legible because they were not brushed but inscribed on scapulae and tortoise shells, with carapaces and plastrons providing a larger flat surface than scapulae (cf. Figure 5.27).

The modelling techniques used to decorate bronzes with relief decoration was actually a form of sculpture, although some vessels were left plain. Some carried quite lengthy inscriptions and this has to be regarded as a form of engraving. Sculptural forms with masses of fine detail are seen in both bronze vessels and jades from the tomb of Fu Hao at Xiaotun (cf. Zheng Zhenxiang 1996) (Figure 5.28).

Sculpture in stone, such as the famous examples from royal tomb 1001 at Xibeigang, Anyang, are highly ritualistic/shamanistic, taking the form of anthropozoomorphs: man-tiger, man-pig, man-toad or frog, etc., cleverly merging the two. Here the condition of being 'taken over' by 'spirit guides' is indicated, as is the menace of the powers tapped by 'going over' into the realm of animal and other nature spirits.

9   *Regular foreign trade, involving comparatively large volumes.*
This is easy at one level – it does not apply to San Dai China. There is no Chinese equivalent to Gulf or Levant trade. There were no doubt uneasy exchanges with pastoralists when they were not actually raiding. The cowrie shells used as elite money had to be brought from the coast, and as elsewhere items of elite consumption, such as bronze, were transported considerable distances. But 'trade' means regular exchanges of significant amounts of goods, and of this there is little evidence in the formative periods. In the Iron Age, when there is evidence for sustained exchanges of goods between regions, those regions are provinces of China itself. It is legendary, but true, that there was nothing that China wanted or thought it needed from overseas. Thus silk traders made their way to China when they could. Until the Tang Dynasty (AD 618–906), the Chinese did not go abroad to trade. The Roman drain of gold to Han China (206 BC–AD 221) in payment for silk was repeated by the drain of silver from eighteenth-century Britain to pay for tea as well as silk, and the Opium Wars of the nineteenth century were the consequence.

10 *Peasants, craftsmen and rulers form a community.*
The original, pre-state solidarity was the highly potent solidarity of the clan. So powerful was it that the clan's own ranking mechanisms were employed by certain lineages (see below) to make themselves elite lineages, ultimately subordinating the clan. At least as early as the Longshan, the division of society into three categories of elite, their servitors and the rest became well established, that is, secure. Social divisions were enhanced with the state, but as its advent was an incre-

mental process and not a revolutionary one. The shared beliefs and practices that form culture were never challenged, inducing the bulk of society to continue identifying with the elite strata, through the medium of what all supposedly had in common.

11 *Social solidarity is expressed in the pre-eminence of the temple or sepulchral shrine.*

This obviously connects with point 4 above. *Lijing*, the *Book of Rites*, states that 'All things stem from heaven and man originates from ancestors.' Probably the most common class of temple, and certainly the most politically important, were the ancestral halls, built and maintained by clans for the veneration of their own ancestors. The halls celebrated the rootedness, success and longevity of the clan itself. The more important the clan, the more imposing the temple structure, and the royal ones were certainly the most imposing of all, very much off-limits to others, as indeed were all ancestral halls. Usually located at the centre of the clan's village or town district, the solidarity they represented was corporate and thus segmental.

Community temples expressing general social solidarity also (necessarily) existed, particularly in larger towns and cities, and dating from Zhou times at least. These were the temples of the city god, *chenghuang miao*, which, amongst many other things, protected the city from disease, fire and sack. The countryside was dotted with numerous temples and shrines to protect agriculture and promote unity in the face of calamity:

> In the imperial days before 1911, in every centre of political administration, from national and provincial capitals to county seats, a standard group of altars were dedicated to deities related to agriculture. Few descriptions of Peking omit mentioning the impressive and inspiring architecture of the Temple of Prayer for the Good Year and the associated Altar of Heaven. In provincial capitals and county seats there were the inevitable altars of the creator of agriculture (Xiannongtan), of the earth and grain god (Shejitan), of wind, cloud, thunder, and rain gods, and, at times, of the god of drought (Youtan). On behalf of the peasants, the emperor, provincial governors and county magistrates throughout the country plowed ceremonial fields and offered sacrifices to the agricultural deities at these altars in the spring and sometimes also in the fall, praying for assistance from the supernatural forces to bring 'harmonious winds and timely rain' for the year.
>
> (Yang 1961:65)

Additionally there were temples and altars for specific local cults and to deified meritorious individuals of local or national fame. A conspicuous example of the latter dating from the Three Kingdoms Period (AD 221–265) was the cult of Guan Yu, who died (AD 219) whilst fighting to restore legitimate Han government. Though a historical individual, he came to be regarded as the god of war. His cult, very widespread and very popular thanks to romances, operas and myths, was much associated with magical powers. Traditional Chinese religion is usually described as polytheistic, but is in fact much nearer to animism (Chang 1983a; Yang 1961:23, 65) as powers are held to reside in many kinds of objects, places, persons, animals, artefacts, and natural phenomena.

Religion begins as a method of coping with ecological conditions, through the reduction of anxiety in the individual psyche, and through the promotion of social co-operation in addressing the real forces that beset. Individual salvation is thereby preferred in the context of social reassurance. The bitter irony is that the cultivators, become the subordinate mass of peasants, were then beset not only by the powers of Nature, but also by the powers of the state, or rather by the hierarchy that it underwrites (cf. note 6(c).1).

12 *State organization is dominant and permanent.*

It could be argued that the Xia regime was the coming into being of the state as a permanent institution. By the time of the Shang takeover, however, there is no question but that a fully developed state existed which further dominated adjacent populations. Thereafter China alternated between a unified imperial state and a number of contending states. However, once hierarchy had become established in the Longshan and had become the developed condition of the San Dai, there was no question that Chinese populations would not be state ordered. The transcendent nature of the state was such that the use of an emperor's personal name was taboo not only during his lifetime, but even during his dynasty. Instead a 'reign title' was used during his life and a 'temple name' after his death. It is generally by the temple name that emperors are known to posterity.

For 2.2 millennia, China has had an Emperor, Mao and Deng being the last of more than 200. Presently, there is rule by committee.

Where the economy leads, ideology, politics and culture eventually follow. Four thousand years of state order in China are being transformed for a new millennium. What cannot be doubted is that the twenty-first century will be the Chinese century, so long as economic smash-and-grab and political intransigence do not send the world into a spiral of decline.

6

CONCLUSION: THE EMERGENCE OF SOCIAL COMPLEXITY

HOW USEFUL DO CHILDE'S CRITERIA TURN OUT TO BE?

Table 6.1 sets them out in comparative form. Childe's insight, based only on what was known at mid-century, is clearly remarkable. All the pristine civilizations have key structural attributes in common, and where they differ is signal. Two major contrasts stand out boldly. The first is that the most westerly and easterly civilizations take the form of territorial states. This much is conventional. However, the analysis (which the table only summarizes) shows something quite unexpected: namely that Harappan Civilization took the form of a stateless oecumene.

Relying on organic social solidarity (inderdependency arising from the division of productive labour), it functioned on a grand scale without the presence of a ruling class or a government of centralized administration, taxation and enforcement. Organic social solidarity was also strong in Mesopotamia, which until the middle of the second millennium was a culture area consisting of city-states. They were, however, states with marked social stratification and a ruling class, all rooted in the exigencies of managerialism. What a contemporary society ancient Mesopotamia turns out to be! Thus on the basis of present knowledge, Indus civilization stands out as exceptional in its mode of social integration and control.

It has been apparent for some time now that Service's (1962) sequence of band, tribe, chiefdom and state fails to describe real developments in the centres of pristine civilization (Maisels 1987). Further, it literally has no place for the Indus oecumene or the Halaf distributed, acephalous and a-centric network. Accordingly, the band–tribe–chiefdom–state sequence should be replaced by a more complex one that branches initially in the early Neolithic (one path is blocked), and decisively in the Chalcolithic, the period when complex divisions of labour are established (see Figure 6.1).

The other thing that emerges from Table 6.1 concerns trade, specifically China's (San Dai) trade: there was none, if what is meant is 'foreign' trade.

342

Table 6.1 Attributes of the urban revolution as found in Egypt, Mesopotamia, India and China

	Egypt	Mesopotamia	Indus	China
1. Cities	1	1	1	1
2. Full-time specialists	1	1	1	1
3. Surplus concentration	1	1	1	1
4. Monumental public buildings	1	1	1	1
5. Ruling class and functionaries	1	1	0	1
6. Writing and numerical notation	1	1	?	1
7. Exact and predictive sciences	1	1	1	1
8. Representative art	1	1	1	1
9. Regular foreign trade	1	1	1	0
10. Organic social solidarity	1	1	1	1
11. Temples and shrines pre-eminent	1	1	0	1
12. State organization dominant and permanent	1	1	0	1

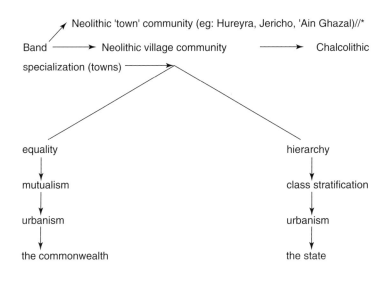

* This path is blocked. Settlements become too big, too soon, upon an Early Neolithic basis.

Figure 6.1 Contrasting evolutionary trajectories from foraging to large-scale complex societies

The early state societies of the central plains were not that extensive, and dealt with contiguous societies not much different from themselves. Eventually all 'became Han', even the so-called barbarians. The important points are, first, that the mode of production (Maisels 1990:262–74) was virtually the same in each of those societies, and, second, that everything needful, even copper and tin, later iron and coal, could be had from within the Chinese culture area without ever going abroad or even trafficking with foreigners. All that social/trade intercourse produced during the Chinese Bronze Age was a more extensive 'internal' exchange system. The costs of this 'closed' system in terms of later stagnation ('the high-level equilibrium trap') have been fully worked out by Mark Elvin (1972, 1973, 1984).

In earlier work (1990, 1993a) I showed that social stratification *preceded* and was the basis for the emergence of the state, which in turn furthered and consolidated the system of stratification. There is no reason in principle, and less in fact, why trade should have anything to do with this. Social (class) stratification is about the majority's loss of control over the resources that sustain life, that is the *basic* subsistence resources, and those are in antiquity always local. Indeed, the more relatively impoverished the majority become, the *less* they can afford traded, and thus more expensive, goods. But the wealth items commanded by the elite – for example, ivory objects, carnelian, copper and turquoise beads – were often traded imports. Is that not proof that 'monopolization by the elite' of foreign trade goods explains their pre-eminence? Not at all.

How did the elite get into a position where they could effectively monopolize the prestige trade goods? *And just what creates prestige in the first place?* Obviously there have to be other, and prior, sources of their power in ritual or warfare. Those, when consolidated ideologically and politically, *would then* license them to make the exceptional demands on traded goods that they were already making on subsistence (basic energy) resources to provide themselves with a superior quality of life.

Indeed, as an alternative or complement to exotic imports, there always existed a range of indigenous resources that could have served as elite prestige goods. Ever finer and decreasingly functional pottery is one possibility, fancy but domestically produced textiles another. The point turns not on the objects themselves, still less upon their utility, but on the *amount of social energy* embodied in them. Key to their display function is the quantity of the energies of *others* that one can command. Something brought a long way is one method of expressing this. But so too is the ability to command the expensively developed and thus scarce skills of professional craftspersons, who, in historical times, tended to be captured and brought back as valuable booty for that reason. Indeed, commanding the labour of others, skilled or unskilled, is the very basis for social stratification, while the state, ostensibly representing the whole society, is able to mobilize labour on an unprecedented scale. This, of course, is what grand palaces, pyramids and royal military campaigns represent: mastery on a grand scale, right into the next life.

Even in historic times and in the best documented early state society, that of Early Dynastic and Akkadian Dynasty Sumer, a recent review by P.R.S. Moorey (1993) found no good evidence for the importance of regular trade in supporting the state, which instead relied on intermittent contacts and raiding to secure goods (cf. Edens 1992). In other words, had trade been either the sinews of the state or at least its economic underpinning, then it would have been organized on a much more thorough basis, as indeed were agriculture and taxation. This shows what the real basis of social stratification and the state was − namely, control over basic subsistence resources such as land, water and, of course, the labour that makes them productive.[1]

In sum, Childe's checklist reveals structural parallels on the basis of what we do know, while highlighting what we do not, and directing us accordingly to what must be tackled as a priority.

Given that the Harappan Civilization stands out as anomalous in several related and crucial respects, this demands that attention be focused on searching for confirming or disconfirming data from excavation in Pakistan and India. This is practically rather than merely conceptually urgent, given the rates of population expansion and extensive irrigation, road and other developments across the sub-continent.

CHILDE'S OTHER REVOLUTION

But Childe's concept was of 'Two Revolutions' − the Neolithic and the Urban − as transition levels in the emergence of social complexity. Table 6.1 concerns just the urban or Bronze Age stage.

Settled farming villages are what defines the Neolithic. We should see villagers as motivated by two complementary and contrasting principles: that of genealogy or kinship and that of shared membership of the village community. Which pre-dominates will depend upon ecological circumstances, specifically those of climate, soils and range of available domesticates, plant and animal. This in turn determines whether, as with the alluvial soils of Egypt, Sumer and the Indus, villages can be fixed for many generations, or whether they have to relocate within a single or a few generations.

Totally fixed villages lead to the dominance of the territorial principle where control over/rights in land are of paramount concern. Relatively mobile settlements lead to the dominance of the genealogical or lineage principle, since this keeps people in relationship over time and space. Accordingly it has social control − control of people − as the overriding principle. By contrast, the necessity of living with the same neighbours, or rather with neighbouring families, over the generations stresses what fellow villagers have in common socially and economically, namely a continuing concern with the viability of the settlements.

Therefore, as settlement consolidated and expanded with the development of the Neolithic, either the lineage principle prevailed (a clear, strong and corporate form of the descent principle) or the settlement itself formed the unit of cooperation and support, rendering the descent principle secondary. Accordingly, in Egypt, village solidarity prevailed, and village clusters were the basis of chiefdoms and ultimately the state, whilst in Sumer, *oikos* households, clustered into nucleated settlements, gave rise to cities, urban culture and civic solidarity. Sumer and later Babylonia look so 'modern' to us in comparison to the other pristine civilizations, because there cities, containing the overwhelming majority of the population, were both at the heart of early formative processes and practised an urban way of life through historic periods. It was by any measure the world's first, and for millennia only, urban society. By this is meant not merely the presence of cities, but that city living *and thinking* are the dominant and natural way of life, as they were to become (and explicity be stated) in first-millennium BC Greece.

In contrast to Egypt and China, which were essentially agrarian village states (Maisels 1987), in Mesopotamia neither cities nor state organizations merely sat atop a rural society with traits fundamentally unchanged from the late Neolithic. In Mesopotamia heterogeneity and hierarchy crystallized uniquely into regimes (city-states) structured around 'mass production' (sustained surpluses generated by capital-intensive means), bulk transfers and sophisticated manufacturing – all controlled by rigorous book-keeping that tracked inputs and outputs, profits and losses and overall efficiencies.

In Meluhha, occupationally specialized lineages/clans developed broad social solidarity through interdependence in the division of labour. A complex but relatively unstratified society emerged without rulers and ruled. The lineages that still exist in Indian rural society are embodied within sub-castes (*jati*)

In China, the very framework of society was formed by the lineage/clan, and it generated the state. In turn Chinese culture has been predicated on the existence of the state at least to the extent to which medieval European culture was predicated on the existence of the Christian Church.

> Given the tremendous changes that took place in later Chinese history, the fundamental threads of unity were the imperial mode of governance itself, the state based on extraction of taxes or services from the rural population, and the dominance of the authoritarian, patriarchal household at the local level.
>
> (Lewis 1990:247)

In China, extending over the greatest distances and possessing the largest populations, perhaps it was that villages were either too large or too impermanent to form an effective unit of cooperation, or the populations may just have expanded too rapidly, generating new lineages that had to move to find land. Here support from established lineages of one's clan could be invaluable. But in most circumstances of flux it may be that the descent principle provides the only sure motive for cooperation and support. In a situation of population mobility, those lending aid to neighbours would not have it reciprocated should those neighbours move on. Also perhaps, without the metaphysical sanctions of consanguinity, support and its reciprocation were less assured, and 'free-rider' problems accentuated. Perhaps, then, the Chinese apotheosis of the lineage seen in ancestor worship, transcendentally extolling continuity and 'rootedness', was (in origin) required precisely because impermanence of settlement patterns was the norm.

The imperative of aid in a landscape of social and natural flux would also explain the centrality of the lineage/clan/tribal (LCT) structure and its values to pastoral nomads (at the mercy of rains, agricultural conditions, politics and other nomadic groups) in the ancient and modern Near East. Beyond this, as in sub-Saharan Africa, tribal society is the form taken for political cohesion where, because of ecological conditions, people and not territory are the major resource. This is in contrast to areas of intensive agriculture (such as San Dai China) where arable terrain is the major resource and a territorial state controls it. In other words, although the Chinese state arose on the basis of the clan system, its very existence as a territorial state *precluded* the historical development of tribal society there, since that is an alternative form of overarching political organization.[2] Accordingly, if territorial power arose to secure valuable arable land, one would logically expect to find no tribal organization in that territory. In Egypt and in Mesopotamia this is clear. Amorite and earlier settlers on the alluvium, who were originally tribally organized, quickly lost this characteristic on settling down. Families continued to trace lineages and allocate property accordingly. However, this took place at the civil, private level, and did not represent the political state structure.

What, then, might Mesopotamian society have looked like if Samarran-Ubaidian society had not been composed of *oikos* households, but instead had remained, like Hassuna and Halaf, at the level of unstratified 'dry' farming villages? The immediate answer is that they would have been unable to colonize the alluvium to the extent and in the way in which they did, using nucleated settlements that upon expansion became cities. Thus there could have been no 'heartland of cities' (Adams 1981) on the southern alluvium; there would have been (at the most) dispersed villages along rivercourses.

In Mesopotamia the *oikos* was a particularly well-adapted vehicle for tackling the alluvium, able to cope with almost all exigencies. Hassuna and Halaf villages, farming naturally watered or rain-fed zones, needed no further developments and so could remain egalitarian. By contrast, the *oikos* house-hold seems a unique product of the need to manage, concentrate and capitalize resources tightly (which the temples did for society as a whole) in a regime where the rivers were unpredictable, unhelpful in the timing of their seasonal maxima relative to the growing season, and which did not provide self-irrigation as did the Ghaggar-Hakra, Indus and Nile. This meant that *oikos* households were stratified internally and relative to one another, and further differentiated into private and public households (temples and palaces). Such circumstances were virtually a forcing ground for the rise of the state, but a particular form of the state in which all household heads had some political muscle.

The sort of state to which this gave rise was the city-state, which, like its exemplars in ancient Greece, remained a 'community state' in the sense that citizens' representative bodies had decision-making functions alongside the king (Jacobsen 1957; Diakonoff 1983a; Yamada 1994). This obviously makes the contrast between city-states and the oecumene less stark than between it and territorial states like Egypt and China.

Patterns become clear in the Chalcolithic, for that is the time of occu-pational specialization, the basis of social complexity. Specialization is either driven by elite demands as it crystallizes into an emerging ruling class, or economic needs drive specialization. In the latter case, either the producers exchange amongst themselves, as in Halaf Mesopotamia or on the Indus, leaving no space for a ruling/administering class, or the specializations are components of productive enterprises, internally and externally stratified, as were the *oikos* households of southern Mesopotamia. The political regime in the economic instances becomes relatively democratic (in the Indus case highly democratic), while those driven ideologically by elite requirements become, unsurprisingly, autocracies.

POLITICAL ECONOMIES

From about the middle until the end of the third millennium, Mesopotamia had regular contact with the Indus Civilization, mostly through the entrepot island (modern Bahrain) that the Sumerians called Dilmun. However, contacts between the Western or South Asian civilizations and China during the fourth and third millennia were virtually non-existent and seem to amount to little more than the adoption by China of some technology through intermediate peoples. Even in the Iron Age, which for convenience can be thought of as beginning at 1000 BC (although its advent varies across regions), China was by far the most isolated of all the pristine civilizations (though iron-casting began there around 900 BC). Its strong cultural (and thus political and economic) continuity until the present indicates just how powerful the formative influences of natural and cultural ecology can be.

The pattern of roles established in the Neolithic sets the social structure, which engenders the social order (the pattern of organizations) in the Chalcolithic from which the state emerges in the Bronze Age,[3] or doesn't in the Harappan case.

Consider the politico-economic possibilities along a continuum. At one extreme there is forced extraction: producers work under duress and hand over the fruits of their labour, being allocated enough for survival or a bit more if they are lucky. Goods are taken from the majority by the minority and some goods for majority consumption are substituted ('exchanged') for others, e.g. fish for cloth. But most production beyond subsistence minima goes to serve the ruling class. This is a regime of generalized slavery, even if the formalized apparatus of slavery is absent.

At the other extreme, producers work for the market in which a token of account (money) serves as the universal medium, the tokens received representing the value produced and thus facilitating (equal) exchange. Money then represents an entitlement to a specific quantity of the produce of others, deemed to be equivalent to the value of one's own labour.

In the middle, then, without forced extraction on the one hand or money circulation on the other, lies the area of a kind of barter of goods for goods or goods for services. No matter that some of the services are imma-terial – for instance entertainment or religion as against material services such as the making and maintenance of machinery – what matters is that the services are actually wanted by the producers and therefore that they are prepared to participate in an exchange, say, of food and clothing for musical performances. The material exchanges are easier to comprehend. Everyone needs a range of goods: food and clothing, pots and pans, a house, etc. In the post-Neolithic (Chalcolithic), producers specialize, which means that they develop skills and processes necessitating full-time concentration upon the activity.

A full-time potter, for example, must engage in exchanges or there will be little to put in one's own pots. But how does one know how many and what quality of one's own pots should be exchanged for a certain amount of grain or fish or cloth or metal goods? Initially by a kind of trial and error: how much fish is the fisherman prepared to give me for a single pot? This in turn depends on the abundance of fish, how easy they are to catch, how far they have to be transported and so forth. Conversely, if a pot takes me a whole day to make, I want sufficient fish for it (perhaps dried) that will last me about a week, since I have to exchange pots for other items on other working days. By such means, sets of equivalences establish them-selves. If consistent over time, they become customary, but nevertheless remain flexible within known limits. Unseasonal storms, for example, increase the price of fish or a season of drought that of grain.

Here then there is neither enforced extraction nor money exchange but an exchange network that is both equitable and flexible. It also allows for new specializations to emerge, such as transport workers moving the fish to the potters, so allowing the fishermen to spend longer at sea, or curing the fish or building better boats. Of course, boat building, net making and fish curing can each become specialized occupations. All that is required is that each new specialism allows other producers to become more productive than the extra cost represented by the upkeep of the new specialist and his family. This too is a matter of experimentation. If successful, everyone gains as overall social productivity increases.

Forced extraction in a condition akin to that of slavery, even without its formal trappings so clearly seen under imperial Rome. It is what obtained most nearly in ancient China and to some extent in Egypt and Mesopotamia also. Societies approaching the Chalcolithic could either go the oppressive-exploitative or the egalitarian-exchange route. The latter, however, proved to be exceptional. What made the difference was whether an elite was already emerging to become a ruling class. This in turn depended on conditions in the respective Neolithics. I have gone into the conical clan in great depth to demonstrate that such a mechanism existed in China. This role was filled by the floodplain hierarchic village in Egypt and by the stratified patriachal (*oikos*) household in Mesopotamia. I have also argued that the basis for this was the local ecology, natural and human; the natural comprising the local geography, climate, fauna and flora; the human, the desire to obtain as much benefit for oneself as possible at the expense of others. This, of course, is rooted in the mechanism by which the genotype (the gene package) gets the phenotype (the biological individual) to maximize its reproductive potential, so favouring the spread of that set of genes. This can and usually does become institutionalized as a regime of negative reciprocity, in which one party does all the giving, the other all the taking, as seen in the three Old World civilizations mentioned. The Harappan regime of balanced reciprocity does not mean that the Harappan regional and occupational groups were not acting in their own best interests. On the contrary, their best interests were indeed served by not having one of those groups become superior, subordinating the rest and so becoming a ruling class.

But why did superordination not arise in northwest India? Probably as a consequence of the relative lateness and patchiness of the Neolithic there. Its confinement to certain stretches of certain rivers over a wide terrain that had to be shared with other groups pursuing other ways of life that we conventionally pigeonhole into 'pastoral' and hunter–gathering, resulted in non-homogeneity which could be bridged only by mutual accommodation and agreement. Within the variety of villages and camps there can have been no single mechanism sufficiently compelling (such as lineage/ shamanism/ancestor worship) and sufficiently uniform in its application (thus supplying initial legitimacy), to allow one group special privileges. Special privilege can, of course, serve as 'founding capital' sufficient to launch a ruling class claiming, then enforcing, deeper and wider powers throughout the locality and within an expanding perimeter.

The qualitative alternative to those and to the market economy, approximating to the 'middle-condition' described above, is that represented by the political economy of the Harappan oecumene. Earlier, and on a smaller scale, it was also characteristic of the Halaf network of northern Mesopotamia. Since this mode of social integration is indeed a novelty, in the contemporary as much as in the ancient world, there exists no appropriate name for it. I am therefore calling this mechanism the 'distributed social network', where groups and individuals plug into a set of social connections, economic and cultural. They put in some of their resources and skills and receive a proportion of what others have likewise done, on a voluntary basis. There is no command structure of and for non-producers and thus no exploitation.

The system of equivalence exchange (it is not barter) involved in the distributed network I call the 'equivalence economy', and the type of society embodying it the 'mutuality society'. Obviously such a society will be qualitatively different in its cultural, institutional and organizational attributes from those we are used to.

This explains, I contend, the Harappan 'anomalies' around the absence of the state and its various apparatuses, including warfare; extensive specialization and social complexity; the apparent ubiquity of trading relationships; and the subsequent devolution from mutuality society into caste organization, a type of social organization not met with anywhere else in anything like the Indian form. Indeed, this one model seems to account for all the features, such as the lack of development of Indus script, that scholars find so puzzling. Thus Harappan society has centres, but no dominating centre and consequently no controlling administration.

POLITICS AND THE STATE

The clan gave rise to the state (in East Asia) because both are political institutions. 'Political' here refers to institutions for guaranteeing private or sectional interests: first those of the powerholders as individuals, then the interests of their families (however defined), then the interests of their class as a whole, and lastly, if at all, of the society as a whole (cf. Keightley 1977:408). The state has previously been defined as control over people and territory from a centre through specialized apparatuses of power: (1) military; (2) administrative (mostly tax raising); (3) legal; and (4) ideological.

For the state to be secure there 'has to be something in it' for at least the key social groups, who are those in control of key resources, material, ideological and military (typically: top generals/palace guards; priests/ shamans; large landowners/local potentates). Indeed, for positive support, the value of the assets of the key resourceholders must be enhanced by the

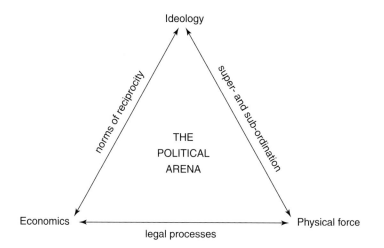

Figure 6.2 The political domain as the arena of contest-exchange

regime, while the standards of life of the majority should at least not be perceived as deteriorating.

Politics is the field of contest-exchange operating at all social levels, from the individual's daily interpersonal relationships right up to the struggles around government. The contest is always about getting what one wants, and at state level is over public furtherance of private interests. No matter what the level, however, the contest-exchange involves the 'trading' of ideological, economic and physical force resources by means of certain rules. Of course, the amount of such resources at one's command determines at what level, from familial or village to governmental, one can participate in the political game. To enter the political game as a player one must come to it with one's own resources. Those, however, can be various: not just economic resources, but bodily strength or beauty, intelligence or cunning, ideological, rhetorical and other skills; the loyalty of a following, kin or charisma derived; some combination of those. The point is that one brings what one has to get what one wants. And there is no free lunch: this is the arena of contest-exchange where there are rival bidders and blockers, and where everyone wants to maximize benefit to themselves. Thus, exchanges will be as unequal and forced as possible, and it can be argued that it is to institutionalize unequal exchanges in favour of certain restricted groups that the state comes into being.

However, the political field in which those resources are deployed is by no means confined to the public realm (which itself has many levels), but inheres in all interpersonal relationships: sexual, intra-familial, intra peer-group and so forth, wherever people interact. Indeed, R.D. Laing's point (pers. comm.) was that contest-exchange was ultimately a struggle going on *within* each person: a conflict of wants and needs, means and ends, available resources and wished for goals, instrumental actions versus existential satisfactions.

This has to be understood in a fractal context (see Glossary). At whatever level one looks from the most private to the most public, from the personal to the organizational, there is a domain of contest-exchange. There is even a politics of the self. Within our own mental/emotional states we are continuously making difficult transactions between our economic, ideological and energy/force/skill reserves in the attempt to optimize our situation. This ongoing process sets our targets (most being necessarily provisional) in our relationships with others.

Politics is then a continuous game – one of life and death and everything between – played not only at all levels of society but in every kind of society, even hunter–gatherer (cf. Leacock and Lee 1982). It is not that political practices are unknown to band-level societies, rather that they have no specifically political organizations. Thus

> Lee demonstrates that former assumptions that authority amongst [the !Kung] was held by chiefs or headmen do not stand up to further research. Like the G/wi, the !Kung arrive at group decisions and handle potential or actual interpersonal conflict through a variety of techniques that range from discussion, through 'rough humour' and 'put downs', to interpersonal fighting when these are not successful, and in extreme cases the execution through community decision of persistently aggressive and arrogant individuals. Lee indicates that both women and men participate in decision-making and conflict resolution and are influential in accordance with their age, experience and wisdom.
>
> (ibid.:10)

Band-level societies generally have no formal organizations (Australian aborigines do, however; cf. Maisels 1990:221–30), but to demonstrate that the same three factors – ideology, economy and force – suffice to explain the operation of all organizations (as well as interpersonal relationships), picture a small triangle intersecting the large one at the 'force' corner to represent the military (or police) organization. At the apex of this (small) 'military' triangle, then, ideology is again located, similarly 'economy' and 'force' at the other vertices. Here the operative ideology would be 'defence' or 'security'; 'economy' – the state monies allocated to the organization as its 'own' resources to be conferred differentially according to rank; plus systems of internal discipline that the organization can itself enforce. Trafficking in those three same resources – ideology, rank with its perquisites and force – thus constitutes the internal politics of those organizations. They mesh with but are distinct from the broader political arena, forming their own domains. One such is the university, with an overall set of ideo-logical, force and economic resources at top level forming a shell domain within which the various heads of department with their own resources make their tri-componential plays in their sub-domains, while each member of staff tries to consolidate their position and obtain promotion.

Mutatis mutandis the same holds true of organizations at the economy vertex, whether the economic unit in question be family farms, family firms or multinational industrial corporations. With industrial and commercial enterprises, force is the market pressure on survival (and the management bearing down on the workers), the economy is embodied in costs and sales revenues, with the ideology that of giving the customer what he wants and thereby the shareholders what they want, namely profits.

A church is a political field represented by another small triangle located at the ideology vertex of the big triangle. The 'church triangle' has its own hierarchy enforcing discipline, its own revenues from capital and contribu-tions, and of course its own archetypal ideology of salvation.

The state, treated like any other organization, likewise has its own set of ideologies, armed forces and revenue sources. Modern professional politi-cians are brokers for the different interests constituting the political class, and between them and the diverse interests of the rest of the population.

Where resources are widely distributed, the means for the peaceful regu-lation of contest-exchanges is a priority. Accordingly, it is not a historical accident that the first codes of law, bearing the names of *Ur-Nammu* (2112–2095 BC), *Lipit-Ishtar* (1934–1924 BC) and, most famously, *Hamm-urabi* (1792–1750 BC) are those of the Mesopotamian city-states. For they were the very first state-level societies in which significant economic power remained with the citizenry (actually heads of households) and where the public power, though centred on kingship, still represented them (through councils), while the cosmology was polytheistic, and thus also distributed.

SOCIAL EVOLUTION

Not only is there an egalitarian alternative to the path from band to state, but within the latter there is no 'standard' trajectory for the emergence of the state. Two ideal types that I have previously contrasted are the city-state and village state paths (1987, 1990), the former characteristic of Mesopotamia and the latter of China (and Egypt) in their earliest and form-ative phases. Nonetheless, Johnson and Earle (1987:247–8) have conflated those contrasting forms into an 'Asiatic mode of production', which according to them is characterized by 'staple finance, often associated with the "Asiatic mode of production", [and which] formed the financial base of most primary states, including those of Mesopotamia and Egypt'. Well, we have seen what the real situation was. If one wishes to know the evolutionary trajectory of Mesopotamia or Egypt (or China or anywhere) one must study each in all its detailed particularity; one cannot hypothesize it from an *a priori* scheme, especially an 'all-purpose' one.

I hope to have shown that social evolution is indeed a process of advancing complexity, so much so that a great deal is retained even when overarching politico-economic structures collapse. 'Regression' to the status quo ante does not occur (e.g. to egalitarian Neolithic society in the Indian case). Rather, the new social configuration incorporates cultural attributes elaborated previously, or indeed even develops them further in the very process of adjusting to post-High Civilization conditions. In other words, while the previous mode of production (as a political economy) collapsed, the social structure (the grid of social positions, which are role-bearing locations; Maisels 1990:223) remained largely intact by adapting.

Accordingly, it may be that social evolutionary theory as a system of integrated and operational concepts can be forged only through 'middle-range operational theory', as Binford (1977, 1983) has said.

In his extended discussion of the concept, Bruce Trigger (1995b:455–6) declares, rightly in my view, that 'the controls exerted by a well-honed body of middle-range theory are what establish the difference between fantasy and archaeology'. The imperative then is 'to expand and develop middle-range theory to provide methodological rigour to a broader range of techniques for attributing human behaviour and ideas to archaeological data'.

One that has proved particularly useful in the study of complex societies is that developed by Robert Redfield (1953) and McKim Marriot (1955), which turns on the contrast between Great and Little Traditions. The Great Tradition is a specialist, literary or elite construct, 'embodied in "sacred books" or "classics", sanctified by a cult, expressed in monuments, sculpture, painting and architecture, served by the other arts and sciences' (Redfield and Singer 1954:63). Nonetheless, it arises out of the oral, folk or Little Tradition, which is hegemonized but not supplanted by the Great Tradition. As Marriott (1955b:196) puts it, while the elite tradition integrates and rationalizes the themes from the common source(s) to make its cosmological schemes, in the Little Tradition 'we see evidence of accretion and of transmutation in form without apparent replacement and without rationalization of the accumulated and transformed elements'. On the one hand, sources of the common culture resident in the folk tradition are taken up and universalized by the Great Tradition, while down below elements of that elite culture are 'parochialized' and given material expression in the villages. In fact the Little Tradition is a lot of local traditions in which some themes are shared, others are variations on common themes, while other strands are restricted to a locality.

Paradoxically, however, the hegemony of the Great Tradition and the elite class interests it reflects depend for legitimation upon the continuity of the folk tradition, which at least has to accept and incorporate a 'trickled down' version of the elite culture (cf. Stewart 1996:267–8 for a concise review).

As Cohn writes of an Untouchable Uttar Pradesh caste who were traditionally leatherworkers and agricultural labourers:

> While the Camars are organizing and fighting for social, political and economic equality with the higher castes, they are also trying to borrow and to revive for themselves elements of a culture that the higher castes are shedding. As the higher castes of Madhopur become secularized and are increasingly drawn into an urban economy and culture, the Camars seem to be trying not only to benefit by the loosening of some old restrictions but also to buttress their own position by adapting these old restrictions to new uses.
>
> (Cohn 1955:76)

In the original formation of elite culture the spontaneous folk tradition gets 'summarized' by having *cardinal tenets* formulated, which encapsulate the key concepts essential to the structure (thus, 'divine/virgin birth', 'son of God', 'died for our sins/redeemer/resurrection' as cardinal tenets central to all versions of Christianity).

These are then subject to comprehensive elaboration at 'high level' by intellectual specialists, so producing new departures. The Chinese and Hindu classics are just such products, as are the Cosmogony of *Iwnw* = On (the Ennead of Heliopolis) and all the other Egyptian cosmogonies plus the Hebrew/Christian Bible:

> From time to time many of the cosmological and cosmogonical materials in the possession of the various Egyptian cults or religions were assimilated, integrated, and interwoven by skilled persons who knew what they were doing. Their task was philosophical and theological [but fundamentally political!]. Their mode of expression was mythological.
>
> (Lesko 1991:90)

Myths 'explain' social and natural phenomena by telling stories about agents (cf. p. 388).

It was the perspective originally induced by the contrast between the Bible (with its commentaries) and the Graeco-Roman classics (and physical remains) that both fed the Renaissance and gave rise to the discipline of archaeology in the wake of the Enlightenment, an intellectual transformation which was, in the broadest sense, anthropological, as it provided impulse and resources for reflective overview (Hampson 1968:218–50). Between the two, of course, came the Reformation and the mercantile revolution, plus Newton, the whole institutionalizing the 'open society' by the naturalization of thought (and practice). Humankind was thereby re-inserted into nature as a consequent part of it, no longer held to be Nature's very purpose and centre.

Finally, as middle-range theory, Childe's Checklist is doubly instrumental: it organizes disparate data and in so doing it generates concepts for higher-order theory (theory properly so-called). In applying the checklist to the originating Old World civilizations, we see confirmation of the Santa Fe Institute's approach to complex adaptive systems (Waldrop 1992) namely, that societies, like all living systems exist in that most narrow area, the boundary between chaos and frozen order.

Societies exist at the edge of chaos

Their permanent precariousness comes from multiple uncertainties:

1 from the dynamics of the environment;
2 from the dynamics of social organization;
3 from the dynamics between individual human beings, their ideological and technological innovations.

Accordingly, social reproduction is always highly conditional, especially:

1 because a relatively successful society is an expanding one, demanding ever greater inputs from its environment;
2 because the divisions of control and labour in society generate interests and demands in society that cannot effectively be met;
3 because societies exist in relation to others, and, linked as they are in cooperation, competition and conflict, changes in one affect the others.

Due to the high number of independent variables, a balance is historically rare and is always highly contingent. The tendency is thus to attempt to 'close down change and uncertainty' by instituting a closed society controlled from above; or to resort to *laissez faire* where it is everyone for themselves. Of course neither of those are viable in the longer term. Living systems exist in that all too narrow zone where there is enough order for cumulative gains to be made, but where the order is just parametric, providing the space for autonomy and innovation.

Societies with too much order freeze and stagnate, like Soviet Russia and Togukawa Japan (1600–1868). Societies with insufficient order destroy the material, cultural and psychological quality of life of their members, as seen all too clearly in Nigeria, Congo and much of the rest of Africa. It has to be said, however, that this is usually a consequence of the ruling elite acting in their own most selfish interests, and unable therefore to command any kind of social consensus. Sudan is a good (bad) example of this. For the entire period since independence in 1956 it has regressed due to continuous civil war caused by the north demanding the complete subjection of the south.

With total control from above, Mao's China necessarily lurched from overweaning order to instigated chaos, and back again. This totalitarian/ millenarian cycle had to be broken for China to take any leap forward.

To advance the quality of life of the majority what is required is a sufficiency of order – effective and efficient government genuinely and continually answerable to the people – preventing society from tumbling over into chaos and dissolving, or freezing up into paralysing hierarchy, usually enforced by military terrorism (as in contemporary Burma).

Becoming modern

For a millennium, in the face of all odds including sack by Crusaders, Byzantium maintained the structure of an ancient Empire in the Eastern Mediterranean. By the century of its collapse, the city-states of Italy, at the crossroads of Eastern and Western Mediterranean, North Africa and North Europe, had succeeded in producing through the Renaissance some definitively modern structures of thought. The balance between stability and dynamism could not be struck by Byzantium, doomed as it was to spend its thousand-year existence (AD 395–1453) just trying to survive while elaborating what it had inherited as the eastern Rome at Constantinople. Even though a university was established there in 425 and literacy was continuous and relatively widespread, Byzantium contributed more to social evolution by its collapse, with the consequent dispersal of that inheritance, than it had when intact. For, despite the faltering of Byzantine scholarship after 1350,

> enough scholars continued to follow, albeit at a distance, in the footsteps of their great predecessors to be able to transmit to the west, when the west was ready to receive it, not merely a body of texts but a critical and rigorous approach to them and their contents, which can be traced back without interruption to the Museum and the Library of Alexandria.
>
> (Browning 1980:197–8)

The library had been destroyed by religious fundamentalists in AD 415.

Founded as the eastern capital by Constantine I in AD 330, it is fitting that Byzantium's last Emperor was also called Constantine (XI). So on 29 May 1453, when he died fighting as the Turks stormed Constantinople, this marked the end of ancient Old World civilizations, with the exception of China which staggered on, changing, but insufficiently transformed. By this time too the developmental phase of Islamic

Civilization was past and Chinese dynamism had settled onto the Ming Dynasty (1368–1644) plateau, there to decline, and with the Qing, decompose. The originating civilizations of the Old World and their immediate successors were thus long gone when a tertiary derivative civilization located at the western extremities of Asia discovered entirely New Worlds.

According to chiliasm within Byzantine Orthodoxy, Christ's Second Coming would occur 7,000 years after the creation of the world, that is, in 1492. On 2 January 1492, the Spanish finally conquered Granada, capital of the Moorish Kingdom (1236–1492), so driving the Moslems from Spain. On 1 August 1492, the Jews were expelled from Spain. On 3 August a Genoese, Christopher Columbus, having obtained finance from the victors at Granada, sailed from Palos de la Frontera in the estuary of the Rio Tinto to establish a direct sea route to the Orient. On 12 October 1492, he made landfall in the Caribbean, so discovering a New World that was well known to the Vikings and on which they had bases centuries before. Now, however, Europe was initiating the first stages of globalization.

On 24 June 1497, John Cabot, sailing from Bristol, by whose merchants he had been financed, reached Cape Breton Island, Nova Scotia, in the *Matthew*, a tiny ship with a crew of only 17. In May 1498, Vasco da Gama reached India, and between September 1519 and September 1522 Magellan's Fleet (he was killed in Guam in 1521) circumnavigated the world. Prior to his setting sail, in 1517 an ordained priest and lecturer at the University of Wittenberg nailed 95 Theses denouncing Indulgences to the door of Wittenberg's principal church. By this and other acts, Martin Luther launched the Reformation. In 1564, John Calvin died, Galileo and Shakespeare were born. Though persecuted by the Inquisition, with Galileo Galilei (d.1642) modern science commenced.

APPENDICES

A: THE GENEALOGICAL PRINCIPLE

Key concepts

Descent is the principle of reckoning relatedness from a common ancestor. Those thus related are held to be members of a descent group such as a lineage or clan. The *descent line* (or 'blood' or consanguinity), which is the basis of the descent group, is formed by a chain of *filiation*. Filiation is legitimated genealogical connection between children and (licensing) parents, who must themselves be proper representatives of the 'line', because *their* parents were.

Descent, then, refers to relatedness based on common ancestry (Lewis 1996: 151) real, imagined or just expedient. Speaking of the role of descent in traditional Arab societies and in contemporary Somalia, Lewis observes that

> In considering its role in such segmentary lineage systems, it has to be remembered that descent is primarily a socio-political (and economic) resource which can be loaded and manipulated in various ways even within one cultural system. It does not in and of itself actually determine action although in these cases it provides an extremely compelling political ideology.
>
> (ibid.:152)

Descent reckoned through males is said to be *patrilineal*, through females *matrilineal*. This is the *unilineal* descent principle, which is one that takes place through a single sex only. Where a person's membership of a patri-lineage and a matrilineage is of equal importance, this is referred to as *dual (or double) descent*. It is, however, extremely rare.

Some writers use the term *agnatic* for patrilineal descent, *uterine* for matri-lineal descent and *cognatic* where both are employed. While the first two terms are traditional usages that cause little confusion, the term 'cognatic' is best reserved for bilateral systems like those of northwestern Europe, where descent through either parent in any generation is the general principle.

Tending to merge *affinal* connections (by marriage) with 'lineal' ones, this system of *cognatic* descent cannot produce true lineages (as, for example, amongst the Nuer, Dinka and other African societies). Instead, *kindred* are recognized, consisting of all the descendants of the four *stocks* deriving from each person's grandparents. Potentially this is a lot of people, since it includes everyone, both male and female, in each generation from each of the stocks. So each person selects from his/her kindred those with whom s/he wishes to associated closely – the *kindred of cooperation* – effectively 'forgetting' the rest. This is necessary for the numbers to be manageable. Providing a large measure of choice, the kindred system is thus a loose and flexible one, especially for the transmission of property. As Lewis succinctly puts it, here 'group cohesion tends to be loose and uncommitting' (ibid.:154).

In general, *kinship* is a system of *ego-focused* relationships ulitizing both descent and affinity, the latter being relationships established by marriage. Thus a kinship network is always a particular person's (an *ego's*) set of relations, because kinship relations are asymmetrical, the corollary of descent positions being unique: 'the oldest son of the youngest daughter', for example. 'Kinship', as Fortes (1953:201) says, 'is used to define and sanction a personal field of social relations for each individual'.

Everything starts from *spouseship* (recognized marriage) producing legitimate = licensed *offspring* = filiation, thus *descent* (serial filiation) and *siblingship*; thence *co-lineal descent* producing *collateral relatives* and thus kinship.

How does a lineage actually work?

As we have seen, a lineage is a line of descent traced through men (patrilineal) or women (matrilineal). It consists of its dead as well as its living members, which is why Neolithic households buried predecessors under the living floors. This relationship with ancestors is crucial. Being nearer to the 'origin', ancestors are thought to be nearer to the source of the powers that ensure or withhold productive and reproductive success. If properly treated, the ancestors will be eager to intercede on behalf of their descendants.

By contrast, the only living members of a specific lineage are:

1   the procreative spouse, male or female and their siblings;
2   their children;
3   if married, their children.

All other members of the lineage are memories, real or invented. The members will be co-resident, living together until the siblings depart with their wives and children to start their own lineages. Thus lineages at any particular point in time are represented by only a three-generational unit of living people. Mayer (1960:169) calls the co-residential or effective lineage grouping of three to four generations (*bhaibandh* or *khandan*) the 'lineage of cooperation', while he calls 'the lineage of recognition' that which 'is based simply on recognition of a previous agnatic link; this link may not be known in any detail to members, but it can be traced through the records of the genealogist. . . . It extends to about ten generations from the founder' (ibid.). Thus at around five to six generations the lineage of recognition 'passes into the clan' (*gotra*), just as the *khutumb*, or kindred, specifically

> the cooperating kindred, meaning those cognates and affines who regard themselves as related and have some sort of interaction . . . is distinct from what one might call the kindred of recognition, which includes all those with whom a kin tie is calculated by a particular person.
>
> (ibid:171–2)

that is, by a particular *ego*, the singular defining centre of any set of kindred.

Meyer's instances are from Central India. More generally we can see that co-lineages, that is similar three-generational units each headed, for instance, by one of three brothers, recognize their relationship from their *Deceased Father* and call themselves 'the DF Lineage'. It is after the death of the three sons of DF, namely Senior, Middle and Junior, that a clan or sub-clan begins. The grandchildren of DFS, DFM and DFJ will then form the respective lineages – DFS, DFM and DFJ – of the DF and in most circumstances this will also be their status ranking. A clear example is given in Figure (A).1.

> The large Farmer (Caste) population is organized with somewhat greater complexity [than other kinship groupings in the village]. Overall, it forms a single kin-group, as the accompanying diagram shows. But within there are three main clan groups (marked A, B and C). Two form large extended families, and one is a smaller extended family based on a man, his son and grandson. These three are prior because they stem from the first Farmers to come to Ramkheri at the end of the nineteenth century. The remainder are affines and uterine kin, some descendants of those who followed the founders to the village.
>
> (ibid:173)

What does a lineage actually do?

The lineage exists to assist the reproducers, namely the procreative family unit, which would not be able to survive the vagaries of nature on its own. The lineage does this in the first instance by transmitting rights in productive resources, especially land. It assists in the second instance by producing

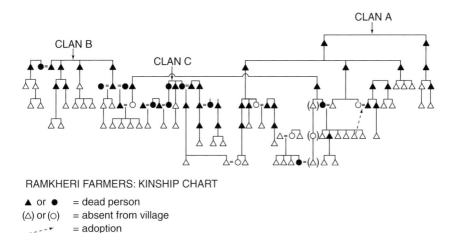

RAMKHERI FARMERS: KINSHIP CHART

▲ or ● = dead person
(△) or (○) = absent from village
---→ = adoption

Figure 6 (A). 1: A Intermarriage within the *jati* (sub-caste)

a set of relatives who are obliged to provide economic or political help, without which the first instance is inoperable. In sum, the family is the individual's life-support system and the lineage is the family's.

A clan comprises a number of lineages who reckon their descent from a common ancestor, and whose name, accordingly, is the clan name. It is here that dead members of the lineage become crucial. For the further back the deceased originator is reckoned to be, the *wider* or more inclusive of lineages can the clan be. A common 'ancestor' only four generations back will not provide as many male or female lines of descent, namely lineages of the clan, as one fourteen generations back, the lineages of which can be so widespread as to reckon a whole country as clan territory.

Since lineages are about ensuring success for their component families, a consistently successful lineage of a corporate clan – one controlling territory – will come to be reckoned the 'senior' lineage, with the shortest line of ascent to the founding ancestor. The other lineages will be reckoned to 'branch away' from this senior lineage, their degree of 'juniority' or inferiority reckoned by the descent distance from the senior line. Thus although all lineages can be represented by only a three-generational living unit, and all such contemporary units in every lineage have the same time depth, the one that has magnified its success and seniority and shortened its lines of communication to the founding ancestor becomes the dominant lineage. The clan becomes a conical clan if this lineage is able to concentrate politico-ritual and economic power, in the process subordinating formerly parallel lineages. By such means status can be transformed into power which can be used to grasp more power, building class stratification.

An ancestor can himself become divine if his lineage becomes politically important enough, as does the dominant lineage of a conical clan when it becomes the lineage ruling over a number of conical clans. By this stage, the human ancestry itself is usually lost in a merger with divine natural forces, such as the sun in Egypt or the sky (heaven) in China.

B: OCCUPATION, KINSHIP AND CASTE

Using modern (and his own) ethnology, Frederick G. Bailey (1963:107–9) has described a system that he finds characteristic of India, namely one that he calls 'closed social stratification'. As his argumentation is thorough, and involves an explanation of caste, it is necessary to quote him quite extensively. The whole system turns on *jati*, sub-castes that are simultaneously kinship and occupational groups:

> Caste as *jati*. This is the main sociological referent of the word 'caste'. In order to expound clearly on the principles on which it is based, I must be permitted the gross oversimplification of 'traditional Indian society'. This society was divided into countless small political units which I shall call 'blocks' because they could be arranged to make larger units. While the larger units were segmentary (in the sense that any feudal state is segmentary, in the particular sense used by Southall 1953), the blocks were organic, relatively stable and relatively indestructable. Blocks had these characteristics because ritual, political and economic systems reinforced one another and to some extent coincided, and because kinship links did not cross the boundaries of the unit.
>
> Both these facts are aspects of the caste system, and each block itself constituted a caste system. The population of each block (call it a 'chiefdom') was divided vertically into villages and horizontally into castes, and each caste is dispersed throughout the village of the chiefdom.
>
> The caste system, in this fourth sense [1 = varna; 2 = caste categories; 3 = caste associations; 4 = caste as *jati*] meets all the criteria suggested by Nadel [in his *Foundations of Social Anthropology*, 1951] for the recognition of social stratification. These groups were exhaustive, since everyone belonged to a caste: they were exclusive, since no one belonged to more than one caste. Castes were groups, in that members not only had common attributes, but interacted with one another in a way that they interacted with no member of another group. The castes were ranked, and, finally, they were organically related to form a system.
>
> (ibid.)

This system was not egalitarian but stratified. However, such a continuous system of finely graded ranks makes it exceedingly difficult for transcendent leadership to emerge that could crystallize into an overarching state. Instead there was (and is) local and regional, but nonetheless oppressive, dominance.

Bailey describes such an outcome as the constitution of an *involute* system:

> To say that a system is involute is to say that there is no special-isation of command: the same man, or the same group, hold positions of command in all different fields of activity. For this system to work it would mean that, by and large, leadership jobs must be simple enough for one man to master them all and, indeed, to have time to attend to all of them. In other words, involute systems are found only in simple societies, or in relatively insu-lated enclaves of complex societies.
>
> (ibid.:120)

And, indeed, recent ethnological work has found even contemporary Indian villages to be thus.

The full autonomy of a village in the cultural or political sphere is as much a myth as its total economic autarky. It is, however, largely a myth created by its critics. The Indian village known to ethnology has its cleav-ages and its solidarities, its external interdependencies and its relative agrarian autarky (cf. Meyer 1960:22–3; Srinivas 1975:71). After all, the exploitation of local resources is the very *raison d'être* of the rural village, and its absence marks out many contemporary British villages as not really villages at all, but simply small settlements.

Thus, especially in regard to pre-British India, where labour was scarce in relation to land available

> village society was divided into a series of production pyramids with the landlord at the apex, the artisan and servicing castes in the middle, and landless labourers at the bottom. Rivalry between patrons was minimised by institutionalized relationships, and by the existence of external threats to the community as whole.
>
> (Srinivas 1975:68)

Indeed, in the contemporary Hindu heartlands,

> each village around Kishan Garhi is regarded as a fictional agnatic group. People use agnatic terms for each other systematically, taking note of fictional generational standing throughout the village, ignoring all actual differences of caste and lineage. All villagers in Kishan Garhi tend accordingly to observe the same rules of inter-village hypergamy.
>
> (Marriott 1955b:177)

(Hypergamy is when a man of a certain status marries a woman of somewhat lower status, the difference, or 'balance', being 'made up' with a substantial dowry.) And as Meyer states in the opening pages of his influential study of a village and its region (Malwa):

> the caste group is based to a large extent on kinship relations within the population of a number of adjacent villages . . . all castes in the village studied ['Ramkheri'] are internally organized along patrilineal virilocal lines, with an emphasis, though not complete insistence, on village exogamy.
>
> (Mayer 1960:6)

Thus caste (*jati*) endogamy, marrying within the (sub-) caste, is effectively village exogamy, marriage partners coming from one's *jati* in other villages. Further, 'an analysis of kinship is at the same time largely an analysis of the internal structure of the sub-caste . . . and [it is] an effective local sub-caste population which I call the kindred of cooperation' (ibid.:3–4). See Appendix A for more detail on 'kindred of cooperation'.

C: THE SUMERIAN KING LIST AS A HISTORICAL SOURCE

Michalowski (1983) again reminds us that the Sumerian King List was far away from being a relatively complete record based on then extant inscriptional material (though some of its information was copied from triumphal inscriptions set up in the Ekur at Nippur). On the contrary, he claims, it was an exercise in 'legitimacy-mongering' by the (Amorite) rulers of Isin in the Isin-Larsa Period. This explains the exclusion of their rivals, Larsa from the List. Michalowski's hypothesis (1983:242–3) is that not being from the 'main' ruling lines of Amorite tribal descent, the kings of Isin resorted to a historical fiction to bolster their claims, the fiction being that at any point in Mesopotamian history one particular city (and thus one ruling house) had hegemony over all the rest. Fate and the gods decreed how long such rulership over 'the land' would last before, 'smitten with weapons' or some other disaster, rulership passed to another city. Thus the List is constructed as a sequence of 'turns', with Isin now receiving its turn (*bala*). It is then the very structure of the King List that constitutes the propaganda for the legitimacy of the rulers of Isin. Lagash is also ignored in the King List, even though it had provided 'paramount kings' such as 'Ay.ana-tumu. The King List's manifest partiality even provoked a Lagash scribe to satirize it by producing a parody in the form of a Lagash King List, with 'the attribution of an impossibly long reign to every single ruler, and the purely imaginary names of most of them; and perhaps also the

detailed biographical notes as compared with the terse statements occasionally found in the King List' (Sollberger 1967:279).

We know that extensive territorial control is the short-lived exception
(Sargon/Naram Sin; Ur III; Hammurabi/Samsu-iluna) and city-state rivalry,
warfare and cooperation the rule. Thus the King List is partial in both
senses. Furthermore, there are many versions. Its efficacy resided, however,
in correctly accessing Sumero-Akkadian cultural sensibilities. Even if they
had wanted to, those composing a written version could scarcely have stood
outside of their own cultural milieu. Indeed, from the King List, Wilcke
(1989:568) has convincingly argued for the concept of 'positional succession' among the rulers of Sumer and Akkad, wherein successors not only
occupy their predecessor's office but also assume some of their persona, in
particular parentage. This process provides a divine genealogy for the Ur
III kings:

> The lengthy enumeration of kings functions as chains linking the
> present kings to the very beginning of kingship in the single cities,
> once in mythic times and again in periods still vivid in memory,
> for the Gutian oppression lasted until Utuhegal's time [initiator of
> the Ur III, Neo-Sumerian dynasty] and Urnammu still had to fight
> them. The genealogical argument underlying the King List connects
> the single lines of rulers in the different cities and thus allows the
> kings of Ur to establish their ties to the beginning of kingship
> after the flood, whereby the kings listed apparently formed lines
> of ancestors.
>
> (ibid.)

Positional succession is, of course, related to 'identity transference' from a
deity or illustrious predecessor to a living individual.

Thus, while not denying the use made of the King List by the Isin
Dynasty, Wilcke (1989:558) makes a very strong and anthropologically
informed argument for its existence in the time of Urnammu, king of Ur
2114–2096 BC. And this makes a great deal of sense, since Ur III was the
second great centralizing period. Indeed, what is surprising is that the King
List was not (though discoveries may reveal to have been in origin) a product
of the first great centralizing initiative, that of Sargon, who had to make
enormous efforts to construct some legitimacy both for himself and even
more so, for his project. Cooper (1993:22–3) observes that the

> Sumerian King List . . . was co-opted by the rulers of Isin, and it
> is with their names that all copies of the list end. From being a
> document that legitimated the notion of hegemony as practiced by
> the Third Dynasty of Ur, it became the charter that legitimized
> Isin as the successor to Ur.

Vincente (1995:267), in her discussion of a version found at Tell Leilan (written in O.B. script), remarks that 'in the final analysis, holding power confers legitimacy to the power holder. The openness of the pattern of succession gives acceptance to any city which has de facto gained, or even claimed, pre-eminence'. While this might be true of a single city claiming merely pre-eminence under normal circumstances, it could not be true of empire-builders wishing to subordinate cities within a centralized territorial state. Some highly resonant ideology would be required to bolster a naked power seeking to remove sovereignty from the individual city-state.

The antediluvian portion of the King List is actually an independent tradition embodying much 'cultural memory', notably of culture heroes like the deified 'shepherd' Dumuzi. Indeed, the antediluvian portion is related to the epics such as the Deluge story and Lugal-e (Sollberger 1967:279), notably through the person of Ziusudra/Atrahasis/Utanapištim (=Noah), who features in some versions as the last king before the Flood (Finkelstein 1963:49). It also retains a memory of the earliest (priest-)kingship in such names as En-me-en-lu-an-na and En-me-(en-)dur-an-ma (cf. Edzard 1959). The first ruler of Kish *after* the Flood was Enmenunna. Finkelstein concludes with an observation of great value to the study of all traditions:

> When a scribe wrote down a version of the antediluvian tradition he was almost certainly never 'copying' a text, but giving something of an *ad hoc* written form to a tradition that was mostly oral, although known to him also in written form as parts of different literary compositions.
>
> (Finkelstein 1963:51)

The 'myths', then, which were accounts of the nature of things, were necessarily live and active.[1] Though studied and copied in the eduba, they were not cut-and-dried literary or theological texts, but ones involved in exchanges between Little and Great Traditions.

So although one's neighbours and contemporary rivals could be excluded from a particular dynasty's version of the King List, the political purpose for which the redaction was undertaken does not render worthless the historical material used in its construction, and still less its value for cultural reconstruction. And while some of its confusion will have been deliberate, some, such as that concerning the Gutians, almost certainly results from lack of contemporary documentation or access to it, something shared by today's scholars of the Kassite period (1595–1155 BC).

NOTES

1 HOW DOES THE PAST ILLUMINATE THE PRESENT?

1 This is the anthropological definition of culture that derives from Tylor (1871:1). The most succinct and operational definition of archaeological culture, recognizable in the material record as a 'constantly recurring assemblage of artifacts' comes from Renfrew (1972:19). For the interactions of archaeology and anthropology in the attempt to reconstruct a functioning society (with the constraints of the 'Hawkes Ladder' of inference), see Maisels 1990:1–6.

2 The state is formed by specialized ideological, administrative, military and revenue apparatuses, coordinated from a central place (capital city or district) by a central person (ruler).

3 Revised and expanded to two volumes, with a rejoinder to critics, 1795.

4 This was refuted in Austen's paper (1842) 'On the Geology of south-east Devonshire' in the Transactions of the Geological Society of London (6:433–89).

5 Only in the last half of the twentieth century have scholarly conferences become frequent enough to provide routine exchanges of the latest information, and to enable the providers to be questioned directly. Prior to this, most face-to-face interaction was through visits by individuals and small groups to persons and places of interest. Many fewer journals likewise encouraged the exchange of ideas through the medium of private letters, facilitated by the spread of railways across Europe and North America in the early Victorian period. With railways and steamships, correspondence became fast, reliable and cheap, and therefore worth the effort. Thus many of the period's scholars have left collections of letters from correspondents plus copies of their own.

6 Hence my suggestions in Maisels 1993a:195–206. Even now Gopher and Gophna have to preface a major review of the Pottery Neolithic period in the Levant, that area which indeed has been most intensively researched, with the following truly amazing reservations:

> First, the grid units (which were not used at all in Israel until the late 1950's) and context definitions are too large to permit detailed analysis of intrasite variability. This limits our reconstruction of social structure and of behaviour through the study of households, activity areas, communal areas etc. Second, excavated sediments were rarely sieved in the past, causing major problems for quantitative analysis. This has improved recently but is still not universal (sic). Flotation, for example, is very infrequent, thus limiting the potential for both radiocarbon dating and reconstruction of the economy. Thus, excavations of PN sites are limited either in scale or in level of recovery, resulting in poor spatial control and the loss of important data. Assemblages are very rarely

contextually secure (sic!), and it is sometimes impossible to assign them to taxonomically ordered and quantitatively defined archaeological units.

(Gopher and Gophna 1993:302)

7 In this he was following the Scottish antiquarian and traveller Alexander Henry Rhind (1833–63) whose *Thebes, its Tombs and Their Tenants* (1862) Petrie would have known from his preparatory reading and Scottish connections. The invited lectures in archaeological subjects at Edinburgh University, where Rhind studied, were established in his memory. In his turn Rhind was following in the footsteps of another Scot, James Bruce (1730–17), known as The Abyssinian, who in 1770, via Thebes and Aswan, reached the Abbai River in Ethiopia, headstream of the Blue Nile. From his observations at Thebes, Bruce argued that three script systems had been employed in ancient Egypt: hieroglyphic, hieratic and demotic. His *Travels to Discover the Sources of the Nile* appeared in 1790, and contained much ethnological observation.

8 For whom Robert Keldewey led the excavation of Babylon from 1899 to 1917, while Walter Andrae dug at Qal'at Sherqat from 1902 until 1914 to reveal the city of Ashur.

9 The getting of the material evidence minimally requires:

a Area and site survey.

b The site excavated by grid-planning/triangulation, stratigraphy and exact three-dimensional recording (especially of artefacts in relation to architecture, each other, and specific features such as wells, pits and ditches which are likely to penetrate through strata).

In sum, the ground being excavated must be conceived of as a three-dimensional block of frozen time and space. The time is represented by the different strata or horizons, the space by the extent of features and by the exact location of artefacts in those strata. Computer Aided Design packages enable the excavated block to be treated as a piece of solid geometry. In the three-dimensional space of, say, a cuboid, it can display the relationships between all the features and artefacts plotted. For detailed examination it can rotate the block on a number of axes to reveal different aspects.

c Sieving (preferably wet) to recover all artefacts and fragments, including seeds and bones.

d The use of lithics and ceramics as culturological indicators.

e The use of specialists to analyse faunal, floral, mineral, skeletal and other finds.

f Site-Catchment Analysis, with its modification, Site Territory Analysis (site exploitation territory, based on time–distance and social information considerations; see Hovers 1989, especially his Table 1).

g Finally, speedy publication of an interim report and full publication of a final report (or series) that does not appear decades after the original excavation when archaeology has already moved on.

Even something as basic as grid-planning was not used in Israel until the 1950s. Sieving was rarely practised and even now (in the 1990s) is still not universal, while flotation is very infrequent (Gopher and Gophna 1993:302; see Note 6 above).

10 See, for instance, K.C. Chang's Preface to the fourth edition of his *Archaeology of Ancient China* (1986a). As will be seen below, my debt to him is at least as great as his to Childe.

11 Of course a day is a single rotation of the earth on its axis as it moves in its orbit, lasting a year, round the sun. The month is the time it takes for the moon to circle the earth, 29.5 days from a full moon to the next; while the earth's seasons are a consequence, not of its distance from the sun, but of the angle that the earth's polar axis (a line through the poles) makes with the plane of the earth's (annual) orbit round the

sun. The plane of the earth's orbit is formed by regarding the ellipse traced as a solid flat surface. In other words, the seasons are a function of the 'tilt' of the earth to the sun, above or below the equator (thus with either northern or southern hemispheres most exposed to the sun's rays) as if the planet was pivoted at its centre. This is the mechanism that makes for varying lengths of day and night during the year all over the planet except within the Equatorial Belt, which extends to 10 degrees north and south of the Equator (a great circle). Within the Equatorial Belt day and night are almost equal and seasonal variation minimal.

2 SEMA-TAWY: THE LAND OF THE PAPYRUS AND LOTUS

1 Students are recommended to read this chapter in association with the *Atlas of Ancient Egypt*, by John Baines and Jaromir Malek (1980 and reprints). This work has particularly fine maps. Also the *British Museum Dictionary of Ancient Egypt*, by Ian Shaw and Paul Nicholson (1995).

   Sema-Tawy: the lotus and papyrus entwined symbolized the united realm. Although both were originally found all along the Nile (and papyrus thickets are now common only in southern Sudan), the lotus (three species of water lily) was the symbol of the god Re (the 'Great Lotus') and became most associated with Upper Egypt (the south), whilst the papyrus flowers were associated with Lower Egypt, particularly the Delta. Many deities were shown in association with papyrus flowers. Like other reeds, papyrus was useful for a range of tasks other than paper-making. Around 5 metres high, the papyrus plant was used for boats, sails, rope, mats, bedding and clothing. Young shoots were eaten like asparagus and the root was used for fuel and containers. In conventionalized form, its image was used for decorative and architectural purposes and is often found on tomb and temple walls.

   Hermopolis in Middle Egypt, the city Khmun, modern Ashmunein, is associated with the 'Ogdoad' or 'Eight' theogony, describing the forces present prior to the emergence of the creator. In formative processes akin to those conceptualized in Mesopotamia, matter is created from nebulous forces through the agency of will and utterance, a primeval mound appears out of the dark waters, and in general world-formation appears by the process of differentiation into complementary opposites: dark:light, wet:dry, hidden:revealed, inchoate:created. From eight characterized conditions (i.e. four pairs of gods and goddesses), Atum creates himself.

2 Uruk connections with the Amuq in the northern Levant, thence to a seaport like Buto (where Amuq F type small bowls with flat bases, thin rims and a highly unusual series of light stripes parallel to the rim were found in layer 1), finally knocks on the head claims about a sea-link with Mesopotamia around the Arabian peninsula (Von der Way 1992b:221).

3 'Pharaoh' is a term for the divine king, not pre-dating the mid-second millennium, and not part of his original and complex titulary. For example, while the king, *nesu* (*nesit*, queen) could earlier be routinely referred to as *neter nefer*, the perfect god, the term Pharaoh refers to his palace *per-aa*, the great house. (cf. Sumerian *e-gal*, great house, palace; *lu-gal*, great man, king).

4 Similar 'bunding' of fields to retain water long enough to soak the soil thoroughly has also been argued to be a feature of Mesopotamian *canal* irrigation, as a means of making the most of water delivered by this complex and costly means: 'If fields were regularly placed between bunds, it implies that basin irrigation was the norm; some of the banks were at least a metre high, and this throws some light on the nature of the initial autumn flooding of the field mentioned by the texts' (Pemberton *et al.* 1988:216). The iku (Akk.) is an areal field measure of 60×60 metres. Iku is generally agreed to derive from the Sumerian *eg*, an earth bank or bund (ibid.:214).

5 It is likely, however, that ancient, especially predynastic, grain storage practices in Egypt encouraged the growth of *Streptomycetes*, resulting in the population ingesting continuous low-level doses of the antibiotic tetracycline, conferring significant, if unrealized, therapeutic benefits (Mills 1992). Thin sections of human trabecular bone shows tetracycline labelling in osteons (Keith and Armelagos 1988).

6 The first part (N'r) of the full name – N'r-mr – of Horus Narmer, the last king of Dynasty 0, is represented by a catfish.

7 So ingrained was the south to north direction of Nile flow, that the north to south current in the Red Sea that took Egyptian ships to Punt, was called 'the great sea of inverted water' (Kitchen 1993:608).

8 A full King List is given in Baines and Malek (1980:36–7) along with the hieroglyphics for the most important.

9 For a discussion involving the results of recent climatic modelling, see H.E. Wright (1993).

10 Ritual is repeated, conventionalized symbolic behaviour, externally (publicly) and internally (psychologically) actualizing aspects of the belief-system (ideology).

11 For discussion of the King List and Ramesside Inscriptions, see Kitchen (1993).

12 Indeed, Butzer (1984) sees four episodes in the long-term variation in Nile flow being implicated in periods of socio-political collapse. The first is a 1 metre (30 per cent) reduction in discharge between 3000 and 2900 BC: the second is in fact two periods of Nile failure 2200 BC and 2002 BC; the third is an erratically high or 'wild' Nile with a recurrence interval of one year in three between 1840 and 1770 BC; while the fourth is caused by the dramatic fall in East African lake levels *c.* 1260+–50 BC, causing agriculture in Nubia to cease almost entirely after the reign of Ramesses II, i.e. after 1212 BC (ibid.:107). Butzer calls those episodes 'Anomalies' and he sees them as implicated in socio-political decline and cultural change, as follows:

> The four periods of decline are: (1) the Second Dynasty (*ca.* 2970–2760 BC), coincident with Anomaly I; (2) the Seventh and Eighth dynasties and the First Intermediate period (*ca.* 2250–2035 BC), coincident with Anomaly II; (3) the Thirteenth Dynasty and Second Intermediate Period (1784–1560 BC), following Anomaly III; (4) the Twentieth Dynasty, following the food riots of 1153 BC, and the assassination of Ramesses III in 1151 BC, coincident with Anomaly IV.
>
> (ibid.:108)

'Coincident with' is rather overstretching the case; 'a consequence of' better expresses the delay between ecological change and political upheaval. Butzer (1980:272) also posits a 'wild' Nile during the Late Palaeolithic; Vermeersch *et al.* (1989:108) put this between 12,690+–60 bp and 11,940+–90 bp, commencing therefore about midway through the occupational life of the Makadma sites.

13 The British Museum has an incomplete 8.8 centimetre figurine carved from ivory of a First Dynasty king dressed in the knee-length jubilee cloak.

14 Although the episodes are not connected, the onset of the First Intermediate Period closely matches that of the 'Gutian' interregnum/Uruk-Lagash period in Mesopotamia; but the breakdown there lasted only a matter of decades.

15 Nonetheless, true paper, that made from retted vegetable fibres, was not produced in Europe until the twelfth-century renaissance. Since the eighth century AD, Europe had acquired its paper by purchase from the Arabs, who had learned paper manufacture from the Chinese (Temple 1986:84). It seems that true paper – made by pounding, disintegrating, floating and settling hemp fibres – was invented in China during the second century BC, but only assumed importance as a writing medium there in the second century AD (ibid.:81). By the ninth century there were printed books in China.

Paper of the Gutenberg period (fifteenth century) was made from the fibres of hemp and linen rags and has proved very durable.

Papyrus manufacture has the pounding but not the disintegration and flotation stages of true paper: 'It was prepared by stripping the outer rind (of *Cyperus papyrus*) and cutting the pith into strips which were then laid parallel, slightly overlapping each other. Then a second layer of strips was laid on top of the first at right angles. Moistened and hammered, the two layers of pith adhered together and formed one homogenous sheet of thin writing material' (Emery 1961:234–5). The horizontally laid strips formed the recto side of the sheet, the vertical the verso. Sheets, about 48 by 43 centimetres when full size, could then be edge-joined along the longer sides to form a standard roll of 20 sheets, and rolls in their turn joined, if required. The British Museum has a roll, the Harris Papyrus, extending to 41 metres. When rolled, the preferred recto side was inside. Then it was tied with a length of papyrus string and sealed with a lump of clay. Indeed, the roll laid horizontally with its sealed knot on top was the sign for book-roll, a word, and abstract concepts like 'plan'.

To have a surface smooth enough for writing (with a reed or rush pen), a special round-edged smoother was required, and thus was a standard part of the writing kit. Tutankhamun took his splendid set to the grave with him. A palette consisted of a wide central slot for a number of reed pens, and shallow circular depressions for cakes of ink, usually black and red, for headings.

16 See Maisels (1990, 1995, Appendix E) for the emergence of alphabetic script; Gelb (1963) for types of writing systems.

17 Nut won those extra five days in a game of dice from her opponent Thoth, the god of time, according to the theology of *On* (Heliopolis). Nut personified the vault of heaven. She was the wife of the earth god Geb and the daughter of Shu, god of the atmosphere and his consort Tefenet.

The *On* theogony (which should really be called the Delta theogony) calls Nuu or Nun the primordial ocean or the formless waters of origin in which the sun-god Atum creates himself. From his spittle or semen, Shu and Tefenet emerge. They produce Geb and Nut, who in turn are the parents of Osiris and the fratricide Seth (the pharaoh hound) and the goddesses Isis and Nephthys. Horus, the falcon, symbol of royal divinity and an early sky god, was the son of Isis and Osiris. Atum and his eight descendants (therefore The Nine) were worshipped at Heliopolis as the Great Ennead.

3 THE LEVANT AND MESOPOTAMIA

1 Students are recommended to read this chapter in association with Michael Roaf's *Cultural Atlas of Mesopotamia and the Ancient Near East* (1990).

2 In parts of Lebanon rainfall presently exceeds 1000 millimetres annually, 500–800 millimetres in Western Galilee, less than 50 millimetres over two-thirds of the Negev and Sinai and in the southeast of the Azraq Basin.

3 For definitions of 'evapotranspiration' and 'isohyet' see Glossary, page xiv.

4 Meanders, which are the large wide loops formed only when a river reaches its middle-course, also have the property of 'migration', that is, the tendency to move progressively downstream (sinusoidal phase shifting).

5 Building measures involved the yardstick, *nindan* (literally 'reed') of 5.94 metres and the 'cord', *ese*, of 59.40 metres. The *iku* was then the square of the chord, or 3528.36 square metres (Jacobsen 1987:9 n12).

6 This restoration is indeed a major achievement, since the line described is the west-ernmost of the two spinal watercourses running north–south down the whole length of Sumer and Akkad (= Babylonia). It has a take-off from the Euphrates just north of Sippar, and runs due south through Kish, Abu Salabikh, Nippur, Shuruppak, Uruk and

on to Eridu. The easterly spine through Tell Uqair and Jemdet Nasr receives a feeder from the Tigris through Tell al-Wilyayah, joining the main trunk at Adab, then south to Umma, where it splits, west to Larsa and Ur, east to Girsu and Lagash (cf. Postgate 1992:26). There were, of course, many subsidiary connections.

7 Harlan points out (ibid.:25) on the basis of his experimental work, that harvesting (collecting) wild grains does not cause their domestication, only *planting* does this, for 'it is then that mutations for non-shattering, synchronous ripening, loss of dormancy, and larger seed size receive positive selection pressures. . . . As a consequence of self-pollination, in as few as three generations of planting/harvesting the frequency of genes for seed retention (non-shattering) and for the fertility of lateral florets and spikelets, can come to predominate. Such features are controlled by one or two genes only (Zohary 1992:85). Domesticated barley thereby becomes six-rowed (all three spikelets female-fertile), in contrast with the two-rowed wild form which has sterile lateral spikelets. As many as eight additional fertile spikelets in pearl millet have evolved from sterile inflorescent branches that have no rudimentary structures. Florets (rudimentary scale-like structures in panicoid grasses) recover fertility in some cultivars of sorghum, zea and panicum.

8 This is determined by the proportion of unfused limb bone epiphyses (see Glossary, page xiv) which occurs between 10 and 18 months (Davis 1991:386). The first phalanx fuses at 6–8 months, the *calcaneum* process, or heel bone, to which a tendon is attached, fuses at 14 months. Another indicator is the third permanent molar, which in gazelle erupts at 12 months, about the same time as the milk molars are replaced by permanent premolars (Legge and Rowley-Conwy 1987:90), prior to which they are classed as juveniles. Measuring the third molar's subsequent crown height gives an indication of the animal's age at death.

9 The 'wide-definition' of the Epipalaeolithic includes all of the Kebaran *plus* the Natufian. To Gilead (1989a; 1989b), however, this makes little sense, for the Kebaran and Geometric Kebaran are continuous in lifestyle with their Upper Palaeolithic antecedents, whereas the Natufian 'breakthrough' to a semi-sedentary society marks a qualitative change. Accordingly, for the Levant, Gilead would confine the term Epipalaeolithic to the Natufian, with the Geometric Kebaran and Kebaran being seen as an extension and part of the Late Upper Palaeolithic.

10 The consequences of intensification have been rigorously examined by Winterhalder (1993). 'In general, the relationship between sustainable yield and resource population size is parabolic' (ibid.:323). Maximum sustainable yield of prey species is half of its carrying capacity level (K/2). Deviations from this, notably by increased predation, cause disruptive stress to the population, interfere with its reproduction and can cause its numbers to crash, threatening the very existence of the population, especially where it is accompanied by habitat damage. Paradoxically then, 'low to intermediate values of effort (w) are associated with the largest sustainable human population and with higher food acquisition rates' (ibid.:327).

11 This has, *inter alia*, allowed Kislev *et al.* to refine the criteria differentiating wild from domesticated barley, formerly thought to be characterized by single internodes with a fragment of the upper internode still attached to the connecting node. However, it is now apparent that 'when barley rachis remnants with attached, fragmented internode are recovered in Pre-pottery Neolithic settlements in small percentage, they belong to the wild type' (ibid.:162–3). In other words a proportion (*c.* 10 per cent) of the *wild* type is of the sort that hitherto was thought to indicate domesticated forms. Contrary, then, to indicating the presence of domesticated cereals, when *this proportion* is part of a wild group of grains, *the whole population is wild*. This has been experimentally checked at Jales and published as Kislev (1992) and Zohary (1992 Postscript). It has been shown, however, that when harvested barley was left to sun-dry for twenty-four hours, the broken fragment of the internode still attached to the plane of disarticulation fell to between 2 and 3 per cent of the sample. Accordingly, Zohary (1992) and Hillman and

Davies (1992) still maintain that two-row barley was being cultivated at Netiv Hagdud, Gilgal 1 and Jericho.

12 Interestingly, Gopher (1989a) has argued for a technically dynamic mid-Euphrates (Mureybet-Hureyra) area in the Pre-Pottery Neolithic Period. In his view it served as a source of innovations like Helwan and El Khiam points, diffused through the Damascus Basin (Tell Aswad at the beginning of the eighth millennium) then across the Upper Jordan Valley and Galilee down into Israel, reaching the south about five hundred years later.

13 The presence of wild cereal grains at Hureyra and Mureybet on the Euphrates, over 100 kilometres from their present natural habitats, causes Anderson (1991:550–1) to 'suggest that there may have been displacement of wild grain to nearer the site, involving sowing in an area where a spontaneous field did not previously exist'. However, with present rainfall of 200 millimetres in the vicinity, it would not need to be much wetter for stands of wild cereal to appear on the steppe (Willcox 1995:15). Interior areas have the most variable rainfall both in the short and the long term.

14 Establishing the place of pulses in the diet and in the evolutionary process is in general very difficult, as Gary Rollefson (pers. comm.) makes plain:

> One of the major sources of error in estimating the amount of pulses vs. cereals is the problem of sample bias, in this case the processes that lead to preservation by charring. Cereals may have been routinely roasted in order to remove the husks (especially if they were harvested semi-green), and naturally this exposure to heat would lead to an increased chance of charring [and thus survival]; not so for peas and lentils, which probably rarely were exposed to heat until at supper time. At 'Ain Ghazal we've had some enormous amounts of charred pulses turn up, but only because the houses caught fire, accidentally scorching the stored material (cf. Rollefson and Simmons 1986:152 and Kafafi and Rollefson 1995:24 . . . in the 1995 publication we've floated only about half of the samples from the LPPNB house, and we have more than a quarter-million lentils already).

15 For the complexities of wheat taxa identification and evolution, see Miller (1992), and also Willcox (1995).

16 Bar-Yosef and Belfer-Cohen (1989b:60–1) think that the initial domestication of sheep and goat took place not in the Levant, but on the flanks of the Zagros ranges. Horwitz (1989:174) disputes this, arguing for localized domestication in the Levant. This seems to be the general view and is shared by I. Kohler-Rollefson and G. Rollefson (pers. comm.).

17 Rollefson and Kafafi (1996a:2) suggest that, because there are so many similarities between 'Ain Ghazal and Jericho in architecture, ritual and art, it is very likely that in the middle of the 7th millennium, when Jericho was temporarily abandoned, a part of its population emigrated to 'Ain Ghazal.

18 The preceding Wadi Raba ware shows Halaf connections (Kaplan 1960:32–6). At Ard Tlaili in the central Beqaa Valley, Wadi Raba and Byblos Neolithique Moyen pottery is found along with Halaf painted wares (Kirkbride 1969:53–9; Elliott 1978:38). Notwithstanding the characteristic Ghassul cornet-cups, pottery there is much inferior to Halaf wares.

19 Strictly speaking, the term Semitic relates to language, as does the term 'Indo-European'. Semitic is a branch of the Afrasian or Semito-Hamitic language family, which comprises: Semitic, Cushitic, Berbero-Libyan, Egyptian and Chadic. Their origins lie in North Africa (Diakonoff 1981:67). Within Semitic the divisions are into: (1) SNP – Northern Peripheral (Akkadian); (2) SNC – Northern Central: (a) Eblaite, Ugaritic, Amorite; (b) Early Canaanite, Hebrew (which is probably a Canaanite dialect with an Amorite

superstratum), Phoenician *et al.*; (c) Aramaic; (3) SSC – South Central (Arabic); SSP – Southern Peripheral: (a) Old South Arabian dialects; (b) the modern South Arabian dialects of Mehri, Sahri, Suqutri *et al.*; (c) the Northern Ethio-Semitic dialects; (d) the numerous modern Southern Ethio-Semitic dialects, of which Amharic is the most important as it has traditionally been the state language of Ethiopia (Diakonoff 1981:28).

20 Summing up his review of the Yarmoukian in Jordan, Zeidan Kafafi concludes that the groups settled in the Jordanian mountain zone

> may have had relations with populations that lived in Mesopotamia. This can be seen in the type of decor, the incised chevrons, of one kind of pottery; they are similar to those excavated at the site of Hassuna (Lloyd and Safar 1945:10). The 'coffee-bean eyes' figurines are like the figurines found, among other sites, at Choga Mami [a Samarran site].
>
> (Kafafi 1993:113)

In *The Emergence of Civilization* (Appendix B: 'Inanna and Dumuzi of the Dates') I argued that the 'coffee-bean eyes' were much more likely to have been 'date-stone eyes', given the enormous importance of dates in Iraq, ancient and modern, and the fact that the two deities most intimately concerned with fecundity in ancient Mesopotamia, Inanna and Dumuzi (Usumgalanna in Sumerian), were the patron deities of dates (although his primary role was as patron of flocks). This being so, it does indeed seem that the *influences* identified by Kafafi flowed from Mesopotamia to the Levant, rather than west to east. This would then be indicative that the baton of pioneering new lifestyles, ultimately of complex society and the state, had passed to Mesopotamia by the beginning of the sixth millennium, that is, by the end of the PPNB.

21 This is a profile with a sharp angle in it, resulting in a projecting angle at the top.

22 Indeed, Tell Hassuna is the site that established the modern periodization of Mesopotamian prehistory, defining the relationships between Hassuna, Samarra, Halaf and Ubaid. As I have previously (1993a:114–24) discussed the Hassuna in some detail, I shall not do so here.

Hijara *et al.* (1980:151) supply the following dates for the Samarran Culture (from Tell es-Sawwan – below) and for the Halaf Culture from Banahilk on the headwaters of the Greater or Upper Zab; Girikihaciyan in Turkey (discussed below) and Chagar Bazar in the middle of the Habur Plains:

Tell es-Sawwan	P–855	7456 +– 37 bp.	5506 BC Level I floor
Tell es-Sawwan	P–856	7299 +– 86 bp.	5349 BC Level III
Tell es-Sawwan	P–857	6806 +– 82 bp.	4858 BC Level III
Banahilk	P–1501	4359 +– 79 BC	DII, 1.3 metres down
Banahilk	P–1502	4801 +– 85 BC	DI floor 6, feature 1
Banahilk	P–1503	4904 +– 72 BC	DI floor 6, feature 1
Girikihaciyan		4515 +– 100 BC	
Chagar Bazar	P–1487	4715 +– 77 BC	levels 11–12.

Akkermans' (1991:124) Halaf site in the Balikh Valley, Tell Sabi Abyad, has dates that (excluding the extremes) range from 4980 +– 80 BC Conventional Date (like those above) calibrated to 5954–5664 BC, to 5275 +– 30 Conventional, which calibrates to 6097–6003 BC (both from charcoal). Sawwan calendar dates are around 6000 BC. Oates (1993a:408) states that irrigation farming was well established as early as the seventh millennium cal. BC. Charcoal has particular radiocarbon problems; see p. 47.

23 It has been suggested that this was done with the use of the ox-pulled plough. However, the first attested evidence for the plough appears on Late Uruk seals and as signs on Uruk IV tablets (see below). The first actual soil evidence appears in adjoining Elam

in the Susa I period. And in many respects this southeastern enclave seems to have a technical lead (e.g. in notation) over the rest of the alluvium during the Uruk V period.

24 This does not apply to Nilotic cattle which are particularly adapted to arid conditions and were probably domesticated in the tenth millennium bp (Close and Wendorf 1992:69). They were used primarily not for meat but for milk and blood, in the tradition of contemporary Nilotic and East African cattle keepers.

25 Indeed, the 'proto-Hassuna' also appears to be such a cluster of localized Neolithic cultures.

26 I owe this reference to Stuart Campbell.

27 Shendge (1985). The number system of Harappa is most similar to that of Susa; cf. Proto-Elamite numerical notation illustrated in Vallat (1986:337). Elam also has several 'great baths' like the famous one at Mohenjo-daro (Gropp 1992). Despite stating that 'most Indus inscriptions . . . were engraved on seals used in administration and trade', Parpola (1986:407) without any argument, peremptorily dismisses (as 'inadmissible') Shendge's (1985) well-argued case that 'inscribed calculi' (so-called 'miniature tablets' or 'amulets') had similar functions in Harappan society as in the Near East: namely they were economic recording devices. But Parpola himself (1986:401) records Indus clay sealings, 'most of (which) are tags which had been attached to bales of goods, for the reverse sides usually show traces of packing materials'. His dismissal is thus inadmissible.

The Acropolis at Susa in Levels 18, 17 and 16 of Le Brun's (1978) excavations, with its clear stratification, shows the intimate association of numerological recording (including *calculi* and *bullae*) with the emergence of script during the second half of the fourth millennium.

28 Accordingly, it is facile to see the hand of 'elites' in every instance of increased complexity, as Yoffee (1993:265) does when he assumes that 'a wide-scale, interregional exchange sphere can be inferred in the Halaf in which local elites sought to control the circulation of goods across vast geographical and social distances'. Specialization in the production of high-quality, large, standardized flint blades from naviform cores, *fossile directeur* for the PPNB, occurs at 'Ain Ghazal without any hint of the presence of 'elites' (Quintero and Wilke 1995:27–9). The production of lime plaster there was probably also a specialist product (ibid.).

29 There are sources of ashphalt/bitumen from the south all the way up to Mosul, and the overlaps of 'Oueilian material with that analysed from Larsa, Sawwan and Susa indicate separate but southern sources, and definitely not Hit-Abu Jir (ibid.: Figure D). However, the bitumen used for waterproofing contemporary boats in the marshes did come from Hit, according to Thesiger (1964:126–7). Further, 'there was no wood suitable for canoes in Southern Iraq. The boat-builders favoured mulberry from Kurdistan for the ribs, and for the planks they used woods imported from abroad' (ibid.).

30 Students are recommended to read this section in association with Postgate (1992) and Crawford (1991).

31 Tepe Gawra is a small, roughly one hectare site, originally Ubaidian, on a tributary of the Khosr River on the Zagros piedmont northeast of Nineveh, excavated by Speiser (1935) and Tobler (1950). Composed largely of tripartite buildings on the now 'classical' pattern, and located on the rainfed soils at the western end of a pass through the Jebel Maqlub linking Assyria to Iran, Tepe Gawra (from Gawra XI) is one of the now famous Uruk period trading stations 'in the far north', yielding the uniquely characteristic coarse 'bevel-rimmed bowls', which look like wide flower pots and were used as bread-moulds (Millard 1988). Another aspect of its 'southern-ness' is the extensive use of seals on goods and storerooms, just as in Sumer. Those round stamp seals (or rather their imprint on clay) have been studied by Rothman (1994:118) inquiring into the sorts of administrative and thus political control represented by the uses of sealing. He concludes that

If Arslantepe is used as a possible model of a state administration, Gawra was not the centre of a state in the fourth millennium BC. Nor is there any clear evidence that Gawra was formally incorporated into a larger state structure as a secondary centre.

Despite the fact that Gawra could therefore be classified as part of a chiefdom throughout the period from phase XI through level VIII, the nature of administration was quite variable through time.

(ibid.)

This is completely wrong. Gawra was a Uruk outpost, and as such a part of the emergence of city-states on the southern alluvium. Rothman (ibid.:112–13) lists Gawra's Activity Areas as follows:

1 Residential;   5 Seal and Bead Cutting;   9 Religious;
2 Clothmaking;   6 Storage;   10 Animal Pen;
3 Ceramic Craft;   7 Kitchen;   11 Receiving (and Processing);
4 Woodworking;   8 Administrative;   12 Trash.

Clearly Gawra is a craft centre, using its sophisticated southern skills to add value to materials available in the north, exchanging their manufactured goods for the raw materials available at Gawra, with the express purpose of transmitting a proportion of them to the south, so deficient in minerals, woods, etc.

No society as sophisticated as this can possibly be a chiefdom. Even the earlier Halaf domain does not represent a chiefdom, but something much more advanced: an autonomous network.

32 This for the built-up area of the capital city. For Girsu in the Ur III period, Maekawa (1987a:89) has established [from BM 25055 and BM 28407 texts] that the total area of the *domain land* (see below) to be cultivated by *all* the public households there amounted to about 26,147 hectares (4,034 *bur*, 17 3/4 *iku*).

Gelb (1986:159–60) seems to suggest that the entire cultivated area of Lagash in the Ur III period was in the hands of only fifteen temple-estates, whose combined acreage was '119,514.2 iku or 41,830 hectares or 418 square kilometres or, roughly, an area of slightly more than 20 by 20 kilometers'. He further suggests that this (or a somewhat larger 522 square kilometres) was close to the entire area of the independent (Pre-Sargonic) city–state of Lagash.

Though there was little waste or grazing land in the state of Lagash, those dimensions seem too small to me, especially in the light of Gelb's insistence upon *three* economic sectors: temple, private and state. The area of the Sargonic province of Lagash is given by Gelb himself (ibid.:160) as being 1,569 square kilometres or about 40 × 40 kilometres.

33 See Maisels (1993b) Appendix A, for details. Ningirsu = Ninurta, the god of thunderstorms. His other name of Abu, 'Father Pasture', 'stresses his role as the power in the thundershowers to call forth pasture in the desert in Spring' (Jacobsen 1989b:129). The early form of this god was Imdugud – the Anzu bird – an enormous black eagle floating on outstretched wings like a dark thundercloud.

34 Millard (1988); Maisels (1990): Appendix D; Chazan and Lehner (1990); Geller (1992). There is no doubt that the mass-produced bevelled-rim bowls of the Uruk period (and the variants like 'flower-pots' and pinched-rim bowls) used for baking bread were the instantly discarded pizza-containers of their day; they are Urukian litter, dropped wherever they went.

35 How patrilines were able to keep hold of elite positions in temple and state over the generations, is discussed for the Ur III period in the context of the 'House of Urmeme' by Hallo (1972) and by Zettler (1984). By the latter it is observed that 'the

governorship of the city of Nippur would appear to have been the preserve of one line of Ur-Me-me's family. A second branch followed Ur-Me-me himself in control of a much smaller institution, the temple of Inanna' (Zettler 1984:5). One of the sons of Ur-Me-me is Lugal-a-zi-da and someone with that name is described as an 'elder of the city' (ab-ba uru).

36 Explaining why temple-building could be done only in peacetime, Jacobsen (1987:4) observes that

> the manpower needed for building was provided by the army and it would, of course, be needed for fighting in times of war. Samsuiluna, for instance, had to postpone building the temple for Shamash in Sippar which the god had asked for because a rebellion broke out in the south of the country and had to be put down.

37 For a concise and well-illustrated review of early warfare in the Near East, see Watkins (1989) and Wiseman (1989).

38 Thus Ur-Nanshe, founder of the highly important dynasty at Lagash, referred to himself as lugal, but later UruKAgina (Uruinimgina) of Lagash, after five years as lugal, assumed the title of ensi.

39 Indeed, of the hundred or so **mes**, which are the norms and techniques defining Sumerian civilization (and which are listed in the myth *Inanna and Enki: the Transfer of the Arts of Civilization from Eridu to Uruk*) the **en**-ship comes first, long before kingship, which is merely number nine. Paradoxically, 'royal' appurtenances rate higher than kingship itself; perhaps it is that they sacralize the *office*, which an individual merely fills.

The first fifteen **mes** are then:

1	**en**-ship	9	kingship
2	godship	10	lasting ladyship
3	the exalted and enduring crown	11	(the priestly office) 'divine lady'
4	the throne of kingship	12	(the priestly office) **ishib**
5	the exalted sceptre	13	(the priestly office) **lumah**
6	the royal insignia	14	(the priestly office) **guda**
7	the exalted shrine [on a ziggurat?]	15	truth
8	shepherdship		(Kramer 1963:116)

Not only does **en**-ship head the list, with godship next, but at least nine of the fifteen refer to priestly offices and attributes. Inanna, as 'Queen of Heaven', is also 'Queen of all the **me**', and there are in fact many more than one hundred. 'The possession of the totality of the **me** (**me.nig.nam.ma**) entails not only absolute power but also absolute responsibility towards their realization and implementation in the world' (Leick 1991:117). Apparently only An and Enlil (with Inanna) possessed this sort of power and responsibility, which included the power to bestow me (*parṣū* in AKK)

Enlil, chief executive of the Sumerian pantheon, was described as 'the en who makes the grain grow . . . the en of heaven, the en of bounty, and the en of the earth art thou' (Jacobsen 1953:181).

40 Recent studies of this most important Sumerian concept are by G. Farber (1990) in *Reallexikon der Assyriologie* 7:610–13; and by G. Leick (1991) *A Dictionary of Ancient Near Eastern Mythology*, p.117. It is also referred to in an important article by I.M. Diakonoff (1983b), which has the descriptive title: Some reflections on numerals in Sumerian: Towards a history of mathematical speculation (*JAOS* 103.1:83–93).

41 Edzard (1959:9–11) provides a photograph of this fragment, and also a palaeographic table for some kings (figures with crowns) of the Early Dynastic period (c.3000–2350 BC). Mesilim (Me-salim), though also 'King of Kish' (lugal Kiš = hegemon) is not actually mentioned in the King List.

42 The famous 'theorem of Pythagorus'. While there were certainly 'Pythagoreans', a school or cult mystically interested in numbers and musical theory, there is no evidence that an individual called Pythagoras 'discovered' the relationships between the sides of right-angled triangles. 'He' left no writings and 'his' theorem is in fact set out in Euclid. 'Pythagoras' rather appears to be a name attached to the Greek 'discovery' of features of Babylonian mathematics during the sixth century BC.

43 Thus the lexical series U uru.an.na = U mastakal, which is a pharmacopoeia.

44 By extension, cylinder seals were badges of office. Both of Sargon's sons, Rimush and Manishtushu, were killed in palace revolutions, probably on account of their incessant warfare and destruction of cities. Having secured Elam, Manishtushu even set sail on the Gulf to fight '32 cities beyond the sea'. The number and the geography may not be exact, but the preoccupations of Rimush and Manishtushu are well reflected in the claim. One tradition maintains that Rimush was killed by his courtiers stabbing him with the long copper pins that passed through the centre of the cylinder and attached it to clothing.

45 Magan is usually taken to be the Oman Peninsula (Crawford 1998). However, Hansman (1973) argues that Magan and Meluhha refer respectively to western and eastern Baluchistan (Greater Makran) and that Bampur is the site of the 'city of Magan' (western Makran), the residence of Manui, Lord of Magan, who was defeated by Naram-Sin. Eastern Makran (i.e. Meluhha) was by contrast part of the Harappan oecumene and the ports of Sutkagen-dor, Sotka-koh and Bala Kot are found there (see Chapter 4).

   Those are the Mesopotamian designations up to the middle of the second millennium BC; thereafter Makkan (Magan) is identified with Egypt and Meluhha with areas to its south. Shifting geographical designations are commonplace. Thus, the 'East Indies' (Indonesia), the 'West Indies' (in the Caribbean) and native American 'Indians' are all named from a term originally referring to South Asia.

4 THE INDUS/'HARAPPAN'/SARASVATI CIVILIZATION

1 There is a schematic map of Lagash state in Heimpel (1994:18).

2 Xu Chaolong (1994:68–70), by contrast, thinks that there is a primary period at Mohenjo-daro, as early, indeed, as the first half of the fourth millennium. As a consequence, 'the Harappans had been developing for a considerable period before the Kot Dijian and Amrian cultures make their appearance'. This rather overlooks the connections of early Amrian and Kot Dijian ceramics with Hakra wares, which occupy the first half of the fourth millennium.

   Nonetheless, Xu says that

> [his] ceramic comparisons seem to indicate that the development of the Harappan culture during the first half of the third millennium BC was occurring at Mohenjo-daro itself and in coexistence with the Amrian Culture some 100 miles to the south and the Kot Dijian Culture to the east. [However] these groups had limited interactions with each other until the time [mid-third millennium] when the Harappans become dominant and established their hegemony over the area.
>
> (ibid.:68, 70)

   This interpretation is certainly novel, both in pushing the occupation of Mohenjo-daro back into the fourth millennium and in omitting to explain whence those occupants came and how they acquired such a lead. What was their cultural background? In the text I have indicated a catalysis/fusion/transmission mechanism, whereby catalytic sites transform the various cultural elements into a higher-order fusion (Early Harappan) which is then retransmitted to sites of the originating cultures. Catalytic sites must either have a high population of their own or be lodged within a dense network that functions as a high population.

3   On hill slopes run-off of both moisture and soil can be checked by 'gabarbands' (stone or earth retaining walls) such as were extensively employed in the Kirthar region. It is also useful, on a small scale, for retaining water on plains.

> In the lowlands, however, both water and stoneless alluvium were (and are) in almost limitless supply, although the scale of potential destruction was (and is) immeasurably greater as well. Nevertheless, the ancient farmers could take advantage of the shallow gradients of the lowlands alluvial zones to carry some of the perennially flowing water or standing moisture trapped in backswamps or tanks to their fields in small, annually reconstructed canals. Evidence for just such a canal network has been uncovered at Mehrgarh in a period IV (late fourth millennium) context in zone MR1.
>
> (Jarrige and Meadow 1992:165)

4   An early first-millennium cross-ploughed field, belonging to the Northwestern or Ghandara Grave Culture, has been excavated by Sebastiano Tusa (1990) at Aligrama in Swat. This leads him into a broader examination of ploughs and ploughing that has general relevance. The article also has excellent illustrations.
    Misra summarizes data on Harappan agriculture as:

> wheat (*Triticum compactum* and *T. sphaerococcum*) in Pakistan Punjab (Harappa), Sind (Mohenjo-daro and Chanhu-daro) and Haryana (Banawali); barley (*Hordeum vulgare*) in Pakistan Punjab (Harappa) and north Rajastan (Kalibangan); millet (*Eleusine coracana* and *Setaria italica*) in Kutch (Surkotada); and rice in Saurashtra (Rangpur and Lothal). It is thus seen that, except in Saurashtra and Kutch, the Harappan agricultural economy was based on barley, wheat and winter crops. Today too, the same crops are grown in these areas, mainly with the help of artificial irrigation. However, the same crops can be *and are grown* without artificial irrigation in areas where annual monsoon floods provide adequate moisture and fresh fertile silt to the land. Since there is no evidence of artificial irrigation during Harappan times, it follows that these crops were grown with the aid of moisture and silt provided by river floods.
>
> (Misra 1984:474, my emphasis)

5   With Dani (1988:37) 'it is reasonable to believe that the Kot Diji culture was actually a Gomal complex, which in due course spread out into the whole of Panjab and to at least one site, [that] of Kot Diji [itself] in Sind'.
    Regarding Rehman Dheri, Chakrabarti (1995:34–5) notes that 'the silos have yielded mostly wheat and some barley as well. The bones of buffalo, cattle, sheep, goat and fish have been identified ... The area has about 10 inches [250mm] of annual rainfall; the vegetation is sparse and dry, and cultivation depends on what is locally called the "barani dagar" method of irrigation. This is a method by which, during the period of heavy rains, fields covering a wide area are embanked on the lower sides with the upper sides kept open. Water can thus flow in, and when the surface is dry, the land can be ploughed, sown with crops and levelled with the help of a wooden plank. The levelling leads to the sealing of the capillary line of the soil and thus preserves soil moisture and [prevents] quick evaporation'.

6   But not necessarily at pre-Harappan Kot Diji, where the citadel probably had a defensive function (Khan 1965:29). This may well be a consequence of its position: the Chalcolithic site lies on what became the Grand Trunk Road in the lee of a medieval fort, hence its name (Diji fort).

7   The only known source of gold in peninsular India is from the Hatti mines near Mysore (Shinde 1991:95).

8 Mound KLB-3, about 80 metres east of the 'lower town', is a subsidiary ritual complex with four to five fire-altars, but may not be contemporary with the main 'citadel' ritual complex (Lal 1979:85).

9 In Mesopotamia, the amount of silt transported and deposited by the river systems causes them to have only minor gradients over much of their length, and given seasonal surges and the mass of water contained, changes in river courses are statistically inevitable. So although the geological causes are different, several important Mesopotamian cities were left high and dry, and thus died, by shifts in rivercourses, which have continued throughout the historical periods. The city of Shuruppak on a western branch of the Euphrates, which early in the third millennium covered 100 hectares (Martin 1988: 117), virtually disappeared when Harappan Civilization did (i.e. at the end of the third millennium) due to water being concentrated in the eastern branch of the Euphrates (ibid.:125). Shuruppak was one of the 'antidiluvian' cities.

10 Mencher's (1974:470–1) point is well taken that historically the artisan castes, which are middle-range castes, amount to only 10–15 per cent of the total population. However, the biggest caste in any locality is usually the main agricultural caste, and 'this caste will normally recognise other agriculturalist castes and most of the artisan castes as more or less equal' (Zinkin 1962:65), thus forming a core bloc. Further, once the system has formed around an occupational nucleus, 'newcomers' to it (unless an incoming elite) will be added to the lower reaches and 'outcaste' levels, where indeed, as Mencher argues, they will form an oppressed pool of dependent labour. Conversely, new ruling strata simply impose themselves at or over the top of the existing order, which need not be otherwise affected. The *Rigveda*, most ancient and sacred of Hindu 'Scriptures', composed at about the time of the Aryan entry to India, does not even mention the caste system.

11 It should be noted that Hinduism does not form a 'Church' or system of organized religion, but is a matter for localities, individuals, clans or castes, especially the latter. Indeed,

> Theologically Hinduism is not a single religion, but many religions, tolerating one another within the shifting social framework of caste. To see them as a unified or coherent whole would be as difficult as to find unity and coherence in the total landscape of the subcontinent.
>
> (Brown 1961:280)

Further,

> there is no equivalent to sin in Hinduism, which has no revealed divine laws, only a tradition and a philosophic discourse . . . custom has assumed the strength of ritual, indeed has become ritual, and is enforced ruthlessly by means of boycott, excommunication and outcasting. . . . Pollution is at the root of the Hindu social system. And pollution is not a private but a corporate matter.
>
> (Zinkin 1962:11–12,18)

12 Pingree (1989:445), concluding his discussion of the influence of the MUL.APIN and other astronomical texts on Vedic astronomy early in the first millennium BC, remarks that

> MUL.APIN, written in about 1000 BC, summarizes the astronomical knowledge that had accumulated in Mesopotamia in the previous half millennium, but whose roots presumably lie in the civilization of Sumer, since so much of the technical vocabulary of MUL.APIN and other Akkadian astronomical texts is, in fact, Sumerian.

Since Mesopotamian mathematics were originally problem based and since the problems of quantities, areas and angles go right back to the late fourth millennium, then a third-millennium Sumerian mathematics is almost certain. Friberg (1978–9 I:51–2) in fact concludes his first volume with the statement that

> it is a remarkable and distressing fact that although almost the entire vocabulary used in Babylonian mathematical texts is of an unmistakable Sumerian origin, practically no Sumerian mathematical texts have been preserved. ... It is therefore inconceivable that Sumerian 'mathematical texts' have never existed. It is just that we have not yet had the luck to find more than a few texts of this type.

In an important and fascinating article that includes worked problems, Powell (1976:420) argues that the Sumerian system of number words along with a system of number symbols indicating those number words are attested as early as about 2800 BC.

He suggests (ibid.:433) that by the Fara period (c.2500 BC), in addition to plane geometry, 'the Sumerians were working problems involving the use of reciprocals calculated to the fourth place', and subsequent to it, in the Akkadian period, further powerful advances were made in calculations involving sexagesimal ratios (ibid.:424). Accordingly he comes to a couple of important conclusions. The first is that the Sumerians evinced considerable interest in abstract numerical relationships; the second that

> the origins of Babylonian mathematics go back much further than anyone has heretofore realized. In the first place, the sexagesimal place notation was in existence during the Third Dynasty of Ur, by ca. 2050 BC. Secondly, mathematical instruction can be documented from 2500 to 2200 BC. Thirdly, two problem texts from ca. 2500 and one from 2200 BC seem to indicate the use of a mental construct analogous to place notation and the use of sexagesimal reciprocals.
>
> (ibid.:434)

5 THE CENTRAL KINGDOM, ZHONG-GUO

1 Students are recommended to read this chapter in association with *The Archaeology of China*, by Kwang-chih Chang (fourth edition, 1986a), plus the *Companion to Chinese History* by Hugh B. O'Neill (1987), which also contains a Wade-Giles/pinyin concordance (as do the major Chinese dictionaries). A comprehensive and thorough overview of developments in East Asia is to be found in *China, Korea and Japan: The Rise of Civilization in East Asia*, by Gina L. Barnes (1993). Much more than just a catalogue of a travelling exhibition covering the period from about 4500 BC to the second century BC, is *Mysteries of Ancient China: New Discoveries from the Early Dynasties*, edited by Jessica Rawson (1996). Excellent photography is complemented by annotation and analysis. Rawson provides a broad introduction and contributes a specialist essay to the eight that comprise the second part of the book.

Since the 1950s, the system used in China to transcribe Chinese characters into Roman script has been *pinyin*. This supplants (and is much more efficient than) the Wade-Giles system, in general use since its introduction during the nineteenth century. *Pinyin* is instantly recognizable by its absence of the apostrophes and hyphens, so characteristic of Wade-Giles. For example Yang-shao becomes Yangshao and Lung-shan becomes Longshan, while compound phonemes are simplified, as Hsia to Xia and Ch'in to Qin (whence our word 'China'). Despite its reliance upon apostrophes and hyphens, however (thus the important Early Neolithic site of Tz'u-shan = Cishan), Wade-Giles is still very useful for consulting printed sources, since basic reference works, library indexes, etc. normally employ it. And the doyen of the Chinese archaeological interpretation in the west, Kwang-chih Chang (K.C. Chang), always employs Wade-Giles, as do many eminent scholars. Nonetheless, current work published by mainland archaeologists uses *pinyin*, so for the sake of consistency I have taken the liberty of changing all Wade-Giles transcriptions to *pinyin*.

2 Settlements are referred to by province, county (*xian*) and village (*cun*). Thus *Henan Xinzheng Shawoli* (xinshiqi shidai yizhi): the Neolithic site at *Shawoli* in *Xinzheng* county, *Henan* (province); cited first, largest to smallest unit.

3 Never city-states, cf. Schwartz (1985:28):

> The city gods of Mesopotamia were, to be sure, not gods of the masses, yet they provided concrete symbolic foci for the loyalty to cities as discrete socio-political entities. It seems to me that ancestor worship as a religious orientation on both the popular and upper-class level did little to develop cities as foci of identity [in China]. Even in modern China where lineage organizations have been important, they have often been more important than identity with the city or even the village as such.

In China cities were centres of domination over the surrounding countryside for a ruling lineage. Even where, as often, the cities were independent *guo* in their own right, the nature of the regime – elite within the walls, subject peasantry without – made them small territorial states and not city-states (cf. Lewis 1990:48 and n.146).

4 It is not clear what sources and controls Beijing has used to assemble these figures.

5 Though usually attributed to upwelling caused by divergence, water flowing towards the Equator forms cold currents. Winds blowing over cold currents deliver little rain. The largest cold water current system is the West Wind Drift, flowing west to east around the world in the south of the southern hemisphere. Where it meets the southern tips of continents it drives cold water north towards the Equator along the western coasts of South America (Peru Current), Africa (Benguela Current) and Australia (West Australia Current). A combination of temperature and coastwise flow are thus responsible for the Atacama Desert, the Namib and Kalahari Deserts, and the West Australia deserts. Low water temperatures result in low moisture pick-up by winds, which in the areas mentioned generally blow in the 'wrong' directions anyway.

   In the northern hemisphere straightforward Equator-return flows are responsible for the California Current and hence the Sonora and Mohave Deserts, while the Canaries Current is largely responsible for the western margins of the Sahara on the Atlantic. However, the eastward extension of the Sahara across Africa and Arabia and into Central Asia is a function of interiority, that is, distance from oceans.

   The Sahara also shows that aridity due to rainshadowing (by mountains) is generally exaggerated, for the effects are relatively localized. The Atlas Mountains are not responsible for the Sahara Desert, even in the west. Spain's aridity is not a consequence of rainshadowing, and neither is the relative dryness of southern and eastern England. This last is accounted for by the generally southwest/northeast progression of the rainbearing winds off the Atlantic. Spain's aridity is a consequence of the Canaries Current. The Alps do not cast a significant rainshadow. The Himalayas do to their north, but that is a function of their height, length, shape and the interior location of the northern shadow.

6 The loess plateau experiences the most rapid rate of soil erosion in the world. Denuded of trees, the summer monsoon rains have been eroding the surface equivalent to 1 centimetre per year, resulting in an estimated 1.6 *billion* tonnes of soil reaching the Huanghe during *each* summer flood! The river is now 10 metres above its floodplain

because no less than 6 centimetres of silt settles *annually* on its bed. So silty is the Huanghe that dams built for flood control and hydro-electric purposes have silted up before they could even start operating. The Huanghe carries three times as much silt as the Yangzi with only a twentieth its water volume. This against only 1 kilogram per cubic metre in the Nile before the building of the High Dam at Aswan.

7 Beyond the purely chronological interest, the Nivison and Pankenier articles cited contain a wealth of ethnological information. See also Keightley (1978).

8 The peninsula long retained its cultural distinctness, and did not even form part of the core area of Zhou, the latest of the San Dai (Three Dynasty) regimes. Shandong contains China's most sacred mountain, Tai Shan, and the province was the home of the philosophers Confucius and Zou Yan.

9 It will be seen that this is similar to the model of Egypt in the Chalcolithic, where chiefdoms in the process of becoming small kingdoms become amalgamated by alliance and conquest into regional kingdoms that are then united under a dominant one. Territorial states form by this means in the Chinese Bronze Age, but the unification of China is an Iron Age phenomenon.

10 Ritual is repeated, conventionalized symbolic behaviour, externally (publicly) and internally (psychologically) actualizing aspects of the belief-system (ideology).

11 Although primarily concerned with later periods (Spring and Autumn/Warring States) the work from which this is cited – *Sanctioned Violence in Early China* – represents as much of a landmark in anthropology and sociology as it does in ancient history.

12 *Ding, li, xian, zeng, fu* and *hu* are all bronze cooking vessels; *zao* is the stove, made of pottery. 'Ding, li, and hu were probably for boiling and simmering-stewing: xian, zeng and fu, for steaming' (Chang 1977b:34). In general, following Bussagli (1969:59–64), ritual bronzes can be grouped into half a dozen functional categories:

1 Vessels for the preparation and cooking of sacrificial food: notably the tripods and the rectangular four-footed *ding*.

2 Vessels for storing sacrificial food: *gui* and *yu*.

3 Vessels for heating 'wine' (fermented millet); *jia* and *jue*, both with pointed tripod legs, used also for libations. The *he*, by contrast, is shaped like a flattened teapot, but with three or four cylindrical legs (and feet!), a long tubular spout, handle and lid. It is not for tea, however, which came much later, but for mixing water with wine.

4 Vessels for storing wine: the *zun* and the *guang* are the most sculptural of all bronzes, the vessel form being fully cast into an animal shape.

5 Vessels for tasting wine: *gu* or *zhi* are circular or square in cross-section.

6 Vessels for ritual ablutions. All have a circular base, are handleless, wide and shallow.

The *yue* is a bronze battle axe, while the *ge* is a halberd (in this form like a dagger on the end of, and fastened at right angles to, a pole). They were major weapons of Shang infantry. See note 17.

In addition to ritual vessels and weapons, bronze was used for horse and chariot fittings, mirrors and belt fasteners, plus musical instruments – all elite goods.

13 This fabric can be as thin as 1 millimetre. Interestingly, the Chalcolithic Kot Diji Culture of northwest India also featured a very fine ware, wheel-made, well levigated, in paste and ground varying from pinkish to red (Khan 1965:43). A very prominent form was dish-on-stand, with both long and short necks, a form common across Chalcolithic western Asia. This does not necessarily imply any connection between the Kot Diji and Longshan forms, but rather suggests that parallel Chalcolithic processes of craft specialization result in similarly fine products.

14 The reasons for which are discussed in the final chapter. It is important to note that the ferocious loyalty to lineage, such that 'the political pattern was almost wholly

assimilated to that of the kinship system', as Creel (1964:167) put it, was a particularly 'northern' or Central Plains phenomenon. It does not seem to have obtained in the south, for instance in the large, powerful and prosperous state of Chu in the Yangzi Valley (see also Yu Weichao 1996).

Instead of ruling by feudal/lineage mechanisms, the Chu state operated bureaucratically by means of centrally controlled administrative units called *xian* (a county; xiancheng is a county town), run by experienced and rotated officials. Chu was an independent state from the earliest times; it is mentioned until conquered by Qin in 223 BC. Upon unification, the Qin empire divided the country into provinces and counties, and this obtains today. See note 2.

15 Despite occasional affixes, there is in general no distinction between singular and plural in Chinese ('Mandarin') nouns. Chinese is a consistently uninflected language.

16 The idea of a 'mandate from heaven' was well known a millennium earlier in Mesopotamia, where it too was implicated in the legitimacy of political process. Discussing the idea of history in Mesopotamia, Speiser observes that

> there had to be of course a reason for the dynastic changes consistent with the theocratic principle of state. The gods would forsake a mortal ruler and turn against him because he had offended them in some way (the technical Akkadian term *qullulu*). The offender is said to have transgressed his solemn oath of office (*mamīta etēqu*) or overstepped the bounds set for him by his god (*itê ili etēqu*).
>
> (Speiser 1983: 56–7)

The coronation oath invokes the god of justice, the vigilant sun-god Shamash:

> He who oversteps the bounds of Shamash, may Shamash surrender him for evil to the executioner! He who oversteps the bounds of Shamash, may the mountain withold from him its passage! May the darting weapon of Shamash overthrow and catch him!
>
> (Speiser 1983:58)

Justice in general and the enforcement and rectification of laws in particular were a prime task for the 'mandated' ruler in Mesopotamia.

17 According to Hsu and Linduff (1988:27), following Shih Chang-ju, each chariot was drawn by two, sometimes four, horses, and carried in addition to the driver an archer with compound bow, plus a soldier with halberd. This complement must apply only to the largest four-horse vehicles such as the Western Zhou example they list in their Table 3.1 (ibid.:86) from Xian (jiaoxian county, Shandong Province) which, exceptionally, had a platform 164 centimetres wide and 97 centimetres deep. A much more typical platform width was around 135 centimetres and about 80 centimetres deep (ibid.). Chariots seem to have been organized into squadrons of five vehicles attached to units of infantry; a 'close-support' and leadership function not common in chariot warfare in other Bronze Age societies. Chariot warfare was supplanted by mass infantry during the Spring and Autumn/Warring States periods, as 'total war' became the norm. The unit of warfare shifted from the lineage and the individual warrior's heroism in serving it to the 'squad of five' (*wu*) in groups of five. The squad was five strong (the character is just the ordinary numeral five) to accommodate each of the infantry weapons working together: long: lances and bows; short: halberds and swords (Lewis 1990:107–8). In theory and in the hands of professional commanders, the army was to serve as a unified extension of the will of the commander and instrument of state; individualism, even individual heroism, was repressed.

18 Anyang was first 'discovered' in 1899. From then until 1929 various 'digs' took place, most of which was just looting, providing bronzes and oracle bones for the international antiquities market. Only after 1927 did proper excavation take place.

19 Ethnographic parallels for early shamanism in mainland East Asia are best sought in Mongolia, in parts of which the tradition is alive, despite many centuries of Buddhism there (cf. Pentikainen 1994).

Chang (1983a) has stressed the key political-catalytic roles played by shamanism and divination (cf. Loewe 1995 for the Han periods). The best succinct description of the latter's methods I know of comes from Ann Guinan's (1989) discussion of the Mesopotamian omen collection called *Summa Alu*: 'Divinatory logic appears to pursue formal lines of reasoning but in fact achieves its effects through indirection, ambiguity, equivocation, contradiction, and subtle shifts from the logical to the figurative.' In other words, it is a paradigm of ideological discourse.

20 In marked contrast is the English term from the Latin with its Greek cognates (such as 'politics'), expressing not the prerogatives of the literary elite but 'city living' (*synoikismos* = living together) and thus citizenship.

21 It was for their knowledge of mathematics and astronomy, demonstrated by their successful prediction of the solar eclipse of 1629, that Jesuits were admitted to posts in the newly formed (Imperial) Calendrical Bureau, despite their earlier persecution in China. Later, Jesuits were appointed to the Board of Astronomy, of which, despite some further xenophobic persecution in the 1660s, the Jesuits remained in charge until the Society itself was terminated in 1773 by order of Pope Clement XIV.

22 As early as 1926, Li Chi (1977:160) observed that Yangshao pottery from the site of Xiyinzun was painted with a hair brush (*maobi*, also used as a pen), and that incision was a *later* mode of decoration applied to (Longshan) Black Pottery, such as underlies Yin-Shang remains at Anyang. He further (ibid.:170–3) thinks that writing with ink on perishable materials explains the absence of characters prior to their appearance incised on oracle bones. See also Postgate, Wang and Wilkinson (1995).

23 Amongst the most common ancient Egyptian documents are the so-called *ostraka*, which are not sherd fragments but flakes of white limestone bearing hieratic inscriptions in ink. For an illustration of hieratic script see Figure 2.9.

6 CONCLUSION: THE EMERGENCE OF SOCIAL COMPLEXITY

1 In the Uruk Period, that enormous city did indeed organize colonies on the edge of Anatolia to secure, it seems, mineral resources from that area. However, the fact that those colonies were fairly short-lived suggests that this effort was not cost-effective, even for a city of Uruk's exceptional size, and that less organized and less costly procurement would thereafter suffice (cf. Algaze 1993).

2 Thus the strong tribalism of the Marsh Arabs in southern Iraq is a consequence of the traditional absence of state control of the 'Sealand' *and* of the tribal organization of the pastoralists around the marshes.

3 Organizations are just structures of offices, which are positions requiring the performance of specified roles. Similarly, social structures are just patterns of roles, licensed by certain statuses (gender, age, class, etc.). Status is always ascriptive (notably by birth to the right parents) while prestige (with which status is usually confused) can be achieved by individual effort. For detailed discussion see Maisels 1990:221–30.

APPENDIX C

1 A myth is a story which purports to relate experiences or powers or events beyond the palpable and present. What myth relates may or may not have had some basis in fact. The purpose of myth, however, is to 'give an account', thereby to fill a cognitive space and so an emotional need. *Myth does not record facts, but tells stories as if they were true.* Structured around actions and their consequences, stories measure the human implications of causes and effects as the basic principle in Nature.

A fantasy is the violation or ignorance of determinate chains of cause and effect. Magic, for instance, imagines it can produce effects by will, associative procedures and verbal means; that is, without any demonstrable instrumentality. By contrast, science resides in the demonstration of mechanism (cf. n.5.19)

Religion is belief in, deference to, and reverence of, unknown or transcendental powers.

BIBLIOGRAPHY

Adams, B. (1974) *Ancient Hierakonpolis: Supplement*. Warminster, Aris and Phillips.

Adams, B. (1987) *The Fort Cemetery at Hierakonpolis*. London, Kegan Paul International.

Adams, B. and Friedman, R.F. (1992) Imports and influences in the Predynastic and Protodynastic settlement and funerary assemblages at Hierakonpolis. In Van den Brink 1992c, pp.317–338.

Adams, R. McC. (1978) Strategies of maximisation, stability and resilience in Mesopotamian society, settlement and agriculture. *Proceedings of the American Philosophical Society* 122:329–335.

Adams, R. McC. (1981) *The Heartland of Cities: Studies of Ancient Settlement and Land Use on the Central Floodplain of the Euphrates*. Chicago and London, University of Chicago Press.

Adams, R. McC. (1983) The Jarmo stone and pottery vessel industries. In Braidwood *et al.*, pp.209–232.

Adams, R. McC. (1989) Discussion on Nissen. In Henrickson and Thuesen, pp.250–255.

Adams, R. McC. (1990) Introduction to Gunter, pp.3–7.

Agrawal, D.P. (1982) *The Archaeology of India*. London and Malmo, Curzon Press.

Agrawal, D.P. and Chakrabarti, D.K. (1979) (eds) *Essays in Indian Protohistory*. Delhi, B.R. Publishing Corporation.

Agrawal, D.P. and Gosh, A. (1973) (eds) *Radiocarbon and Indian Archaeology*. Bombay.

Akkermans, P.M.M.G. (1989a) The Neolithic of the Balikh Valley, Northern Syria: a first assessment. *Paleorient* 15(1):122–134.

Akkermans, P.M.M.G. (1989b) Tradition and social change in Northern Mesopotamia during the later fifth and fourth millennium BC. In Henrickson and Thuesen, pp.339–364.

Akkermans, P.M.M.G. (1989c) *Excavations at Tell Sabi Abyad: Prehistoric Investigations in the Balikh Valley, Northern Syria*. Oxford, BAR 468.

Akkermans, P.M.M.G. (1990) *Villages in the Steppe: Later Neolithic Settlement and Subsistence in the Balikh Valley, Northern Syria*. Leiden, Rijks Museum van Oudheden.

Akkermans, P.M.M.G. (1991) New radiocarbon dates for the Later Neolithic of Northern Syria. *Paleorient* 17(1):121–125.

Akkermans, P.M.M.G. (1995) An image of complexity: the burnt village at Late Neolithic Sabi Abyad, Syria. *American Journal of Archaeology* 99:5–32.

Al-Adami, K.A. (1968) Excavations at Tell Es-Sawwan. *Sumer* 24:54–94.

Albright, W.F. (1960) *The Archaeology of Palestine*, Harmondsworth, Penguin.

Aldred, C. (1980) *Egyptian Art in the Days of the Pharaohs, 3100–320 BC*. London, Thames & Hudson.

Algaze, G. (1989) The Uruk expansion: cross-cultural exchange in Early Mesopotamian Civilization. *Current Anthropology* 30(5):571–608.

Algaze, G. (1993) Expansionary dynamics of some early pristine states. *American Anthropologist* 95(2):304–333.

Allchin, B. (1979) Stone blade industries of early settlements in Sind as indicators of geographical and socio-economic change. In Taddei, I:173–211.

Allchin, B. (1984) (ed.) *South Asian Archaeology 1981: Proceedings of the 6th International Conference of the Association of South Asian Archaeologists in Western Europe*. Held in Cambridge. Cambridge University Press.

Allchin, B. (1994) *Living Traditions: Studies in the Ethnoarchaeology of South Asia*. Oxford, Oxbow and IBH.

Allchin, B. and Allchin, F.R. (1982) *The Rise of Civilization in India and Pakistan*. Cambridge, Cambridge University Press.

Allchin, B., Goudie, A. and Hegde, K. (1978) *The Prehistory and Palaeogeography of the Great Indian Desert*. London and New York, Academic Press.

Allchin, F.R. (1992) City and state formation in early historic South Asia. *Pakistan Archaeology* 27:1–16.

Allchin, F.R. (1995) (ed.) *The Archaeology of Early Historic South Asia: The Emergence of Cities and States*. Cambridge, Cambridge University Press.

Al-Radi, S. and Seeden, H. (1980) The AUB rescue excavations at Shams ed-Din Tannira. *Berytus* 28:88–126.

Al-Soof, B.A. (1968) Tell Es-Sawwan: Excavation of the fourth season (spring 1967). *Sumer* 24:3–15.

Al-Soof, B.A. (1969) Excavations at Tell Qalinj Agha (Erbil); summer, 1968. *Sumer* 25:3–42.

Alster, B. (1975) Studies in Sumerian proverbs. *Mesopotamia* Vol. 3, Copenhagen, Akademisk Forlag.

Alster, B. (1991–93) The Sumerian folktale of the three ox-drivers from Adab. *Journal of Cuneiform Studies* 43–45:27–38.

Amiet, P. (1993) The period of Irano-Mesopotamian contacts 3500–1600 BC. In Curtis, pp.23–30.

Amiran, R. (1970) The beginning of urbanization in Canaan. In Sanders, pp.83–100.

Ammerman, A.J. and Cavalli-Sforza, L.L. (1984) *The Neolithic Transition and the Genetics of Populations in Europe*. Princeton, Princeton University Press.

An, C.H. (1986) The Shang City at Chen-chou [Zhengzhou] and related problems. In K.C. Chang 1986b, pp.15–48.

Anderson, P.C. (1991) Harvesting of wild cereals during the Natufian as seen from the experimental cultivation and harvest of wild einkorn wheat and microwear analysis of stone tools. In Bar-Yosef and Valla 1991b, pp.521–556.

Anderson, P.C. (1992a) Experimental cultivation, harvest and threshing of wild cereals and their relevance for interpreting the use of Epipalaeolithic and Neolithic artefacts. In Anderson 1992b, pp.179–209.

Anderson, P.C. (1992b) (ed.) *Préhistoire de l'Agriculture: Nouvelles Approches Expérimentales et Ethnographiques*. Paris, Editions du CNRS, Monographie du CRA no. 6.

Anderson, W. (1992) Badarian burials: Evidence of social inequality in Middle Egypt during the early Predynastic era. *Journal of the American Research Centre in Egypt*. 29:51–66.

Anderson-Gerfaud, P.C. (1983) A consideration of the uses of certain backed and lustred stone tools from the late Mesolithic and Natufian levels of Abu Hureryra and Mureybet (Syria). In M.-C. Cauvin, pp.77–106.

Andersson, J.G. (1934) *Children of the Yellow Earth*, London, Kegan Paul, Trench & Trubner.

Andersson, J.G. (1943) Researches into the prehistory of the Chinese. *BMFEA* 15.

Andres, W. and Wunderlich, J. (1992) Environmental conditions for early settlement at Minshat Abu Omar, Eastern Nile Delta, Egypt. In Van den Brink 1992c, pp.157–166.

Anthes, R. (1961) Mythology in Ancient Egypt. In S.N. Kramer 1961b, pp.15–92.

Antonova, E. (1992) Images on seals and the ideology of the state formation process. *Mesopotamia* 27:77–87.

An Zhimin (1980) The Neolithic archaeology of China. *Early China* 5: 35–45.

An Zhimin (1982–3) Some problems concerning China's early copper and bronze artifacts. Translated by Julia K. Murray, *Early China* 8:53–75.

An Zhimin (1989) Prehistoric agriculture in China. In Harris and Hillman, pp.643–649.

An Zhimin (1991) Radiocarbon dating and the prehistoric archaeology of China. *World Archaeology* 23(2):193–200.

Archi, A. (1987a) Ebla and Eblaite. In Gordon *et al.*, pp.7–18.

Archi, A. (1987b) Reflections on the system of weights from Ebla. In Gordon *et al.*, pp.47–90.

Archi, A. (1987c) The 'Sign-list' from Ebla. In Gordon *et al.*, pp.91–114.

Archi, A. (1987d) Gifts for a princess. In Gordon *et al.*, pp.115–124.

Archi, A. (1987e) More on Ebla and Kish. In Gordon *et al.*, pp.125–140.

Ardeleanu-Jansen, A. (1989) A short note on a steatite sculpture from Mohenjo-Daro. In Frifelt and Sorensen, pp.196–210.

Arensburg, B. and Hershkovitz, I. (1989) Artificial skull 'treatment' in the PPNB Period: Nahal Hemar. In Hershkovitz, pp.115–131.

Assman, J., Burkard, G. and Davies, V. (1987) (eds) *Problems and Priorities in Egyptian Archaeology*. London, Kegan Paul International.

Asthana, S. (1979) Indus-Mesopotamian trade: Nature of trade and structural analysis of operative system. In Agrawal and Chakrabarti, pp.31–47.

Asthana, S. (1982) Harappan trade in metals and minerals: A regional approach. In Possehl, pp.271–285.

Astrom, P. (ed.) *High, Middle or Low. Acts of International Colloquium in Absolute Chronology Held at the University of Gothenburg, 20th–22nd August 1987*. Gothenburg, Astroms Verlag.

Ataman, K. (1992) Threshing sledges and archaeology. In P.C. Anderson 1992b, pp.305–319.

Atre, S. (1989) Toward an economico-religious model for Harappan urbanism. *South Asian Studies* 5:49–58.

Aurenche, O. (1981) L'Architecture Mésopotamienne du 7e au 4e millénaires. *Paleorient* 7(2):43–55.

Aurenche, O., Evin, J. and Hours, F. (1987) (eds) *Chronologies in the Near East: Relative Chronologies and Absolute Chronology, 16,000–4,000 B.P. C.N.R.S. International Symposium, Lyon, 24–28 Nov. 1986*. Oxford, BAR 379(i, ii).

Azoury, I. and Bergman, C. (1980) The Halafian lithic assemblage of Shams ed-Din Tannira. *Berytus* 28:127–143.

Bader, N.O. (1993a) Tell Maghzaliyah: An early Neolithic site in Northern Iraq. In Yoffee and Clark, pp.7–40.

Bader, N.O. (1993b) The early agricultural settlement of Tell Sotto. In Yoffee and Clark, pp.41–54.

Bader, N.O. (1993c) Results of the excavations at the early agricultural site of Kultepe in Northern Iraq. In Yoffee and Clark, pp.55–62.

Bader, N.O. (1993d) Summary of 'The Earliest Agriculturalists of Northern Mesopotamia (1989)'. In Yoffee and Clark, pp.63–72.

Bader, N.O., Merpert, N.Ya. and Munchaev, R.M. (1981) Soviet expedition's surveys in the Sinjar Valley. *Sumer* 37(1–2):55–110.

Bagley, R.W. (1977) P'an-lung-ch'eng [Panlongcheng] A Shang city in Hupei. *Artibus Asiae* 39:165–219.

Bagley, R.W. (1980) The beginnings of the Bronze Age: The Erlitou Culture Period. In Fong, pp.67–77.

Bailey, F.G. (1963) Closed social stratification in India. *Archives Européenes de Sociologie* IV:107–124.

Baines, J. (1983) Literacy and Ancient Egyptian society. *Man* (N.S.) 18:572–599.

Baines, J. (1989) Communication and display: The integration of early Egyptian art and writing. *Antiquity* 63:471–482.

Baines, J. (1989) Egyptian myth and discourse: Myth, gods and the early written and icono-
graphic record. *JNES* 50:81–105.

Baines, J. (1995a) Kingship, definition of culture, and legitimation. In O'Connor and
Silverman, pp.3–47.

Baines, J. (1995b) Origins of Egyptian kingship. In O'Connor and Silverman, pp.95–156.

Baines, J. and Malek, J. (1980) *Atlas of Ancient Egypt*. Oxford, Andromeda/Facts on File.

Baird, D. (1993) *Neolithic Chipped Stone Assemblages of the Azraq basin, Jordan, and the Significance
of the Neolithic Arid Zones from the Southern Levant*. PhD Dissertation, Edinburgh, University
of Edinburgh, Dept of Archaeology.

Baird, D., Campbell, S. and Watkins, T. (1996) *Excavations at Kharabeh Shattani, Vol. II.
Occasional Papers No. 18*. Edinburgh University Dept of Archaeology.

Baker, H.D.R. (1979) *Chinese Family and Kinship*. London, Macmillan.

Banks, K.M. (1989) The appearance and spread of cattle-keeping in Saharan North Africa.
In Krzyzaniak and Kobusiewicz, pp.57–60.

Banning, E.B. and Byrd, B.F. (1989) Alternative approaches for exploring Levantine Neolithic
architecture. *Paleorient* 15(1):154–160.

Bard, K. (1987) The geography of excavated Predynastic sites and the rise of complex society.
JARCE 24:81–93.

Bard, K. (1988) A quantitative analysis of the Predynastic burials in Armant cemetery
1400–1500. *Journal of Egyptian Archaeology* 74:39–55.

Bard, K. (1989) The evolution of complexity on Predynastic Egypt: An analysis of the
Naqada cemeteries. *Journal of Mediterranean Archaeology* 2: 233–248.

Bard, K. (1990) Review of B.J. Kemp's 'Ancient Egypt: Anatomy of a civilization'. *Journal
of Field Archaeology* 17:481–485.

Bard, K. (1992) Origins of Egyptian writing. In Friedman and Adams, pp.297–306.

Barnard, A. and Spencer, J. (1996) (eds) *Encyclopaedia of Social and Cultural Anthropology*.
London, Routledge.

Barnard, N. (1986) A new approach to the study of clan-sign inscriptions of Shang, In K.C.
Chang 1986b, pp.141–183.

Barnes, G. (1993) *China, Korea and Japan*. London, Thames and Hudson.

Barocas, C., Fattovich, R. and Tosi, M. (1989) The Oriental Institute of Naples expedition
to Petrie's South Town (Upper Egypt), 1977–83: an interim report. In Kryzyzaniak and
Kobusiewicz, pp.295–301.

Baruch, U. and Bottema, S. (1991) Palynological evidence for climatic changes in the Levant
ca. 17,000–9000 B.P. In Bar-Yosef and Valla 1991b, pp.11–20.

Bar-Yosef, O. (1980) Prehistory of the Levant. *Annual Review of Anthropology* 9:101–133.

Bar-Yosef, O. (1981) The Epi-palaeolithic complexes in the southern Levant. In Cauvin and
Sanlaville, pp.389–408.

Bar-Yosef, O. (1989a) The PPNA in the Levant – an overview. *Paleorient* 15(1):57–63.

Bar-Yosef, O. (1989b) Introduction to section on archaeology. In Hershkovitz, pp.1–5.

Bar-Yosef, O. (1991a) The archaeology of the Natufian layer at Hayonim Cave. In Bar-Yosef
and Valla 1991b, pp.81–92.

Bar-Yosef, O. (1991b) Changes in the selection of marine shells from the Natufian to the
Neolithic. In Bar-Yosef and Valla 1991b, pp.629–636.

Bar-Yosef, O. and Belfer-Cohen, A. (1989a) The origins of sedentism and farming communities in the Levant. *Journal of World Prehistory* 3(4):447–498.

Bar-Yosef, O. and Belfer-Cohen, A. (1989b) The Levantine 'PPNB' interaction sphere. In
Hershkovitz, pp.59–72.

Bar-Yosef, O. and Belfer-Cohen, A. (1992) From foraging to farming in the Mediterranean
Levant. In Gebauer and Price, pp.21–48.

Bar-Yosef, O., Gopher, A. and Goring-Morris, A.N. (1980) Netiv Hagdud: a 'Sultanian'
mound in the Lower Jordan valley. *Paleorient* 6:201–206.

Bar-Yosef, O., Gopher, A. and Nadel, D. (1987) 'The Hagdud Truncation' – a new tool type from the Sultanian industry at Netiv Hagdud, the Jordan Valley. *Mitekufat Haeven* 20:151–157.

Bar-Yosef, O., Gopher, A., Tchernov, E. and Kislev, M.E. (1991) Netiv Hagdud: an early Neolithic village site in the Jordan valley. *Journal of Field Archaeology* 18:405–424.

Bar-Yosef, O. and Khazanov, A. (1992) (eds) *Pastoralism in the Levant*. Madison, Prehistory Press.

Bar-Yosef, O. and Kislev, M. (1989) Early farming communities in the Jordan Valley. In Harris and Hillman, pp.632–642.

Bar-Yosef, O. and Valla, F.R. (1991a) The Natufian Culture – An introduction [to 1991b:1–10].

Bar-Yosef, O. and Valla, F.R. (1991b) (eds) *The Natufian Culture in the Levant*. Ann Arbor, Michigan. International Monographs in Prehistory: Archaeological Series 1.

Bar-Yosef, O. and Vandermeersch, B. (1989) (eds) *Investigations in South Levantine Prehistory*. Oxford, Bar Int. Series 497.

Bar-Yosef, O., Vandermeersch, B., Arensburg, B., Belfer-Cohen, A., Goldberg, P., Laville, H., Meignen, L., Rak, Y., Speth, J.D., Tchernov, E., Tillier, A-M. and Weiner, S. (1992) The excavations in Kebara Cave, Mt. Carmel. *Current Anthropology* 33(5):497–550.

Basham, A.L. (1989) *The Sacred Cow: The Evolution of Classical Hinduism*. London, Rider.

Bashilov, V.A., Bolshakov, O.G. and Kouza, A.V. (1980) The earliest strata at Yarim Tepe I. *Sumer* 36:43–64.

Baugh, D.A. (1975a) The social basis of stability. Introduction to Baugh (1975b), pp.1–28.

Baugh, D.A. (1975b) (ed.) *Aristocratic Government and Society in Eighteenth Century England*. New York, Franklin Watts.

Baumgartel, E.J. (1970) *Petrie's Naqada Excavation: A Supplement*. London, Quaritch.

Beattie, J.H.M. and Lienhardt, G. (1975) *Studies in Social Anthropology: Essays in Memory of E.E. Evans-Pritchard by his Former Oxford Colleagues*. Oxford, Clarendon Press.

Becker, C. (1991) The analysis of mammalian bones from Basta, a Pre-Pottery Neolithic site in Jordan: problems and potential. *Paleorient* 17(1):59–75.

Behrens, H., Loding, D. and Roth, M.T. (1989) (eds) *DUMU-E₂-DUB-BA-A: Studies in Honour of Ake W. Sjoberg*. Philadelphia, S.N. Kramer Fund, 11.

Belcher, W.R. (1994) Riverine fisheries and habitat exploitation of the Indus valley tradition: an example from Harappa, Pakistan. In Parpola and Koskikallio, pp.71–80.

Belfer-Cohen, A. (1989) The Natufian issue: a suggestion. In Bar-Yosef and Vandermeersch, pp.297–307.

Belfer-Cohen, A. (1990) The origins of sedentism and agricultural communities in the Levant. *Mitekufat Haeven* 23:176–178.

Belfer-Cohen, A. (1991) Art items from layer B, Hayonim Cave: A case study of art in a Natufian context. In Bar-Yosef and Valla 1991b, pp.569–588.

Belfer-Cohen, A., Arensburg, B., Bar-Yosef, O. and Gopher, A. (1990) Human remains from Netiv Hagdud – A PPNA site in the Jordan Valley. *Mitekufat Haeven* 23:79–85.

Belfer-Cohen, A., Schepartz, L.A. and Arensburg, B. (1991) New biological data for the Natufian populations in Israel. In Bar-Yosef and Valla 1991b, pp.411–424.

Berger, M.A. (1992) Predynastic animal-headed boats from Hierakonpolis and Southern Egypt. In Friedman and Adams, pp.107–120.

Bernbeck, R. (1992) Migratory patterns in early nomadism: a reconsideration of Tepe Tula'i. *Paleorient* 18(1):77–88.

Bernbeck, R., Coursey, C. and Pollock, S. (1996) Excavations of Halaf Levels at Kazane, SE Turkey. *Neo-Lithics* 2/96:4–5.

Berreman, G. (1983) The evolutionary status of caste in India. In Mencher, pp.237–250.

Betts, A. (1989) The Pre-Pottery Neolithic B Period in Eastern Jordan. *Paleorient* 15(1):147–153.

Betts, A. (1991) The Late Epipalaeolithic in the Black Desert, eastern Jordan. In Bar-Yosef and Valla 1991b, pp.217–234.

Bibby, G. (1957) *The Testimony of the Spade*. Glasgow, Collins.

Bierbrier, M.L. (1986) (ed.) *Papyrus: Structure and Usage*. British Museum Occasional Paper No. 60, London.

Bietak, M. (1975) *Tell el-Dab'a II. Der Fundort im Rahmen einer archäologisch-geographischen Untersuchungen über das Ägyptische Ostdelta. Österreichische Akademie der Wissenschaften, Denkschriften der Gesamtakademie, Band IV*. Vienna, Verlag der Österreichischen Akademie der Wissenschaften.

Biggs, R. (1967) Semitic names in the Fara period. *Orientalia* N.S. 36:55–66.

Biggs, R. (1969) Medicine in Ancient Mesopotamia. *History of Science* 8:94–105.

Binford, L.R. (1977) *For Theory Building in Archaeology*. New York, Thomas Crowell.

Binford, L.R. (1980) Willow smoke and dogs' tails: Hunter-gatherer settlement systems and archaeological sites. *American Antiquity* 45(1):4–20.

Binford, L.R. (1983) *In Pursuit of the Past: Decoding the Archaeological Record*. London, Thames and Hudson.

Binford, L.R. (1989) The 'New Archaeology', then and now. In C.C. Lamberg-Karlovsky, pp.50–62.

Bintliff, J.L. (1982) Palaeoclimatic modelling of environmental changes in the East Mediterranean region since the last glaciation. In Bintliff and Van Zeist, pp.485–527.

Bintliff, J.L. and Van Zeist, W. (1982) (eds) *Palaeoclimates, Palaeo-Environments and Human Communities in the Eastern Mediterranean Region in Later Prehistory*, Oxford, BAR Int. Series 133.

Birrell, A. (1988) *Popular Songs and Ballads of Han China*. London, Unwin Hyman.

Biscione, R. (1984) Baluchistan presence in the ceramic assemblage of Period I at Shahr-i Sokhta. In B. Allchin, pp.69–80.

Bisht, R.S. (1982) Excavations at Banawali: 1974–77. In Possehl, pp.113–124.

Bisht, R.S. (1984) Structural remains and town-planning of Banawali. In Lal *et al.*, pp.89–98.

Bisht, R.S. (1990) Dholavira: New horizons of the Indus Civilization. *Puratattva: Bulletin of the Indian Archaeological Society* 20:71–82.

Bisht, R.S. and Asthana, S. (1979) Banawali and some other recently excavated sites in India. In Taddei, I:223–240.

Black, J. and Green, A. (1992) *Gods, Demons and Symbols of Ancient Mesopotamia*. London, British Museum Press.

Bodde, D. (1961) Myths of Ancient China. In Kramer 1961b, pp.369–408.

Bodde, D. (1979) Introduction to the history of China. In B. Smith and Weng, pp.10–13.

Boehmer, R.M. (1991) Uruk 1980–1990: A progress report. *Antiquity* 65(248):465–478.

Bokonyi, S. (1982) The climatic interpretation of macrofaunal assemblages in the Near East. In Bintliff and van Zeist, pp.149–163.

Bor, N.L. and Guest, E. (1968) *Flora of Iraq, Vol. 9: Graminae*. Bagdad, Ministry of Agriculture.

Bostanci, E.Y. (1959) Researches on the Mediterranean coast of Anatolia: A new Palaeolithic site at Beldibi near Antalya. *Anatolia* 4(9):127–167.

Bottema, S. (1992a) Palynological investigations of the Ibrahim Awad deposits (Northeastern Nile Delta): Preliminary report. In van den Brink 1992b, pp.123–125.

Bottema, S. (1992b) Cereal-type pollen in the Near East as indicators of wild or domestic crops. In P.C. Anderson 1992b, pp.95–106.

Bottero, J. (1992) *Mesopotamia: Writing, Reasoning and the Gods*. Chicago and London, University of Chicago Press.

Bowden, M. (1991) *Pitt Rivers: The Life and Archaeological Work of Lieutenant-General Augustus Henry Lane Fox Pitt Rivers, DCL, FRS, FSA*, Cambridge, Cambridge University Press.

Braidwood, L.S. (1983) Appendix: additional remarks on the Jarmo obsidian. In Braidwood *et al.*, pp.285–288.

394

Braidwood, L.S. and Braidwood, R.J. (1960) Excavation on the Plain of Antioch. Vol. 1: *The Earlier Assemblages, Phases A-J*. Oriental Institute Publications, Vol. 61. Chicago, University of Chicago Press.

Braidwood, L.S. and Braidwood, R.J. (1982) (eds) *Prehistoric Village Archaeology in South-Eastern Turkey: The Eighth Millennium* B.C. *Site at Cayonu: its Chipped and Ground Stone Industries and Faunal Remains*. Oxford, British Archaeology Reports.

Braidwood, L.S., Braidwood, R.J., Howe, B., Reed, C.A. and Watson, P.J. (1983) (eds) *Prehistoric Investigations along the Zagros Flanks*. Oriental Institute Publications, No. 105. Chicago: The Oriental Institute of the University of Chicago.

Braidwood, R.J. (1983a) The site of Jarmo and its archaeological remains. In Braidwood *et al.*, pp.155–208.

Braidwood, R.J. (1983b) Jarmo chronology. In Braidwood *et al.*, pp.537–540.

Braidwood, R.J. and Howe, B. (1960) *Prehistoric Investigations in Iraqi Kurdistan*. Oriental Institute Publications No. 31. Chicago: The Oriental Institute of the University of Chicago.

Breniquet, C. (1989) Les origines de la culture d'obeid en Mésopotamie du nord. In Henrickson and Thuesen, pp.325–338.

Breniquet, C. (1991) Tell es-Sawwan – realités et problèmes. *Iraq* 53:75–90.

Breniquet, C. (1992) Rapport sur deux campagnes de fouilles à Tell Es-Sawwan, 1988–1989. *Mesopotamia* 27:5–30.

Brewer, D.J. (1989a) *Fisherman, Hunters and Herders: Zooarchaeology in the Fayum, Egypt (ca.8200–5000 bp)*. Oxford, BAR Int. Series 478.

Brewer, D.J. (1989b) A model for prehistoric resource exploitation in the prehistoric Fayum. In Krzyzaniak and Kobusiewicz, pp.127–137.

Brewer, D.J. and Wenke, R.J. (1992) Transitional late Predynastic – early Dynastic occupation at Mendes: A preliminary report. In Van den Brink 1992c, pp.191–198.

Brice, W.C. (1955) The Anatolian village (Harran). *Geography* 40:161–168.

Brice, W.C. (1966) *South-West Asia: A Systematic Regional Geography*. London, University of London Press.

Brockington, J. (1981) *The Sacred Thread: Hinduism in its Continuity and Diversity*. Edinburgh, Edinburgh University Press.

Brockington, J. (1993) Imperial India. In Cotterell, pp.193–236.

Brown, W.N. (1961) Mythology of India. In Kramer 1961b, pp.277–330.

Browning, R. (1980) *The Byzantine Empire*. London, Weidenfeld & Nicholson.

Bryant, J. (1992) *Robert Adam: Architect of Genius*. London, English Heritage.

Buchanan, B. (1967a) The prehistoric stamp seal: A reconsideration of some old excavations, Part I. *JAOS* 87:265–279.

Buchanan, B. (1967b) The prehistoric stamp seal: A reconsideration of some old excavations, Part II. *JAOS* 87:525–540.

Buckingham, J.S. (1825) *Travels Among the Arab Tribes*. London, Longman & Co.

Buckingham, J.S. (1827) *Travels in Mesopotamia*. 2 vols. London, Henry Colburn.

Bussagli, M. (1969) *Chinese Bronzes*, London, Paul Hamlyn.

Bussagli, M. (1987) *Chinese Bronzes*. London, Cassell.

Butler, A. (1992) Pulse agronomy: Traditional systems and implications of early cultivations. In P.C. Anderson (1992b), pp.67–78.

Butler, C. (1989) The plastered skulls from 'Ain Ghasal: Preliminary findings. In Hershkovitz, pp.141–145.

Butzer, K.W. (1976) *Early Hydraulic Civilization in Egypt: A Study in Cultural Ecology*. Chicago, University of Chicago Press.

Butzer, K.W. (1980) Pleistocene History of the Nile Valley in Egypt and Lower Nubia. In Williams and Faure, pp.253–280.

Butzer, K.W. (1984) Long-term Nile flood variation and political discontinuities in Pharaonic Egypt. In Clark and Brandt, pp.102–112.

Buxo i Capdevila, R. (1992) Quelques aspects des restes palaeobotaniques prélevés sur la terrasse de Hayonim (Haute Galilee). In P.C. Anderson 1992b, pp.225–229.

Byrd, B.F. (1988) The Natufian of Beidha: Report on renewed field research. In Garrard and Gebel Vol I, pp.175–197.

Byrd, B.F. (1989) The Natufian: Settlement variability and economic adaptations in the Levant at the end of the Pleistocene. *Journal of World Prehistory* 3(2):159–197.

Byrd, B.F. (1991) Beidha: An Early Natufian encampment in southern Jordan. In Bar-Yosef and Valla 1991b, pp.245–264.

Byrd, B.F. (1992) The dispersal of food production across the Levant. In Gebauer and Price, pp.49–62.

Byrd, B.F. and Colledge, S.M. (1991) Early Natufian occupation along the edge of the southern Jordanian Steppe. In Bar-Yosef and Valla 1991b, pp.265–276.

Calvet, Y. (1985–86) The new deep sounding x36 at Tell el-'Oueili. *Sumer* 44(1–2):67–87.

Calvet, Y. (1987) L'apport de Tell el 'Oueili à la chronologie d'Obeid. In Aurenche *et al.*, part ii: pp.465–472.

Campana, D. (1991) Bone implements from Hayonim Cave: Some relevant issues. In Bar-Yosef and Valla 1991b, pp.459–466.

Campbell, S. (1992) The Halaf Period in Iraq: Old sites and new. *Biblical Archaeologist* Dec. 1992:182–187.

Campbell, S. and Baird, D. (1990) Excavations at Ginnig: the Aceramic to Early Ceramic Neolithic sequence in North Iraq. *Paleorient* 16(2):65–78.

Campbell, S. and Healey, E. (1996) Domuztepe: A Late Pottery Neolithic Site in Southeast Turkey. *Neo-Lithics* 2/96:3–4.

Caneva, I. (1992) Predynastic Cultures of Lower Egypt: The Desert and the Nile. In Van den Brink 1992c, pp.217–224.

Caneva, I., Frangipane, M. and Palmieri, A. (1987) Predynastic Egypt: New data from Maadi. *African Archaeology Review* 5:105–114.

Caneva, I., Frangipane, M. and Palmieri, A. (1989) Recent excavations at Maadi (Egypt). In Krzyzaniak and Kobusiewicz, pp.287–293.

Carter, E. (1990) Elamite exports. In Vallat 1990, pp.89–100.

Casal, J.M. (1961) *Fouilles de Mundigak, 2 vols. Mémoires de la Délégation Archéologique Française en Afghanistan, 17*. Paris, Librairie C. Klinksieck.

Casal, J.M. (1964) *Fouilles d'Amri, 2 vols. Publications de la Commission des Fouilles Archéologique. Fouilles de Pakistan*. Paris, Librairie C. Klinksieck.

Casal, J.M. (1966) Nindowari: A Chalcolithic site of South Baluchistan. *Pakistan Archaeology* 3:10–21.

Casal, J.M. (1979) Amri: An introduction to the history of the Indus Civilization. In Agrawal and Chakrabarti, pp.99–112.

Casanova, M. (1994) Lapis lazuli beads in Susa and Central Asia: A preliminary study. In Parpola and Koskikallio, pp.137–145.

Cashdan, E. (1990a) Information costs and customary prices. In Cashdan 1990b, pp.259–278.

Cashdan, E. (1990b) *Risk and Uncertainty in Tribal and Peasant Economies*, Boulder, San Francisco and London, Westview Press.

Caton-Thompson, G. (1926) The Neolithic industry of the northern Fayum Desert. *Journal of the Royal Anthropological Institute* 56:309–323.

Caton-Thompson, G. (1928) Recent excavations in the Fayum, *MAN* 28:109–113.

Caton-Thompson, G. and Gardner, E.W. (1926) Research in the Fayum. *Ancient Egypt 1926*, pp.1–4.

Caton-Thompson, G. and Gardner, E.W. (1929) Recent work on the problem of Lake Moeris. *Geographical Journal* 73:20–60.

Caton-Thompson, G. and Gardner, E.W. (1934) *The Desert Fayum*. London, Royal Anthropological Institute.

Cauvin, J. (1989) La stratigraphie de Cafer Hoyuk-Est (Turquie) et les origines du PPNB du Taurus. *Paleorient* 15(1):75–86.

Cauvin, J. (1992) Problèmes et méthodes pour les débuts de l'agriculture: point de vue de l'archéologie. In Anderson 1992b, pp.265–268.

Cauvin, J and Sanlaville, P. (1981) (eds) *Préhistoire du Levant*. Paris, Editions du CNRS.

Cauvin, M. C. (1983) (ed.) *Traces d'utilisation sur les outils néolithiques du Proche-Orient*. Lyons, Travaux de la Maison de l'Orient 5.

Cauvin, M.-C. (1991) De Natoufien au Levant Nord? Jayroud et Mureybet (Syrie). In Bar-Yosef and Valla 1991b, pp.295–314.

Cauvin, M.-C. and Cauvin, J. (1993) La séquence Néolithique PPNB au Levant Nord. *Paleorient* 19(1):23–31.

Chadwick, J. (1994) Review of Parpola (1994). *The Times Higher Educational Supplement*, Dec. 9.

Chakrabarti, D.K. (1979) Size of the Harappan settlements. In Agrawal and Chakrabarti, pp.205–215.

Chakrabarti, D.K. (1995) *The Archaeology of Ancient Indian Cities*. Oxford, Oxford University Press.

Chandler, G.M. (1994) Petrographic analysis of some Early Harappan ceramics from the Bugti region, Baluchistan. In Parpola and Koskikallio, pp.147–155.

Chang, C.L. (1986) A brief discussion of Fu Tzu. In K.C. Chang 1986b, pp.103–120.

Chang, K.C. (1974) Urbanism and the King in ancient China. *World Archaeology* 6(1):pp.1–14.

Chang, K.C. (1977a) (ed.) *Food in Chinese Culture*. New Haven, Yale University Press.

Chang, K.C. (1977b) Food in Ancient China. In K.C. Chang 1977a, pp.23–52.

Chang, K.C. (1977c) *The Archaeology of Ancient China*, 3rd edition. New Haven, Yale University Press.

Chang, K.C. (1980a) *Shang Civilization*. New Haven, Yale University Press.

Chang, K.C. (1980b) The Chinese Bronze Age: A modern synthesis. In Fong, pp.35–50.

Chang, K.C. (1983a) *Art, Myth and Ritual: The Path to Political Authority in Ancient China*. New Haven, Yale University Press.

Chang, K.C. (1983b) Settlement patterns in Chinese archaeology: A case study from the Bronze Age. In Vogt and Leventhal, pp.361–374.

Chang, K.C. (1986a) *The Archaeology of Ancient China* (4th edn). New Haven, Yale University Press.

Chang, K.C. (1986b) (ed.) *Studies of Shang Archaeology: Selected Papers from the International Conference on Shang Civilization*. New Haven and London, Yale University Press.

Chang, K.C. (1986c) Yin-hsu Tomb Number Five and the question of the P'an Keng, Hsiao Hsin, Hsian Yi Period in Yin-hsu archaeology. In K.C. Chang 1986b, pp.65–80.

Chang, P.C. (1986) A brief description of the Fu Hao oracle bone inscriptions. In K.C. Chang 1986b, pp.121–140.

Chang, T.T. (1989) Domestication and the spread of cultivated rices. In Harris and Hillman, pp.408–417.

Chao, L. (1983) *Chinese Kinship*. London, Kegan Paul International.

Charvat, P. (1988) Archaeology and social history. The Susa sealings, ca. 4000–2340 B.C. *Paleorient* 14(1):57–63.

Charvat, P. (1992) On sealings and officials: Sumerian DUB and SANGA, c.3,500–2,500 B.C. In Vavrousek and Zemanek, (eds).

Chazan, M. and Lehner, M. (1990) An ancient analogy: Pot baked bread in ancient Egypt and Mesopotamia. *Paleorient* 16(2):21–35.

Chen, C.-Y. and Xi, Z. (1993) The Yao Dian and the origins of Astronomy in China. In Ruggles and Saunders, pp.32–66.

Chen, Chun (1984) The Microlithic of China. *Journal of Anthropological Archaeology* 3:79–115.

Chen, Chun and Olsen, J.W. (1990) China at the last glacial maximum. In Soffer and Gamble, I:276–295.

Chen, Lie (1996) The ancestor cult in Ancient China. In Rawson 1996a, pp. 269–272.

Chen Zhucai (1985) (translator) *China Handbook Series: Life and Life Styles.* Beijing, Foreign Languages Press.

Cheng, C.H. (1986) A study of the bronzes with the 'Ssu T'u Mu' inscriptions excavated from the Fu Hao Tomb. In K.C. Chang 1986b, pp.81–102.

Childe, V.G. (1928) *The Most Ancient East: The Oriental Prelude to European Prehistory.* London, Kegan Paul.

Childe, V.G. (1934) *New Light on the Most Ancient East: The Oriental Prelude to European Prehistory.* London, Kegan Paul.

Childe, V.G. (1950) The urban revolution. *Town Planning Review* 21(1):3–17.

Chlodnicki, M., Fattovich, R. and Salvatori, S. (1992) The Nile Delta in transition: A view from Tell el-Farkha. In Van den Brink 1992c, pp.171–190.

Chu, T.C. (1972) *Han Social Structure.* Seattle, University of Washington Press.

Chung Chih (1978) *An Outline of Chinese Geography.* Peking, Foreign Languages Press.

Cialowicz, K.M. (1989) Predynastic mace-heads in the Nile valley. In Krzyzaniak and Kobusiewicz, pp.261–266.

Cialowicz, K.M. (1992) La composition, le sens et la symbolique des scènes zoomorphes prédynastiques en relief. Les manches de couteaux. In Friedman and Adams, pp.247–258.

Civil, M. (1976) Lexicography. In Lieberman, pp.123–157.

Civil, M. (1987) Ur III bureaucracy: Quantitative aspects. In Gibson and Biggs, pp.43–53.

Civil, M. (1989) The Statue of Šulgi-Ki-ur$_5$-sag$_9$-kalam-ma. Part One: The Inscription. In Behrens, Loding and Roth 1989, pp.49–63.

Claessen, H.J.M. and Skalnik, P. (1978a) Limits: The beginning and end of the early state. In Claessen and Skalnik 1978b, pp.619–635.

Claessen, H.J.M. and Skalnik, P. (1978b) (eds) *The Early State.* The Hague, Mouton.

Clagett, M. (1989) *Ancient Egyptian Science: A Source Book. Vol. 1: Knowledge and Order.* Philadelphia, American Philosophical Society, Memoir 184.

Clagett, M. (1995) *Ancient Egyptian Science, A Source Book. Vol. 2: Calendars, Clocks and Astronomy.* Philadelphia, American Philosophical Society, Memoir 214.

Clark, J.D. and Brandt, S.A. (1984) (eds) *From Hunters to Farmers.* Berkeley, University of California Press.

Clayton, P. and Price, M. (1988) (eds) *The Seven Wonders of the Ancient World.* London, Routledge.

Clermont, N. and Smith, P.E.L. (1990) Prehistoric, prehistory, prehistorian . . . Who invented the terms? *Antiquity* 64(242):97–102.

Close, A.E. (1980) (ed) Wendorf, F. and Schild, R. (assemblers) *Loaves and Fishes: The Prehistory of Wadi Kubbaniya.* Dallas, SMU Press.

Close, A.E. (1984a) (ed.) Wendorf, F. and Schild, R. (assemblers) *Cattle-Keepers of the Eastern Sahara: The Neolithic of Bir Kiseiba.* Dallas, SMU Press.

Close, A.E. (1984b) (ed.) *Prehistory of Arid North Africa: Essays in Honor of Fred Wendorf.* Dallas, SMU Press.

Close, A.E. (1989) Lithic development in the Kubbaniyan (Upper Egypt). In Krzyzaniak and Kobusiewicz, pp.117–125.

Close, A.E. and Wendorf, F. (1992) The beginnings of food production in the Eastern Sahara. In Gebauer and Price, pp.63–72.

Clutton-Brock, J. (1971) The primary food animals of the Jericho tell from the Proto-Neolithic to the Byzantine Period. *Levant* 3:41–55.

Clutton-Brock, J. (1979) The mammalian remains from the Jericho tell. *Proceedings of the Prehistoric Society* 45:135–157.

Clutton-Brock, J. (1981) *Domesticated Animals from Early Times.* London, British Museum/ Heinemann.

Clutton-Brock, J. (1989a) Cattle in Ancient North Africa. In Clutton-Brock 1989b, pp.200–206.

Clutton-Brock, J. (1989b) (ed.) *The Walking Larder: Patterns of Domestication, Pastoralism, and Predation*. London, Unwin Hyman.

Clutton-Brock, J. (1993) The spread of domestic animals in Africa. In Shaw *et al.*, pp.61–70.

Coe, M.D. (1995) On *not* breaking the Indus Code. Review of Parpola 1994. *Antiquity* 69:393–395.

Cohen, C. and Hublin, J.-J. (1989) *Boucher de Perthes 1788–1868: Les Origines Romantiques de la Préhistoire*. Paris, Belin.

Cohen, M.E., Snell, D.C. and Weisberg, D.B. (1993) (eds) *The Tablet and the Scroll: Near Eastern Studies in Honor of William W. Hallo*. Bethesda, Maryland, CDL Press.

COHMAP MEMBERS (1988) Climatic changes of the last 18,000 years: observations and model simulations. *Science* 241:1043–1052.

Cohn, B.S. (1955) The changing status of a depressed caste. In Marriott 1955a (1969b), pp.53–77.

Colledge, S.M. (1991) Investigations of plant remains preserved in Epipalaeolithic sites in the Near East. In Bar-Yosef and Valla 1991b, pp.391–398.

Collon, D. (1987) *First Impressions: Cylinder Seals in the Ancient Near East*. London, British Museum Publications.

Collon, D. and Reade, J. (1983) Archaic Nineveh. *Baghdader Mitteilungen* 14:33-41.

Connan, J. and Deschesne, O. (1992) Origine et altération de quelques bitumes archaé-ologiques de tell Es-Sawwan (5500–5000 av. J.C.). *Mesopotamia* 27:47–61.

Constantini, L. (1981) Palaeoethnobotany at Pirak: A contribution to the 2nd millenium BC agriculture of the Sibi-Kachi Plain. *South Asian Archaeology* 1979, pp.271–277.

Constantini, L. (1984) The beginning of agriculture in the Kachi Plain: The evidence of Mehrgarh. In B. Allchin, pp.29–33.

Constantini, L. (1990) Harappan agriculture in Pakistan: The evidence of Naushuro. *South Asian Archaeology* 1987, pt 1. pp.321–332.

Cooper, J.S. (1983) *The Curse of Agade*. Baltimore, Johns Hopkins University Press.

Cooper, J.S. (1986) *Sumerian and Akkadian Royal Inscriptions, I: Presargonic Inscriptions*. New Haven, American Oriental Society.

Cooper, J.S. (1989) Enki's member: Eros and irrigation in Sumerian literature. In Behrens *et al.*, pp.87–89.

Cooper, J.S. (1990) Mesopotamian historical consciousness and the production of monu-mental art in the third millennium BC. In Gunter, pp.39–51.

Cooper, J.S. (1993) Paradigm and propaganda. The dynasty of Akkade in the 21st century. In Liverani 1993c, pp.11–24.

Cope, C. (1991) Gazelle hunting strategies in the southern Levant. In Bar-Yosef and Valla 1991b, pp.341–358.

Copeland, L. (1991) Natufian sites in Lebanon. In Bar-Yosef and Valla 1991b, pp.27–42.

Copeland, L. and Hours, F. (1987) The Halafians, their predecessors and their contempo-raries in Northern Syria and the Levant: Relative and absolute chronologies. In Aurenche *et al.*, pt ii:401–425.

Coqueugniot, E. (1991) Tell Es-Sawwan (1988–1989): Note concernant les outils de Pierre Taillée. *Mesopotamia* 27:31–46.

Cotterell, A. (1980) (ed.) *The Encyclopedia of Ancient Civilizations*. New York, Mayflower Books.

Cotterell, A. (1993) (ed.) *The Penguin Encyclopedia of Classical Civilizations*. Harmondsworth, Viking.

Courty, M.A. (1989) Integration of sediment and soil information in the reconstruction of protohistoric and historic landscapes of the Ghaggar Plain, North-west India. In Frifelt and Sorensen, pp.255–259.

Cowan, C.W. and Watson, P.J. (1992) (eds) *The Origins of Agriculture: An International Perspective*. Washington, Smithsonian Institution Press.

Crabtree, P.J., Campana, D.V., Belfer-Cohen, A. and Bar-Yosef, D.E. (1991) First results of the excavations at Salibiya I, lower Jordan Valley. In Bar-Yosef and Valla 1991b, pp.161–172.

Crawford, G.W. (1992) Prehistoric plant domestication in East Asia. In Cowan and Watson (eds), pp.7–38.

Crawford, H.E.W. (1991) *Sumer and the Sumerians*. Cambridge, Cambridge University Press.

Crawford, H.E.W. (1998) *Dilmun and its Gulf Neighbours*. Cambridge, Cambridge University Press.

Creel, H.G. (1964) The Beginnings of Bureaucracy in China: The Origin of the Hsien. *Journal of Asian Studies* 23(3):155–84.

Creel, H.G. (1970) *The Origins of Statecraft in China*. Chicago, University of Chicago Press.

Curtis, J. (1982) (ed.) *Fifty Years of Mesopotamian Discovery*. London, British School of Archaeology in Iraq.

Curtis, J. (1993) (ed.) *Early Mesopotamia and Iran: Contact and Conflict c.3500–1600* BC. London, British Museum Press.

Cziesla, E. (1989) Sitra and related sites at the western border of Egypt. In Krzyzaniak and Kobusiewicz, pp.255–260.

Dabbagh, T. (1966) Halaf pottery. *Sumer* 22:23–43.

Dalal, K.F. (1980) A short history of archaeological explorations in Bikaner and Bahawalpur along the 'lost' Sarasvati River. *Indica* 17(1):3–40.

Dales, G.F. (1974) Excavations at Balakot, Pakistan, 1973. *Journal of Field Archaeology* 1:3–22.

Dales, G.F. (1979) The Balakot Project: Summary of four years excavations in Pakistan. In Taddei, I:241–274.

Dales, G.F. (1981) Reflections on four years of excavations at Balakot. In Dani, pp.25–32.

Dales, G.F. and Kenoyer, J.M. (1990) Excavations at Harappa 1989. *Pakistan Archaeology* 25:241–280.

Dalley, S. (1984) *Mari and Karana: Two Old Babylonian Cities*. London, Longman.

Dalley, S. (1989) *Myths from Mesopotamia*. Oxford, Oxford University Press.

Damerow, P. and Englund, R.K. (1989) The Proto-Elamite texts from Tepe Yahya. *American School of Prehistoric Research* 39, Cambridge MA.

Dani, A.H. (1981) (ed.) *Indus Civilization: New Perspectives*. Islamabad, CSCCA.

Dani, A.H. (1988) *Recent Archaeological Discoveries in Pakistan*. Paris, Unesco, with The Centre for East Asian Cultural Studies, Tokyo.

Daniel, G. (1975) *One Hundred and Fifty Years of Archaeology*. London, Duckworth.

Daniel, G. (1981) (ed.) *Towards a History of Archaeology*. London, Thames and Hudson.

D'Argence, R.Y.L. (1977) *Bronze Vessels of Ancient China in the Avery Brundage Collection*. San Francisco, Asian Art Museum of San Francisco.

David, R. (1982) *The Ancient Egyptians: Religious Beliefs and Practices*. London, Routledge & Kegan Paul.

Davidson, T.E. (1977) *Regional Variation within the Halaf Ceramic Tradition*. Unpublished PhD thesis, University of Edinburgh.

Davidson, T.E. (1981) Pottery manufacture and trade at the prehistoric site of Tell Aqab. *Journal of Field Archaeology* 8:65–77.

Davidson, T.E. and McKerrell, H. (1976) Pottery analysis and Halaf Period trade in the Khabur headwaters region. *Iraq* 38:45–56.

Davidson, T.E. and McKerrell, H. (1980) Neutron activation of Halaf and Ubaid pottery from Tell Arpachiya and Tepe Gawra. *Iraq* 42:155–167.

Davidson, T.E. and Watkins, T. (1981) Two seasons of excavations at Tell Aqab in the Jezireh, N.E. Syria. *Iraq* 43:1–18.

Davis, P.H. (1965) (ed.) *Flora of Turkey and the East Aegean Islands*, Vol. 1 [Vol. 4 1972]. Edinburgh, Edinburgh University Press.

Davis, S.J.M. (1989) Hatoula 1980–1986: Why did prehistoric peoples domesticate food animals? In Bar-Yosef and Vandermeersch, pp.43–59.

Davis, S.J.M. (1991) When and why did prehistoric people domesticate animals? Some evidence from Israel and Cyprus. In Bar-Yosef and Valla 1991b, pp.381–390.

Davis, W. (1982) Artists and patrons in the Predynastic and Early Dynastic period. *Studien zur altägyptischen Kultur* 10.

Davis, W. (1983) Cemetery T at Nagada. *MDAIK* 39:17–28.

Debono, F. and Mortensen, B. (1990) (eds) El Omari: A Neolithic settlement and other sites in the vicinity of Wadi Hof, Helwan. *AVDAIK 82*. Mainz am Rhein.

De Cardi, B. (1984) Some third and fourth millennium sites in Sarawan and Jhalawan, Baluchistan, in relation to the Mehrgarh sequence. In B. Allchin, pp.61–67.

De Contenson, H. (1989) L'Aswadien, un nouveau faciès du Néolithique Syrien. *Paleorient* 15(1):259–262.

De Contenson, H., Cauvin, M.-C., van Zeist, W., Bakker-Heeres, J.A.H. and Leroi-Gourhan, A. (1979) Tell Aswad (Damascene). *Paleorient* 5:152–153.

Defen, H. and Chunhua, X. (1985) Pleistocene mammalian faunas of China. In Rukang and Olsen, pp.267–289.

Delougaz, P. (1934) *The Temple Oval at Khafaje*. Chicago, Oriental Institute Publications, No. 53.

De Moulins, D. (1993) Les restes de plantes carbonisés de Cafer Hoyuk. *Cahiers de l'Euphrate* 7:191–234.

De Moulins, D. (1994) Agricultural change at Euphrates and steppe sites in the mid-8th millennium B.C. PhD Thesis, University College London.

Dentan, R.C. (1983) (ed.) *The Idea of History in the Ancient Near East*. New Haven, American Oriental Society [1954].

Des, S.B. (1972) (ed.) *Archaeological Congress and Seminar Papers*. Nagpur.

De Roller, G.J. (1992) The archaeobotanical remains from Tell Ibrahim Awad, seasons 1988–1990. In Van den Brink 1992c, pp.111–116.

Desse, J. (1985–86) Analysis of bones from Tell el-'Oueili, Lower Levels (Obeid 0,1,2,3), 1983 Campaign. *Sumer* 44(1–2):123–134.

De Wit, H.E. (1993) The evolution of the eastern Nile Delta as a factor in the development of human culture. In Krzyzaniak *et al.*, pp.305–320.

De Wit, H.E. and Pawlikowski, M. (1992) Comparison of Palaeoenvironmental data from Neolithic and Early Dynastic sites of Upper Egypt, the Fayum and the Nile Delta (Abstract). In Van den Brink 1992c, pp.289–292.

Dhavalikar, M.K. (1992) Kuntasi: A Harappan port in Western India. In C. Jarrige, pp.73–81.

Dhavalikar, M.K. (1995) *Cultural Imperialism: Indus Civilization in Western India*. New Delhi, Books and Books.

Dhavalikar, M.K. and Atre, S. (1989) The fire cult and virgin sacrifice. Some Harappan rituals. In Kenoyer 1989b, pp.193–205.

Diakonoff, I.M. (1969a) (ed.) *Ancient Mesopotamia: A Socio-Economic History. A Collection of Studies by Soviet Scholars*. Moscow, Nauka Publishing House.

Diakonoff, I.M. (1969b) Editor's preface. In Diakonoff 1969a, pp.8–16.

Diakonoff, I.M. (1969c) The rise of the despotic state in Ancient Mesopotamia. In Diakonoff 1969a, pp.173–203.

Diakonoff, I.M. (1976) Ancient writing and ancient written language: Pitfalls and peculiarities in the study of Sumerian. In Lieberman, pp.99–121.

Diakonoff, I.M. (1981) Earliest Semites in Asia: Agriculture and animal husbandry according to linguistic data (VIIIth–IVth millennia B.C.). *Altorientalische Forschungen* 8:23–67.

Diakonoff, I.M. (1983a) The structure of Near Eastern society before the middle of the second millennium BC. *Oikumene* 3:7–100.

Diakonoff, I.M. (1983b) Some reflections on numerals in Sumerian: Towards a history of mathematical speculation. *JAOS* 103 (1):83–93.

Diakonoff, I.M. (1985) Extended families in Old Babylonian Ur. *ZA* 75: 47–65.

Dikshit, K.N. (1984) The Sothi complex: Old records and fresh observations. In Lal *et al.*, pp.531–537.

Diot, M.-F. (1992) Etudes palynologiques de blés sauvages et domestiques issus de cultures expérimentales. In P.C. Anderson 1992b, pp.107–111.

Donaldson, M.L. (1985) The plant remains. In Rollefson *et al.*, pp.96–104.

Donovan, A.L. (1975) *Philosophical Chemistry in the Scottish Enlightenment: The Doctrines and Discoveries of William Cullen and Joseph Black.* Edinburgh, Edinburgh University Press.

Dreyer, G. (1992a) Recent discoveries at Abydos Cemetery U. In Van den Brink 1992c, pp.293–299.

Dreyer, G. (1992b) Horus Krokodil, ein Gegenkönig der Dynastie 0. In Friedman and Adams, pp.259–263.

Drower, M.S. (1982) The early years. In James, pp.9–36.

Drower, M.S. (1985) *Flinders Petrie: A Life in Archaeology.* London, Gollancz.

Ducos, P. (1992) La faune de Tell Es-Sawwan (1988–1989). *Mesopotamia* 27:63–70.

Ducos, P. (1993) Proto-élevage au Levant Sud au VIIe millénaire B.C. Les données de la Damascene. *Paleorient* 19(1):153–173.

Dunnell, R.C. (1980) Evolutionary theory and archaeology. *Advances in Archaeological Method and Theory* 3:35–99.

Dunnell, R.C. (1989) Aspects of the application of evolutionary theory in archaeology. In Lamberg-Karlovsky, pp.35–49.

Dunnell, R.C. and Wenke, R.J. (1980) Cultural and scientific evolution: Some comments on 'The Decline and Rise of Mesopotamian Civilization' [by Norman Yoffee]. *American Antiquity* 45(3):605–609.

Durante, S. (1979) Marine shells from Balakot, Shahr-I Sokhta and Tepe Yahya: Their significance for trade and technology in Ancient Indo-Iran. In Taddei, I:317–343.

Durrani, F.A. (1981a) Indus Civilization: Evidence west of Indus. In Dani, pp.133–138.

Durrani, F.A. (1981b) Rehman Dheri and the birth of civilization in Pakistan. *Bulletin of the Institute of Archaeology,* University of London 18:191–207.

Durrani, F.A. (1988) Excavations in the Gomal Valley: Rehman Dheri excavation report No. 1. *Ancient Pakistan* 6:1–204.

Durrani, F.A. and Wright, R.P. (1992) Excavation at Rehman Dheri: The pottery typology and technology. In Possehl, pp.145–162.

Dyson, R.H. (1987) The relative and absolute chronology of Hissar II and the Proto-Elamite horizon of Northern Iran. In Aurenche *et al.*, pt ii:647–678.

Edens, C. (1992) Dynamics of trade in the Ancient Mesopotamian 'world system'. *American Anthropologist* 94:118–139.

Edens, C. (1994) On the complexity of complex societies: structure, power and legitimation in Kassite Babylonia. In Stein and Rothman, pp.209–224.

Edwards, I.E.S. (1972) *The Pyramids of Egypt.* London, Ebury Press and Michael Joseph.

Edwards, I. and Hope, C.A. (1989) A note on the Neolithic ceramics from the Dakleh Oasis (Egypt). In Krzyzaniak and Kobusiewicz, pp.233–242.

Edwards, P.C. (1989) Revising the broad spectrum revolution: And its role in the origins of Southwest Asian food production. *Antiquity* 63:225–246.

Edwards, P.C. (1991) Wadi Hammeh 27: An Early Natufian site at Pella, Jordan. In Bar-Yosef and Valla 1991b, pp.123–148.

Edzard, D.O. (1959) Enmebaragesi von Kis. *Zeitschrift für Assyriologie* (N.F.) 19:9–26.

Edzard, D.O. (1974) La royauté dans la période présargonique. In Garelli, pp.141–149.

Edzard, D.O. (1987) Deep-rooted skyscrapers and bricks: Ancient Mesopotamian architecture and its imaging. In Mindlin *et al.*, 13–24.

Eichler, B.L. (1976) (ed.) Kramer Anniversary Volume. Studies in Honor of Samuel Noah Kramer. Neukirchen-Vluyn, *AOAT* 25.

Eichler, B.L. (1987) Literary structure in the laws of Eshnunna. In Rochberg-Halton, pp.71–84.

Eigner, D. (1992) A temple of the Early Middle Kingdom at Tell Ibrahim Awad. In Van den Brink 1992c, pp.69–78.

Eisenstadt, S.N. (1986) (ed.) *The Origins and Diversity of Axial Age Civilizations*. Albany, State University of New York Press.

Eiwanger, J. (1984) *Merimde-Benisalame 1: Die Funde der Urschicht*. Mainz, von Zabern.

El-Alfi, M. (1992) Means of transport in Neolithic Egypt. In Van den Brink 1992c, pp.399–444.

Eldar, I. and Baumgarten, Y. (1985) Neve Noy: A Chalcolithic site of the Beer-sheba Culture. *Biblical Archaeologist* 48:134–139.

El-Gamili, M.M., Hassanian, A.Gh. and El-Mahmoudi, A.E. (1992) Geoelectric resistivity contribution to the mode of occurrence of sand islets 'turtle backs' in the Nile Delta, Egypt. In Van den Brink 1992c, pp.269–288.

El-Hadidi, M.N. (1992) Notes on Egyptian weeds in antiquity:1. Min's lettuce and the Naqada plant. In Friedman and Adams, pp.323–326.

Elliott, C. (1978) The Ghassulian Culture in Palestine: Origins, influences and abandonment. *Levant* 10:37–54.

Ellis, C. (1992) A statistical analysis of the protodynastic burials in the 'Valley' Cemetery of Kafr Tarkhan. In Van den Brink 1992c, pp.241–258.

Ellis, M. de J. (1989) Observations on Mesopotamian oracles and prophetic texts: Literary and historiographic considerations. *Journal of Cuneiform Studies* 41(2):127–186.

Elvin, M. (1972) The high-level equilibrium trap: The causes of the decline in the traditional Chinese textile industries. In Willmott, pp.137–172.

Elvin, M. (1973) *The Pattern of the Chinese Past: A Social and Economic Interpretation*. Stanford, California, Stanford University Press.

Elvin, M. (1984) Why China failed to create an endogenous industrial capitalism: A critique of Max Weber's explanation. *Theory and Society* 3(3):379–391.

Elvin, M. (1986) Was there a transcendental breakthrough in China? In Eisenstadt, pp.325–359.

El-Wailly, F. and Abu es-Soof, B. (1965) The excavations at Tell es-Sawwan. First preliminary report. *Sumer* 21:17–32.

Emery, W.B. (1961) *Archaic Egypt*. Harmondsworth, Penguin.

Englund, R.K. (1988) Administrative timekeeping in Ancient Mesopotamia. *JESHO* 31:121–185.

Englund, R.K. (1996) *Proto-Cuneiform Texts from Diverse Collections. Series: Materialien zu den frühen Schriftzeugnissen des Vorderen Orients {MSVO} Vol. 4*. Berlin, Gbr. Mann Verlag.

Englund, R.K. and Gregoire, J.P. (1991) *The Proto-Cuneiform texts from Jemdet Nasr: Copies, Transliterations and Glossary. MSVO, Vol.1*. Berlin, Mann Verlag.

Erdosy, G. (1987) Early historic cities in N. India. *South Asian Studies* 3:1–23.

Evans, J. (1956) *A History of the Society of Antiquaries*. Oxford, Oxford University Press.

Evans, J.D., Cunliffe, B. and Renfrew, C. (1981) (eds) *Antiquity and Man: Essays in Honour of Glyn Daniel*. London, Thames and Hudson.

Ewald, P.W. (1991a) Transmission modes and the evolution of virulence; with special reference to cholera, influenza and Aids. *Human Nature* 2(1):1–30.

Ewald, P.W. (1991b) Waterborne transmission and the evolution of virulence among gastrointestinal bacteria. *Epidemiology and Infection* 106:83–119.

Ewald, P.W. (1993a) The evolution of virulence. *Scientific American* 268(4):86–93.

Ewald, P.W. (1993b) *Evolution of Infectious Disease*: Chap. 5. Oxford, Oxford University Press.

Fairservis, W.A. (1975) *The Roots of Ancient India* (2nd edn). London, Allen & Unwin.

Fairservis, W.A. (1984) Harappan Civilization according to its writing. In B. Allchin, pp.154–161.

Fairservis, W.A. (1989) An epigenetic view of the Harappan Culture. In Lamberg-Karlovsky, pp.205–217.

Fairservis, W.A. (1992) *The Harappan Civilization and its Writing. A model for the Decipherment of the Indus Script.* Leiden/Oxford, E.J. Brill and IBH.

Fairservis, W.A. (1994) The Harappan script. Is it deciphered or can it be deciphered? In Kenoyer 1994b, pp.173–178.

Falkenhausen, L. von (1993) On the historiographical orientation of Chinese archaeology. *Antiquity* 67:839–849.

Farber, W. (1983) Der Vergöttlichung Naram-Sins. *Orientalia N.S.* 52:67–72.

Fei, H.T. (1939) *Peasant Life in China.* London, Routledge.

Fellner, R.O. (1995) *Cultural Change and the Epipalaeolothic of Palestine.* Oxford, BAR S599.

Feng, H. and Tong, E. (1979) The jade objects found in Guanghan. *Wenwu* 2:31–36.

Fentress, M. (1982) From Jhelum to Yamuna: City and settlement in the second and third millennium BC. In Possehl, pp.245–260.

Finkbeiner, U. (1991) Uruk, Kampagne 35–37, 1982–1984: Die archäologische Ober-flachenuntersuchung (Survey), Ausgrabungen in Uruk-Warka Endberichte 4, Mainz am Rhein.

Finkel, I.L. (1988) The Hanging Gardens of Babylon. In Clayton and Price, pp.38–58.

Finkelstein, I. (1995) Two notes on Early Bronze Age urbanization and urbanism. *Tel Aviv* 22:47–69.

Finkelstein, I. and Gophna, R. (1993) Settlement, demographic and economic patterns in the highlands of Palestine in the Chalcolithic and Early Bronze Periods and the beginning of urbanism. *BASOR* 289:1–22.

Finkelstein, J.J. (1961) Ammisaduqa's edict and the Babylonian 'law codes'. *Journal of Cuneiform Studies* 15:91–104.

Finkelstein, J.J. (1963) The Antediluvian Kings: A University of California tablet. *Journal of Cuneiform Studies* 17:39–51.

Finkelstein, J.J. (1970) On some recent studies in Cuneiform Law (review article). *Journal of the American Oriental Society* 90(2):243–256.

Fisher, W.B. (1978) *The Middle East* (7th edn). London, Methuen.

Flam, L. (1987) Recent explorations in Sind: Palaeogeography, regional ecology, and prehistoric settlement patterns (ca. 4000–2000 B.C.). In Jacobson 1987b, pp.65–89.

Flannery, K.V. (1971) Origins and ecological effects of early domestication in Iran and the Near East. In Streuver (ed.), pp.50–79.

Flannery, K.V. (1972) The origins of the village as a settlement type in Mesoamerica and the Near East: A comparative study. In Ucko *et al.*, pp.23–53.

Flannery, K.V. and Wheeler, J.C. (1967) Animal bones from Tell es-Sawwan, Level III (Samarran Period). *Sumer* 23:179–182.

Fong, W. (1980) (ed.) *The Great Bronze Age of China.* New York, Metropolitan Museum of Art and Knopf.

Fontain, J. and Tung, W. (1976) *Han and Tang Murals: Discovered in the PRC and Copied by Contemporary Chinese Painters.* Boston, Museum of Fine Arts.

Forest, C. (1984) Kheit Qasim III: The Obeid settlement. *Sumer* 40(1–2):119–121.

Forest, J.D. (1983) Aux origines de l'architecture obéidienne: Les plans de type Samarra. *Akkadica* 34:1–47.

Forest, J.D. (1984) Kheit Qasim III – An Obeid settlement. *Sumer* 40(1–2):85.

Forest, J.D. (1985–86) Tell el-'Oueili preliminary report on the 4th Season (1983): Stratigraphy and architecture. *Sumer* 44(1–2):55–66.

Forest-Foucault, C. (1980) Rapport sur le fouilles de Kheit Qasim III. *Paleorient* 6:221–224.

Fortes, M. (1953) The structure of unilineal descent groups. *American Anthropologist* 55:17–41.

Fortes, M. (1959) Descent, filiation and affinity. *Man* 59:193–197 and 206–212.

Foster, B.R. (1982a) *Umma in the Sargonic Period*. Hampden, Conn., Memoirs of the Connecticut Academy of Sciences.

Foster, B.R. (1982b) Archives and recording-keeping in Sargonic Mesopotamia. *Zeitschrift für Assyriologie* 72(1):1–27.

Foster, B.R. (1982c) *Administration and Use of Institutional Land in Sargonic Sumer. Mesopotamia 9: Copenhagen Studies in Assyriology*. Copenhagen, Akademisk Forlag.

Foster, B.R. (1985) The Sargonic victory stele from Telloh. *Iraq* 47:15–30.

Foster, B.R. (1986) Agriculture and accountability in Ancient Mesopotamia. In Weiss 1986c, pp.109–128.

Foster, B.R. (1993a) Management and administration in the Sargonic Period. In Liverani 1993c ed., pp.25–40.

Foster, B.R. (1993b) Select bibliography of the Sargonic Period. In Liverani 1993c, pp.171–182.

Foster, B.R. (1993c) *Before the Muses: An Anthology of Akkadian Literature. Vol. 1: Archaic, Classical, Mature. Vol. 2: Mature, Late*. Bethesda, Maryland. CDL Press.

Fox, R.G. (1969) *Varna* schemes and ideological integration in Indian society. *Comparative Studies in Society and History* 2:27–45.

Foxvog, D.A. (1994) A new Lagas text bearing on Uruinimgina's reforms. *Journal of Cuneiform Studies* 46:11–15.

Franke-Vogt, U. (1994) The 'Early Period' at Mohenjo-Daro. In Kenoyer 1994b, pp.27–49.

Francfort, H.-P. (1989) The Indo-French Archaeological Project in Haryana and Rajasthan. In Frifelt and Sorensen 1989, pp.260–264.

Frankfort, H., Lloyd, S. and Jacobsen, T. (1940) *The Gimil-Sin Temple and the Palace of the Rulers at Tell Asmar*. Chicago, Oriental Institute.

Frayne, D.R. (1992) *The Early Dynastic List of Geographical Names*. American Oriental Series Vol. 74. New Haven, Yale University Press.

Freedman, M. (1966) *Chinese Lineage and Society*. London, Athlone Press.

Frere, J. (1800) Account of flint weapons discovered at Hoxne in Suffolk. *Archaeologia* 13:204–5.

Friberg, J. (1978–79) *The Third Millennium Roots of Babylonian Mathematics. Research Report 2 Vols*. Sweden, Dept. of Mathematics, Chalmers University of Technology and the University of Goteberg, Sweden.

Friberg, J. (1982) *A Survey of Publications on Sumero-Akkadian Mathematics, Metrology, and Related Matters (1954–1982)*. Research Report No. 1982:17, Dept. of Mathematics, Chalmers University of Technology, the University of Goteberg, Sweden.

Friberg, J. (1984) Numbers and measures. *Scientific American* 250:110–118.

Friedman, R.F. (1992a) The early dynastic and transitional pottery of Mendes. The 1990 season. In Van den Brink 1992c, pp.199–206.

Friedman, R.F. (1992b) Pebbles, pots and petroglyphs: Excavations at Hk64. In Friedman and Adams, pp.99–106.

Friedman, R.F. and Adams, B. (1992) (eds) *The Followers of Horus: Studies Dedication to Michael Allen Hoffman (1944–1990)*. Oxford, Oxbow Monographs in Archaeology.

Friedman, J. and Rowlands, M.J. (1977) (eds) *The Evolution of Social Systems*. London, Duckworth.

Frifelt, K. (1989) 'Ubaid in the Gulf Area. In Henrickson and Thuesen, pp.405–419.

Frifelt, K. and Sorensen, P. (1989) (eds) *South Asian Archaeology, 1985*. London, Curzon Press.

Fujiwara, H., Mughal, M.R., Sasaki, A. and Matano, T. (1992) Rice and ragi at Harappa: Preliminary results by plant opal analysis. *Pakistan Archaeology* 27:129–142.

Gadd, C.J. (1963) Two sketches from the life at Ur. *Iraq* 25:183–188.

Galili, E., Weinstein-Evron, M., Hershkovitz, I., Gopher, A., Kislev, M., Lernau, O., Kolska-Horwitz, L. and Lernau, H. (1993) Atlit-Yam: A prehistoric site on the sea floor off the Israeli coast. *Journal of Field Archaeology* 20:133–157.

Gallery Kovacs, M. (1989) *The Epic Of Gilgamesh*. Stanford, Stanford University Press.

Gardin, J.C. (1980) *Archaeological Constructs*. Cambridge, Cambridge University Press.

Gardner, C.S. (1961) *Chinese Traditional Historiography*. Cambridge, Harvard University Press.

Garelli, P. (1974) (ed.) *Le Palais et la Royauté*. Paris, Compte Rendu, XIXe Rencontre Assyriologique International.

Garfinkel, Y. (1987a) Yiftahel: a Neolithic village from the seventh millennium BC in lower Galilee, Israel. *Journal of Field Archaeology* 14:199–212.

Garfinkel, Y. (1987b) Burnt lime products and social implications in the Pre-Pottery Neolithic B villages of the Near East. *Paleorient* 13(1):69–76.

Garfinkel, Y. (1993) The Yarmoukian Culture in Israel. *Paleorient* 19(1):115–134.

Garrard, A.N. (1991) Natufian settlement in the Azraq Basin, eastern Jordan. In Bar-Yosef and Valla 1991b, pp.235–244.

Garrard, A.N. and Byrd, B.F. (1992) New dimensions to the Epipalaeolithic of the Wadi el-Jilat in Central Jordan. *Paleorient* 18(1):47–62.

Garrard, A.N. and Gebel, G. (1988) (eds) The Prehistory of Jordan: The state of research in 1986. 2 pts. *BAR International Series* 396 (i,ii).

Garrod, D.A.E. (1932) A new Mesolithic industry: The Natufian of Palestine. *Journal of the Royal Anthropological Institute* 62:257–270.

Garrod, D.A.E. (1942) Excavation at the cave of Shukbah, Palestine, 1928. *Proceedings of the Prehistoric Society* 8:1–20.

Gawarecki, S.L. and Perry, S.K. (1992) Late Pleistocene human occupation in the Suez Rift, Egypt: A key to landform development and climatic regime. In Friedman and Adams (eds), pp.139–146.

Ge, Yan (1989) Sanxingdui: The Early Shu civilisation. MA thesis, University of Pittsburgh, unpublished manuscript.

Ge, Yan and Linduff, K.M. (1990) Sanxingdui: a new Bronze Age site in southwest China. *Antiquity* 64:505–513.

Gebauer, A.B. and Price, T.D. (1992) (eds) *Transitions to Agriculture in Prehistory*. Madison, Prehistory Press: Monographs in World Archaeology No. 4.

Gebel, H.G. (1988) Late Epipalaeolithic – Aceramic Neolithic sites in the Petra-Area. In Garrard and Gebel, pp.67–100.

Gebel, H.G., Kafafi, Z. and Rollefson, G. (1997) (eds) *The Prehistory of Jordan II. Perspectives from 1996*. Berlin, Ex Oriente.

Gebel, H.G. and Koszlowski, S.K. (1994) (eds) Neolithic chipped stone industries of the Fertile Crescent. Proceedings of the First Workshop on PPN Chipped Lithic Industries, Berlin 1993. Berlin studies in the early production subsistence and environment. Zaklad Graficzny, Uniwersytet Warszawaski, Warszawa.

Gebel, H.G., Muheisen, M.S., Nissen, H.J., Qadi, N. and Starck, J.M. (1988) Preliminary report on the first season of excavations at the Late Aceramic Neolithic site of Basta. In Garrard and Gebel, I:101–134.

Gebhardt, A. (1992) Micromorphological analysis of soil structure modifications caused by different cultivation implements. In P.C. Anderson 1992b, pp.373–381.

Gelb, I.J. (1961) *Old Akkadian Writing and Grammar*, (2nd edn) Chicago, University of Chicago Press.

Gelb, I.J. (1963) *A Study of Writing*. Berkeley, University of California Press.

Gelb, I.J. (1965) The ancient Mesopotamian ration system. *Journal of Near Eastern Studies* 24:230–243.

Gelb, I.J. (1969) On the alleged temple and state economies in ancient Mesopotamia. *Studi in Onore di Eduardo Volterra* 6:137–154. Rome, Guiffre Editore.

Gelb, I.J. (1970) Makkan and Meluhha in Early Mesopotamian sources. *Revue d'Assyriologie* 64:1–8.

Gelb, I.J. (1972) The Arua institution. *Revue d'Assyriologie* 66:1–32.

Gelb, I.J. (1979) Household and family in Ancient Mesopotamia. In Lipinski, I:1–98.

Gelb, I.J. (1980) Comparative method in the study of the society and economy of the Ancient Near East. *Rocznik Orientalistyczeny* 41(II):29–36.

Gelb, I.J. (1986) Ebla and Lagash: Environmental contrast. In Weiss 1986c, pp.157–167.

Gelb, I.J. (1987) Compound divine names in the Ur III Period. In Rochberg-Halton, pp.125–138.

Gelb, I.J. (1992) Mari and the Kish Civilization. In Young, pp.121–215.

Gelb, I.J. and Kienast, B. (1990) *Die Altakkadischen Königsinschriften des dritten Jahrtausends v. Chr.* Stuttgart, Freiburger Altorientalische Studien 7.

Gelb, I.J., Steinkeller, P. and Whiting, R.M. (1991) *Earliest Land Tenure Systems in the Near East: Ancient Kudurrus (Text)*. Chicago, Oriental Institute Publications Vol. 104.

Geller, M.J. (1987) The Lugal of Mari at Ebla and the Sumerian King List. In Gordon *et al.*, pp.141–145.

Geller, M.J. (1992) From Prehistory to History: Beer in Egypt. In Friedman and Adams, pp.19–26.

Gibson, McG. (1972) *The City and Area of Kish.* Coconut Grove, Florida, Field Research Projects.

Gibson, McG. and Biggs, R.D. (1987) (eds) *The Organization of Power: Aspects of Bureaucracy in the Ancient Near East. Studies in Ancient Oriental Civilization No. 46.* Chicago, The Oriental Institute.

Gibson, McG. and McMahon, A. (1995) Investigation of the Early Dynastic-Akkadian transition: Report of the 18th and 19th seasons of excavation in Area WF, Nippur. *Iraq* 57:1–39.

Gilead, I. (1984) The micro-endscraper: a new tool-type of the Chalcolithic period. *Tel Aviv* 11:3–10.

Gilead, I. (1988) The Chalcolithic Period in the Levant. *Journal of World Prehistory* 2(4):397–443.

Gilead, I. (1989a) The Upper Palaeolithic to Epi-Palaeolithic transition in the Levant. *Paleorient* 14:177–182.

Gilead, I. (1989b) The Upper Palaeolithic in the Southern Levant: Periodization and terminology. In Bar-Yosef and Vandermeersch, pp.231–254.

Gilead, I. (1990a) The Neolithic-Chalcolithic transition and the Qatifian of the northern Negev and Sinai. *Levant* 22:47–63.

Gilead, I. (1990b) The Natufian as seen from the Upper Paleolithic Period. *Mitekufat Haeven* 23:179.

Gillispie, C.C. (1959) *Genesis and Geology: The Impact of Scientific Discoveries upon Religious Beliefs in the Decades before Darwin.* New York, Harper.

Gimpel, J. (1988) *The Medieval Machine* (2nd edn). London, Wildwood House.

Goedicke, H. (1991) Jurisdiction in the Pyramid Age. *MDAIK* 47:135–141.

Goepper, R. (1996) Precursors and early stages of the Chinese script. In Rawson 1996a, pp.273–281.

Goetze, A. (1962) Two Ur-Dynasty tablets dealing with labour. *Journal of Cuneiform Studies* 16:13–16.

Goody, J. (1986) *The Logic of Writing and the Organization of Society.* Cambridge and New York, Cambridge University Press.

Gopher, A. (1989a) Diffusion processes in the Pre-Pottery Neolithic Levant: The case of the Helwan Point. In Hershkovitz, pp.91–106.

Gopher, A. (1989b) Neolithic arrowheads of the Levant: Results and implications of a seriation analysis. *Paleorient* 15(1)43–56.

Gopher, A. (1989c) Horvat Galil and Nahal Betzet I: Two Neolithic sites in the Upper Galilee. *Mitekufat Haeven* 22:82–92.

Gopher, A. (1990) Mujahiya, an Early Pre-Pottery Neolithic B site in the Golan Heights. *Tel Aviv* 17(2):115–143.

Gopher, A. (1993) Sixth–fifth millennia B.C. settlements in the coastal plain, Israel. *Paleorient* 19(1):55–63.

Gopher, A. and Gophna, R. (1993) Cultures of the eighth and seventh millennia B.P. in the southern Levant: A review for the 1990s. *Journal of World Prehistory* 7 (3):297–353.

Gordon, C.H. (1987) Eblaitica. In Gordon *et al.*, pp.19–28.

Gordon, C.H., Rendsberg, G.A. and Winter, N.H. (1987) (eds) *Eblaitica: Essays on the Ebla Archives and Eblaite Language. Vol. 1.* Winona Lake, Eisenbrauns.

Gordon, E.I. (1959) *Sumerian Proverbs: Glimpses of Everyday Life in Ancient Mesopotamia.* Philadelphia, Museum Monographs.

Gordon, E.I. (1960) A new look at the wisdom of Sumer and Akkad. *Biblotheca Orientalis* 17:122–152.

Goring-Morris, A.N. (1989) Developments in terminal Pleistocene hunter-gatherer sociocultural systems: A perspective from the Negev and Sinai Deserts. In Hershkovitz, pp.7–28.

Goring-Morris, A.N. (1991) The Harifian of the southern Levant. In Bar-Yosef and Valla 1991b, pp.173–216.

Goring-Morris, N. (1993) From foraging to herding in the Negev and Sinai: The early to late Neolithic Transition. *Paleorient* 19(1):65 –89.

Gosline, S.L. (1994) Instrumentalists or devotees? Three 'female' figurines from Nippur. In Kenoyer 1994b, pp.193–198.

Gourou, P. (1975) *Man and Land in the Far East.* London, Longman.

Grayson, D.K. (1983) *The Establishment of Human Antiquity.* New York and London, Academic Press.

Green, M.W. (1981) The construction and implementation of the cuneiform writing system. *Visible Language* 15:345–372.

Gregoire, J.-P. (1992) Les grandes unités de transformation des céréales. L'example des minoteries de la Mésopotamie du sud à la fin du IIIe millénaire avant notre ère. In P.C. Anderson 1992b, pp.321–339.

Grimal, N. (1992) *A History of Ancient Egypt.* trans. I. Shaw. Oxford, Blackwell.

Griswold, W.A. (1992) Measuring social inequality at Armant. In Friedman and Adams, pp.193–198.

Gropp, G. (1992) A 'great bath' in Elam. In C. Jarrige, pp.113–118.

Grove, A.T. (1993) Africa's climate in the Holocene. In Shaw *et al.*, pp.32–42.

Guest, E. (1966) (ed.) *Flora of Iraq. Vol. 1. Introduction.* Baghdad, Ministry of Agriculture.

Guinan, A. (1989) The perils of high living: Divinatory rhetoric in *Summa Alu.* In Behrens *et al.*, pp.227–235.

Guisso, R.W.L., Pagani, C. and Miller, D. (1989) *The First Emperor of China.* Toronto, Stoddart.

Gunter, A.C. (1990) (ed.) *Investigating Artistic Environments in the Ancient Near East.* Washington, Smithsonian Institution Press.

Guo, D.-S. (1995a) Hongshan and related cultures. In Nelson 1995c, pp.21–64.

Guo, D.-S. (1995b) Lower Xiajiadian Culture. In Nelson 1995c, pp.147–181.

Gustavson-Gaube, C. (1981) Shams ed-Din Tannira: The Halafian pottery of Area A. *Berytus* 29:9–182.

Hackett, J. (1989) (ed.) *Warfare in the Ancient World.* London, Sidgwick and Jackson.

Hadidi, A. (1985) (ed.) *Studies in the History and Archaeology of Jordan, II.* Amman and London, Routledge.

Hadidi, A. (1987) (ed.) *Studies in the History and Archaeology of Jordan, III.* Amman and London, Routledge.

Hale, J. (1993) *The Civilization of Europe in the Renaissance.* London, HarperCollins.

Halim, M.A. (1970–71) Excavation at Sarai Khola (Part 1). *Pakistan Archaeology* 7:23–89.

Halim, M.A. (1972) Excavation at Sarai Khola (Part 2). *Pakistan Archaeology* 8:1–112.

BIBLIOGRAPHY

Hall, H.R. (1930) *A Season's Work at Ur, Al-'Ubaid, Abu Shahrain (Eridu), and Elsewhere.* London, Methuen.

Hallo, W.W. (1972) The House of Urmeme. *Journal of Near Eastern Studies* 31:87–95.

Hallo, W.W. (1976) Toward a history of Sumerian literature. In Lieberman, pp.181–203.

Hallo, W.W. (1990) The limits of skepticism. *JAOS* 110:187–199.

Halstead, P. (1990) Quantifying Sumerian agriculture: Some seeds of doubt and hope. In Postgate and Powell, pp.187–195.

Hammond, N. (1973) (ed.) *South Asian Archaeology: Papers from the First International Conference of South Asian Archaeologists held in the University of Cambridge.* London, Duckworth.

Hampson, N. (1968) *The Enlightenment.* Harmondsworth, Penguin Books.

Hamrouch, H.A. and Abu Zeid, H. (1990) Petrological and chemical analyses of some Neolithic ceramics from El Omari, Egypt. In Debono and Mortensen, pp.117–128.

Hanbury Tenison, J. (1983) The 1982 flaked stone assemblage at Jebel Aruda, Syria. *Akkadica* 33:27–33.

Hansen, D.P. (1970) Al-Hiba, 1968–69: A Preliminary Report. *Artibus Asiae* 32:243–250.

Hansen, D.P. (1992) Royal building activity at Sumerian Lagash in the Early Dynastic Period. *Biblical Archaeologist* Dec. 1992:206–211.

Hansen, J. (1992) Franchthi Cave and the beginnings of agriculture in Greece and the Aegean. In P.C. Anderson 1992b, pp.231–247.

Hansman, J. (1973) A periplus of Magan and Meluhha. *Bulletin of the School of Oriental and African Studies* (University of London) 36:554–587.

Harlan, F. (1992) Wadi and desert settlement at Predynastic Hierakonpolis. In Friedman and Adams, pp.15–18.

Harlan, J.R. (1967) A wild wheat harvest in Turkey. *Archaeology* 20:197–201.

Harlan, J.R. (1989) The tropical African cereals. In Harris and Hillman, pp.335–343.

Harlan, J.R. (1992a) Wild grass seed harvesting and implications for domestication. In P.C. Anderson 1992b, pp.21–27.

Harlan, J.R. (1992b) Indigenous African agriculture. In Cowan and Watson, pp.59–70.

Harlan, J.R. (1993) The tropical African cereals. In Shaw *et al.*, pp.53–60.

Harley, J.B. and Woodward, D. (1987) (eds) *Cartography in Prehistoric, Ancient and Mediaeval Europe and the Mediterranean.* Chicago, University of Chicago Press.

Harris, D.R. (1994) *The Archaeology of V. Gordon Childe: Proceedings of the Childe Centennial Conference held at the Institute of Archaeology, University College, London, 1992.* London, UCL Press.

Harris, D.R. (1996) (ed.) *The Origins and Spread of Agriculture and Pastoralism in Eurasia.* London, UCL Press.

Harris, D.R. and Hillman, G.C. (1989) (eds) *Foraging and Farming: The Evolution of Plant Exploitation.* London, Unwin & Hyman.

Harrison, T.P, (1993) Economics with an entrepreneurial spirit: Early Bronze trade with Late Predynastic Egypt. *Biblical Archaeologist* 56.2:81–93.

Hartel, H. (1981) (ed.) *South Asian Archaeology 1979.* Berlin, Dietrich Reimer.

Hassan, F.A. (1984) Environment and subsistence in Predynastic Egypt. In Clark and Brandt, pp.57–64.

Hassan, F.A. (1986) Desert environment and the origins of agriculture in Egypt. *Norwegian Archaeological Review* 19(2):63–76.

Hassan, F.A. (1988) The Predynastic of Egypt. *Journal of World Prehistory* 2(2):135–185.

Hassan, F.A. (1993) Town and village in ancient Egypt: Ecology, society and urbanization. In Shaw *et al.*, pp.551–569.

Hassan, F.A. and Matson, R.G. (1989) Seriation of predynastic potsherds from the Nagada region. In Krzyzaniak and Kobusiewicz, pp.303–323.

Hassan, M.A. (1989) Ras-Koh: A crossroads of ancient civilizations. In Frifelt and Sorensen, pp.189–195.

Hawass, Z.A. (1992) A burial with an unusual plaster mask in the western cemetery of Khufu's Pyramid. In Friedman and Adams, 327–336.

Hawass, Z.A., Hassan, F.A. and Gautier, A. (1987) Chronology, sediments, and subsistence at Merimda Beni Salama. *Journal of Egyptian Archaeology* 74:31–38.

Hawkes, K. (1990) Why do men hunt? Benefits for risky choices. In Cashdan 1990b, pp.145–166.

Hawkins, J.D. (1977) (ed.) Trade in the Ancient Near East: Papers presented to the XXIII Rencontre Assyriologique Internationale, 1976. *Iraq*, Vol. 39.

Hayes, T.R. (1984) A reappraisal of the Egyptian Predynastic. In Clark and Brandt, pp.65–73.

Hegmon, M. (1985) *Exchange in Social Integration and Subsistence Risk: A Computer Simulation.* Doctoral qualifying paper, Dept of Anthropology, University of Michigan.

Hegmon, M. (1986) *Sharing as Social Integration and Risk Reduction: A Computer Simulation Involving the Hopi.* Manuscript, Museum of Anthropology, University of Michigan.

Heimpel, W. (1989) The Babylonian background of the term 'Milky Way'. In Behrens *et al.*, pp.249–252.

Heimpel, W. (1994) Towards an understanding of the term Sikkum. *Revue d'Assyriologie* 88:5–31.

Heinrich, E. (1982) *Tempel und Heiligtumer im alten Mesopotamien.* Berlin, Walter de Gruyter.

Helbaek, H. (1965) Early Hassunan vegetable food at Tell es-Sawwan near Samarra. *Sumer* 20:45–48.

Helbaek, H. (1966) Pre-Pottery Neolithic farming at Beidha. *Palestine Exploration Quarterly* 98:8–72.

Helbaek, H. (1972) Samarran irrigation agriculture at Choga Mami in Iraq. *Iraq* 34:35–48.

Helmer, D. (1991) Etude de la faune de la phase 1A (Natoufien final) de Tell Mureybet (Syrie), Fouilles Cauvin. In Bar-Yosef and Valla 1991b, pp.359–370.

Hendrickx, S. (1989) *De grafvelden der Naqada-cultuur in Zuid-Egypte, met bijzondere aandacht het Naqada III grafveld te Elkab: Interne chronologie en social differentiate.* Unpublished doctoral thesis, Katholieke Universiteit te Leuven.

Hendrickx, S. (1992) The Predynastic cemeteries at Khozam. In Friedman and Adams, pp.199–202.

Henneberg, M., Kobusiewicz, M., Schild, R. and Wendorf, F. (1989) The Early Neolithic, Qarunian burial from the Northern Fayum Desert (Egypt). In Krzyzaniak and Kobusiewicz, pp.181–196.

Hennessy, J.B. (1969) Preliminary report on a first season of excavations at Teleilat Ghassul. *Levant* I:1–24.

Henrickson, E.F. (1981) Non-religious residential settlement patterning in the Late Early Dynastic of the Diyala region. *Mesopotamia* 16:43–140.

Henrickson, E.F. (1982) Functional analysis of elite residences in the Late Early Dynastic of the Diyala region. *Mesopotamia* 17:5–33.

Henrickson, E.F. (1989) Ceramic evidence for cultural interaction between the 'Ubaid tradition and the Central Zagros Highlands, Western Iran. In Henrickson and Thuesen, pp.369–404.

Henrickson, E.F. (1994) The outer limits: Settlement and economic strategies in the Central Zagros Highlands during the Uruk Era. In Stein and Rothman, pp.85–102.

Henrickson, E.F. and Thuesen, I. (1989) (eds) *Upon this Foundation – The 'Ubaid Reconsidered.* Copenhagen, Carsten Niebuhr Institute Publications 10, Museum Tusculanum Press.

Henrickson, E.F. and Vitalli, V. (1987) The Dalma tradition: Prehistoric inter-regional cultural integration in Highland Western Iran. *Paleorient* 13(2):37–45.

Henry, D.O. (1983) Adaptive evolution within the Epipalaeolithic of the Near East. *Advances in World Archaeology* 2:99–160.

Henry, D.O. (1985) Preagricultural sedentism: The Natufian example. In Price and Brown, pp.365–381.

Henry, D.O. (1989) *From Foraging to Agriculture: The Levant at the End of the Ice Age*. Philadelphia, University of Pennsylvania Press.

Henry, D.O. (1995) *Prehistoric Cultural Ecology and Evolution: Insights from Southern Jordan*. New York, Plenum.

Henry, D.O. and Garrard, A.N. (1988) Tor Hamar: An Epipalaeolithic rockshelter in Southern Jordan. *Palestine Excavation Quarterly* 120:1–25.

Henry, D.O. and Leroi-Gourhan, A. (1976) The excavation of Hayonim Terrace: An interim report. *Journal of Field Archaeology* 3:391–406.

Henry, D.O., Leroi-Gourhan, A. and Davis, S. (1981) The excavation of Hayonim Terrace: An examination of terminal Pleistocene climatic and adaptive changes. *Journal of Archaeological Science* 8:33–58.

Hermansen, D. and Gebel, H.G. (1996) More 'pillow-shaped pieces' from LPPNB Basta. *Neo-Lithics* 2/96:11.

Hershkovitz, I. (1989) (ed.) *People and Culture in Change*. Oxford BAR International Series 508.

Hershkovitz, I. and Gopher, A. (1990) Palaeodemography, burial customs and food-producing economy at the beginning of the Holocene: A perspective from the Southern Levant. *Mitekufat Haeven* 23:9–47.

Herzfeld, E.E. (1930) *Die Ausgrabungen von Samarra, Band V: Die Vorgeschichtlichen Topferein von Samarra*. Berlin.

Hijara, I.H. (1973) Fouilles de Tell Qalinj Agha. *Sumer* 29:13–34.

Hijara, I.H., Hubbard, R.N.L.B., Watson, J.P.N. and Davies, C. (1980) Arpachiya, 1976. *Iraq* 42:131–154.

Hillman, G.C. (1989) Late Palaeolithic plant foods from Wadi Kubbaniya in Upper Egypt: Dietary diversity, infant weaning, and seasonality in a riverine environment. In Harris and Hillman, pp.207–239.

Hillman, G.C., Colledge, S.M. and Harris, D.R. (1989) Plant-food economy during the Epipalaeolithic period at Tell Abu Hureyra, Syria: dietary diversity, seasonality, and modes of exploitation. In Harris and Hillman, pp.240–268.

Hillman, G.C. and Davies, M.S. (1990) Measured domestication rates in wild wheats and barley under primitive cultivation, and their archaeological implications. *Journal of World Prehistory* 4(2):157–222.

Hillman, G.C. and Davies, M.S. (1992) Domestication rate in wild wheats and barley under primitive cultivation: Preliminary results and archaeological implications of field measurements of selection coefficient. In P.C. Anderson 1992b, pp.113–158.

Ho, Ping-Ti (1977) The indigenous origins of Chinese agriculture. In Reed, pp.413–484.

Hodder, I. (1987) (ed.) *The Archaeology of Contextual Meanings*. Cambridge, Cambridge University Press.

Hodder, I., Isaac, G and Hammond, N. (1981) (eds) *Patterns of the Past: Essays in Honour of David Clarke*. Cambridge, Cambridge University Press.

Hoffman, M.A. (1979) *Egypt Before the Pharaohs: The Prehistoric Foundations of Egyptian Civilization*. New York, Dorset Press [1990].

Hoffman, M.A. (1980) An Amratian house from Hierakonpolis and its significance for prehistoric research. *Journal of Near Eastern Studies* 39:119–137.

Hoffman, M.A. (1982) *The Predynastic of Hierakonpolis*. Egyptian Studies Association, Publication No. 1, Cairo, Cairo University Herbarium.

Hoffman, M.A. (1987) (ed.) *A Final Report to the National Endowment for the Humanities on Predynastic Research at Hierakonpolis 1985–86*. Colombia, Earth Sciences and Resources Institute, University of South Carolina.

Hoffman, M.A. (1989) A stratified Predynastic sequence from Hierakonpolis (Upper Egypt). In Kryzyzaniak and Kobusiewicz, pp.317–323.

Hoffman, M.A., Hamroush, H.A. and Allen, R.O. (1986) A model of urban development for the Hierakonpolis region from Predynastic through Old Kingdom times. *Journal of the American Research Centre in Egypt* 23:175–187.

Hoffman, M.A., Hamroush, H.A. and Allen, R.O. (1987) The environment and evolution of an Early Egyptian urban centre: Archaeological and geochemical investigations at Hierakonpolis. *Geoarchaeology* 2(1):1–13.

Hoffman, M.A. and Mills, J.O. (1993) Problems of assessing environmental impact on the Predynastic settlements of Hierakonpolis. In Kryzyzaniak *et al.*, pp.359–370.

Hole, F. (1984) A reassessment of the Neolithic revolution. *Paleorient* 10(2):49–60.

Hole, F. (1987a) Issues in Near-Eastern chronology. In Aurenche *et al.*, ii:559–563.

Hole, F. (1987b) (ed.) *The Archaeology of Western Iran: Settlement and Society from Prehistory to the Islamic Conquest*. Washington, DC and London, Smithsonian Institution Press.

Hole, F. (1994) Environmental instabilities and urban origins. In Stein and Rothman, pp.121–152.

Hole, F. and Flannery, K.V. (1967) The prehistory of south-western Iran: A preliminary report. *Proceedings of the Prehistoric Society* 33:147–206.

Holmen, K. (1990) Identification of some plant remains in the El Omari Pottery. In Debono and Mortensen, pp.129–130.

Holmes, D.L. (1988) The Predynastic lithic industries of Badari, Middle Egypt: New perspectives and inter-regional relations. *World Archaeology* 20(1):70–86.

Holmes, D.L. (1989) Inter-regional variability in Egyptian Predynastic lithic assemblages. In Krzyzaniak and Kobusiewicz, pp.243–253.

Holmes, D.L. (1992a) Chipped stone-working craftsmen, Hierakonpolis and the rise of civilization in Egypt. In Friedman and Adams, pp.37–44.

Holmes, D.L. (1992b) The evidence and nature of contacts between Upper Egypt and Lower Egypt during the Predynastic: A view from Upper Egypt. In Van den Brink 1992c, pp.301–316.

Honigmann, J.J. (1973) (ed.) *Handbook of Social and Cultural Anthropology*. Chicago, Rand McNally.

Hopf, M. and Bar-Yosef, O. (1987) Plant remains from Hayonim Cave. *Paleorient* 13:117–120.

Horwitz, L.K. (1989) A reassessment of caprovine domestication in the Levantine Neolithic: Old questions, new answers. In Hershkovitz, pp.153–181.

Hovers, E. (1989) Settlement and subsistence patterns in the Lower Jordan Valley from Epipalaeolithic to Neolithic times. In Hershkovitz, pp.37–51.

Howard-Carter, T. (1989) Voyages of votive vessels in the Gulf. In Behrens *et al.*, pp.253–266.

Hsu, C.Y. (1965) *Ancient China in Transition*. Stanford, Stanford University Press.

Hsu, C.Y. (1980) *Han Agriculture*. Seattle, University of Washington Press.

Hsu, C.Y. (1986) Historical conditions of the emergence and crystallization of the Confucian system. In Eisenstadt, pp.306–324.

Hsu, C.Y. and Linduff, K.M. (1988) *Western Chou Civilization*. New Haven, Yale University Press.

Hsu, F.L.K. (1949) *Under the Ancestors' Shadow*. London, Routledge & Kegan Paul.

Huang, Tsui-mei (1992) Liangzhu: A Late Neolithic jade-yielding culture in southwestern coastal China. *Antiquity* 66:75–83.

Hubbard, R.N.L.B. (1980) Halafian agriculture and environment at Arpachiya. *Iraq* 42:153–154.

Huber, L.G.F. (1988) The Bo capital and questions concerning Xia and Early Shang. *Early China* 13:46–77.

Hunt, R.C. (1987) The role of bureaucracy in the provisioning of cities: a framework for analysis in the Ancient Near East. In Gibson and Biggs, pp.161–192.

Hunt, R.C. (1988) Hydraulic management in Southern Mesopotamia in Sumerian times. In Postgate and Powell, pp.189–206.

412

Hunt, R.C. (1995) On dry farming in Upper Mesopotamia. [Discussion of T.J. Wilkinson 1994]. *Current Anthropology* 36:289–290.

Huot, J.-L. (1989) 'Ubaidian village of Lower Mesopotamia. Permanence and evolution from 'Ubaid 0 to 'Ubaid 4 as seen from Tell el'Oueili. In Henrickson and Thuesen, pp.19–42.

Huot, J.-L. (1992) The first farmers at Oueili. *Biblical Archaeologist* Dec. 1992:188–195.

Huot, J.-L. and Vallet, R. (1990) Les habitations aux salles hypostyles d'Epoque Obeid 0 de Tell el-Oueili. *Paleorient* 16(1):125–130.

Hutton, J. (1788) Theory of the Earth: Or an investigation of the laws observable in the composition, dissolution, and restoration of land upon the globe. *Transactions of the Royal Society of Edinburgh*, I.

Inizan, M.-L. (1985–96) Tell el'Oueili: The knapped stone finds. *Sumer* 44(1–2):120–122.

Issawi, B. and McCauley, J.F. (1992) The Cenozoic rivers of Egypt: The Nile problem. In Friedman and Adams, pp.121–138.

Iversen, E. (1990) Metrology and canon [in Egyptian art]. *MDAIK* 46:113–125.

Jacobsen, T. (1939) *The Sumerian Kinglist. (Oriental Institute) Assyriological Studies No. 11*, Chicago, University of Chicago Press.

Jacobsen, T. (1953) The myth of Inanna and Bilulu. *Journal of Near Eastern Studies* 12:160–187.

Jacobsen, T. (1957) Early political development in Mesopotamia. *Zeitschrift für Assyriologie, Neue Folge* 18(52):91–140.

Jacobsen, T. (1976) *The Treaasures of Darkness: A History of Mesopotamian Religion*. New Haven, Yale University Press.

Jacobsen, T. (1978–9) Iphur-Kishi and his times. *Archiv für Orientforschung* 26:1–14.

Jacobsen, T. (1980) Sumer and Akkad. In Cotterell, pp.72–89.

Jacobsen, T. (1987) Pictures and pictorial language (The Burney Relief). In Mindlin *et al.*, pp.1–11.

Jacobsen, T. (1989a) Lugalbanda and Ninsuna. *Journal of Cuneiform Studies* 41(1):69–86.

Jacobsen, T. (1989b) God or worshipper. In Leonard and Williams: chapter 9.

Jacobsen, T. (1993) The descent of Enki. In Cohen *et al.*, pp.120–123.

Jacobson, J. (1987a) The Harappan Civilization: An early state. In Jacobson 1987b, pp.137–173.

Jacobson, J. (1987b) (ed.) *Studies in the Archaeology of India and Pakistan*. Warminster, Aris & Phillips with the American Institute of Indian Studies.

James, T.G.H. (1979) *An Introduction to Ancient Egypt*. London, British Museum Publications.

James, T.G.H. (1982) (ed.) *Excavating in Egypt: The Egypt Exploration Society, 1882–1982*. Chicago, University of Chicago Press.

James, T.G.H. (1983) Early travellers in Egypt. In Smith and Hall, pp.11–24.

James, T.G.H. (1984) *Pharaoh's People, Scenes from Life in Imperial Egypt*. London, Bodley Head.

Jansen, M. (1979) Architectural problems of the Harappa Culture. In Taddei, I:405–431.

Jansen, M. (1989a) Some problems regarding the *forma urbis* Mohenjo-Daro. In Frifelt and Sorensen, pp.247–254.

Jansen, M. (1989b) Water supply and sewage disposal at Mohenjo-daro. *World Archaeology* 21(2):177–192.

Jansen, M. (1992) Non-contemporeity of the contemporaneous in the Indus Culture. In Possehl, pp.209–222.

Jansen, M. (1994) Mohenjo-Daro, type site of the earliest urbanizing process in South Asia: Ten years of research at Mohenjo-daro, Pakistan. In Parpola and Koskikallio, I:263–280.

Jarrige, C. (1992) (ed.) *South Asian Archaeology 1989*. Madison, Wisconsin, *Monographs in World Archaeology*, No. 14.

Jarrige, C. (1994) The Mature Indus phase at Nausharo as seen from a block of period III. In Parpola and Koskikallio, I:295–313.

Jarrige, J.F. (1981) Economy and society in the early Chalcolithic Bronze Age of Baluchistan: New perspectives from recent excavations at Mehrgarh. In Hartel, pp.93–114.

Jarrige, J.F. (1982) Excavations at Mehrgarh: Their significance for understanding the background of the Harappan Civilization. In Possehl, pp.79–84.

Jarrige, J.F. (1984) Chronology of the earlier periods of the Greater Indus as seen from Mehrgarh, Pakistan. In B. Allchin, pp.21–28.

Jarrige, J.F. (1989) Excavations at Nausharo 1987–88. *Pakistan Archaeology* 24:21–67.

Jarrige, J.F. (1990) Excavations at Nausharo 1988–89. *Pakistan Archaeology* 25:193–240.

Jarrige, J.F. (1994) The final phase of the Indus occupation at Nausharo and its connection with the following cultural complex of Mehrgarh VIII. In Parpola and Koskikallio, I:295–313.

Jarrige, J.F. and Hassan, M.U. (1989) Funerary complexes in Baluchistan at the end of the third millennium in the light of recent discoveries at Mehrgarh and Quetta. In Frifelt and Sorensen, pp.150–166.

Jarrige, J.F. and Lechevalier, M. (1979) Excavations at Mehgarh, Baluchistan: Their significance in the prehistorical context of the Indo-Pakistan borderlands. In Taddei, II:463–536.

Jarrige, J.F. and Meadow, R.H. (1980) The antecedents of civilization in the Indus Valley. *Scientific American* 243:102–110.

Jarrige, J.F. and Meadow, R.H. (1992) Melanges Fairservice: A discourse on relations between Kachi and Sindh in Prehistory. In Possehl, pp.163–178.

Jasim, S.A. (1985) *The Ubaid Period in Iraq: Recent Excavations in the Hamrin Region.* Oxford, BAR International Series No. 267. 2 vols, text and figs.

Jasim, S.A. (1989) Structure and function in an 'Ubaid village. In Henrickson and Thuesen, pp.79–90.

Jasim, S.A. and Oates, J. (1986) Early tokens and tablets in Mesopotamia: New information from Tell Abada and Tell Brak. *World Archaeology* 17(3): 348–360.

Jenkins, P.C. (1994a) Cemetery R37: New perspectives on style and chronology. In Kenoyer 1994b, pp.105–112.

Jenkins, P.C. (1994b) Continuity and change in the ceramic sequence at Harappa. In Parpola and Koskikallio, I:315–328.

Johnson, A.W. and Earle, T. (1987) *The Evolution of Human Societies: From Foraging Group to Agrarian State.* Stanford, California, Stanford University Press.

Jones, T.B. and Snyder, J.W. (1961) *Sumerian Economic Texts from the Third Ur Dynasty: A Catalogue and Discussion of Documents from Various Collections.* Minneapolis, University of Minnesota Press.

Joshi, J.P. (1979) The nature of settlement of Surkotada. In Agrawal and Chakrabarti, pp.59–64.

Joshi, J.P., Bala, M. and Ram, J. (1984) The Indus Civilization: A reconsideration on the basis of distribution maps. In Lal *et al.*, pp.511–530.

Kafafi, Z.A. (1988) Jebel Abu Thawwab. A Pottery Neolithic village in north Jordan. In Garrard and Gebel, pp.451–471.

Kafafi, Z.A. (1993) The Yarmoukians in Jordan. *Paleorient* 19(1):101–114.

Kafafi, Z.A. and Rollefson, G. (1995) The 1994 Excavation Season at 'Ayn Ghazal: Preliminary Report. *Annual of the Department of Antiquities of Jordan* 39:13–29.

Kaiser, W. (1957) Zur innern Chronologie der Naqadakultur. *Archaeologia Geographica* 6:69–77.

Kaiser, W. (1985) Zur Sudausdehnung der vorgeschichtlichen Delta-Kulturen und zur frühen Entwicklung Oberägyptens. *Mitteilungen des Deutschen Archäologischen Instituts, Abteilung Kairo* 41:61–71.

Kaiser, W. (1990) Zur Enstehung des gesamtägyptischen Staats. *MDAIK* 47:287–299.

Kao, C.H. (1986) An introduction to Shang and Chou Bronze *Nao* excavated in South China. In K.C. Chang 1986b, pp.275–300.

Kaplan, J. (1960) The relation of the Chalcolithic pottery of Palestine to Halafian ware. *BASOR* 159:32–36.

Katz, D. (1987) Gilgamesh and Akka: Was Uruk ruled by two assemblies? *Revue d'Assyriologie* 81:105–114.

Kaufman, D. (1986) A reconsideration of adaptive change in the Levantine Neolithic. In Straus, pp.117–128.

Kaufman, D. (1988) New radiocarbon dates for the Geometric Kebaran. *Paleorient* 14(1): 107–109.

Kaufman, D. (1989) Observations on the Geometric Kebaran: A view from Neve David. In Bar Yosef and Vandermeersch, pp.275–285.

Kaufman, D. (1990) The transition to the Natufian, *Mitekufat Haeven* 23:180.

Keay, J. (1991) *The Honourable Company: A History of the English East India Company*. London, HarperCollins.

Keeley, L.H. (1988) Hunter-gatherer economic complexity and 'population pressure': A cross-cultural analysis. *Journal of Anthropological Archaeology* 7:373–411.

Keeley, L. (1992) The use of plant foods among hunter-gatherers: a cross-cultural survey. In P.C. Anderson 1992b, pp.29–38.

Kees, H. (1961) *Ancient Egypt: A Cultural Topography*. London, Faber & Faber.

Keightley, D.N. (1977) Ping-Ti Ho and the origins of Chinese civilization (Review Article). *Harvard Journal of Asiatic Studies* 37:381–411.

Keightley, D.N. (1978a) *Sources of Shang History*. Berkeley and Los Angeles, University of California Press.

Keightley, D.N. (1978b) The Bamboo Annals and Shang chronology. *Harvard Journal of Asiatic Studies* 38:423–438.

Keightley, D.N. (1983) (ed.) *The Origins of Chinese Civilization*. Berkeley, University of California Press.

Keightley, D.N. (1987) Archaeology and mentality: The making of China. *Representations* 18:91–128.

Keightley, D.N. (1995) Review of Nelson (ed.) *The Times Higher Education Supplement*, 6 Dec. p.24.

Keith, M.S. and Armelagos, G.L. (1988) An example of in vivo tetracycline labelling: Reply to Piepenbrink. *Journal of Archaeological Science* 15:595–601.

Kemp, B.J. (1966) Abydos and the royal tombs of the First Dynasty. *JEA* 52:13–22.

Kemp, B.J. (1967) The Egyptian First Dynasty royal cemetery. *Antiquity* 41:22–32.

Kemp, B.J. (1972) Temple and town in Ancient Egypt. In Ucko *et al.*, pp.657–680.

Kemp, B.J. (1975) Dating Pharaonic cemeteries. Part 1: non-mechanical approaches to seriation. *MDAIK* 31:259–291.

Kemp, B.J. (1977) The early development of towns in Egypt. *Antiquity* 51:185–200.

Kemp, B.J. (1982a) Automatic analysis of predynastic cemeteries: A new method for an old problem. *Journal of Egyptian Archaeology* 68:5–15.

Kemp, B.J. (1982b) Abydos. In James, pp.71–88.

Kemp, B.J. (1989) *Ancient Egypt: Anatomy of a Civilization*. London, Routledge.

Kendall, D.G. (1963) A statistical approach to Flinders Petrie's sequence dating. *Bulletin of the International Statistical Institute* 40:657–680.

Kennedy, K.A.R. and Lovell, N. (1989) Morphology, diet and pathology. *Pakistan Archaeology* 24:94–107.

Kenoyer, J.M. (1989a) Socio-economic structures of the Indus civilization as reflected in specialized crafts and the question of ritual segregation. In Kenoyer 1989b, pp.183–192.

Kenoyer, J.M. (1989b) (ed.) *Old Problems and New Perspectives in the Archaeology of South Asia. Wisconsin Archaeological Reports Vol. 2*. Madison, University of Wisconsin, Dept of Anthropology.

Kenoyer, J.M. (1991a) The Indus Valley tradition of Pakistan and Western India. *Journal of World Prehistory* 5(4):331–385.

Kenoyer, J.M. (1991b) Urban process in the Indus tradition: A preliminary model from Harappa. In Meadow 1991b, pp. 29–60.

Kenoyer, J.M. (1994a) The Harappan State, was it or wasn't it? In Kenoyer 1994b, pp.71–80.

Kenoyer, J.M. (1994b) (ed.) *From Sumer to Meluhha: Contributions to the Archaeology of South and West Asia in Memory of George F. Dales, Jr. Wisconsin Archaeological Reports, Vol. 3.* Madison, Wisconsin, Prehistory Press.

Kenoyer, J.M., Vidale, M. and Bhan, K.K. (1991) Contemporary stone beadmaking in Khambat, India: Patterns of craft specialization and organization of production as reflected in the archaeological record. *World Archaeology* 21(1):44–63.

Kerner, S. (1991) (ed.) *The Near East In Antiquity: German Contributions to the Archaeology of Jordan, Palestine, Syria, Lebanon and Egypt, Vol. II.* Amman, German Protestant Institute for Archaeology of the Holy Land.

Kersten, A.M.P. (1989) The Epipalaeolithic ungulate remains from Ksar'Akil: Some preliminary results. In Hershkovitz, pp.183–198.

Kesarwani, A. (1984) Harappan gateways: A functional reassessment. In Lal *et al.*, pp.63–73.

Khan, F.A. (1965) Excavations at Kot Diji. *Pakistan Archaeology* 2:11–85.

Kilmer, A.D. (1960a) Two new lists of key numbers for mathematical operations. *Orientalia* 29:273–308.

Kilmer, A.D. (1960b) Sumerian and Akkadian names for designs and geometric shapes. In Gunter, pp.83–91.

Kilmer, A.D. (1987) The symbolism of the flies in the Mesopotamian flood myth and some further implications. In Rochberg-Halton, pp.175–180.

Kim, S.O. (1994) Burials, pigs, and political prestige in Neolithic China. *Current Anthropology* 35(2):119–141.

King, D.A. (1993) Folk astronomy in the service of religion: The case of Islam. In Ruggles and Saunders, pp.124–138.

Kirch, P.V. (1991) Prehistoric exchange in Western Melanesia. *Annual Review of Anthropology* 20:141–165.

Kirchhoff, P. (1935) The principles of clanship in human society. In M. Fried, *Readings in Anthropology*, II:260–270. New York, Thomas Y. Crowell [1968].

Kirkbride, D. (1966) Five seasons at the Pre-Pottery Neolithic site of Beidha in Jordan: A summary. *Palestine Exploration Quarterly* 98:8–61.

Kirkbride, D. (1967) Beidha 1965: an interim report. *Palestine Exploration Quarterly* 99:5–13.

Kirkbride, D. (1968) Beidha: Early Neolithic village life south of the Dead Sea. *Antiquity* 42:263–274.

Kirkbride, D. (1969) Early Byblos and the Beqa'a. *MUSJ* 45:53–59.

Kirkbride, D. (1972) Umm Dhabaghiya. *Iraq* 34:3–15.

Kirkbride, D. (1973a) Umm Dhabaghiya, 1972: A second preliminary report. *Iraq* 35:1–7.

Kirkbride, D. (1973b) Umm Dhabaghiya 1973: A third preliminary report. *Iraq* 35:205–209.

Kirkbride, D. (1974) Umm Dhabaghiya: A trading outpost? *Iraq* 36:85–92.

Kirkbride, D. (1975) Umm Dhabaghiya 1974: A fourth preliminary report. *Iraq* 37:3–10.

Kislev, M.E. (1985) Early Neolithic horsebean from Yiftah'el, Israel. *Science* 228:319–330.

Kislev, M.E. (1988) Nahal Hemar cave, desiccated plant remains: An interim report. *'Atiqout* 18:76–81.

Kislev, M.E. (1989) Pre-domesticated cereals in the Pre-Pottery Neolithic A Period. In Hershkovitz, pp.147–151.

Kislev, M.E. (1992) Agriculture in the Near East in the 7th millennium BC. In P.C. Anderson 1992b, pp.87–93.

Kislev, M.E., Bar-Yosef, O. and Gopher, A. (1986) Early Neolithic domesticated and wild barley from the Netiv Hagdud region in the Jordan Valley. *Israel Journal of Botany* 35:197–201.

Kislev, M.E., Nadel, D. and Carmi, I. (1992) Epipalaeolithic (19,000 BP) cereal and fruit diet at Ohalo II, Sea of Galilee, Israel. *Review of Paleobotany and Palynology* 73:161–166.

Kitchen, K.A. (1964) Some new light on the Asiatic wars of Ramesses II. *Journal of Egyptian Archaeology* 50:47–70.

Kitchen, K.A. (1975) *Ramesside Inscriptions, I*. Oxford, Blackwell Publishers. Vol. VIII (1990).

Kitchen, K.A. (1987) The basics of Egyptian chronology in relation to the Bronze Age. In Astrom, pp.37–55.

Kitchen, K.A. (1991) The chronology of ancient Egypt. *World Archaeology* 23(2):201–208.

Kitchen, K.A. (1993) The land of Punt. In Shaw *et al.*, pp.587–608.

Knight, C. and Maisels, C.K. (1994) An instinct for revolution (on selfish-gene theory and the origins of culture). *Anthropology Today* 10(6):20–22.

Knight, C., Power, C. and Watts, I. (1995) The human symbolic revolution: A Darwinian account. *Cambridge Archaeological Journal* 5(1):75–114.

Knox, R. (1994) Review of Parpola 1994. *The Times Higher Education Supplement*, 9 Dec.

Koeppel, R. (1940) *Teleilat Ghasul II*. Rome, Pontifical Biblical Institute.

Kohl, P. (1989) The use and abuse of world systems theory: The case of the 'pristine' West Asian state. In C.C. Lamberg-Karlovsky, pp.218–240.

Kohl, P. (1992) The Jura-Araxes 'chiefdom/state': The problems of evolutionary labels and imperfect analogies. In Possehl, pp.223–232.

Kohler, C. (1992) The Pre- and Early Dynastic Pottery of Tell el-Fara'in (Buto). In Van den Brink 1992c, pp.11–22.

Kohler-Rollefson, I. (1988) The aftermath of the Levantine Neolithic revolution in the light of the ecological and ethnographic evidence. *Paleorient* 14(1):87–93.

Kohler-Rollefson, I. (1989) Changes in goat exploitation at 'Ain Ghazal between the early and late Neolithic: a metrical analysis. *Paleorient* 15(1):141–146.

Kohler-Rollefson, I., Gillespie W. and Metzger, M. (1988) The fauna from Neolithic 'Ain Ghazal. In Garrard and Gebel, II: 423–430.

Kohler-Rollefson, I., Quintero, L. and Rollefson, G.O. (1993) A brief note on the fauna from Neolithic 'Ain Ghazal. *Paleorient* 19(2):95–96.

Kozlowski, J.K. (1989) Nemrik 9, a PPN Neolithic site in Northern Iraq. *Paleorient* 15(1):25–31.

Koslowski, J.K. and Ginter, B. (1989) The Fayum Neolithic in the light of new discoveries. In Krzyzaniak and Kobusiewicz, pp.157–179.

Koslowski, J.K. and Ginter, B. (1993) Holocene changes in the Fayum: Lake Moeris and the evolution of climate in northeastern Africa. In Krzyzaniak *et al.*, pp.327–336.

Koslowski, J.K. and Kempisty, A. (1990) Architecture of the pre-pottery Neolithic settlement in Nemrik, Iraq. *World Archaeology* 21(3):348–362.

Koslowski, J.K. and Szymczak, K. (1989) Flint industry from House 1/1A/1B at the PPN site in Nemrik 9, Northern Iraq. *Paleorient* 15(1):32–42.

Kovacs, M.G. (1989) *The Epic of Gilgamesh*. Stanford, Stanford University Press.

Kramer, S.N. (1949) Schooldays, a Sumerian composition relating to the education of a scribe. *Journal of the American Oriental Society* 69:199–215.

Kramer, S.N. (1961a) Mythology of Sumer and Akkad. In Kramer 1961b, pp.95–137.

Kramer, S.N. (1961b) (ed.) *Mythologies of the Ancient World*. New York, Doubleday.

Kramer, S.N. (1963) *The Sumerians: Their History, Culture, and Character*. Chicago and London, Chicago University Press.

Krispijn, Th.J.H. (1993) The Early Mesopotamian lexical lists and the dawn of linguistics. *Jaarbericht Ex Oriente Lux* 32:12–22.

Kristiansen, K. (1981) A social history of Danish archaeology (1805–1975). In Daniel, pp.20–44.

Kroeper, K. (1992) Tombs of the elite in Minshat Abu Omar. In Van den Brink 1992c, pp.127–150.

Kroeper, K. and Kryzyzaniak, L. (1992) Two ivory boxes from Early Dynastic graves in Minshat Abu Omar. In Friedman and Adams, pp.207–214.

Kropelin, S. (1989) Untersuchungen zum Sedimentationsmilieu von Playas im Gilf Kebir (Sudwest-Ägypten). In Kuper, pp.183–230.

Krzyzaniak, L. (1989) Recent archaeological evidence on the earliest settlement in the eastern Nile delta. In Krzyzaniak and Kobusiewicz, pp.267–285.

Krzyzaniak, L. (1992) Again on the earliest settlement at Minshat Abu Omar. In Van den Brink 1992c, pp.151–156.

Krzyzaniak, L. (1993) New data on the late prehistoric settlement at Minshat Abu Omar, Eastern Nile Delta. In Krzyzaniak et al., pp.321–325.

Krzyzaniak, L. and Kobusiewicz, M. (1989) (eds) *Late Prehistory of the Nile Basin and the Sahara. Studies in African Archaeology Vol. 2*. Poznan, Poznan Archaeological Museum.

Krzyzaniak, L., Kobusiewicz, M. and Alexander, J. (1993) (eds) *Environmental Change and Human Culture in the Nile Basin and Northern Africa until the Second Millennium* B.C.. Poznan, Poznan Archaeological Museum.

Kuijt, I. (1996) Where are the microlithics? Lithic technology and Neolithic chronology as seen from the PPNA occupation at Dhra', Jordan. *Neo-Lithics* 2/96:7–8.

Kuijt, I., Mabry, J. and Palumbo, G. (1991) Early Neolithic use of upland areas of Wadi el-Yabis: Preliminary evidence from the excavations of 'Iraq ed-Dubb, Jordan. *Paleorient* 17(1):99–108.

Kuper, R. (1989) (ed.) *Forschungen zur Umweltgeschichte der Ostsahara; Africa Praehistorica 2*. Cologne, Heinrich-Barth-Institut.

Lal, B.B. (1970–1) Perhaps the earliest ploughed field so far excavated anywhere in the world. *Puratattva: Bulletin of the Indian Archaeological Society* 4:1–3.

Lal, B.B. (1979) Kalibangan and Indus Civilization. In Agrawal and Chakrabarti, pp.65–97.

Lal, B.B. (1984) Some reflections on the structural remains at Kalibangan. In Lal et al., pp.55–62.

Lal, B.B. (1994) Chronological horizon of the mature Indus Civilization. In Kenoyer 1994b, pp.15–25.

Lal, B.B., Gupta, S.P, and Asthana, S. (1984) (eds) *Frontiers of the Indus Civilization: Sir Mortimer Wheeler Commemoration Volume*. New Delhi, Books & Books.

Lamberg-Karlovsky, C.C. (1989) (ed.) *Archaeological Thought in America*. Cambridge, Cambridge University Press.

Lambert, W.G. (1967) *Babylonian Wisdom Literature*. Oxford, Clarendon Press.

Lambert, W.G. (1987a) Devotion: The languages of religion and love. In Mindlin et al., pp.25–39.

Lambert, W.G. (1987b) A further attempt at the Babylonian 'Man and His God'. In Rochberg-Halton, pp.187–202.

Lambert, W.G. (1989) Notes on a work of the most ancient Semitic literature. *Journal of Cuneiform Studies* 41(1):1–33.

Lambrick, H.T. (1964) *Sind: A General Introduction (History of Sind Series, Vol. 1)*. Hyderabad.

Lamdan, M. and Ronen, A. (1989) Middle and Upper Palaeolithic blades in the Levant. In Hershkovitz, pp.29–36.

Lanpo, J. and Weiwen, H. (1985a) The Late Palaeolithic of China. In Rukang and Olsen, pp.211–223.

Lanpo, J. and Weiwen, H. (1985b) On the recognition of China's Palaeolithic cultural traditions. In Rukang and Olsen, pp.259–265.

Lapidus, I.M. (1969) (ed.) *Middle Eastern Cities*. Berkeley and Los Angeles, University of California Press.

LaPlaca, P.J. and Powell, M.A. (1990) The agricultural cycle and the calendar at Pre-Sargonic Girsu. In Postgate and Powell, pp.75–104.

Larsen, M.T. (1976) The Old Assyrian City-State and its Colonies. *Mesopotamia* Vol. 4. Copenhagen, Akademisk Forlag.

Larsen, M.T. (1987) The Mesopotamian lukewarm mind: Reflections on science, divination and literacy. In Rochberg-Halton, pp.203–225.

Latham, R. (1951) *The Nature of the Universe (Lucretius' De Rerum Natura)*. Harmondsworth, Penguin.

Layard, A.H. (1849) *Nineveh and its Remains*, 2 vols. London, John Murray.

Layard, A.H. (1853) *Discoveries in the Ruins of Nineveh and Babylon; with travels in Armenia, Kurdistan and the desert: Being the Result of a Second Expedition Undertaken for the Trustees of the British Museum*. London, John Murray.

Layard, A.H. (1867) *Nineveh and its Remains. A Narrative of an Expedition to Assyria during the years 1845, 1846 and 1847*. New edition of the abridgement of *Nineveh and its Remains* [1851]. London, John Murray.

Leacock, E. and Lee, R. (1982) *Politics and History in Band Societies*. Cambridge, Cambridge University Press.

Lebeau, M. (1985–86) A first report on pre-Eridu pottery from Tell el-'Oueili. *Sumer* 44(1–2):88–119.

LeBlanc, S.A. and Watson, P.J. (1973) A comparative statistical analysis of painted pottery from seven Halafian sites. *Paleorient* 1:117–133.

Le Brun, A. (1978) Chantier de l'Acropole I. *Paleorient* 4:177–192.

Le Brun, A. and Vallat, F. (1978) L'origine de l'écriture a Suse. *Cahiers de la Délégation Archéologique Française en Iran* 8:11–70.

Lechevallier, M. (1984) The flint industry of Mehrgarh. In B. Allchin, pp.41–51.

Lechevallier, M., Philibert, D., Ronen, A. and Samzun, A. (1989) Une Occupation Khiamienne et Sultanienne à Hatoula (Israel)? *Paleorient* 15(1):1–10.

Lechevallier, M. and Ronen, A. (1985) Le Site Natoufien-Khiamien de Hatoula, près de Latroun, Israel. *Le cahiers de C.R.F.J. No. 1*. Jerusalem, C.R.F.J.

Leemans, W.F. (1975) The role of landlease in Mesopotamia in the early second millennium BC. *JESHO* 18:134–145.

Leemans, W.F. (1986) The family in the economic life of the Old Babylonian period. *Oikumene* 5:15–22.

Legge, A.J. and Rowley-Conwy, P.A. (1987) Gazelle killing in Stone Age Syria. *Scientific American* 257:76–83.

Lei Congyun (1996) Neolithic sites of religious significance. In Rawson 1996a, pp.219–224.

Leick, G. (1988) *A Dictionary of Near Eastern Architecture*. London, Routledge.

Leick, G. (1991) *A Dictionary of Near Eastern Mythology*. London, Routledge.

Leick, G. (1994) *Sex and Eroticism in Mesopotamian Literature*. London, Routledge.

Le Mort, F. (1989) PPNA burials from Hatoula (Israel). In Hershkovitz, pp.133–140.

Leonard, A. and Williams, B. (1989) (eds) *Essays in Ancient Civilization Presented to Helen J. Kantor*. SAOC 47, Chicago, Oriental Institute.

Leroi-Gourhan, A. and Darmon, F. (1991) Analyses polliniques de stations natoufiennes au Proche-Orient. In Bar-Yosef and Valla 1991b, pp.21–26.

Leshnik, L.S. (1973) Land use and ecological factors in prehistoric North-West India. In N. Hammond, pp.67–84.

Lesko, L.H. (1991) Ancient Egyptian cosmogonies and cosmology. In Shafer, pp.89–122.

Levy, T. (1983) The emergence of specialized pastoralism in the southern Levant. *World Archaeology* 15:15–36.

Levy, T. (1986) The Chalcolithic period. *Biblical Archaeologist* 49:82–108.

Lewis, I.M. (1996) 'Descent'. In Barnard and Spencer, pp.151–154.

Lewis, M.E. (1990) *Sanctioned Violence in Early China*. Albany, State University of New York Press.

Lewis, O. (1955) Peasant culture in India and Mexico: A comparative analysis. In Marriott 1955a, pp.145–170.

Li Chi (1977) *Anyang*. Washington, University of Washington Press.

Liancheng, L. (1993) Chariot and horse burials in Ancient China. *Antiquity* 67:824–838.

Lieberman, D.E. (1991) Seasonality and gazelle hunting in Hayonim Cave: New evidence for 'sedentism' during the Natufian. *Paleorient* 17(1):47–57.

Lieberman, S.J. (1976) (ed.) *Sumerological Studies in Honor of Thorkild Jacobsen*. The Oriental Institute of the University of Chicago, Assyriological Studies No. 20. Chicago and London, The University of Chicago Press.

Limbrey, S. (1990) Edaphic opportunism? A discussion of soil factors in relation to the beginnings of plant husbandry in south-west Asia. *World Archaeology* 22(1):45–52.

Limet, H. (1986) Croyances, superstitions, et débuts de la science en Mésopotamie ancienne. *Oikumene* 5:67–90.

Linduff, K.M. (1995) Zhukaigou, steppe culture and the rise of Chinese civilization. *Antiquity* 69:133–145.

Lipinski, E. (1979) (ed.) *State and Temple Economy in the Ancient Near East*. 2 vols. Leuven, Orientalia Lovaniensa Analecta 6.

Little, D. (1989) *Understanding Peasant China*. New Haven, Yale University Press.

Litynska, M. (1993) Plant remains from the Neolithic site at Armant: preliminary report. In Krzyzaniak *et al.*, pp.351–354.

Liu, Jun (1985) Some observations on the archaeological site of Hemudu, Hejiang province, China. *Bulletin of the Indo-Pacific Prehistory Association* 6:40–45.

Liverani, M. (1990) The shape of Neo-Sumerian fields. In Postgate and Powell, pp.147–186.

Liverani, M. (1993a) Akkad: An introduction. In Liverani 1993c, pp.1–10.

Liverani, M. (1993b) *Model and Actualization. The Kings of Akkad in the Historical Tradition*. In Liverani 1993c, pp.41–67.

Liverani, M. (1993c) (ed.) *Akkad, the First World Empire: Structure, Ideology, Traditions*. Padua, History of the Ancient Near East/Studies – 5 (Hane/S – Vol.5).

Liverani, M. (1996) Reconstructing the rural landscape of the Ancient Near East. *Journal of the Economic and Social History of the Orient. (JESHO)* 39(1):1–41.

Lloyd, S. (1978) *The Archaeology of Mesopotamia: From the Old Stone Age to the Persian Conquest*. London, Thames & Hudson.

Lloyd, S. (1980) *Foundations in the Dust: The Story of Mesopotamian Exploration*. Revised edn, London, Thames & Hudson.

Lloyd, S. and Safar, F. (1945) Tell Hassuna: Excavations by the Iraq Government Directorate General of Antiquities in 1943 and 1944. *Journal of Near Eastern Studies* 4:255–289.

Loewe, M. (1974) *Crisis and Conflict in Han China*. London, Allen & Unwin.

Loewe, M. (1995) *Divination, Mythology and Monarchy in Han China*. Cambridge, Cambridge University Press.

Loftus, W.K. (1857) *Travels and Researches in Chaldea and Susiana: With an Account of Excavations at Warka, the 'Erech' of Nimrod, and Shush, 'Shushan the palace' of Esther, in 1849–52*. London, James Nisbet & Co.

Lovell, N.C. and Kennedy, K.A.R. (1989) Society and disease in prehistoric South Asia. In Kenoyer 1989b, pp.89–92.

Low, B.S. (1990) Human responses to environmental extremeness and uncertainty: A cross-cultural perspective. In Cashdan 1990b, pp.259–278.

Lucas, A. (1962) *Ancient Egyptian Materials and Industries*. 4th rev. edn by J.R. Harris, London, Edward Arnold.

Lucretius (Titus Lucretius Carus) *De Rerum Natura (On the Nature of Things)*. See Latham 1951 (trans.).

Lukacs, J.R. (1992a) CA comment on 'The Osteological Paradox'. *Current Anthropology* 33(4).

Lukacs, J.R. (1992b) Dental palaeopathology and agricultural intensification in South Asia: New evidence from Bronze Age Harappa. *American Journal of Physical Anthropology* 87(1):133–150.

Lukacs, J.R. (1994) The osteological paradox and the Indus Civilization: Problems inferring health from human skeletons at Harappa. In Kenoyer 1994b, pp.143–155.

Lukacs, J.R. and Joshi, M.R. (1992) Enamel hypoplasia prevalence in three ethnic groups of northwest India: A test of daughter neglect and a framework for the past. *Journal of Palaeopathology, Monographic Publications No. 2*, A.H. Goodman and L.L. Capasso (eds).

Lukacs, J.R. and Minderman, L. (1992) Dental pathology and agricultural intensification from Neolithic to Chalcolithic Periods at Mehrgarh (Baluchistan, Pakistan). In C. Jarrige, pp.167–179.

Lupton, A. (1996) *Stability and Change: Socio-political Development in North Mesopotamia and South-East Anatolia 4000–2700 BC.* Oxford, BAR/Tempus Reparatum Int. Series 627.

McAdam, E. (1997) The Figurines from the 1982–5 Seasons of Excavations at Ain Ghazal. LEVANT 29:115–145.

McArdle, J. (1990) Halafian fauna at Girikihaciyan. In Watson and Le Blanc, pp.109–120.

McArdle, J.E. (1992) Preliminary observations on the mammalian fauna from Predynastic localities at Hierakonpolis. In Friedman and Adams, pp.53–56.

McCorriston, J. (1992) The Halaf environment and human activities in the Khabur drainage, Syria. *Journal of Field Archaeology*, 19(3):315–333.

McCorriston, J. (1994) Acorn eating and agricultural origins: California ethnographics as analogues for the ancient Near East. *Antiquity* 68:97–107.

McCorriston, J. and Hole, F. (1991) The ecology of seasonal stress and the origins of agriculture in the Near East. *American Anthropologist.* 95:46–69.

McCown, D.H. and Haines, R.C. (1967) *Nippur I. Temple of Enlil, Scribal Quarter and Soundings.* Chicago, Oriental Institute of the University of Chicago, OIP 78.

Ma Chengyuan (1980) The splendour of Ancient Chinese bronzes. In Fong, pp.1–19.

McIntosh, R.J. (1991) Early urban clusters in China and Africa: The arbitration of social ambiguity. *Journal of Field Archaeology* 18(2):199–212.

Mackay, E.J.H. (1935) *The Indus Civilization.* London, Lovat, Dickinson & Thompson.

Mackay, E.J.H. (1938) *Further Excavations at Mohenjo-daro, I–II.* Delhi, Government of India Press.

Mackay, E.J.H. (1943) *Chanhu-daro Excavations, 1935–36.* New Haven, Connecticut, American Oriental Series, 20.

McKinnon, M. (1990) *Arabia.* London and New York, Guild Publishing.

Maeda, T. (1979) On the agricultural festivals in Sumer. *Acta Sumerologica* 1:19–33.

Maeda, T. (1984) 'King of the Four Regions' in the Dynasty of Akkad. *Orient (Journal of the Society for Near Eastern Studies in Japan)* 20:67–82.

Maeda, T. (1985) 'King as Law Giver' in the Ur III Dynasty. *Orient* 21:31–45.

Maekawa, K. (1976) The erin-people in Lagash in Ur III times. *RA* 70:9–44.

Maekawa, K. (1980) Female weavers and their children in Lagash. *ASJ* 2:81–125.

Maekawa, K. (1981) The Agricultural Texts of Ur III Lagash of the British Museum. *Acta Sumerologica* 3:37–61.

Maekawa, K. (1982) The Agricultural Texts of Ur III Lagash of the British Museum (II). *Acta Sumerologica* 4:85–127.

Maekawa, K. (1986) The Agricultural Texts of Ur III Lagash of the British Museum (IV). *Zinbun: Memoirs of the Research Institute for the Humanistic Studies, Kyoto University (Kyoto)* 21:91–157.

Maekawa, K. (1987a) The Agricultural Texts of Ur III Lagash of the British Museum (V). *Acta Sumerologica* No. 9. Middle Easter Culture Centre in Japan (Mitaka).

Maekawa, K. (1987b) Collective labor-service in Girsu-Lagash. In Powell, pp.49–71.

Maekawa, K. (1988) New texts on the collective labor service of the erin-people of Ur III Girsu. *ASJ* 10:37–94.

Maekawa, K. (1989a) Rations, wages and economic trends in the Ur III period. *Altorientalische Forschungen (AOF)* 16:42–50.

Maekawa, K. (1989b) The Agricultural Texts of Ur III Lagash of the British Museum (VI). *Acta Sumerologica* 11:113–144.

Maekawa, K. (1990) Cultivation methods in the Ur III period. In Postgate and Powell, pp.115–145.

Mahadevan, I. (1977) *The Indus Script: Texts, Concordance and Tables*. New Delhi, Archaeological Survey of India.

Maisels, C.K. (1984) *The Origins of Settlement, Agriculture and the City-State in Mesopotamia*. PhD thesis, University of Edinburgh.

Maisels, C.K. (1987) Models of social evolution: Trajectories from the Neolithic to the state. *MAN* 22(2):331–359.

Maisels, C.K. (1990) *The Emergence of Civilization: From Hunting and Gathering to Agriculture, Cities and the State in the Near East*. London, Routledge.

Maisels, C.K. (1991) Trajectory versus typology in social evolution. *Cultural Dynamics* 4(3):251–269.

Maisels, C.K. (1993a) *The Near East: Archaeology in the 'Cradle of Civilization'*. London, Routledge.

Maisels, C.K. (1993b) *The Emergence of Civilization: From Hunting and Gathering to Agriculture, Cities and the State in the Near East*. Revised paperback edition. London, Routledge.

Majer, J. (1992) The Eastern Desert and Egyptian Prehistory. In Friedman and Adams, pp.227–233.

Malamat, A. (1989) *Mari and the Early Israelite Experience: The Schweich Lectures 1984*. Oxford, The British Academy/Oxford University Press.

Mallon, A., Koeppel, R. and Neuville, R. (1934) *Teleilat Ghassul I*. Rome, Pontifical Biblical Institute.

Mallowan, M.E.L. (1933) The Prehistoric Sondage at Nineveh, 1931–1932. *Annals of Archaeology and Anthropology* 20:127–177.

Mallowan, M.E.L. (1936) The excavations of Tell Chagar Bazar and an archaeological survey of the Habur region 1934–5. *Iraq* 3:1–87.

Mallowan, M.E.L. (1947) Excavations at Brak and Chagar Bazar. *Iraq* 9:1–258.

Mallowan, M.E.L. and Rose, J.C. (1935) Excavations at Tell Arpachiyah, 1933. *Iraq* 2: 1–178.

Malul, M. (1988) Studies in Mesopotamian legal symbolism. *Neukirchen-Vluyn, Alter Orient und Altes Testament* 221.

Mandel, R.D. and Simmons, A.H. (1988) A preliminary assessment of the geomorphology of 'Ain Ghazal. In Garrard and Gebel, II:431–436.

Marechal, C. (1991) Elements de parure de la fin du Natufien: Mallaha niveau I, Jayroud 1, Jayroud 3, Jayroud 9, Abu Hureyra et Mureybet 1A. In Bar-Yosef and Valla 1991b, pp.589–612.

Marriott, McKim (1955a) (ed.) *Village India: Studies in the Little Community*. Chicago and London, The University of Chicago Press.

Marriott, McKim (1955b) Little communities in an indigenous civilization. In Marriott 1955a, pp.171–222.

Marriott, McKim (1959) Interactional and attributional theories of caste ranking. *Man In India* 39(2):92–107.

Marshall, J. (1931) (ed.) *Mohenjo-daro and the Indus Civilization I–III*. London, Arthur Probsthain.

Martin, H.P. (1988) *Fara: A Reconstruction of the Ancient Mesopotamian City of Shuruppak*. Birmingham (UK), Chris Martin & Associates.

Matthews, R.J. (1990) Excavations at Jemdet Nasr, 1989. *Iraq* 52:25–59.

Matthews, R.J. (1991) Fragments of officialdom from Fara. *Iraq* 53:1–15.

Matthews, R.J. (1992) Jemdet Nasr: The site and the period. *Biblical Archaeologist*, Dec. 1992:196–202.

Matthews, R.J. (1993) *Cities, Seals and Writing: Archaic Seal Impressions from Jemdet Nasr and Ur. Materialien zu den Frühen Schriftzeugnissen des Vorderen Orients, Vol. 2*; Berlin, Gebr. Mann Verlag.

Matthews, R.J. and Wilkinson, T.J. (1991) Excavations in Iraq. 1989–90. *Iraq* 53:169–182.

Mauer, G. (1986) Agriculture of the Old Babylonian Period. *JANES (Journal of the Ancient Near Eastern Society)* 15:63–78.

Mayer, A.C. (1960) *Caste and Kinship in Central India: A Village and its Region*. Berkeley and Los Angeles, University of California Press.

Maxwell, G. (1957) *A Reed Shaken by the Wind*. London, Longmans, Green & Co.

Meacham, W. (1990) Review of the 4th ed. of *The Archaeology of Ancient China*, by K.C. Chang. *Asian Perspectives* 27(2):215–216.

Meadow, R.H. (1984) Notes on the faunal remains from Mehrgarh, with a focus on cattle. In B. Allchin, pp.34–40.

Meadow, R.H. (1989a) A note on the distribution of faunal remains during the later periods of Mehrgarh (Baluchistan, Pakistan). In Frifelt and Sorensen, pp.167–175.

Meadow, R.H. (1989b) Agriculture and the Greater Indus Valley: The palaeoethnobotanical and zooarchaeological evidence. In Kenoyer 1989b, pp.61–74.

Meadow, R.H. (1991a) Faunal remains and urbanism at Harappa. In Meadow 1991b, pp.89–106.

Meadow, R.H. (1991b) (ed.) *Harappa Excavations 1986–1990: A Multidisciplinary Approach to Third Millennium Urbanism. Monographs in World Archaeology No. 3*. Madison, Wisconsin, Prehistory Press.

Meadow, R.H. and Kenoyer, J.M. (1994) Harappa excavations 1993: The city wall and inscribed materials. In Parpola and Koskikallio, II:451–470.

Mencher, J.P. (1974) The caste system upside down, or the not-so-mysterious East. *Current Anthropology* 15(4):469–493.

Mencher, J.P. (1983) (ed.) *Social Anthropology of Peasantry*. Bombay, Somaiya Publishers.

Merpert, N.Ya. and Munchaev, R.M. (1973) Early agricultural settlements in the Sinjar Plain, N. Iraq. *Iraq* 35:93–119.

Merpert, N.Ya, and Munchaev, R.M. (1984) Soviet expedition's research at Yarim Tepe III Settlement in Northwestern Iraq, 1978–1979. *Sumer* 43(1–2):54–68.

Merpert, N.Ya, and Munchaev, R.M. (1987) The earliest levels at Yarim Tepe I and Yarim Tepe II in Northern Iraq. *Iraq* 49:1–36.

Merpert, N.Ya., Munchaev, R.M. and Bader, N.O. (1981) Investigations of the Soviet expedition in Northern Iraq, 1976. *Sumer* 37:22–54.

Mery, S. (1994) Excavation of an Indus potter's workshop at Nausharo (Baluchistan), Period II. In Parpola and Koskikallio, II:471–482.

Meyer, A.C. (1960) *Caste and Kingship in Central India*. Berkeley, University of California Press.

Michalowski, P. (1983) History as charter: Some observations of the Sumerian Kinglist. *Journal of the American Oriental Society* 103:237–248.

Michalowski, P. (1986) Mental maps and ideology: Reflections on Subartu. In Weiss 1986c, pp.129–156.

Michalowski, P. (1987) Charisma and control: On continuity and change in Early Mesopotamian bureaucratic systems. In Gibson and Biggs, pp. 55–68.

Michalowski, P. (1989) *The Lamentation over the Destruction of Sumer and Ur*. Winona Lake, Indiana, Eisenbrauns.

Michalowski, P. (1990) Early Mesopotamian communicative systems: Art, literature and writing. In Gunter, pp.53–69.

Michalowski, P. (1993) Memory and deed: The historiography of the political expansion of the Akkad State. In Liverani 1993c, pp.69–90.

Michalowski, P. and Walker, C.B.F. (1989) A new Sumerian 'Law Code'. In Behrens *et al.*, pp.383–396.

Milano, L. (1987) Barley for rations and barley for sowing (ARET II and related matters). *Acta Mesopotamica* 9:177–201.

Millard, A.R. (1987) Cartography in the Ancient Near East. In Harley and Woodward, pp.107–116.

Millard, A.R. (1988) The bevelled-rim bowls: Their purpose and significance. *Iraq* 50:49–57.

Miller, D. (1985a) Ideology and the Harappan Civilization. *Journal of Anthropological Archaeology* 4:31–71.

Miller, D. (1985b) *Artifacts as Categories: A Study of Ceramic Variability in Central India.* Cambridge, Cambridge University Press.

Miller, H.M.-L. (1994) Metal processing at Harappa and Mohenjo-Daro: Information from non-metal remains. In Parpola and Koskikallio, II:497–510.

Miller, N.F. (1984) The use of dung as fuel: An ethnographic example and an archaeological application. *Paleorient* 10(2):71–79.

Miller, N.F. (1992) The origins of plant cultivation in the Near East. In Cowan and Watson, pp.39–58.

Miller, N.F. and Smart, T.L. (1984) Intentional burning of dung as fuel: A mechanism for the incorporation of charred seeds into the archaeological record. *Journal of Ethnobiology* 4:15–28.

Miller, R. (1980) Water use in Syria and Palestine from the Neolithic to the Bronze Age. *World Archaeology* 11(3):331–341.

Miller, T.E. (1992) A cautionary note on the use of morphological characters for recognising taxa in wheat (genus *Triticum*). In P.C. Anderson 1992b, pp.249–253.

Milles, A., Williams, D. and Gardner, N. (1989) (eds) *The Beginnings of Agriculture. Symposia for the Association of Environmental Archaeology* Oxford, BAR S496.

Millet, N.B. (1990) The Narmer Macehead and related objects. *JARCE* 27:53–59.

Mills, J.O. (1992) Beyond nutrition: Antibiotics produced through grain storage practices, their recognition and implications for the Egyptian Predynastic. In Friedman and Adams, pp.27–35.

Mindlin, M., Geller, M.J. and Wansbrough, J.E. (1987) (eds) *Figurative Language in the Ancient Near East.* London, SOAS.

Misra, V.N. (1973) Bagor: A late Mesolithic settlement in Northwest India. *World Archaeology* 5(1):92–110.

Misra, V.N. (1984) Climate, a factor in the rise and fall of the Indus Civilization – evidence from Rajastan and beyond. In Lal *et al.*, pp.499–503.

Misra, V.N. (1994) Indus Civilization and the Rgvedic Sarasvati. In Parpola and Koskikallio, II:511–525.

Moholy-Nagy, H. (1983) Jarmo artifacts of pecked and ground stone and of shell. In L.S. Braidwood *et al.*, pp.289–346.

Momigliano, A. (1987) An Introduction to K.O. Muller's Prologemena Zur Einer Wissenschaftlichen Mythologie. In Rochberg-Halton, pp.231–243.

Mond, R. and Myers, O.H. (1937) *Cemeteries of Armant I.* London, Egyptian Exploration Society 42.

Montet, P. (1965) *Eternal Egypt.* London, Weidenfeld & Nicholson.

Moore, A.M.T. (1979) A Pre-Neolithic farmer's village on the Euphrates. *Scientific American* 241(2):62–70.

Moore, A.M.T. (1989) The transition from foraging to farming in Southwest Asia: Present problems and future directions. In Harris and Hillman, pp.620–631.

Moore, A.M.T. (1991) Abu Hureyra 1 and the antecedents of agriculture on the Middle Euphrates. In Bar-Yosef and Valla 1991b, pp.277–294.

Moore, A.M.T. and Hillman, G.C. (1992) The Pleistocene transition and human economy in Southwest Asia: The Impact of the Younger Dryas. *American Antiquity* 57(3):483–494.

Moorey, P.R.S. (1964) The 'plano-convex building' at Kish and Early Mesopotamian Palaces. *Iraq* 26:83–98.

Moorey, P.R.S. (1971) The Loftus hoard of Old Babylonian tools from Tell Sifr in Iraq. *Iraq* 33:61–86.

Moorey, P.R.S. (1976) The late prehistoric administrative building at Jamdat Nasr. *Iraq* 38:95–106.

Moorey, P.R.S. (1978) *Excavations at Kish 1923–33*. Oxford, Oxford University Press.

Moorey, P.R.S. (1982) (ed. and intro.) *Ur of the Chaldees by Sir Leonard Woolley: revised and updated*. London, Herbert Press.

Moorey, P.R.S. (1987) On tracking cultural transfers in prehistory. The case of Egypt in the fourth millennium B.C. In Rowlands *et al.*, pp.36–46.

Moorey, P.R.S. (1991) *A Century of Biblical Archaeology*. Cambridge, Lutterworth.

Moorey, P.R.S. (1993) Iran: A Sumerian El-Dorado? In Curtis, pp.31–43.

Moorey, P.R.S. (1994) *Ancient Mesopotamian Materials and Industries: The Archaeological Evidence*. Oxford, Clarendon Press.

Morales, V.B. (1983) Jarmo figurines and other clay objects. In Braidwood *et al.*, pp.369–424.

Mortensen, B. (1992) Carbon-14 dates from El Omari. In Friedman and Adams, pp.173–174.

Mughal, M.R. (1970) The Early Harappan Period in the Greater Indus Valley and Northern Baluchistan (3000–2400 BC). PhD dissertation, Anthropology Department, University of Pennsylvania.

Mughal, M.R. (1982) Recent archaeological research in the Cholistan Desert. In Possehl, pp.85–95.

Mughal, M.R. (1984) The Post-Harappan Phase in Behawalpur District, Pakistan. In Lal *et al.*, pp.499–503.

Mughal, M.R. (1990a) The protohistoric settlement patterns in the Cholistan Desert. *South Asian Archaeology* 1987 pt 1:pp.143–156.

Mughal, M.R. (1990b) Further evidence of the Early Harappan culture in the Greater Indus Valley: 1971–90. *South Asian Studies* 6:175–200.

Mughal, M.R. (1990c) The Harappan settlement patterns in the Greater Indus Valley. *Pakistan Archaeology* 25:1–72.

Mughal, M.R. (1992a) The consequences of river changes for the Harappan settlements in Cholistan. *Eastern Anthropologist* 45(1–2):105–116.

Mughal, M.R. (1992b) The geographical extent of the Indus Civilization during the Early, Mature and Late Harappan times. In Possehl, pp.123–143.

Muheisen, M. (1988) The Epipalaeolithic phases of Kharaneh IV. In Garrard and Gebel, II:353–367.

Muheisen, M., Gebel, H.G., Hanns, C. and Neef, R. (1988) Excavations at 'Ain Rahub, a final Natufian and Yarmoukian site near Irbid (1985). In Garrard and Gebel, II:473–502.

Munchaev, R.M., Merpert, N.Ya. and Bader, N.O. (1984) Archaeological studies in the Sinjar valley, 1980. *Sumer* 43(1–2):32–53.

Nadel, D. (1990a) Ohalo II – A preliminary report. *Mitekufat Haeven* 23:48–59.

Nadel, D. (1990b) The Khiamian as a case of Sultanian intersite variability. *Mitekufat Haeven* 23:86–99.

Nadel, D., Bar-Yosef, O. and Gopher, A. (1991) Early Neolithic arrowhead types in the Southern Levant: A typological suggestion. *Paleorient* 17(1):109–119.

Nadel, D., Danin, A., Werker, E., Schick, T., Kislev, M.E. and Stewart, K. (1994) 19,000-year-old twisted fibres from Ohalo II. *Current Anthropology* 35(4):451–457.

Nadel, D. and Hershkovitz, I. (1991) New subsistence data and human remains from the earliest Levantine Epipalaeolithic. *Current Anthropology* 32(5):631–635.

Nadel, S.F. (1942) *A Black Byzantium: The Kingdom of Nupe in Nigeria. International African Institute*. Oxford, Oxford University Press.

Nadel, S.F. (1951) *The Foundations of Social Anthropology*. London, Cohen & West.

Nadel, S.F. (1957) *The Theory of Social Structure*. London, Cohen & West.

Nai, H. (1986) The classification, nomenclature and usage of Shang Dynasty jades. In K.C. Chang 1986b, pp.207–236.

Neeley, M.P. and Barton, C.M. (1994) A new approach to interpreting Late Pleistocene microlith industries in Southwest Asia. *Antiquity* 68:275–288.

Nelson, S.M. (1990) The Neolithic of Northeastern China and Korea. *Antiquity* 64:234–248.

Nelson, S.M. (1995a) Introduction to Nelson 1995c, pp.1–18.

Nelson, S.M. (1995b) Conclusion to Nelson 1995c, pp.251–253.

Nelson, S.M. (1995c) (ed.) *The Archaeology of Northeast China: Beyond the Great Wall*. London and New York, Routledge.

Netting, R.McC. (1990) Population, permanent agriculture, and politics: Unpacking the evolutionary portmanteau. In Upham, pp.21–61.

Neugebauer, O. (1938) Die Bedeutungsloskeit der 'Sothisperiode' für die älteste ägyptische Chronologie. *Acts Orientalia* 17:169–195.

Neugebauer, O. (1939) La période sothique. *Chronique d'Egypte* 28:258–260.

Neugebauer, O. (1942) The origin of the Egyptian calendar. *Journal of Near Eastern Studies* 1:396–403.

Neugebauer, O. (1947) The water clock in Babylonian astronomy. *Isis* 37:37–43.

Neugebauer, O. (1949) The early history of the astrolabe. *Isis* 40:240–256.

Neugebauer, O. (1969) *The Exact Sciences in Antiquity*. (2nd edn), New York, Dover Publications.

Neugebauer, O. (1975) *A History of Mathematical Astronomy. Part 2*. Berlin, Springer.

Neumann, K. (1989) Vegetationsgeschichte der Ostsahara im Holozan: Holzkohlen aus prähistorischen Fundstellen. In Kuper, pp.13–182.

Nibbi, A. (1989) Some remarks on two very early but enduring symbols in ancient Egypt. In Krzyzaniak and Kobusiewicz, pp.340–351.

Nigam, J.S. (1979) Harappan pottery. In Agrawal and Chakrabarti, pp.135–161.

Nissen, H.J. (1987) The chronology of the proto- and early history periods in Mesopotamia and Susiana. In Aurenche *et al.*, part 2:607–614.

Nissen, H.J. (1988) *The Early History of the Ancient Near East*. Chicago, University of Chicago Press.

Nissen, H.J. (1989) The 'Ubaid Period in the context of the early history of the Ancient Near East. In Henrickson and Thuesen, pp.245–255.

Nissen, H.J. (1993a) The context of the emergence of writing in Mesopotamia and Iran. In Curtis, pp.54–71.

Nissen, H.J. (1993b) Settlement patterns and material culture of the Akkadian Period: Continuity and discontinuity. In Liverani 1993c, pp.91–106.

Nissen, H.J., Damerow, P. and Englund, R.K. (1989) Zur rechnergestützen Bearbeitung der archaischen Texte aus Mesopotamien (ca. 3200–300 v. Chr.). *Mitteilungen der Deutschen Orient-Gesellschaft zu Berlin*, 121:139–152.

Nissen, H.J. and Renger, J. (1982) (eds) *Mesopotamien und seine Nachbarn*. Berlin, Berliner Beiträge zum Vorderen Orient, 1.

Nissen, H.J., Damerow, P. and Englund, R.K. (1990) *Frühe Schrift und Techniken der Wirtschaftsverwaltung im alten Vordern Orient. Informationsspeicherung und -verarbeitung vor 5000 Jahren*. Berlin, Franzbecker.

Nivison, D. (1982–83) 1040 as the date of the Chou Conquest. *Early China* 8:76–78.

Nivison, D. (1983) The dates of Western Chou. *Harvard Journal of Asiatic Studies* 43(2):482–580.

Noy, T. (1989a) Gilgal – a Pre-Pottery Neolithic site, Israel – the 1985–1987 seasons. *Paleorient* 15(1):11–18.

Noy, T. (1989b) Some aspects of Natufian mortuary behaviour at Nahal Oren. In Hershkovitz, pp.53–57.

Noy, T. (1991) Art and decoration of the Natufian at Nahal Oren. In Bar-Yosef and Valla 1991b, pp.557–568.

Noy, T., Legge, A.J. and Higgs, E.S. (1973) Recent excavations at Nahal Oren, Israel. *Proceedings of the Prehistoric Society* 39:75–99.

Noy, T., Schuldrein, J. and Tchernov, E. (1980) Gilgal, a Pre-Pottery Neolithic A site in the Lower Jordan Valley. *Israel Exploration Journal* 30:63–82.

Oates, D. (1982) Tell Brak. In Curtis, pp.62–71.

Oates, D. and Oates, J. (1976) Early irrigation agriculture in Mesopotamia. In Sieveking *et al.*, pp.109–135.

Oates, D. and Oates, J. (1981) The Near East: A personal view. In Evans, *et al.*, pp.28–34.

Oates, D. and Oates, J. (1991) Excavations at Tell Brak 1990–91. *Iraq* 53:193–211.

Oates, J. (1969) Choga Mami, 1967–68. A preliminary report. *Iraq* 31:115–152.

Oates, J. (1973) The background and development of early farming communities in Mesopotamia and the Zagros. *Proceedings of the Prehistoric Society* 39:147–181.

Oates, J. (1977) Mesopotamian social organisation: Archaeological and philological evidence. In Friedman and Rowlands, pp.457–485.

Oates, J. (1982) Choga Mami. In Curtis 1982, pp.22–29.

Oates, J. (1983) Ubaid Mesopotamia reconsidered. In Young *et al.*, pp.251–281.

Oates, J. (1987) 'Ubaid chronology. In Aurenche *et al.*, part ii:473–482.

Oates, J. (1993a) Trade and power in the fifth and fourth millennia BC: New evidence from northern Mesopotamia. In J. Oates 1993b, pp.403–440.

Oates, J. (1993b) (ed.) *World Archaeology Vol. 24(3): Ancient Trade: New Perspectives.*

O'Connor, D. (1972) The geography of settlement in Ancient Egypt. In Ucko *et al.*, pp.681–704.

O'Connor, D. (1987) The earliest pharaohs and the University Museum: Old and new excavations – 1900–1987. *Expedition* 29(1): 27–39.

O'Connor, D. (1989) New funerary enclosures (Talbezirke) of the Early Dynastic period at Abydos. *JARCE* 26:51–86.

O'Connor, D. (1992) The status of Early Egyptian temples: An alternate theory. In Friedman and Adams, pp.83–98.

O'Connor, D. (1993) Urbanism in Bronze Age Egypt and Northeast Africa. In Shaw *et al.*, pp.570–587.

O'Connor, D. and Silverman, D.P. (1995a) Introduction. In O'Connor and Silverman 1995b, xvii–xxvii.

O'Connor, D. and Silverman, D.P. (1995b) (eds) *Ancient Egyptian Kingship.* Leiden, Brill.

Oldham, C.F. (1874) Notes on the lost river of the Indian Desert. *Calcutta Review* 59:1–27.

Oldham, C.F. (1893) The Saraswati and the Lost River of the Indian Desert. *Journal of the Royal Asiatic Society* (N.S.) 34:49–76.

Olszewski, D.I. (1991) The lithic evidence from Abu Hureyra I, in Syria. In Bar-Yosef and Valla 1991b, pp.433–444.

Olszewski, D.I. (1993) Subsistence ecology in the Mediterranean forest: Implications for the origins of cultivation in the Epipalaeolithic Levant. *American Anthropologist* 95:420–435.

Olszewski, D.I., Clark, G.A. and Fish, S. (1990) WHS 784X (Yutil al-Hasa): A Late Amharian site in the Wadi Hasa, west-central Jordan. *Proceedings of the Prehistoric Society* 56:33–49.

Olszewski, D.I. and Dibble, H.L. (1994) The Zagros Aurignacian. *Current Anthropology* 35(1):68–75.

Olszewski, D.I., Stevens, M., Glass, M., Beck, R.F., Cooper, J. and Clark, G.A. (1994) The 1993 excavations at Yutil al-Hasa (WHS 784), an Upper/Epipalaeolithic site in west-central Jordan. *Paleorient* 20(2):129–141.

O'Neill, H. (1987) *Companion to Chinese History.* New York and Oxford, Facts on File.

Oppenheim, A.L. (1969) Mesopotamia – land of many cities. In I.M. Lapidus, pp.3–16.

Oppenheim, A.L. (1975) The position of the intellectual in Mesopotamian society. *Daedalus* Spring, pp.37–46.

Oppenheim, A.L. (1978) Man and nature in Mesopotamian Civilization. *Dictionary of Scientific Biography* 15:6.

Oppenheim, M. von (1931) *Tell Halaf: A New Culture in Oldest Mesopotamia.* London and New York, G.P. Putnam's Sons.

Orthmann, W. (1986) The origin of Tell Chuera. In Weiss 1986c, pp.61–70.

Otte, M., Yalcinkaya, I., Leotard, J.-M., Kartal, M., Bar-Yosef, O., Kozlowski, J., Bayon, I.L. and Marshak, A. (1995) The Epi-Palaeolithic of Okuzini cave (SW Anatolia) and its mobiliary art. *Antiquity* 69:931–944.

Ozdogan, M. and Ozdogan, A. (1989) Cayonu: A conspectus of recent work. *Paleorient* 15(1):65–74.

Pal, Y., Sahai, B., Sood, R.K. and Agrawal, D.P. (1984) Remote sensing of the 'Lost' Sarasvati River. In Lal *et al.*, pp.491–497.

Palmieri, A. (1981) Excavations at Arslantepe (Malatya). *Anatolian Studies* 31:101–119.

Pankenier, D. (1981–82) Astronomical dates in Shang and Western Chou. *Early China* 7:1–37.

Park, T.K. (1992) Early trends toward class stratification: Chaos, common property, and flood recession agriculture. *American Anthropologist* 94:90–117.

Parpola, A. (1986) The Indus script: A challenging puzzle. *World Archaeology* 17: 399–419.

Parpola, A. (1994) *Deciphering the Indus Script.* Cambridge, Cambridge University Press.

Parpola, A. and Joshi, J.P. (1987) (eds) Corpus of Indus seals and inscriptions: Collections in India. *Memoirs of the Archaeological Survey of India, No. 86.* Helsinki, Soumalainen Tiedeakatemia.

Parpola, A. and Koskikallio, P. (1994) (eds) *South Asian Archaeology 1993: Proceedings of the Twelfth International Conference of the European Association of South Asian Archaeologists held in Helsinki University 5–9 July 1993,* 2 vols. Helsinki, Soumalainen Tiedeakatemia.

Parpola, A. and Shah, S.G.M. (1987) (eds) Corpus of Indus seals and inscriptions: Collections in Pakistan. *Memoirs of the Dept. of Archaeology and Museums, Govt. of Pakistan, No. 5.* Helsinki, Suomalainen Tiedeakatemia.

Parpola, S. (1987) The forlorn scholar. In Rochberg-Halton, pp.257–275.

Pastner, S. and Flam, L. (1982) (eds) *Anthropology in Pakistan: Recent Socio-Cultural and Archaeological Perspectives.* Cornell University, South Asia Occasional Papers and Theses.

Patterson, T.C. (1989) Pre-State societies and cultural styles in Ancient Peru and Mesopotamia: A comparison. In Henrickson and Thuesen, pp.293–321.

Pawlikowski, M. (1993) Mineralogy of the Nile sediments as an indicator of changes in climate: The Armant-Luxor area, Upper Egypt. In Krzyzaniak *et al.*, pp.355–357.

Payne, J.C. (1968) Lapis lazuli in Early Egypt. *Iraq* 30:58–61.

Payne, J.C. (1992) Predynastic chronology at Naqada. In Friedman and Adams, pp.185–192.

Pearce, L.E. (1993) Statements of purpose: Why the scribes wrote. In Cohen *et al.*, pp.185–190.

Pearson, R. (1981) Social complexity in Chinese coastal Neolithic sites. *Science* 213: 1078–1086.

Pearson, R. (1983) [with Shyh Charng Lo] The Ch'ing-lien-kang Culture and the Chinese Neolithic. In Keightley, pp.119–145.

Pearson, R. (1988) Chinese Neolithic burial patterns: Problems of method and interpretation. *Early China* 13:1–45.

Pei, G. (1985) Microlithic industries in China. In Rukang and Olsen, pp.225–241.

Pemberton, W., Postgate, J.N. and Smyth, R.F. (1988) Canals and bunds, ancient and modern. In Postgate and Powell, pp.207–221.

Pentikainen, J. (1996) (ed.) *Shamanism and Northern Ecology.* Berlin, Walter de Gruyter.

Perles, C. and Phillips, J. (1991) The Natufian Conference – Discussion. Conclusion to Bar-Yosef and Valla 1991b, pp.637–644.

Perrot, J. (1955) The Excavation of Tell Abu Matar near Beersheba. *Israel Exploration Journal* 5:17–40, 73–84, 167–189.

Perrot, J. (1966) La troisième campagne de fouilles à Munhatta (1964). *Syria* 43:49–63.

428

Peterson, J. (1996) The 'other' lithics: Ground stone from Tor al-Tareeq, Jordan. *Neo-Lithics* 2/96:8–9.

Petrie, W.M.F. (1900) *Royal Tombs of the Earliest Dynasties I*. London, EES 18.

Petrie, W.M.F. (1903) *Abydos II 1903*. London, EEF 24.

Petrie, W.M.F. (1904) *Methods and Aims in Archaeology*. London, Macmillan.

Petrie, W.M.F. and Quibell, J.E. (1896) *Naqada and Ballas*. London, BSAE 1.

Pettinato, G. (1991) *Ebla: A New Look at History*. Trans. C.F. Richardson. Baltimore and London, Johns Hopkins University Press.

Pichon, J. (1991) Les oiseaux au natoufien, avifaune et sedentarite. In Bar-Yosef and Valla 1991b, pp.371–380.

Pingree, D. (1963) Astronomy and astrology in India and Iran. *Isis* 54:229–246.

Pingree, D. (1987) Venus omens in India and Babylon. In Rochberg-Halton, pp.293–315.

Pingree, D. (1989) MUL.APIN and Vedic astronomy. In Behrens *et al.*, pp.439–445.

Pitt Rivers, A.H. Lane Fox (1887, 1888, 1892, 1898) *Excavations in Cranborne Chase*. Four volumes, privately printed.

Podzorski, P.V. (1988) Predynastic Egyptian seals of known provenience in the R.H. Lowie Museum of Anthropology. *Journal of Near Eastern Studies* 47:259–268.

Pollock, S. (1989) Power politics in the Susa A Period. In Henrickson and Thuesen, pp.281–292 (includes discussion).

Pollock, S. (1991) Of priestesses, princes and poor relations: The dead in the Royal Cemetery of Ur. *Cambridge Archaeological Journal* 1(2):171–189.

Pollock, S. (1992) Bureaucrats and managers, peasants and pastoralists, imperialists and traders: Research on the Uruk and Jemdet Nasr Periods in Mesopotamia. *Journal of World Prehistory* 6(3):297–336.

Popkin, S.L. (1979) *The Rational Peasant*. Berkeley, University of California Press.

Porada, E. (1987) On the origins of 'Aquarius'. In Rochberg-Halton, pp.279–191.

Porada, E. (1990) Animal subjects of the Ancient Near Eastern artist. In Gunter, pp.71–79.

Porada, P. (1993) Seals and related objects from Early Mesopotamia and Iran. In Curtis, pp.44–53.

Portugali, J. and Gophna, R. (1993) Crisis, progress and urbanization: The transition from Early Bronze I to Early Bronze II in Palestine. *Tel Aviv* 20(2):164–186.

Possehl, G.L. (1982) (ed.) *Harappan Civilization: A Contemporary Perspective*. Warminster, Aris & Phillips.

Possehl, G.L. (1991) The Harappan Civilization in Gujarat: The Sorath and Sindhi Harappans. *Eastern Anthropologist* 45(1–2):117–135.

Possehl, G.L. (1992) (ed.) *South Asian Archaeological Studies: Essays in Honour of Walter A. Fairservice*. Publisher not named.

Possehl, G.L. (1994) (ed.) Of men. In Kenoyer 1994b, pp.179–186.

Possehl, G.L. and Mehta, D.P. (1994) Excavations at Rojdi, 1992–93. In Parpola and Koskikallio, II:603–614.

Possehl, G.L. and Raval, M.H. (1989) *Harappan Civilization and Rojdi*. New Delhi, Oxford and IBH.

Postgate, J.N. (1982) Abu Salabikh. In Curtis, pp.48–61.

Postgate, J.N. (1990) Excavations at Abu Salabikh, 1988–89. *Iraq* 52:95–106.

Postgate, J.N. (1992) *Early Mesopotamia: Society and Economy at the Dawn of History*. London, Routledge.

Postgate, J.N. and Moon, J. (1984) Excavations at Abu Salabikh, a Sumerian city. *National Geographic Reports* 17 (Year 1976):721–743.

Postgate, J.N. and Powell, M.A. (1985) (eds) *Bulletin on Sumerian Agriculture, Vol. 2 [Cereals and Pulses]*. Cambridge.

Postgate, J.N. and Powell, M.A. (1987) (eds) *Bulletin on Sumerian Agriculture, Vol. 3 [Trees and Vegetables]*. Cambridge.

Postgate, J.N. and Powell, M.A. (1988) (eds) Irrigation and Cultivation in Mesopotamia, part 1. Cambridge, *Bulletin on Sumerian Agriculture, Vol. 4.*

Postgate, J.N. and Powell, M.A. (1990) (eds) Irrigation and Cultivation in Mesopotamia, part 2. Cambridge, *Bulletin on Sumerian Agriculture,* Vol. 5.

Postgate, J.N. and Powell, M.A. (1992) (eds) Trees and Timber in Mesopotamia. Cambridge, *Bulletin on Sumerian Agriculture, Vol. 6.*

Postgate, J.N., Wang, T. and Wilkinson, T. (1995) The evidence for early writing: Utilitarian or ceremonial. *Antiquity* 69: 459–80.

Potts, D.T. (1982) The Zagros Frontier and the problem of relations between the Iranian Plateau and Southern Mesopotamia in the third millennium BC. In Nissen and Renger 1982, pp.33–55.

Potts, D.T. (1990) *The Arabian Gulf in Antiquity, Vol. 1.* Oxford, Clarendon Press.

Potts, D.T. (1993) Rethinking some aspects of trade in the Arabian Gulf. In J. Oates 1993b, pp.423–440.

Potts, T.F. (1993) Patterns of trade in third-millennium BC Mesopotamia and Iran. In J. Oates 1993b, pp.379–402.

Potts, T.F. (1994) *Mesopotamia and the East.* OUCA Monograph, No. 37.

Powell, M.A. (1971) Sumerian numeration and metrology. Dissertation, University of Minnesota.

Powell, M.A. (1976) The antecedents of Old Babylonian place notation and the early history of Babylonian mathematics. *Historia Mathematica* 3:417–439.

Powell, M.A. (1981) Three problems in the history of cuneiform writing: origins, direction of script, literacy. *Visible Language* 15:419–440.

Powell, M.A. (1986) Economy of the extended family according to Sumerian sources. *Oikumene* 5:9–13.

Powell, M.A. (1987) (ed.) *Labor in the Ancient Near East.* American Oriental Series 68, New Haven.

Powell, M.A. (1988) Evidence for agriculture and waterworks in Babylonian mathematical texts. In Postgate and Powell, pp.161–172.

Powell, M.A. (1994) Elusive Eden: Private property at the dawn of history (review article). *Journal of Cuneiform Studies* 46:99–104.

Prag, K. (1986) Byblos and Egypt in the fourth millennium B.C. *Levant* 18:59–74.

Price, T.D. and Brown, J.A. (1985) (eds) *Prehistoric Hunter Gatherers: The Emergence of Cultural Complexity.* London and New York, Academic Press.

Pumpelly, R. (1908) (ed.) *Exploration in Turkestan.* 2 vols. Washington, Carnegie Institution.

Puskas, I. (1984) Society and religion in the Indus Valley civilization. In B. Allchin, pp.162–165.

Quibell, J.E. (1900) *Hierakonpolis I. Egyptian Research Account Vol. 4.* London, Bernard Quaritch.

Quibell, J.E. and Green, F.W. (1902) *Hierakonpolis II. Egyptian Research Account Vol. 5.* London, Bernard Quaritch.

Quintero, L.A. and Wilke, P.J. (1995) Evolution and economic significance of naviform core-and-blade technology in the Southern Levant. *Paleorient* 21(1):17–33.

Quintero, L.A., Wilke, P.J. and Waines, J.G. (1997) Pragmatic studies of Near Eastern Neolithic sickle blades. In Gebel, Kafafi and Rollefson 1997.

Quirke, S. (1992) *Ancient Egyptian Religion.* London, British Museum Press.

Quirke, S. and Spencer, J. (1992) *The British Museum Book of Ancient Egypt.* London, British Museum Press.

Quivron, G. (1994) The pottery sequence from 2700 to 2400 BC at Naushario, Baluchistan. In Parpola and Koskikallio, pp.629–644.

Raikes, R.L. (1966) Beidha: Prehistoric climate and water supply. *Palestine Exploration Quarterly* 98:68–72.

Raish, C. (1992) *Domestic Animals and Stability in Pre-State Farming Societies.* Oxford, BAR S579.

Ramachandran, K.S. (1984) Dating the Indus Civilization. In Lal *et al.*, pp.538–539.

Rao, S.R. (1973) *Lothal and the Indus Civilization*. New York, Asia Publishing House.

Rao, S.R. (1979) Lothal, A Harappan port town, 1955–62, I. New Delhi, *Memoirs of the Archaeological Survey of India* 78, Vol. 1.

Rao, S.R. (1984) New light on Indus script and language. In Lal *et al.*, pp.193–199.

Rao, S.R. (1985) Lothal. A Harappan Port Town, 1955–62, II. New Delhi, *Memoirs of the Archaeological Survey of India* 78, Vol. 2.

Ratnagar, S. (1981) *The Westerly Trade of the Harappa Civilization*. New Delhi, Oxford University Press.

Ratnagar, S. (1982) The location of Harappa. In Possehl, pp.261–264.

Ratnagar, S. (1986) An aspect of Harappan agricultural production. *Studies in History* 2(2) n.s. pp.137–153. New Delhi/London, Sage Publications.

Rawson, J. (1980) *Ancient China: Art and Archaeology*. London, British Museum Publications.

Rawson, J. (1993) Ancient Chinese ritual bronzes: The evidence from tombs and hoards of the Shang (c.1500–1050 BC) and Western Zhou (c.1050–771 BC) periods. *Antiquity* 67:805–823.

Rawson, J. (1996a) (ed.) *The Mysteries of Ancient China: New Discoveries from the Early Dynasties*. London, British Museum Press.

Rawson, J. (1996b) Introduction. In Rawson 1996a, pp.11–30.

Rawson, J. (1996c) The ritual bronze vessels of the Shang and the Zhou. In Rawson 1996a, pp.248–265.

Ray, J.D. (1986) The emergence of writing in Egypt. *World Archaeology* 17(3):307–316.

Reade, J.E. (1968) Tell Taya: Summary report. *Iraq* 30:234–264.

Reade, J.E. (1973) Tell Taya: Preliminary report. *Iraq* 35:155–187.

Reade, J.E. (1982) Tell Taya. In Curtis, pp.72–78.

Redfield, R. (1947) The folk society. *American Journal of Sociology* 52(4):293–308.

Redfield, R. (1953) The natural history of the folk society. *Social Forces* 31(3):224–228.

Redfield, R. (1955) The social organization of tradition. *Far Eastern Quarterly* 15(1):13–21.

Redfield, R. (1960) *The Little Community and Peasant Society and Culture*. Chicago, University of Chicago Press.

Redfield, R. and Singer, M. (1954) The cultural role of cities. *Economic Development and Cultural Change* 3:53–73.

Redman, C.L., Berman, M., Curtin, F., Langhorne, W., Versaggi, N. and Wanser, J. (1978) *Social Archaeology: Beyond Subsistence and Dating*. London and New York, Academic Press.

Reed, C.A. (1977) (ed.) *Origins of Agriculture*. The Hague, Mouton.

Reese, D.S. (1991) Marine shells in the Levant: Upper Palaeolithic, Epipalaeolithic, and Neolithic. In Bar-Yosef and Valla 1991b, pp.613–628.

Rendell, H.H., Dennel, R.W. and Halim, M.A. (1989) *Pleistocene and Palaeolithic Investigations in the Soan Valley, North Pakistan. British Archaeological Mission to Pakistan Series 2*. Oxford, BAR S544.

Renfrew, C. (1972) *The Emergence of Civilization*. London, Methuen.

Renfrew, C. and Bahn, P. (1991) *Archaeology: Theories, Methods and Practice*. London, Thames and Hudson.

Renfrew, C. and Cherry, J.F. (1986) *Peer Polity Interaction and Socio-Political Change*. Cambridge, Cambridge University Press.

Renfrew, C. and Zubrow, E.B.W. (1995) *The Ancient Mind: Elements of Cognitive Archaeology*. Cambridge, Cambridge University Press.

Renger, J. (1990) Rivers, watercourses and irrigation ditches. In Postgate and Powell, pp.31–46.

Reynolds, P.J. (1992) Crop yields of the prehistoric cereal types emmer and spelt: The worst option. In P.C. Anderson 1992b, pp.383–393.

Ridley, R.T. (1992) *The Eagle and the Spade: The Archaeology of Rome during the Napoleonic Era, 1809–1814*. Cambridge, Cambridge University Press.

Rizkana, I. and Seeher, J. (1984) New light on the relation of Maadi to the Upper Egyptian cultural sequence. *MDAIK* 40:237–252.

Rizkana, I. and Seeher, J. (1985) The chipped stones at Maadi: Preliminary reassessment of a predynastic industry and its long-distance relations. *MDAIK* 41:235–255.

Rizkana, I. and Seeher, J. (1987) Maadi I. Excavations at the predynastic site of Maadi and its cemeteries conducted by Mustapha Amer and Ibrahim Rizkana on behalf of the Department of Geography, Faculty of Arts of Cairo University, 1930–1953. The Pottery of the Predynastic Settlement. *Archäologische Veröffentlichungen DAIK* 64. Mainz, Philip von Zabern.

Rizkana, I. and Seeher, J. (1988) Maadi II. The lithic industries of the predynastic settlement. *Archäologische Veröffentlichungen DAIK* 65. Mainz, Philip von Zabern.

Rizkana, I. and Seeher, J. (1989) Maadi III. The non-lithic small finds and the structural remains of the pre-dynastic settlement. *Archäologische Veröffentlichungen DAIK* 80. Mainz, Philip von Zabern.

Rizkana, I. and Seeher, J. (1990) Maadi IV. The predynastic cemeteries of Maadi and Wadi Digla. *Archäologische Veröffentlichungen DAIK* 81. Mainz, Philip von Zabern.

Roaf, M.D. (1989) 'Ubaid social organization and social activities as seen from Tell Madhhur. In Henrickson and Thuesen, pp.91–146.

Roaf, M.D. (1990) *Cultural Atlas of Mesopotamia and the Near East*. Oxford, Equinox/Facts on File.

Roaf, S. (1982) Tell Madhur: Isometric partial reconstruction. In Curtis, p.43.

Rochberg-Halton, F. (1987) (ed.) Language, literature and history: Philological and historical studies presented to Erica Reiner. *American Oriental Series* No. 67.

Rodden, J. (1981) The development of the three age system: Archaeology's first paradigm. In Daniel, pp.51–68.

Rodwell, S. (1984a) China's earliest farmers: the evidence from Cishan. *Bulletin of the Indo-Pacific Prehistory Association* 5:55–63.

Rodwell, S. (1984b) The common fowl in early China. *Journal of the Hong Kong Archaeological Society* 11:124–127.

Rollefson, G.O. (1983) Ritual and ceremony at Neolithic 'Ain Ghazal (Jordan). *Paleorient* 9(2):29–38.

Rollefson, G.O. (1986) Neolithic 'Ain Ghazal (Jordan): ritual and ceremony II. *Paleorient* 12(1)25–52.

Rollefson, G.O. (1987) Local and external relations in the Levantine PPN period: 'Ain Ghazal as a regional centre. In Hadidi, III, pp. 29–32.

Rollefson, G.O. (1988) Stratified burin classes at 'Ain Ghazal: Implications for the Desert Neolithic of Jordan. In Garrard and Gebel, II, pp.437–449.

Rollefson, G.O. (1990) Neolithic chipped stone technology at 'Ain Ghazal, Jordan: The status of the PPNC phase. *Paleorient* 16(1):119–124.

Rollefson, G.O. (1993) The origins of the Yarmoukian at 'Ain Ghazal. *Paleorient* 19(1):91–100.

Rollefson, G.O. (1996) 'Ain Ghazal Excavations 1996. *Neo-Lithics* 2/96:5–6.

Rollefson, G.O. (n.d.) *Neolithic 'Ain Ghazal in its Landscape. Studies in the History and Archaeology of Jordan VI* (in press, due 1998). Amman, Department of Antiquities.

Rollefson, G.O. and Kafafi, Z. (1994) The 1993 Season at 'Ain Ghazal: Preliminary Report. *Annual of the Department of Antiquities of Jordan* 38:11–32.

Rollefson, G.O. and Kafafi, Z. (1996a) 'Ain Ghazal: Ten seasons of discovery. American Centre of Oriental Research (ACOR), Amman. *Newsletter* 8(1):1–4.

Rollefson, G.O. and Kafafi, Z. (1996b) The 1995 season at 'Ain Ghazal: Preliminary report. *ADAJ* 40:1–17.

Rollefson, G.O., Kafafi, Z.A. and Simmons, A.H. (1991) The Neolithic village of 'Ain Ghazal, Jordan: Preliminary report on the 1988 season. *Basor Supplement* 27:95–116; published by Johns Hopkins University Press for ASOR. *Preliminary Reports of ASOR-Sponsored Excavations 1982–89*. E. Rast and M. Zeiger eds.

Rollefson, G.O. and Kohler-Rollefson, I. (1989) The collapse of Early Neolithic settlement in the Southern Levant. In Hershkovitz, pp.73–89.

Rollefson, G.O. and Kohler-Rollefson, I. (1993) PPNC adaptations in the first half of the 6th millennium BC. *Paleorient* 19(1):33–42.

Rollefson, G.O. and Simmons, A.H. (1988) The Neolithic settlement at 'Ain Ghazal. In Garrard and Gebel, II, pp.393–421.

Rollefson, G.O., Simmons, A.H., Donaldson, M.L., Gillespie, W., Kafafi, Z.A., Kohler-Rollefson, I.U., McAdam, E., Rolston, S.L. and Tubb, M.K. (1985) Excavation at the Pre-Pottery Neolithic B village of 'Ain Ghazal (Jordan), 1983. *Mitteilungen der Deutschen Orient-Gesellschaft (MDOG)* 117:69–134.

Rollefson, G.O., Simmons, A.H. and Kafafi, Z. (1992) Neolithic cultures at 'Ain Ghazal, Jordan. *Journal of Field Archaeology* 19:443–471.

Romer, W.H. Ph. (1980) Das sumerische Kurzepos 'Gilgames und Akka'. *Neukirchen-Vluyn, Alter Orient und Altes Testament* 209.

Ronen, A. (1984) *Sefunim Prehistoric Sites, Mount Carmel, Israel.* Oxford, BAR 230.

Ronen, A. and Kaufman, D. (1976) Epi-Palaeolithic sites near Nahal Hadera, central coastal plain of Israel. *Tel Aviv* 3:16–30.

Ronen, A. and Lechevallier, M. (1985) The Natufian-Early Neolithic site at Hatula, near Latrun, Israel. *Quartar* 35/36:141–164.

Ronen, A. and Lechevallier, M. (1991) The Natufian of Hatula. In Bar-Yosef and Valla 1991b, pp.149–160.

Rosen, A.M. (1992) Phytoliths as indicators of ancient irrigation farming. In P.C. Anderson 1992b, 281–288.

Rosen, S.A. (1983) Tabular scraper trade: a model of material cultural dispersion. *BASOR* 249:79–86.

Rosen, S.A. (1989) The origins of craft specialization: Lithic perspectives. In Hershkovitz, pp.107–114.

Rosen, S.A. (1990) Excavations at Givat Hayil 33, an Epipalaeolithic site in the Western Negev. *Mitekufat Haeven* 23:60–78.

Rosenberg, M. and Davis, M. (1992) Hallam Cemi Tepesi, an early aceramic neolithic site in eastern Anatolia: Some preliminary observations concerning material culture. *Anatolica* 18:1–18.

Rosner, U. and Schabitz, F. (1991) Palynological and sedimentological evidence for the historic environment of Khatouniye, Eastern Syrian Djezire. *Paleorient* 17(1):77–87.

Rossignol-Strick, M. (1993) Late Quaternary climate in the Eastern Mediterranean region. *Paleorient* 19(1):135–152.

Roth, A.M. (1993) Social change in the fourth dynasty: The spatial organization of pyramids, tombs and cemeteries. *JARCE* 30:33–55.

Rothman, M.S. (1994) Sealings as a control mechanism in prehistory: Tepe Gawra XI, X and VIII. In Stein and Rothman, pp.103–120.

Rowlands, M., Larsen, M. and Kristiansen, K. (1987) (eds) *Centre and Periphery in the Ancient World.* Cambridge, Cambridge University Press.

Rowton, M.B. (1987) The role of ethnic invasion and the chiefdom regime in dimorphic interaction: The post-Kassite period (ca.1150–750 BC). In Rochberg-Halton, pp.367–378.

Ruggles, C.L.N. and Saunders, N.J. (1993) (eds) *Astronomies and Cultures: Papers derived from the third 'Oxford' International Symposium on Archaeoastronomy, St Andrews, UK, Sept. 1990.* Colorado, University Press of Colorado.

Rukang, W. and Olsen, J.W. (1985) (eds) *Palaeoanthropology and Palaeolithic Archaeology in the People's Republic of China.* New York and London, Academic Press.

Runciman, S. (1965) *The Fall of Constantinople.* Cambridge, Cambridge University Press.

Runciman, S. (1970) *The Last Byzantine Renaissance.* Cambridge, Cambridge University Press.

Safar, F., Mustafa, M.A. and Lloyd, S. (1981) *Eridu*. Baghdad, State Organisation of Antiquities and Heritage.

Sambursky, S. (1962) *The Physical World of Late Antiquity*. London, Routledge and Kegan Paul.

Sanders, J.A. (1970) (ed.) *Near Eastern Archaeology in the Twentieth Century, Essays in Honour of Nelson Glueck*. New York.

Sanlaville, P. (1996) Changements climatiques dans la région levantine à la fin du Pléistocène supérieur et au début de l'Holocène. Leurs relations avec l'évolution des sociétés humaines. *Paléorient* 22/1:7–30.

Santoni, M. (1984) Sibri and the South Cemetery of Mehrgarh: Third millennium connections between the northern Kachi Plain (Pakistan) and Central Asia. In B. Allchin, pp.52–59.

Santoni, M. (1989) Potters and pottery at Mehrgarh during the third millennium B.C. (Periods VI and VII). In Frifelt and Sorensen, pp.176–185.

Sarcina, A. (1979) The private house at Mohenjo-daro. In Taddei, I, pp.433–447.

Sasson, J.M. (1972) Some comments on record keeping at Mari. *Iraq* 34:55–67.

Scheffler, H.W. (1966) On ancestor worship in anthropology: or, observations on descent and descent groups. *Current Anthropology* 7:541–551.

Scheffler, H.W. (1967) On concepts of descent and descent groups. *Current Anthropology* 8:506–509.

Scheffler, H.W. (1973) Kinship, descent and alliance. In Honigman, pp.747–793.

Schepartz, L.A. (1989) Modelling the effects of subsistence pattern change on prehistoric populations. In Hershkovitz, pp.199–219.

Schick, T. (1986) Perishable remains from the Nahal Hemar Cave. *Journal of the Israel Prehistoric Society* 10:95–97.

Schmandt-Besserat, D. (1988) Tokens at Uruk. *Baghdader Mitteilungen* 19:1–175.

Schmandt-Besserat, D. (1992) *Before Writing*. Austin, Texas, University of Texas Press.

Schmidt, K. (1992a) Tell el-Fara'in/Buto and Tell el-Iswid (south): The lithic industries from the Chalcolithic to the Early Old Kingdom. In Van den Brink 1992c, pp.31–42.

Schmidt, K. (1992b) Tell Ibrahim Awad: A preliminary report on the lithic industries. In Van den Brink 1992c, pp.79–96.

Schmidt, K. (1993) Comments on the lithic industry of the Buto-Maadi culture in Lower Egypt. In Kryzyzaniak *et al.*, pp.267–277.

Schmidt, K. and Beile-Bohn, M. (1996) A LPPNB-variant of Byblos points from Gurcutepe II – 'Palmyra points'? *Neo-Lithics* 2/96:9–11.

Schoeninger, M. (1982) Diet and the evolution of modern human form. *American Journal of Physical Anthropology* 58:37–52.

Schroeder, B. (1991) Natufian in the Central Beqaa Valley, Lebanon. In Bar-Yosef and Valla 1991b, pp.43–80.

Schuldenrein, J. and Clark, G.A. (1994) Landscape and prehistoric chronology of West-Central Jordan. *Geoarchaeology* 9.1:31–55.

Schwartz, B. (1985) *The World of Thought in Ancient China*. Cambridge, Mass., Harvard University Press.

Schwartz, G.M. (1986) Mortuary evidence and social stratification in the Ninevite V period. In Weiss 1986c, pp.45–60.

Scott, J.C. (1976) *The Moral Economy of the Peasant*. New Haven and London, Yale University Press.

Seeden, H. (1982) Ethnoarchaeological reconstruction of Halafian occupational units at Shams ed-Din Tannira. *Berytus* 30:55–95.

Seeher, J. (1992) Burial customs in Predynastic Egypt: A view from the Delta. In Van den Brink 1992c, pp.225–234.

Sellars, J. (1991) An examination of lithics from the Wadi Judayid Site. In Bar-Yosef and Valla 1991b, pp.445–458.

Selz, G.J. (1990) Studies in early syncretism: The development of the Pantheon in Lagas. *Acta Sumerologica* 12:111–142.

Service, E. (1962) *Primitive Social Organization: An Evolutionary Perspective*. New York, Random House.

Shafer, B.E. (1991) (ed.) *Religion in Ancient Egypt*. London, Routledge.

Shaffer, J.G. (1982) Harappan commerce: An alternative perspective. In Pastner and Flam, pp.166–201.

Shaffer, J.G. and Lichtenstein, D.A. (1989) Ethnicity and change in the Indus Valley cultural tradition. In Kenoyer 1989b, pp.117–126.

Shah, F.G.H. and Parpola, A. (1991) (eds) *Corpus of Indus Seals and Inscriptions. II: Collections in Pakistan*. Helsinki, Annales Academiae Scientarium Fennicae B 240/Memoirs of the Dept of Archaeology and Museums, Govt of Pakistan 5.

Shaughnessy, E.L. (1989) Historical Geography and the Extent of the Earliest Chinese Kingdoms. ASIA MAJOR, Vol II (2), pp.1–22.

Shaw, T., Sinclair, P., Andah, B. and Okpoko, A. (1993) (eds) *The Archaeology of Africa*. London, Routledge.

Shelagh, G. (1994) Social complexity in North China during the Early Bronze Age: A comparative study of the Erlitou and Lower Xiajiadian Cultures. *Asian Perspectives* 33(2):261–292.

Shendge, M.J. (1985) The inscribed calculi and the invention of writing: The Indus view. *JESHO* 28(1):50–80.

Sherratt, A. (1980) Water, soil and seasonality in early cereal cultivation. *World Archaeology* 11(3):313–330.

Sherratt, A. (1981) Plough and pastoralism: Aspects of the secondary products revolution. In Hodder *et al.*, pp.261–305.

Shinde, V. (1991) The Late Harappan Culture in Maharashtra, India: A study of settlement and subsistence patterns. *South Asian Studies* 7:91–96.

Shinde, V. (1992) Padri and the Indus Civilization. *South Asian Studies* 8:55–66.

Sieveking, G. de G., Longworth, I.H. and Wilson, K.E. (1976) *Problems in Economic and Social Archaeology*. London, Duckworth.

Sigaut, F. (1992) Rendements, semis et fertilité: Signification analytique des rendements. In P.C. Anderson 1992b, pp.395–403.

Sillen, A. and Lee-Thorp, J.A. (1991) Dietary change in the Late Natufian. In Bar-Yosef and Valla 1991b, pp.399–410.

Silverman, D.P. (1995) The nature of Egyptian kingship. In O'Connor and Silverman 1995b, pp.49–92.

Simmons, A., Bolton, A., Butler, C., Kafafi, Z. and Rollefson, G. (1990) A plastered skull from Neolithic 'Ain Ghazal, Jordan. *Journal of Field Archaeology* 17:107–110.

Simmons, A.H. and al-Najjar, M. (1996) Current investigations at Ghwair I, a Neolithic Settlement in Southern Jordan. *Neo-Lithics* 2/96:6–7.

Simmons, A.H., Kafafi, Z., Rollefson, G. and Moyer, K. (1989) Test excavations at Wadi Shu'eib, a major Neolithic settlement in Central Jordan. *Annual of the Dept of Antiquities of Jordan* 33:27–42.

Sinha, P. (1989) Economic and subsistence activities at Baghor III, India: A microwear study. In Kenoyer 1989b, pp.47–52.

Sjoberg, A.W. (1975) In-nin-sa₃-gur₄-ra. A hymn to the Goddess Inanna by the en-Priestess Enheduanna. ZA 65:161–253.

Sjoberg, A.W. (1976) The Old Babylonian Eduba. In Lieberman, pp.159–179.

Sjoberg, A.W. and Bergmann, E. (1969) *The Collection of the Sumerian Temple Hymns. Texts from Cuneiform Sources Vol. 3*. Locust Valley, New York, J.J. Augustin.

Skinner, G.W. (1964) Marketing and social structure in rural China, part 1. *Journal of Asian Studies* 24:3–43.

Skinner, G.W. (1971) Chinese peasants and the closed community: An open and shut case. *Comparative Studies in Society and History* 13:270–281.

Smith, B. and Weng, W.G. (1979) *China: A History in Art*. New York, Gemini Smith Inc.

Smith, E.A. and Boyd, R. (1990) Risk and reciprocity: Hunter-gatherer socioecology and the problem of collective action. In Cashdan 1990b, pp.167–191.

Smith, E.A. and Winterhalder, B. (1992) (eds) *Evolutionary Ecology and Human Behavior*. Hawthorne, NY, Aldine de Gruyter.

Smith, H.S. (1972) Society and settlement in ancient Egypt. In Ucko *et al.*, pp.705–719.

Smith, H.S. (1992) The making of Egypt: A review of the influence of Susa and Sumer on Upper Egypt and Lower Nubia in the 4th millennium B.C. In Friedman and Adams, pp.235–246.

Smith, H.S. and Hall, R. (1983) (eds) *Ancient Centres of Egyptian Civilization*. London, Egyptian Education Bureau.

Smith, P. (1991) The dental evidence for nutritional status in the Natufians. In Bar-Yosef and Valla 1991b, pp.425–430.

Smith, R.J. (1992) *Chinese Almanacs*. Hong Kong, Oxford University Press.

Smith, S. (1969) Babylonian time reckoning. *Iraq* 31:74–81.

Snell, D.C. (1982) *Ledgers and Prices: Early Mesopotamian Merchant Accounts. Yale Near Eastern Researches, 8*. New Haven and London, Yale University Press.

Snell, D.C. (1988) The allocation of resources in the Umma silver account system. *JESHO* 31:1–13.

Soffer, O. and Gamble, C. (1990) The World at 18,000 BP. Vol. 1, *High Latitudes*; Vol. 2, *Low Latitudes*. London, Unwin Hyman.

Solecki, R.L. and Solecki, R.S. (1983) Late Pleistocene–early Holocene cultural traditions in the Zagros and the Levant. In Young *et al.*, pp.123–127.

Sollberger, E. (1967) The rulers of Lagash. *Journal of Cuneiform Studies* 21: 279–291.

Soundara Rajan, K.V. (1982) Motivations for early Indian urbanization: An examination. In Possehl, pp.69–75.

Southworth, F.C. (1992) Linguistics and archaeology: Prehistoric implications of some South Asian plant names. In Possehl, pp.81–85.

Speiser, E.A. (1952) Some factors in the collapse of Akkad. *Journal of the American Oriental Society* 72:97–101.

Speiser, E.A. (1983) Ancient Mesopotamia. In Dentan, pp.35–76.

Spencer, A.J. (1982) *Death in Ancient Egypt*. Harmondsworth, Penguin.

Spencer, A.J. (1993) *Early Egypt: The Rise of Civilization in the Nile Valley*. London, British Museum Press.

Srinivas, M.N. (1955) The social system of a Mysore village. In Marriott 1955a, pp.1–35.

Srinivas, M.N. (1975) The Indian village: Myth and reality. In Beattie and Lienhardt, pp.41–85.

Stampfli, H.R. (1983) The fauna of Jarmo, with notes on animal bones from Matarrah, the Amuq and Karim Shahir. In L.S. Braidwood *et al.*, pp.431–434.

Starck, J.M. (1988) Stone rings from Baga and Basta: Geographical and chronological implications. In Garrard and Gebel, I.137–174.

Steegman, J.S. (1986 [1936]) *The Rule of Taste from George I to George IV*. London, Century/Hutchinson/The National Trust of Great Britain.

Stein, A. (1917) On some river names in the Rgveda. *Journal of the Royal Asiatic Society*, 1917, pp.91–99.

Stein, A. (1942) A survey of ancient sites along the 'lost' Sarasvati River. *Geographical Journal* 99:173–182.

Stein, G. (1990) On the Uruk Expansion (Critique of Algaze 1989). *Current Anthropology* 31(1):66–67.

Stein, G. (1994) Economy, ritual and power in 'Ubaid Mesopotamia. In Stein and Rothman, pp.35–46.

Stein, G. and Rothman, M.S. (1994) (eds) *Chiefdoms and Early States in the Near East*. Madison, Wisconsin, Prehistory Press.

Steinkeller, P. (1981) The renting of fields in early Mesopotamia and the development of the concept of interest in Sumerian. *JESHO* 24:113–145.

Steinkeller, P. (1982) The question of Marhasi: A contribution to the historical geography of Iran in the third millennium B.C.. *ZA* 72:237–265.

Steinkeller, P. (1987) The administrative and economic organization of the Ur III State. In Gibson and Biggs, pp.19–41.

Steinkeller, P. (1988) Notes on the irrigation system in third millennium Southern Babylonia. In Postgate and Powell, pp.73–92.

Steinkeller, P. (1989) *Sale Documents of the Ur III period*. Stuttgart, Freiburger Altorientalische Studien 17.

Steinkeller, P. (1993) Early political development in Mesopotamia and the origins of the Sargonic Empire. In Liverani 1993c, pp.107–130.

Steinkeller, P. (1995) *Third Millennium Legal and Administrative Texts in the Iraq Museum, Baghdad*. Winona Lake, Indiana, Eisenbrauns.

Stekelis, M. (1972) *The Yarmoukian Culture of the Neolithic Period*. Jerusalem, Magnes Press.

Stekelis, M. and Yisraeli, T. (1963) Excavations at Nahal Oren, preliminary report. *Israel Exploration Journal* 13:1–12.

Stephens, D.W. (1990) Risk and incomplete information in behavioral ecology. In Cashdan 1990b, pp.19–46.

Stewart, C. (1996) Great and little traditions. In Barnard and Spencer 1996, pp.267–268.

Stieglitz, R.R. (1987) Ebla and Dilmun. In Gordon *et al.*, pp.43–46.

Stocking, G.W. (1987) *Victorian Anthropology*. New York, The Free Press.

Stockton, E.D. (1971) Non-Ghassulian flint elements at Teleilat Ghassul. *Levant* 3:80–81.

Stoddart, S. (1992) Towards a historical ethnology of the Mediterranean. *Current Anthropology* 33(5): 599–600.

Stoddart, S. and Malone, C. (1994) (eds) *Territory, Time and State: The Archaeological Development of the Gubbio Basin*. Cambridge, Cambridge University Press.

Stol, M. (1988) Old Babylonian fields. In Postgate and Powell, pp.173–188.

Stol, M. (1995) Women in Mesopotamia. *Journal of the Economic and Social History of the Orient* 38(2):123–144.

Stordeur, D. (1989) El Kowm 2 Caracol et le PPNB. *Paleorient* 15(1):102–110.

Stordeur, D. (1991) Le natoufien et son évolution à travers les artefacts en os. In Bar-Yosef and Valla 1991b, pp.467–482.

Stordeur, D. (1993) Sédentaires et nomades du PPNB final dans le désert de Palmyre (Syrie). *Paleorient* 19(1):187–203.

Stordeur, D., Jammous, B., Helmer, D. and Willcox, G. (1996) Jerf el-Ahmar: a new Mureybetian site (PPNA) on the Middle Euphrates. *Neo-Lithics* 2/96:1–2.

Straus, L.G. (1986) *The End of the Paleolithic in the Old World*. BAR-S284.

Streuver, S. (1971) (ed.) *Prehistoric Agriculture*. American Museum Sourcebook in Anthropology Q 15. New York, Natural History Press.

Stronach, D. (1982) Ras al 'Amiya'. In Curtis, pp.37–39.

Strouhal, E. (1973) Five plastered skulls from Pre-Pottery Neolithic B Jericho. *Paleorient* 1(2):231–247.

Stuiver, M., Kromer, B., Beckker, B. and Ferguson, C.W. (1986) Radiocarbon age calibration back to 13,300 years B.P. and the 14C age matching of the German oak and U.S. bristlecone pine chronologies. *Radiocarbon* 28(2B):969–979.

Stuiver, M. and Reimer, P.J. (1986) *Radiocarbon* 28:1022–1030.

Suraj Bhan, (1972) Changes in the course of the Yamuna and their bearing on the proto-historic cultures in Haryana. In Deo pp.125–128.

Suraj Bhan, (1973) The sequence and spread of prehistoric cultures in the upper Sarasvati Basin. In Agrawal and Gosh pp.252–263.

Surenhagen, D. (1986a) The dry farming belt: The Uruk period and subsequent developments. In Weiss 1986c, pp.7–43.

Surenhagen, D. (1986b) Archaische Keramik aus Uruk-Warka. *Baghdader Mitteilungen* 17:7–95.

Surenhagen, D. (1987) Archaische Keramik aus Uruk-Warka. *Baghdader Mitteilungen* 18:1–92.

Szarzynska, K. (1987–8) Some of the oldest cult symbols in Archaic Uruk. *Ex Oriente Lux* 30:3–21, Leiden.

Szarzynska, K. (1994) Archaic Sumerian tags. *Journal of Cuneiform Studies* 46:1–10.

Taddei, M. (1979) (ed.) *South Asian Archaeology 1977: 2 Vols.* Naples, Instituto Universitario Orientale, Seminario Di Studi Asiatici.

Taddei, M. (1990) (ed.) *South Asian Archaeology 1987.* Rome, ISMEO.

Tchernov, E. (1991) Biological evidence for human sedentism in Southwest Asia during the Natufian. In Bar-Yosef and Valla 1991b, pp.315–340.

Temple, R.K.G. (1986) *China: Land of Discovery and Invention.* Wellinborough, Patrick Stephens.

Thanheiser, U. (1992) Plant-food remains at Tell Ibrahim Awad: Preliminary report (Season 1990). In Van den Brink 1992c, pp.117–122.

Thapar, B.K. (1973) New traits of the Indus Civilization at Kalibangan: An appraisal. In Hammond, pp.85–104.

Thapar, B.K. (1984) Six decades of Indus studies. In Lal *et al.*, pp.1–25.

Thapar, B.K. (1985) *Recent Archaeological Discoveries in India.* Paris, UNESCO, with the Centre for East Asian Cultural Studies, Tokyo.

Thesiger, W. (1964) *The Marsh Arabs.* Harmondsworth, Penguin.

Thiebault, S. (1989) A note on the ancient vegetation of Baluchistan based on charcoal analysis of the latest periods from Mehrgarh, Pakistan. In Frifelt and Sorensen, pp.186–188.

Thomas, K.D. and Allchin, F.R. (1986) Radiocarbon dating of some early sites in N.W. Pakistan. *South Asian Studies* 2:37–44.

Thompson, M.W. (1977) *General Pitt-Rivers: Evolution and Archaeology in the Nineteenth Century.* Bradford-on-Avon, Moonraker Press.

Thorp, R.L. (1980) Burial practices of Bronze Age China. In Fong, pp.51–64.

Thorp, R.L. (1983) Origins of Chinese architectural style: The earliest plans and building types. *Archives of Asian Art* 36:22–39.

Thorp, R.L. (1985) The growth of Early Shang Civilization: New data from ritual vessels. *Harvard Journal of Asiatic Studies* 45(1):5–75.

Thorp, R.L. (1991) Erlitou and the search for the Xia. *Early China* 16:1–38.

Thuesen, I. (1989) Diffusion of 'Ubaid pottery into Western Syria. In Henrickson and Thuesen, pp.419–440.

Tosi, M. and Vidale, M. (1990) Fourth millennium BC lapis lazuli working at Merhgarh, Pakistan. *Paleorient* 16(2):89–99.

Townsend, C.C. and Guest, E. (1966) (eds) *Flora of Iraq: Vol. 2. Classification, Sequence and General Systematic Text.* Baghdad, Ministry of Agriculture.

Tregear, T.R. (1965) *A Geography of China.* London, University of London Press.

Trigger, B.G. (1974) The archaeology of government. *World Archaeology* 6(1):95–106.

Trigger, B.G. (1980) *Gordon Childe: Revolutions in Archaeology.* London, Thames & Hudson.

Trigger, B.G. (1989) *A History of Archaeological Thought.* Cambridge, Cambridge University Press.

Trigger, B.G. (1991) Distinguished lecture in archaeology: Constraint and freedom – a new synthesis for archaeological explanation. *American Anthropologist* 93:551–569.

Trigger, B.G. (1995a) *Early Civilizations: Ancient Egypt in Context.* New York, Columbia University Press.

Trigger, B.G. (1995b) Expanding middle-range theory. *Antiquity* 69:449–458.

Trigger, B.G., Kemp, B.J., O'Connor, D. and Lloyd, A.B. (1983) *Ancient Egypt: A Social History*. Cambridge, Cambridge University Press.

Tubb, M.K. (1985) Preliminary report on the 'Ain Ghazal statues. In Rollefson *et al.*, pp.117–134.

Tulane, E. (1944) A repertoire of the Samarran painted pottery style. *Journal of Near Eastern Studies* III: 57–65, 69ff.

Turnbull, P. and Reed, C.A. (1974) The fauna from the Terminal Pleistocene of Palegawra Cave: A Zarzian occupation site in Northeast Iraq. *Fieldiana: Anthropology* 63:81–146.

Turville-Petre, F. (1932) Excavations in the Mugharet el Kebarah. *Journal of the Royal Anthropological Institute*. 62:270–276.

Tusa, S. (1990) Ancient ploughing in Northern Pakistan. In Taddei, pp.348–376.

Tutundzic, S.P. (1989) The problem of foreign north-eastern relations of Upper Egypt, particularly in the Badarian period: An aspect. In Krzyzaniak and Kobusiewicz, pp.255–260.

Tutundzic, S.P. (1993) A consideration of differences between the pottery showing Palestinian characteristics in the Maadian and Gerzean cultures. *Journal of Egyptian Archaeology* 79:33–55.

Tylor, E.B. (1871) *Primitive Culture: Researches into the Development of Mythology, Philosophy, Religion, Language, Art, and Custom*. London, John Murray.

Ucko, P.J. and Dimbleby, G.W. (1969) (eds) *The Exploitation and Domestication of Plants and Animals*. London, Duckworth.

Ucko, P.J., Tringham, R. and Dimbleby, G.W. (1972) (eds) *Man, Settlement and Urbanism*. London, Duckworth.

Uerpmann, H. (1982) Faunal remains from Shams ed-Din Tannira, a Halafian site in Northern Syria. *Berytus* 30:3–52.

Underhill, A.P. (1991) Pottery production in chiefdoms: The Longshan period in northern China. *World Archaeology* 23(1):12–27.

Underhill, A.P. (1994) Variation in settlements during the Longshan period of Northern China. *Asian Perspectives* 33(2):197–28.

Unger-Hamilton, R. (1989) The Epi-Palaeolithic Southern Levant and the origins of pastoralism. *Current Anthropology* 30(1):88–103.

Unger-Hamilton, R. (1991) Natufian plant husbandry in the southern Levant and comparison with that of the Neolithic periods: The lithic perspective. In Bar-Yosef and Valla 1991b, pp.483–520.

Unger-Hamilton, R. (1992) Experiments in harvesting wild cereals and other plants. In P.C. Anderson 1992b, pp.211–224.

Upham, S. (1990) (ed.) *The Evolution of Political Systems*. Cambridge, Cambridge University Press.

Uphill, E. (1972) The concept of the Egyptian palace as a 'ruling machine'. In Ucko *et al.*, pp.721–734.

Valla, F.R. (1981) Les établissements naroufiens dans le nord d'Israel. In J. Cauvin and Sanlaville, pp.409–420.

Valla, F.R. (1991) Les natoufiens de Mallaha et l'espace. In Bar-Yosef and Valla 1991b, pp.111–122.

Valla, F.R., Le Mort, F. and Plisson, H. (1991) Les fouilles en cours sur la Terrace d'Hayonim. In Bar-Yosef and Valla 1991b, pp.93–110.

Vallat, F. (1978) Le matériel épigraphique des couches 18 à 14 de l'Acropole. *Paleorient* 4:193–195.

Vallat, F. (1986) The most ancient scripts of Iran: The current situation. *World Archaeology* 17(3):335–347.

Vallat, F. (1990) (ed.) *Contribution à l'histoire de l'Iran: Mélanges offerts à Jean Perrot*. Paris, Editions Recherche sur les Civilisations.

Van Beek, G.W. (1982) A population estimate for Marib: A contemporary tell village in North Yemen. *BASOR* 248:61–67.

Van de Mieroop, M. (1989) Gifts and tithes to the temples in Ur. In Behrens *et al.*, pp.397–401.

Van den Brink, E.C.M. (1992a) Corpus and numerical evaluation of 'thinite' potmarks. In Friedman and Adams, pp.265–296.

Van den Brink, E.C.M. (1992b) Preliminary report on the excavations at Tell Ibrahim Awad, seasons 1988–1990. In Van den Brink 1992c, pp.43–68.

Van den Brink, E.C.M. (1992c) (ed.) *The Nile Delta in Transition: 4th–3rd Millennium B.C.* Tel Aviv, E.C.M. van den Brink.

Van den Brink, E.C.M. (1993) Settlement patterns in the northeastern Nile Delta during the fourth–second millennia B.C. In Krzyzaniak *et al.*, pp.279–304.

Van den Brink, E.C.M., Schmidt, K., Boessneck, J. and Von den Dreisch, A. (1989) A transitional late Predynastic–Early Dynastic settlement site in the northeastern Nile Delta, Egypt. *MDAIK* 45:55–108.

Van Driel, G. (1995) Nippur and the Inanna Temple during the Ur III Period (Review article on Zettler 1992). *JESHO* 38(3):393–406.

Van Gijn, A. (1992) The interpretation of 'sickles': A cautionary tale. In P.C. Anderson 1992b, pp.363–372.

Van Neer, W. (1989) Fishing along the prehistoric Nile. In Krzyzaniak and Kobusiewicz, pp.49–56.

Vanstiphout, H.L.J. (1990) The Mesopotamian debate poems. A general presentation (Part 1). *Acta Sumerologica* 12:271–318.

Van Wijngaarden-Bakker, L.H. (1989) The animal remains of Tell Sabi Abyad – square P14. In Akkermans 1989c, pp.301–323.

Van Zeist, W. (1969) Reflections on prehistoric environments in the Near East. In Ucko and Dimbleby, pp.35–46.

Van Zeist, W. (1979–80) Plant remains from Girikihaciyan, Turkey. *Anatolica* 7:75–89.

Van Zeist, W. (1985) Past and present environments of the Jordan Valley. In Hadidi, pp.199–204.

Van Zeist, W. (1986) Some aspects of Early Neolithic plant husbandry in the Near East. *Anatolica* 15:49–67.

Van Zeist, W. and Bakker-Heeres, J.A.H. (1975) Evidence for linseed cultivation before 6000bc. *Journal of Archaeological Science* 2:215–219.

Van Zeist, W. and Bakker-Heeres, J.A.H. (1979) Some economic and ecological aspects of plant husbandry at Tell Aswad. *Paleorient* 5:161–169.

Van Zeist, W. and Bakker-Heeres, J.A.H. (1982) Archaeobotanical studies in the Levant I. Neolithic sites in the Damascus Basin: Aswad, Ghoraife, Ramad. *Palaeohistoria* 24:165–256.

Van Zeist, W. and Bakker-Heeres, J.A.H. (1984/6a) Archaeobotanical studies in the Levant 2. Neolithic and Halaf levels at Ras Shamra. *Palaeohistoria* 26:151–169.

Van Zeist, W. and Bakker-Heeres, J.A.H. (1984/6b) Archaeobotanical studies in the Levant 3. Late Palaeolithic Mureybit. *Palaeohistoria* 26:171–199.

Van Zeist, W. and Bottema, S. (1982) Vegetational history of the Eastern Mediterranean and the Near East during the last 20,000 years. In Bintliff and Van Zeist, pp.277–321.

Van Zeist, W., Bottema, S., Woldring, H. and Stapert, D. (1975) Late Quarternary vegetation and climate of southeastern Turkey. *Palaeohistoria* 17:53–143.

Van Zeist, W. and Buitenhuis, H. (1983) A palaeobotanical study of Neolithic Erbaba, Turkey. *Anatolica* 10:47–89.

Van Zeist, W. and Casparie, W.A. (1968) Wild einkorn wheat and barley from Tell Mureybit in Northern Syria. *Acta Botanica Neerlandica* 17:44–53.

Van Zeist, W. and de Roller, G. (1994) The plant husbandry of aceramic Cayonu, SE Turkey. *Palaeohistoria* 33/34:65–96.

Van Zeist, W., Smith, P.E.L., Palfenier-Vegter, R.M. and Casparie, W.A. (1986) An archaeobotanical study of Ganj Dareh Tepe, Iran. *Palaeohistoria* 26:201–224.

Van Zeist, W. and Waterbolk-van Rooijen, W. (1985) The palaeobotany of Tell Bouqras, Eastern Syria. *Paleorient* 11(2)·131–147.

Van Zeist, W. and Waterbolk-van Rooijen, W. (1989) Plant remains from Sabi Abyad. In Akkermans 1989c, pp.325–335.

Vats, M.S. (1940) *Excavations at Harappa I: Text; II: Plates*. Delhi, Government of India Press.

Vavronset, P. and Zemanet, P. (1992) (eds) *Karel Petracek Memorial Volume*. Prague, Charles University.

Veenhof, K.R. (1987) 'Dying Tablets' and 'Hungry Silver': Elements of figurative language in Akkadian commercial terminology. In Mindlin *et al.*, pp.41–75.

Vermeersch, P.M. and Paulissen, E. (1993) Palaeolithic chert quarrying and mining in Egypt. In Krzyzaniak *et al.*, pp.327–336.

Vermeersch, P.M., Paulissen, E., Huyge, D., Newmann, K., Van Neer, W. and Van Peer, P. (1992) Predynastic hearths in Upper Egypt. In Friedman and Adams, pp.163–172.

Vermeersch, P.M., Paulissen, E. and Van Neer, W. (1989) The Late Palaeolithic Makhadma sites (Egypt): Environment and subsistence. In Krzyzaniak and Kobusiewicz, pp.87–114.

Vertesalji, P.P. (1987) The chronology of the Chalcolithic in Mesopotamia (6,200–3,400 B.C.). In Aurenche *et al.*, part ii:483–523.

Vertesalji, P.P. (1989) Transitions and transformations: 'Ubaidizing tendencies in Early Chalcolithic Mesopotamia. In Henrickson and Thuesen, pp.227–255.

Vincente, C.-A. (1995) The Tall Leilan Recension of the Sumerian King List. *Zeitschrift für Assyriologie* 85:234–237.

Vishnu-Mittre (1989) Forty years of archaeobotanical research in South Asia. *Man and Environment* 14(1):1–16.

Vishnu-Mittre, and Savithri, R. (1982) Food economy of the Harappans. In Possehl, pp.205–222.

Vogt, E.Z. and Leventhal, R.M. (1983) (eds) *Prehistoric Settlement Patterns: Essays in Honor of Gordon R. Willey*. University of New Mexico Press and Peabody Museum of Archaeology and Technology, Harvard University.

Voigt, M. (1987) Relative and absolute chronologies for Iran between 6,500 and 3,500 cal. BC. In Aurenche *et al.*, part ii:615–633.

Von der Way, T. (1986) Tell el-Fara'in – Buto 1. Bericht. *Instituts abt. Kairo (MDAIK)* 42:191–212.

Von der Way, T. (1987) Tell el-Fara'in – Buto 2. Bericht. *MDAIK* 43:241–249.

Von der Way, T. (1988) Tell el-Fara'in – Buto 3. Bericht. *MDAIK* 44:283–249.

Von der Way, T. (1989) Tell el-Fara'in – Buto 4. Bericht. *MDAIK* 45:275–307.

Von der Way, T. (1991) Investigations concerning the pre- and early Dynastic periods in the Northern Delta of Egypt. In Kerner, pp.47–62.

Von der Way, T. (1992a) Excavations at Tell el-Fara'in/Buto in 1987–1989. In Van den Brink 1992c, pp.1–10.

Von der Way, T. (1992b) Indications of architecture with niches at Buto. In Friedman and Adams, pp.217–226.

Von Wickede, A. (1990) *Prähistorische Stempel Glyptik in Vorderasien*. Munich, Profil Verlag.

Waldrop, M.M. (1992) *Complexity: The Emerging Science at the Edge of Chaos and Complexity*. Harmondsworth, Penguin [1994].

Wang, N. (1988–9) Yangshao burial customs and social organization. *Early China* 11–12:6–32.

Ward, W.A. (1992) The present status of Egyptian chronology. *BASOR* 288:53–66.

Waslikowa, K., Harlan, J.R., Evans, J., Wendorf, F., Schild, R., Close, A.E., Krolik, H. and Housley, R.A. (1993) Examination of botanical remains from Early Neolithic houses at Nabta Playa, Western Desert, Egypt, with special reference to sorghum grains. In Shaw *et al.*, pp.154–164.

Wasse, A. (1997) Preliminary results of an analysis of the sheep and goat bones from 'Ain Ghazal, Jordan. In Gebel, Kafafi and Rollefson 1997.

Watkins, T. (1989) The beginnings of warfare. In Hackett, pp.15–35.

Watkins, T. (1990) The origins of house and home? *World Archaeology* 21(3):336–347.

Watkins, T. (1992) Pushing back the frontiers of Mesopotamian prehistory. *Biblical Archaeologist* Dec. 1992:176–181.

Watkins, T. (1995) *Qermez Dere, Tell Afar: Interim Report No. 3*. Edinburgh, Edinburgh University Press.

Watkins, T., Baird, D. and Betts, A. (1989) Qermez Dere and the Early Aceramic Neolithic of N. Iraq. *Paleorient* 15(1):19–24.

Watkins, T. and Campbell, S. (1986) *Kharabeh Shattani, Vol. 1*. University of Edinburgh, Dept of Archaeology Occasional Paper No. 14.

Watkins, T. and Campbell, S. (1987) The chronology of the Halaf Culture. In Aurenche *et al.*, pp.427–460.

Watson, J.L. (1976) Anthropological analyses of Chinese religion. *China Quarterly* 66: 355–364.

Watson, J.L. (1977) Hereditary tenancy and corporate landlordism in traditional China: A case study. *Modern Asian Studies* 11(2):161–182.

Watson, J.L. (1982) Chinese kinship reconsidered: Anthropological perspectives on historical research. *China Quarterly* 92:589–622.

Watson, J.P.N. (1980) The vertebrate fauna from Arpachiyah. *Iraq* 42:15–23.

Watson, P.J. (1978) Architectural differentiation in some Near Eastern Communities, prehistoric and contemporary. In Redman *et al.*, pp.131–158.

Watson, P.J. (1983a) The Halafian Culture: A review and synthesis. In T.C. Young *et al.*, pp.231–250.

Watson, P.J. (1983b) A note on the Jarmo plant remains. In L.S. Braidwood *et al.*, pp.501–504.

Watson, P.J. and Le Blanc, S.A. (1990) (eds) *Girikihaciyan: A Halafian Site in Southeastern Turkey*. Los Angeles, UCLA Institute of Archaeology, Monograph 33.

Wattenmaker, P. (1990) On the Uruk expansion (Critique of Algaze 1989). *Current Anthropology* 31(1):67–69.

Wattenmaker, P. (1994) Political fluctuations and local exchange systems: Evidence from the Early Bronze Age settlements at Kurban Hoyuk. In Stein and Rothman, pp.193–209.

Weadock, P.N. (1975) The Giparu at Ur. *Iraq* 37:101–128.

Weber, S.A. (1992) South Asian archaeobotanical variability. In C. Jarrige, pp.283–290.

Webley, D. (1969) A note on the pedology of Teleilat Ghassul. In Hennessy, pp.21–23.

Wei-Ming, T. (1986) The structure and function of the Confucian intellectual in Ancient China. In Eisenstadt, pp.360–373.

Weinstein-Evron, M. (1991) New Radiocarbon dates for the Early Natufian of El-Wad Cave, Mt. Carmel, Israel, *Paleorient* 17(1):95–98.

Weiss, H. (1985) (ed.) *Ebla to Damascus: Art and Archaeology of Ancient Syria*. Washington, DC, Smithsonian Institution.

Weiss, H. (1986a) The origins of cities in dry-farming Syria and Mesopotamia in the third millennium BC. In Weiss 1986c, pp.1–6.

Weiss, H. (1986b) The origins of Tell Leilan and the conquest of space in third millennium Mesopotamia. In Weiss 1986c, pp.71–108.

Weiss, H. (1986c) (ed.) *The Origins of Cities in Dry-Farming Syria and Mesopotamia in the Third Millennium B.C.* Guilford, Conn., Four Quarters Publishing Co.

Weiss, H. and Courty, M.-A. (1992) The genesis and collapse of the Akkadian Empire: The accidental refraction of historical law. In Liverani 1993c, pp.131–156.

Weiss, H., Courty, M.-A., Wetterstrom, W., Guichard, F., Senior, L., Meadow, R. and Curnow, A. (1993) The genesis and collapse of the third millennium North Mesopotamian civilization. *Science* 261:995–1004.

Weiss, H. and Young, T.C. (1975) The merchants of Susa. *Iran* 13:1–17.

Wendorf, F. and Close, A.E. (1992) Early Neolithic food economies in the Eastern Sahara. In Friedman and Adams, pp.155–162.

Wendorf, F., Close, A.E. and Schild, R. (1989) Early domestic cattle and scientific methodology. In Krzyzaniak and Kobusiewicz, pp.61–67.

Wendorf, F. and Marks, A.E. (1975) (eds) *The Pleistocene Prehistory of the Southern and Eastern Mediterranean Basin*. Dallas, Southern Methodist University Press.

Wendorf, F. and Schild, R. (1975) The Palaeolithic of the Lower Nile Valley. In Wendorf and Marks, pp.127–170.

Wendorf, F. and Schild, R. (1976) *Prehistory of the Nile Valley*. New York, Academic Press.

Wendorf, F. and Schild, R. (1980) *Prehistory of the Eastern Sahara*. New York, Academic Press.

Wendorf, F. and Schild, R. (1984) The emergence of food production in the Egyptian Sahara. In Clark and Brandt, pp.93–101.

Wenke, R.J. (1989) Egypt: Origins of complex societies. *Annual Review of Archaeology* 18:129–155.

Wenke, R.J. (1991) The evolution of Early Egyptian Civilization: Issues and evidence. *Journal of World Prehistory* 5:279–329.

Wenke, R.J. and Brewer, D.J. (1992) The Neolithic–Predynastic transition in the Fayum Depression. In Friedman and Adams, pp.175–184.

Wenke, R.J. and Casini, M. (1989) The Epipalaeolithic–Neolithic transition in Egypt's Fayum Depression. In Krzyzaniak and Kobusiewicz, pp.139–155.

Wenke, R.J., Long, J.E. and Buck, P.E. (1988) Epipalaeolithic and Neolithic subsistence and settlement in the Fayum oasis of Egypt. *Journal of Field Archaeology* 15:29–51.

Westenholz, A. (1977) Old Akkadian school texts. *AfO* 25:95–110.

Westenholz, A. (1987) *Old Sumerian and Old Akkadian Texts in Philadelphia, Part Two: The 'Akkadian' Texts, the Enlilemaba Texts, and the Onion Archive*. Copenhagen, Carsten Niebuhr Institute Publications 3, Museum Tusculanum Press.

Westenholz, A. (1993) The world view of Sargonic officials: Differences in mentality between Sumerians and Akkadians. In Liverani 1993c, pp.157–169.

Westenholz, J.G. (1989) Enheduanna, En-Priestess, Hen of Nanna, Spouse of Nanna. In Behrens, *et al.*, pp.539–556.

Western, A.C. (1971) The ecological interpretation of ancient charcoals from Jericho. *Levant* 3:31–40.

Wetterstrom, W. (1993) Foraging and farming in Egypt: The transition from hunting and gathering to horticulture in the Nile Valley. In Shaw *et al.*, pp.165–226.

Wheatley, P. (1971) *The Pivot of the Four Quarters*. Edinburgh, Edinburgh University Press.

Wheeler, M. (1954) *Archaeology from the Earth*. Harmondsworth, Penguin.

Wheeler, M. (1955) *Still Digging: Interleaves from an Antiquary's Notebook*. London, Michael Joseph.

Wheeler, M. (1968) *The Indus Civilization* (3rd edition). Cambridge, Cambridge University Press.

Wigley, T.M.L. and Farmer, G. (1982) Climate of the Eastern Mediterranean and the Near East. In Bintliff and Van Zeist, pp.3–37.

Wilcke, C. (1987) A riding tooth: Metaphor, metonymy and synecdoche, quick and frozen in everyday language. In Mindlin *et al.*, pp.77–102.

Wilcke, C. (1989) Genealogical and geographical thought in the Sumerian King List. In Behrens *et al.*, pp.557–569.

Wilhelmy, H. (1969) Das Urstromtal am Ostrand der Indusebene und das 'Sarasvati-Problem'. *Zeitschrift fur Geomorphologie, Supplement-Band* 8:76–93.

Wilkinson, R.H. (1985) The Horus name and the form and significance of the serekh in the royal Egyptian titulary. *Journal of the Society for the Study of Egyptian Antiquities* 15:98–104.

Wilkinson, Toby A.H. (1994–5) A new comparative chronology for the Predynastic–Early Dynastic transition. *Journal of the Ancient Chronology Forum* 7:5–26.

Wilkinson, T.J. (1990a) Soil development and early land use in the Jazira region, Upper Mesopotamia. *World Archaeology* 22(1):87–103.

Wilkinson, T.J. (1990b) The development of settlement in the North Jazira between 7th and 1st millennia BC. *Iraq* 52:49–62.

Wilkinson, T.J. (1994) The structure and dynamics of dry-farming states in Upper Mesopotamia. *Current Anthropology* 35(5):483–520.

Willcox, G.H. (1992a) Some differences between crops of Near Eastern origin and those from the Tropics. In C. Jarrige, pp.291–308.

Willcox, G.H. (1992b) Archaeobotanical significance of growing Near Eastern progenitors of domestic plants at Jales (France). In P.C. Anderson 1992b, pp.159–177.

Willcox, G.H. (1995) Wild and Domestic Cereal Exploitation: New Evidence from Early Neolithic Sites in the Northern Levant and South-Eastern Anatolia. ARX 1(1):9–16.

Willcox, G.H. (1996) Evidence for plant exploitation and vegetation history from three Early Neolithic pre-pottery sites on the Euphrates (Syria). *Vegetation History and Archaeobotany* 5:143–152.

Williams, M.A.J. and Faure, H. (1980) (eds) *The Sahara and the Nile*. Rotterdam, A.A. Balkema.

Willmott, W.E. (1972) (ed.) *Economic Organization in Chinese Society*. Stanford, Calif., Stanford University Press.

Wilshusen, R.H. and Stone, G.D. (1990) An ethnoarchaeological perspective on soils. *World Archaeology* 22(1):104–111.

Wilson, J.A. (1951) *The Culture of Ancient Egypt* (originally published as *The Burden of Egypt*). Chicago, University of Chicago Press.

Winkelmann, S. (1994) Intercultural relations between Iran, Central Asia and Northwestern India in the light of squatting stone sculptures from Mohenjo-Daro. In Parpola and Koskikallio, II:815–831.

Winterhalder, B. (1993) Work, resources and population in foraging societies. *Man* (N.S.) 28(2):321–340.

Winterhalder, B. and Smith, E.A. (1981) (eds) *Hunter-Gatherer Foraging Strategies: Ethnographic and Archaeological Analyses*. Chicago, University of Chicago Press.

Wiseman, D.J. (1989) (ed.) The Assyrians. In Hackett, pp.36–53.

Wittfogel, K. (1957, 1981 new edn.) *Oriental Despotism: A Comparative Study of Total Power*. New York, Vintage Books.

Woolley, C.L. (1934) The prehistoric pottery of Carchemish. *Iraq* 1:146–162.

Woolley, C.L. (1953) *Spadework: Adventures in Archaeology*. Cambridge, Lutterworth.

Woolley, C.L. (1982) *Ur 'of the Chaldees'* P.R.S. Moorey (ed.) London, The Herbert Press.

Worsaae, J.A. (1849) *The Primeval Antiquities of Denmark* [trans. W.J. Thoms]. London, John Henry Parker.

Wright, H.E. (1993) Environmental determinism in Near Eastern prehistory. *Current Anthropology* 34(4):458–469.

Wright, H.E., Kutzbach, J.E., Webb, T. III, Ruddiman, W.F., Street-Perrott, F.A. and Bertlein, P.J. (1993) (eds) *Global Climates Since the Last Glacial Maximum*. Minneapolis, University of Minnesota Press.

Wunderlich, J. (1989) Untersuchungen zur Entwicklung des westlichen Nildeltas im Holozan. *Marburger Geographische Schriften* 114:164–172.

Wunderlich, J. (1993) The natural conditions for Pre- and Early Dynastic settlement in the Western Nile Delta around Tell el-Fara'in, Buto. In Kryzyaniak *et al.*, pp.259–266.

Wunderlich, H., Von der Way, T. and Schmidt, K. (1989) Neue Fundstellen der Buto-Maadi-Kultur bei Ezbet el-Qerdahi. *MDAIK* 45:309–318.

Xia, Nai (1977) Carbon-14 dating and China's prehistorical archaeology. *Kaogu* 4: 217–232.

Xigui, Q. (1989) An examination of whether the charges in Shang oracle bone inscriptions are questions. *Early China* 14:77–114.

Xu, C. (1994) Cultural changes in Sindh prior to the mature Harappan period? A clue drawn from a comparative study of the pottery. In Kenoyer 1994b, pp.71–80.

Xu, Y.-L. (1995) The Houwa site and related issues. In Nelson 1995c, pp.65–88.

Yamada, M. (1994) The dynastic seal and Ninurta's seal: Preliminary remarks on sealing by the local authorities of Emar. *Iraq* 56:59–62.

Yan, W. (1991) China's earliest rice agricultural remains. *Bulletin of the Indo-Pacific Prehistory Association* 10:118–126.

Yang, C.K. (1961) *Religion in Chinese Society*. Berkeley and Los Angeles, University of California Press.

Yang, H.C. (1986) The Shang Dynasty cemetery system. In K.C. Chang 1986b, pp.49–64.

Yang, M.C. (1948) *A Chinese Village: Taitou, Shantung Province*. London, Kegan Paul, Trench, Trubner & Co.

Yang, Yang (1996) The Chinese Jade Culture. In Rawson 1996a, pp.225–231.

Yasin, W. (1970) Excavations at Tell es-Sawwan, 1969. *Sumer* 26:3–20.

Yin, W.C. (1986) A re-examination of Erh-li-t'ou Culture. In K.C. Chang 1986b, pp.1–14.

Yoffee, N. (1993) Mesopotamian interaction spheres. In Yoffee and Clark, pp.257–269.

Yoffee, N. and Clark, J.L. (1993) (eds) *Early Stages in the Evolution of Mesopotamian Civilization: Soviet Excavations in Northern Iraq*. Tucson and London, University of Arizona Press.

Yoffee, N. and Sherratt, A. (1993) (eds) *Archaeological Theory: Who Sets the Agenda?* Cambridge, Cambridge University Press (New Directions in Archaeology).

Young, G.D. (1992) (ed.) *Mari in Retrospect: Fifty Years of Mari and Mari Studies*. Winona Lake, Indiana, Eisenbrauns.

Young, T.C., Smith, P.E.L. and Mortensen, P. (1983) (eds) *The Hilly Flanks and Beyond: Essays on the Prehistory of Southwestern Asia (Presented to Robert J. Braidwood)*. Studies in Ancient Oriental Civilization, No. 36. Chicago, The Oriental Institute.

Yu, Weichao (1996) The State of Chu. In Rawson 1996a, pp.266–268.

Yu, Y.H. (1977) Food in Han China. In K.C. Chang 1977a, pp.53–84.

Yun, L. (1986) A re-examination of the relationship between bronzes of the Shang Culture and of the Northern Zone. In K.C. Chang 1986b, pp.237–274.

Zagerell, A. (1989) Pastoralism and the early state in Greater Mesopotamia. In Lamberg-Karlovsky, pp.268–301.

Zarins, J. (1989) Ancient Egypt and the Red Sea trade: The case for obsidian in the Predynastic and Archaic Periods. In Leonard and Williams, pp.339–368.

Zarins, J. (1990) Early pastoral nomadism and the settlement of Lower Mesopotamia. *BASOR* 280:31–65.

Zeder, M.A. (1994a) After the revolution: Post-Neolithic subsistence in Northern Mesopotamia. *American Anthropologist* 96:97–126.

Zeder, M.A. (1994b) Of kings and shepherds: Specialized animal economy in Ur III Mesopotamia. In Stein and Rothman, pp.175–192.

Zettler, R.M. (1987) Administration of the Temple of Inanna at Nippur under the Third Dynasty of Ur: Archaeological and documentary evidence. In Gibson and Biggs, pp.117–131.

Zettler, R.L. (1992) *The Ur III Temple of Inanna at Nippur. The operation and organization of urban religious institutions in Mesopotamia in the late third millennium* BC. Berlin, Berliner Beiträge zum Vorderen Orient 11.

Zettler, R.L. with Roth, M.T. (1984) The genealogy of the House of UR-ME-ME: A second look. *Archiv für Orientforschung* 31:1–14.

Zhang, Zhong-pei (1985) The social structure reflected in the Yuanjunmiao cemetery. *Journal of Anthropological Archaeology* 4:19–33.

Zhao, Dianzheng (1996) The sacrifical pits of Sanxingdui. In Rawson 1996a, pp.248–265.

Zhao, Songqiao and Wu, Wei-Tang (1988) Early Neolithic Hemodu culture along the Hangzhou Estuary and the origin of domestic paddy rice in China. *Asian Perspectives* 27:29–34.

Zheng, Zhenxiang (1996) The royal consort Fu Hao and her tomb. In Rawson 1996a, pp.248–265.

Zhou, Ben Xiong (1981) Animal remains from Cishan village, Wuan, Hebei Province, China. *Kaogu Xuebao* 3:339–347.

Zinkin, T. (1962) *Caste Today*. London, Institute of Race Relations/Oxford University Press.

Zohary, D. (1969) The progenitors of wheat and barley in relation to domestication and agricultural dispersal in the Old World. In Ucko and Dimbleby, pp.47–66.

Zohary, D. (1972) The wild progenitor and place of origin of the cultivated lentil: *Lens culinaris*. *Economic Botany* 26:326–332.

Zohary, D. (1989) Domestication of the Southwest Asian Neolithic crop assemblage of cereals, pulses, and flax: The evidence from the living plants. In Harris and Hillman, pp.358–373.

Zohary, D. (1992) Domestication of the Neolithic Near Eastern crop assemblage. In P.C. Anderson 1992b, pp.81–88.

Zohary, D. and Hopf, M. (1973) Domestication of pulses in the Old World. *Science* 182:887–894.

Zohary, D. and Hopf, M. (1988) *Domestication of Plants in the Old World: The Origin and Spread of Cultivated Plants in West Asia, Europe and the Nile Valley*. Oxford, Oxford University Press.

Zohary, D. and Spiegel-Roy, P. (1975) Beginnings of fruit growing in the Old World. *Science* 187:319–327.

INDEX